# AMERICAN SHOWCASE

# PHOTOGRAPHY
## AMERICAN SHOWCASE
### VOLUME 7

American Showcase, Inc.
New York

# CONTENTS

## SPECIAL FEATURE
### Articles and Interviews

| | |
|---|---|
| A Funny Thing Happened on My Way to the Studio<br>by Carl Fischer | 12,13 |
| "Surprise Me!"<br>by Ernst Haas | 14,15 |
| Nobody asked me, but…<br>by Jay Maisel | 16,17 |
| Changes<br>by Phil Marco | 18,19 |
| The Real Thing<br>by Joel Meyerowitz | 20,21 |
| Dilution<br>by Michael O'Neill | 22,23 |
| Francesco Scavullo: An Interview<br>by Amy Schiffman with Francesco Scavullo | 24,25 |
| Seeing and Feeling: An Interview with Bert Stern<br>by Amy Schiffman with Bert Stern | 26,27 |
| Turbeville on Turbeville<br>by Deborah Turbeville | 28,29 |

## PHOTOGRAPHY NEW YORK CITY

| | |
|---|---|
| Mulligan, Joseph | 32 |
| Bartone, Laurence | 33 |
| Elkins, Joel | 34 |
| Hedrich, David | 35 |
| Mervar, Louis | 36,37 |
| Aubry, Daniel | 38 |
| Standart, Joe | 39 |
| Rusing, Rick | 40,41 |
| Wilcox, Shorty | 42,43 |
| Photofile International, Ltd. | 44,45 |
| Ochi | 46 |
| Alexander, Jules | 47 |
| Allen, Jim | 48 |
| Alt, Howard | 49 |
| Baker, Joe | 50 |
| Barrow, Scott | 51 |
| Beaudin, Ted | 52 |
| Berkun, Phil | 53 |
| Bevilacqua | 54 |
| Bezushko | 55 |
| Byers, Bruce | 56 |
| Cadge, Bill | 57 |
| Cannon, Gregory | 58 |
| Cantor, Phil | 59 |
| Carroll, Don | 60,61 |
| Certo, Rosemarie | 63 |
| Clifford, Geoffrey C. | 64,65 |
| Clough, Terry | 66,67 |
| Cook, Irvin | 68 |
| Crane, Tom | 69 |
| De Lessio, Len | 70 |
| D'Innocenzo, Paul | 71 |
| Dunn, Phoebe | 72 |
| Dunoff, Rich | 73 |
| Elmore, Steve | 75 |
| Fishbein, Chuck | 76,77 |
| Fishman, Chuck | 78 |
| Flatow, Carl | 79 |
| Forelli, Chip | 81 |
| Francekevich, Al | 82,83 |
| Fraser, Douglas | 85 |
| Funk, Mitchell | 86,87 |
| Furman, Michael | 88,89 |
| Giese, Al | 91 |
| Gladstone, Gary | 92,93 |
| Gordon, Joel | 95 |
| Green-Armytage, Stephen | 96,97 |
| Greenberg, David | 98 |
| Gscheidle, Gerhard | 99 |
| Harrington, Phillip A. | 100 |
| Harris, Brownie | 101 |
| Hashi | 102,103 |
| Haviland, Brian | 104 |
| Horowitz, Ryszard | 105 |
| Joern, James | 106 |
| Johansky, Peter | 107 |
| Kalfus, Lonny | 108 |
| Kaplan, Peter B. | 109 |
| Kent, Karen | 110 |
| Korsh, Ken | 111 |
| Landsman, Gary D. | 112,113 |
| Lane, Whitney | 114 |
| Leeds, Karen | 115 |
| Leighton, Thomas | 116,117 |
| Lerner, Richard | 104 |
| Leung, Jook | 118 |
| Luria, Dick | 119 |
| Marchese, Jim | 120,121 |
| Maresca, Frank | 122,123 |
| Marshall, Lee | 124 |
| Martin, Butch | 125 |
| McGrail, John | 126 |
| Mellor, D.W. | 127 |
| Meola, Eric | 128-133 |
| Miller, Donald L. | 134,135 |
| Munson, Russell | 136 |
| Musto, Tom | 137 |
| Myers Studios, Inc. | 138 |
| Nadelson, Jay | 139 |
| Nathan, Simon | 141 |

| | |
|---|---|
| **Obremski, George** | 142,143 |
| **Orenstein, Ronn** | 144 |
| **Palmer, Gabe** | 145 |
| **Parik, Jan** | 146 |
| **Peacock, Christian** | 147 |
| **Peltz, Stuart** | 148 |
| **Photoscope** | 149 |
| **Pottle, Jock** | 150 |
| **Powers, Guy** | 151-156 |
| **Pribula, Barry** | 157 |
| **Rezny, Aaron** | 159 |
| **Rizzo, Alberto** | 160 |
| **Rosner, Eric H.** | 161 |
| **Roth, Peter** | 162 |
| **Rysinski, Edward** | 163 |
| **Sandone, A.J.** | 164 |
| **Shore, Stephen** | 165 |
| **Simpson, Jerry** | 166 |
| **Skalski, Ken** | 167 |
| **Smith, Gordon E.** | 168 |
| **Smith, William Edward** | 169 |
| **Smyth, T. Kevin** | 170 |
| **Sochurek, Howard** | 171 |
| **Sööt, Olaf** | 173 |
| **Stratos, Jim** | 174,175 |
| **Strongin, Jeanne** | 176 |
| **Stuart, John** | 177 |
| **Stuart, Stephen** | 179 |
| **Tcherevkoff, Michel** | 180,181 |
| **Togashi** | 183 |
| **Waine, Michael** | 184,185 |
| **Watson, H. Ross** | 187 |
| **Weidman, H. Mark** | 188,189 |

| | |
|---|---|
| **Weigand, Tom** | 190 |
| **Weinberg, Michael** | 191 |
| **Weitz, Allan** | 192 |
| **West, Charles** | 193 |
| **Wick, Walter** | 194,195 |
| **Zenreich, Alan** | 196 |

## NORTHEAST

| | |
|---|---|
| **Joachim, Bruno** Boston | 198,199 |
| **King, Ralph** Boston | 200,201 |
| **The Studio, Inc.** Pittsburgh | 202 |
| **Northlight Group** Newark NJ | 203 |
| **Rockhill, Morgan** Providence RI | 205 |
| **brt Photographic Illustrations** Lancaster PA | 206,207 |
| **Bedford Photo-graphic** Bedford NY | 208 |
| **Collins, Fred** Boston | 209 |
| **Dreyer, Peter** Boston/Westwood MA | 210 |
| **Dwiggins, Gene** Providence RI | 211 |
| **Foster, Frank** Boston | 213 |
| **Hansen, Steve** Boston | 214,215 |
| **Jones, Lou** Boston | 217 |
| **Kawalerski, Ted** Rochester NY | 218,219 |
| **La Riche, Michael** Philadelphia | 220,221 |
| **Martin, Marilyn** Boston | 222 |
| **McCoy, Dan** Housatonic MA | 223 |
| **McKean, Tom** Wynnewood PA | 224 |
| **Photography Associates** Hartford CT | 225 |
| **Robinson, George A.** Jericho VT | 226 |
| **Rotman, Jeffrey L.** Sommerville MA | 227 |
| **Sauter, Ron** Rochester NY | 228 |
| **Schleipman, Russ** Charlestown MA | 229 |
| **Simmons, Erik Leigh** Boston | 230 |
| **Steiner, Peter** Rochester NY | 231 |

| | |
|---|---|
| **Vaughan, Ted** Manheim PA | 232,233 |
| **Yablon, Ron** Exton PA | 234 |

## MID-ATLANTIC

| | |
|---|---|
| **Pohuski, Michael** Baltimore MD | 237 |
| **Noble Inc.** Baltimore MD | 238,239 |
| **Benn, Nathan** Washington DC | 240 |
| **Morgan, Frank** Virginia Beach VA | 241 |
| **Pease, Greg** Baltimore MD | 242,243 |
| **Schoon, Tim** Lancaster PA | 244 |
| **Touchton, Ken** Washington DC | 245 |

## SOUTHEAST

| | |
|---|---|
| **Kohanim, Parish** Atlanta | 248,249 |
| **Chapple, Ron** Charlotte NC | 250 |
| **Kearney, Mitchell** Charlotte NC | 251 |
| **Smith, Richard W.** Greensboro NC | 252 |
| **Jamison, Chipp** Atlanta | 253 |
| **Katz, Arni** Atlanta | 254 |
| **Hood, Robin** Franklin TN | 255 |
| **Abel, Wilton** Charlotte NC | 256 |
| **Barley, Bill** Columbia SC | 257 |
| **Bilby, Glade II** New Orleans LA | 258 |
| **Carriker, Ronald C.** Winston-Salem NC | 259 |
| **DeVault, Jim** Nashville TN | 260,261 |
| **Gleasner, Bill** Denver NC | 262 |
| **Gupton, Lee** Cary NC | 263 |
| **Henderson, Chip** Raleigh NC | 264 |
| **Johns, Douglas** St Petersberg FL | 265 |
| **Miller, Randy** Miami | 266,267 |
| **Murray, Steve** Raleigh NC | 268 |
| **Petrey, John** Winter Park FL | 269 |
| **Sherman, Ron** Atlanta | 271 |
| **Vance, David** Miami | 272,273 |

## CHICAGO

| | |
|---|---|
| **Deahl, David** | 276,277 |
| **Elliott, Peter** | 278,279 |
| **Manarchy, Dennis** | 280,281 |
| **Scott, Denis** | 282 |
| **Keeling, Robert** | 283 |
| **DeBold, Bill** | 284 |
| **Harris, Bart** | 285 |
| **Tucker, Bill** | 286 |
| **Welzenbach, John** | 287 |
| **Rubin, Laurie** | 288 |
| **Click! Chicago** | 289-291 |
| **Cowan, Ralph** | 292 |
| **Hetisimer, Larry** | 293 |
| **Kazu** | 294,295 |
| **Warkenthien, Dan** | 296 |
| **Zann, Arnold** | 297 |

## MIDWEST

| | |
|---|---|
| **Bartz, Carl** St Louis | 301 |
| **Brimacombe, Gerald** | 302,303 |
| **Hix, Steve** Kansas City MO | 304 |
| **Pitzner, Al** Kansas City MO | 305 |
| **Rohman, Jim** Toledo OH | 306 |
| **Sanderson, Glenn** Green Bay WI | 307 |
| **Schridde, Charles** Madison Hts MI | 308 |
| **Smith, R. Hamilton** St Paul MN | 309 |
| **Westerman, Charlie** Louisville KY | 310,311 |
| **Kahn, Dick** Waukesha WI | Back Cover |

## SOUTHWEST

| | |
|---|---|
| **Duran, Mark** Phoenix AZ | 314 |
| **Kaluzny, Zigy** Austin TX | 315 |
| **Peterson, Bruce** Phoenix AZ | 316 |
| **Bagshaw, Cradoc** Albuquerque NM | 317 |
| **Baker, Kipp** Ft Worth TX | 318 |
| **Clintsman, Dick** Dallas | 319 |
| **Digital Transparencies, Inc.** Houston | 320 |
| **Faustino** Houston | 321 |
| **Gayle, Rick** Phoenix AZ | 322 |
| **Gerczynski, Tom** Phoenix AZ | 323 |
| **Glentzer, Don** Houston | 324 |
| **Hamilton, Jeffrey Muir** Tucson AZ | 325 |
| **Jones, Jerry** Houston | 326 |
| **Marshall, Jim** Carefree AZ | 327 |
| **Meyler, Dennis** Houston | 328 |

## WEST COAST

| | |
|---|---|
| **Zak, Ed** SF | 330,331 |
| **Becker Bishop Studios, Inc.** SF | 332,333 |
| **Blakeley, Jim** SF | 334,335 |
| **Heffernan, Terry** SF | 336,337 |
| **Werts Studios, Inc.** LA | 338,339 |
| **Springmann, Christopher** Point Reyes CA | 340 |
| **O'Brien, Tom** LA | 341 |
| **Dunbar, Clark** Mountain View CA | 342 |
| **Young, Ed** SF | 343 |
| **Abraham, Russell** SF | 344 |
| **Ambrose, Paul** Sunnyvale CA | 345 |
| **Bator, Joe** Golden CO | 347 |
| **Blaustein, John** Berkeley CA | 348,349 |
| **Browne, Warren** SF | 350 |
| **Buchanan, Craig** SF | 351 |
| **Carroon, Chip** Mill Valley CA | 352 |
| **Cassidy Photographic Design** Santa Clara CA | 353 |
| **Chaney, Brad** SF | 354,355 |
| **Cook, Kathleen Norris** Laguna Hills CA | 356 |
| **Dahlstrom Photography, Inc.** Portland OR | 357 |
| **Davidson, Jerry** LA | 358,359 |
| **de Gennaro, George** LA | 360,361 |
| **De Sciose, Nicholas** Denver | 362 |
| **Fader, Bob** Denver | 363 |
| **Ferro, Daniel J.** La Jolla CA | 364 |
| **Gardner, Robert** LA | 365 |
| **Gottlieb, Mark** Palo Alto CA | 367 |
| **Harrington, Marshall** San Diego CA | 368,369 |
| **Keenan, Larry** SF | 370 |
| **Lee, Larry** North Hollywood CA | 371 |
| **Livzey, John** Hollywood CA | 372,373 |
| **Masterson, Ed** San Diego CA | 375 |
| **McAllister, Bruce** Denver | 376,377 |
| **Melgar Photographers, Inc.** Santa Clara CA | 378 |
| **Mishler, Clark** Anchorage AK | 379 |
| **Percey, Roland** LA | 380 |
| **Peregrine, Paul** Denver | 381 |
| **Perry, David** Seattle | 382 |
| **Photographic Communications** Santa Clara CA | 383 |
| **Ressmeyer, Roger** SF | 384 |
| **Sadlon, Jim** SF | 385 |
| **Schoenfeld, Michael** Salt Lake City UT | 386 |
| **Smith, Charles J.** San Diego CA | 387 |
| **Solomon, Marc** LA | 388,389 |
| **Steinberg, Bruce** SF | 391 |
| **Swarthout, Walter** SF | 392,393 |
| **Wood, James B.** LA | 394 |
| **Wortham, Robert** LA | 395 |

## STOCK

| | |
|---|---|
| **Arnold, Peter** NYC | 398,399 |
| **Heilman, Grant** Lititz PA | 400 |
| **La Ferla, Sandro** NYC | 401 |
| **Long, James L.** Fort Lauderdale FL | 402 |
| **Southern Stock Photos** Miami | 403 |
| **Sports Illustrated Pictures** NYC | 404 |
| **Stock Imagery** Denver | 405 |
| **The Stock Market** Denver | 406 |

## VIEWPOINTS

**On Trying to be Good** — 62
Paula Scher
Designer
New York City

**Only Financially Sound Studios Will Survive** — 74
Lawrence Robins
President
Advertising Photographers of America (APA)
New York City

**"Hello, Deli!" (A Pre-Broadway Musical)** — 80, 84
Peter LeDonne
Executive Vice President/
Creative Director
Ash/LeDonne, Inc.
New York City

**You Don't Have to be Crazy But...** — 90, 94
Alvin Hampel
Chairman/New York
D'Arcy-MacManus & Masius, Inc.
New York City

**Call Call Call** — 140
Sal de Rouin
Senior Vice President/
Creative Director
Rolf Werner Rosenthal, Inc.
New York City

**The "Good Ol' Days"** — 158
Ellen Johnson
Manager of Art Buying
Ogilvy & Mather Advertising
New York City

**How to Handle an Art Director** — 172, 178
Peter S. Kellogg
Copywriter
SSC&B/Lintas Worldwide
New York City

**What is a Creative Ad?** — 182, 186
Dick Jackson
Dick Jackson, Inc.
New York City

**It's Your Talent—Use It or Lose It** — 204
Kurt Haiman
Co-Director
Fashion/Soft Goods/Retail
Grey Advertising, Inc.
New York City

**Wallpaper is More Impressive than a Portfolio** — 212
Judy Guerin de Neco
President
The Advertising Club of New York
New York City

**You Meet the Nicest People in this Business** — 216
Robert A. Paige
President/Creative Director
Evans, Garber & Paige, Inc.
Utica, N.Y.

**How I Spent Your Summer Vacation** — 236
Betty Reynolds
Art Director
Spiro & Associates
Philadelphia

**Fairy Tales Can Come True, It Can Happen to You...or, It's Still a Thrill!** — 246
Vicki Joyce
Senior Art Director
Frankel and Company
Chicago

**Simplified Art Buying** — 270
John Long
Supervisor of Art Buying
and The Art Buying Staff
Leo Burnett Company, Inc.
Chicago

**The Greatest Things** — 274
Robert Qually
President/Creative Director
Qually & Company, Inc.
Chicago/Evanston

**Education by Emulation** — 312
Ron Anderson
Executive Creative Director-Midwest
Bozell & Jacobs, Inc.
Minneapolis

**Ira** — 346
Tom Sexton
Creative Director
Young & Rubicam
San Francisco

**Strategizing, Philosophizing and Other Ways a Creative Director Can Avoid Work** — 366
Robert Black
Senior Vice President
Group Creative Director
Foote, Cone, Belding/Honig
San Francisco

**How to Avoid Doing Bad Advertising** — 374
Jay Chiat
President
Chiat/Day Inc.
New York City

**Silence, Please!** — 390
Dudley Maddox
Art Director
Sieber & McIntyre, Inc.
Chicago

## GRAPHIC ARTS ORGANIZATIONS

| | |
|---|---|
| **Address/Telephone** | 298, 300 |

## PHONE LISTINGS

| | |
|---|---|
| **Telephone Listings/Index** | Grey Pages |

## INDEX

| | |
|---|---|
| **Index** | 407, 408 |

President and Publisher:
**Ira Shapiro**

Production Manager:
**Fiona L'Estrange**

Director of Marketing and New Projects:
**Chris Curtis**

Operations/Credit Manager:
**Wendl Kornfeld**

Distribution and Advertising Sales Manager:
**Julia Morris**

Book Sales Manager:
**Chuck Novotny**

Production Assistant:
**Kyla Kanz**

Grey Pages:
**Julia Bahr**

Bookkeeper:
**Cathy Arrigo**

Assistant Operations Manager:
**Daria Dodds**

---

Sales Representatives:

New York:
**John Bergstrom, Deborah Darr, Stacey Gold, Kate Hoffman, Donna Levinstone, Wendy Saunders.**

West Coast:
**Bob Courtman, Ralph Redpath.**

---

Book Design:
**Weeks & Toomey, Inc., NYC**

Mechanical Production:
**The Mike Saltzman Group, NYC**

---

Typesetting:
**Ultra Typographic Services, Inc., NYC**
**Automatech Graphics Corporation, NYC**

---

Color Separation, Printing and Binding:
**Dai Nippon Printing Co. Ltd., Tokyo, Japan**

---

U.S. Book Trade Distribution:
**Van Nostrand Reinhold Co.** VNR
135 West 50th Street, New York, New York 10020

---

Published by
American Showcase, Inc.
724 Fifth Avenue, 10th Floor
New York, New York 10019
(212) 245-0981

Copyright 1984, American Showcase, Inc. All Rights Reserved
American Photography Showcase, Volume Seven, 1984
ISBN 0-931144-21-3 (Softback)
ISBN 0-931144-22-1 (Spiral)
ISSN 0278-8314 (Softback & Spiral)

This textbook is for educational and reference purposes only.
The pages are neither designed nor suitable for framing.

# AMPHETAMINE FOR THE SOUL. $40.

You are not alone.

Every advertising art director and copywriter in the world has—at one time or another—gotten the awful feeling that no decent idea was going to come this time.

When that happens, inexperienced creative people panic.

Experienced ones reach for the One Show Annual.

Not to copy from it.

To be inspired by it. To give their spirit a jolt.

Because a very interesting phenomenon occurs when a creative person is confronted by great work.

He or she begins to think better.

It's like Gresham's Law in reverse. Contact with good ideas drives away bad ideas, and triggers good ones. No one knows why it happens, but it does.

Suddenly, your creative juices start to flow, your spirits are lifted, you're more confident, and you couldn't do hack work if you tried.

Is that worth $40?

What's a good ad worth to you? (Probably a couple of grand.)

What's your *career* worth?

It's got to be worth as much as an account man spends on lunch every day.

We're talking about food for the spirit. We're talking about amphetamine for the soul. VOLUMES 1 & 2 ARE PERMANENTLY SOLD OUT. THEY ARE NOW COLLECTOR'S ITEMS. SO DON'T WAIT UNTIL IT SLIPS YOUR MIND. ORDER NOW.

## AMERICAN SHOWCASE
724 5TH AVE., N.Y., N.Y. 10019

Please send me the following at a DISCOUNT.
Quantity
☐ Volume #5 at $36 plus tax and $3 per book shipping and handling (Reg. price $40)
☐ Volume #4 at $29 plus tax and $3 per book shipping and handling (Reg. price $40)
☐ Volume #3 at $21 plus tax and $3 per book shipping and handling (Reg. price $35)
(Sorry, we cannot fill orders which do not include postage and handling.)

NAME_____
COMPANY_____
ADDRESS_____
CITY_____ STATE\_\_\_\_\_ ZIP\_\_\_\_\_
American Express, Visa, Master Charge (Circle one.)
#_____ Exp. Date_____
☐ I am enclosing a check.

PHOTOGRAPH © 1983 COLIN COOKE

## EDITORIAL

Ever since we began publishing American Showcase, we have been interested in promulgating visual and verbal ideas for the worldwide graphics community. Our lofty ambition has been to establish a visual standard against which the creators of photographs could compare, grow, experiment and improve. And as the pictures in each volume get stronger, and we see them—or others like them—disseminated through the media, we feel that we have made some small contribution to progress.

Right from the start, we invited art directors, graphic designers, ad agency art buyers and industry leaders to share their experiences, suggestions, criticisms, dreams and anecdotes. Their efforts have been appreciated and acknowledged by the hundreds of letters and conversations praising this aspect of each issue.

We looked for other ways to offer insights and serve the graphics community. So this issue includes our latest ripple to the visual communications pond: an editorial section featuring the ideas, stories, recommendations, and philosophies of some of America's best known photographers. The articles are written primarily by the photographers themselves.

Most of the nine photographers featured this year are frequently written about in the photography magazines. A few have been famous for decades and continue to influence younger generations. Some are also known in the photography gallery and museum worlds.

All chose the pictures which accompany their words. A few questioned whether what they had to say would be of interest to the advertising/graphics/photographic community that reads and sees Showcase. We think their doubts are hardly warranted, now that the words and pictures are on the pages. We believe you'll be touched by some of these articles. Others will make you chuckle, think twice, smile knowingly...or even change your ways.

## Articles and Interviews

| | |
|---|---:|
| **A Funny Thing Happened on My Way to the Studio**<br>by Carl Fischer | 12,13 |
| **"Surprise Me!"**<br>by Ernst Haas | 14,15 |
| **Nobody asked me, but...**<br>by Jay Maisel | 16,17 |
| **Changes**<br>by Phil Marco | 18,19 |
| **The Real Thing**<br>by Joel Meyerowitz | 20,21 |
| **Dilution**<br>by Michael O'Neill | 22,23 |
| **Francesco Scavullo: An Interview**<br>by Amy Schiffman<br>with Francesco Scavullo | 24,25 |
| **Seeing and Feeling: An Interview with Bert Stern**<br>by Amy Schiffman<br>with Bert Stern | 26,27 |
| **Turbeville on Turbeville**<br>by Deborah Turbeville | 28,29 |

**SPECIAL FEATURE**

12

# Carl Fischer

### A Funny Thing Happened on My Way to the Studio

Except for the absence of Novocaine and The New York Times, there were some advantages to the artist living in medieval times compared to the artist living today. In that earlier day, a carver or a stained-glass maker was as necessary to society as a baker or a carpenter, and his work was highly valued.

As an ordinary member of the community, he was not treated differently than any other worker, and more important, *he* did not consider himself any different. There was no fine art in the Middle Ages—all art was commercial art. It must have been a less stressful environment in which to work. Except, of course, for The Plague.

Today, fine artists are a unique, often distrusted class, and their art is viewed with suspicion or neglect. Mostly art is considered a cosmetic addition to our lives, an embellishment that we can do without, if necessary. That is a great loss. So much hoopla and so much public relations attends being an artist today, that the stress to provide something unique, arcane or outrageous pressures fine artists to provide work that panders to an enigmatic market. Add to that an artist's reputation as an abstruse person, plus the hyperbole that artists themselves like to engage in, and life can become a staggering burden.

That's why I am satisfied with the current state of commercial art, which somewhat parallels the role of the arts in the Middle Ages. Salaried artists do not have tenured employment, neither are they given grants in financial aid, but they *are* offered exhilarating opportunities in which to work. For an artist, work is the bottom line. True, much of the work that wins awards (including my own) in the cacophony of exhibitions often is not the most worthy. True, the proportion of good to bad in commercial art is a great deal of bad to very little good—perhaps the same proportion as in fine art, politics or automobile repair. But that is another subject, isn't it?

An advantage of doing unsanctioned commercial art, rather than established fine art, is that commerical art is an important ingredient of our culture. It is widely understood and appreciated without the need for art appreciation courses, or esthetic diagnosis. The artist can therefore eschew notoriety, and can develop within a system that regards him as a necessary producer of useful things, and not as a melancholy outsider.

No one has been able to show that the Bohemian life has produced work of a more lasting nature than that of the unknown piece-workers of Chartres, say, who did not feel constrained to sign their work. (It has been suggested that the masons who *did* sign their work during the building of St. Sophia did so in order to get paid.) Andy Warhol's drawings of shoes for Andrew Geller advertising were as good as anything he has done for art galleries since.

Commercial art has been abused, because it can make artists economically comfortable: a hopelessly middle-class failing. But Herbert Muller has written that "Plumbing is not necessarily fatal to the good life, or poverty or misery essential to spiritual elevation." Or, as Tevye has said, more wistfully, "It is not a great shame to be poor. On the other hand, it's not a great honor, either."

My experience in the business end of advertising has been sanguine: I have not seen the predatory behavior that is endemic in the garment and in the entertainment businesses. Compared to them, working in advertising is like working in a monastery.

Which was another clever medieval invention.

14

# Ernst Haas

**"Surprise Me!"**

I have a dream!

The telephone rings. It's an ad agency, and the creative director says, "Ernst, we have a project with a difficult problem, and we hope you can help us. We want to tell you what we need, we hope you can solve it, and surprise us. Knowing your work and books for many years we trust your creative instinct and experience. We will give you an art director as an adviser to tell you the idea, scope and approximate deadline. But we want to know where you want to do it and how long it should take. We want to surprise our client and, hopefully, you will surprise yourself and us in a most positive way."

If asked like that, I would give my utmost. Forget any day rate, I would throw myself into the project with the most joyful enthusiasm—for me, a necessary ingredient to achieve the most positive results. I would be inspired merely by being trusted. You see, as a photographer, I love the unexpected. But even the unexpected must be anticipated, otherwise it can't be realized, and thus reactions come too late. That goes for pictures as well as for telephone calls, and one could say it becomes a way of life, instinct. To expect the unexpected is a paradox, but it is also a direction to avoid. To avoid the calculated, the repetitious, the obvious, the overly graphic, the over-directed. One should *deserve* to be called art director, creative director.

Can art and creativity really be directed? Yes, they can. But one should use the word "inspired" rather than directed, for even the best technique without inspiration is never enough. Even within the most staged situations there are those rare moments which surprise us and others if we are only open enough to receive them. Moments which cannot be copied or repeated.

Nothing increases my insecurity or frustrates me more than the fear and insecurity of others, or contradicting orders from a committee.

"Do it, but don't do it. Be far out, but not too far."

"Be daring, but don't dare too much—Here is our sketch—you understand, we are between you and the client (the grey eminence?) You know, it's a business, it's market, you are a professional, you understand."

I do. And I don't.

For me, the highest example of an art director was Sergei Diaghilev, director-producer of the Ballet Russe Company during the '20's. He neither danced nor sang, nor painted nor played an instrument, but he had a keen feeling for people who could do what was needed. He found new talent everywhere and gave opportunities to young artists barely known during that time. Debussy, Ravel, Stravinsky, Picasso, Braque, Anna Pavlova, Nijinsky are only part of a long list. He also sold tickets to fill his own theatre, and often there was not enough money around. But what an ingenious feeling he cultivated that led him to the greatest talent so often, in so many fields. When asked for direction, he only replied with the most inspiring words an artist wants to hear. He simply said, "Surprise me!" He expected the unexpected and succeeded in it.

I still have that dream—I am still expectant.

Surprise me.

# Jay Maisel

**Nobody asked me, but...**

When I was about 16 years old, Jimmy Cannon was a great sportswriter for the *New York Post,* back when *The Post* was a real New York newspaper. Occasionally he used the following format as a catch-all for random thoughts: "Nobody asked me, but..."

So, with apologies to Mr. Cannon's memory, and in the hope that I won't come off sounding like photography's answer to Andy Rooney, I offer these random observations about life in our often puzzling industry.

Nobody asked me, but...

...Why can't art directors conceive of a photographer's ability to photograph something not already in his or her portfolio?

...What's the name of the guy who has the job of tearing transparencies apart at the separators?

...It seems to me that art director's ability to coax good work from me is in direct proportion to how much he trusts himself and me. If you hire a top photographer and tell him exactly what to do, you're wasting your money. If you don't understand that remark, your boss is wasting his.

...It really knocks me out when good, non-New York City art directors call up and act as though they're asking a favor by offering me a "plum" job. Do they think I sit in New York advertising my work, just waiting for a chance to turn them down?

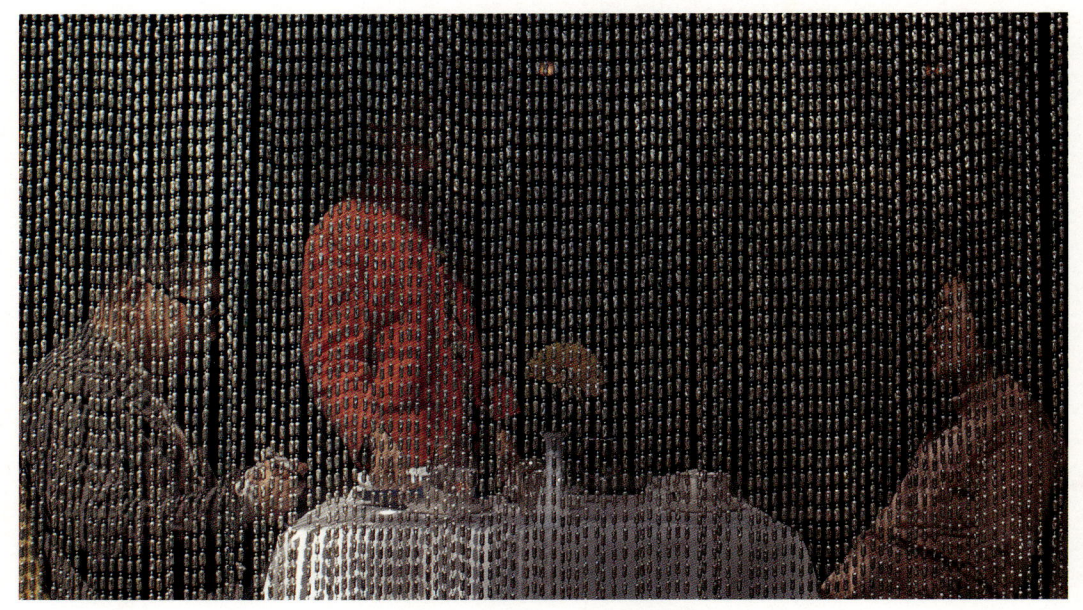

...Just once I'd like to hear the words, "We have a budget" uttered in a positive rather than a negative context.

...There's nothing more depressing than getting word that the client loved it, but the company's being reorganized.

...Out-of-town and out-of-the-country people (in other words, non-New Yorkers) suffer from undeserved inferiority complexes. There's superb work done in really out-of-the-way places.

...There's a special place in heaven for the art director who watched me agonize over his shot and said, "Come on, creep, I only need one good one—what are you worried about?"

...The law of location shooting: "If you forget anything, it won't be some optional piece of equipment; it will be your sync cords."

...Every once in a while I see something that's been done with a shot of mine and I'm thrilled; I remember what good art direction is. It adds another dimension to the work.

...Most beginning photographers who try to get jobs as assistants think that a good portfolio will do the trick. Wrong. What gets you hired is your ability to convince someone of your burning desire to sweep floors.

...I always take an assistant with me on a job. I feel I'm shortchanging the client if I don't, since time and efficiency are of prime importance. When I work on my own things, I never take one. Traveling alone leaves me exhausted and depressed, but it encourages introspection and intensity.

...I'm not well-rounded. I've never wanted a sports car or a pleasure boat. I'm more inclined to yearn for one more dye transfer print or a helicopter available for shooting.

...Why is it that the film you have gets better as you approach the last hundred rolls or so of your emulsion?

...If all you're interested in is money, that's all you get...if you get that.

...If you love your work and you shoot on your own, then you realize how lucky we photographers are. There are very few doctors, lawyers, or art directors whose vocation is also their avocation.

...Satisfying the client is not enough. If I don't satisfy myself, I'm shortchanging the client.

...Being a professional photographer is like having a license to steal experience.

...When you're out shooting, you often get more by waiting than by walking.

...If you never fail, you're not trying hard enough.

17

ALL PHOTOGRAPHS THIS PAGE ©1984 JAY MAISEL

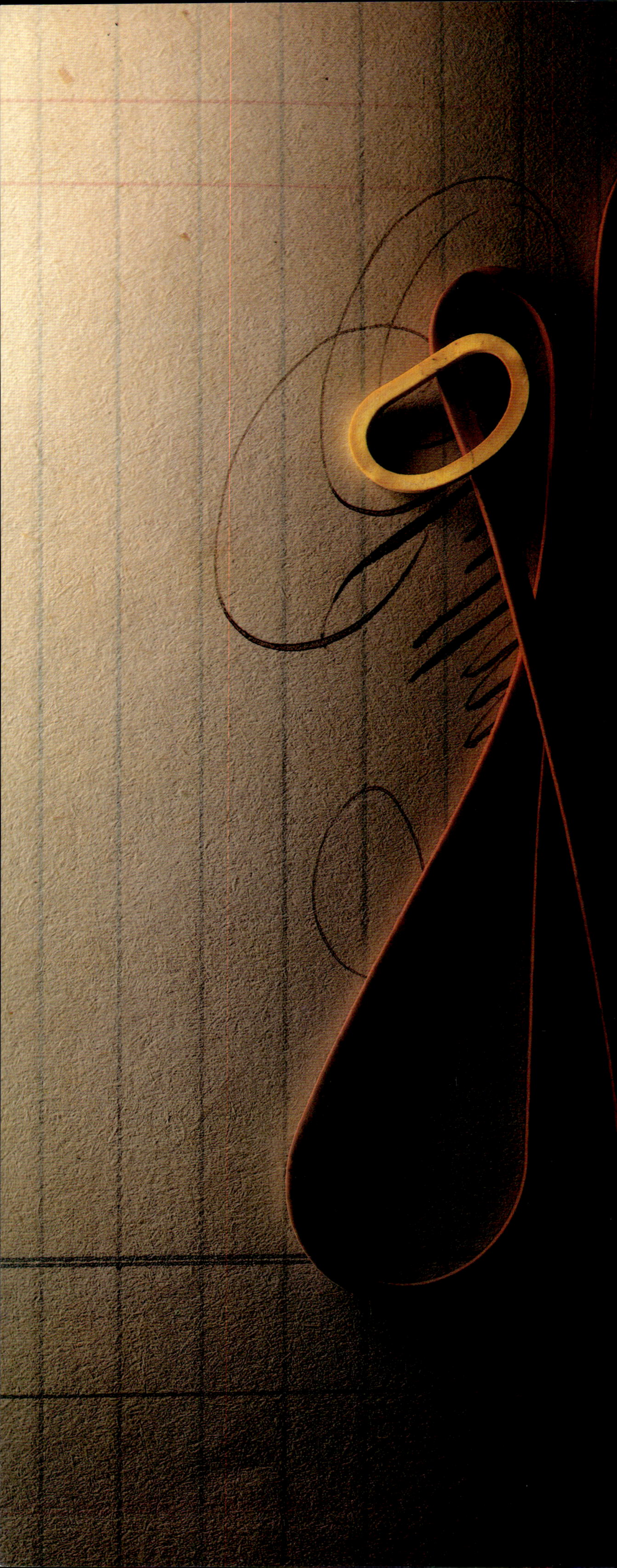

# Phil Marco

**"Changes"**

"Personally, I am now at a very exciting crossroad of my career. One path is leading my print imagery in a gallery and museum direction, while the other is involving me in television commercials and film. What is even more interesting is that I am following both paths simultaneously, and I am genuinely equally enthusiastic about each. Although the final outcome remains to be seen, when you are through changing, you are through."

The preceding paragraph is an excerpt from an article I wrote for American Showcase in 1978. As I write this, it is late August 1983 and I must say in all honesty, that I have found it very difficult if not impossible to follow both paths simultaneously. The fact is that the nature and the sheer logistics of shooting motion film are by far more complicated than print. This brought me to the realization that if I wanted to pursue film and bring it to the level of quality that I achieved in print, I simply had to make a choice. That is not to say that I am through with print, or that I will not on occasion now or in the future photograph stills. I will continue to plan shows and perhaps publish a few books, but the majority of my energy and thought is now on motion film.

A few years back, after arriving at a solution for a visual problem, I reflected: "That's an interesting idea, but how do I make it move?" I knew at that point the transition was complete.

I do miss the intimacy and the autonomy of shooting print; the one-to-one working relationship of myself and an Art Director. More so I miss the layouts that were sent down or literally called in on the phone where I was just given the product and totally designed the visuals myself. Now at times there are so many people in the studio for a film shoot or a pre-production meeting that I sometimes wonder if there is anyone left back at the Agency. Be that as it may I am at this point in my life in love and very much involved with motion film.

The next five years may witness other alterations, but through the changes I am sure that one thing will always remain constant: the pursuit of a strong and beautiful graphic simply stated.

# Joel Meyerowitz

**The Real Thing**

My life as a photographer began in much the same way that a photograph comes into being: something is instantly recognized and acted upon. For me it was seeing the photographer Robert Frank make photographs, on assignment, of two young, coming-of-age girls. It was his behavior, the way he moved; he was effortless and decisive, persistent, watchful and yet invisible. He burned an idea into my mind; one could move *and* photograph. What could be done with that? I bought a camera with the intention of finding out. I was innocent of preconceptions. There was no photographic history that I was aware of. I knew that commercial photography existed, that portraits and fashion and still-lifes were things that photographs were used for, but they held no deep interest for me. I wanted to see what was nearly invisible—the life that slipped by in front of our eyes everyday, what only a camera might hold onto if one might be quick enough to meet it, to anticipate it.

Stung by that desire, I went into the streets and practiced being there, in the right place at the right time, ready for the unexpected. The willingness to put oneself out in chaos builds trust, trust in the medium and its grasp of things and trust in one's instincts. Instinct (as well as luck) is the photographer's divining rod; it points the way. By watching life, I've come to love life. The gifts it offers, I have learned to accept, taking them in with the camera and studying them for the understanding they might bring.

It never occured to me, though, that I might ever earn a living with this tool. Quite by chance, a few years after I began, I was offered an opportunity to make a photograph for an ad. It came out—well enough for me to be offered another one and later other offers followed that. I was lucky in that these jobs were right for me to do, jobs for me to make a distinction between my personal work and the work I did to earn a living. This distinction continually clarifies my values and allows me to come freshly to the work I do. One should not be too easily seduced by the lure of money, for it is there that desire can be turned away from one's original intentions.

Maintaining this duality between the personal and commercial aspects of my life has also shown me a way of viewing the world. Duality offers a choice between things or raises differing things to a plane of equality. It also can be looked at as defining the line that separates choices. My preference for maintaining this tightrope between choices has given me a vantage point from where I might stand and look for the real thing.

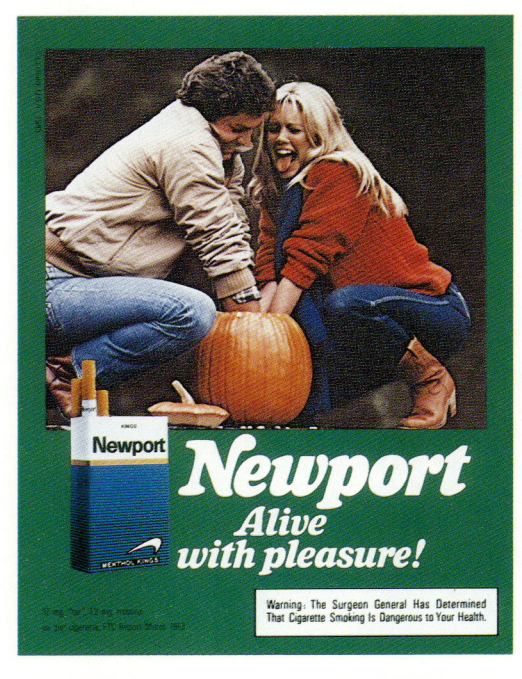

21

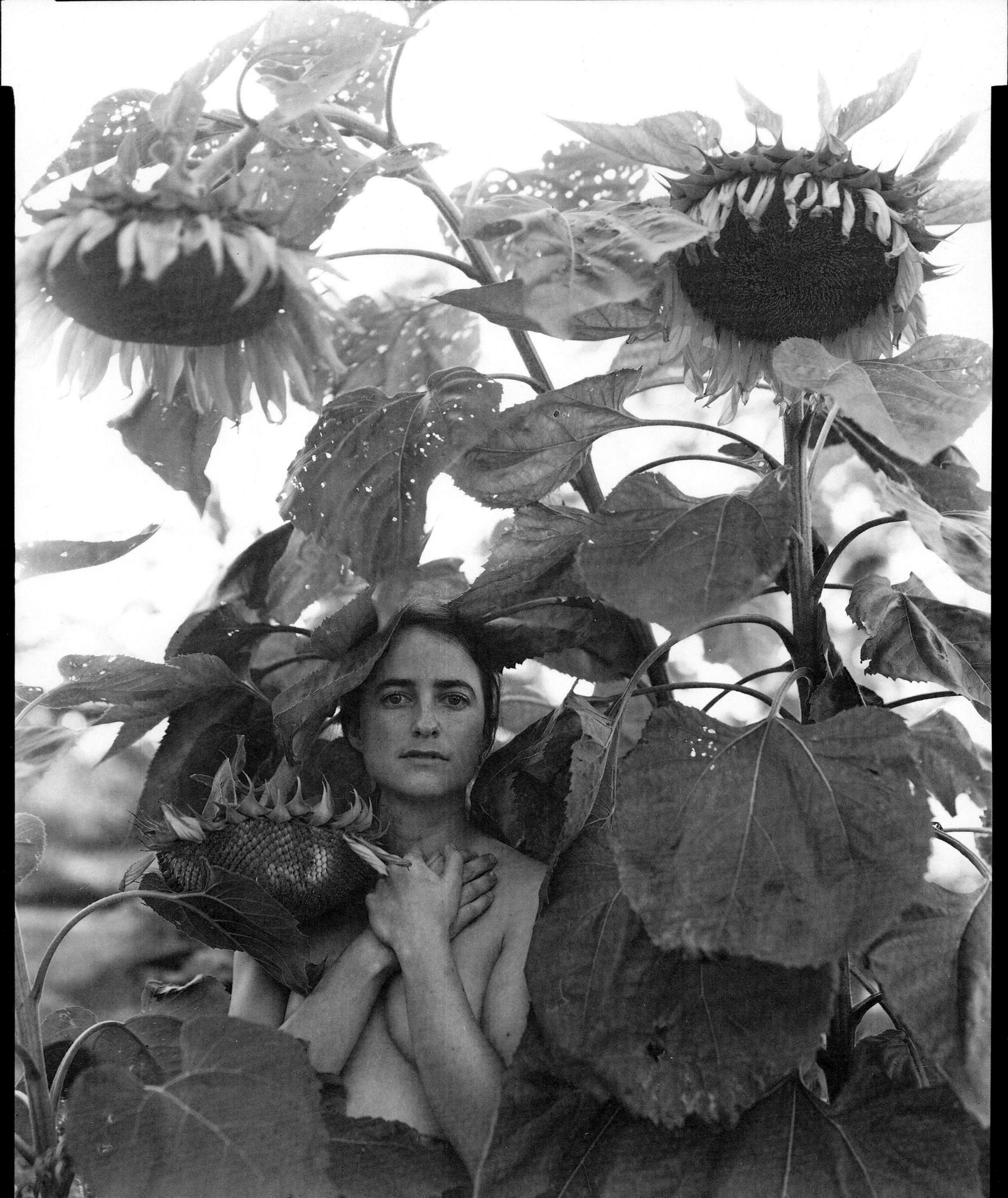

# Michael O'Neill

**Dilution**

Phones ring—requests for the portfolio, the reel—"Can you send up the portfolio?" "Do you have photographs of this kind of fruit or that kind of drink?" "Do you have a picture of a mother hugging a child or a desert road at night?" "Could you do this job?" "Are you available? We want you. We want *you* to do this job. It has to be special, different, spectacular, superb exquisite. Can you make it look like a jewel? You know, like that photo you did for so 'n' so, but… *better!*" "It has to be just like that one but better; in fact, the *best* thing you've ever done. And we'll enter it in all the shows."

And now the economic process begins …"Can you make an estimate?" "Oh, it's a bid," and the tedium begins. Justify this—"Why is this so expensive?"—Justify that, etc. Inevitably there is someone on the other end cutting away…deleting diminishing. The process starts with the competition for the job, heightens with the numbers, and magnifies each step of the way.

We become involved. Yes, there are people who care about producing good work and satisfying clients. We style, assemble the elements, produce, tediously cast, build sets and, often overlooked, put together a group of people in an environment for the sole purpose of making these images with the spirit, energy, and all with the desire to deliver a fine job.

From here on the process becomes subtractive. These same people who asked for the best, for something new or different, instigate a process of deletion based on, at least from my viewpoint, *fear*.

Art Directors over-direct. Account people direct photography based on their market research and the conservative attitudes of the clients. Often the work is "Too far out." Or "Let's do it two ways to be safe." All input deletes, dilutes, and diminishes the original purpose of hiring one of us—people who not only could, but *wanted* to give you more.

Where did the creativity and freedom go???

*Homogeneity reigns.*

What purpose to give the accolade, spend the money, ask for the best, and then shove it into neat pre-packaged, pre-analyzed, plastic bordered, tested-to-death layouts for pages?

Rumor has it that I quit the business. Not true. My availability diminished, because more of my time gets spent these days pulling platinum prints and working for the magazines, where creativity is expected, not diluted.

# Francesco Scavullo

**Francesco Scavullo:
An Interview**
by Amy Schiffman

**AS:** Two years ago you had an exhibition of portraits of members of the *American Ballet Theatre.* Was that your only gallery show?

**FS:** Yes. I haven't had time to do others. But my work is in the permanent collection of the *Metropolitan Museum.* And the *Museum of Modern Art* has called up asking for a complete set of *Cosmo* covers.

**AS:** Do you ever take "personal pictures" that are not assigned or not for public consumption?

**FS:** I think every picture is a personal picture.

**AS:** What about advertising photographs?

**FS:** I do ads all the time. I do fashion. I do soap. I did Brooke Shields when she was 11 months old for Ivory soap. I do hairspray, I do make-up, I do everything.

**AS:** Is there a difference between the problem-solving you are asked to do in advertising and that which is required for editorial work?

**FS:** Every problem is different. Every problem has to be solved. You have to turn on your *Vogue* eyes, your *Good Housekeeping* eyes, your Ivory soap eyes. You know what I mean? If I made everything look alike, I could only do one thing. I do everything.

**AS:** Do art directors present you with different demands in advertising than they do in editorial?

**FS:** It's totally different. With advertising, the layouts are done first, and then we shoot the picture. With magazines you shoot the pictures first and do the layouts later.

**AS:** What process takes place when you shoot an ad?

**FS:** The art directors have a concept which they want me to interpret, from a layout. They know what they want, but they leave it up to me to interpret it.

**AS:** Do you do corporate portraits or annual reports?

**FS:** Yes. I did Lee Iacocca and David Mahoney, the president of Norton Simon (which owns Max Factor and Halston). I do all of Mary Kaye's personal portraits and annual reports. I do lots of work for the major corporations.

**AS:** Apparently you do all sorts of things.

**FS:** I love fabulous experiences. I like challenges. I like to jump into things, get my juices running. I do TV commercials. I directed Crystal Gayle's first one hour CBS musical special. I was the visual consultant on the movie "Lipstick." I am a member of the directors guild of America.

**AS:** Do you think your photographs have an effect on fashion?

**FS:** Very much so, but also on the look for women. My pictures are for women who want to be liberated women. My photographs have helped women believe they can be working women with a brain—intelligent and exciting—and they can be gorgeous, too. I think there is no such thing as an ugly woman, or a homely woman. There are no ugly ducklings growing up to be ugly ducks. People grow with their minds and their spirits, their bodies. Everyone can develop the most and best of themselves, the positive.

**AS:** Will you shoot ads for jeans?

**FS:** I love to do them. I love jeans. Look at me, I wear Levi Strauss jeans because they fit me the best. With the buttons—I don't like zippers. The best designer in America ever was Levi Strauss.

**AS:** One of the things you're renowned for is your Cosmo covers. How did "That Cosmo Woman" evolve?

**FS:** The Cosmo woman originated with Helen Gurly Brown. The sexy woman with large bosoms was Helen's idea. It took 15 years to develop the Cosmo look of today. The creative styling for the last 10 years has been done by Sean Byrnes.

**AS:** Do you ever have a day when inspiration fails you?

**FS:** I can't allow that to happen. Sometimes I get nervous, depressed, frightened, or I might not feel well that day, but I put all that aside and get right to work in the studio. I photographed Rose Kennedy less that a week after my kidney stone operation. I shot a fabulous portrait for her 92nd birthday. Nothing will stop me. I think even when I'm dying, I will somehow get one last picture in.

INTRODUCING
L'Artiste
ENDURING LIPSTICK
PARIS L'ORÉAL NEW YORK
THE NEW SPIRIT OF CHIC

THE MAGAZINE FOR TODAY'S BLACK WOMAN
OCTOBER 1982
ESSENCE
IN PRAISE OF BLACK STYLE

MAY
HARPER'S
BAZAAR
YOUR SHAPE-UP ISSUE!
low to have
sensational
body at
ny age
eautiful Breasts
us breast
ancer update
ersonal secrets of
America's
Sexiest Beauties
air, makeup
xercise, diet
pecial section:
Wake up your sex life
exclus
Christie Brinkley
Seducti
Body Guid
the best & the barest!
85 BODY-REVEALING LOOK

AMERICAN
BALLET
THEATRE

Pure jeanius. We've taken our traditional double stitched, copper riveted, heavyweight cotton blue jeans and made them *in colors other than blue!* Levi's Painted Denims. It's a whole new Levi's look for good old Levi's jeans.
Painted Denims. Strokes Of Levi's Jeanius.
Levi's
QUALITY NEVER GOES OUT OF STYLE

TIME
HOMECOMING
"Turn the Page"
The '80s Look
Brooke Shields

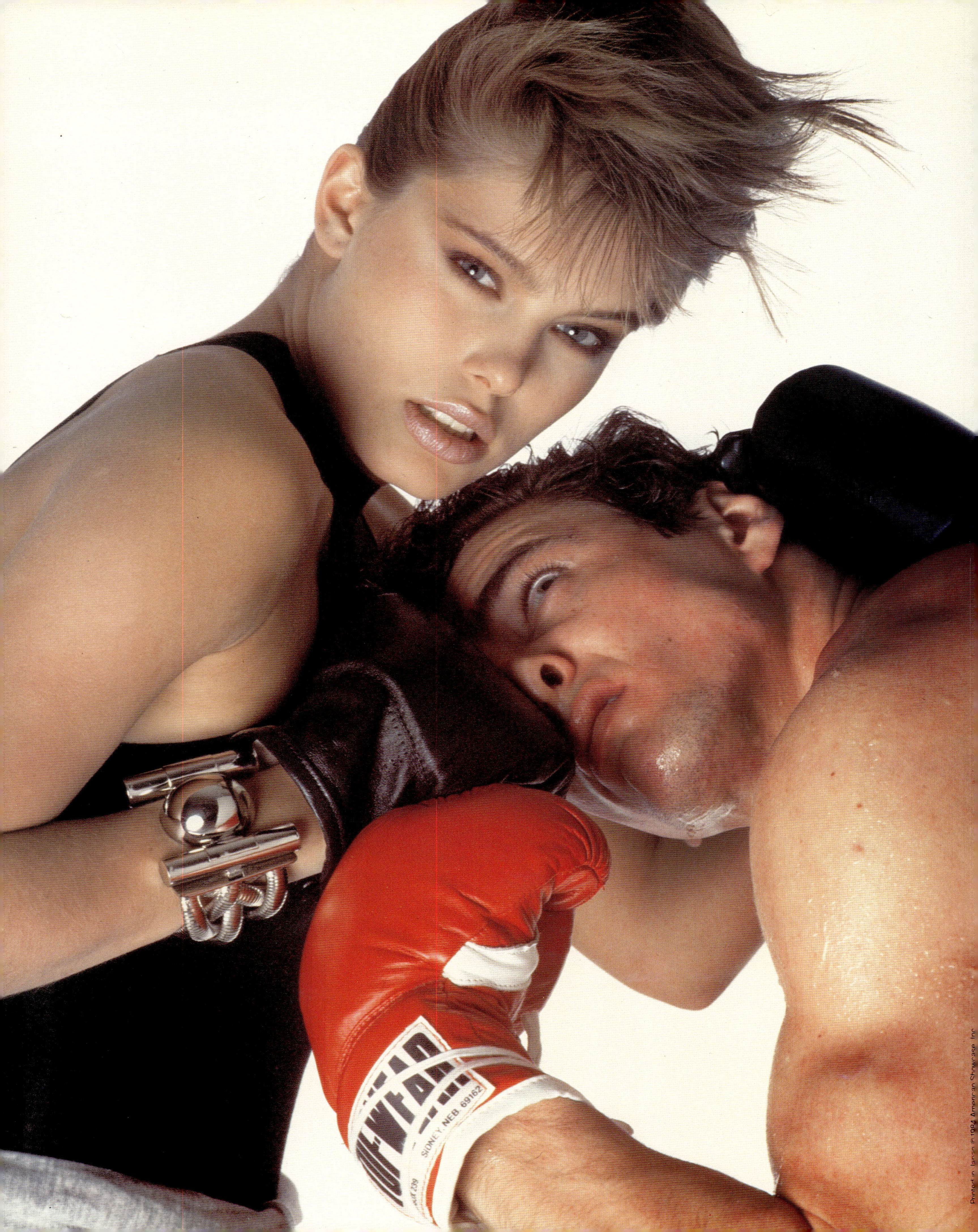
SIDNEY, NEB. 69162

# Bert Stern

**Seeing and Feeling:
An Interview with Bert Stern**
by Amy Schiffman ©1983

**AS:** Were you always interested in photography?

**BS:** When I was in school I didn't think about photography. Guys who took pictures had big cameras and talked loud and later got to smoke cigars. After high school, when I was working in the mailroom at LOOK, I began to see pictures in magazines that opened up a whole new world of ideas in my mind.

**AS:** How did you go from mailroom boy to professional photographer?

**BS:** At LOOK I met Herschel Bramson who was an art director there. I worked as his assistant at various times, and when I got out of the army, he offered me a job to assist him in designing the original Smirnoff campaign.

**AS:** Were you taking pictures at the time?

**BS:** I was, but just for myself. I looked on photography as something very special. It was like being in love and having a record of it, and I had made up my mind never to do it for money.

**AS:** How then did you manage to become one of the world's most celebrated commercial photographers?

Photograph at left by Bert Stern. Courtesy VOGUE. Copyright © 1983 The Condé Nast Publications.

**BS:** I had helped design the Smirnoff campaign, and the photographers who were being considered either said it was impossible to do or wanted to shoot it in the studio. We had layouts and a concept, but we wanted real pictures. So Bramson asked me if I thought I could do it, and it was an opportunity I couldn't pass up. So I went off to the desert with a camera and a car and props and film, and I struggled with it and learned photography, as they say, in the field.

**AS:** You make it sound so easy.

**BS:** It wasn't that simple. In fact, the optical aspect was so complex that I really felt I wasn't going to get it. But I worked slowly and kept at it. I didn't give myself a two-hour deadline. I actually spent a good part of a week working on that picture.

**AS:** How did you pull off such a difficult picture with no formal experience in photography?

**BS:** The fact that I knew nothing worked to my advantage. It allowed me to create a kind of clarity that someone with more visual training might have thought too elementary. I've always tried to maintain that kind of simple direct relationship with my subject and felt that if I could see something, I could take a picture of it. I just put the camera in front of my eyes and take a picture, and the picture turns out to be what I see.

**AS:** That notion may be baffling to some people. Can you elaborate on how you establish that "relationship?"

**BS:** Photography is a highly instinctual process: You have to use your intuitive side in order to find the many wonderful opportunities out there in front of your camera. For me, it has always seemed that there is a force following me around, making sure that the pictures came out the way it wanted them, not so much the way I wanted them. If I felt stumped by a photograph, I would just start to laugh, or sit down and relax for a while and wait for an idea to come, or something to happen. If I was chased from a location, instead of being disappointed, I would think "OK, where can I shoot?" They would send me someplace wonderful. It wasn't that they were yelling at me, it's that I was shooting in the wrong place, and some great opportunity would be right around the corner. In photography, you can plan, but you also have to be open and be able to plan as you go along.

**AS:** Can you give me a specific example of that principle at work? Such as when you photographed Marilyn Monroe?

**BS:** I think Monroe was a good example of that. At first I said, "Wow, I just want to look at her," and as much as I had planned everything to the hilt, every picture became a happening. There was no way I was going to tell her what to do—it just occurred. I think that spontaneity is in the pictures and makes them alive.

**AS:** But Monroe was a very unusual subject.

**BS:** Yes, and photographing her was a challenge, but the challenge was two-sided. She had tremendous feelings about what she did, she worked it her own way, but she brought as much energy to it as I did, maybe even more. She may have come late, but once she was there, she was really there. She was a sensitive human being, who wanted to get so much out of every-

continued on page 30

# Deborah Turbeville

**Turbeville on Turbeville**

I think photography has to do with the individual photographer. It's almost a portrait of the photographer. I would say in personality I'm like the women in my photographs—a little bit anxious and spooked and insecure. In certain ways out of balance with my times.

Perhaps the most interesting thing about my work is that it's a little bit of an enigma; it's hard to place. Perhaps it's done for the wrong medium. I like the idea of making images that are cinematic, or like book illustrations—photographs that evoke a mood. Environments take me over. When I work, there is never very much conversation. It's quiet and still. And we all seem to get involved. I walk around and the women just sort of look around, and turn, and move. And I just say "continue." When you're very quiet something else takes over. Unfamiliar environments can have an almost spellbinding effect if you are drawn to them as I am.

There isn't a very fast pace to my work. I don't even work every day. There is time between jobs to think and take it easy. My work evolves slowly, because I like to look at things and have them around awhile. I'm not the kind of photographer who's always wanting to take my camera out. I almost have to have assignments. I often go for long periods of time without photographing. I just look, observe and watch…

I work best with found things. The most surreal looking things are things that exist in life, and that's why I've always been drawn toward Paris. Paris looks like a series of sets. Much of the time it's hard to believe it's not a set. You have this in downtown New York. The buildings look like theater sets. I love set design, but I don't happen to work well with it. There's no spontaneity…I always try to leave an open point for things that come up that are interesting and are not planned, because if you limit yourself to what you've planned, sometimes you miss something incredible. You have to be open…

My first attempt to do a photographer essay was for a small magazine no longer in existence. I was to photograph the prêt-à-porter collections of several French designers, so we decided it would be fun to do a girl on a holiday in clothes that would attract attention. It was 1966—all the girls were in short skirts. We went to towns that were rather restrictive, like Dubrovnik in Yugoslavia. You didn't see many young women walking down that street in miniskirts. We wanted to show what a girl does on her own when she goes on holiday—a modern, contemporary girl who has some interest in clothes. What would she do with people following her, staring at her, with men picking her up? What accidents would happen?—We just played with that. We let her wander through the streets and sit in cafés, and we would stand around, take pictures and watch. But there was a definite theme. We were placing her in specific places to see what would happen to her. It became like a film. That's the quality I look for in film making. It's a mood, a mystery, a sense of surrealism. Of all the mediums, I would say I have been influenced by film the most.

I was once asked by a French magazine to do a series of pictures with models interpreting a certain designer. I was told I could do what I wanted, but it had to be about death. So I went to a glass factory, and I did the pictures. I liked them very much and turned them in. But the magazine wasn't satisfied because it wasn't clear how the girls died. So we had to go back and put pieces of glass by the girls' wrists. I felt the art director had missed the point. He should hire photographers for what they are. For me it was an enigma how the girls died. He missed the whole point of his own assignment, and of me, and what I would bring to it…

Because of my experience as an editor at *Harper's Bazaar*, certain art directors trust me. At *Mademoiselle* and *Vogue* I was allowed to work as an editor and photographer on my own assignments. They would say, "Well, you have an idea, you take the clothes and go out and photograph them."… The girls I use are not perfect. They are much more personal looking than most of the models you see. They're not slick-looking girls…

My way has been to stick to what I believe in, and what I want to do, and not compromise it. That's the way I work. My style was so well evolved by the time I became a professional that it was impossible for me to compromise it. When it comes to being successful, I do think it's important to learn about yourself, learn about what you want to do with a camera, and develop it strongly in your way. Certainly, the more it develops your way, the more definite it will be, and the more attention you can expect to get from it—and interest.

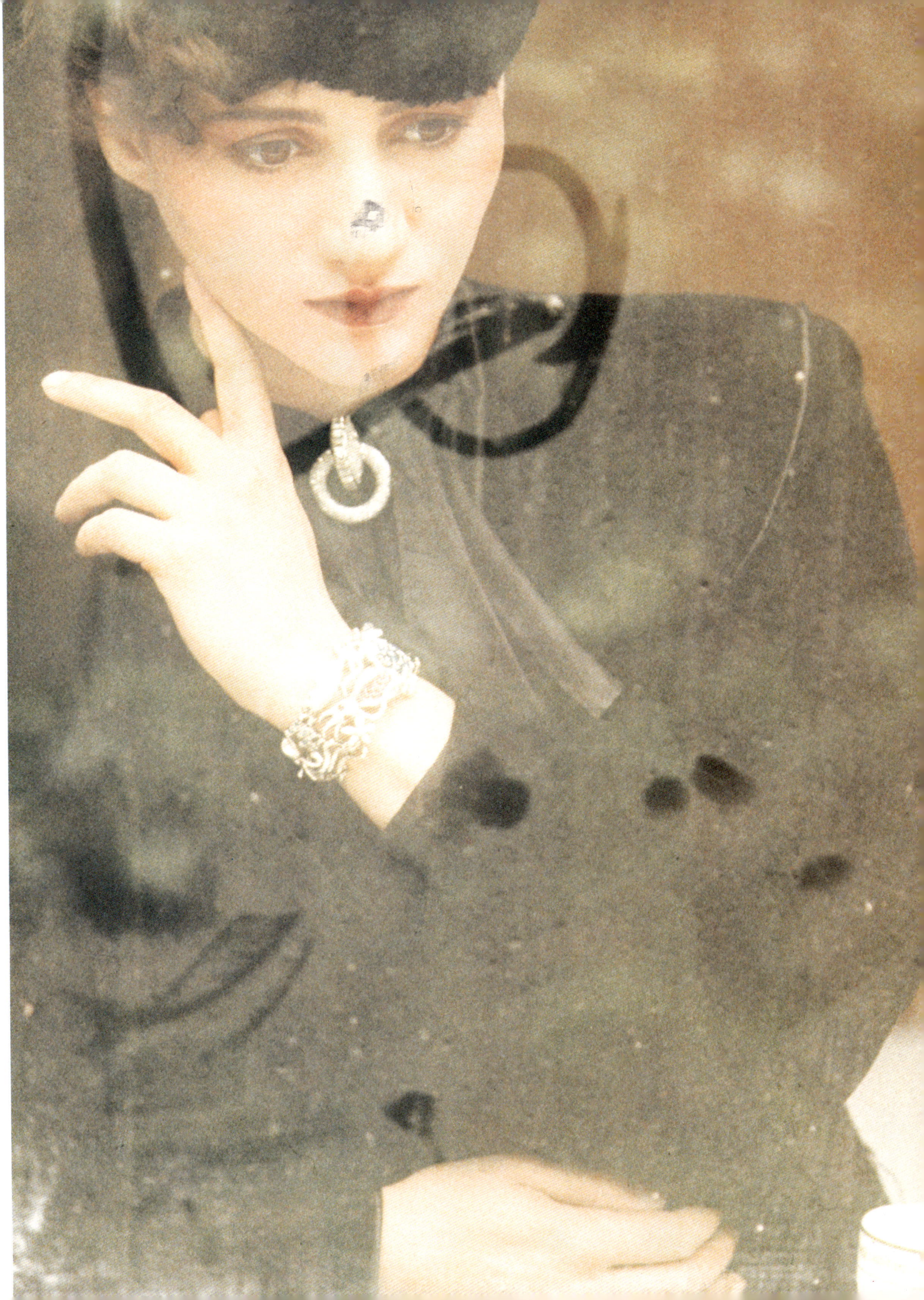

continued from page 27

**thing she did. She was a really creative human being.**

**AS:** But you were really interested in Monroe. What about someone you've never met before. How do you go about photographing them?

**BS:** Well, it's possible to love a stranger. I sometimes seduce myself into being in love with a person while I'm photographing them. Especially with fashion. A beautiful girl comes into the room, and she's all yours, to talk to, to light, to photograph...it's a short relationship, but it's intimate. You can make it as intimate as you like.

**AS:** But can a model bring as much to a shoot as someone like Monroe?

**BS:** A great model isn't just beautiful. She knows how to use herself, how to respond, how to trust the photographer.

**AS:** Is there a difference between photographing people and photographing things?

**BS:** With people, things can happen. They can change in front of the camera, their emotions and expressions can be affected by the light or can affect the light. With an object, you have to use the light to make the appearance change. Dripping water would be more interesting than just the bottle, because it's moving and you catch it. If you were photographing a rock, the first thing that would come to mind is a shadow—the rock could block the light. Or you could look at the texture of the rock or create a sense of locale. Something that's totally static, like a rock, you have to light, and work with, so that its power comes from the environment.

**AS:** The ability to make a rock interesting is a rare talent. Do you think that your degree of creativity is common?

**BS:** It's natural to be creative. A lot of people are not creative simply because they don't allow themselves to be. When you're creative, you're natural. You feel normal and alive, because life is a creative experience. People block their creative channels by worrying, by being nervous, by doubting themselves, by not pleasing themselves, or trying to please others at the expense of themselves.

**AS:** Is making a picture pleasing to you?

**BS:** Making pictures feels good. I think I learned that when I was on my first assignment. I was having a lot of trouble the first couple of days. Being in Egypt where it was hot was not as easy as being in New York dreaming about the pyramids. About the fourth day something happened that made me feel good, I felt I got something, and sure enough, that picture won an award. I've always felt that if I please myself when I take a picture, I'm pleasing you. If I'm unhappy, you're bound to be unhappy with the picture.

**AS** Is taking pictures satisfying?

**BS:** Taking a picture is a different experience than anything else. It's very satisfying, but in other ways it's frustrating. I think painting a picture would be more satisfying, because it's longer and slower. Photography's very fast, but it gives you instant gratification.

**AS:** What about lasting gratification?

**BS:** It's rare that you get a picture you really love. But when you do, every time you look at it, you get a little touch of instant gratification. I find that if I do a picture I really like, I come back to it later and still like it.

**AS:** You began your career in the sixties, when photography was flourishing. Is photography a creative medium today?

**BS:** I think the nature of photography in our electronic age is important, because photography is the base, or the clay, that everything is made out of. Photographers are the eyes of the public, or the eyes of the art director. And that's a very interesting—and creative—job, being someone's eyes. Photography is visual, and the visual world is what we all share.

**AS:** Does your work reflect changes that have taken place in the world since you began photographing?

**BS:** I'm trying to make better pictures, which is hard, because the better picture is the simpler picture, to a great extent. I work at it, and every now and then I get close to it. I think a good example is the girl wearing the bracelet punching the guy out. It reflects the fact that today women are fighting back, have fought back, and there is a perennial battle between the sexes.

**AS:** What aspect of your photography transcends fashion and current events?

**BS:** Photography can be a reflection of the greatness of life, the majesty of life, the divineness of life, and so, in its many ways, photography is a very spiritual experience. But it's also simple, a marvelously simple idea that can go beyond clichés. A picture can express what is contemporary—or what is classical, like the look of love between two people. Things that are always being reborn, like flowers. We see a zillion flowers in our lives, then we see another gorgeous rose—and we gasp!

| Name | Page |
|---|---|
| Mulligan, Joseph | 32 |
| Bartone, Laurence | 33 |
| Elkins, Joel | 34 |
| Hedrich, David | 35 |
| Mervar, Louis | 36,37 |
| Aubry, Daniel | 38 |
| Standart, Joe | 39 |
| Rusing, Rick | 40,41 |
| Wilcox, Shorty | 42,43 |
| Photofile International, Ltd. | 44,45 |
| Ochi | 46 |
| Alexander, Jules | 47 |
| Allen, Jim | 48 |
| Alt, Howard | 49 |
| Aubry, Daniel | 38 |
| Baker, Joe | 50 |
| Barrow, Scott | 51 |
| Bartone, Laurence | 33 |
| Beaudin, Ted | 52 |
| Berkun, Phil | 53 |
| Bevilacqua | 54 |
| Bezushko | 55 |
| Byers, Bruce | 56 |
| Cadge, Bill | 57 |
| Cannon, Gregory | 58 |
| Cantor, Phil | 59 |
| Carroll, Don | 60,61 |
| Certo, Rosemarie | 63 |
| Clifford, Geoffrey C. | 64,65 |
| Clough, Terry | 66,67 |
| Cook, Irvin | 68 |
| Crane, Tom | 69 |
| DeLessio, Len | 70 |
| D'Innocenzo, Paul | 71 |
| Dunn, Phoebe | 72 |
| Dunoff, Rich | 73 |
| Elkins, Joel | 34 |
| Elmore, Steve | 75 |
| Fishbein, Chuck | 76,77 |
| Fishman, Chuck | 78 |
| Flatow, Carl | 79 |
| Forelli, Chip | 81 |
| Francekevich, Al | 82,83 |
| Fraser, Douglas | 85 |
| Funk, Mitchell | 86,87 |
| Furman, Michael | 88,89 |
| Giese, Al | 91 |
| Gladstone, Gary | 92,93 |
| Gordon, Joel | 95 |
| Green-Armytage, Stephen | 96,97 |
| Greenberg, David | 98 |
| Gscheidle, Gerhard | 99 |
| Harrington, Phillip A. | 100 |
| Harris, Brownie | 101 |
| Hashi | 102,103 |
| Haviland, Brian | 104 |
| Hedrich, David | 35 |
| Horowitz, Ryszard | 105 |
| Joern, James | 106 |
| Johansky, Peter | 107 |
| Kalfus, Lonny | 108 |
| Kaplan, Peter B. | 109 |
| Kent, Karen | 110 |
| Korsh, Ken | 111 |
| Landsman, Gary D. | 112,113 |
| Lane, Whitney | 114 |
| Leeds, Karen | 115 |
| Leighton, Thomas | 116,117 |
| Lerner, Richard | 104 |
| Leung, Jook | 118 |
| Luria, Dick | 119 |
| Marchese, Jim | 120,121 |
| Maresca, Frank | 122,123 |
| Marshall, Lee | 124 |
| Martin, Butch | 125 |
| McGrail, John | 126 |
| Mellor, D.W. | 127 |
| Meola, Eric | 128-133 |
| Mervar, Louis | 36,37 |
| Miller, Donald L. | 134,135 |
| Mulligan, Joseph | 32 |
| Munson, Russell | 136 |
| Musto, Tom | 137 |
| Myers Studios, Inc. | 138 |
| Nadelson, Jay | 139 |
| Nathan, Simon | 141 |
| Obremski, George | 142,143 |
| Ochi | 46 |
| Orenstein, Ronn | 144 |
| Palmer, Gabe | 145 |
| Parik, Jan | 146 |
| Peacock, Christian | 147 |
| Peltz, Stuart | 148 |
| Photofile International, Ltd. | 44,45 |
| Photoscope | 149 |
| Pottle, Jock | 150 |
| Powers, Guy | 151-156 |
| Pribula, Barry | 157 |
| Rezny, Aaron | 159 |
| Rizzo, Alberto | 160 |
| Rosner, Eric H. | 161 |
| Roth, Peter | 162 |
| Rusing, Rick | 40,41 |
| Rysinski, Edward | 163 |
| Sandone, A J | 164 |
| Shore, Stephen | 165 |
| Simpson, Jerry | 166 |
| Skalski, Ken | 167 |
| Smith, Gordon E. | 168 |
| Smith, William Edward | 169 |
| Smyth, T. Kevin | 170 |
| Sochurek, Howard | 171 |
| Sööt, Olaf | 173 |
| Standart, Joe | 39 |
| Stratos, Jim | 174,175 |
| Strongin, Jeanne | 176 |
| Stuart, John | 177 |
| Stuart, Stephen | 179 |
| Tcherevkoff, Michel | 180,181 |
| Togashi | 183 |
| Waine, Michael | 184,185 |
| Watson, H. Ross | 187 |
| Weidman, H. Mark | 188,189 |
| Weigand, Tom | 190 |
| Weinberg, Michael | 191 |
| Weitz, Allan | 192 |
| West, Charles | 193 |
| Wick, Walter | 194,195 |
| Wilcox, Shorty | 42,43 |
| Zenreich, Alan | 196 |

NEW YORK CITY

JOSEPH MULLIGAN
239 CHESTNUT STREET
PHILADELPHIA, PA 19106
215 592-1359

LAURENCE BARTONE STUDIO 20 EAST 20th ST. NEW YORK NY 10003 212·254·6430

# BARTONE
### PHOTOGRAPHY

# joel elkins

**5 EAST 16 ST., N.Y., N.Y. 10003**
**989-4500**

# DAVID HEDRICH

7E. 17th St. New York 10003 (212) 924-3324
Represented By Barbara Gordon

Partial Client List: AT&T, Alka-Seltzer, Amaretto di Saronno, American Airlines, American Express, American Tourister, Aunt Jemima, Avon, Ban, Beefeaters, Best Foods, Bell System, Bird's Eye, Brim, Buitoni, Bulova, Canada Dry, Champale, Charles of the Ritz, Chivas Regal, Citibank, Clairol, Cling Free, Close-up, Coca Cola, Colgate-Palmolive, Cosmopolitan, Cunard, Dunhill, Dynamo, El-Al, Essence, Exxon, Family Circle, Finnair, GTE, General Electric, General Foods, General Mills, General Tire, Good Seasons, Goodyear, Gorton's Clams, Gordon's Gin, Monsieur Henri Wines Ltd., Hershey's, Heublein, Imperial Margarine, Inver House Scotch, Jean Naté, J&B Scotch, Ken-L-Ration, Knirps, Ladies Home Journal, Lanvin, Lever Bros., Lord Calvert, Luden's, M&M/Mars, MCA Video, Macleans, Martini & Rossi, Matchabelli, Maxell, Maxim, Maxwell House, Mazola, Mennen, Myers Rum, Minute-Maid, Mobil, NAPA, Nice'n Easy, Noilly Prat, Orange-plus, Ore Ida, Owens-Corning, Pan Am, Passport Scotch, Penthouse, Pepsi Cola, Playtex, Polaroid, Prell, Prestone, Procter & Gamble, Progresso, Puss'n Boots, Quaker Oats, RCA, Ralston Purina, ReaLemon, Revlon, Royal Canadian, Helena Rubinstein, SCM, Safeguard Soap, Sansui, Sara Lee, Savin Copiers, Sharp, Schaefer Beer, Schenley, Schick, Scope, Seagram's, Sears, Sony, Speidel, Spray'n Vac, Squibb, Standard Brands, Sucrets, Swift & Co., Sylvania, TDK, Texaco, Time-Life, Uniroyal, Vick's NyQuill, Vitabath, Volkswagon, Johnny Walker, Welch's, Western Electric, Western Union, Woman's Day.

© David Hedrich 1984

## LOUIS MERVAR STUDIO
## 29 WEST 38 STREET, NEW YORK, NEW YORK 10018   212-354-8024

*Representative: Susan Moss*
*Portfolio on request*

Member ASMP © 1983 Louis Mervar

LES INDULGENCES

Individually, these six photographs are strong, effective print ads of top quality, high priced merchandise which not only sell one featured item, but all the merchandise which define the ambience of each photograph.

Then, as a group, these six print ads tell a story of a couple's romantic liaison as each photograph captures a particular "moment-in-time." We follow this "unseen" couple from a late afternoon lunch to an evening champagne toast at a Country Inn outside Paris.

*Concept Team:*
  *Barbara Borejko, 212-308-9362 &*
  *Alexandra Self, 212-794-1466*
*Photographer: Louis Mervar*
*Art Director & Producer: Barbara Borejko*
*Copywriter: Alexandra Self*
*Stylist & Co-Producer: Nora Lee*
*Project Co-ordinator: Joan Borejko*
*Chrome retoucher: Iva Mervar*
*Men & Women's Jewelry — Gold & Silver*
  *Accessories: Cartier, New York*
*Bed & Table Linens: Porthault, New York*
*Malachite Counter with Washbasin and*
  *Bath Accessories:*
    *Sherle Wagner, New York*
*Room Sets & All Other Merchandise:*
  *Bloomingdales' New York*

**1.** SHE: You've made me look so beautiful!
HE: I can't take all the credit...not with that face and this pen!

**4.** HE: What do you call that silk underthing?
SHE: A camisole, why? You like?
HE: Mmmm, I like!

2. HER: Madame, your rings...trés elegante. Oh, don't forget them.
SHE: I could never forget these rings!

3. SHE: These sheets are going to feel so gorgeous!
HE: We're wasting time.

5. SHE: You're still wearing that beautiful watch I gave you.
HE: I can't get along without it...or you!

6. SHE: Sweetheart, please pour me another glass of champagne, I'm just starving!

# EXPECT THE UNEXPECTED

**DANIEL AUBRY-PHOTOGRAPHER** 365 FIRST AVENUE
NEW YORK, NEW YORK 10010 212 598-4191

EDWARD DE BONO BY DANIEL AUBRY © 1983 DANIEL AUBRY

Joe STANDART
5 West 19th St.
New York City 10011
Rep: Allison Mitchell
(212) 924-4545

1 COINTREAU:
  INTERMARCO ADVERTISING
2 KARASTAN:
  ALLY GARGANO
3 TARKETT FLOORING:
  SCALI McCABE SLOVES
4 SPRINGMAID:
  WOLFF WHITEHILL
5 GENERAL ELECTRIC:
  BBD&O

JENNIFER CLARK, DESIGN

**ON LOCATION**
Complex Lighting
**ON LOCATION**
People, Products
And Experiences
**ON LOCATION**
Rick Rusing

RUSING PHOTOGRAPHY

Kona Coast of Hawaii for American Hawaii Cruises.

Wind tunnel in Wolfsburg, Germany for the new Audi 5000S.

**RICK RUSING
RUSING PHOTOGRAPHY, INC.**

Phoenix, Arizona
(602) **967-1864**

All photos unretouched

212 246-6367

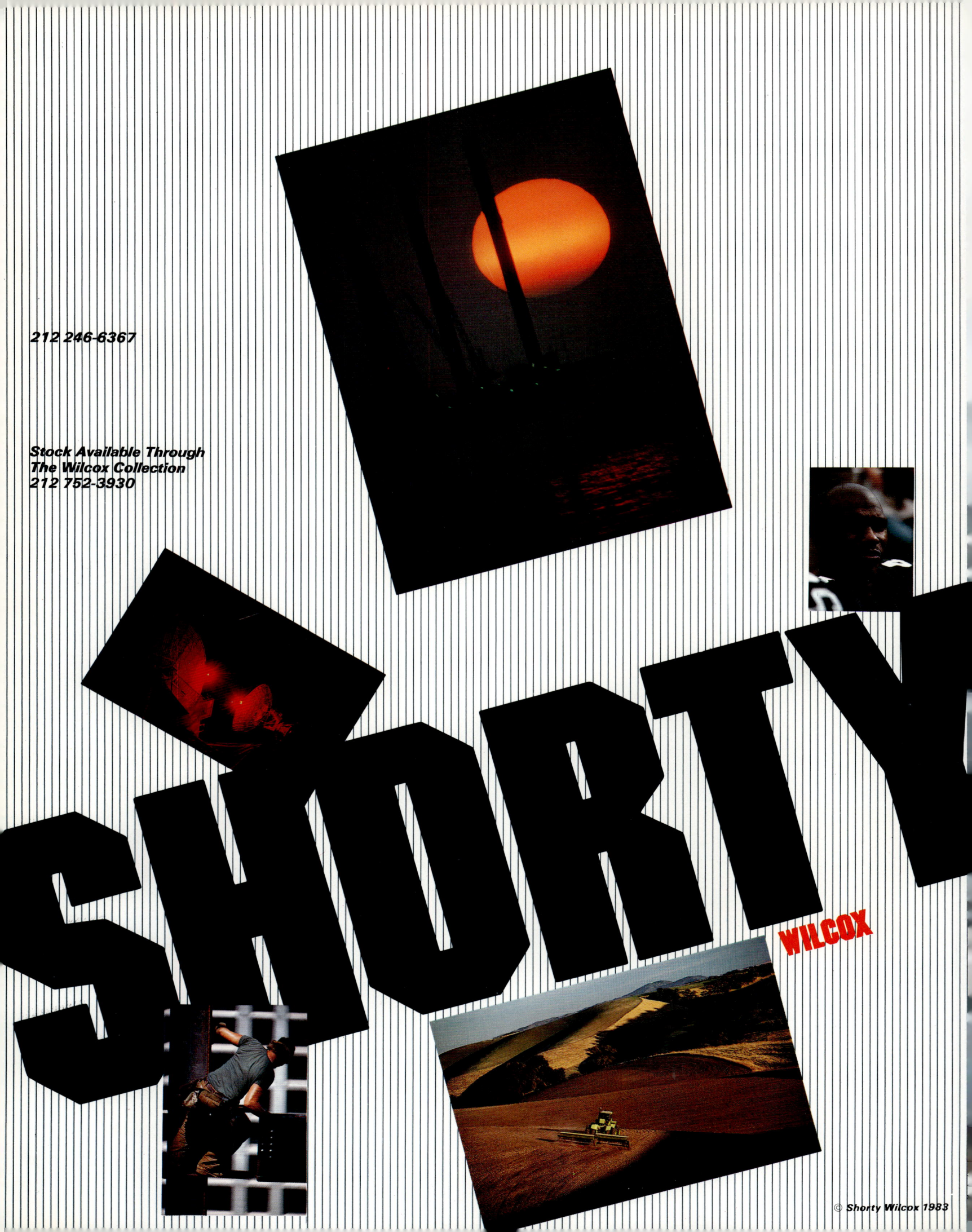

Stock Available Through
The Wilcox Collection
212 752-3930

# SHORTY
**WILCOX**

© *Shorty Wilcox 1983*

# SHORTY WILCOX

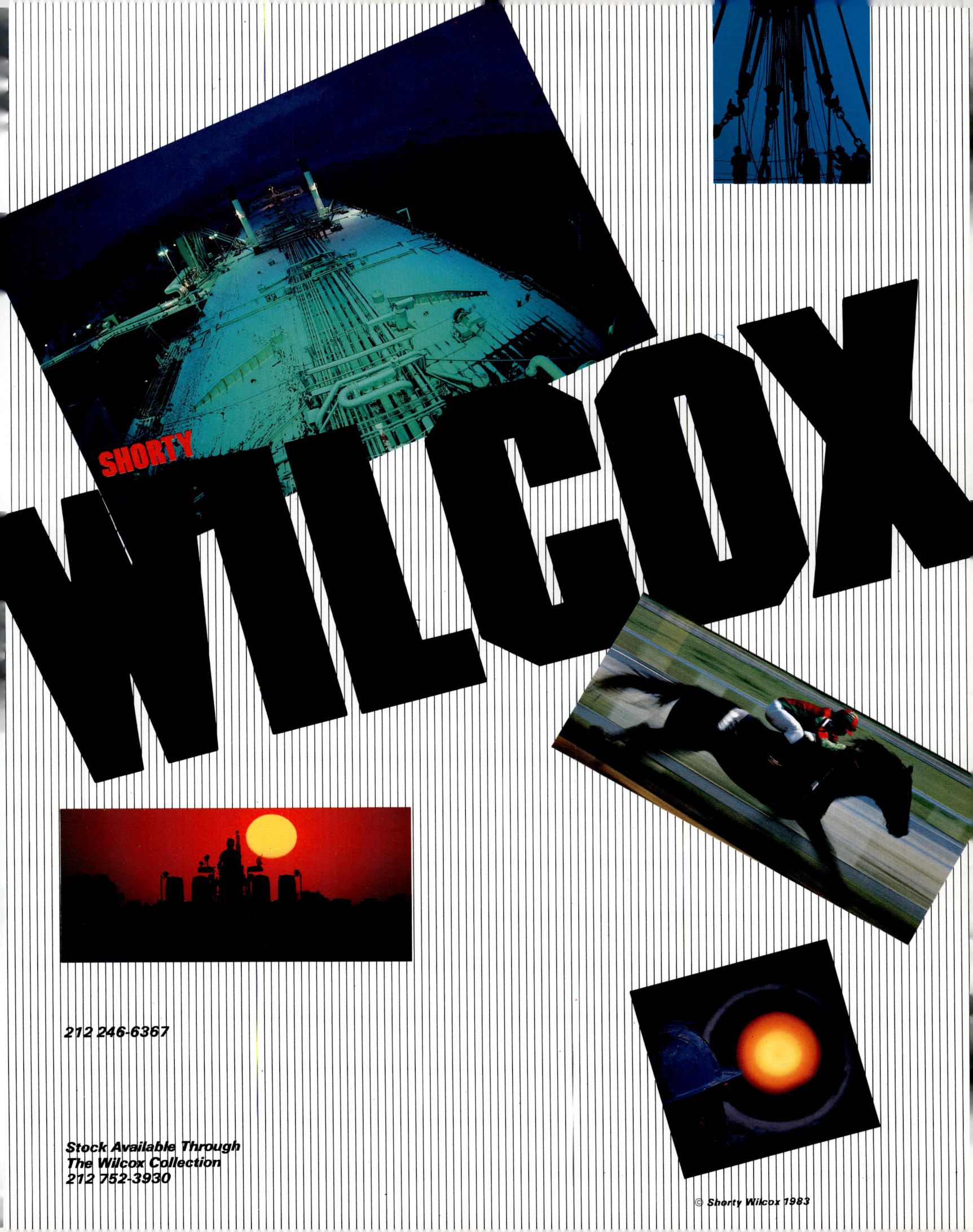

212 246-6367

Stock Available Through
The Wilcox Collection
212 752-3930

© Shorty Wilcox 1983

# photofile

### international ltd.

# HERE'S A GLIMPSE

**—— And our Catalogs are a glimpse from our files ——**
*750,000 of the finest images on Earth.* Not just pretty pictures, but photographs that *work*, that do the job. That's why, since 1975, people who call for stock, call PHOTOFILE first.

©1983, PHOTOFILE INTERNATIONAL, LTD.

# FROM OUR CATALOGS

Are you up-to-date with our free, full color Catalogs?
If not, just let us know. We'll send you one. Free.

**PHOTOFILE**
32 East 31 Street
New York, NY 10016

**TOLL FREE: (800) 225-2727**
IN NEW YORK: (212) 989-0500

# OCHI

636 6th Ave. N.Y.C. 10011
(212) 807-7711

Represented By
Terry DaGrosa

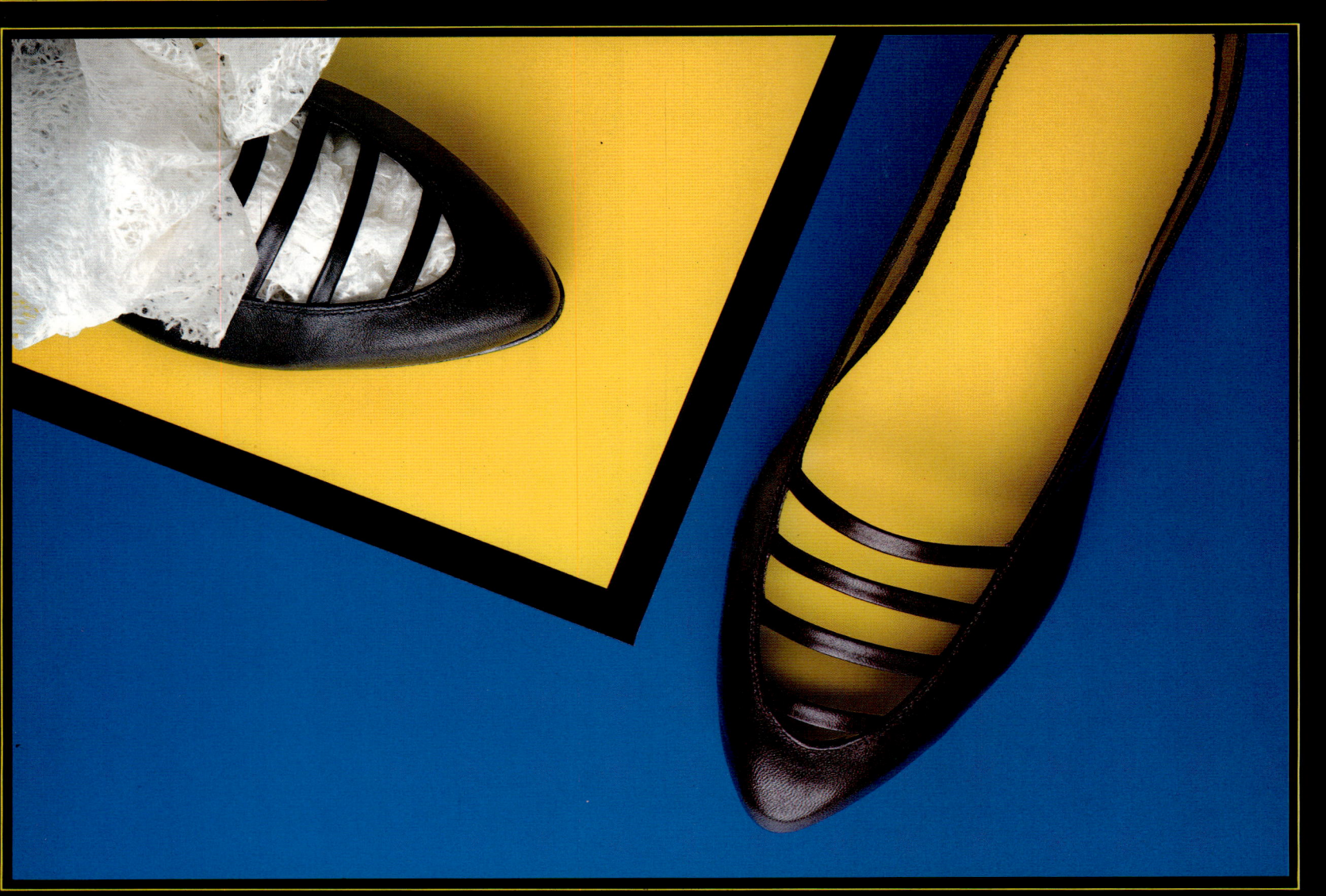

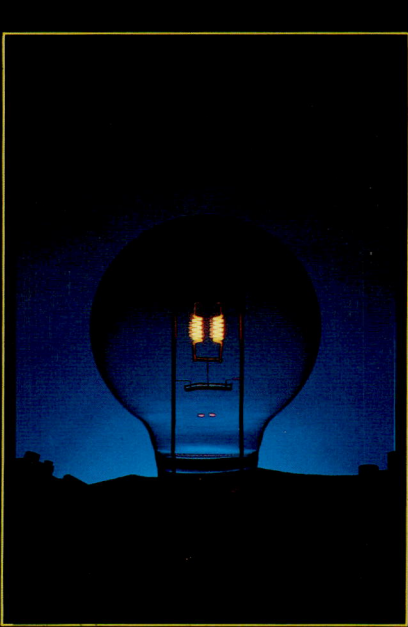

**JULES ALEXANDER**
(212) 533-3150; (914) 967-8985

A special directorial ability and a dedication to the photography of people.

Years of experience with major advertising agencies, major magazines, and Fortune 500 clients.

Brochure and client list on request.

**JIM ALLEN**
Represented by Alexis Dickinson
21 East 22nd Street
New York, New York 10010
(212) 473-8020

Fifteen years of fashion merchandising and marketing lie behind
Jim Allen's confident grasp of fashion photography.

48

**HOWARD ALT**
24 West 31st Street
New York, New York 10001
(212) 594-3300

Represented by: Chris Conroy
(212) 598-9766

Partial Client List: Atari, CBS, Clairol, Coca-Cola, Drambuie, GTE, Milk-Bones, Norelco, Old Smuggler Whisky, Parliament, Passport Scotch, Polaroid, Timex, True.

All Photographs © Howard Alt 1983

49

SELF PROMOTION

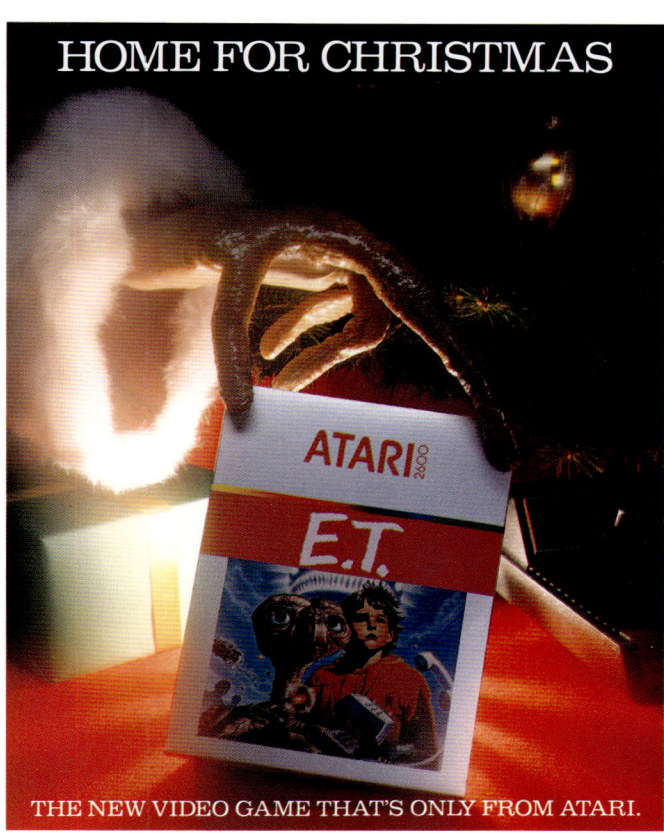

JAY MORALES/DOYLE DANE BERNBACH, INC.

PAUL MAURER/DOYLE DANE BERNBACH, INC.

SELF PROMOTION

**JOE BAKER**
156 Fifth Avenue, Studio 925
New York, New York 10010
(212) 924-3440
Northwest Connecticut
Studio: (203) 824-7942

Medical & industrial advertising photography for American & foreign clients: includes: *Medical World News, Contemporary Surgery, Newsweek, New York Times,* DuPont, Carrier, Sony, Allied Chemical, Bank of New York, Ronson, Ohaus, Superior Cable, GAB, Research-Cottrell, Goodyear, Texaco, GAF, Leitz, ADT, Ayerst Laboratories, JVC, Armour Pharmaceutical Co., Zeiss.

Medical Stock Available.

Portfolio on Request.
See page 15, American Showcase 6

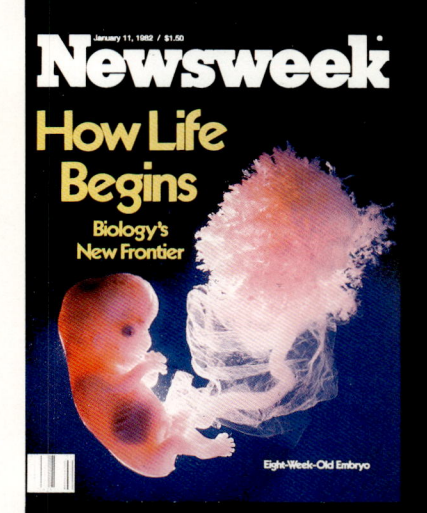

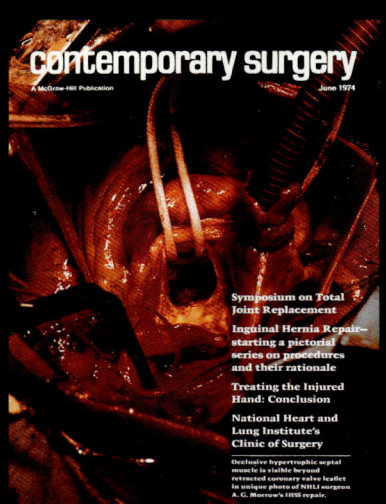

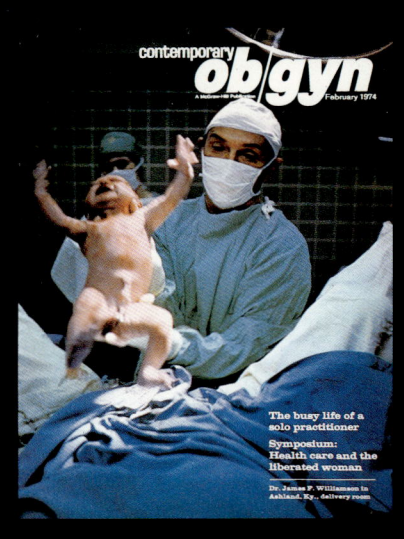

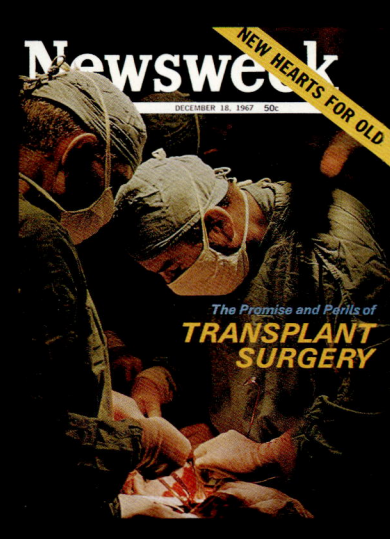

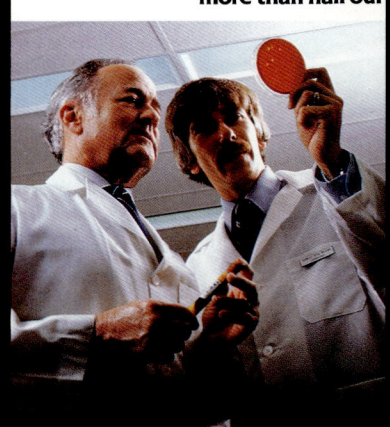

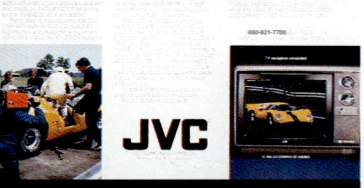

**JOE BAKER   (212) 924-3440**

**SCOTT BARROW**
214 West 30th Street
New York, New York 10001
Studio: (212) 736-4567

Color and Black & White photography for Travel, Advertising and Corporate (See Showcase 6) accounts. Stock available.

Clients: Yes.

# BARROW

**TED BEAUDIN
PHOTOGRAPHER**
6 West 37th Street
New York, New York 10018
(212) 683-5480
(212) 594-4082

Represented in New England
By Kimble Kenney, Studio
Manager, Hartford Studio
(203) 232-6198

Member ASMP

All photos ©1983 Ted Beaudin

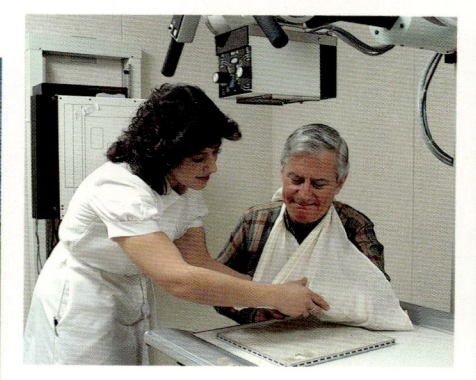

**PHIL BERKUN**
179 Columbia Heights
Brooklyn Heights, New York 11201
(212) 596-0294

All photographs below © 1983 Phil Berkun.

The simplest statement of my service to you: vision.

Insight and imagination to solve your visual problems.
And the ability to bring out the extraordinary in the ordinary.
Specializing in corporate public relations and annual reports,
Illustration, travel and advertising.

I can see things your way.

53

ASMP

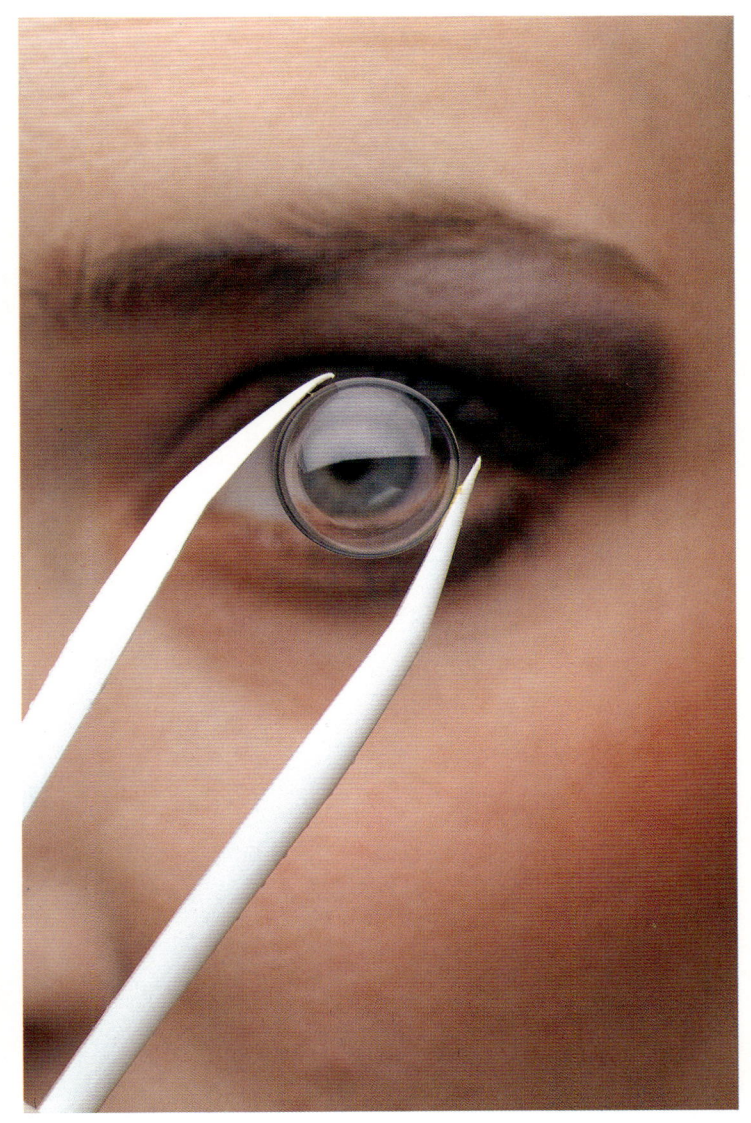

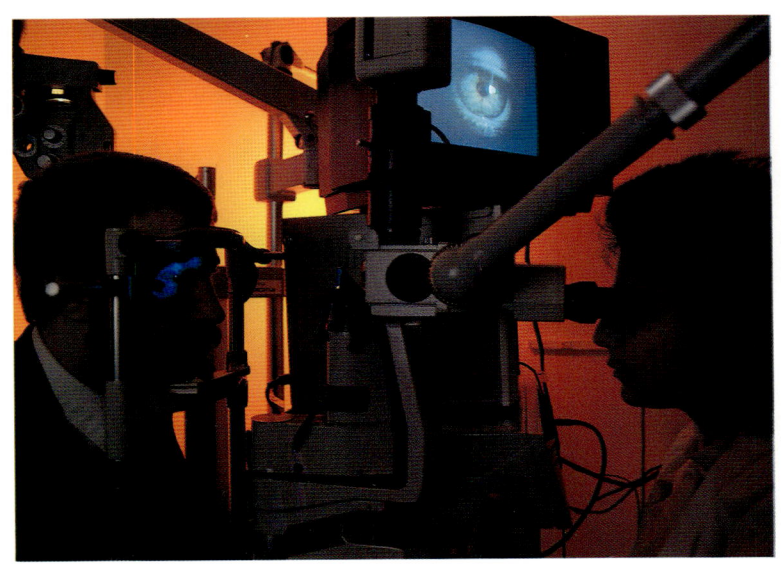

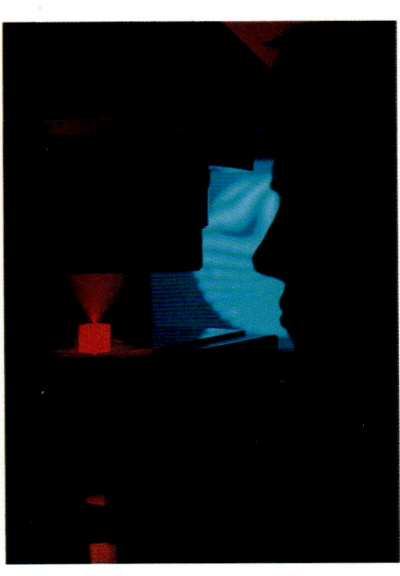

**BEVILACQUA**
202 East 42nd Street
New York, New York 10017
(212) 490-0355

ASMP, APA

In the beginning,
it was all here.
But we didn't know.
We weren't aware
of the wonder,
the majesty.
Until there was light.
A light which shone
to illuminate all.
And all that existed
could be seen
and appreciated
in its splendor.

An object.
With light
one is aware
of its presence,
its being.
But then there is lighting.
And the object
is illuminated.
It shines.
Its every nuance
defined.
Bathed.
In lighting.
Bevilacqua's lighting.
And for the object.
for our appreciation,
this makes all the difference
in the world.

*And Bevilacqua said, "Let There Be Lighting..."*

**BEZUSHKO**
1311 Irving Street
Philadelphia, Pennsylvania 19107
(215) 735-7771

George Bezushko, photographer

Bob Bezushko, photographer

**BRUCE BYERS**
11 West 20th Street
New York, New York 10011
(212) 242-5846

Partial list of clients includes:
Fashion Magazines; Foote, Cone & Belding; Kelly Advertising; Oscar de la Renta; Dr. Scholls; *W Magazine;* American Express; Woolrich; Eisenman & Enock.

For more examples of my work, see American Showcase Volumes 5 and 6; then give me a call.

**BILL & JEFF CADGE**
15 West 28th Street
New York, New York 10001
(212) 685-2435

Representative: Rita Carty

Specializing in people and children illustration.

Clients include: J.W. Thompson, SSC&B, N.W. Ayer, M.C.A., Johnson & Johnson, United Technologies, American Maize Products, Ciba-Geigy, Paramount Pictures, Warner Communications, *McCall's,* Bantam, *Parents.*

Stock: The Image Bank

Members A.S.M.P.

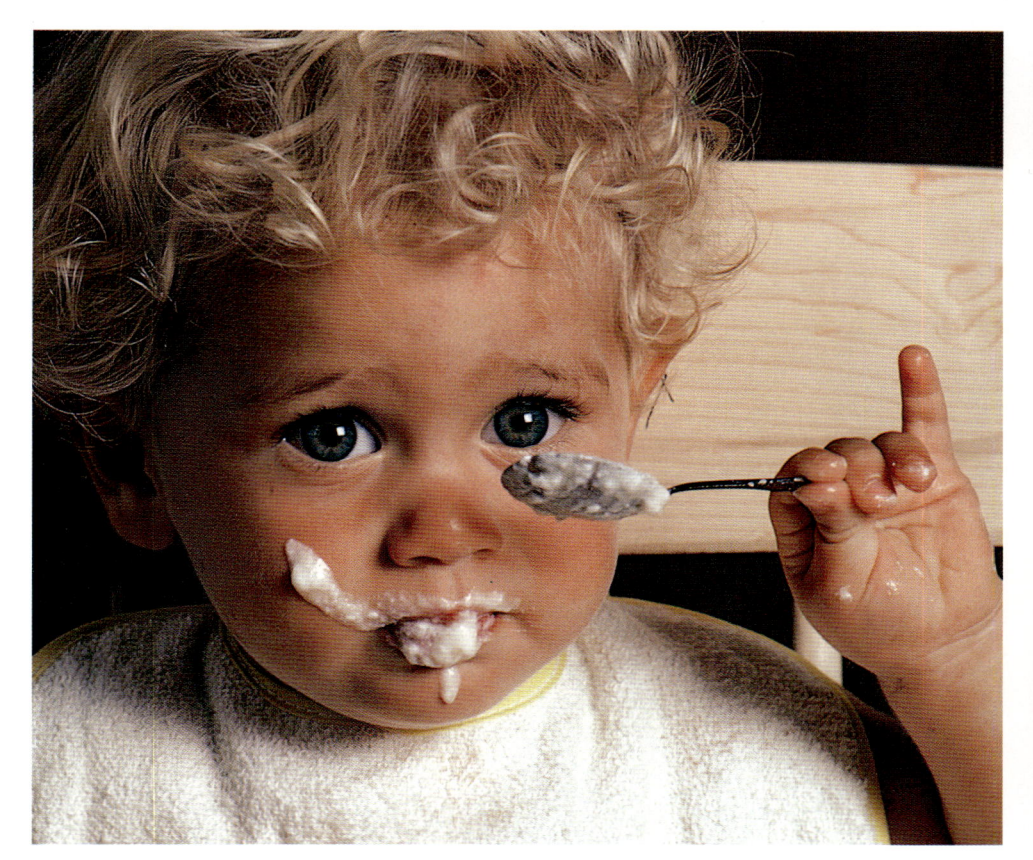

**GREGORY CANNON**
876 Broadway
New York, New York 10003
(212) 228-3190

Still life photography

Clients include: AT&T, Jacques Jugeat, Gloria Vanderbilt Handbags, Stepan, Pierre Cardin, Albert Nipon, Royal Silk, Hart Shafner Marx, Bergdorf Goodman, Emporium-Capwell, Bride's Magazine, Mademoiselle Magazine, Fashion Accessories Magazine, Luggage & Travelware Magazine.

**PHIL CANTOR**
75 Ninth Avenue
New York, New York 10011
(212) 243-1143

Represented by: Ron Basile
(212) 564-3703

Existing photography available through: PhotoUnique
(212) 244-5511

Specializing in people on location: corporate/industrial, advertising, audio-visual and editorial.

Client list upon request.

**DON CARROLL**
188 Grand Street
New York, New York 10013
(212) 371-3648

"In the heart of Little Italy"

The photographs on this page are all camera originals. Don would like to thank the art directors whose concepts made these photographs possible.

The book pictured below, *Focus on Special Effects,* contains many other examples of Don's work, explains his approach to problem solving through a variety of special effects techniques, and gives detailed explanations of how each of 168 photographs were made. It is a comprehensive guide of photographic possibilities for art directors and photographers. Obtainable in bookstores world wide, or from the authors. (Published by Amphoto, New York City.)

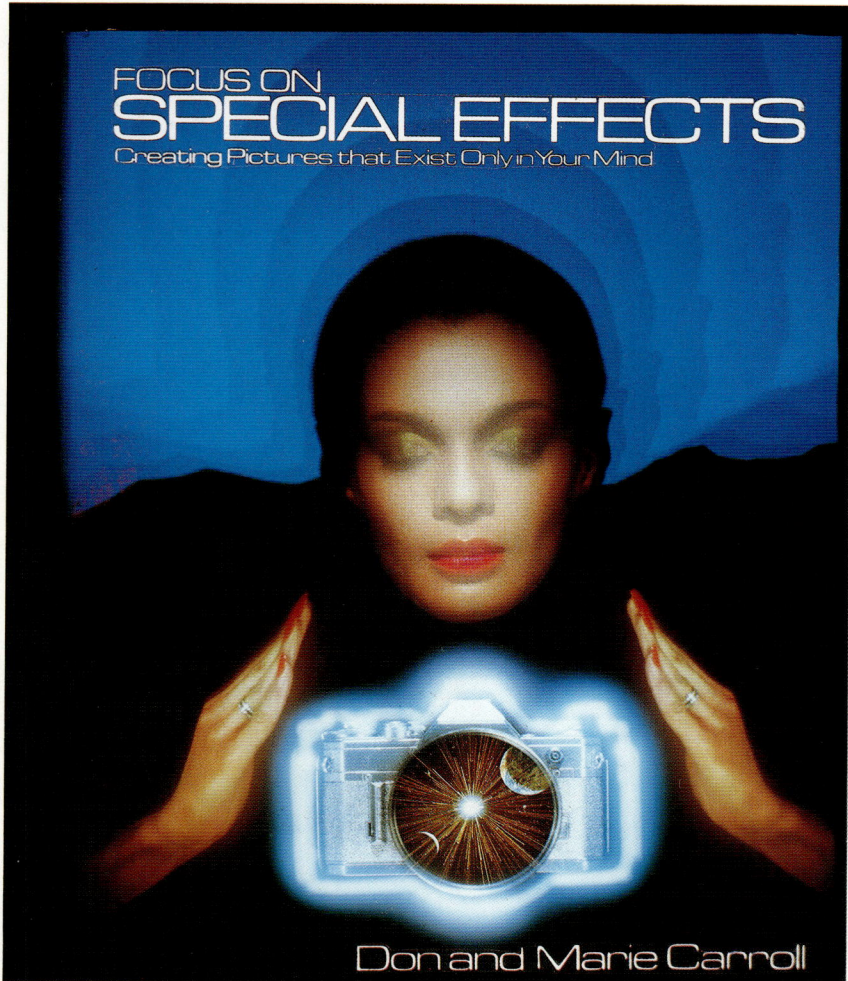

AD: DON CARROLL/DESIGNER: DIANE LYON

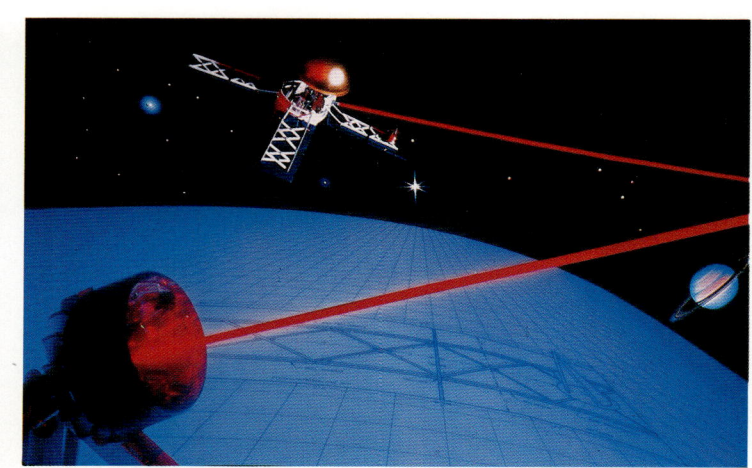

MELINDA THOMPSON/SPEEDRING

JOE BROOKS/PENTHOUSE

JON KARPER/WORLD COMMUNICATIONS

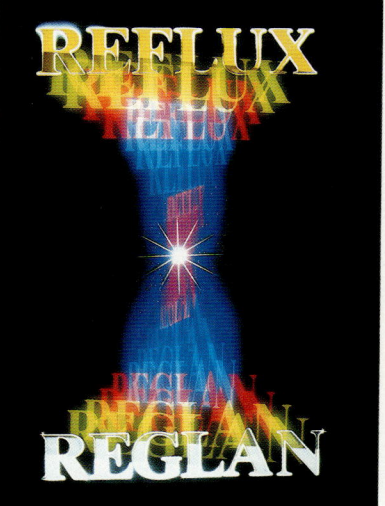

MIKE WILSON/REGLAN

AD: DON CARROLL

60

**DON CARROLL**
188 Grand Street
New York, New York 10013
(212) 371-3648

"In the heart of Little Italy"

Our area of expertise is special effects and problem solving for advertising, industrial, and editorial accounts. We do thermograms and stroboscopic effects against backgrounds other than black, multidimentional images, color enhancement, computer generated and computer enhanced images. Front projection used in the studio can offer a variety of backgrounds, including dangerous, distant, or out-of-season locations that might otherwise be impossible to photograph.

Don is available for consultation to aid in the practical conceptualization of your idea.

Additional samples of Don's work may be seen in Volumes 5 and 6 of American Showcase, and in the book *Focus on Special Effects* by Don and Marie Carroll.

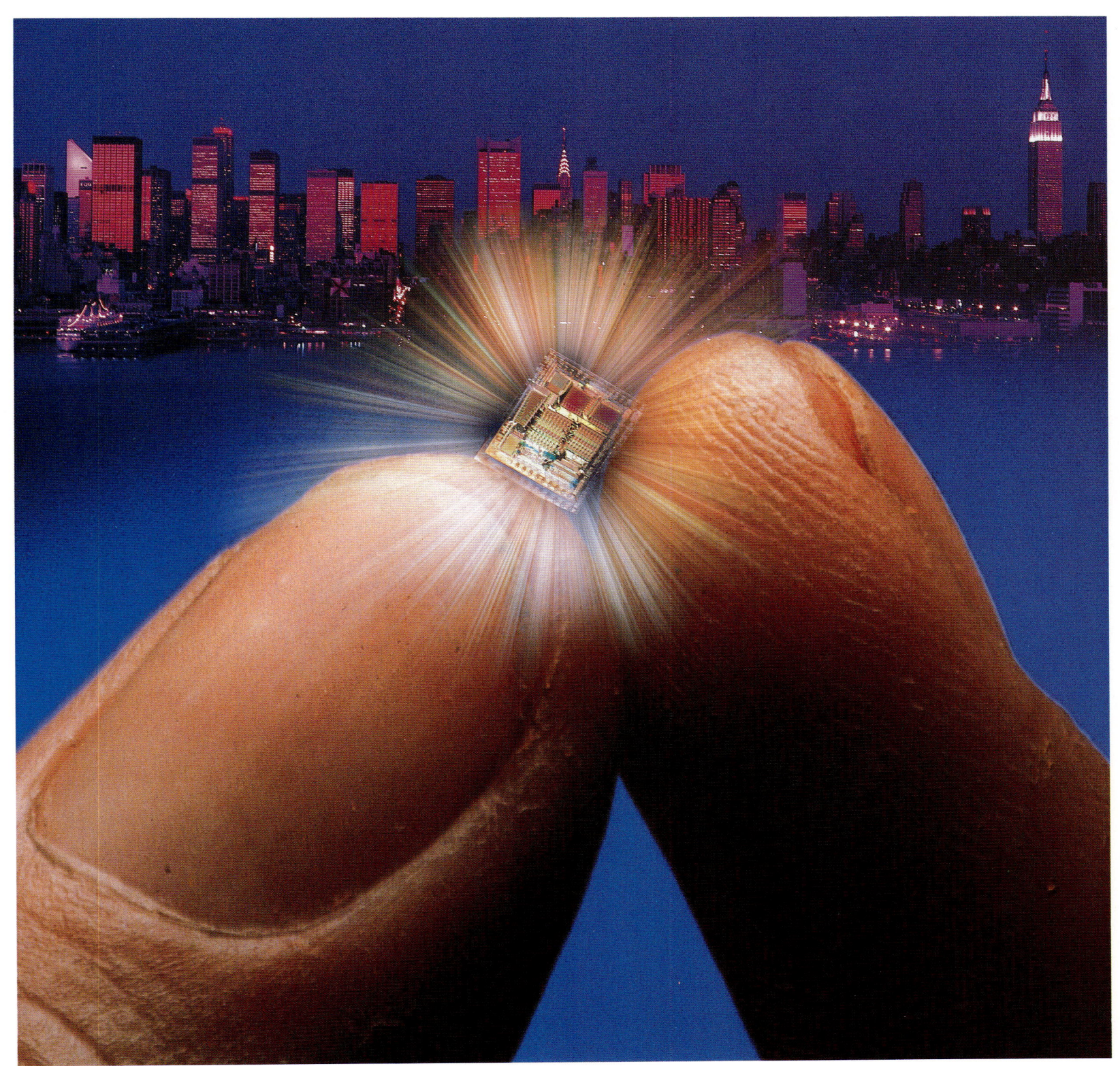

RON PETRELLA/DELCO ELECTRONICS

## ON TRYING TO BE GOOD

**I**t's inspired!" said the client.

"Thank you," I said, "I'm glad that you like it."

I was pleased with myself when I hung up the phone. I had sold a design on the first try. I could send in a nice bill. I had made everybody happy. I had made a design that I had done about seventeen times before in the last three years and it was just what the client wanted. I was finally getting smarter. Not like last week. Last week I did a job over six times because I was trying to be good...

I can't remember when it first dawned on me that trying to be good might be a total waste of time. I do remember the first time that I did a job that I thought was good. "But it's good!" I cried to the client.

Client: "I don't like the blue."

Me: "It's got to be blue. Blue makes the whole design work. If it's not blue, it won't be good."

Client: "Well, I don't know what's good, but I know what I like."

Blue became red, and the client loved it. Maybe it wasn't so bad. I showed the job to another designer.

"That should have been blue," said the designer. "The red doesn't work."

I decided to look for clients who didn't know what they liked. I figured that would make things easier when I decided to try to be good. These were easy clients to find.

Client: "I don't know if I like it or not. What do you think?"

Me: "I think it's good."

Client: "I still don't know if I like it. I don't know what I like. Let me sleep on it and I'll get back to you tomorrow."

He got back to me three weeks later.

Client: "I showed it to my wife, and she didn't like it. My brother-in-law didn't like it either."

I realized that if I was going to continue to try to be good I had to find clients that wanted "good." There were three left in America. One of them hired me.

Client: "We hired you because we want quality work. This is a quality organization. Be innovative. Be imaginative. This is your opportunity to break new ground and grow as an artist."

I broke new ground and grew as an artist. I presented my creation to the client.

Client: "This doesn't look like the other stuff we saw in your portfolio."

Me: "I thought it was very innovative."

Client: "It's too sophisticated. No one can understand it."

Me: "I was trying to grow as an artist."

Client: "This wasn't the kind of growth we had in mind. Do it again. Be inspiring, like the work we saw in your portfolio."

I redesigned the job and made it look like something I had done five years ago.

"Now, this is good," said the client.

I then decided to look for clients who didn't care what the job looked like at all. There were some, and I did some good work for them. The clients didn't notice whether or not the work was good, and none of them questioned the design. But their indifference was complicated by the fact that they did not want to pay me any money for my good work.

Client: "Why should we pay you for something we don't care about. If you want to go running off and trying to be good, that's your business."

I realized that somehow I had been taking the wrong approach with all of my clients. My friends told me that I had no business at all trying to be good, though a few of them confessed to secretly trying to be good when no one was looking.

"I never own up to a good job," said a friend. "Acknowledging that a job may be good is the kiss of death. I say that it 'solves the problem', or 'it's appropriate for the market place', or that 'it's in keeping with the client's philosophy.'"

The next day I did a job in keeping with the client's philosophy.

Client: "Well, this seems to be somewhat in keeping with our philosophy, but that blue bothers me. Do you think you could make it red?"

Me: "Frankly sir, I don't think that red will properly reflect your philosophy."

Client: "Hmm, you may be right. Why don't you try something else, like that design you did last year that we saw in your portfolio. Now, that's our philosophy, exactly."

I gave up on "philosophy" and switched to "problem solving!" The results were the same.

"You're still trying to be good," said my friends. "Give it up. Try to be mediocre. It's easy once you get the hang of it. You'll get more out of life. You'll begin to appreciate nature, a whole new world will unfold for you. You'll feel young again."

They were right. I tried it.

"It's inspired," said the client.

**Paula Scher**
**Designer**

**ROSEMARIE CERTO**
Philadelphia, Pennsylvania
(215) 232-2814

People specialist for advertising, corporate, industrial and annual reports.

1. Arnold Palmer-Spokesperson for State of Pennsylvania National Ad Campaign, Al Paul Lefton, Inc.

2. Safeguard Scientifics, Inc. Annual Report

3. Caloric Corporation, Elkman Advertising

All Photography © Rosemarie Certo

ASMP

**GEOFFREY C. CLIFFORD**
Craggle Ridge
Reading, Vermont 05062
(802) 484-5047

New York Representative:

BLACK STAR
(212) 679-3288

Location Photography: Advertising, Corporate/Annual Reports, Editorial, Travel

64

ASMP

**GEOFFREY C. CLIFFORD**
Craggle Ridge
Reading, Vermont 05062
(802) 484-5047

New York Representative:

BLACK STAR
(212) 679-3288

Location Photography: Advertising, Corporate/Annual Reports, Editorial, Travel

ASMP

65

**TERRY CLOUGH STUDIO**
147 West 25th Street
New York, New York 10001
(212) 255-3040

Represented by

Gail Gaynin
(212) 580-3141

66

APA

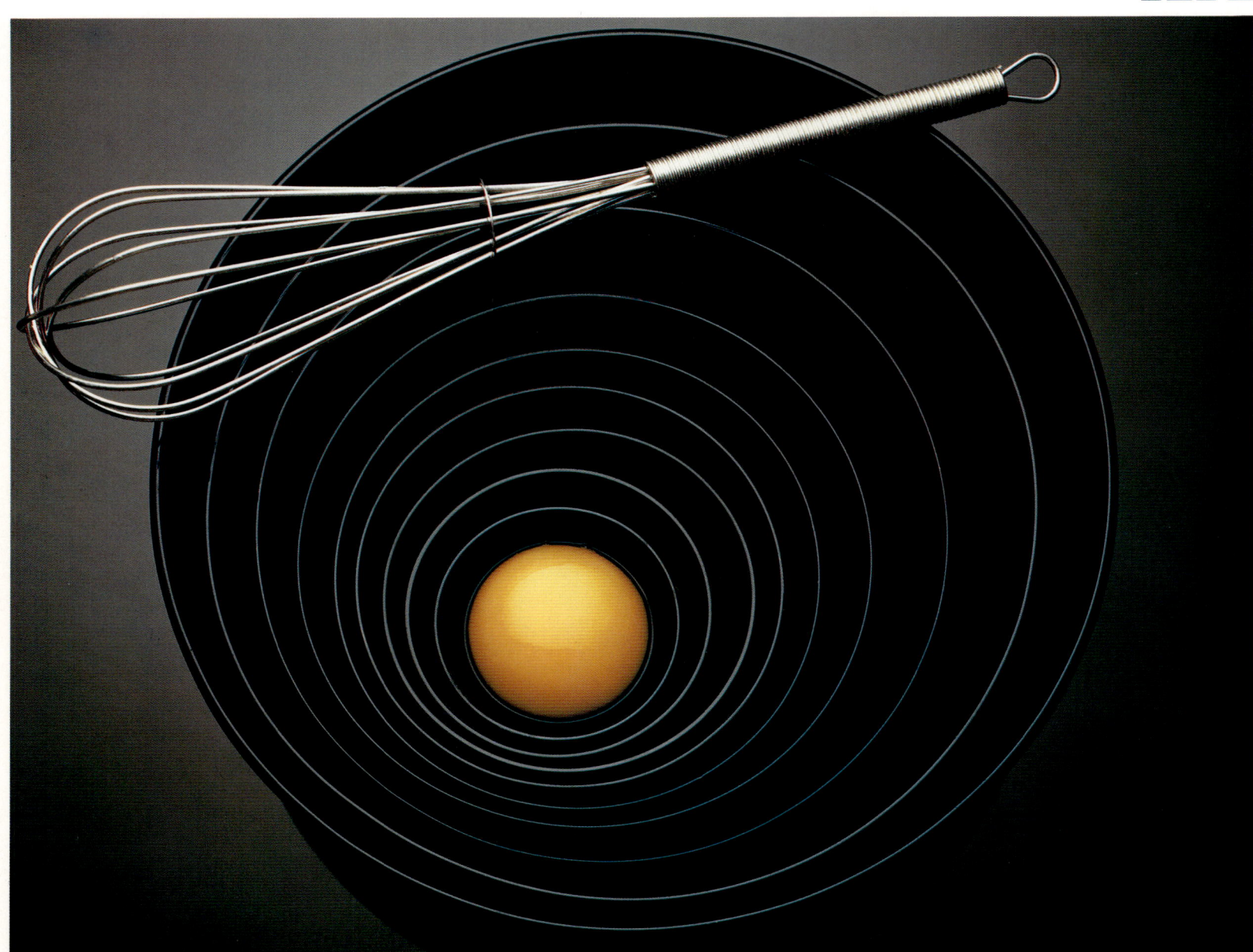

**TERRY CLOUGH STUDIO**
147 West 25th Street
New York, New York 10001
(212) 255-3040

Represented by

Gail Gaynin
(212) 580-3141

IRVIN COOK

68

**LEN DE LESSIO**
49 West 27th Street
New York, New York 10001
(212) 683-3522

Still Life Photography
for print, fotomatic, and TV.

Photographs © 1983 Len DeLessio

AD DALE TANGEMAN, COMPTON / P&G, CASCADE

AD JOSEPH P. TULLY, BESSEN + TULLY / PAINTED EGG BY LINDA FLORIO

**TERRY CLOUGH STUDIO**
147 West 25th Street
New York, New York 10001
(212) 255-3040

Represented by

Gail Gaynin
(212) 580-3141

67

**IRVIN COOK**
(212) 925-6216

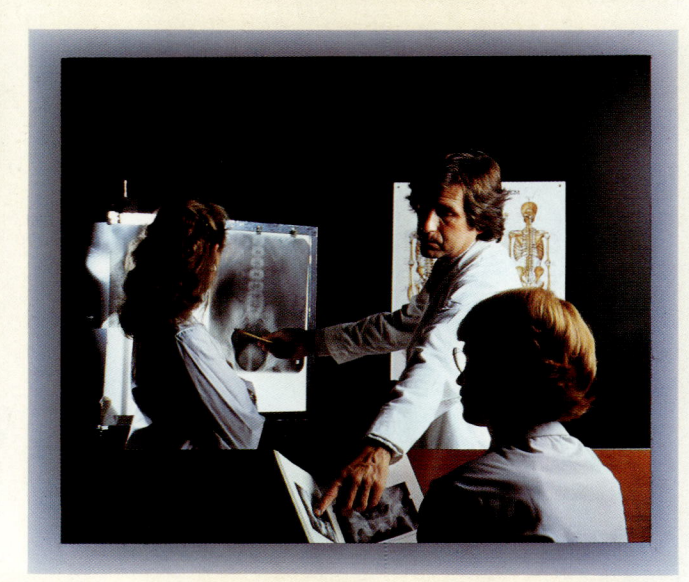

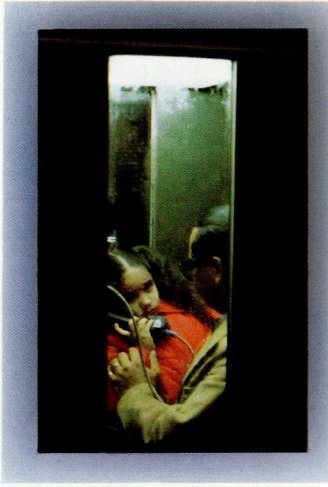

68

**TOM CRANE**
113 Cumberland Place
Bryn Mawr, Pennsylvania 19010
(215) 525-2444

Architecture, Interiors, and Large Studio Photography

Clients in furniture: Hardwood House, JG, Knoll, Stowe Davis, Design Group Inc., Krueger, Conwed

Editorial: Architectural Digest, Architectural Record, Antiques, Interior Design, Interiors, House Beautiful, Progressive Architecture

**LEN DE LESSIO**
49 West 27th Street
New York, New York 10001
(212) 683-3522

Still Life Photography
for print, fotomatic, and TV.

Photographs © 1983 Len DeLessio

AD DALE TANGEMAN, COMPTON / P&G, CASCADE

AD JOSEPH P. TULLY, BESSEN + TULLY / PAINTED EGG BY LINDA FLORIO

**PAUL D'INNOCENZO STUDIO**
13 East 16th Street
New York, New York 10003
(212) 620-0610

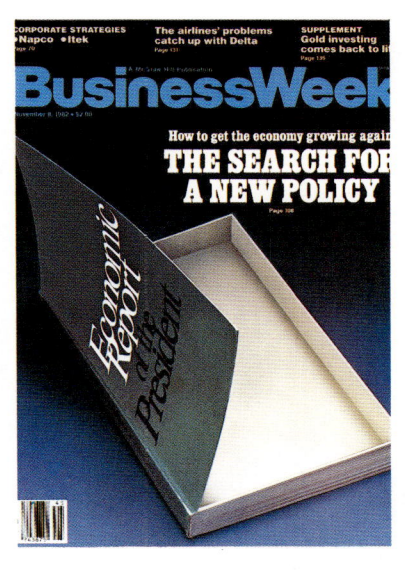

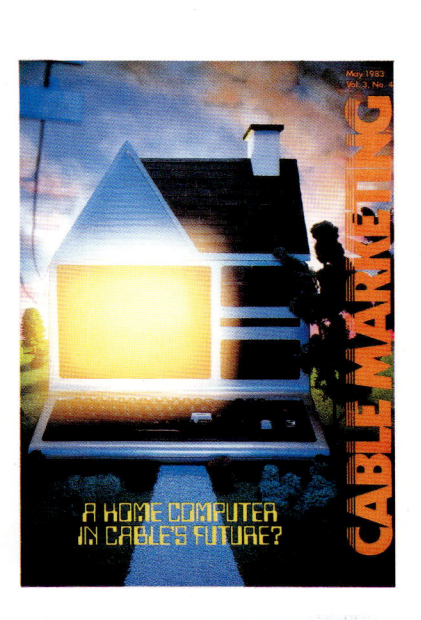

71

**PHOEBE DUNN**
20 Silvermine Road
New Canaan, Connecticut 06840
(203) 966-9791

Babies, children, family relationships, retireds, nature design.
"One of advertising's most sought-after photographers of children." (Photography Annual)

Advertising, magazine illustrations, annual reports, photography for packaging, promotional materials, calendars.

Clients include: Campbell Soup, Chesebrough-Pond's, General Foods, General Mills, Gerber, Hallmark, Hasselblad, J&J, Kimberly-Clark, Kodak, Eli Lilly, Mennen, P&G, 3M Company, Parents Magazine, Reader's Digest, Woman's Day.

Available photographs also: Al Forsythe at DPI (212) PL2-3930

Copyright © 1983 Phoebe Dunn

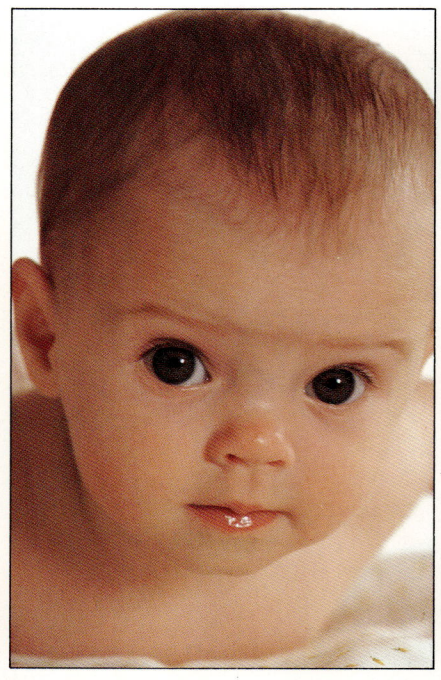

**RICH DUNOFF**
407 Bowman Avenue
Merion Station, Pennsylvania 19066
(215) 627-3690

People
Location
Annual Reports
Advertising

Stock available through: The Stock Market (212) 684-7878

© Richard Dunoff

73

## ONLY FINANCIALLY SOUND STUDIOS WILL SURVIVE

Photographers are easy prey, or so they would have you believe. The big bad agencies tell them where and when and for how much they may work, and the photographers, meek little sheep, are powerless to resist. Everyone knows that if John won't do the job, Jack will. It is, after all, a buyer's market. And it will remain a buyer's market for ever and ever. Or will it?

I would like to propose that some time in the near future this situation may change. Not because of anything that clients or agencies or photographers are consciously doing, but because it is becoming increasingly difficult to remain in the advertising photography business in New York. It's too expensive. It's too expensive to get started and it's too expensive to keep going. It just takes too much money.

Only the largest, and perhaps the smallest, studios will survive. Well capitalized studios are less likely to view business on a job-by-job basis. Rather, they will by necessity look for return on capital commensurate with the risk. Agencies will no longer find photographers willing to work on unprofitable jobs. When an agency hires an individual photographer, that photographer may not have the time or inclination to actualize expenses to find out whether or not he or she is really making money. A $3,000 fee is fantastic, how can you lose? Yet, again and again, photographers are losing. And it's frequently their own fault because they don't do the numbers. It's confounding. How can a reasonably intelligent businessman continue to live in a world where he gives away lunch, assistants, props, supplies, telephones, equipment, floor space, air conditioning, and electricity? How can he give away any or all of these things and still expect that the fee—the un-indexed, mostly unchanged-since-the-sixties-fee—is going to make him a profit? It's lunacy.

However, when an agency seeks to hire a large studio or print production company that uses cost accounting as good as, or better than, the agency's own accounting, there is very little inclination for that studio or production house to work on an unprofitable or even marginally profitable job. The old promises that "we'll make it up to you on the next job" is a reminder that they never have and they never will make it up to you. Financially secure studios do not need or want to discount the present or the future. And it is my contention that only financially sound studios will survive.

In a way, it's ironic that the future of advertising photography may be with large production studios. It was operations such as those that were the predecessors of today's studios. In the sixties, as more miniaturized and affordable equipment became available, it was much easier for anyone and everyone to become a photographer. Cheap space, inexpensive and portable equipment and a booming, loosely structured advertising business made possible the heyday of the one-man studio. Now however, high rents, enormous capital needs, and a highly structured advertising business may combine to sound the death knell for the one-man studio.

It's not that one man can't handle the work. There are plenty of great freelance suppliers around to augment a small staff. One man just cannot handle the overhead. A studio in New York's photo district easily costs $2,500 a month, raw. Equipping a modern studio on a modest scale costs somewhere in the neighborhood of $20,000 for fixtures and another $30,000 or so for equipment. Overhead, including advertising, accounting, bookkeeping, office supplies, heat, taxes and the like add at least another $2,000 a month. In a large studio, it can cost a photographer $300 a day to turn on the air conditioning. What pays for all this? Fees! Those very same fees from which the photographer's rep takes 25%. Those very same fees from which photographers foolishly deduct the cost of assistants, insurance, working lunches and who knows what else. What's left of the fee? Not much.

It's difficult to see where all this is going to end, but it's not hard to see that the direction agencies have been taking in the past few years is having an impact on our business. Many of the successful entrepreneurial agencies have been gobbled up by behemoths. Scali isn't Scali, it's actually Ogilvy. Lord Geller isn't Lord Geller, it's really J. Walter Thompson. And while these monsters keep getting bigger and bigger from their indexed profits and acquisitions, individual photographers are looking relatively smaller and more helpless.

One way photographers may counteract this helplessness is by doing some growing of their own. Such growth might occur when individual photographers get together as a group under one corporate umbrella. Growth might also occur when one or two photographers use their capital to underwrite other photographers in return for a share of the profits. However it happens, this kind of positive growth means that eventually this business will once again become profitable. Without growth, a lot of very talented people will be going out of business.

**Lawrence Robins**
**President**
**Advertising Photographers of America (APA)**
**New York City**

**STEVE ELMORE**
Mithras Images Ltd.
1640 York Avenue
New York, New York 10028
(212) 472-2463

On-location photography around the world: Advertising, Corporate, Editorial, and Travel.

Clients include: American Express, Audubon, Chevron, *Europe Magazine,* European Travel Commission, New York Botanical Gardens, *Sierra, Travel/Holiday, Travel & Leisure, Where,* CBS, and NBC.

Based in New York, Steve travels regularly to Italy and the Southwest, speaks both Italian and Texan and specializes in creating graphic images which reveal the uniqueness of a place or person.

Extensive stock of New York City, the Southwest, and Italy. We'll be glad to send you a copy of our New York 1984 or Italy 1984 calendar. Please request on letterhead.

MITHRAS IMAGES LTD.

**CHUCK FISHBEIN**
49 West 27th Street
New York, New York 10001
(212) 532-4452

Clients include: Somerset Liquors, Midori Liquor, Paramount, MGM, Dual, ABC, NBC, CBS Video, Nimslo Cameras, Ricoh Cameras, Berkey Marketing, Clinique, Estée Lauder, Brown & Williamson, Celanese, Lionel Trains, Binney & Smith Winchester, RCA, Warner Communications, Absolút Vodka, Reunité, Quick Fox Computer Software.

FRUZEN GLÄDJÉ/LEWANDOWSKI ENTERPRISES

CHUCK FISHBEIN PHOTOGRAPHY
49 W. 27 ST.   NEW YORK, N.Y. 10001
212-532-4452

RICOH CORPORATION/JEAN DOYNOW ASSOCIATES

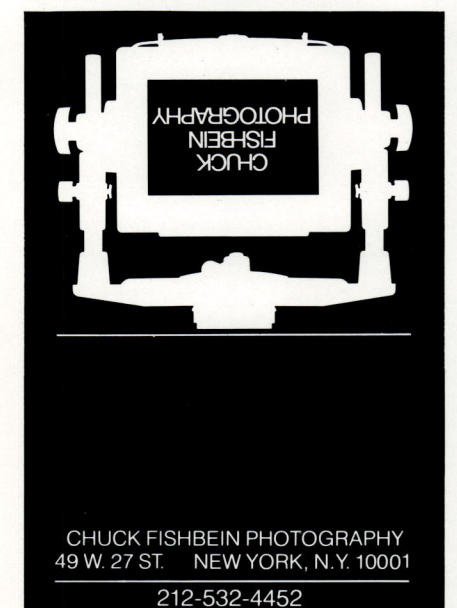

BINNEY & SMITH/DORSHIMER & EVANS, INC.

**CHUCK FISHBEIN**
49 West 27th Street
New York, New York 10001
(212) 532-4452

...Our specialty is making our clients happy,
so that their clients are happy...

77

BEVERAGE INDUSTRY MAGAZINE/LEWANDOSKI ENTERPRISES

SOMERSET LIQUORS/JERRY MOSS, INC.

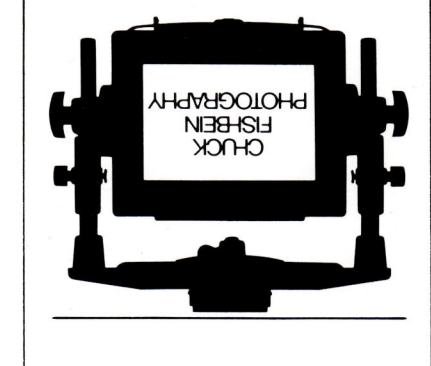

LILLIAN VERNON-PROVENDER/LARRY JENNINGS

CHUCK FISHBEIN PHOTOGRAPHY
49 W. 27 ST.   NEW YORK, N.Y. 10001
212-532-4452

**CHUCK FISHMAN**
69½ Morton Street
New York, New York 10014
(212) 242-3987

Stock Photography: Woodfin Camp & Assoc.
(212) 750-1020

Reportage.....location photography for Annual Reports and Advertising.

Clients include: Ogilvy & Mather; Wells, Rich, Greene; United Technologies; Westinghouse; TWA; *National Geographic; Geo; Life; Fortune; Time.*

© 1984 Chuck Fishman

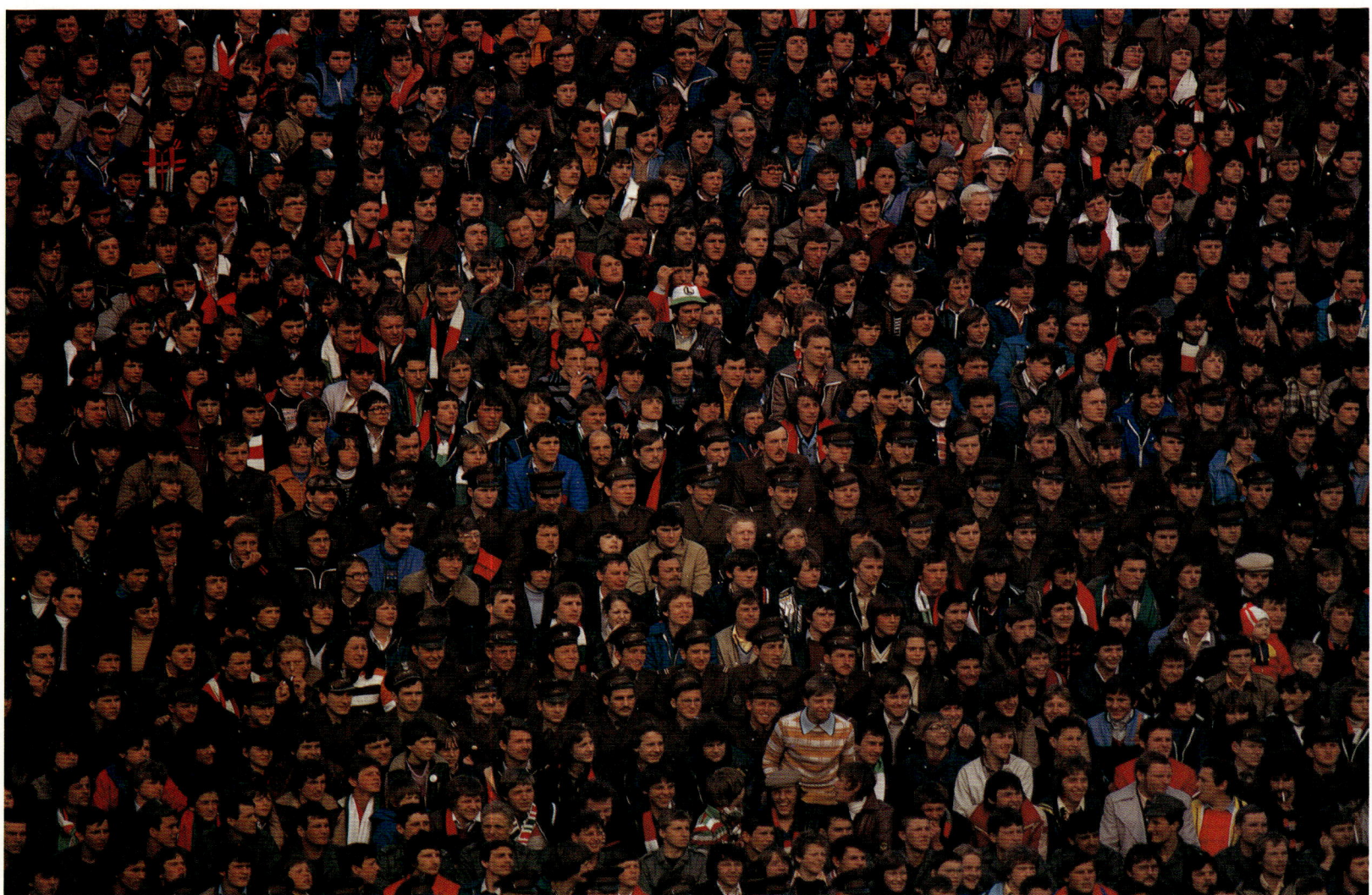

78

POLAND

GREECE

AUSTRALIA

NEW ORLEANS

**CARL FLATOW**
20 East 30th Street
New York, New York 10016
(212) 683-8688

79

| | | | |
|---|---|---|---|
| Adria | Ciba-Geigy | *Fortune* | Peat Marwick |
| *American Photographer* | Coburn Optical | General Foods | Pfizer |
| Ayerst | Datamation | E.F. Hutton | Phctomethods |
| Ballantine Books | Deak-Perera | Ideal Toy | *Psychology Today* |
| Barnes-Hind | Dun & Bradstreet | Irex | Quantum |
| Barnes and Noble | Dunhill | Johnson & Johnson | Seiko |
| Beecham | Empire | Metropolitan Museum of Art | Telecom |
| Boehringer Ingelheim | Ferrero | Olympus | J.B. Williams |
| *Business Week* | Food and Wine | *Omni* | Ziff-Davis |
| Chase Bank | Forbes | Ortho | |

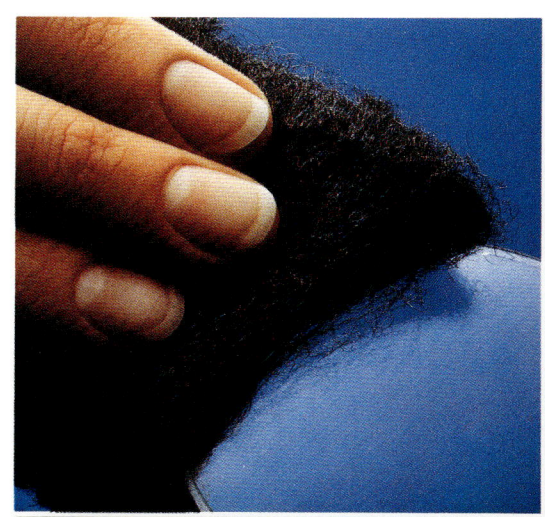

## "HELLO, DELI!"
## (A PRE-BROADWAY MUSICAL)

All my years in advertising have been spent writing copy. I find it appropriate that I've been asked to add some thoughts to *American Showcase*, a publication devoted to the visual rather than the written message. It is in keeping with industry standards and my own experience that it is always best to expound upon that which I know very little or nothing. So...Art.

Art in theatrical advertising and the selection thereof by the client (producers) is the all-important first step that forever links a graphic design to a Broadway show. We call it the window card, because its primary purpose is to hang in the windows of ticket brokers' offices. Most folks just call it "the poster."

If the show itself gets past opening night with good reviews the poster will begin popping up all over: train stations, airports, billboards, buses, of course newspapers—and, in the case of musicals, the album cover. Often the art influences even the television commercial. It's clearly one of the most important tasks to be performed because much of what is done in selling the show reflects the art. In selecting the poster art the producers are determining for all time the signature for their show.

Since the economics of theatre today require more than one major producer, all decisions involve an ever-increasing cast of characters. A typical meeting at the agency to begin selecting logo art would involve all the producers and several agency personnel—something like this:

Present:

The cast:

**Producers:** Abe, Sheila, Ralph, Manny and Eileen

**Agency:** Peter LeDonne, Don Gordon and HoNo, head of mailroom and former Sumo wrestler

**LeDonne**    Let's get started, okay? I've got several designs to show you today. Some were done by our own Sr. Art Director, Don Gordon, others by our staff artists and a few completed by free-lance artists. The first is one of Don's designs.

**Manny**    I hate it. I mean I really hate it! Words cannot describe the truly negative feelings I have. This art lacks style, wit and charm. It has no life!

**Sheila**    I love it. It has style, wit and charm. It's...alive! I don't want to see anymore.

**Eileen**    It's very sexy. I'm getting hot flashes just looking at it.

**Abe**    I've got a very good friend who is a great artist. Why don't I call her?

**Ralph**    When are we shooting the TV spot?

**Sheila**    I'm having second thoughts.

**Manny**    Red! Red is my lucky color. If we add some red someplace it wouldn't be so awful.

**Ralph**    Can we order lunch?

**Don Gordon**    Aargh!

**HoNo**    Ho. No.

**Eileen**    My daughter's favorite color is red! Mine's blue.

**Manny**    Lucky! Not favorite. Lucky. Don't you want us to have a hit?

**Abe**    Yes, favorite is for selfish producers. Manny's talking about luck. Let's get all the help we can, but we need lots of blue. Critics like blue.

**Eileen**    Can I get a tongue and swiss on rye?

**Don Gordon**    Grrrr. Grrr.

**HoNo**    Ho. No.

**Eileen**    You know the problem. It doesn't last. It's not sexy anymore.

**Sheila**    I've got to take these shoes off.

**Abe**    I've got a very good artist friend. I may see her tonight.

**Ralph**    What's today's date? Am I in an advertising meeting? I'm supposed to be in L.A.!

**Manny**    I hope all the art you're going to show us isn't this terrible.

**Don Gordon**    Oooh! Eeow!

**HoNo**    Ho! No!

**Abe**    Since the agency can't deliver good art, I may have to spend all night working with my very good artist friend, doing your job!

**Ralph**    Tuna salad.

**Abe**    I've got to pick up a box of crayolas.

continued on page 84

**CHIP FORELLI**
316 Fifth Avenue
New York New York 10001
(212) 564-1835

Representative: Susan Kay Pauliny

Clients Include:

| | |
|---|---|
| Baccarat Crystal | Norelco |
| Charles of the Ritz | Procter & Gamble |
| Chromatic Corp | Ralph Lauren |
| Cunningham & Walsh | Revlon |
| Equitable Life Insurance | Squibb |
| Geer, DuBois | Stone McCaffery & Ratner |
| Isidore Lefkowitz Elgort | Warner Cosmetics |
| McCaffrey and McCall | Westvaco |
| New York Telephone | Wunderman Ricotta & Kline |

Represented by Susan Kay Pauliny
316 5th Ave. N.Y., N.Y.   212-564-1835

**AL FRANCEKEVICH**
73 Fifth Avenue
New York, New York 10003
(212) 691-7456

A partial list of clients includes:
AT&T, Abbott Laboratories, Aetna Life Insurance, Aim Toothpaste, Alcoa, Alcon, Armour, Avon, Ayerst, Barnes Hind, Bausch & Lomb, Beseler Enlargers, Bio-Search, Boehringer-Ingleheim, Breon, Burroughs Wellcome, Canon Camera, Ciba Giegy, Colgate, Cooke-Waite, Crest Toothpaste, *Discover Magazine,* Dome, Du Pont, Eastman Kodak, Electro Nucleonics, Firestone, *Food & Wine Magazine, Forbes Magazine,* Ford, Fruit-of-the-Loom, General Electric, Goodyear, Head & Shoulders Shampoo, Hydrocurve, IBM, IREX, Irving Trust, Ives Laboratories, Johnson & Johnson, Knoll, Lederle, Lever Brothers, Lilly, Lufkin, Macmillan Publishers, McNeil Laboratories, Mead Johnson, Mennen, Mercedes-Benz, Merck Sharpe Dohme, Merrill, Mighty Star, Miles Laboratories, *Newsweek,* Nicholson Tools, Olympus Corp. of America, Oneida Silverware, Organon, Ortho, Osteonics, Pan Am, *Parent's Magazine,* Parke Davis, Pfizer, Pharmacia, Polaroid, Procter & Gamble, RCA, *Reader's Digest,* Republic Airlines, Revlon, Richardson-Vicks, Roche, Roerig, Rorer, Ross, Sandoz, *Science Digest,* Scope Mouthwash, Sentry Insurance, Shering, Springs Industries, Squibb, Stuart Pharmaceutical, *Time Magazine,* TV Guide, TWA, Upjohn, US Navy, USV, Wallace, Winthrop, *Woman's Day*

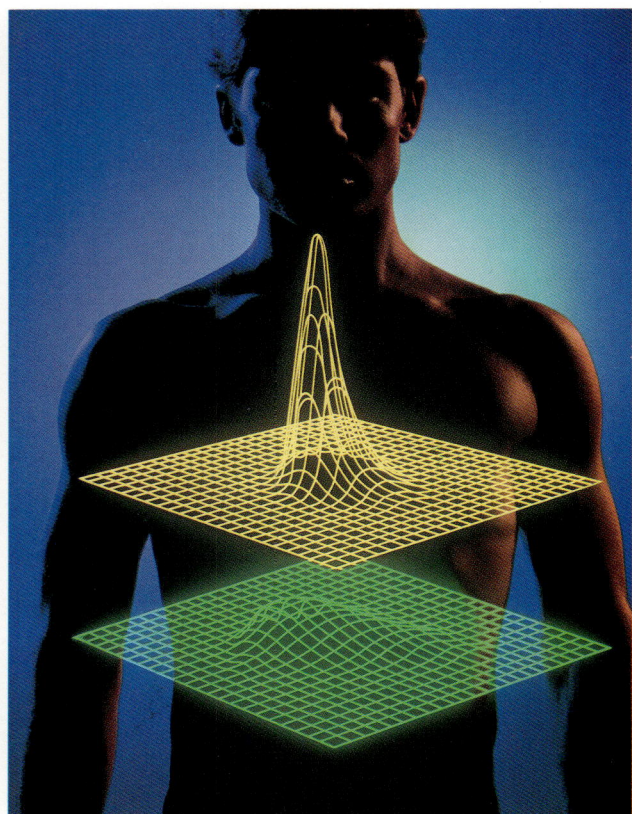

82

**AL FRANCEKEVICH**
73 Fifth Avenue
New York, New York 10003
(212) 691-7456

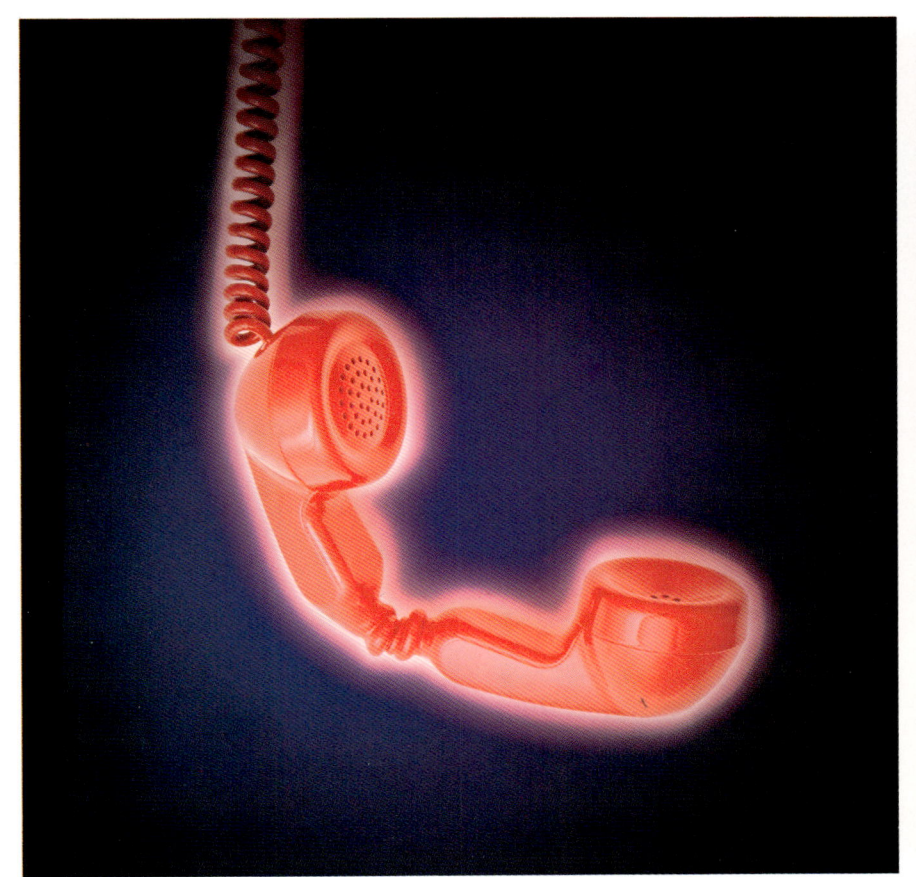

continued from page 80

**Eileen**      *My hot flashes are completely gone.*

**Sheila**      *My kids are coming home from camp this week.*

**Don Gordon**      *Aragh! (Moving toward the producers, he has begun to drool and moan and is lifting his left pant leg to remove the exacto knife strapped to his leg.)*

**HoNo**      *Ho! No! Ho! No! (leaping to intercept Gordon)*

**Don Gordon**      *Oh no, HoNo! You're not stopping me this time. (HoNo wrestles the exacto knife from Gordon, but Gordon manages to sink his teeth into HoNo's toe... ho ho!)*

**Manny**      *That's it! Look at that red stain on the carpet where those two are rolling around. There, by that one's foot. That's my lucky color! Boy, this must be my lucky day!*

**Abe**      *I'm going to see my very good artist friend.*

**Ralph**      *I once met Merv Griffin at a party.*

**Sheila**      *Are there any other advertising agencies we should be talking to?*

After several similar meetings, Abe's very good artist friend has the best shot at delivering art all the producers will like. The show has a real good chance of opening and closing in one night. Bloomingdale's will make a deal with the producers to sell framed copies of the window card at $75.00 cash. Cold compresses and a sympathetic shoulder will have Don Gordon ready for the next meeting. HoNo's limp will last less than a week.

**Peter LeDonne**
**Exec. Vice President**
**and Creative Director**
**Ash/LeDonne, Inc.**
**New York City**

**DOUGLAS FRASER**
9 East 19th Street
New York, New York 10003
(212) 777-8404

85

**MITCHELL FUNK**
500 East 77th Street
New York, New York 10162
(212) 988-2886

Special effects and concepts

Partial list of clients includes: IBM, AT&T, TWA, Nikon, Newmont Mining, Inmont, Litton Industries, *Life, Fortune, Newsweek, New York Magazine,* Polaroid, Western Electric, *Science Digest,* J&B Scotch, Fuji, *Omni,* Johnnie Walker Red, ABC, North American Philips.

86

**MITCHELL FUNK**
500 East 77th Street
New York, New York 10162
(212) 988-2886

Special effects and concepts

Partial list of clients includes: IBM, AT&T, TWA,
Nikon, Newmont Mining, Inmont, Litton Industries,
*Life, Fortune, Newsweek, New York Magazine,*
Polaroid, Western Electric, *Science Digest,* J&B Scotch,
Fuji, *Omni,* Johnnie Walker Red, ABC, North American Philips.

87

**MICHAEL FURMAN**
115 Arch Street
Philadelphia, Pennsylvania 19106
(215) 925-4233

88

**MICHAEL FURMAN**
115 Arch Street
Philadelphia, Pennsylvania 19106
(215) 925-4233

89

## YOU DON'T HAVE TO BE CRAZY BUT...

There is a hard core group of us that continues to believe that creativity and selling are not mutually exclusive...unlike the words "Military Intelligence."

As a judge in advertising awards competitions over the years, I have always thought that picking the winners was rather easy. After a few obvious and unanimous choices, the quality of advertising drops off drastically. Then you begin to wonder about the judgment of those who submitted the remainder of the entries and those who screened it.

That's as much as I'm going to say about the deplorable state of creativity today in advertising. However, I do want to delve into the mystery of creativity itself...and in the process perhaps touch upon some possible explanations why, when we are confronted with so many advertising campaigns, we are able to honor so few.

Adler tells us...and I don't mean Old Man Adler who gave us his famous elevator shoes...that human beings produce art, science and literature to compensate for their own inadequacies.

The oyster producing the pearl to cover up the grain of sand intruding into its shell is often cited as a simple illustration of compensation. Beethoven's deafness is another. Van Gogh had psychotic tendencies. Poe was an alcoholic who wrote and drank to overcome an inferiority complex. Virginia Woolf attempted to write herself out of a serious depression. Carol Burnett said, "I don't think you can truly be funny unless there's some suffering." Her parents were alcoholics. Dudley Moore was born with a clubfoot. Art Buchwald's mother died giving birth to him. Charlie Chaplin did not know where his next meal would come from.

I seem to be focusing on humorists and comedians in my examples of famous people who compensated for their inadequacies by creating....Let me explain.

I think that humor and wit comprise the very core of some of our best advertising. And good copywriters have much in common with comedy writers.

My friend Buddy Hackett was fat and homely as a kid. And as if that weren't enough, "God said, 'Here have some of these, too', and he threw a bunch of pimples at my face."

The older guys in the neighborhood told him the only way he could get rid of those zits was to "get shtupped." Hackett went to a pharmacy and asked the druggist, "Hey, Mister, can I get shtupped here?" The guy said, "Not even with a prescription."

And that's when Buddy Hackett turned to comedy to overcome his looks and his zits and his inability to "get shtupped."

All of which poses some interesting questions:

Does creativity often stem from an effort to overcome inadequacies? Is an inferiority complex helpful to producing creative work? Is creative talent possibly a sort of malfunction? And is creativity linked to neurosis?

Or to put it bluntly...do you have to be a little funny to write great advertising?

If you're old enough to have lived it, you will remember that in the 1960's creative people were tagged with opprobrium. "The lunatics took over the asylum," it was said. We smoked. We drank. We tripped. We experimented lavishly with every fad that came along promising Nirvana. Only account executives got their hair cut. Designer clothes came from army surplus stores.

They called us crazy.

And they called that period..."the crazy 60's." But they also called it "The Golden Age of Creativity." And nostalgia aside, *creativity did flourish in the 1960's.*

But every movement in history carries its own seeds of destruction. We embarked on a program of reform...some of it, I might add, justified.

But of all the cures we undertook, one might just have backfired. And that's the decision by major advertising agencies to include psychoanalysis under medical benefits.

Fifty minutes at a time we talked out our problems and talked away some of the magic. As we became more sane, the advertising became more sanitized. Over a period of time, nothing did more to undermine creative vitality. Not copy research. Not the worst recession. Not even MBA's. The cure became deadlier than the disease. You still can't get anything out of creative during the month of August.

The late John Cheever, a writer I adored, once wrote, "A psychiatrist was meant to cure you of that painful sense of alienation that is, so far as I know, the very beginning of perception. There was once a great deal of excitement at the thought that all of one's limitations and failures were simply symptomatic of mistakes and cruelties that had been inflicted on one earlier in life."

I have always felt that the ability to regress to a more childlike view of the world was a critical necessity to being creative. As one very childish but brilliant art director put it, "Ain't no dude going to fornicate with my head."

Creativity can be characterized by an *intensity of awareness* or *heightened consciousness*. The moment when lightning strikes. Sometimes known as the *intense encounter.* The heart beats faster, the blood pressure races higher, sweat emerges, appetite disappears.

continued on page 94

**AL GIESE**
156 Fifth Avenue
New York, New York 10010
(212) 675-2727

Represented by: Mary Hottelet

© Al Giese

**GARY GLADSTONE**
The Gladstone Studio, Ltd.
237 East 20th Street
New York, New York 10003
(212) 777-7772

Corporate:
Annual Reports,
Capability Brochures,
Institutional Illustration

Stock Photographs:
The Image Bank

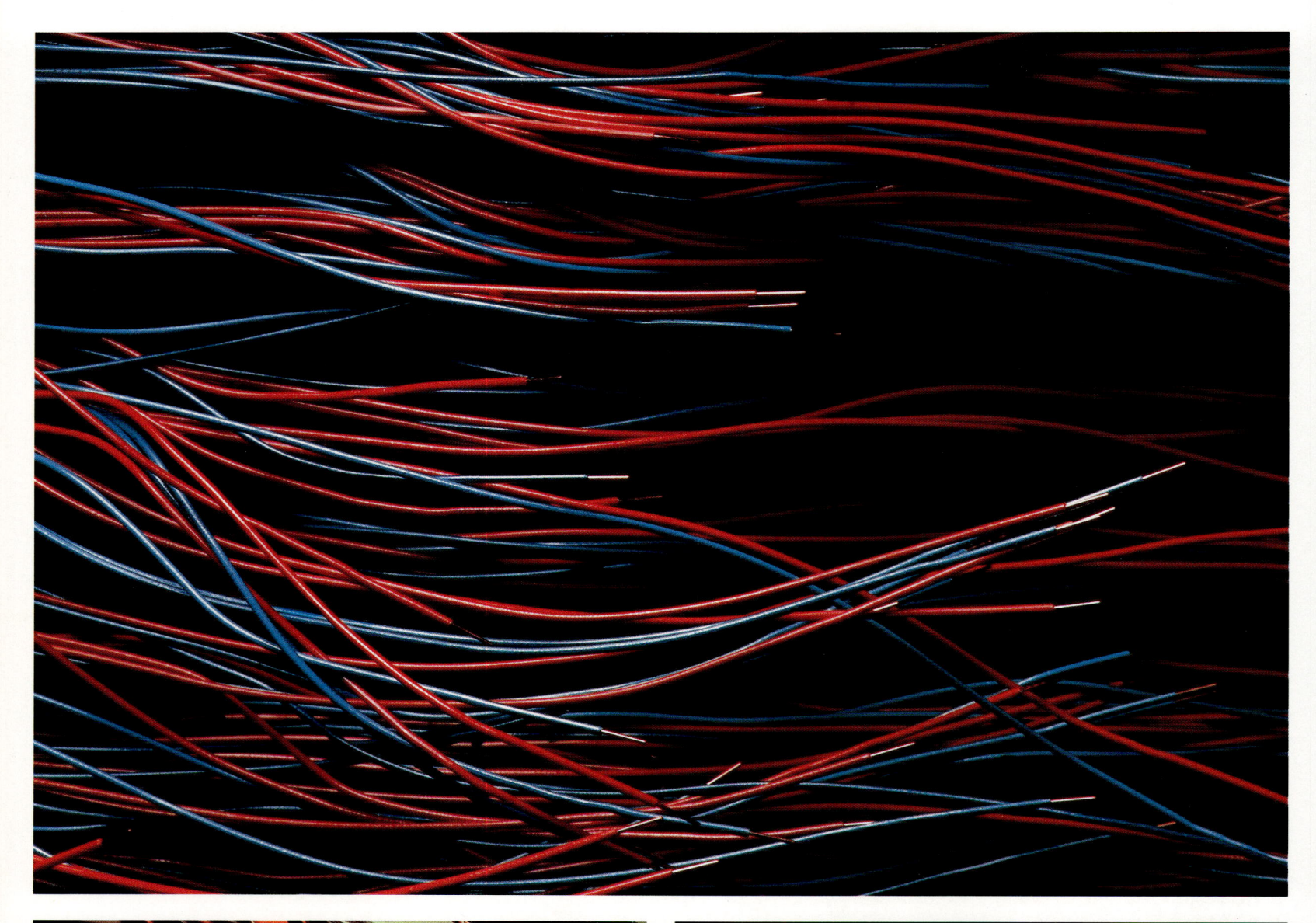

92

**GARY GLADSTONE**
The Gladstone Studio, Ltd.
237 East 20th Street
New York, New York 10003
(212) 777-7772

Corporate:
Annual Reports,
Capability Brochures,
Institutional Illustration

Stock Photographs:
The Image Bank

93

continued from page 90

Creative people are distinguished by the fact that they can live with this anxiety...even though a high price may be paid in insecurity and sensitivity. It's the price you pay for what the classical Greeks called "Divine Madness."

The same symptoms we associate with *fear* and *anxiety* also accompany the *joy* of creativity. For me there are few emotional experiences to compare with the birth of an idea. And isn't it interesting how often we use the word "birth" in connection with idea-getting. "Birth" as in the supreme act of creativity.

Without the pain of creativity there cannot be the pleasure of creating.

I could never understand how creative people could call the writing of advertising "fun." For me it was anguish. Every time I sat down I wanted to write the great American ad. Every time I sat down I was scared to death I *couldn't* write the great American ad. So there were often bouts of melancholy and gasping and lots of expletives and sometimes rage and cries of distress. I mean you could get cramps.

I have often thought that the Clios should be awarded to the families of the copywriters and art directors who do the ads. Ah! But when it's done, it's fun. When you see your ad set in type, then it's fun. When someone on the train discusses your commercial, then it's fun.

It wasn't until long into my career that I realized that self-doubt went with the territory. To like something you create, to fully believe in it, is in no way contradictory with doubt about yourself or your work. It's doubt that sends you careening down the hall with copy hot out of the typewriter...to be read to anyone who will listen. It's doubt that can send you back to your office and into a blue funk if you don't get the desired reaction.

If doubt inspires you to go beyond what you've written, to try harder to make it better, there can be no doubt about the value of doubt. Actually, I think the whole concept of the copywriter/art director team was born out of this doubt and insecurity. When you worked with someone in the same office to generate the idea, in a sense you had instant approval from someone you respected. When both agreed on an idea, there was less room for doubt.

Too many in our business practice what Rollo May calls "escapist creativity." We stop short of what he calls the "creative encounter." It's that high degree of absorption in the problem which produces the insight that leads to the brilliant expression of copy and art that constitute a great ad.

It's so much easier to cop out early and sit back to enjoy the ecstasy of superficial creation. It's pretty well summed up in the words, "Don't Stop," which has sort of become the philosophy of my company.

Someone once asked playwright Alan Jay Lerner why it took him so long to write a show. He said, "It's not that I'm slow to write. I'm just quick to throw out." That says it for me.

**Alvin Hampel**
**Chairman/New York**
**D'Arcy-MacManus & Masius, Inc.**
**New York City**

**JOEL GORDON PHOTOGRAPHY**
5 East 16th Street
New York, New York 10003
(212) 989-9207

"To help you create that special image."

Advertising, Corporate, and Editorial. Studio or location.

Stock list available in color and b/w. Also, selected stock through Al Forsyth at DPI.

ASMP, APA

See ads: Art Directors Index—
　　　　　Vol 9 page 184
　　　American Showcase—
　　　　　Vol 5 page 75
　　　　　Vol 4 page 114
　　　　　Vol 3 page 93

© Joel Gordon 1983

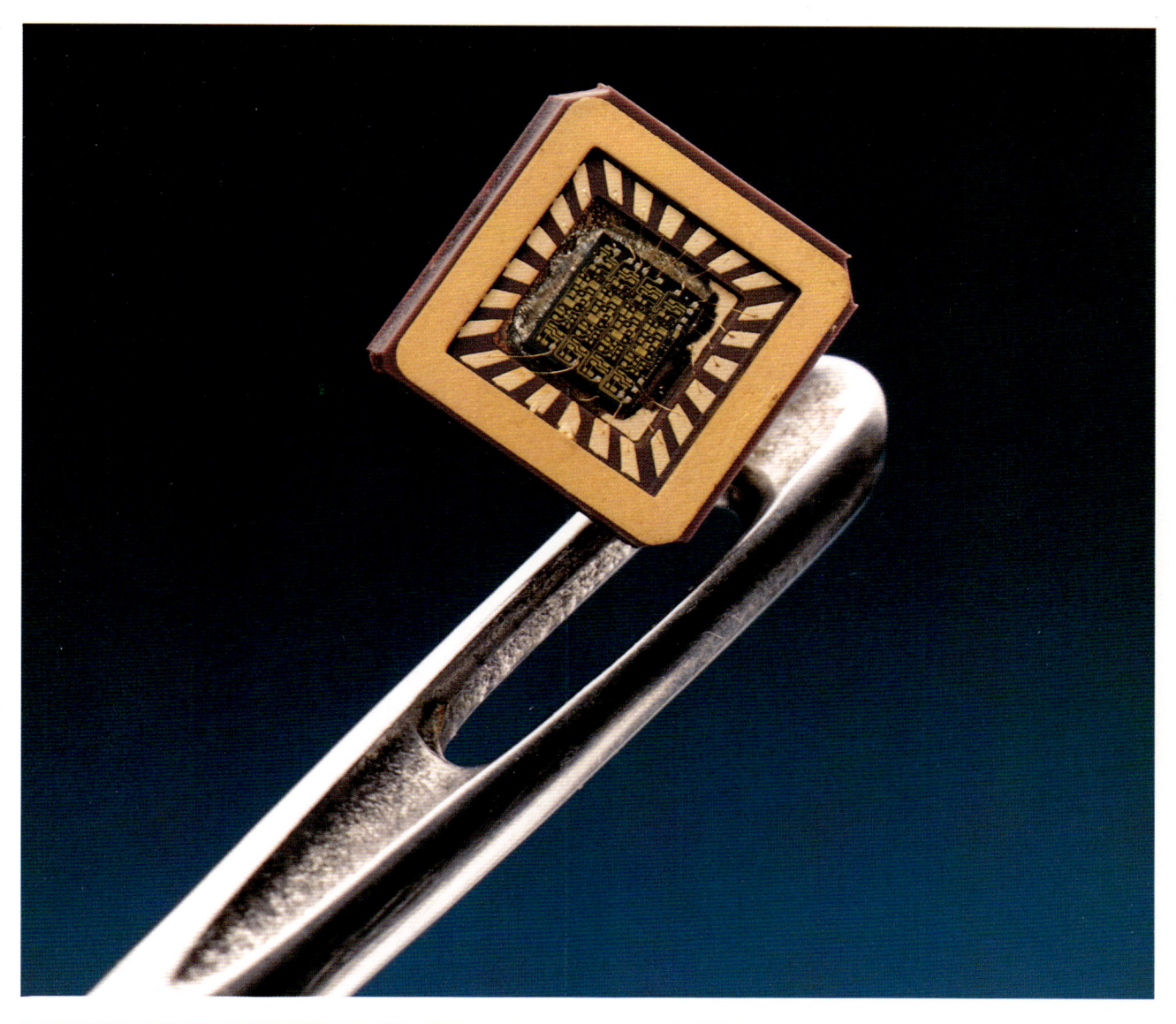

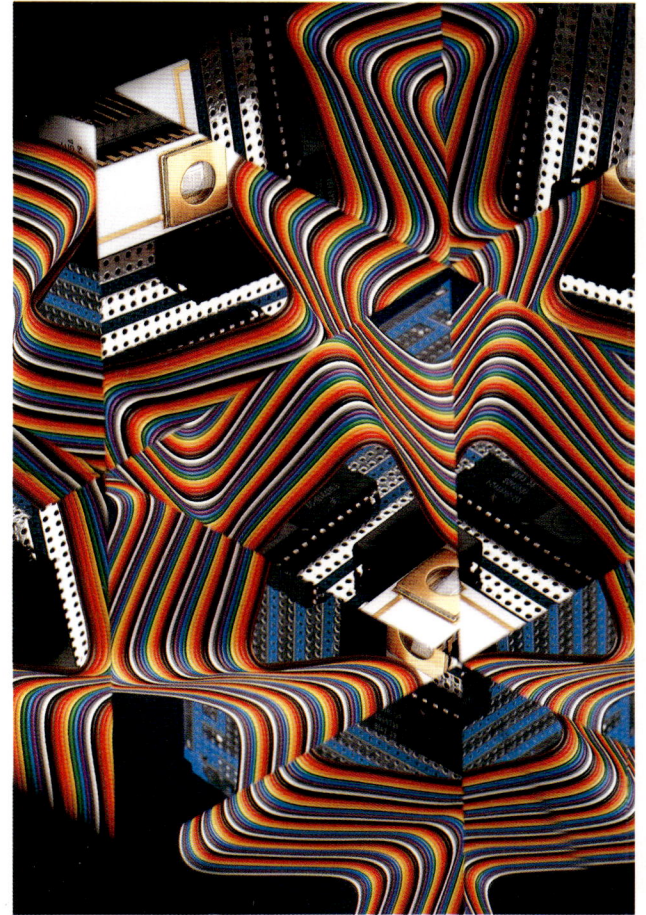

**STEPHEN GREEN-ARMYTAGE**
171 West 57th Street
New York, New York 10019
(212) 247-6314

Represented by: Ursula G. Kreis
(212) 562-8931

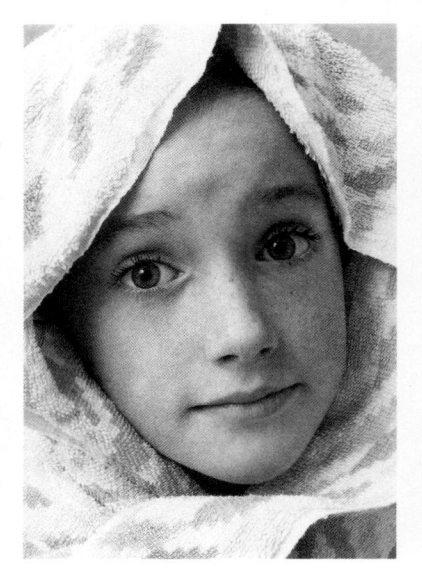

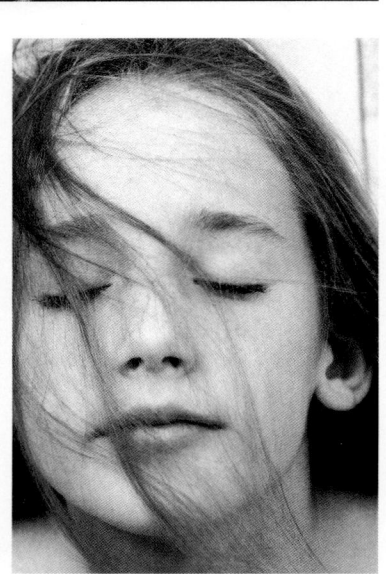

**STEPHEN GREEN-ARMYTAGE**
171 West 57th Street
New York, New York 10019
(212) 247-6314

Represented by: Ursula G. Kreis
(212) 562-8931

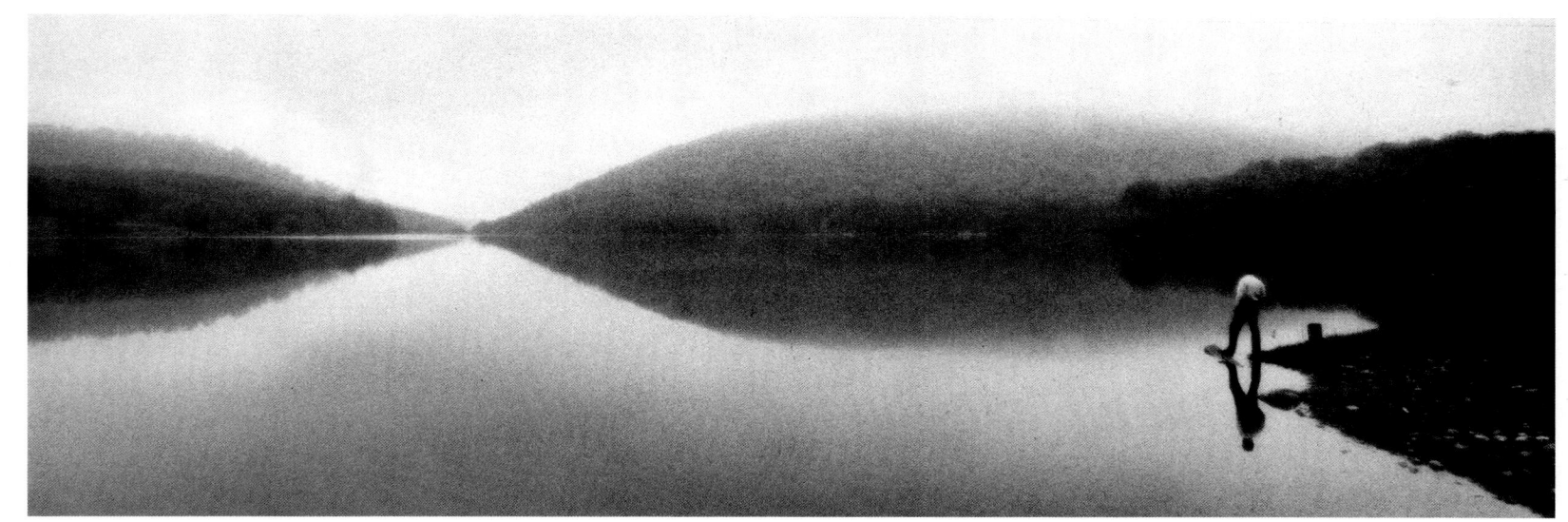

**DAVID GREENBERG**
54 King Street
New York, New York 10014
(212) 243-7351

Represented by:
Ken Abbey
(212) 947-7577

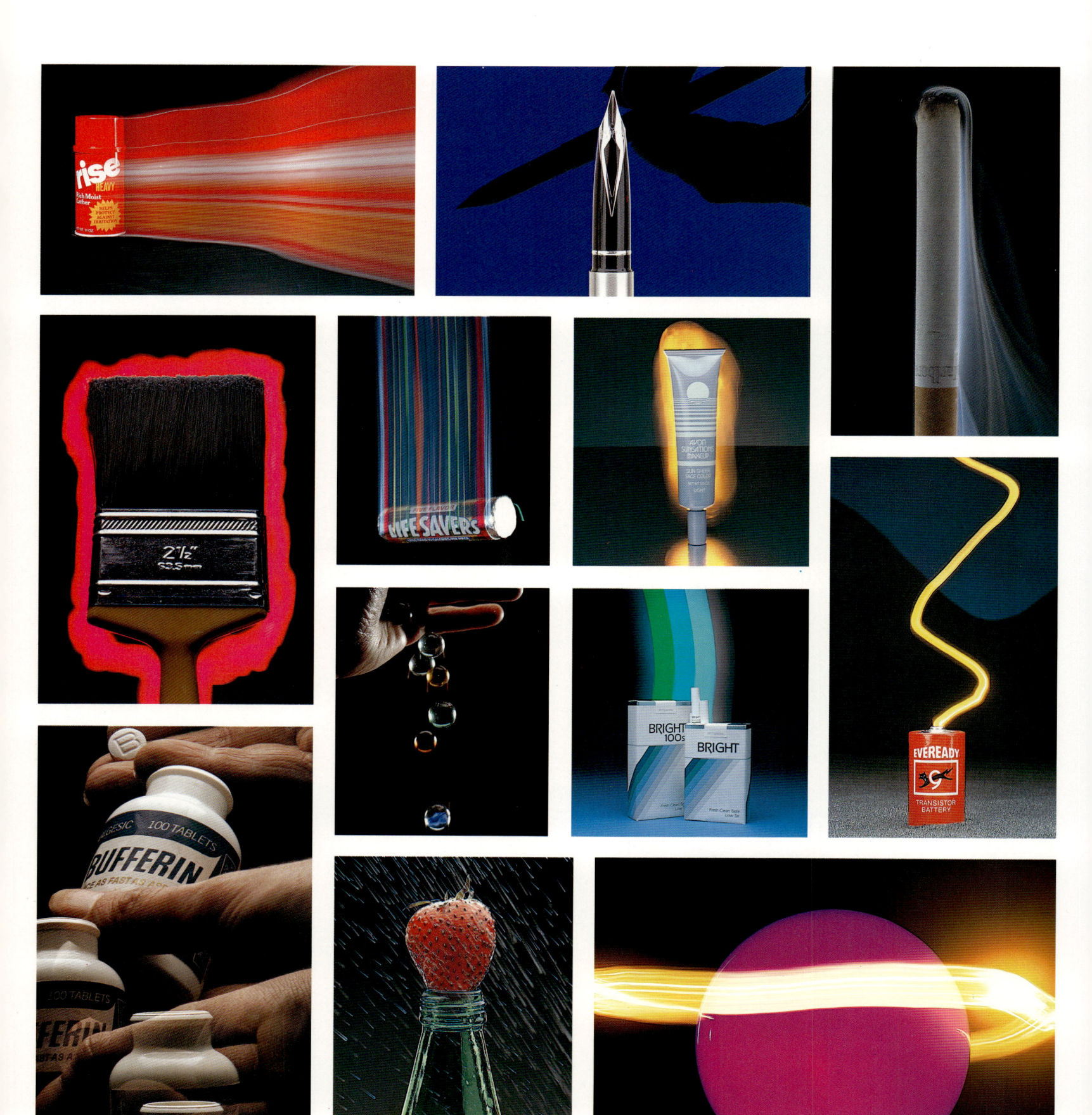

98

**GERHARD GSCHEIDLE**
381 Park Avenue South
New York, New York 10016
(212) 532-1374

Advertising, corporate/industrial and editorial photography.
Location and studio.

Clients include: AT&T, American Can, Amstar, Coca-Cola, Exxon, R/Greenberg Assoc., Harcourt Brace Jovanovich, IBM, ITT, Interstate Amiesite, Main Hurdman, McGraw Hill, New York Stock Exchange, Public Service Electric & Gas, Sterling Drug, Texaco, Western Electric, Western Pacific Industries.

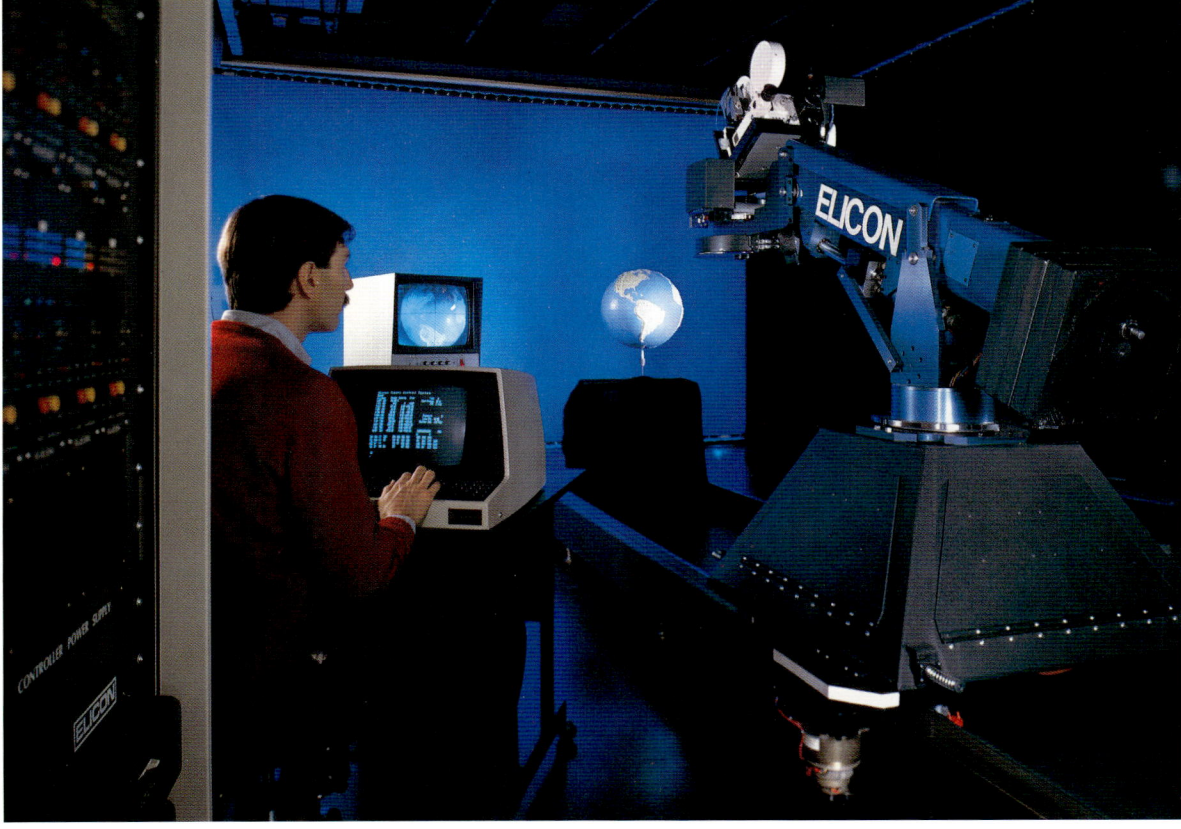

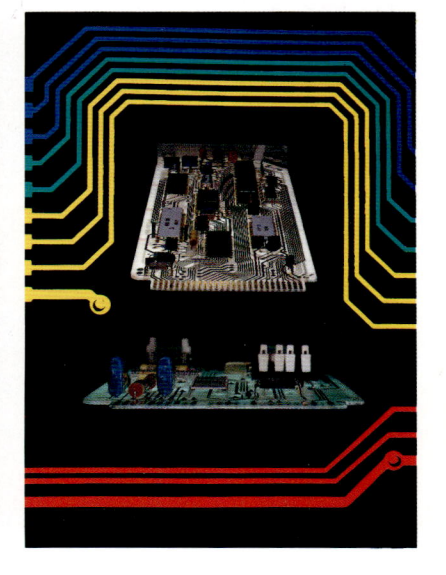

99

**PHILLIP A. HARRINGTON**
New York, New York
(212) 284-0212

PHOTOMICROGRAPHY

Represented by:
**FRAN HEYL ASSOCIATES**
230 Park Avenue
New York, New York 10017
(212) 581-6470

Specializing in photomicrography for the advertising, corporate/industrial, and editorial fields.

Fellow of the Royal Microscopical Society and the New York Microscopical Society.

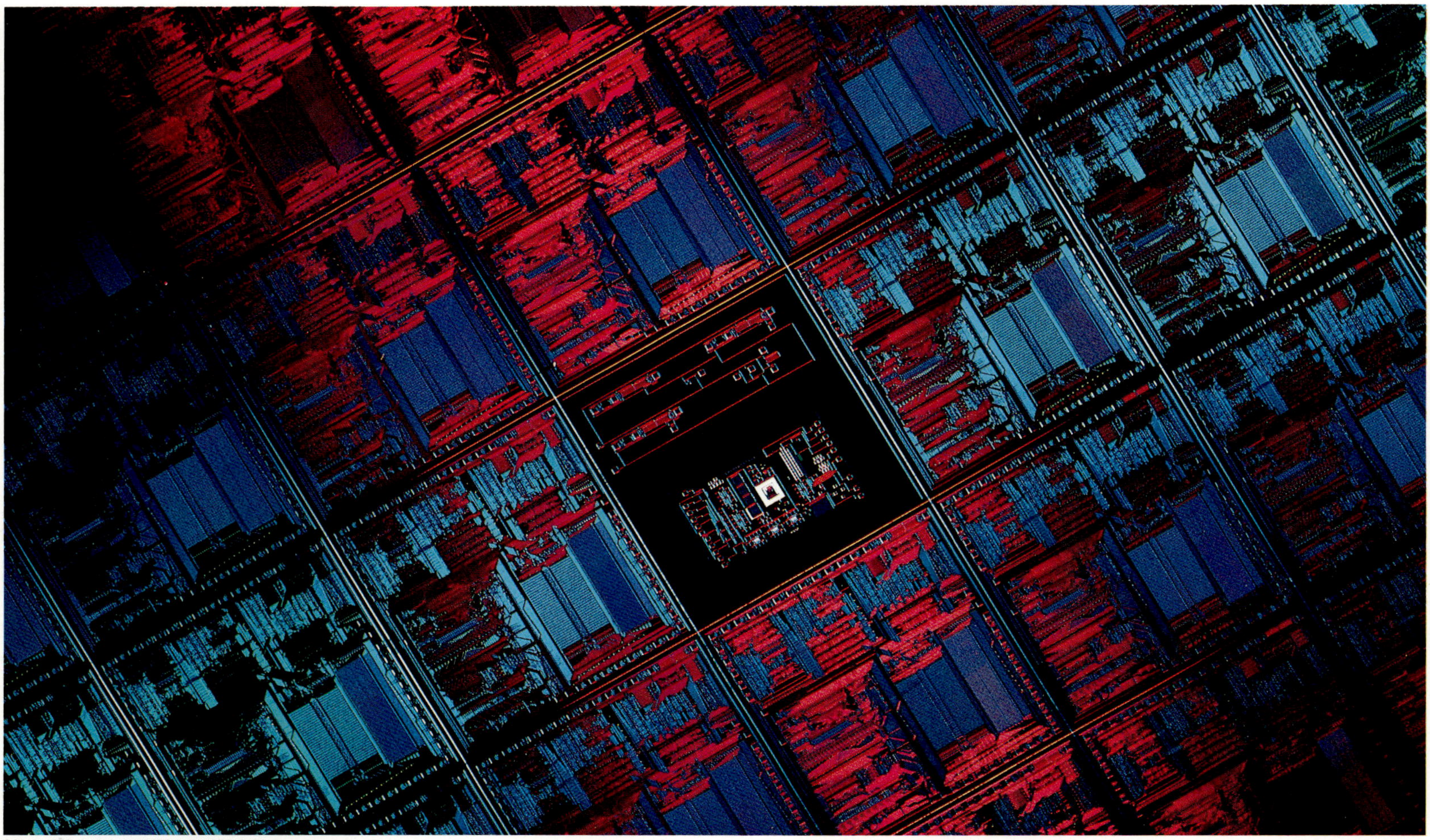

COMPUTER CHIPS: WESTERN ELECTRIC CO.

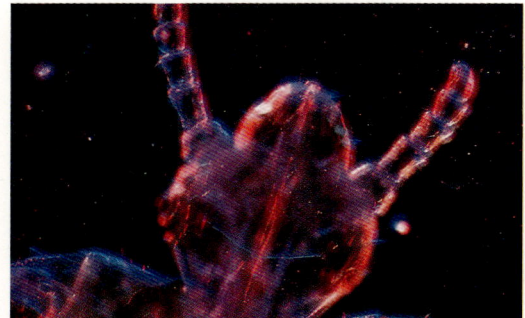

HEAD OF A LOUSE: MEDICAL ECONOMICS

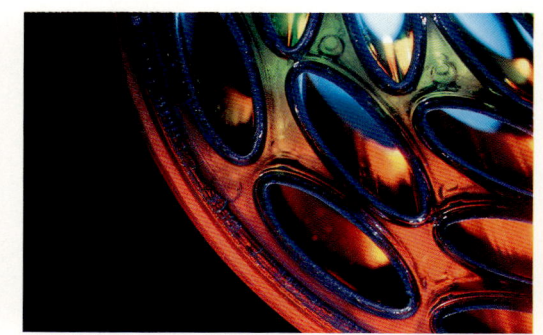

BLOOD OXYGENATOR: C.R. BARD CO.

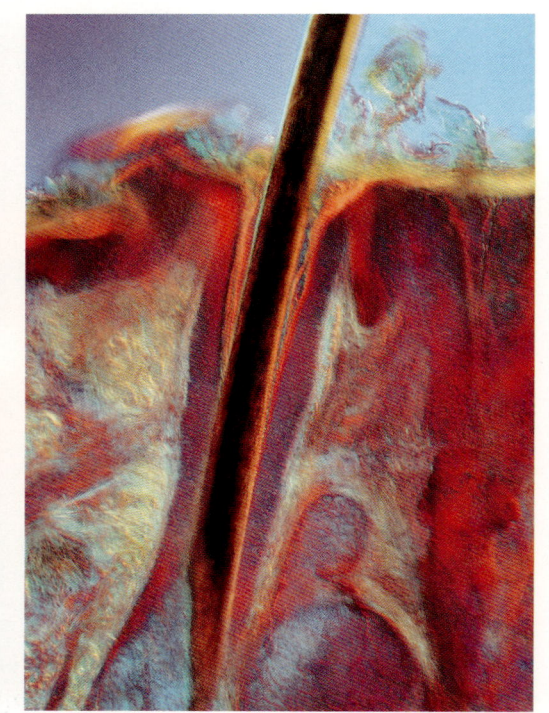

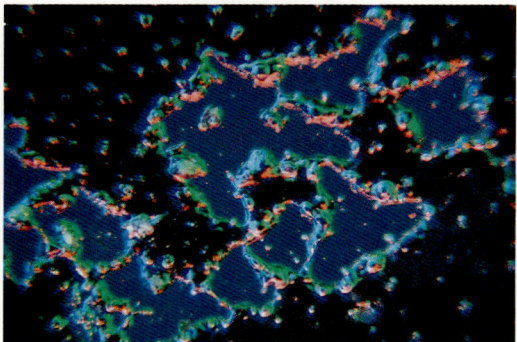

THULLIUM CRYSTALS: ALLIED CHEMICAL

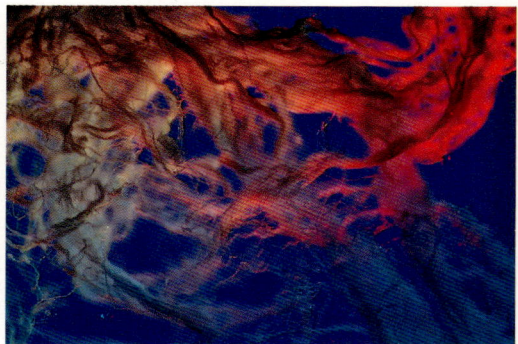

DNA FIBERS: REVLON ANNUAL REPORT

HAIR ROOT IN HEAD BONE

**BROWNIE HARRIS**
459 West 21st Street
New York, New York 10011
(212) 929-1796

1 ter rue Morère
75014 Paris, France
Tel: 540.59.92

Corporate/industrial, editorial and advertising photography

Partial client list: AT&T, *American Health,* ABC, *Business Week,* Chase Manhattan Bank, CBS Publications, *Connoisseur, Fortune,* Genentech Corporation, Hitachi, *Horizon,* I.B.M., Nabisco Brands, *Newsweek, New York Magazine,* Raytheon Corp., *Savvy,* St. Regis Paper, *Smithsonian,* Tandem Computer, *The New York Times,* United Airlines, Volkswagen of America.

Photographs © Brownie Harris, 1983

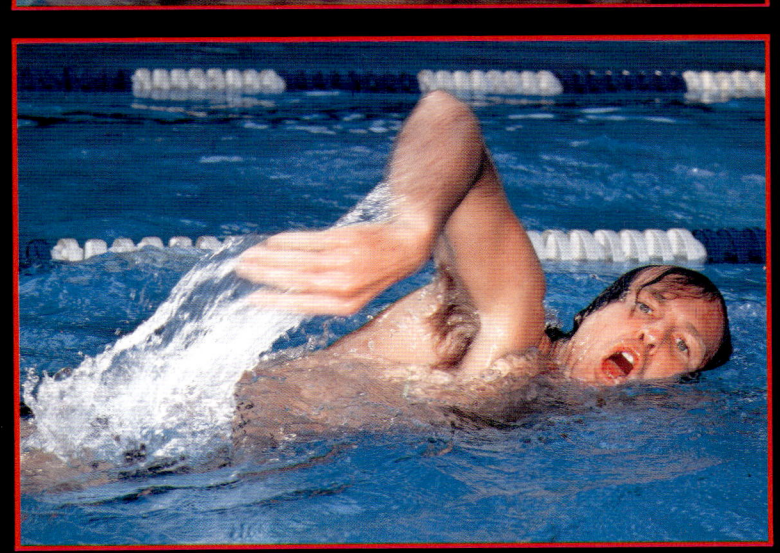

# Brownie Harris

459 West 21 Street
New York, N.Y. 10011
(212) 929·1796

**HASHI**
49 West 23rd Street
New York, New York 10010
(212) 675-6902

Represented by: Ken Mann
(212) 245-3192

**HASHI**
49 West 23rd Street
New York, New York 10010
(212) 675-6902

Represented by: Ken Mann
(212) 245-3192

**BRIAN HAVILAND
ASSOCIATE:
RICHARD LERNER**
34 East 23rd Street
New York, New York 10010
(212) 598-0070

Partial list of clients: Badische Corp., Ted Bates, Berkline, Blue Nun, Bufferin, Chase Manhattan, Creamer, Cunningham & Walsh, Inc., D.F.K., DiMarzio Musical Instruments, Dior, Doner, Doremus, Fiorentino Assocs., Hardwick, Lancaster, Lavey, Wolff & Swift, Martell, M.E.D. Communications, Music Technology Inc., Onkyo, OZ Communications, Sullivan & Brugnatelli, Syntex, Upjohn, Mario Valentino, JB Williams, Zotos International.

OZ COMMUNICATIONS

ONKYO AUDIO COMPONENTS

APA

**RYSZARD HOROWITZ**
103 Fifth Avenue
New York, New York 10003
(212) 243-6440

Representatives:

New York:
Sol Shamilzadeh (212) 532-1977

Paris:
Evelyne Menascè 227.24.82

Tokyo:
PPS (03) 264-3821
    (06) 531-5577

© Ryszard Horowitz 1983

WITH ILLUSTRATION BY ANDRZEJ DUDZINSKI

**JAMES JOERN**
125 Fifth Avenue
New York, New York 10003
(212) 260-8025

106

Stock photography available through James Joern Stock Files & Bruce Coleman, Ltd., NYC, 683-5227

Assignments: James Joern 260-8025 & NYC liaison Stuart Craig at Bruce Coleman, Ltd., 683-5227

Solutions for advertising, corporate, industrial, feature editorial & essay, plus the individual booklet. Your visual problems are my photographic adventures.

Photography produced for: N.W. Ayer; DuPont; *Natural History Magazine;* Trout & Ries; Western Union & Mortgage Guarantee Insurance Corporation; *Town & Country;* A R A Corporation; National C S S; *Datamation Magazine;* Pace; Madison Green; Leo Burnett; Allstate; *Ms. Magazine;* Hadley Lockwood, Inc.; *Independent Insurance Magazine;* Gray & Rogers; Ziff Davis Publishing; Ciba-Geigy; *Folio;* Leitz, E. Inc.; *Avenue;* Compton Adv.; Steve Phillips Design; Dow Chemical; Dun & Bradstreet; Geer DuBois; Atlantic Aviation; Rudolph DeHarak Design; First Pennsylvania Corporation; United Nations Plaza Hotel; *New York Times;* K P R; Wallace & Sandoz Laboratories; Time-Life Books; Micom Systems; Muller Jordan Weiss; Monsanto; Video Mentor; Hastings House; The Family of Children; Peat Marwick & Mitchell; The World.

**PETER JOHANSKY**
108 East 16th Street
New York, New York 10003
(212) 260-4301
(212) 361-7400

© Peter Johansky 1983
ASMP Member

Clients include: ABC Network Radio, Avon, Cunard, Frito-Lay, Noxell Corporation, Phelps Dodge, Putnam Books, Sony.

Portfolio available.

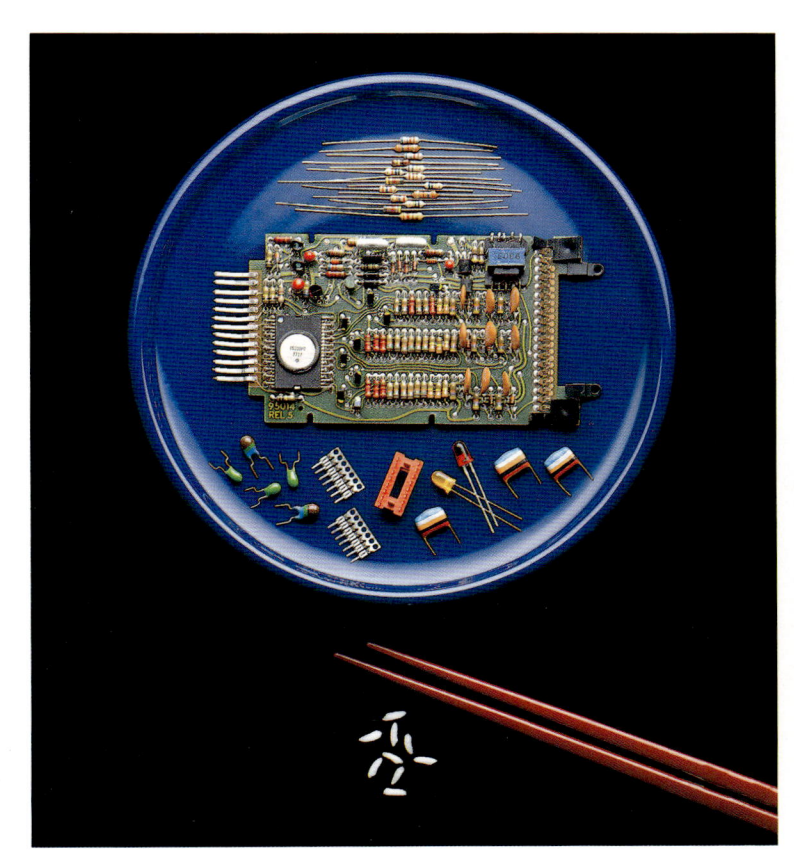

107

**LONNY KALFUS**
36 Myrtle Avenue
Edgewater, New Jersey 07020
(212) 868-3370
(201) 886-0776

Location photography for business and editorial clients worldwide.
People—from kids to CEO's portrayed in a relaxed and natural manner.
Strong Graphics—from aerials to the computer room.
Images for Advertising, Annual Reports, Editorial & Multi-Media

Clients include: ACT/Pace, Allied Corp., American Cyanimid, ASARCO, AT&T, Borg-Warner, Bristol-Myers, Chase Manhattan, Columbia Pictures, DataCom, Dictaphone, Equitable Life, McNeil Pharmaceuticals, Trans Freight Lines, Western Union.

Additional portfolio samples available upon request.

© Lonny Kalfus, 1984.

**PETER B. KAPLAN**
126 West 23rd Street
New York, New York 10011
(212) 206-1362

Some of the corporations that have used that view from a different angle are:

Fortune, Life, Smithsonian, AMOCO, AT&T, Goodyear, Philip Morris, Statue of Liberty Commission, Tenneco.

**KAREN KENT**
29 John Street
New York, New York 10038
(212) 962-6793

Represented by:
Doug Sheer
(212) 732-4216

Location photography for advertising, corporate/industrial and editorial.

Wide variety of unique images available for purchase from stock.

Cibachrome, black and white museum quality prints provided directly to corporate, private collectors and designers.

Member ASMP

Copyright © 1983

**KEN KORSH**
118 East 28th Street
New York, New York 10016
(212) 685-8864

*Client list:*
Burger King
HBO-Cinemax
Exxon
Citibank
Frank B. Hall
Fotomat
Bell System
Irving Trust
T-Bar Inc.
Astoria Federal Savings and Loan
Allied Corp.
Royal Zenith Corp.
Audit Bureau of Circulation
Merrill Lynch
Practising Law Institute
Anthony Russel Design
Mobay Chemical

*Agencies:*
Bryant Press
Grey Advertising
Foote
Cone and Belding
McCaffery and McCall
J. Walter Thompson
Greenstone and Rabasca
Soskin-Thompson
Young and Rubicam
Lubliner/Saltz

*Magazines:*
Redbook
Ladie's Home Journal
New York Magazine
Institutional Investor
Finanical World Mag.
Science '82
Seventeen Magazine

**GARY D. LANDSMAN & ASSOCIATES**
Washington, D.C.
(301) 468-2588

Environmental Photography including:
Architecture
Interiors
Furniture
Room Sets
(Large Accessible Studio)

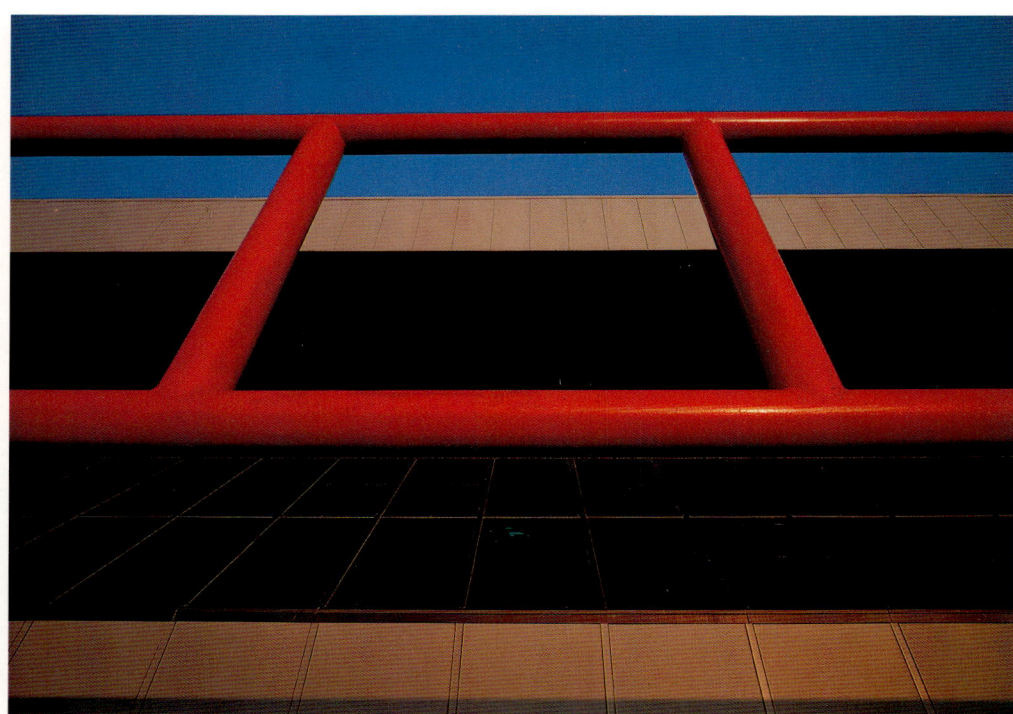

112

**GARY D. LANDSMAN & ASSOCIATES**
Washington, D.C.
(301) 468-2588

Environmental Photography For:
Annual Reports
Advertising
Capabilities Brochures
Your location or... We'll build it for you in our large accessible studio.

113

**WHITNEY LANE**
109 Somerstown Road
Ossining, New York 10562
(914) 762-5335

Stock photography available through The Image Bank:
(212) 953-0303

I specialize in taking whatever picture has to be taken, wherever it must be taken (including underwater).

Not all my clients see things the same way: Anaconda Ericsson, AMF, AT&T, Avon, Ciba-Geigy, Duracell, General Foods, IBM, Ingersoll-Rand, Johnson & Johnson, Lederle, Olin, Osram, Pepsico, Reader's Digest, Savin, Sears Roebuck, Textron, Upjohn, Ziff-Davis and...

My Studio (part of a 200-year-old farmhouse) is located in Westchester, only a short distance from New York City. Unique locations are everywhere.

If you would like to see things a little differently, maybe you should call for my portfolio.

CIBA-GEIGY: RON VARELTZIS AD

INGERSOLL-RAND: DMCD: ED DE MARTIN; WENDY OPPEL AD

UPJOHN: KALLIR, PHILIPS, ROSS: GERALD PHILIPS AD

FAMILIES: NORMAN HOTZ AD

114

**KAREN LEEDS**
119 West 23rd Street
New York, New York 10011
(212) 243-4546

Partial List of Clients:

Benton & Bowles, CBS Publications, Chesebrough-Ponds, Corpcom Services, *Cosmopolitan,* Coty, *Cuisine,* Evyan Fragrances, Germaine Monteil, Grand Marnier, IBM, Macy's, Merrill-Lynch, McGraw-Hill, *New York Magazine,* Perfumer's Workshop, Ltd., *Redbook,* Revlon, *Self,* Uniworld, Wunderman, Ricotta & Kline, Young and Rubicam.

KAREN LEEDS

APA

**THOMAS LEIGHTON**
c/o Penthouse 12
321 East 43rd Street
New York, New York 10017
(212) 370-1835 (office)
(212) 532-2925 (service)

All location photography: industrial/corporate, advertising, editorial, specializing in architecture.

Clients include:
Merrill Lynch
Citibank
Smith Barney
IBM
The Morgan Bank
W.R. Grace
Mobil
Equitable Life
Texaco
C.I.T.
AT&T
European American Bank

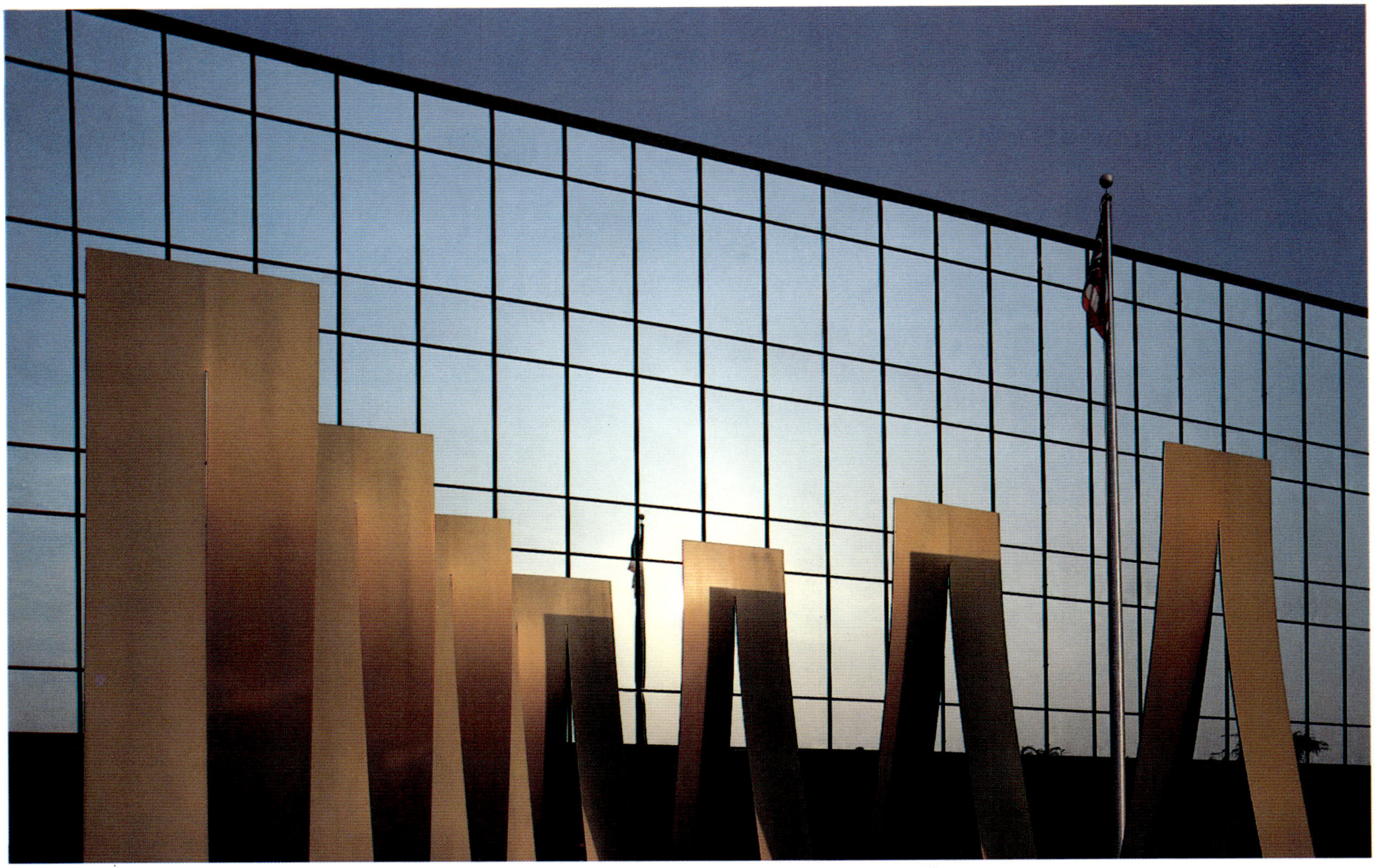

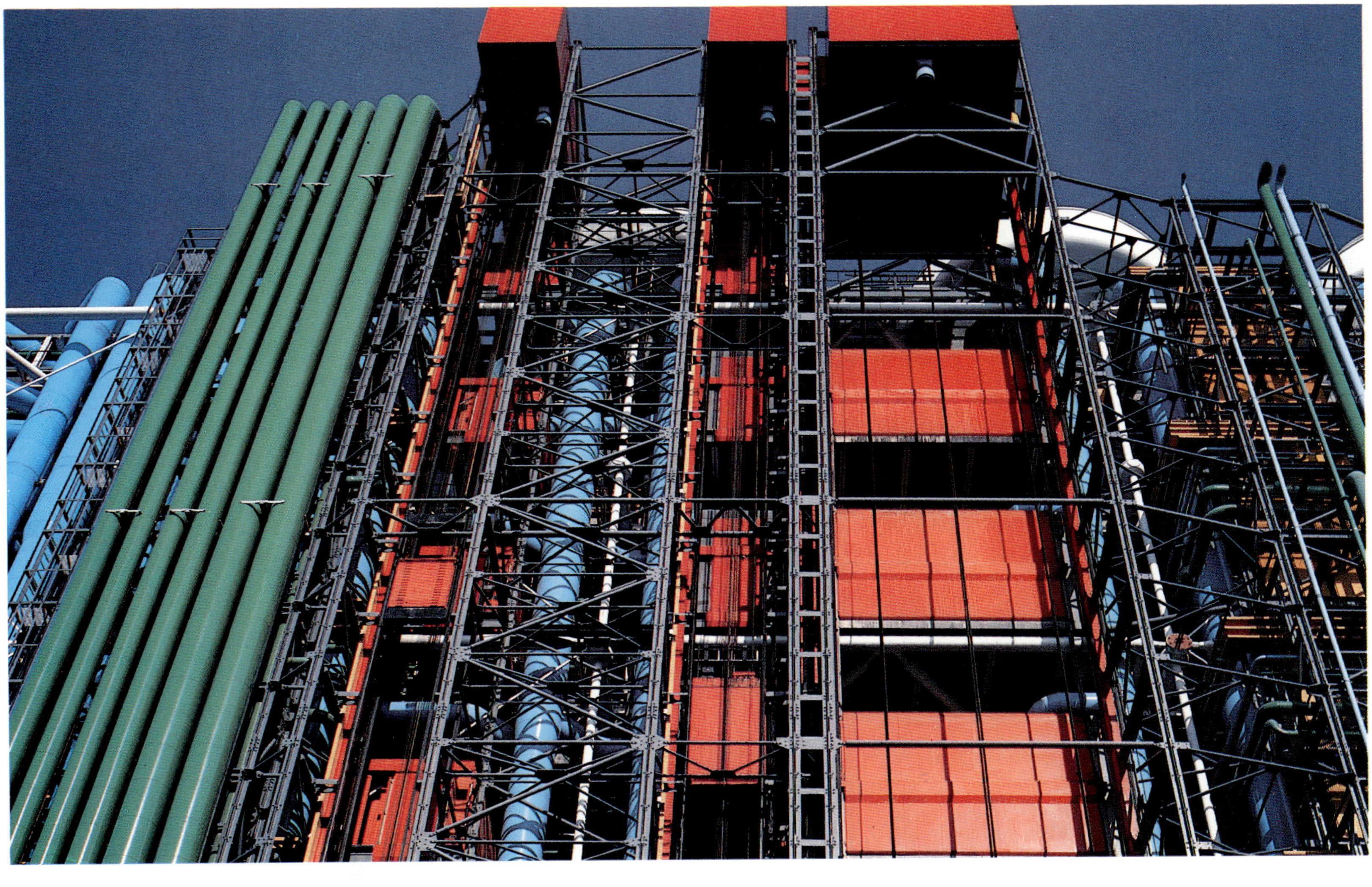

**JOOK LEUNG PHOTOGRAPHY**
110 East 23rd Street
New York, New York 10010
(212) 254-8334

Stock photography available thru:
BLUE CHIP STOCK
(212) 750-1386

Client List includes:

American Express, Baume & Mercier, Bentley Industries, Boris Kroll Fabrics, Clarins, *Datamation Magazine,* Dean Witter Reynolds, Deknatel, General Instrument Corp., Estée Lauder, *Institutional Investor,* Lazare Kaplan & Sons, Mercedes-Benz, Merrill Lynch, Minolta Corp., Oppenheimer & Co., Owens-Corning Fiberglas, Paine Webber, Parfums de Coeur, Playboy Enterprises, Random House, Reuters, Ltd., Simon & Schuster, Sony Corporation, Spectra Video, *Technology Magazine,* The Perfumer's Workshop, United Technologies, Winston International, Ziff-Davis

© 1984 JOOK LEUNG
Member ASMP, PPA

See also Corporate Showcase
Volume 2 page 36

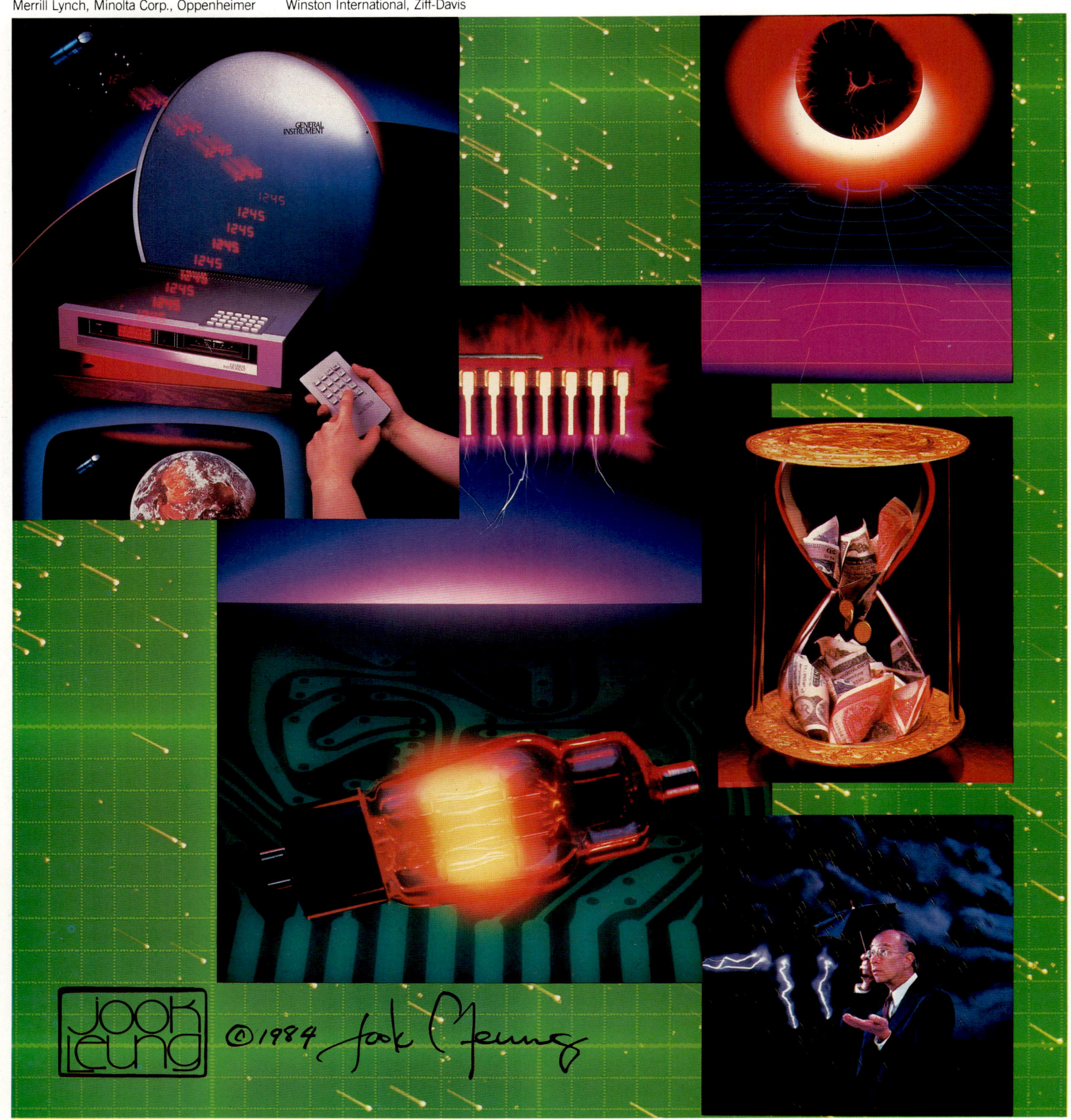

118

**DICK LURIA PHOTOGRAPHY, INC.**
5 East 16th Street
New York, New York 10003
(212) 929-7575

Corporate and industrial photography for major graphic design firms and Fortune 500 companies such as: Allegheny Corporation, Allied Corporation, American Airlines, American Hoechst, Bell Labs, Chemical Bank, Eastern Airlines, Eaton Corporation, Fortune, General Electric, General Signal, Getty Refining, W.R. Grace, Hoffmann-La Roche, E.F. Hutton, IBM, Ingersoll-Rand, ITT, International Paper, Lever Brothers, Merrill Lynch, North American Phillips, Penn Central, Pratt & Whitney, Purolator Courier, Ryder Systems, Savin, TWA, United Technologies, Warner-Lambert, Westvaco.

Stock available.

© Dick Luria 1984

PUROLATOR COURIER

PUROLATOR COURIER

PUROLATOR COURIER

**JIM MARCHESE**
200 West 20th Street
New York, New York 10011
(212) 242-1087

Represented by Mary Lamont

Photography for advertising, annual reports, corporate communications, editorial and travel. AIGA, Andy, Art Directors Club and CA awards. Member ASMP.

Clients have included American Express, Analog & Digital Systems, *Attenzione*, *Avenue*, Ballantine Books, *Barron's*, Capitol/EMI, Colorado Heritage Center, DelMonte Canada, *Discover*, Exxon, Federal Express, Grow Group, Hanover Square Securities, Life of Virginia, Merrill Lynch, *New York Magazine*, OTB New York, Pan Am, *Print*, *Reader's Digest*, Saks Fifth Avenue, Schirmer Music, South Bronx Development Corporation, Bruce Springsteen, T. Rowe Price, Texaco, TWA, Western Union, *Wall Street Journal*.

120

**JIM MARCHESE**
200 West 20th Street
New York, New York 10011
(212) 242-1087

Represented by Mary Lamont

Photography for advertising, annual reports, corporate communications, editorial and travel. AIGA, Andy, Art Directors Club and CA awards. Member ASMP.

© Jim Marchese 1984

121

**JIM MARCHESE's** clients have included American Express, Analog & Digital Systems, Attenzione, Avenue, Ballantine Books, Barron's, Capitol/EMI, Colorado Heritage Center, DelMonte Canada, Discover, Exxon, Federal Express, Grow Group, Hanover Securities, Life of Virginia, Merrill Lynch, New York Magazine, OTB New York, Pan Am, Print, Reader's Digest, Saks Fifth Avenue, Schirmer Music, South Bronx Development Corp., Bruce Springsteen, T. Rowe Price, Texaco, TWA, Western Union, Wall Street Journal (Creative Directors Campaign). Stock available.

**REPRESENTED BY MARY LAMONT 212-242-1087**

**FRANK MARESCA**
236 West 26th Street
New York, New York 10001
(212) 620-0955

Advertising and Editorial
Beauty, Fashion, People

Select Stock with:
International Stock N.Y.C.

Member A.P.A.

Promotional Posters on Request

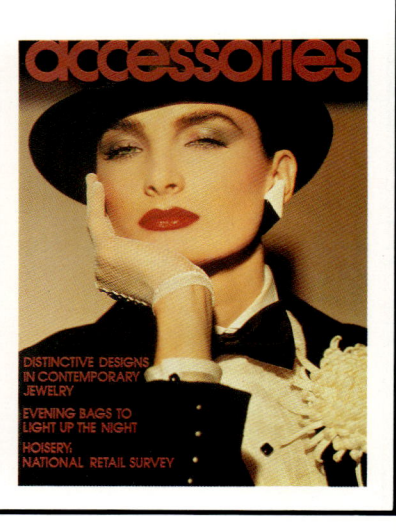

# MARESCA

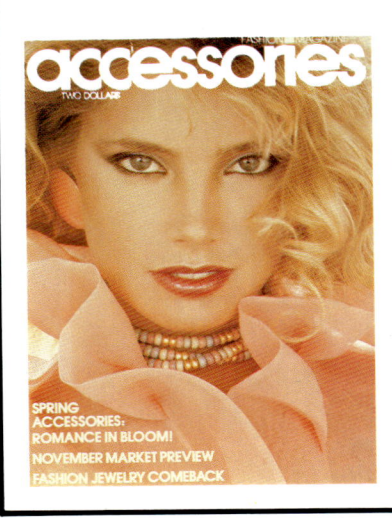

**LEE MARSHALL**
201 West 89th Street
New York, New York 10024
(212) 799-9717

All photographs © Lee Marshall 1984

Advertising, architecture, corporate, industrial, medical, pharmaceutical, product, and travel photography.

Partial list of clients: Apollo Technologies, Inc., Atlantic Records, Avery-Knodel Television, Ballantine Books, Bobbs-Merrill, Dome, Economics Lab, Inc., EMI Records, Foster Wheeler, Gulf & Western Company, Key Pharmaceuticals, Inc., MCA Music, McGraw-Hill, Miles Laboratories, Monsanto, 3M Company, New Directions Books, Pfizer Medical Systems, Inc., RCA Records, Riker Lab, *Signature Magazine,* Sire Records, Solid State Heating Corporation, Telecom Plus, *Time, Inc.,* Time International, Time-Life Video, TVI Energy Corporation.

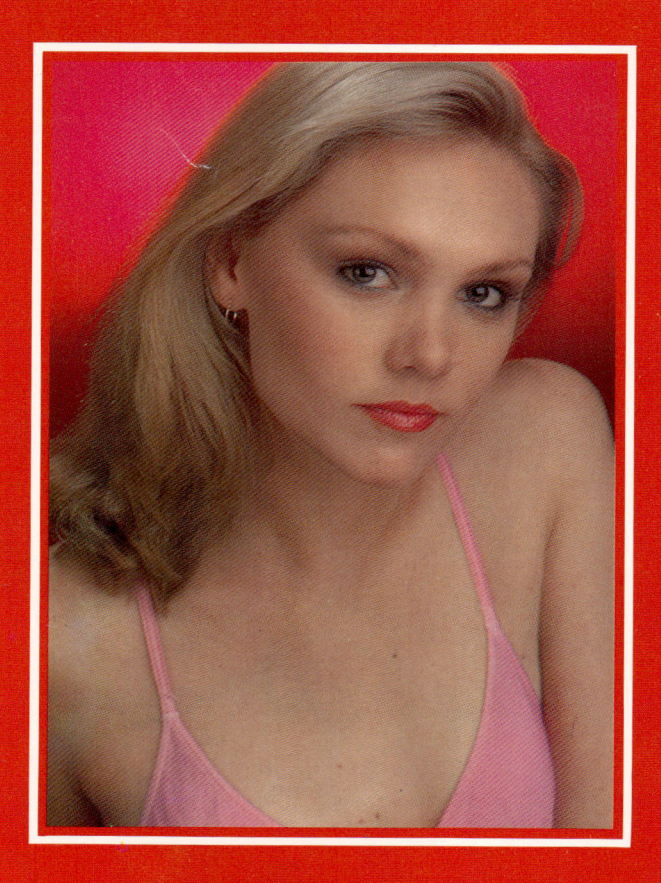

124

**BUTCH MARTIN**
(212) 563-6363

Beauty & Fashion

Editorial work has appeared in:

—British Vogue
—Linea Italiana
—Harper's Bazaar (Italia)
—Zoom

Existing Photography:
The Image Bank
(212) 953-0303

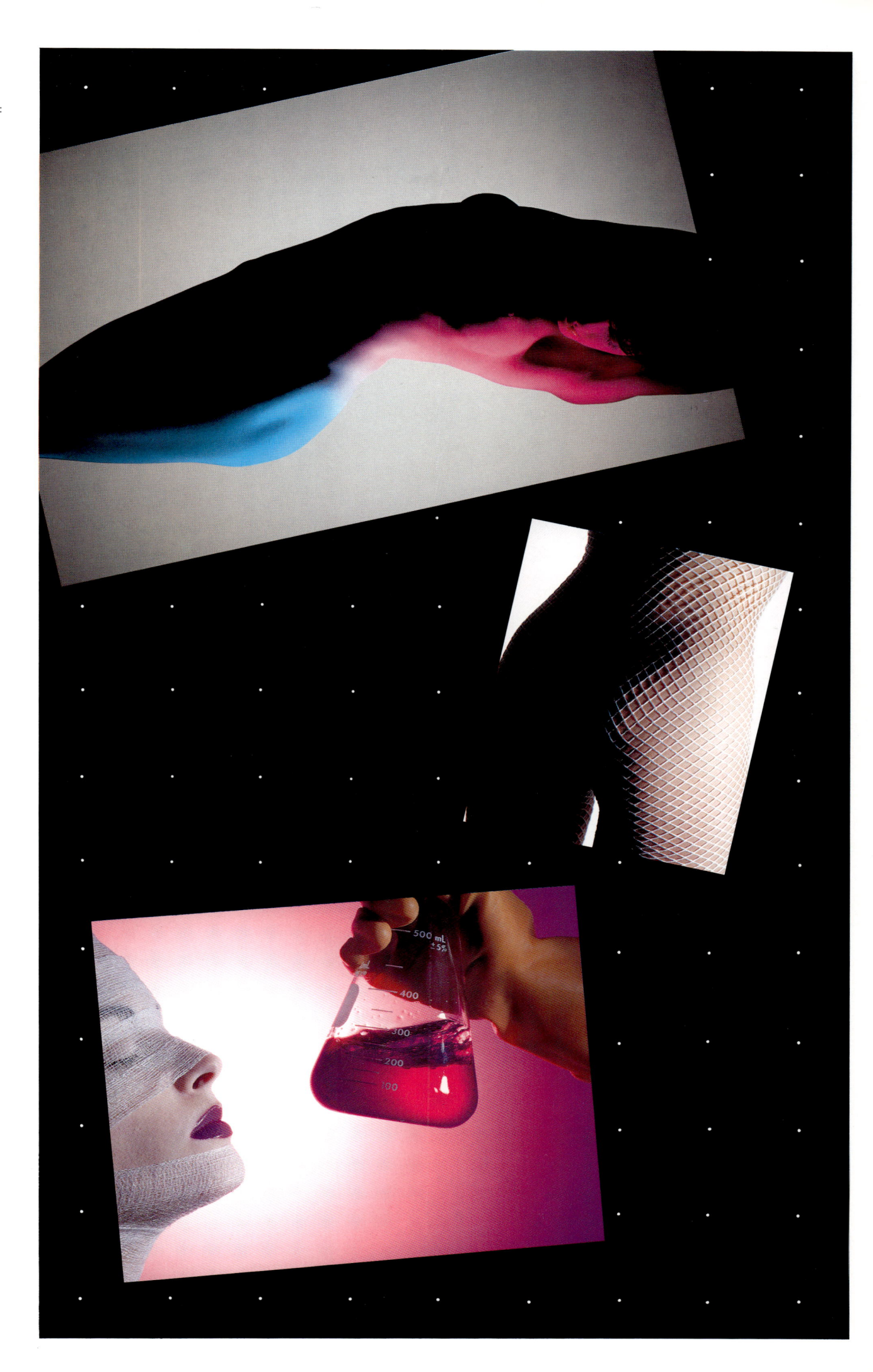

THE IMAGE BANK

**JOHN MCGRAIL**
522 East 20th Street
New York, New York 10009
(212) 475-4927

Worldwide photography for advertising, annual report, corporate, editorial, sports and travel clients.

Specialties include aerial and remote camera photography.

Selected stock available.

© John McGrail 1984. All Rights Reserved.

1. Stock
2. English castles for *National Geographic*
3. Bob Guccione for *Business Week*
4. Winemaking for *Discover*
5. Bath Iron Works for *Fortune*

Clients include: ABC Sports, Abrams Books ("Manhattan" and "Washington, D.C."), *Bunte, Business Week, Changing Times, Connoisseur, Cosmopolitan, Discover, Elle, Forbes, Fortune, Geo,* Grolier, Guest Informant, IBM, *Life, London Sunday Times,* Mobay, *Money, National Geographic, Nation's Business,* Nike, *Parade, Parents,* Pony, Raytheon, *Running,* Scholastic Inc., *Smithsonian, Sports Illustrated, Time, TV-Cable Week,* United Technologies, U.S. Information Agency, *USA Today, U.S. News & World Report,* Warner Communications, *Women's Sports.*

**D.W. MELLOR**
Darby and Marple Roads
Haverford, Pennsylvania 19041
Studio: (215) 649-6087

CLIENT: Douglas, we know you do beautiful still lifes, but do you photograph executives?

DOUGLAS: Of course...

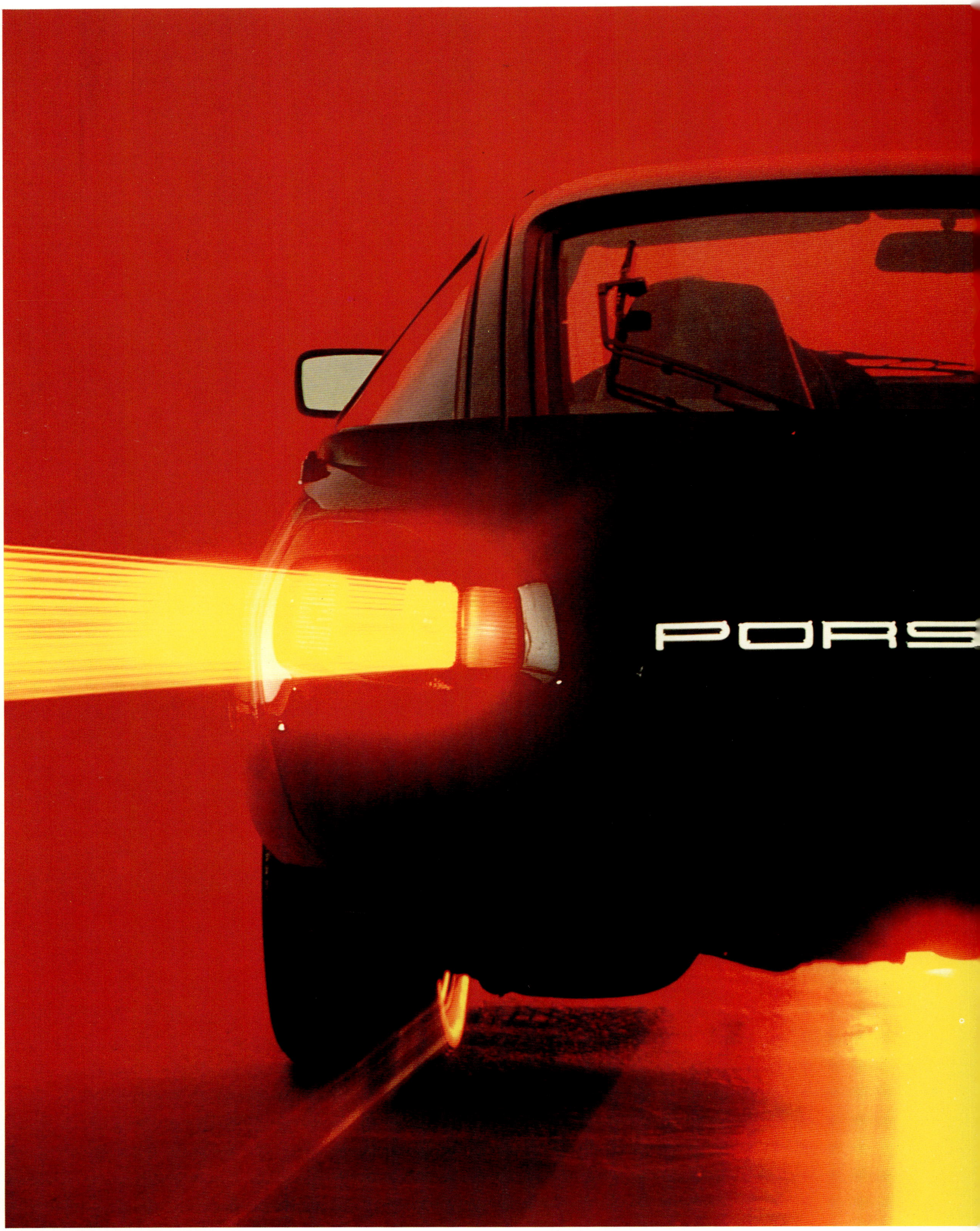
PORS

**ERIC MEOLA STUDIO, INC.**
535 Greenwich Street
New York, New York 10013
(212) 255-5150

Representatives:
New York:
Les Klein (212) 832-7220
Out-of-Town:
Call Studio Direct
Tokyo:
P.P.S. Tsushinsha (03) 264-3821

ROAD WARRIOR
©1984 ERIC MEOLA

ERIC MEOLA

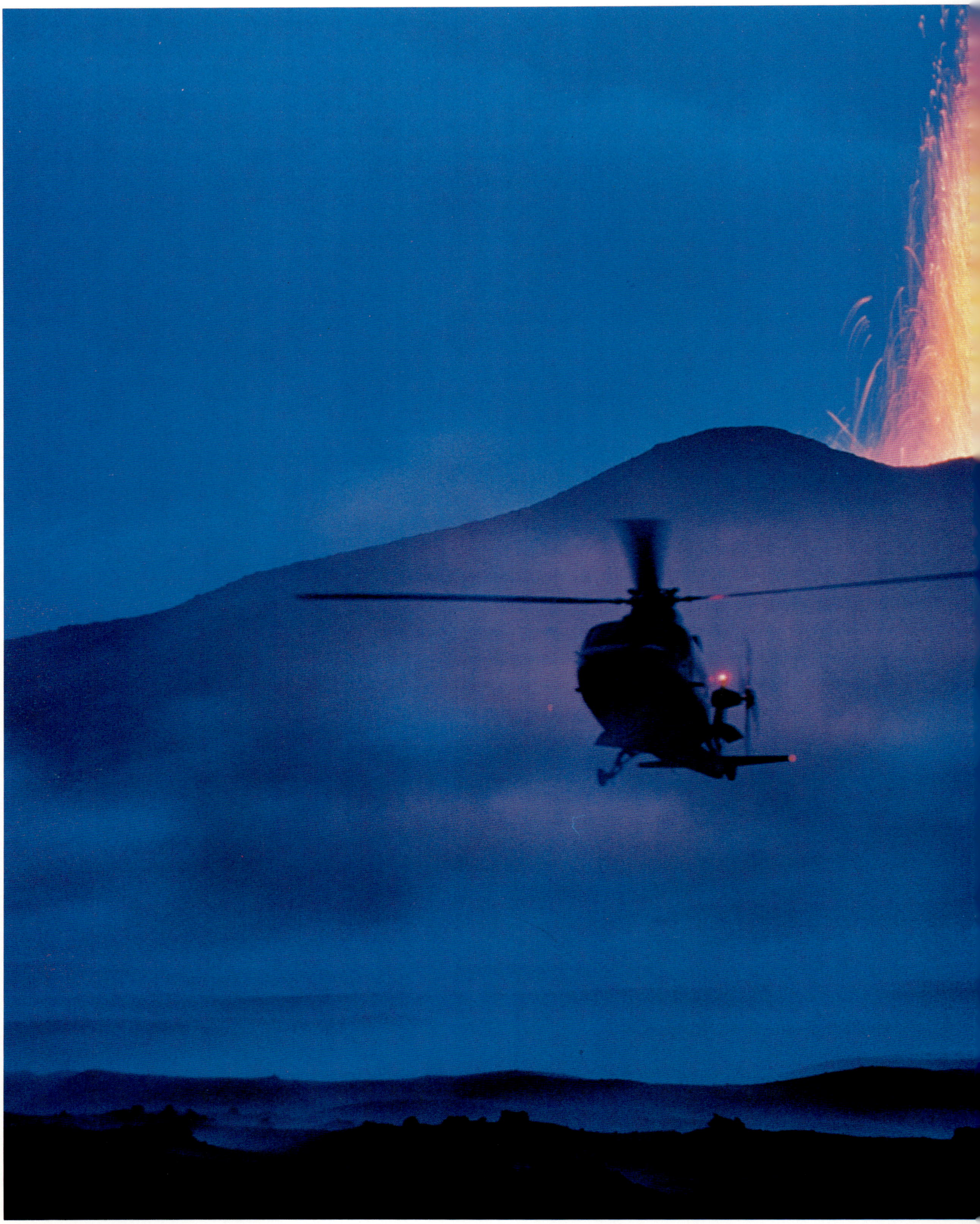

**ERIC MEOLA STUDIO, INC.**
535 Greenwich Street
New York, New York 10013
(212) 255-5150

Representatives:
New York:
Les Klein (212) 832-7220
Out-of-Town:
Call Studio Direct
Tokyo:
P.P.S. Tsushinsha (03) 264-3821

FORBIDDEN ISLAND (KILAUEA)
© 1984 ERIC MEOLA

ERIC MEOLA

ERIC MEOLA
PORSCHE
ERIC MEOLA
ERIC MEOLA
ERIC MEOLA
ERIC MEOLA
MALIBU
MORE FUN THAN RUM...
ERIC MEOLA
LONGER BETWEEN FILL-UPS. LONGER BETWEEN CARS.
THE VOLVO DIESEL
ERIC MEOLA
ERIC MEOLA
ERIC MEOLA
Color me Plus!
Colorplus
ERIC MEOLA
ERIC MEOLA
ERIC MEOLA

**ERIC MEOLA STUDIO, INC.**
535 Greenwich Street
New York, New York 10013
(212) 255-5150

Representatives:
New York:
Les Klein (212) 832-7220
Out-of-Town:
Call Studio Direct
Tokyo:
P.P.S. Tsushinsha (03) 264-3821

Advertising, corporate and editorial photography for domestic and foreign clients, including Almay, AT&T, IBM, LIFE, Nikon, Panasonic, Polaroid, Porsche, Rockwell International, Warner Communications, Winston, Xerox. Color, graphics, and concept applied to travel, still-life, beauty, illustration and corporate communications. Self-promotion booklets available upon request. Direct sales of stock images and prints available through the studio.

Campagnes de grande ampleur, annonces publicitaires, travaux sur brochures d'enterprises et sur magazines pour clients francais et étrangers, dont Porsche, IBM et Polaroid. Réalisation couleur, graphisme et création pour les articles de style nature morte, les voyages, les produits de beauté les illustrations symboliques et les publications des sociétés. Trois brochures auto-publitaires contenant plus de cinquante pages en couleur sont disponibles sur demande. Ventes directes de transferts de couleurs (dimensions 76 cm x 101 cm) aux entreprises, dessinateurs et collectionneurs.

Bedutende Kampagnen, Werbeanzeigen, Aufträge von deutschen und ausländischen Zeitschriften und Internehmen wie Porsche, IBM und Polaroid. Farbvorschläge, graphische Darstellungen und Konzepte für fotographische Stilleben, für die Reise- und die Kosmetikindustrie, symbolische Darstellungen und Veröffentlichungen von Firmen. Drei erläuternde Broschüren über uns selbst mit mehr als fünfzig Farbseiten stehen auf Anfrage zur Verfügung, Direktverkauf von Farbübertragungen (76 cm x 101 cm) an Unternehmen, Designer und Sammler.

ポルシェ、IBM、ポラロイドをはじめ内外のクライアントの広告キャンペーン、企業の広報メディア、一般雑誌など広い制作範囲を持つ。洗練されたグラフィック、濃密なカラー、斬新なコンセプトを駆使し、特に精密機器、女性商品、観光地紹介などの撮影に卓抜な手腕を発揮する 50余ページからなる自己紹介用のパンフレットをご希望の方に提供。また企業、デザイナー、コレクターを対象にダイトランスファープリント（76 x 101cm）の直売を行っている。

©1984 ERIC MEOLA
DESIGN: WEEKS & TOOMEY INC.

**DONALD L. MILLER**
485 Fifth Avenue
New York, New York 10017
(212) 986-9783

Specializing in C.E.O.'s, Chairmen, Presidents,
Directors and top management.

134

**DONALD L. MILLER**
485 Fifth Avenue
New York, New York 10017
(212) 986-9783

Specializing in C.E.O.'s, Chairmen, Presidents,
Directors and top management.

135

**RUSSELL MUNSON**
6 East 39th Street
New York, New York 10016
(212) 689-7672

PHOTOGRAPHY FROM THE AIR.

© Russell Munson 1983

136

**TOM MUSTO**
225 South Main Street
Wilkes-Barre, Pennsylvania 18701
(717) 822-5798

Photography and Film for Industrial and Corporate Training, Annual Reports, Product Ads and Catalogs.

From around the World and Beyond.

**MYERS STUDIOS, INC.**
21 Princeton Place
Orchard Park, New York 14127
(716) 662-6002

Represented in New York by:
Susan Silverman (212) 586-3700

138

WHERE DO YOU SHOOT AN ELEPHANT? Why, you could shoot an entire circus in our spacious studios. With over 20,000 square feet, Myers Studios is one of the largest, best-equipped photographic facilities in the Eastern U.S. We feel that no job is too big for us.

If you happen to be shooting a product that won't walk in on its own, we have a forklift to unload it. If it's big, we can shoot it in our 60-foot cove ('cyc'). If it's edible, we can prepare it to perfection in our studio kitchen. If it's drab, we can bring it alive with creative set design—even building entire rooms or office scenes. And to assure you that you have what you came for, we have a major lab on the premises—so we can show you your results before we tear down your set. (You might want your own copy of our lab's price catalog.)

But our expansive physical capabilities are only the beginning. We've assembled a staff of highly skilled photographers, lab technicians, stylists and support personnel. People who understand the finer subtleties of the art. People who have produced some of the most arresting, award-winning photography you're ever likely to see. People dedicated to excellence.

We won't pretend that such first-rate photography only costs peanuts. But you will find our prices *very* competitive, especially when compared with those charged by studios in major urban centers. Yet our peaceful rural location is quickly accessible—just twenty minutes from the Buffalo International Airport.

Sound impressive? Give us a call. We'd love to discuss your next studio session with you.

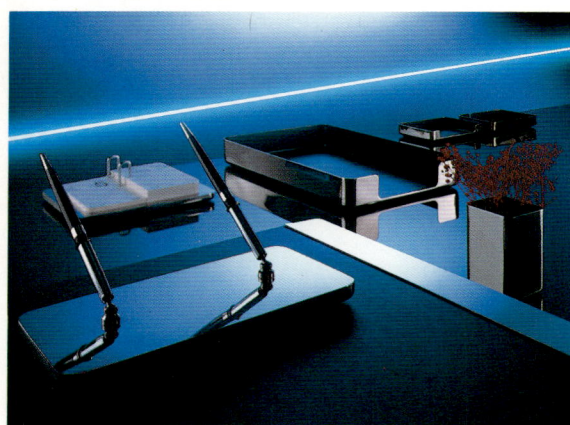

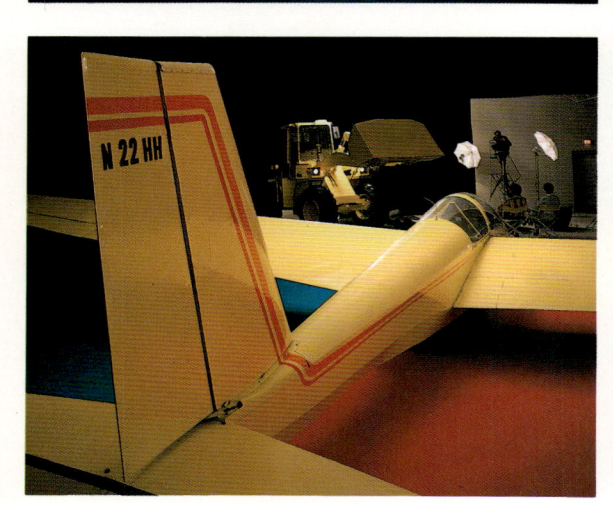

**JAY NADELSON STUDIO**
116 Mercer Street
New York, New York 10012
(212) 226-4266

Color Graphics and Concepts

- Advertising
- Corporate
- Editorial
- Fashion
- Location
- Special Effects
- Call for Book

In New York: Call Studio Direct
(212) 226-4266

In Far East: Call Dave Jampel
Imperial Press
Tokyo, Japan
011-81-3-585-2721

For Stock: The Stock Market
(212) 684-7878

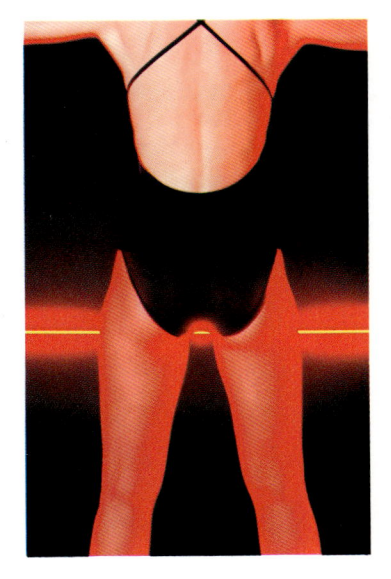

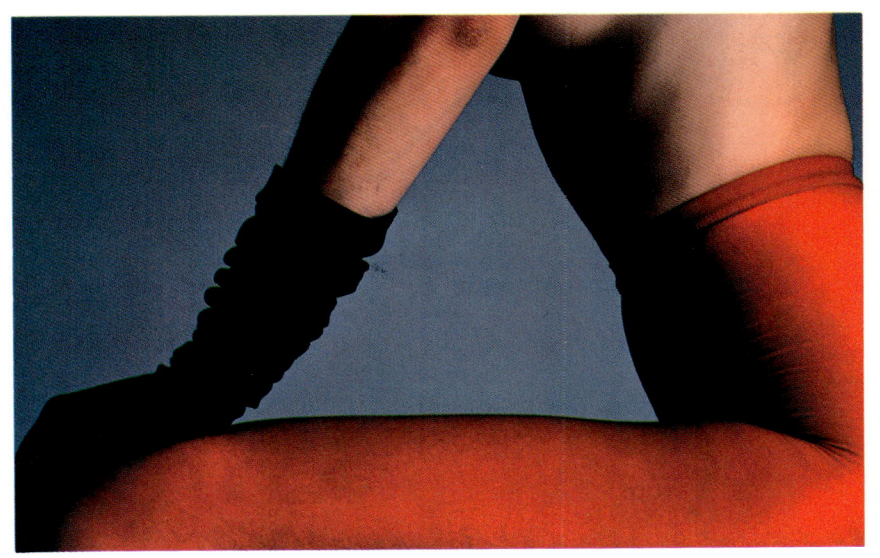

139

## CALL CALL CALL

Three years ago, a close photographer friend of mine was back-packing along, near Grand Central Station. As was his wont, a tennis racquet handle was sticking out of his pack.

"I could hardly believe it," he related to me. "Marching right toward me was Ilie Nastase. We made eye contact as his hand made a sort of salute motion. I stopped. He said, 'Excuse me, can you tell me how to get to Flushing Meadows Stadium?' It was my chance of a lifetime. I looked him straight in the eye and said: 'Practice, practice, practice.'" Nastase enjoyed the moment as much as my friend did. And I enjoyed it even more.

I can't think of when I last thought of my photographer friend as a supplier, and the reasons for this form the basis of my article. My marvelous, witty and wonderful friend might have remained a photographer, a witty problem-solving supplier, a wonderful tennis player—and I never would have had the pleasure of using his professional talent or enjoying his personal friendship (and stories) if he hadn't called me back…about twelve times before I ever found the opportunity to use him!

So that is my message to all of you out there: Please call me, and keep calling. I have one wife. I have three sons. I have three partners. I have six art directors and four associate art directors on my staff, and I have more than fifteen major clients. I also have a studio with twenty people. I work with twelve writers and with another hundred plus employees at the agency—not to mention outside suppliers. Add up the numbers. They should tell you how I do on remembering names and portfolios.

Do I need you? It is highly possible. When I do need you, will I jump on the phone and call you? It is highly improbable; especially if I have only seen your book once and you've never called back. I work regularly with three exceptional photographers, all of whom have become my friends and chances are I will call them first. Or use someone who has called me back recently. All I've ever asked of people who show me their books is that they call me, call me back, and keep calling me—about once a month. Some people think this is embarrassing. Others think they're above this sort of contact.

Anybody who calls me, rep or artist, gets his or her book seen by me. I also call my art directors and writers in to see books. In our agency we share calls. You can see me and see five other people while you're here. When you leave, I'll tell you to call me again. I don't mean that in the "We must get together sometime" syntax. I MEAN IT. CALL ME. CALL ME ONCE A MONTH.

I don't make formal appointments. I tell everybody the same thing: "Yes, I'd like to look at your book. Please call me a half hour before you come."

If I have to cancel, I will let you know before you get on the subway or into the cab. I have to report—sadly—that in the past nine months, of all the books I have seen, and of all the "Keep calling me" messages I have given out, only two photographers have accepted my invitation to call back. As I write this, one of them is getting a call from one of my art directors. It was not timed to meet the deadline for this article. It is the way our business goes.

I previously mentioned both my family and business associates. As I start each day, both of them impact upon me. Your life is no different, I know. But there is one small diference: You know who I am. You know my agency, and, if you've done your homework, you know we buy a great deal of print photographic work.

I may not know you or remember you all that well. If the last time you were in my office was two, four, six or twelve months ago, your book may have been incredible, but I don't remember you. There were many who came before or after you whose books were what I needed some time down the road. There were four or five more whose work I really liked but couldn't use at the time, and on it goes. Did you call me back? I invited you to. Did you call? I told you to check in with me once a month. Did you? Or were you too embarrassed? I'm still here. I don't keep score.

Call me, and call me back. If it takes more than two calls before I need your services (and it probably will) keep calling. If someone stops you in the street and asks you how to get to Sal deRouin, look him straight in the eye and say, "Call. Call. Call."

**Sal de Rouin**
**Senior Vice President**
**Creative Director**
**Rolf Werner Rosenthal, Inc.**
**New York City**

**SIMON NATHAN-PANORAMICS**
275 West 96th Street
New York, New York 10025
(212) 873-5560

Photo file @ The Stock Market
(212) 684-7878

Simon Nathan-Panoramics
275 West 96 Street
New York, N.Y. 10025 USA
(212) 873-5560
Photo file @ The Stock Market (212) 684-7878

Top: Venezuela 2¼" x 7", 75°
Center - Canyon Hotel, Palm Springs
9" Left to Right represent 360°
Bottom - Toronto 120 on 7" 120 Film
All shown actual film size.

**GEORGE OBREMSKI**
1200 Broadway
New York, New York 10001
(212) 684-2933

Represented by:
Susan Steiner
(212) 673-4704

In Copenhagen—contact:
Finn Rosted
(01) 11.65.25

In Rio—contact:
Raul Canto E Mello
274-5559

In Tokyo—contact:
Dave Jampel
585-2721

# GEORGE OBREMSKI

## 1200 BROADWAY NYC 10001 TEL. 212-684-2933

REPRESENTED BY SUSAN STEINER 212-673-4704     IN TOKYO CONTACT DAVE JAMPEL TEL. 585-2721
IN COPENHAGEN CONTACT FINN ROSTED TEL. (01) 11 65 25    IN RIO CONTACT RAUL CANTO E MELLO TEL. 274-5559

**RONN ORENSTEIN**
55 West 26th Street
New York, New York 10010
(212) 685-0563

Advertising, product, and editorial photography.

Producing photographic images for advertising. Bring me your problems...

ASMP

**GABE PALMER**
Palmer/Kane, Inc.
269 Lyons Plains Road
Weston, Connecticut 06484
(203) 227-1477

Advertising and Corporate Photography
on location.

© Palmer/Kane, Inc. 1982

145

**JAN PARIK**
Represented by:
Barbara Gordon Associates
165 East 32nd Street
New York, New York 10016
(212) 686-3514

146

**CHRISTIAN PEACOCK**
28 West 86th Street
New York, New York 10024
(212) 580-1422

All these images were photographed on location for print or audio-visual productions.

*Christian Peacock photography*

**STUART PELTZ**
6 West 18th Street
New York, New York 10011
(212) 929-4600

Agent:
Anita Green
160 East 26th Street
New York, New York 10010
(212) 532-5083

Clients include:
Nikon, Perdue, Cunard, Olivetti, Bendix, Mellon Bank, Pioneer, Singer, Maxell, Cooking Good, General Foods, Sambucca, Procter & Gamble, Hebrew National, Omega, U.P.S., *Geo*, Minolta, American Can.

148

**PHOTOSCOPE**
12 West 27th Street
12th Floor
New York, New York 10001
(212) 696-0880

Metallics, strobe, neon, crystal, zooms, glows, starbursts and an infinite variety of customized special effects for product and logo treatments. No illustration or airbrushing used, all work produced optically directly on film. Average turn around time 3 days. Ask for Photoscoping.™

**JOCK POTTLE**
301 West 89th Street, #15
New York, New York 10024
(212) 874-0216

Architecture, Interiors, Exteriors & Landscapes.

Stock available.

© Jock Pottle 1983

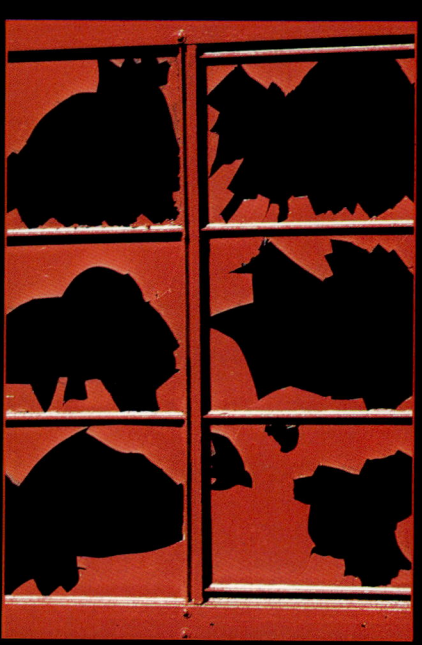

150

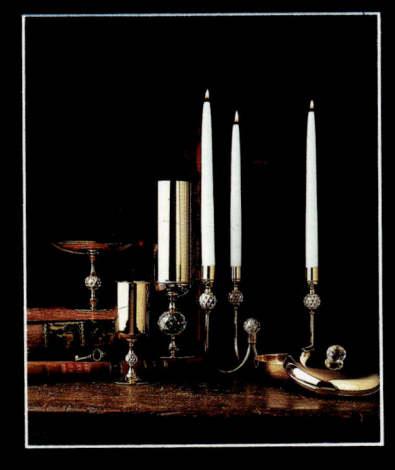

**GUY POWERS**
Represented by Carmel
(212) 925-6216

151

**GUY POWERS**
Represented by: Carmel
(212) 925-6216

152

Susan West—food stylist
(212) 541-7600

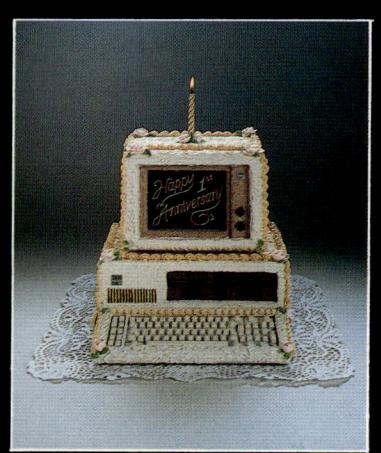

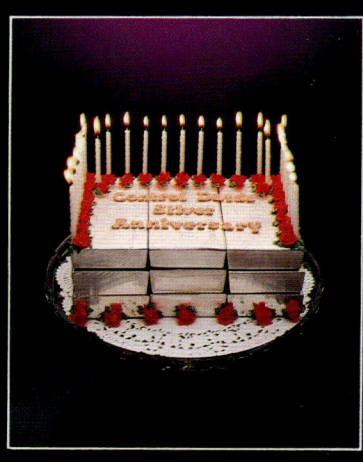

**GUY POWERS**
Represented by Carmel
(212) 925-6216

153

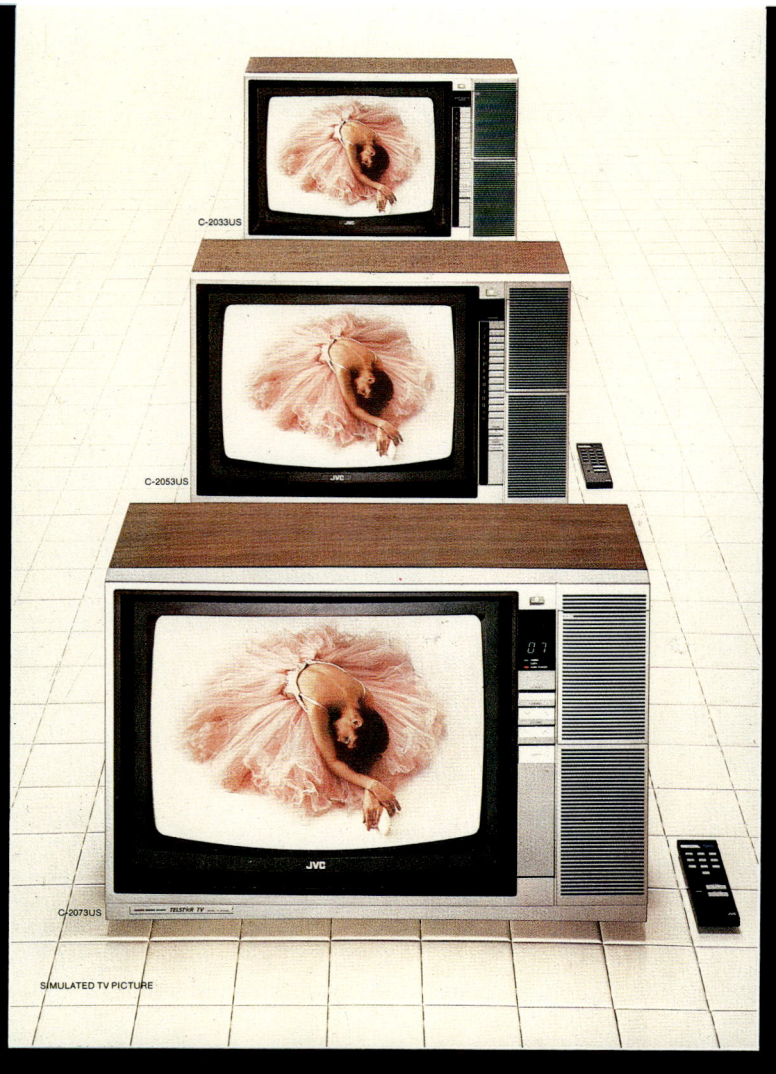

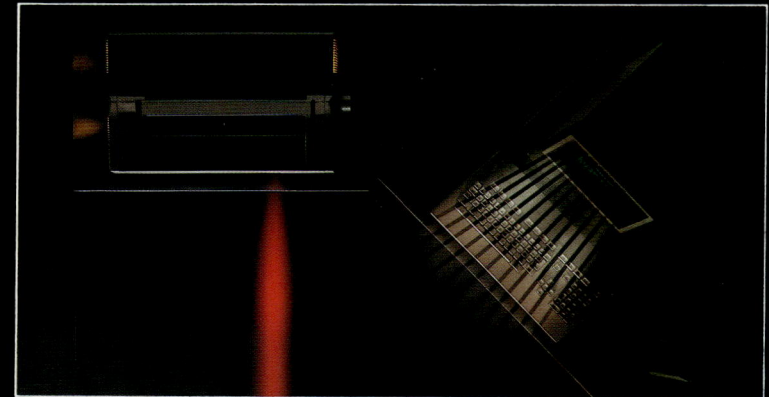

**GUY POWERS**
Represented by Carmel
(212) 925-6216

154

**GUY POWERS**
Represented by Carmel
(212) 925-6216

155

**GUY POWERS**
Represented by Carmel
(212) 925-6216

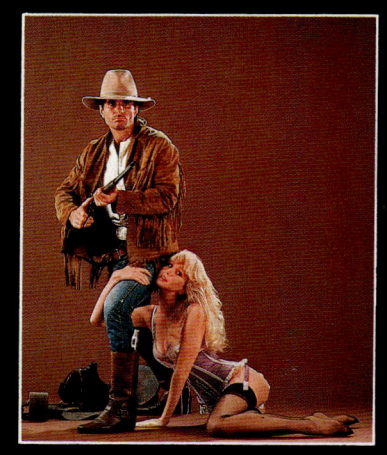

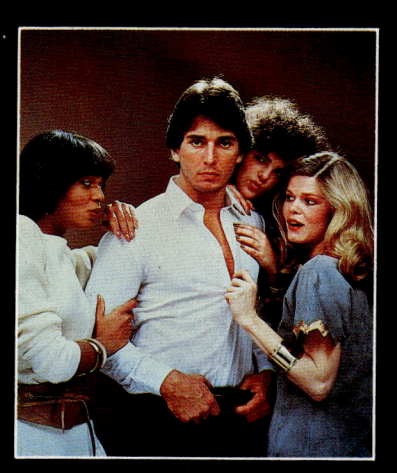

156

**BARRY PRIBULA**
62 Second Avenue
New York, New York 10003
(212) 777-7612

Advertising, corporate
and editorial photography.

© Barry Pribula 1983

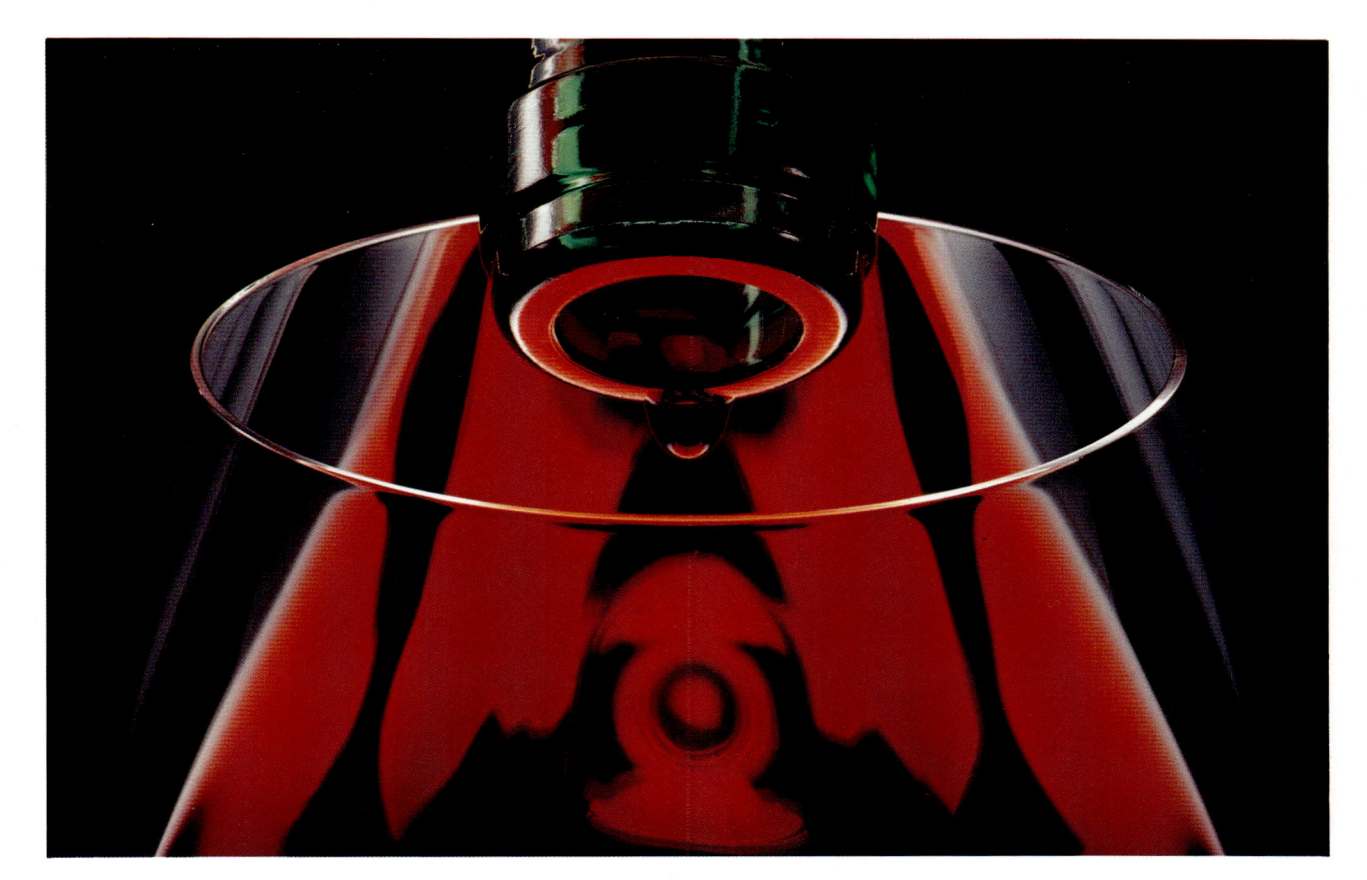

## THE GOOD OL' DAYS

**E**very time my phone rings, I can count on speaking with a creative person; a photographer, an illustrator, a model maker, a retoucher, or an art director. That's not bad for an Art History major who once wondered how she would use all that knowledge about dead painters to make a living.

Some days my phone rings and the conversation is about artists' books: books that I have seen; books that I need to see; books that I didn't have the time to see; books that I love; books that are exceptional and books that are not.

And some days the phone rings and my conversation is about artists' rights: one time rights or trade rights, consumer rights or point of purchase rights, T.V. rights or world rights.

Then there are the days when the phone rings and the conversation is about who has the right to the rights...that's when the trouble begins. And, it is inevitable that during one of these conversations, someone always laments the passing of the "good ol' days."

The "good ol' days," I have been able to ascertain, refer to that carefree period of time prior to 1978, when artists and buyers worked hand-in-hand, each devoted to a common goal. There may be some truth to this wistful claim, but I suspect, for the most part, it's pure myth.

Art Directors refer to the "good ol' days" whenever there is a brouhaha about rights being purchased. The standard line goes something like this: "I never had these problems in the "good ol' days." We'd shoot the assignment, shake hands, and promise to send the purchase order later!" I'll bet there are a few of you still waiting for one.

Account Executives vehemently refer to the "good ol' days" whenever the fee quoted exceeds the budget: "Why, in the 'good ol' days' I could have gotten this photograph for a song."

And then there is the photographer who reluctantly brings it to your attention that the Agency is running his photograph bought for point of purchase in national magazines. This conversation usually closes with a request for a purchase order to cover the additional use and a claim that this is not the time to be a photographer: "In the 'good ol' days' there weren't problems like these."

It must be true that time erases all but the pleasant memories. Nostalgia clouds reality, and only the "good ol' days" are seen floating in the mist. The connections between the events of then and the circumstances of now are lost in the remembering.

The "good ol' days," if the truth is told, were fraught with problems and misunderstandings for both the artist and the agency. The seriousness of these misunderstandings brought us to the copyright law we have today.

Under the old law, work commissioned was considered "work made for hire," and the client owned the copyright in the absence of an agreement to the contrary. Under the new law, the presumption has been reversed. Now, in the absence of an agreement to the contrary, the artist owns the copyright. Artists no longer have to negotiate for copyright, they own it from the instant of creation. Copyright is infinitely divisible under the new law. It is not one right, but a package of individual rights. Any or all of the rights can be assigned by the artist.

The change in the law is easy enough to understand, and so are the reasons for its coming about. The difficulty lies in the manner in which business is conducted.

Traditionally advertising work was done with neither the buyer nor the artist spelling out what was bought or sold. Wording was vague and the "understood" agreement was the rule. Copyright in all its divisibility can no longer be transferred in an "understood" agreement, and therein lies the rub. The problem isn't with the new copyright law, but with those who continue to do business as if it didn't apply to them. Too often, when assignments are discussed, no proper license clarifying terms is drawn. The artist and the buyer blunder along with an agreement which neither of them really understands. Loose arrangements can work, but they rarely do. Inevitably someone gets burned.

The "good ol' days" are gone. Things just aren't what they used to be. In order to purchase photography and illustration, you now have to discuss what you're purchasing and put it in a written agreement. What a clever idea. Now, why couldn't they have thought of that in the "good ol' days?"

**Ellen Johnson**
**Manager of Art Buying**
**Ogilvy & Mather**
**New York City**

**AARON REZNY**
119 West 23rd Street
New York, New York 10011
(212) 691-1894

**REPRESENTED BY: JERRY ANTON (212) 679-4562**

Clients include: Alfred Dunhill, Abraham & Straus, American Diabetes, BSR, Cambells, *Cuisine*, Datamation, *Discover*, E F Hutton, *Folio*, *Glamour*, Grundig, Hammarplast, Hatachi Metals, HBO, International Playtex, Intertec, LJN Toys, *Money*, *New York Magazine*, *Oui*, *Savvy*, *Seventeen*, Showtime, Simon & Schuster, Smucker's, Sony, TDK Electronics, WIX.

159

**ALBERTO RIZZO**
220 East 23rd Street
New York, New York 10010
(212) 684-7440
(212) 684-7441

*Harper's Bazaar, Vogue, Mademoiselle, G., Linea Italiana.*
Bloomingdale's, Bonwit Teller, Bergdorf Goodman, Saks Fifth Avenue, Revlon, Charles of The Ritz, Chanel, Clinique, Max Factor, Bulgari, Seiko, Piaget, Danskin, Wrangler Jeans, Lee Jeans, True Cigarettes

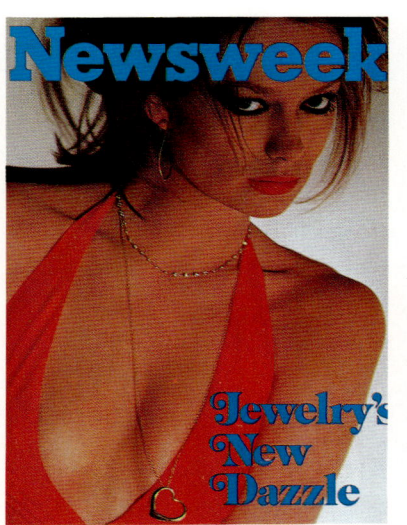

160

**ERIC H. ROSNER INC.**
Photographer
1133 Arch Street, 9th Floor
Philadelphia, Pennsylvania 19107
(215) 567-2758

New York Studio:
234 Fifth Avenue, 5th Floor
New York, New York 10001
(212) 686-1325

Represented by Shelly Merhige

**PETER ROTH**
8 West 19th Street
New York, New York 10011
(212) 242-4853

Clients include:

ADP, Burroughs Wellcome, CBS, The Continental Group, Dansk International Designs, Estée Lauder, *Fortune Magazine,* GAF, Germaine Monteil, Hoffmann-La Roche, Home Insurance, IBM, Industrial Bank of Japan, Johnson & Johnson, Kosta Boda, Macmillan, Marimekko, *The New York Times,* Pfizer, Random House, Simon & Schuster, Squibb, Yamazaki Tableware.

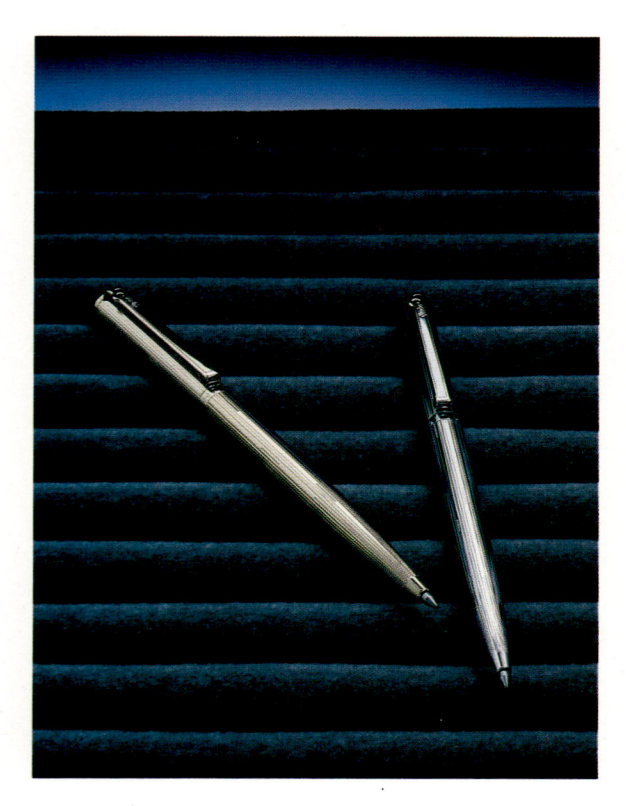

**EDWARD RYSINSKI**
636 Avenue of the Americas
New York, New York 10011
(212) 807-7301

163

**AJ SANDONE**
91 Fifth Avenue
New York, New York 10003
(212) 807-6472

Represented by George Venetos
(212) 431-6771

A.J. specializes in catalogue production, including product stills, home furnishings and fashion, either on location or on studio sets.

He has photographed catalogues and ads for Fieldcrest, J.P. Stevens, Marshall Fields, Gimbels, J.C. Penney, Jordan Marsh, Micar Communications and many others.

164

**STEPHEN SHORE**
RD3, Box 280
Rhinebeck, New York 12572
(914) 876-4450

Clients: *Fortune, Life, New York Times Magazine, GEO, Scientific American, Architectural Digest, AIA* Journal, Tiffany & Co., A.T.&T., Fuji Film Co., Polaroid Corp., Joseph E. Seagram & Sons, Metropolitan Museum of Art, The Frick Collection, The Library of Congress, Venturi & Rauch, and Hardy Holzman & Pfeiffer.

**JERRY SIMPSON STUDIO**
28 West 27th Street
New York, New York 10001
(212) 696-9738

**KEN SKALSKI**
866 Broadway
New York, New York 10003
(212) 777-6207

Member APA

Client List:

Aramis
AT&T
Balducci's
Burroughs Wellcome
Corning Design
J.C. Penney
Johnson & Johnson
Lever Brothers
New York Telephone
Sanyei America
TDK
Warner Communications
Western Union

KEN SKALSKI STUDIO
866 BROADWAY
NEW YORK, NY 10003
212 777 6207

**GORDON E. SMITH**
Studios in New York City and Connecticut
(212) 807-7840
(203) 655-2899—1 hour from New York City

*We have a lot to offer!*

1. A complete studio in New York City with fully equipped kitchen.

    Plus

2. A complete studio in Connecticut with fully equipped kitchen.

    Plus

3. Rural Scenery or formal lawn backgrounds are a step outside the studio, and boating/shore points are minutes away.

    Plus

4. Attractive, traditional, contemporary and Early American rooms for photography in the studio/home.

    Plus

5. Styling (propping) and home economists are readily available.

Gordon's professional career spans many years. He is thoroughly experienced in still-life, people, food, beverages, interiors and travel photography utilizing all camera formats.

He has created images to sell concepts and products for a long list of companies and also images for major national publications. Gordon has received many awards from organizations recognizing distinctive photography including the New York Art Directors Club.

Let Gordon create an image for you.

**WILLIAM EDWARD SMITH**
498 West End Avenue
New York, New York 10024
(212) 877-8456

Stock Photography: The Stock Market

Boston Representative: Martha Kidder
(617) 462-2402

Location/Still Life, Advertising, Architecture, and Industrial

Clients include: IBM, Chivas Regal, Holland America, *Camera 35*, CIGNA, Somerset Importers, U.S. Ski Team, Polaroid, Nintendo, Maersk, Pfizer, Boston Globe, Amcon, Pulsar, CIT, CBS, D.C. Heath, Dallek, Helmsley Spear, St. Regis, Paul Masson, Pitney-Bowes, Westinghouse.

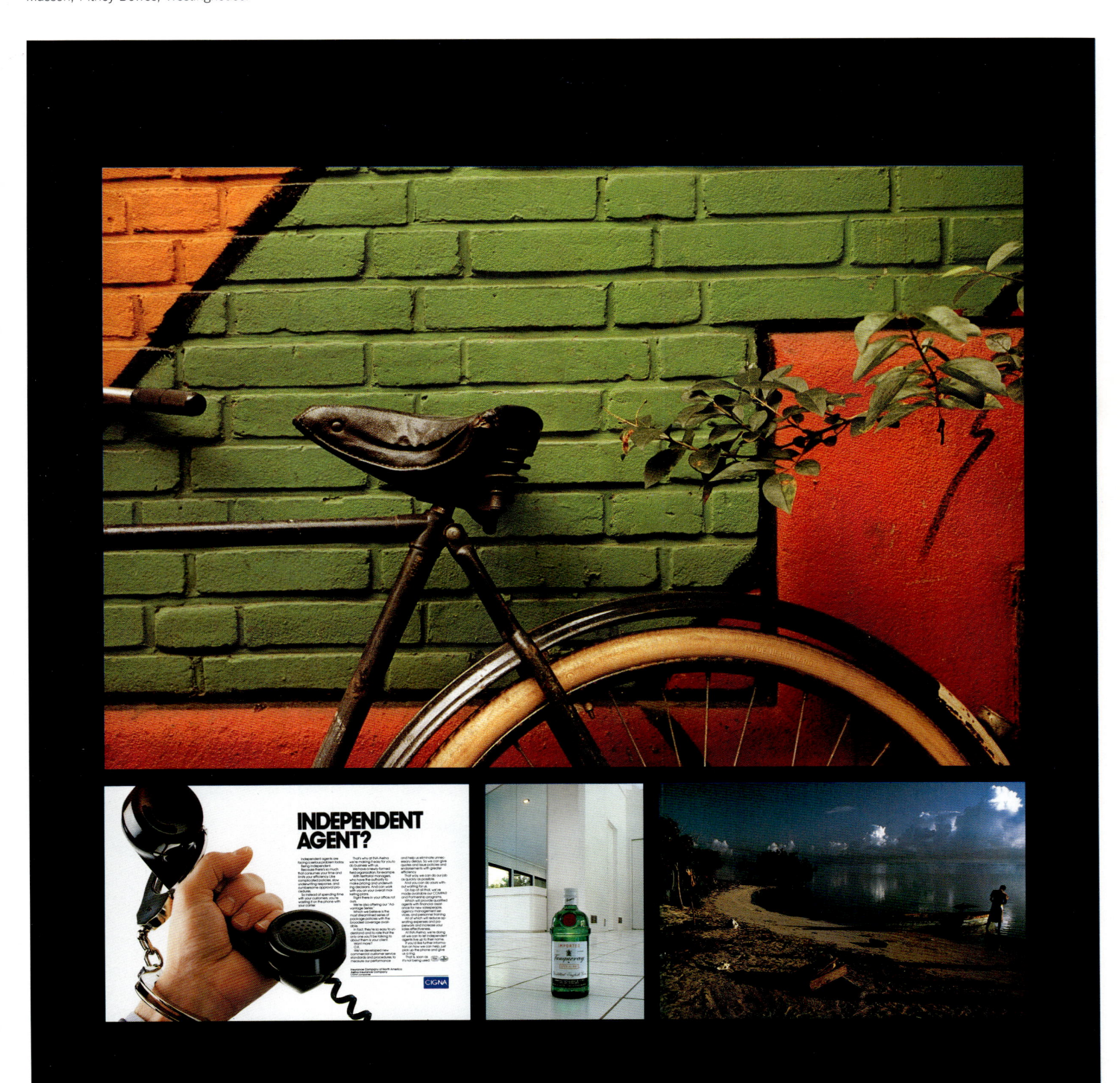

169

**T. KEVIN SMYTH**
604 Main Street
Belmar, New Jersey 07719
(201) 681-2602

Clients include: Becton, Dickinson & Co., ITT, Balan Marketing, E & B Marine, Mobil Oil, Doubleday, Kramer Music and Pennwalt.

Member ASMP

Film and TV Commercials, too. Please call to see our reel or Portfolio.

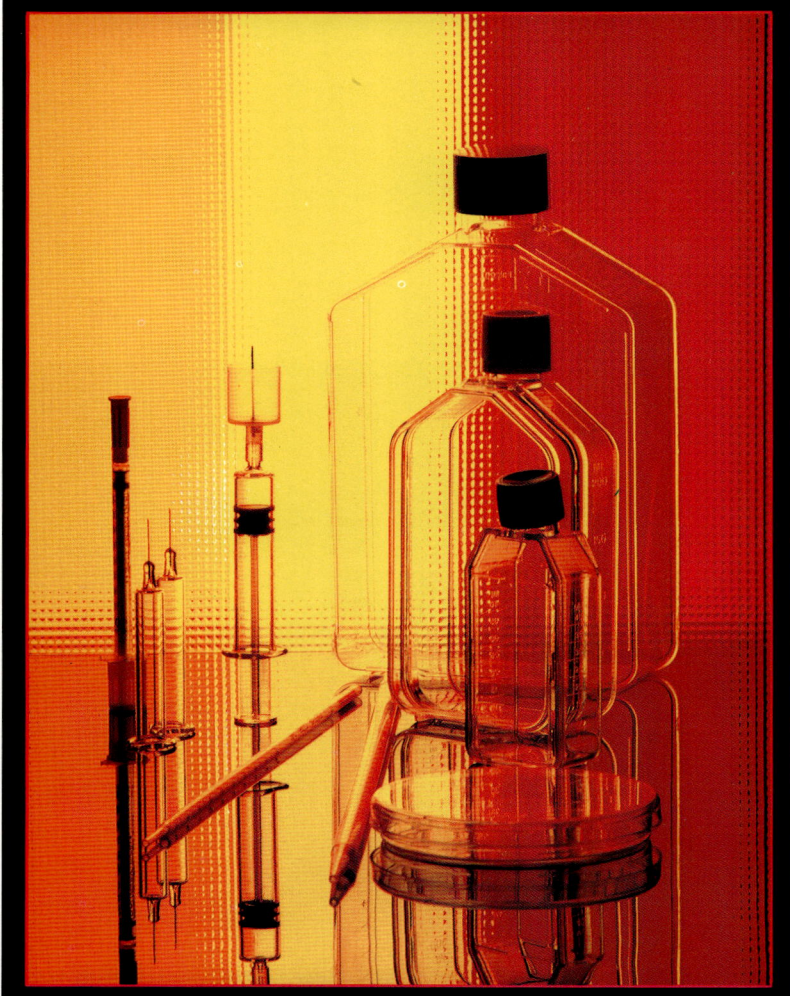

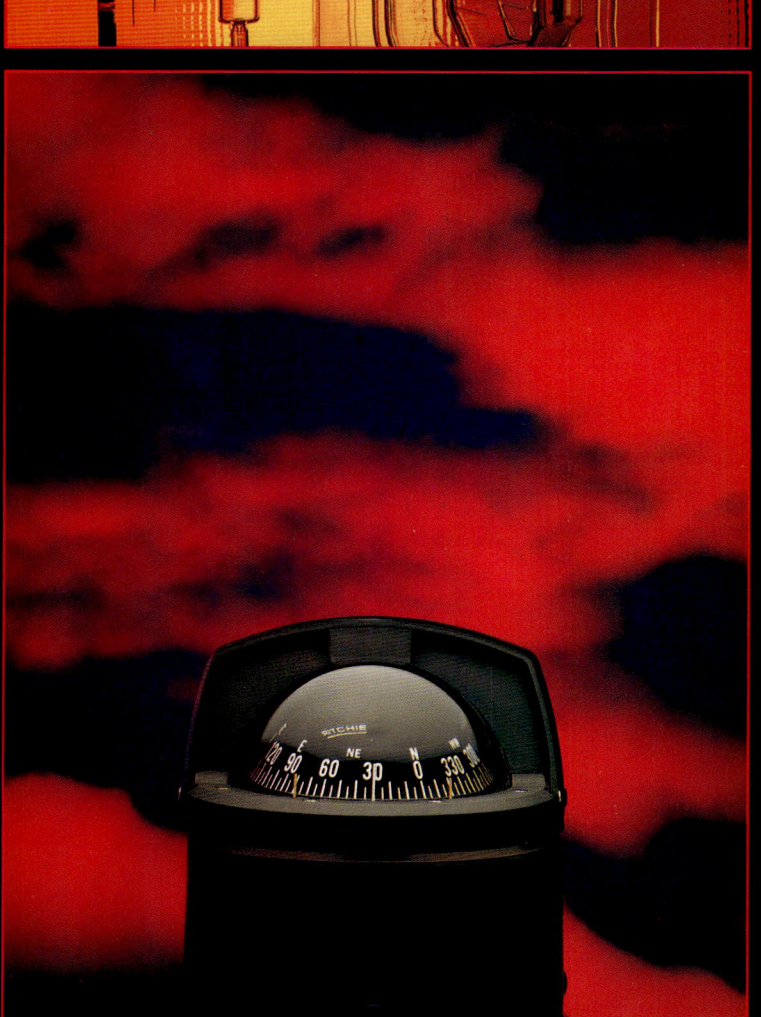

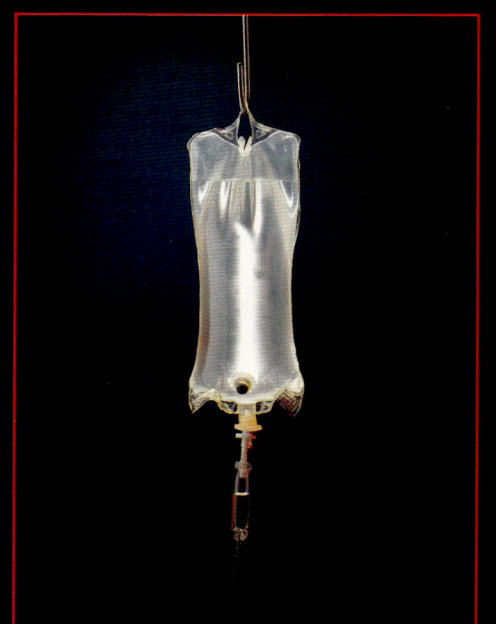

ASMP

**HOWARD SOCHUREK**
680 Fifth Avenue
New York, New York 10019
Office: (212) 582-1860
Home: (914) 337-5014

Represented by: Joe Cahill
(212) 582-1860

Electronic Graphics for both TV and print
Computer Imaging
Thermography
Tomography
Angiography
Color X-rays
Image Enhancement
Density scanning

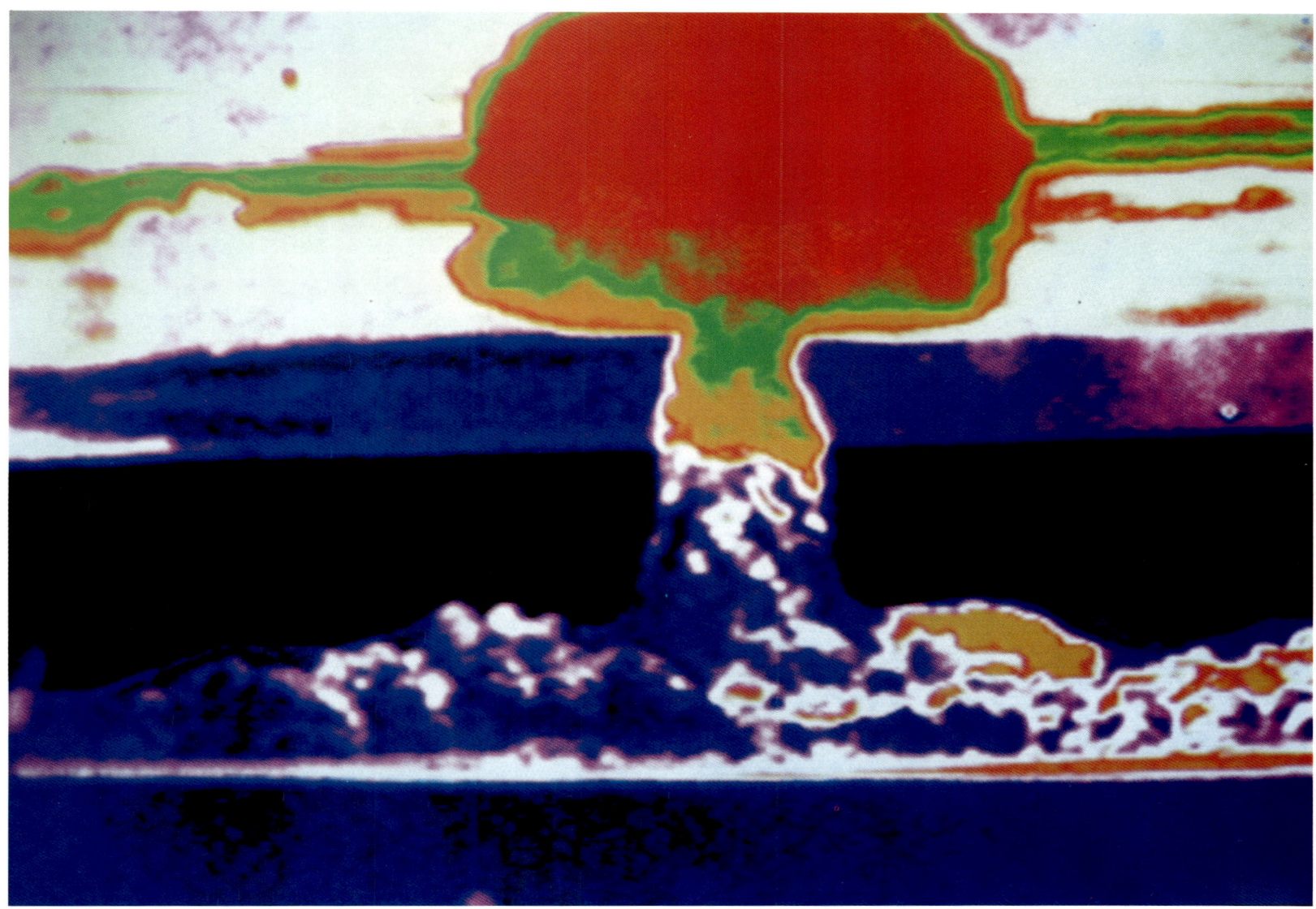

171

COMPUTER GRAPHICS

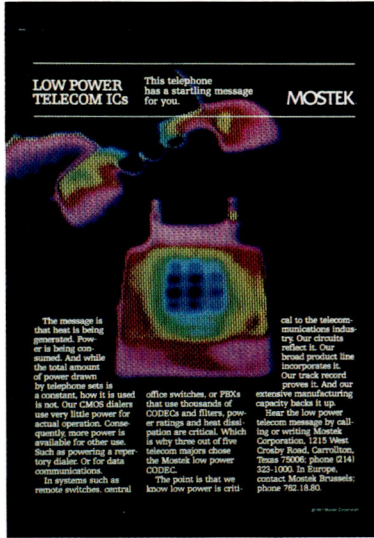

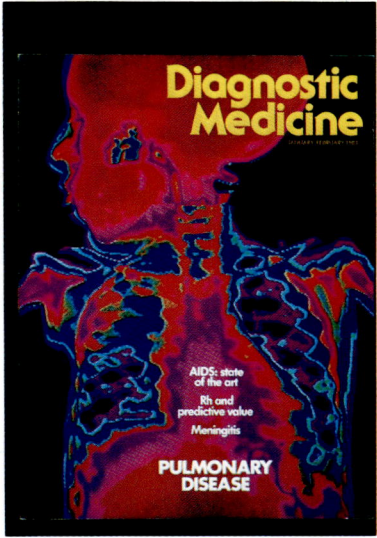

ELECTRONIC IMAGE

THERMOGRAPHY

DENSITY SLICE

TOMOGRAPHY

## HOW TO HANDLE AN ART DIRECTOR

David Ogilvy, that scourge of copywriters everywhere, has done it again. In his latest manifesto on advertising, he claims that the average copywriter spends less than one hour a week actually writing. This untimely disclosure has proved rather embarrassing to me and my colleagues, since it naturally prompts everyone who reads it to exclaim, "An hour! What on earth do you do with the rest of your time?"

My initial reply to this question was to roll my eyes heavenward and to moan, "Ah, if you only knew!" But finding this didn't evoke much sympathy, I decided to do a little investigating, to find out for myself exactly what it is we copywriters do. Accordingly, I spent two weeks monitoring myself, following me wherever I went, counting my trips to the bathroom and logging my exact hours on every task.

The result was astonishing even to me. Subtracting the obligatory time spent drinking coffee, chit-chatting, going to recordings, dodging account people, working on my novel and daydreaming, I found that the great bulk of my time was spent in the difficult, soul-wrenching activity known as "Dealing with an Art Director." (Of course, I have long known how impossible these creatures can be, but hitherto I had no idea how much of my valuable time they consumed.)

To the uninitiated, I realize, this may sound strange. "What's the big deal?" I hear them say. "You walk into an art director's office with an idea, and you say, 'Here it is!'"

Wrong. Wrong. Wrong. That's like saying to a lion tamer, "What's the big deal? You walk into the cage and stick your head in the lion's mouth." It's just not that simple. Even the bravest lion tamer has found it advisable to pet his lion first, and to murmur something soothing—like "nice kitty" or "good kitty." And if kitty is having a bad day, most lion tamers with any experience will opt to come back later.

Well, we copywriters face a similar situation with art directors. If you walk into an art director's office with an idea and say, "Here it is!" you're just asking to get your head chewed off. Art directors, you see, like to think they had some part in the creative process, and as a copywriter, you've got to convince them they did.

In pursuit of this goal, I've found it best to divide "Dealing with an Art Director" into four main stages. The first stage I call, "Testing the Waters."

"Testing the Waters" is a way to gauge the general mood and receptivity of your art director. Art directors, you see, can be touchy, stubborn and irascible. (They call this being "artistic.") Besides, sniffing spray mount and magic markers all day seems to affect their brains. So it's always wise to proceed with caution.

The first step in "Testing the Waters" is to step inside your art director's office, legs braced to spring backwards if necessary, and to hazard a cheery "hello." If your art director doesn't growl in response, you may then proceed to pay him or her a compliment. All art directors, of course, pride themselves on their appearance, so compliments in this direction yield the best results.

If your art director seems pleased by your remark and begins to simper, you may proceed to Stage Two. Stage Two is called "Convincing your Art Director that Your Idea is Our Idea."

Suppose for example that you work on a deodorant tampon account, and you conceive of a demo utilizing a girl in a shark tank. You picture the idea greeted with wild enthusiasm by the creative director, praised by the account people, and applauded by the clients. All you have to do now is get your art director to lay it out.

Not an easy task, believe me. Coming up with the idea was nothing compared to the creative wiles needed to manipulate your art director's ego. The operative word here is "deceit."

For example, you might say to him or her, "Gee, I've got this sort of hazy idea for our tampon ad, but I need your help, your insight, your visual sense to give it focus." (Art directors like to think they have a "visual sense.") "I thought we might do this ad, see, showing a girl swimming in this tank, see, and the tank would be filled with vicious, man-eating polliwogs. What do you think?"

continued on page 178

**OLAF SÖÖT**
419 Park Avenue South
New York, New York 10016
(212) 686-4565

Represented by Carmel
(212) 925-6216

Large stock available:

Land and mountains from Alaska to Patagonia:
Climbing, skiing, flying and boating. Mountain scenes, moods, people and wildlife. Collection includes Alaska, Canada, Western U.S., Mexico, Guatemala, Peru, Bolivia, Argentina and Chile.

Northeast:
New York scenes and mountains, New England coast and mountains. Aerial scenes. Abstract and realistic details of nature.

Cities and places:
New York, California Coast, Vancouver, B.C., Houston, Taxco and other Mexico, Tikal and other Guatemala, Caracas and Maracaibo, Venezuela. Miscellaneous South America, some Europe.

Activities:
Hiking, climbing, skiing, boating, camping, flying, soaring, some hockey and other sports.

Additional portfolio available upon request.

Selective assignments accepted.

173

**JIM STRATOS**
176 Madison Avenue
New York, New York 10016
(212) 696-1133

Clients:
American Hospital Supply
Block Drug Co.
CitiCorp
*Family Weekly*
Gillette
Godiva Chocolates
Heublein
J.P. Stevens
Lever Brothers
McGraw-Hill
MacMillan Publishing
Newgate Importers Inc.
Prentice-Hall
Schweppes
Shaeffer-Eaton
Timex
Viletta China

ASMP

Jim Stratos·Studio Photography·176 Madison Avenue·New York, N.Y. 10016·(212)696·1133

Jim Stratos·Studio Photography·176 Madison Avenue·New York, N.Y. 10016·(212)696·1133

**JEANNE STRONGIN**
61 Irving Place
Gramercy Park
New York, New York 10003
(212) 473-3718

Assignment Photography/Portraits in the studio and on location/Editorial/Annual Report/Travel

See American Showcase Six
page 135

**JOHN STUART**
80 Varick Street
New York, New York 10013
(212) 966-6783

Still life, conceptual, industrial travel.

I can make it happen... for you.

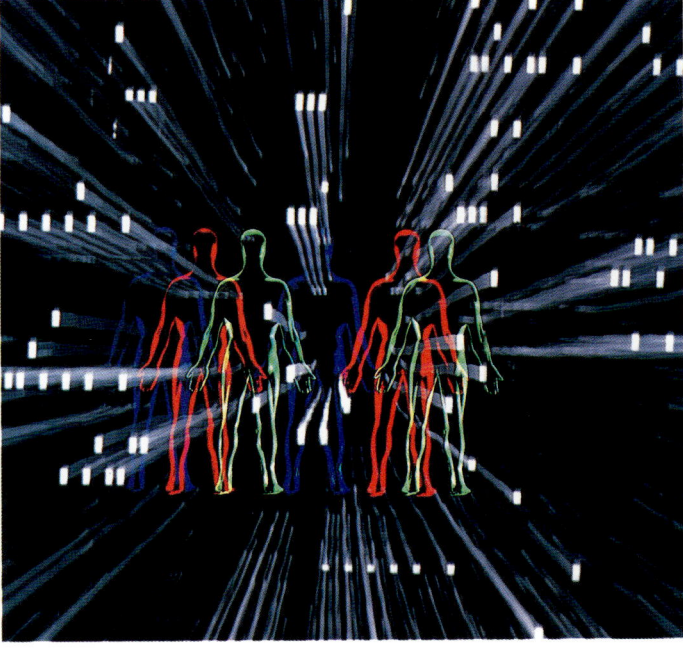

177

continued from page 172

Most people, of course, would catch on right away, but art directors can be suprisingly dense. You may find it helpful to hum the theme from "Jaws" while he or she sits there pretending to think. Eventually your art director will rise to the bait.

"Gee, wouldn't sharks make more sense?"

Here is where reaction becomes important. "Sharks?", you must exclaim, jumping out of your chair. "Sharks? My God, you're brilliant."

Of course, no art director can resist being called brilliant. Once you reach this point, you're well on your way to seeing your idea in print.

But don't be fooled into thinking your job is finished. On the contrary, your job has only begun. Because now, inevitably, your art director will proceed to the third stage of the creative process, a stage I call "Ruining Your Idea."

Years of bitter experience have taught me, despite the most constant vigilance and the most sensible suggestions on your part, most art directors will invariably produce a first layout with a visual filling the entire page and a little squiggle in the lower right-hand corner.

"What's that squiggle?" you ask, doing your best to control your emotion.

"Oh, that," the art director says deprecatingly. "That's the headline."

"Ah, the headline."

Now is no time to lose your cool, copywriter. Diplomacy! It's time to begin Stage Four of the creative process, the stage I call, "Personally I think it's wonderful, but..."

For example, you might say, "Personally I think it's wonderful, but you know those silly, unreasonable clients. They like to see the name of their product in a type-size people can read." With variations on this attack, you can chip away at your art director's layout until you eventually arrive at something you can live with.

So you see, "Dealing with an Art Director" can be an incredibly demanding job. In fact, given the time and effort involved, I think it's remarkable we copywriters find even an hour a week to sit down and write. It's a tribute to our dedication and discipline.

**Peter S. Kellogg**
**Copywriter**
**SSC&B Lintas Worldwide**
**New York City**

**STEPHEN STUART**
9 Legion Drive
Valhalla, New York 10595
(914) 682-1418

JUST NORTH OF WHITE PLAINS
IN WESTCHESTER COUNTY

EXPERIENCE: Chesebrough Ponds; General Foods; American Can; Continental Baking; Pepsi-Cola; Orrefor's; Smuckers; Kodak; Kane-Miller; Cannon Mills; Fieldcrest Mills; M.G.M. Records; J. Walter Thompson; Union Carbide; Avon; National Distillers; Celanese Corporation; and more... much more.

ORREFOR'S

PERSONAL PROMOTION

PERSONAL PROMOTION

CONTINENTAL BAKING

**MICHEL TCHEREVKOFF**
873 Broadway
New York, New York 10003
(212) 228-0540

Portfolio available upon request:
Call Studio (212) 228-0540

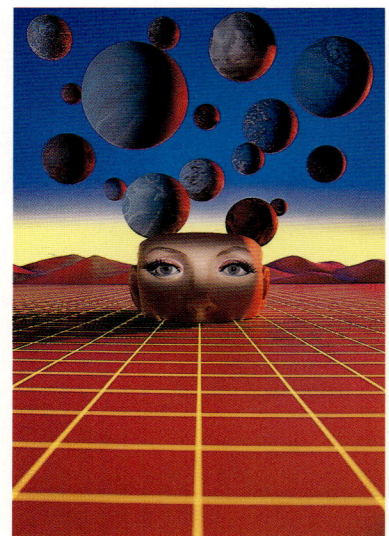

180

AMERICAN SHOWCASE COVER

A.B.C. ANNUAL REPORT COVER/A.D. SUSAN LEEDS

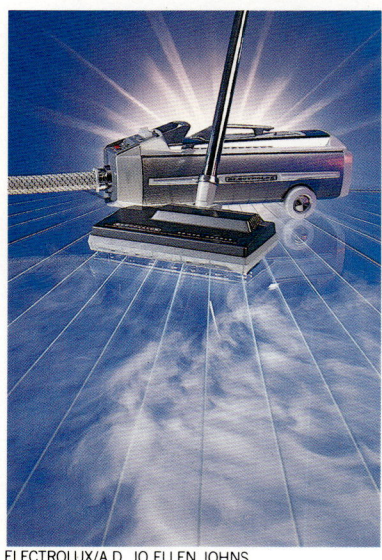

ELECTROLUX/A.D. JO ELLEN JOHNS

FEDERAL EXPRESS ANNUAL REPORT COVER/A.D. STEVEN FERRARI

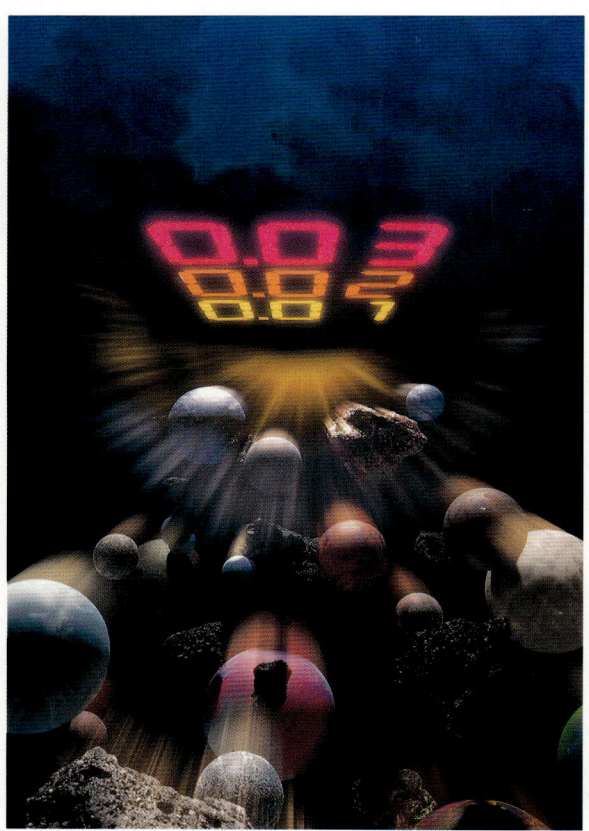

DISCOVER MAGAZINE/A.D. LEONARD WOLF

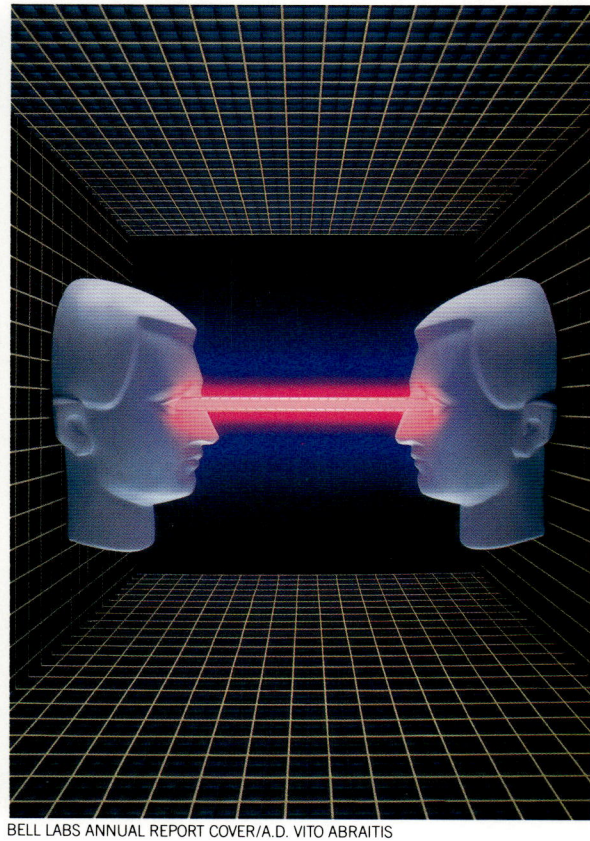

HARMAN KARDON/A.D. MAXINE BRENNER

BELL LABS ANNUAL REPORT COVER/A.D. VITO ABRAITIS

QUASAR/A.D. BUDD SHEHAB

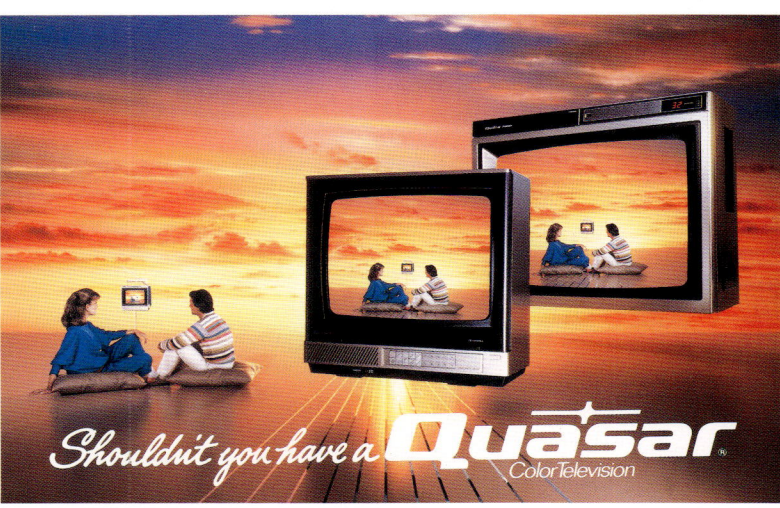

QUASAR/A.D. BUDD SHEHAB

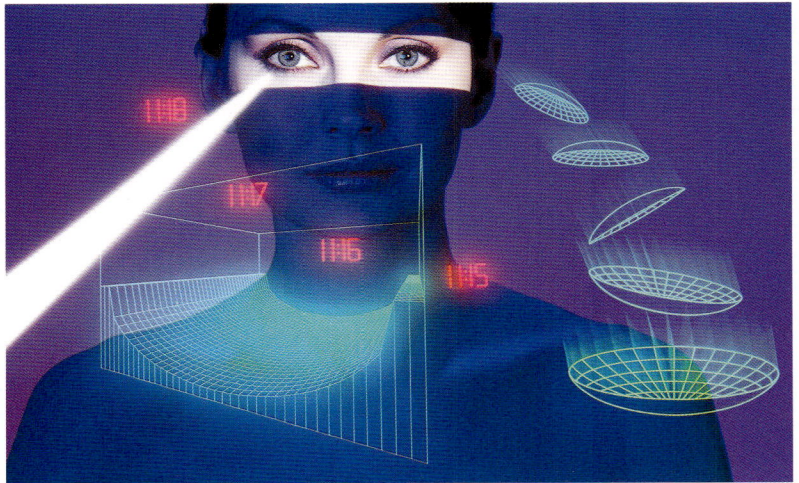

HYDROCURVE/A.D. BARBARA WHITE

FORTUNE MAGAZINE/A.D. LEONARD WOLF

CASIO/A.D. JOHN GARRE

PENTHOUSE MAGAZINE/A.D. RICHARD BLEIWEISS

PENTHOUSE MAGAZINE/A.D. RICHARD BLEIWEISS

NIGHT OF OLAY/A.D. JACQUES BORIS

## WHAT IS A CREATIVE AD?

In a lot of advertising agencies, a good ad is an ad the client buys. Period.

That's not necessarily a cynical point of view. Often it is a genuine, honestly held belief. After all, the customer is always right. And if the customer likes the product we produce for him, then we have done our job, and the ad or commercial is a good one, by definition.

Woe to the art director or copywriter who works for an agency like that.

Some agencies take an even more pragmatic approach.

They define a good ad as an ad that the client buys, *and an ad that works in the marketplace.* "It's not creative unless it sells." Good. As far as it goes. Except that that pat definition is deceptive. The inclination is to turn it around. To say: "If it sells, it must be creative."

That gives us a nice easy litmus test for creativity. And one that has given countless hacks a nice, warm feeling inside.

But the definition is false.

A good ad will sell. And if it doesn't it's not a good ad. But so will a lot of terrible ads. And the truth is, in advertising as in government, the end does not justify the means. People who believe it does deserve each other.

A creative ad must do much more than sell product.

First of all, it must please its creators. If you make an ad and say to yourself, "It will probably work, but I hate it," you should destroy that ad before someone else sees it. For your own good. Which is not to say that a good, creative ad won't cause you some disquiet. A great many do. After all, you are breaking new ground. You are probably breaking a good many rules. And no one has done what you've done in the way you've just done it. But there's a difference between an ad that makes you sweat, and one that makes you retch.

Second, a creative ad should please your peers. Or at least the ones you respect. But don't bet on it. Sometimes, what you do is so new and different, it scares your fellow practitioners. They may not like that. Or they may not understand it. That could mean it's a very creative ad. Or a bad one.

Third, a creative ad should please the client, or it will probably never run—unless you have one hell of a client. But don't be dismayed if your client doesn't jump up and down with excitement when he first sees your ad. Because if it's *really* creative, he's going to need some time to get used to it. And he's going to need to be sold by you. Not by some bag-carrier who doesn't understand what you've done. If your ad is truly creative, and if you do your homework, and your selling job, and if you have an enlightened client, the ad will run.

But that doesn't mean it's good.

And it may even "sell," whatever that means. (Ads don't really "sell" products. They are only part of the process. If the product is good, and the distribution is good, and the price is right, and there's a lot of sampling thrown in just to make sure, the chances are the product will sell. Even, unfortunately, with a bad ad. But if all of those other things are lacking, no ad in the world can save the product. Bill Bernbach said it: "Great ads make bad products fail faster." And, as usual, he was right.)

A good ad should get people to walk into the store and ask to see the product. If it does that, it has done a lot. Unfortunately, that result is not measured by SAMI, or even sales figure. It seems that sometimes people actually look at the product, and walk out of the store with someone else's product. So much for that test.

That leaves the awards shows.

You can leave it up to the judgement of your peers.

That works, but it, too, is not infallible. There are a lot of questionable ads that have won gold medals over the years. The judging panels fell in love with them for one reason or another, but, on reflection, they didn't deserve those medals. Often, the runners-up were far better, by almost any measure.

And things that should have gotten into the show sometimes didn't. Why? Perhaps misjudgement on the part of the screening panel. Or professional jealousy. Or maybe the idea was so new and different, the judges didn't understand it, quite.

Still, the shows aren't the answer, either, it seems.

However, no truly great ad will fail all of the above tests. Or even most of them. The great ads usually get recognized—sometimes a year later, when everyone

continued on page 186

**TOGASHI**
36 West 20th Street
New York, New York 10011
(212) 929-2290

Represented by:
Chris Quaritius

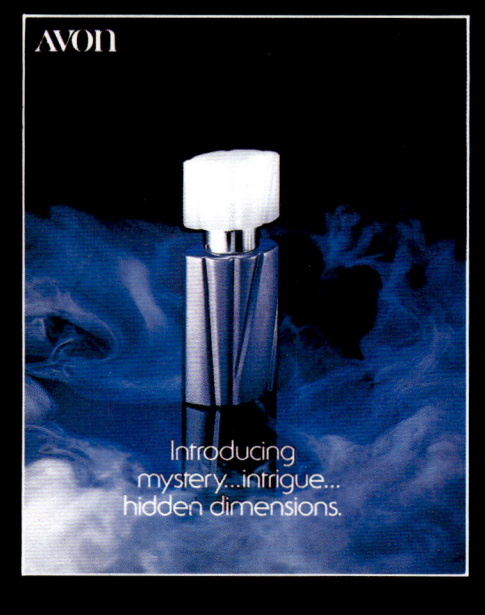

183

**MICHAEL WAINE**
873 Broadway
New York, New York 10003
(212) 533-4200

Print & Film

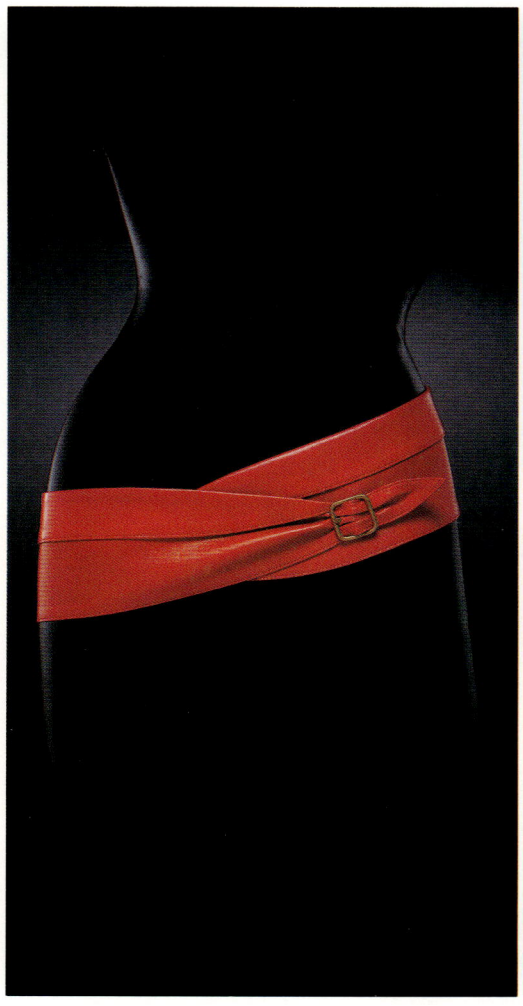

184

**MICHAEL WAINE**
873 Broadway
New York, New York 10003
(212) 533-4200

The Kodak Award for Commercial Photography was given to six Commercial Photographers throughout the world. Michael's work appears at Walt Disney World's Epcot Center, Orlando, Florida, in the Kodak Pavilion "Journey Into Imagination."

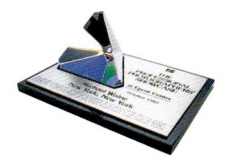

185

continued from page 182

begins to copy them. Or when really good creative people begin to wish they did them.

Then, there's the ultimate test. The same test that applies to the great films that never won the Academy Award, or never broke box-office records. The same test that recognized the Impressionists after they couldn't get any museum or gallery to hang their work.

The test of time.

Great ads stand up. Even ten years later. They set trends, and good people begin to unconsciously borrow from them. No matter a decade or so later, that the type treatment is a bit dated, or the photograph could have been done differently today. The ad is great, and everyone seems to know it.

Art defies quantification. And great, innovative advertising is still much more art than it is science. True, the people with the computers can measure, and test, and even copy a breakthrough—if they recognize it as such. But they can no more create the next innovation than they can create a new orchid with micrometer calipers.

Alas, they can't even tell you when an ad is really creative.

And neither can I.

But if you're thinking that this is a cop-out, take heart. You may lose an ad or a commercial you think is great. You may lose a dozen. But one ad, or a dozen, doesn't make a career. Work of consistently good quality wins out, and is recognized. And the people who produce it are rewarded. Financially and otherwise.

I've been told by some old-timers at Doyle Dane Bernbach—people who helped create the so-called "Golden Age" of the Sixties—that fully 10% of DDB's *best* work never saw the light of day. It was just too far ahead of its time.

Nevertheless, DDB continues to innovate. To break the rules. To produce work that produces for their clients. Work which wins awards. Work which is recognized.

So, if you feel unsung, persevere.

As a truly creative person, you have no choice. You must keep creating, and damn the Philistines.

And when it's *really* great, you'll know.

**Dick Jackson**
**Dick Jackson, Inc.**
**New York City**

**H. ROSS WATSON, JR.**
859 Lancaster Avenue
Bryn Mawr, Pennsylvania 19010
(215) 527-1519

187

**H. MARK WEIDMAN**
2112 Goodwin Lane
North Wales (Philadelphia), Pennsylvania 19454
(215) 646-1745

Represented by Marjorie Ackermann.
Stock photographs available.

© HMW 1984

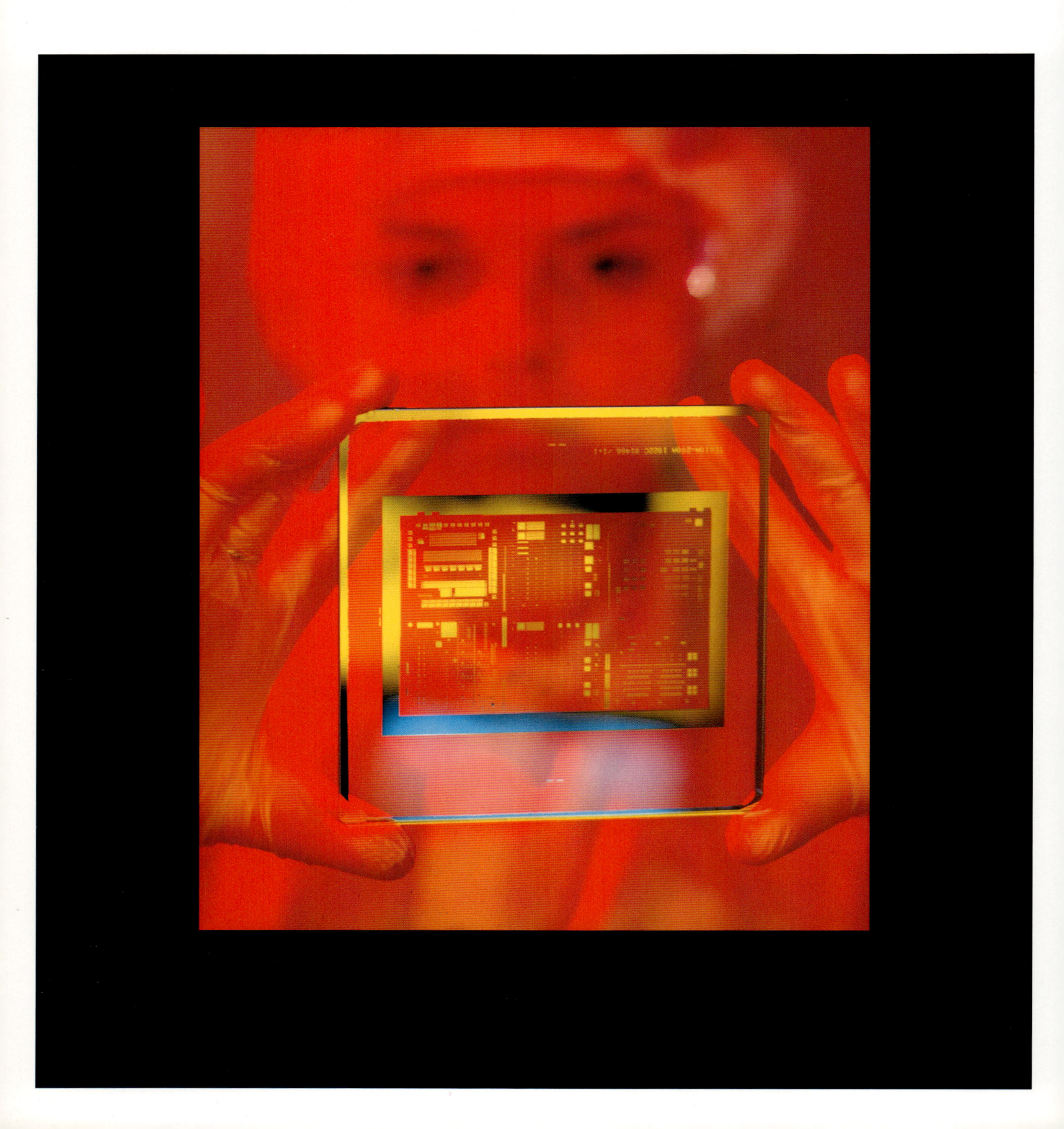

189

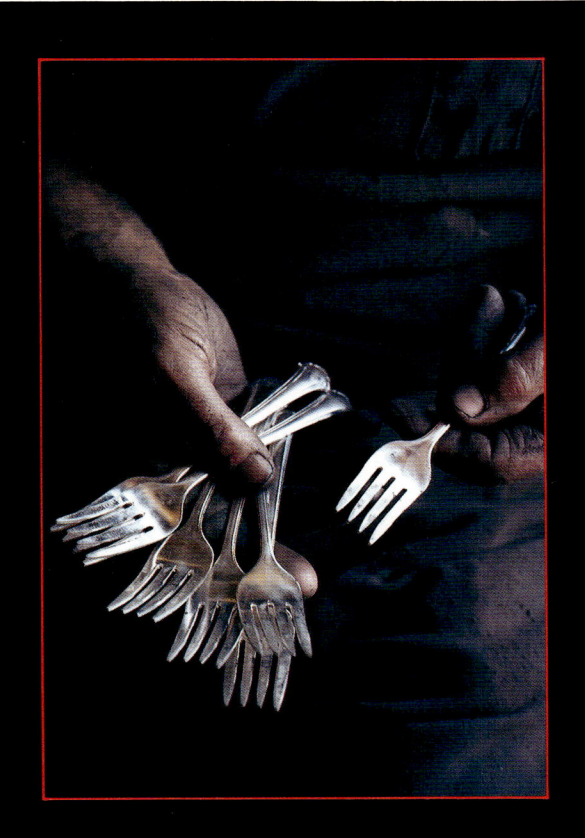

**TOM WEIGAND**
707 North Fifth Street
Reading, Pennsylvania 19601
(215) 374-4431

Advertising, corporate
& still life photography

Classical Photography: Studio
and on location

Accolades: Cleo, Andy, Addy, PIA,
The Art Director's Club of New York,
The Art Director's Club of Philadelphia,
AD 61, and more.

Audition our complete repertoire by calling our representative
Ken Haas at (212) 807-8706.

©1983 Tom Weigand

190

ASMP

AD RUSS SLOCUM

**MICHAEL WEINBERG STUDIO**
5 East 16th Street
New York, New York 10003
(212) 691-0713

© Michael Weinberg 1983

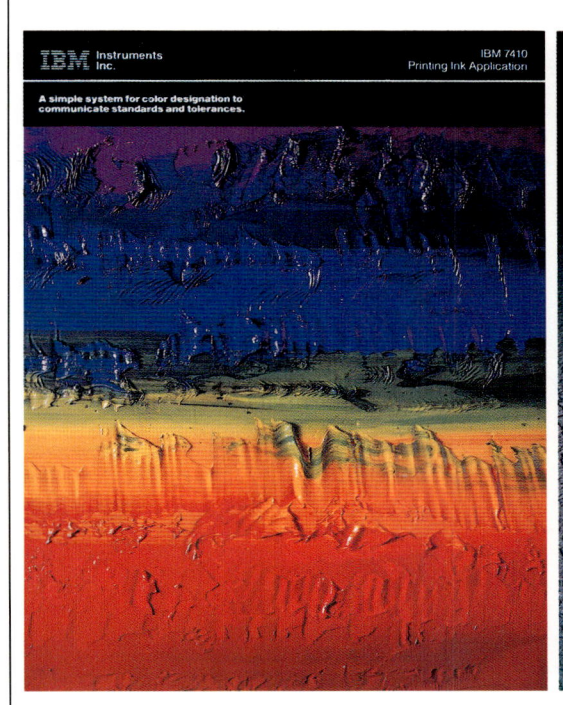

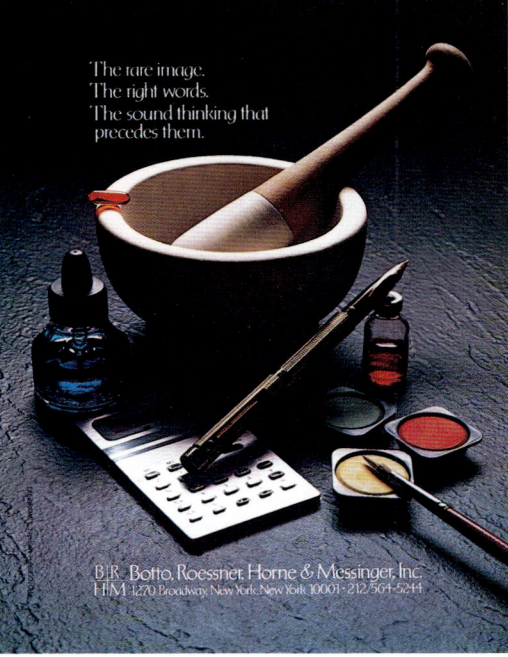

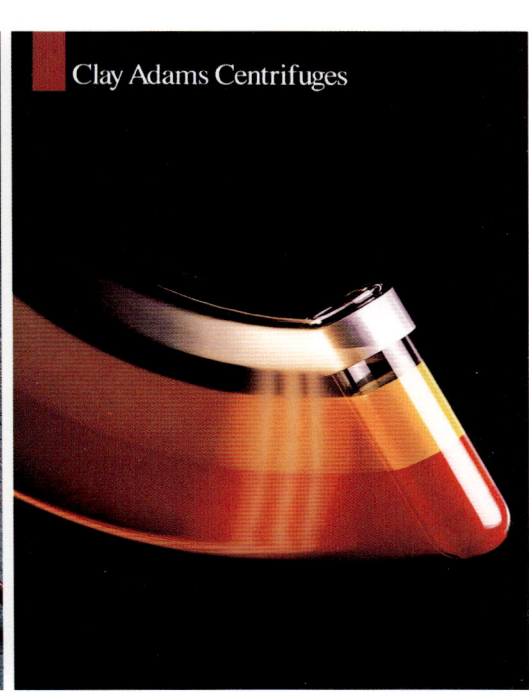

191

APA

**ALLAN WEITZ**
373 Park Avenue South
10th Floor
New York, New York 10016
(212) 725-8041

192

Represented in the Mid-West by: Joel Harlib (312) 329-1370      All Photos ©1983—Allan Weitz

Clients include: American Express, Bell Labs, Ogden Corporation, AT&T Long Lines, Warner Communications, St. Regis Paper, Nikon, American Cyanamid, and others.

Editorial clients include: Nautical Quarterly, New York Magazine, Esquire, Gentleman's Quarterly, Attenzione, Forbes, The New York Times Magazine, and others.

Also see: Art Director's Annuals 57th-60th editions
CA-79, CA Art Annual-'80, AIGA Graphic Design USA—Volumes 1&2
Photographis 80, The One Show—Volume 3

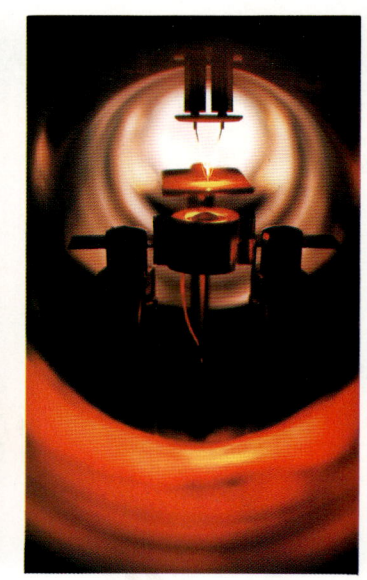

**CHARLES WEST**
New York City
(212) 624-5920

Contact:
Beatrix West

Stock Photography:
The Stock Market
(212) 684-7878

193

**WALTER WICK**
119 West 23rd Street
New York, New York 10011
(212) 243-3448

Represented by:
Michele Vollbracht
(212) 475-8718

# WALTER WICK

119 W. 23RD ST., NEW YORK, NY 10011. (212) 243 3448. REPRESENTED BY MICHELE VOLLBRACHT (212) 475 8718.

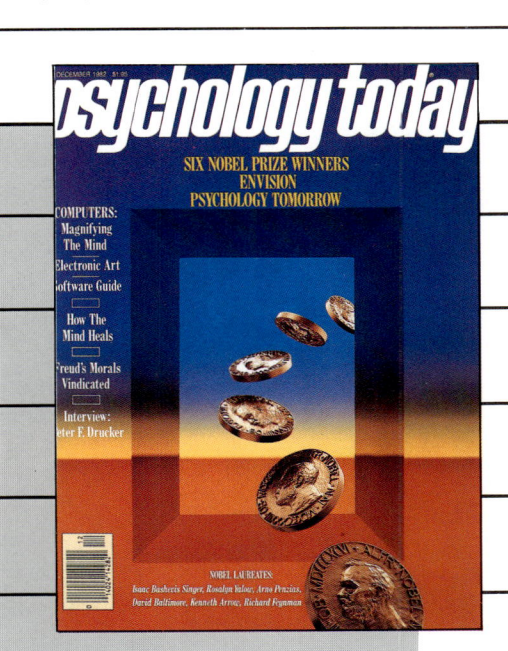

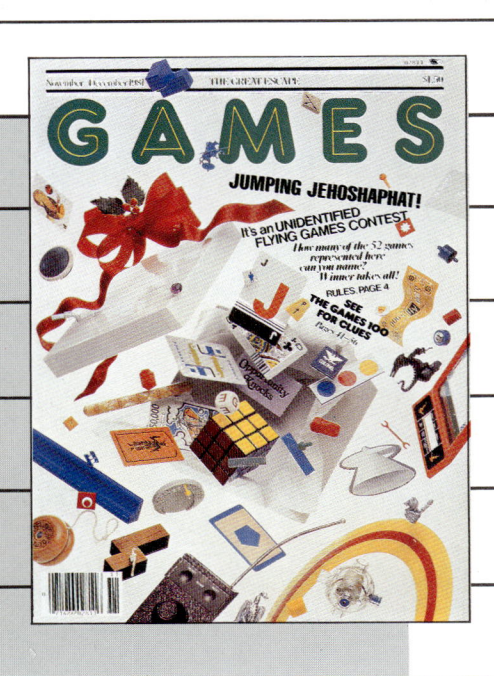

**ALAN ZENREICH**
78 Fifth Avenue
New York, New York 10011
(212) 807-1551

Represented by Lauren Morse

Advertising and editorial photography

Top: Cameras and computers
  Collaboration with Lauretta Jones
Lower left: Cover Video Magazine
Lower right: Fear of Flying—
editorial assignment

© Alan Zenreich 1983

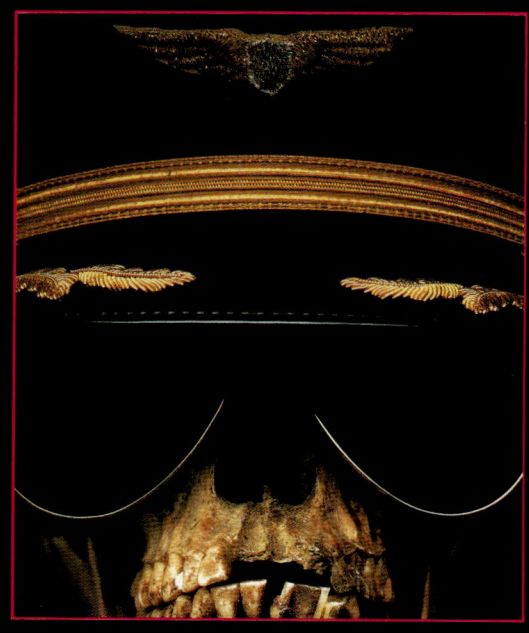

# NORTHEAST

| | |
|---|---|
| **Joachim, Bruno** Boston | 198,199 |
| **King, Ralph** Boston | 200,201 |
| **The Studio, Inc.** Pittsburgh | 202 |
| **Northlight Group** Newark NJ | 203 |
| **Rockhill, Morgan** Providence RI | 205 |
| **brt Photographic Illustrations** Lancaster PA | 206,207 |
| **Bedford Photo-graphic** Bedford NY | 208 |
| **Collins, Fred** Boston | 209 |
| **Dreyer, Peter** Boston/Westwood MA | 210 |
| **Dwiggins, Gene** Providence RI | 211 |
| **Foster, Frank** Boston | 213 |
| **Hansen, Steve** Boston | 214, 215 |
| **Joachim, Bruno** Boston | 198,199 |
| **Jones, Lou** Boston | 217 |
| **Kawalerski, Ted** Rochester NY | 218,219 |
| **King, Ralph** Boston | 200,201 |
| **La Riche, Michael** Philadelphia | 220,221 |
| **Martin, Marilyn** Boston | 222 |
| **McCoy, Dan** Housatonic MA | 223 |
| **McKean, Tom** Wynnewood PA | 224 |
| **Northlight Group** Newark NJ | 203 |

| | |
|---|---|
| **Photography Associates** Hartford CT | 225 |
| **Robinson, George A.** Jericho VT | 226 |
| **Rockhill, Morgan** Providence RI | 205 |
| **Rotman, Jeffrey L.** Somerville MA | 227 |
| **Sauter, Ron** Rochester NY | 228 |
| **Schleipman, Russ** Charlestown MA | 229 |
| **Simmons, Erik Leigh** Boston | 230 |
| **Steiner, Peter** Rochester NY | 231 |
| **The Studio, Inc.** Pittsburgh | 202 |
| **Vaughan, Ted** Manheim PA | 232,233 |
| **Yablon, Ron** Exton PA | 234 |

**Connecticut**
**Delaware**
**Maine**
**Massachusetts**
**New Hampshire**
**New Jersey**
**New York State**
**Pennsylvania**
**Rhode Island**
**Vermont**

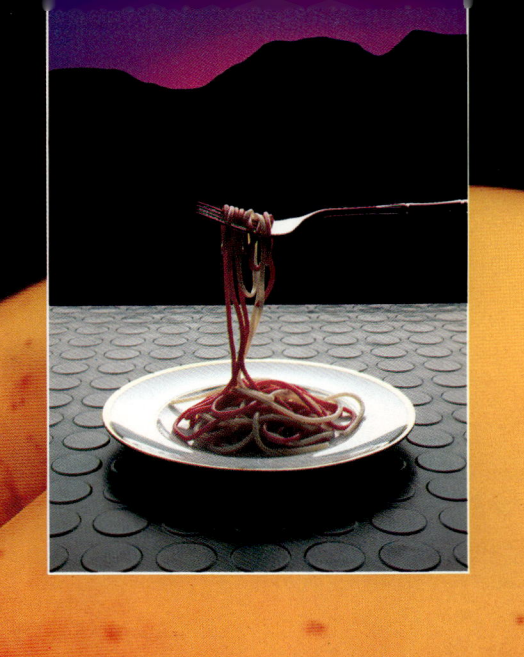

**BRUNO JOACHIM STUDIO**

BOSTON
(617) 451-6156

MAJOR AGENCY
CORPORATE AND EDITORIAL
ACCOUNTS

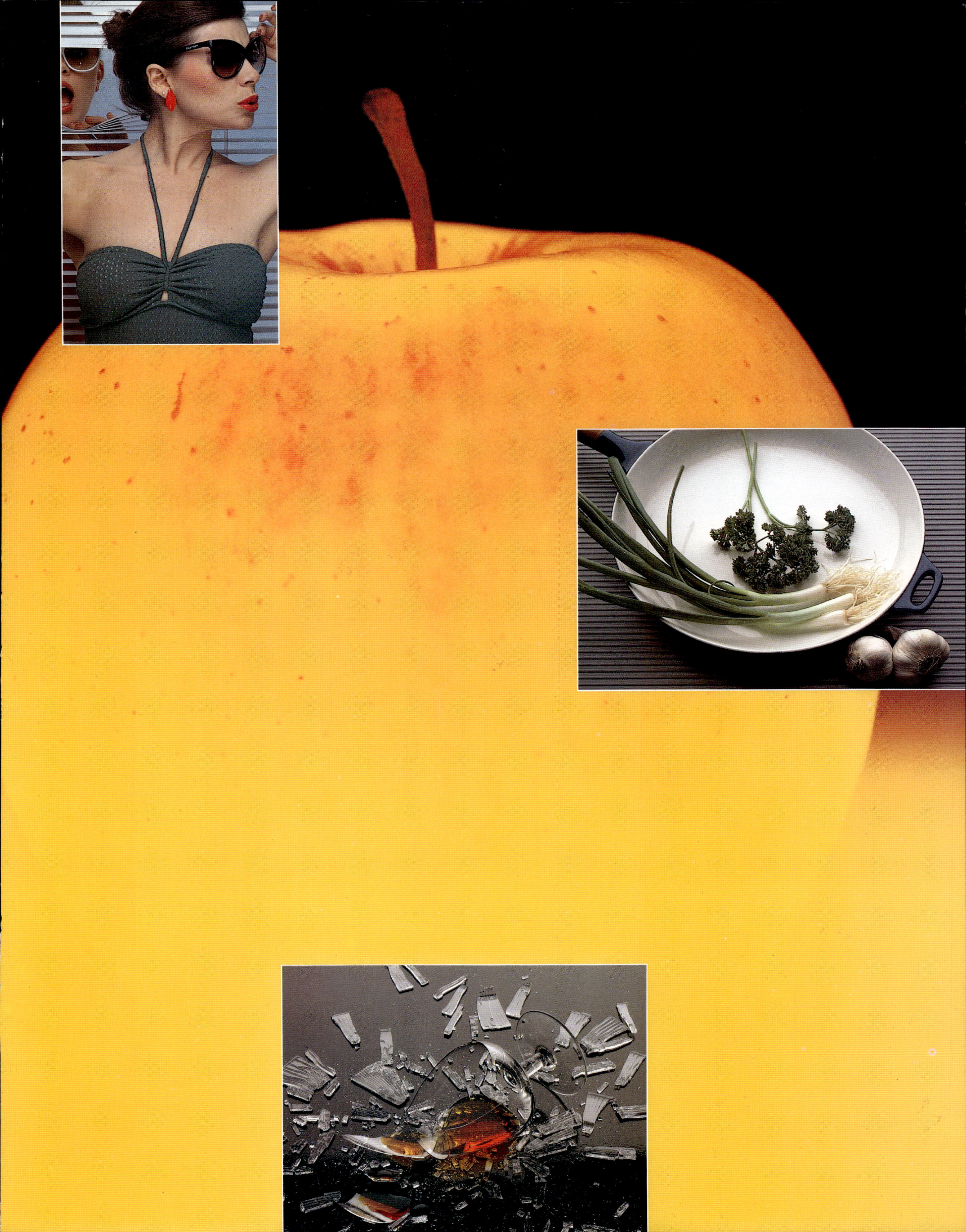

103 BROAD STREET • BOSTON, MA 02110 • (617) 426-3565 • REPRESENTED BY ELLA • (617) 266-3858

# RALPH KING

103 BROAD STREET • BOSTON, MA 02110 • (617) 426-3565 • REPRESENTED BY ELLA • (617) 266-3858

# RALPH KING

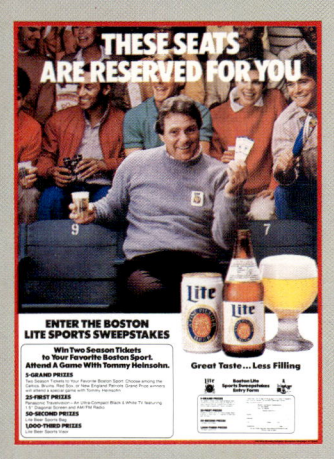

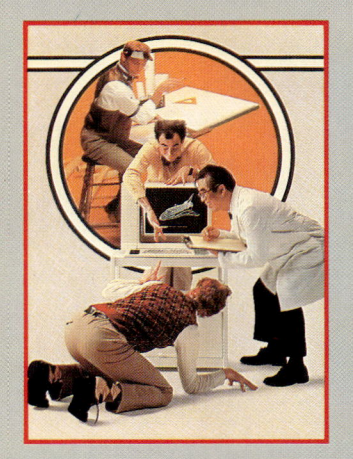

# The Studio inc.
818 Liberty Avenue
Pittsburgh, Pa. 15222
(412) 261-2022

# NORTHLIGHT
## VISUAL COMMUNICATIONS GROUP, INC.

**HOSPITAL UNDERWRITERS MUTUAL INSURANCE COMPANY/Financial and Services Symposium**

**INTERPACE CORPORATION/Annual Report**

**MACY'S AND BAMBERGER'S/Retail Sales Brochure**

**THE ARCHIE SCHWARTZ COMPANY/Facilities Brochure**

Renowned for large format still-life photography Northlight offers a wealth of creative ideas and optimum lighting techniques.

We pride ourselves in our diversification and the ability to get the job done.

Our expertise lies within the areas of product illustration, jewelry, food preparation, corporate portraiture, annual reports, architecture and location photography.

Shed a new light on your next assignment.

Call or write:
**Northlight Visual Communications Group, Inc.
21-23 Quine Street
Cranford, New Jersey 07016
201-272-1155**

## IT'S YOUR TALENT—
## USE IT OR LOSE IT.

I recently gave a speech to a group of creative people at a high school commencement exercise (it's the same speech I give to one person or 500). It said the following:

"I love what I do for a living."

I'm thankful that I had the good fortune to have someone recognize I had a bit of talent way back then. And that someone encouraged me on.

If you've got a God-given talent, please don't throw it away.

Don't waste it.

Nourish it.

Invest in it; continue your education.

There are too many people out there doing dull, mundane things for eight hours a day, 365 days a year, every year for the rest of their lives.

Hating their job.

Knocking it.

Wishing they had done something about it way back when.

There's no turning back for them.

But for you—you're at the turning point.

It's right now.

So don't throw away that God-given talent.

You'll regret it the rest of your life.

That's right.

I love what I do.

I love the profession I work in.

Sure:

We bitch all day long.

We yell.

We fight.

We moan.

We scream.

We even act like animals at times.

We embarrass ourselves in front of others.

We do so many stupid things over the years.

But even so...I still love it.

What other profession puts you into such a creative environment that permits you the creative license to:
- one moment create a vessel to house a client's product in.
- design a graphic which embodies a company's philosophy.
- reshape the corporate identity of a major corporation.
- create a magazine campaign for a client's new product line
- select and work with the most talented photographers on the scene, one talent playing off another, your idea blending with theirs. An end result that gives one the same satisfaction as a painter finishing his creation.
- watch an illustrator take your rough sketch and just bring it to life: What a revelation to be part of.

Then there's the T.V. commercial:

Remember when you were a kid and went to the movies and maybe dreamt about going to Hollywood and being in them.

Well, now you are.

There you are creating a T.V. commercial for a client's product. Selling it to the client as if you were the director.

Then you pick the film company and finally there you are in "Hollywood."

Seeing your creation being filmed.

Being the co-producer,

co-director,

co-editor,

and co-everything.

Now if that's not a dream come true I don't know what is.

What a profession.

It sure as hell ain't boring!

Wouldn't it have been a shame if I had thrown away my talent way back when. I never would have been able to be with you today, give this speech and end it with:

"Thank God, I love what I do."

**Kurt Haiman
Co-Director
Fashion/Soft Goods/Retail
Grey Advertising
New York City**

**MORGAN ROCKHILL**

*204 Westminster Mall*
*Providence, RI 02903*
*(401) 274-3472*

REPRESENTED BY: BOB LENAHAN & MARY CRAIG (617) 327-4968 / KIM CRAGNOLIN (212) 883-1188

## brt PHOTOGRAPHIC ILLUSTRATIONS

911 State Street
Lancaster, Pennsylvania 17603
(717) 393-0918

Brian R. Tolbert, Member ASMP
Representative: Jill Brown

What's one of the largest full-service studios in the northeast doing in Lancaster, Pennsylvania? Providing photographs that tell, sell, illustrate, educate, evaluate, move, groove, ease, please, condense, expand, abstract, epitomize, personify and gratify.

Studio facilities:
- 12,000 sq. ft.
- in-house lab production
- room set construction
- thirty-five foot cyc
- full kitchen, w/food stylist

Our client list runs from… Armstrong, Black & Decker, Creamer Adv., Dentsply, Empire Foods, Frito-Lay, General Battery, Hamilton Watch, ITT, Jones & Laughlin, Ketchum, Litton, Metro Wire, Novatec, Owens-Corning, Pfaltzgraf, Quaker Alloy, RCA, San Giorgio, Thonet, United Way, Victrex LeCarpenter, Woodstream, X/stock, York/Borg-Warner, thru…Zimpro Inc.

Call us…even if it's just to hear the cows mooing at the other end of the phone!

Additional published work may be seen in Corporate Showcase 1 and 2, American Showcase 6, ASMP 2, Art Directions Creativity 80 and 82, Images and Ideas issue one.

brt
© BRIAN R. TOLBERT 1983

# brt

Photographic Illustrations
911 State Street • Lancaster, PA 17603
(717) 393-0918

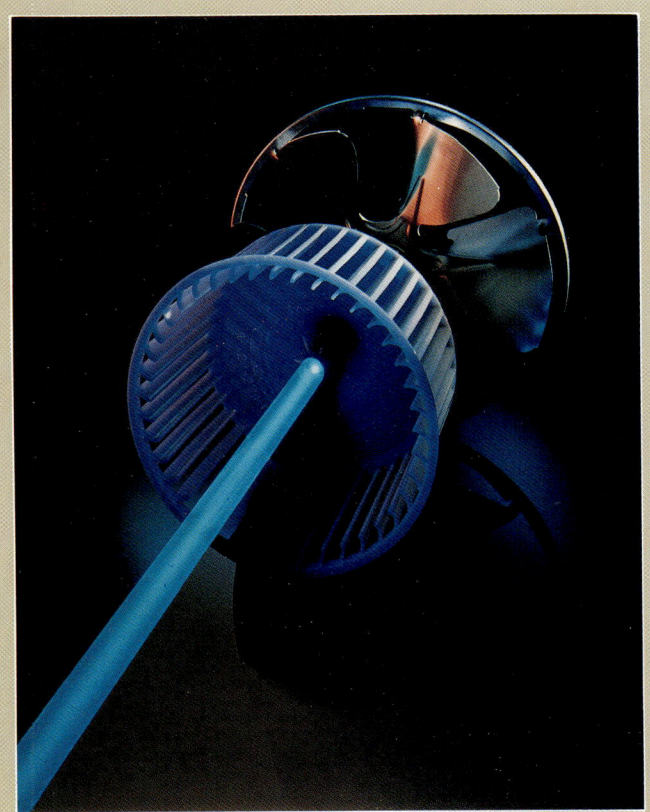

**BEDFORD PHOTO-GRAPHIC STUDIO**
Rt. 22
P.O. Box 64
Bedford Village, New York 10506
(914) 234-3123, 234-6814

Photography by Doug Abdelnour
Represented by Jeff Spaulding

Technical services: Chuck Keogh

Major work performed for advertising, industrial, and corporate purposes includes concept and product illustration, architectural and culinary photography, and photography for multi-image slide presentations. We maintain a fully equipped studio with full color and black-and-white processing facilities. We welcome location assignments.

The studio is located in Westchester County, N.Y., bordering Fairfield County at Stamford, Ct. We serve clients nationally as well as those in the New York metropolitan area.

Clients include: American Can Company, Arnold Bakers, Bing & Grondahl Porcelain, Copper Development Association, Curtis Instruments, Dansk International Designs, GTE, General Foods, ITT Continental Baking, Merrill Lynch Relocation, Murata-Erie, Olin, Perkin-Elmer, Pfizer, PepsiCo, Reader's Digest, Reinhold Publishing, Southland Corporation, and Waldenbooks.

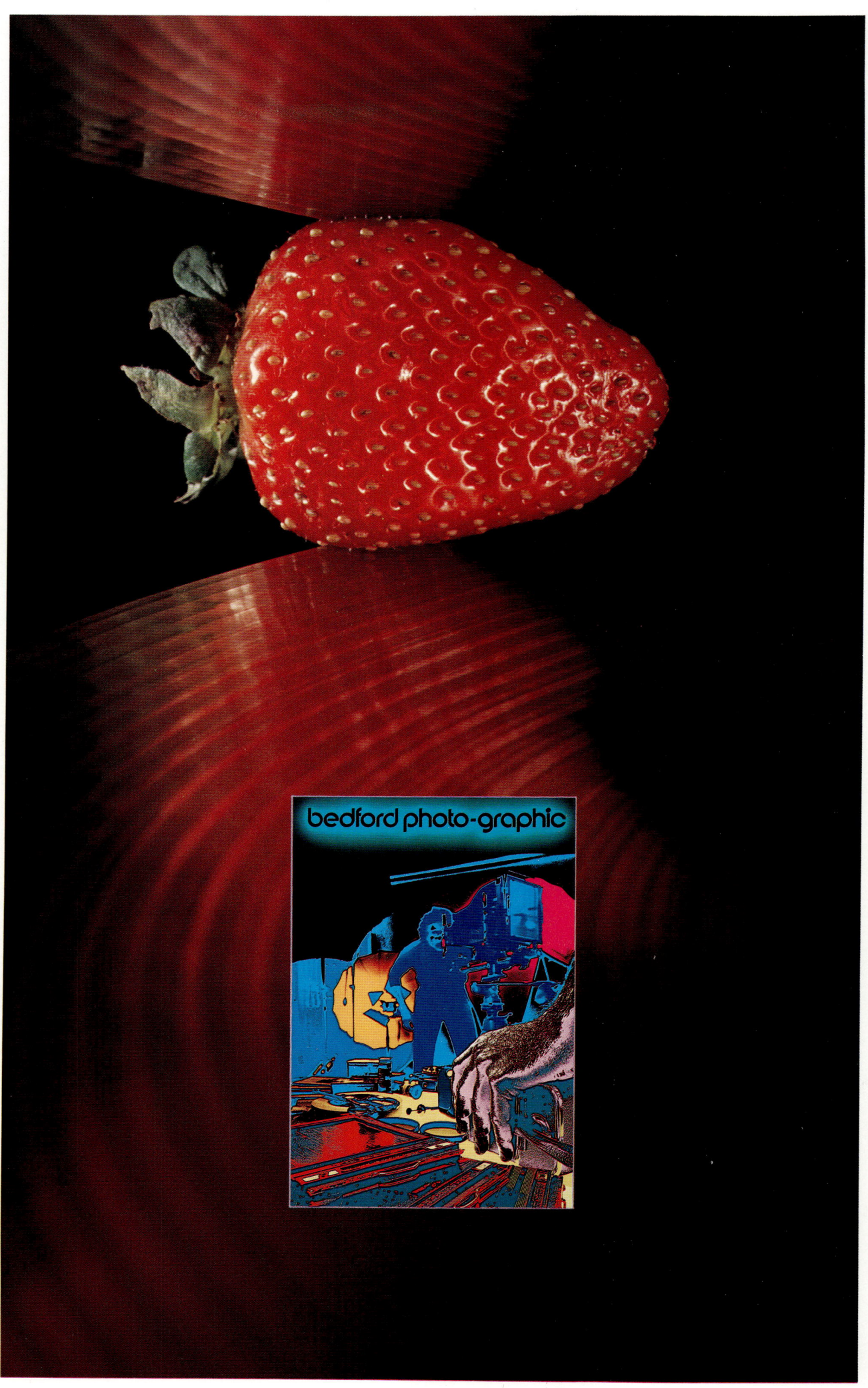

**FRED COLLINS STUDIOS, INC.**
186 South Street
Boston, Massachusetts 02111
(617) 426-5731
Member ASMP
Represented by: Alison Fisher

Clients Include: BASF, Bill Rodgers & Co., Carter's, Commercial Union, ComputerVision, Converse, Dexter Shoe Co., Digital, Honeywell, Liberty Mutual, McCormack & Dodge, Polaroid, Providence Gravure, Providence Journal Bulletin, Roger Tory Petersen, Shawmut, Spalding, Teradyne, Trak/Kneissl, United Technology.

209

McCORMICK AND DODGE/COMPUTER SOFTWARE

TRAK/KNEISSL SKIS

TRAK/KNEISSL SKIS

HOUGHTON MIFFLIN/ROGER TORY PETERSON

COMMERCIAL UNION ASSURANCE COMPANY

**PETER DREYER**
166 Burgess Avenue
Westwood, Massachusetts 02090
(suburban Boston)
(617) 762-8550

Corporate/industrial, advertising, and editorial photography.

Clients include: American Optical, Analog Devices, Compugraphic, Cullinet Software, Digital Equipment, Gillette, IBM, LTX Corp., Nixdorf Computer, Polaroid, Raytheon Data Systems, Thermo Electron, Wang Laboratories.

Stock photos available.

Design: David Grotrian

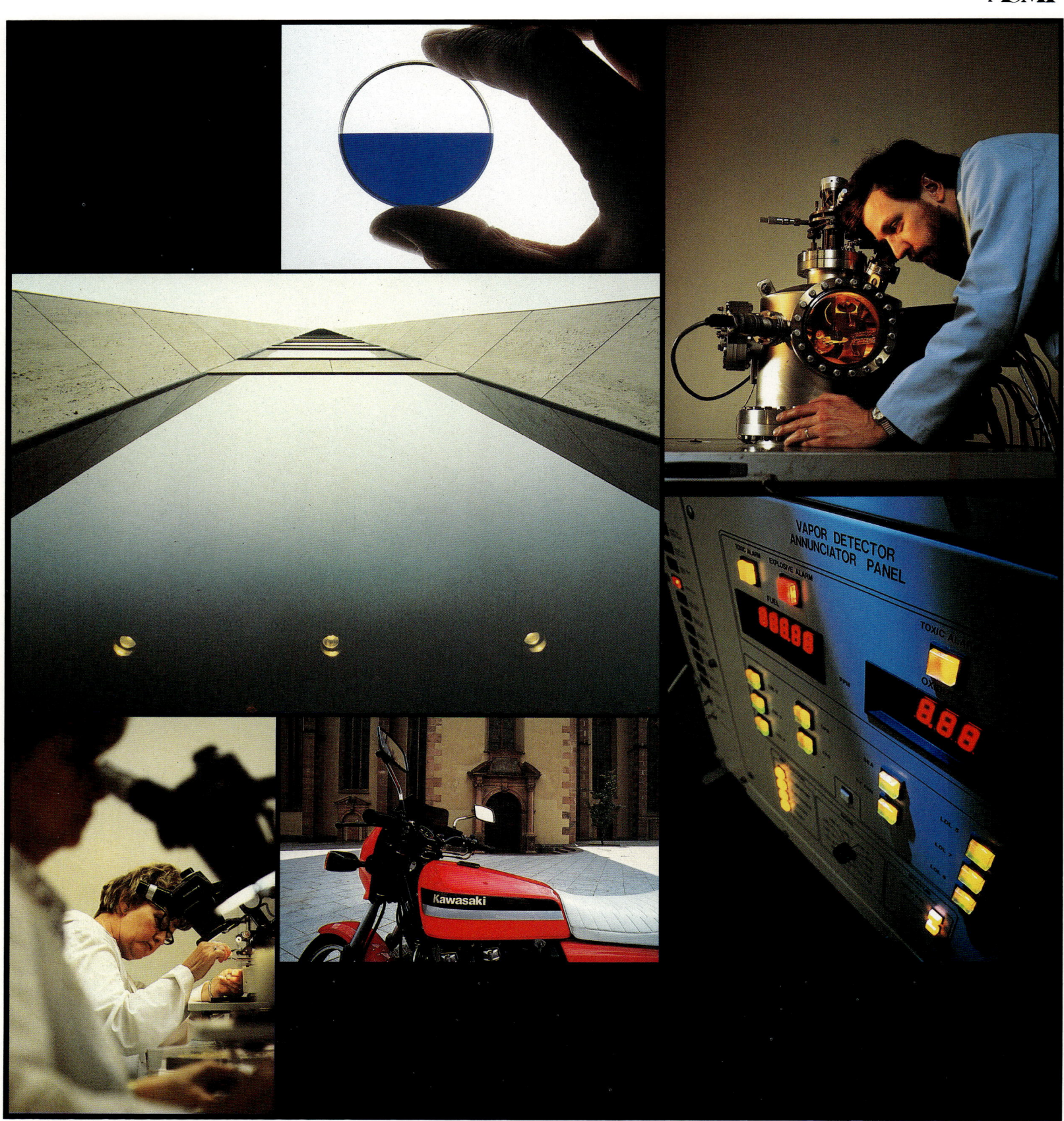

210

ASMP

**GENE DWIGGINS**
Gene Dwiggins Photography, Inc.
204 Westminster Mall
Providence, Rhode Island 02903
(401) 421-6466

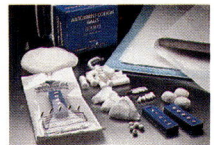

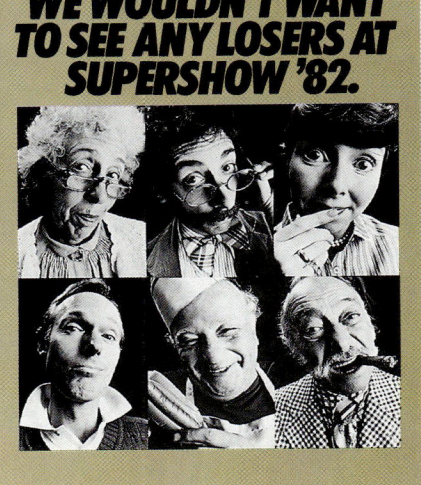

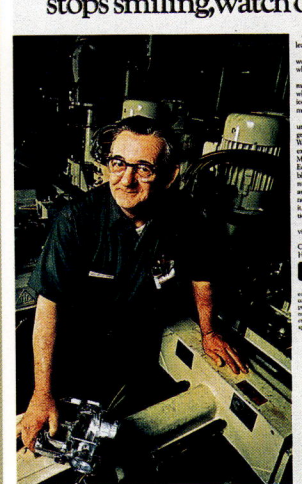

211

## WALLPAPER IS MORE IMPRESSIVE THAN A PORTFOLIO

My husband calls me a squirrel. I love to store things: school-day diaries and yearbooks; miscellaneous treasures; recipes; slides, maps and guide books from all my travels, divided by country and city; business files on every client I've had in 25 years; even the warranties on every electrical/mechanical item in home or office. And they're all beautifully organized. If I lost my eyesight tomorrow, I'd still be able to put my hands on anything. Evidence of organizational skills? Yes. But perhaps it's truly the ultimate streak of laziness. By putting each item away in its proper place, I then never waste time later searching for it. It's just where it belongs.

Perhaps that's why I have a respect for portfolios. The kind all art directors build, photographers' reps lug around, and those ad and PR agencies develop for their clients. They're historical, representational of talent, and also a recognition of that talent; recognition by a client approving work to run, or of a publisher or editor choosing work to appear, or even awards received for excellence singled out in competition.

My 12-year old Ad/PR agency is the largest internationally in the beauty salon/hairstyling field. We maintain portfolios for each client; annual portfolios for clients such as Wella Balsam, mounting press clips on product publicity, press parties, trade press items, corporate matters, their beauty spokeswomen, etc.

For our beauty salon clients, our big job is keeping one portfolio on each. This means constant editing—retaining perhaps 2-6 pages of press pick-up on a series of photos—and sending the salon 20 pages to keep as a memory/report/impression scrapbook.

To build a good client's portfolio, we have to teach them photographic hairstyling. He or she may do great work in their salon, but a photographer's studio may be another matter. The pressures are different. Meters are running—the photographer's, makeup artist's, photo and wardrobe stylists', and above all—the models'!! Thousands of dollars are riding on even a half day's work. And the hairstyles they create aren't for the day or a week/month as they are in the salon. They can live on in photography for a year, a decade, or more. We have two goals for each photo session: 1) to produce photos representative of a stylist's talent that will hopefully achieve press pick-up/recognition and 2) to provide the client with photographic hairstyling experience so we can recommend him/her to magazine editors/manufacturers/ad agencies to style models for their shootings.

The results? Gratifying indeed. How much more impressive than a color photo is a color *cover* in a portfolio? And how much more impressive than photos are the photos' pick-up in French *Vogue,* British *Cosmo,* American *Vogue's* "Hair Now," *Harper's Bazaar, Seventeen,* etc.; and descriptions of a hairstylist's work in French, Italian, German, Japanese, etc.—not just in English!

We see photographers' portfolios constantly, but only those who have a good book on beauty (we can't gamble clients' thousands of hard-earned dollars on a photographer's learning experience), and only if they'll include contacts from at least one shooting. I need to see how much work—and good or bad lighting, went into producing the one or two great shots he's put in his portfolio. We do co-op, though, on test shootings during which photographers, models, and hairstylists gain experience and occasionally photos worth releasing.

Do I have a portfolio for my agency? Well, no—I guess it's a repeat of the story of the shoemaker's child having no shoes. We get too busy doing our clients' PR to concentrate on our own. But we do have a good portfolio "substitute." About eight years ago, one of my photographers laminated magazine covers featuring his work and hung them on his studio wall. I followed suit. When prospective clients come in to visit, it's often enough for them to see the results of our talent/skills by just looking at this wall of covers achieved from photo sessions we've guided for past clients.

I used to say I'd close up shop when my cover wall got too full. But I'll probably never do this as long as I still get the thrill I do out of seeing each new magazine cover. My wall got full last year. We moved to new offices, one with a larger wall to fill. I love my "cover wall." It saves on wallpaper and is easier than mounting portolio pages!

**Judy Guerin de Neco
The Advertising Club of New York
New York City**

**FRANK FOSTER/BOSTON**
323 Newbury Street
Boston, Massachusetts 02115
(617) 536-8267

Award winning photography including first place in the New York "The One Show."

Clients include P. Lorillard, Spaulding, Carling, Heublein, S.D. Warren, Pillsbury, Parker Brothers and Sheraton Hotels. Stock Photography available on Boston/New England area.

Represented by Stephanie Holmes

213

*World Middleweight Boxing Champion Marvelous Marvin Hagler and his mother, Ida Mae Lang.*

ONE MEAN BEAN.
Jack Rabbit Brand
Pillsbury THE PILLSBURY COMPANY

BOSTON MARATHON

PAUL SZEP/PULITZER PRIZE

**STEVE HANSEN PHOTOGRAPHY, INC.**
40 Winchester Street
Boston, Massachusetts 02116
(617) 426-6858

ASMP Member
Represented by: Rita Hansen

Advertising/Annual Reports/Architecture
Executive Portraits/Special Effects
Client list and mailers on request

© 1983 Steve Hansen

Your place…

**STEVE HANSEN PHOTOGRAPHY, INC.**
40 Winchester Street
Boston, Massachusetts 02116
(617) 426-6858

ASMP Member
Represented by: Rita Hansen

Advertising/Annual Reports/Architecture
Executive Portraits/Special Effects
Client list and mailers on request

© 1983 Steve Hansen

or mine?

## YOU MEET THE NICEST PEOPLE IN THIS BUSINESS.

There was a time when I wanted to be a baseball player. That came after wanting to be a fireman, a cowboy and a long fantasy about owning a candy store.

I used to sit and draw pictures and think about what I'd do later in life.

As it turns out, those pictures I used to draw turned me away from the ballpark and into the direction of art school, a job teaching art, and finally into advertising.

My heroes changed from ballplayers to art directors, photographers and illustrators. The only pinstripes I would end up wearing would be tailored at Paul Stuart or Brooks Brothers. Instead of a bat, I carried a briefcase.

I have no regrets because there is as much satisfaction in coming up with a good ad as there used to be in winning a game in the bottom of the ninth. I get as much of a kick out of watching a good photographer put together a great shot as I did watching a spectacular catch or a ball being launched into the stands.

I have as much respect for "All Stars" of our business as I used to have for both the National and American Leagues' finest.

I feel very fortunate to have worked with some of the best talent in our industry. I've met some of the nicest people in this very special business and I'm a snob about it.

Having lunch with Lou Dorfsman made me feel as proud as I felt when I shook Jackie Robinson's hand in Cooperstown. It's not that there is a different degree of talent, it's just that my heroes have changed.

The photographer who can make an idea become real, the designer who can put everything exactly where it belongs, the writer who can employ the right words, or the illustrator who can put on canvas a combination of color, line and feeling—just the proper elements that make it—are my new heroes.

I must confess that there are others who have put me into the "groupie" category. I really like reps. I haven't met one I don't like. There are a few who are even very special to me; I admire their good sense and their judgment of talent. I envy them their ability to work for their people and their tenacity.

It's a nice business in spite of the pressures of impossible deadlines and the day to day struggles of trying to please so many people.

Yes, I'd rather be in this business than playing baseball. My arm never really was all that great; and I was a sucker for a curve ball. I even tried chewing tobacco once—got sick as a dog (you can't make it to the big leagues if you can't chew).

When the day comes that I can no longer do what I do well, I know I'll hang up my briefcase. Like baseball, this is a young person's business. There are a lot of things I'll miss, but most of all it will be the people who make it fun. The people whose talent inspires others to do better things. The people who make you look good. The rush of watching everything come together and even that let-down that comes when the job is over.

I'm not going to think of that now...I think I still have a few more seasons in me, and I look forward to working with some of those heavy hitters again.

I've met some of the nicest people in this business, and there are a few of them in this book.

**Robert A. Paige
President/Creative Director
Evans, Garber & Paige
Utica, N.Y.**

**LOU JONES**
22 Randolph Street
Boston, Massachusetts 02118
(617) 426-6335

*Specializing in location & illustration photography*

Clients include:
Pan Am
Chase Manhattan
Bose
Data General
New Balance
Xerox
Polaroid
PBS
Gillette
*Time*
*Nation's Business*

International representation by the Image Bank

Member ASMP/APA

**TED KAWALERSKI**
52 San Gabriel Drive
Rochester, New York 14610
(716) 244-4656

Location photography for annual reports and corporate advertising.

A partial list of clients: Bausch & Lomb, Corning Glass, Eastman Kodak, First of America Bank Corporation, *Fortune,* Gannett Co., Inc., Holiday Inn, Lincoln First Banks Inc., Security New York State Corporation, Time-Life Books, Washington Post Company, Xerox.

Stock photography: The Image Bank

Member ASMP

All photographs © Ted Kawalerski 1982-1983

**TED KAWALERSKI**
52 San Gabriel Drive
Rochester, New York 14610
(716) 244-4656

All photographs © Ted Kawalerski 1982-1983

219

**MICHAEL LA RICHE**
30 South Bank Street
Philadelphia, Pennsylvania 19106
(215) 922-0447
(212) 690-1677

Advertising, Corporate/Industrial and Editorial Photography (studio and location)

Represented by: Robert Rotella
(215) 922-1681

Clients include: Armotek, Blue Cross & Blue Shield, Bookbinders, Cable Today, Dimensions, Eagle's Eye, Fitz and Floyd, Girard Bank, IMM, International Envelope Co., John Wanamaker, Krementz, London Fog, Mannington Mills, Mattheyprint, Mitchell Daroff, Mrs. Smith's, NFL Films, Okidata, Penn Maid, Philadephia Magazine, Presto Lock, Rhone-Polenc, Rhom & Haas, Sperry Univac, Strawbridge & Clothier, Scott Paper, SGL Industries, Slazenger, Syntex, University of Pennsylvania, Wood River Village.

**MICHAEL LA RICHE**
30 South Bank Street
Philadelphia, Pennsylvania 19106
(215) 922-0447
(212) 690-1677

Represented by: Robert Rotella
(215) 922-1681

**MARILYN MARTIN**
560 Harrison Avenue
Boston, Massachusetts 02118
(617) 426-0064

Representative: Robert E. Raftery

Fashion, Industrial, People, and Product Photography
fulfilling all of your photographic needs in our studio
or on location anywhere in the world.

222

**DAN McCOY**
c/o Rainbow
Main Street
Housatonic, Massachusetts 01236
(413) 274-6211

Contact: Coco

On-location photography for annual reports, brochures, corporate communications and editorial.

Specialty: High technology
Can also bring along airplane and microscope

Stock photos available through:
Rainbow (see above)
Black Star, New York City
Colorific, London
Rapho, Paris
Pacific Press Service, Japan

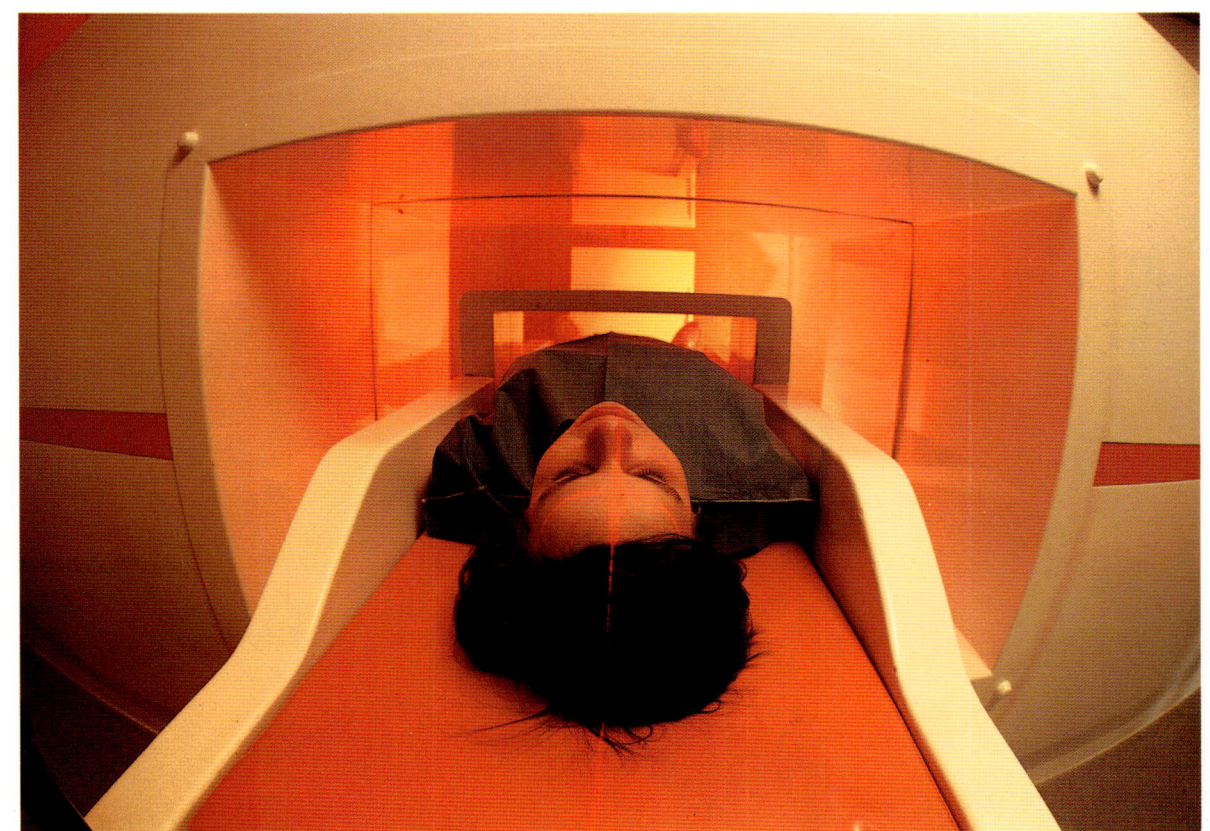

223

SOLAR ONE HELIOSTATS

NUCLEAR MAGNETIC RESONANCE

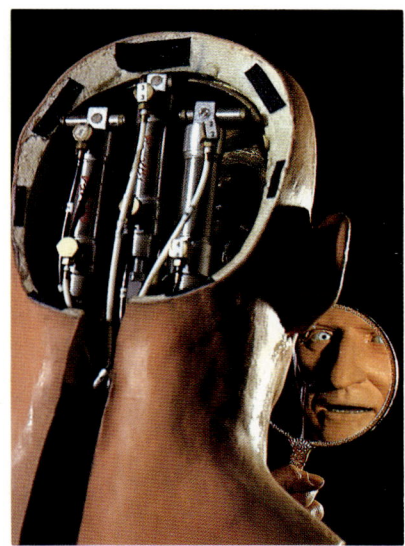

VAIN ROBOT

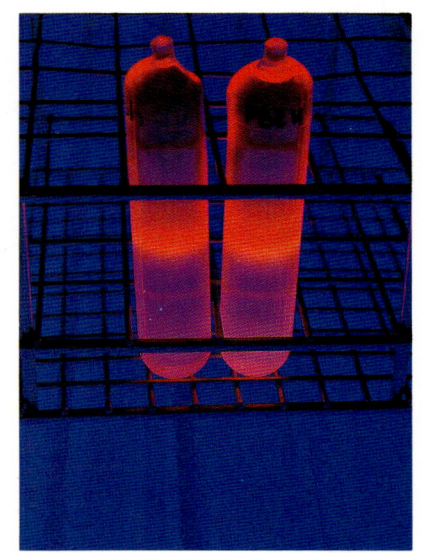

DNA BANDS

HEART PUMP

**TOM McKEAN PHOTO STUDIO, INC.**
742 Cherry Circle
Wynnewood, Pennsylvania 19096
(215) 642-0966

Advertising-Still Life, Editorial Photography.

Member ASMP.

All Photographs © Tom McKean 1983.

Call or Write For Samples, and Client List.

224

ASMP

**PHOTOGRAPHY ASSOCIATES/BILL TCHAKIRIDES**
140-150 Huyshope Avenue
Hartford, Connecticut 06106
(203) 249-1105

Represented by: Ellen Smith
(203) 525-5117

Product still life, food, interiors, industrial and location photography. Full kitchen facilities. 2 shooting studios.

Some recent clients: Abbott Ball Co.; American Saw; Bassick Casters; Coleco; Connecticut Valley Arms; Corbin Hardware; Dennison National Co.; Dexter Corp.; Erving Paper; *Fine Woodworking Magazine*; Frigitronics; Heritage Savings Bank; Infranour, Inc.; Munson Candies; National Telephone Co.; Ramada Inns; Sheet Metal and Air Conditioning Contractors Nat'l Association; Stanley Hardware; Traditions, Inc.; Whedon Products Co.

Photographs © 1983 Bill Tchakirides

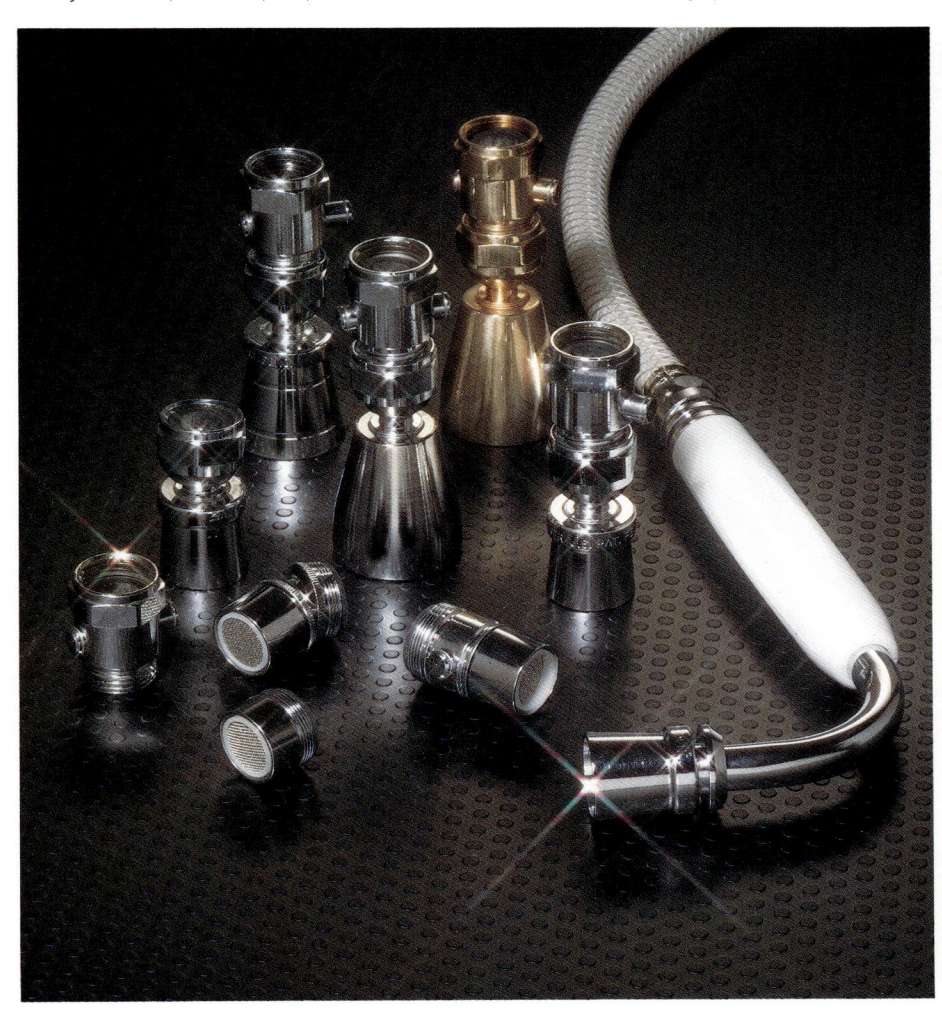

225

ASMP

**GEORGE A. ROBINSON**
377 Old Pump Road
Jericho, Vermont 05465
(802) 899-3703

Specializing in location photography for industry, corporate, editorial, and annual reports.

Graduate of Brooks Institute of Photography, BA.

Stock photography available.

Credits include: IBM, General Electric, *Newsweek, Garden Way, Country Journal, Reader's Digest,* U.S. Dept. of the Interior, U.S. Dept. of Agriculture, *Yankee,* Dartmouth College, Eastman Kodak, *Natural History, Vermont Life, Country Living,* Foremost Book Publishers, Argus Posters, Gibson Greeting Cards, *Billy Graham Decision, Organic Gardening,* U.S. Air, Bo Tree, *Quest,* United Methodist, *Family Journal,* National Library Association, *Modern Photography,* Delta Airlines.

GENERAL ELECTRIC/MONOGRAM

ACID RAIN RESEARCH/COUNTRY JOURNAL

NEWSWEEK

DARTMOUTH COLLEGE

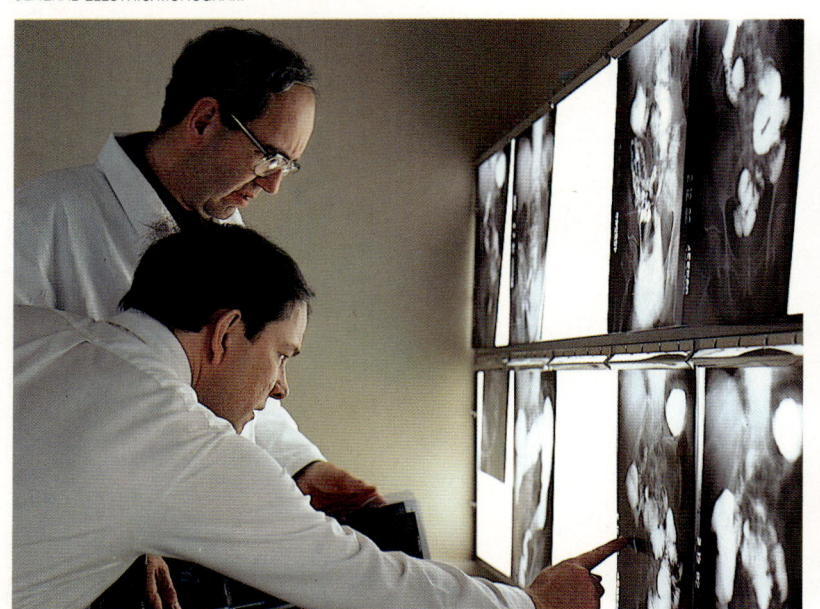

DARTMOUTH MEDICAL SCHOOL

**JEFFREY L. ROTMAN**
14 Cottage Avenue
Somerville, Massachusetts 02144
(617) 666-0874

On-location photography around the world: advertising, corporate/industrial, editorial, travel, specializing in underwater.

Extensive marine life stock

Editorial clients include: Audubon, *Discover, Geo, Life, National Geographic, National/International Wildlife, New York Times, Omni, People, Science Digest,* and *Smithsonian.*

DIVER—CORAL REEF

SAND TIGER SHARK

TRIGGER FISH

SEA ANEMONE

**RON SAUTER**
183 Saint Paul Street
Rochester, New York 14604
(716) 232-1361

In New York (212) 757-8987

© Ron Sauter 1983

SAUTER

**RUSS SCHLEIPMAN**
Zero Nearen Row
Charlestown (Boston)
Massachusetts 02129
(617) 242-9298

Advertising, annual report, corporate, editorial, industrial, photo-journalism, travel.

AMCA International, Bausch & Lomb, Digital, Ernst & Whinney, United Airlines, Polaroid, Raytheon.

*American Photographer, Forbes, Fortune, Life, Money, Outside.*

Nikon Photo Contest International 1983 Honorable Mention.

**ERIK LEIGH SIMMONS**
259 A Street
Boston, Massachusetts 02210
(617) 482-5325

Specializing in location, annual report and corporate/industrial photography

Stock photography available through The Image Bank

Partial client list: Amtrak, Avon, Boise-Cascade, CBS, Case-Hoyt, Deere & Company, Digital Equipment Corporation, EG&G, Fairchild, Goodyear, Grumman Aerospace, Heublein, IBM,, Kimberly-Clark, Polaroid, Prime Computer, Rollei of American, Scott Paper, St. Regis, TWA, Time-Life, Touche-Ross, Westinghouse Electric Corp.

**PETER STEINER**
183 Saint Paul Street
Rochester, New York 14604
(716) 454-1012

Advertising, product, annual report, editorial and travel photography.

Partial list of clients:

Eastman Kodak, Xerox Corp., Seneca Foods, Blair Advertising, GM DuBois Corp., Hutchins Y & R, Parlec Inc.

Stock available.

**TED VAUGHAN**
423 Doe Run Road
Manheim, Pennsylvania 17545
(717) 665-6942

Assignments & Stock

Clients:
Shell
John Deere
FMC
International Harvester
*Forbes*
Stauffer Chemical
DuPont

"Nature and Man working with care & understanding"

**TED VAUGHAN**
423 Doe Run Road
Manheim, Pennsylvania 17545
(717) 665-6942

Assignments & Stock

Clients:
Shell
John Deere
FMC
International Harvester
*Forbes*
Stauffer Chemical
DuPont

"Nature and Man working with care & understanding"

**RON YABLON**
Box 128
Exton (Suburban Philadelphia), Pennsylvania 19341
(215) 363-2596

234

I don't specialize in any particular industries.
I don't limit myself to any one or more types of photography.
I don't work exclusively out of a studio, or for that matter,
I don't take just location assignments.
I don't even use one specific style to answer every problem.

I do consistently create unique images to graphically enrich
and attract maximum attention to your project.

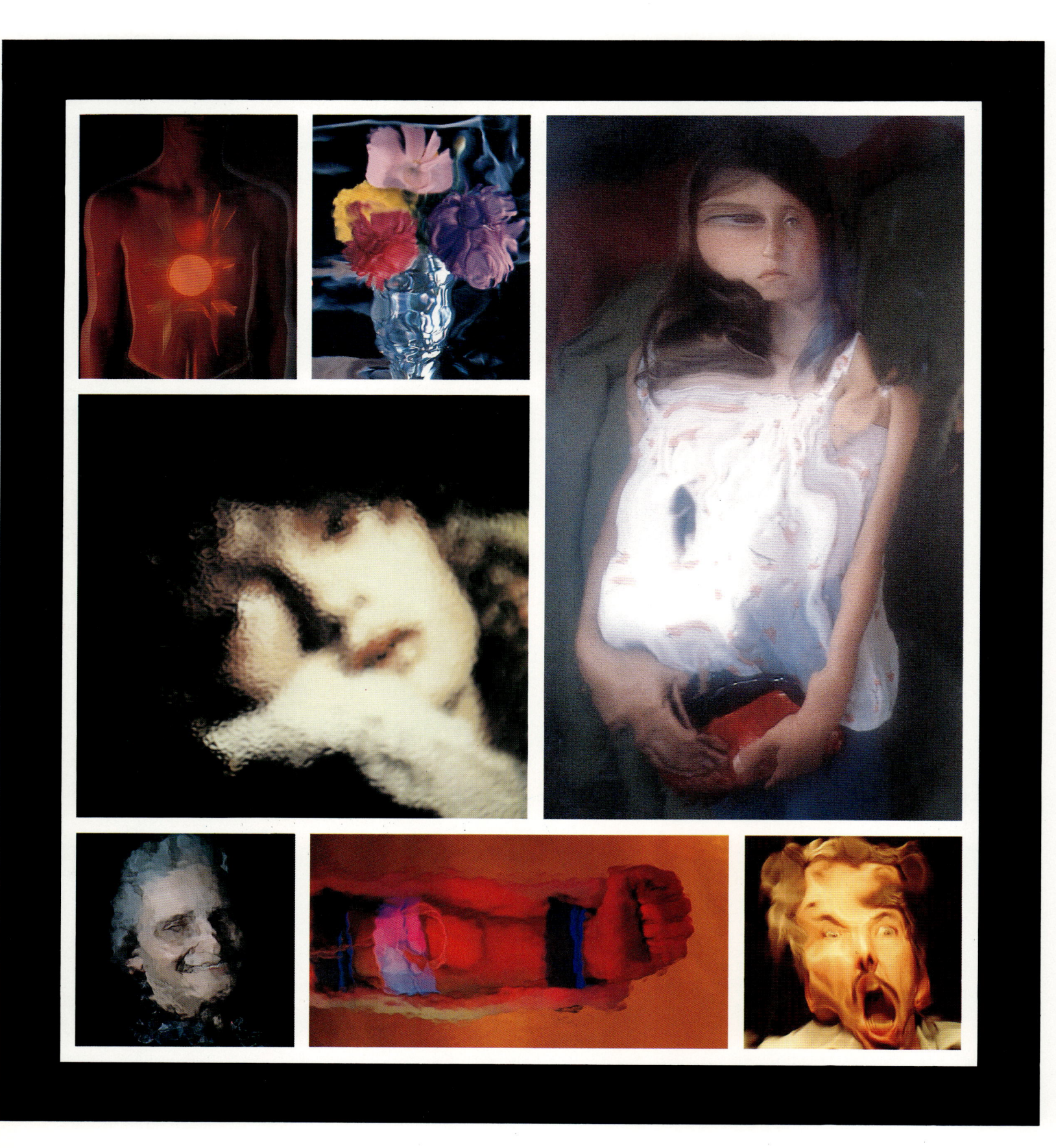

# MID-ATLANTIC

| | |
|---|---:|
| **Pohuski, Michael** Baltimore MD | 237 |
| **Noble Inc.** Baltimore, MD | 238,239 |
| **Benn, Nathan** Washington DC | 240 |
| **Morgan, Frank** Virginia Beach VA | 241 |
| **Noble Inc.** Baltimore MD | 238,239 |
| **Pease, Greg** Baltimore MD | 242,243 |
| **Pohuski, Michael** Baltimore MD | 237 |
| **Schoon, Tim** Lancaster PA | 244 |
| **Touchton, Ken** Washington DC | 245 |

**Maryland**
**Pennsylvania**
**Virginia**
**Washington, D.C.**
**West Virginia**

## HOW I SPENT YOUR SUMMER VACATION

**S**hooting on location at resort hotels is an art director's idea of a paid vacation. Until you actually have to live through one.

For openers, while everyone else has nothing more strenuous to do than raise a Pina Colada to their lips, I have to wear my sneakers thin chasing after overdue props, clearing guests out of the hotel pool, wrestling with 200-lb. planters, struggling through cascading waterfalls to strategically plant a bougainvillea, soothing a half dozen fragile egos and generally keeping spirits up.

The hours are not too terrific either.

First there are the disco shots. No respectable resort would dream of being caught in the pages of *Travel and Leisure* without one. But it means working from 11 p.m. until after midnight with models who are only getting paid a day rate. And then getting up at 4 a.m. the next morning for the inevitable sunrise shots on the beach or the golf course. What's more, on hotel shoots there are simply no weekends. And to make matters worse, you're always there in the off season.

Then there are the people problems.

There are models who don't follow your advice and eat ceviche in Mexico. Photographers who simply refuse to believe that tropical blue waters are still appealing to landlocked people in the northeast and midwest. Account executives who insist you can photograph both the pool and the ocean if you only use a wide-enough angle lens. And of course the locals who work in the hotels who think that a deadline is simply a phone that's out of order.

Weather, of course, can create problems too.

Once in Acapulco at the height of the rainy season (when else?), we could always tell when a storm was coming—not by watching the sky but by watching the Mexicans. The hotel lobby was totally open for five stories in the front facing the ocean. Which makes for a spectacular effect, but one that in the stormy season is a little impractical. When a storm was coming, the hotel employees would swarm into the lobby, rolling up the carpeting, moving the furniture, slipping in puddles, laying down runners and piling up sandbags on the ocean side, all to rousing Mariachi music from a 10-piece brass Mexican band. At that point we would pack up our equipment and head for Margaritaville. The Mexicans were never wrong in their predictions.

Hotel shoots are not without their pleasant moments, of course. Like the time the class of vacationing Georgia schoolboys fells in love with our model en masse, trailing her around like a flock of ducklings and calling her room just to hear the sound of her voice.

Of course, there was also the time, in a country which shall go unnamed, when one after another the models, photographer and crew all came down with raging fevers and intestinal upsets and had to be nursed through the entire shoot by the intrepid art director who persevered and brought the project in on schedule. And then came down with the sickness herself—on her weekend home, naturally.

All in all, I'd rather be in Philadelphia.

Or out West, on vacation, with just a tent and the stars over my head and not another living soul for miles around.

**Betty Reynolds**
**Art Director**
**Spiro & Associates**
**Philadelphia**

PŌ'HŨ'SKĪ

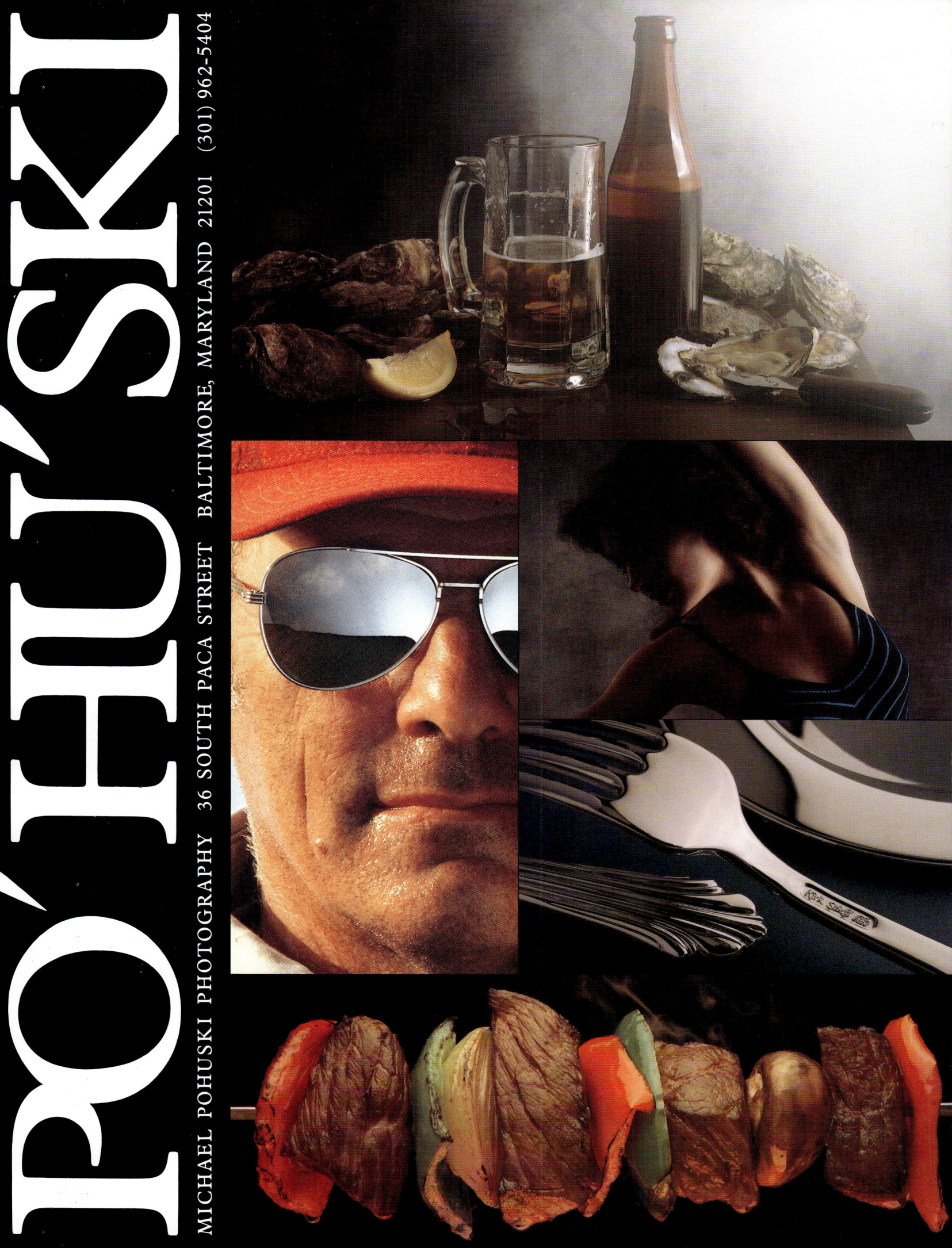

MICHAEL POHUSKI PHOTOGRAPHY  36 SOUTH PACA STREET  BALTIMORE, MARYLAND 21201  (301) 962-5404

# NOBLE THIRST.

Your photography can be common.
Or it can be Noble.

Jim Noble / Noble, Inc. / 611 Cathedral St. / Baltimore, Md 21201
Represented by Richard Geer
301-244-0292

# NOBLE SOUNDS.

Your photography can be common.
Or it can be Noble.

Jim Noble / Noble, Inc. / 611 Cathedral St. / Baltimore, Md. 21201
Represented by Richard Geer
301-244-0292

**NATHAN BENN**
c/o Woodfin Camp, Incorporated
925½ F Street, Northwest
Washington, D.C. 20004
(202) 638-5705

For stock photos contact:
Woodfin Camp, Incorporated
(202) 638-5705

For assignments contact:
Gail W. Troussoff
(202) 393-2658

Contract photographer for National Geographic Magazine. Available for editorial, corporate and architectural assignments.

240

**FRANK MORGAN**
Assignment and Existing Photography

Frank Morgan, Inc.
2414 Arctic Avenue #5
Virginia Beach, Virginia 23451
(804) 422-9328

For a free folio, phone or write.

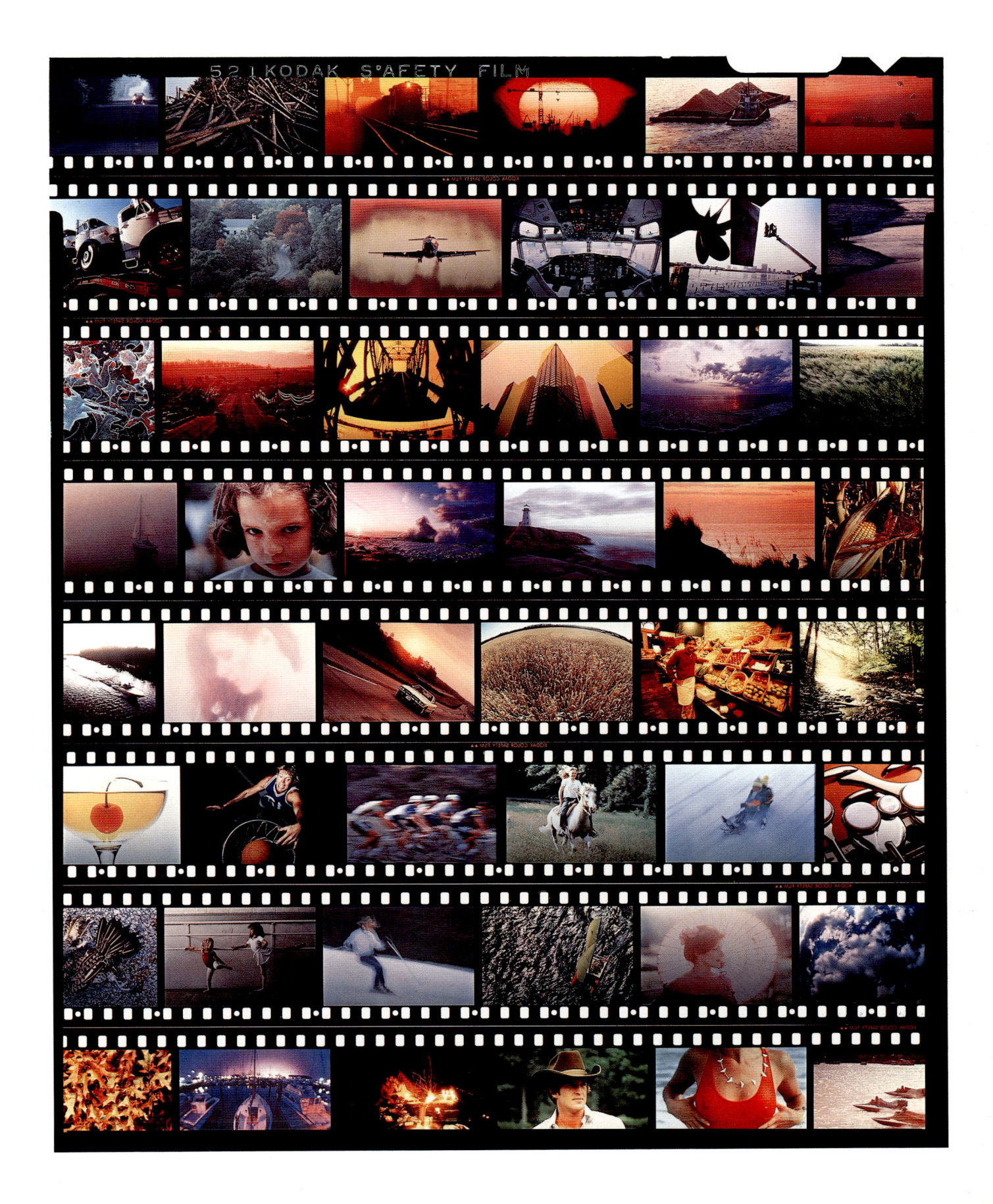

241

**GREG PEASE**
23 East 22nd Street
Baltimore, Maryland 21218
(301) 332-0583

Studio Manager/Kelly Baumgartner
(301) 332-0583

New York Representative/Franz Furst
(212) 753-3148

Also see:
CA Art Annual 1977, 78, 79, 80, 82 & 83
Creativity 1977, 79, 81, 82
American Showcase 4, 5 and 6
Corporate Showcase 1

Corporate/Industrial, advertising, editorial:
location and studio

Studios in Washington, D.C. and Baltimore

Stock photography available

Partial list of clients: American Airlines, Armco Steel, Arctec, Bio-Chem Tech., Black & Decker, Carborundum, Chevron, Citicorp, Commercial Credit, Consolidated Coal, Control Data, Cosmair, E. I. Du Pont de Nemours, Easco, General Electric, Gould, W. R. Grace Chemical, I.B.M., Lancôme, Mitsui, Monumental Life Insurance, Phillips Petroleum, Simpson Paper, Steiff Silver, Sun Life Insurance, Texas International Airlines, U.S.F.&G., Western Electric.

© Greg Pease 1983

**GREG PEASE**
23 East 22nd Street
Baltimore, Maryland 21218
(301) 332-0583

Studio Manager/Kelly Baumgartner
(301) 332-0583

New York Representative/Franz Furst
(212) 753-3148

Also see:
CA Art Annual 1977, 78, 79, 80, 82 & 83
Creativity 1977, 79, 81, 82
American Showcase 4, 5 and 6
Corporate Showcase 1

Corporate/Industrial, advertising, editorial:
location and studio

Studios in Washington, D.C. and Baltimore

Stock photography available

Partial list of clients: American Airlines, Armco Steel, Arctec, Bio-Chem Tech., Black & Decker, Carborundum, Chevron, Citicorp, Commercial Credit, Consolidated Coal, Control Data, Cosmair, E. I. Du Pont de Nemours, Easco, General Electric, Gould, W. R. Grace Chemical, I.B.M., Lancôme, Mitsui, Monumental Life Insurance, Phillips Petroleum, Simpson Paper, Steiff Silver, Sun Life Insurance, Texas International Airlines, U.S.F.&G., Western Electric.

© Greg Pease 1983

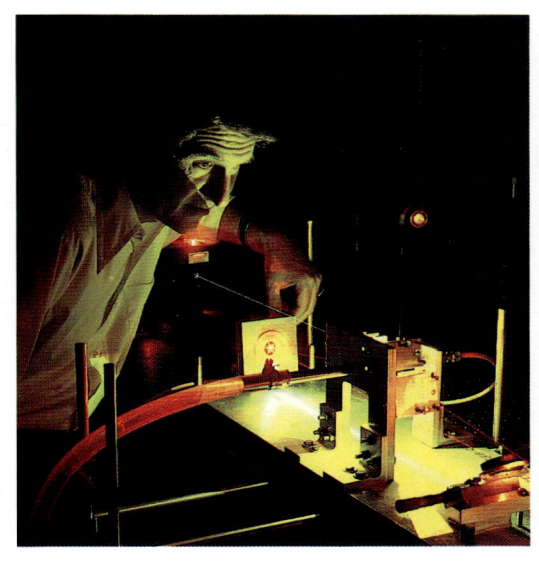

243

**TIM SCHOON**
P.O. Box 7446
Lancaster, Pennsylvania 17604
(717) 291-9483

Photography on location for advertising, corporate and industrial assignments.

Represented by Deborah Labonty
(717) 291-9483

© Tim Schoon, 1983

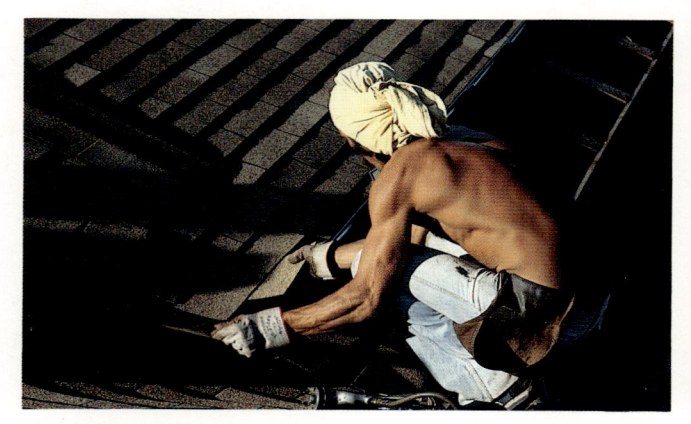

244

**KEN TOUCHTON**
Post Office Box 9435
Washington, D.C. 20016
(703) 534-4497

Specialties:
Location photography for annual reports, corporate/industrial, advertising and editorial. Stock photography available.

Member ASMP

See also American Showcase 6

© Ken Touchton 1984

245

OK. You're ready to select a photographer who can visually communicate your message. An annual report? Corporate capability brochure? Advertising campaign? Editorial coverage? Diversity, competence and creativity may be the key. On this one page, you can see medical technology, solar energy, telecommunications, a casual executive portrait and the beginning of a marathon. Yet, seeing these images may not be enough for you. If you need to see more, just call and you can receive overnight a carousel tray for a closer look.

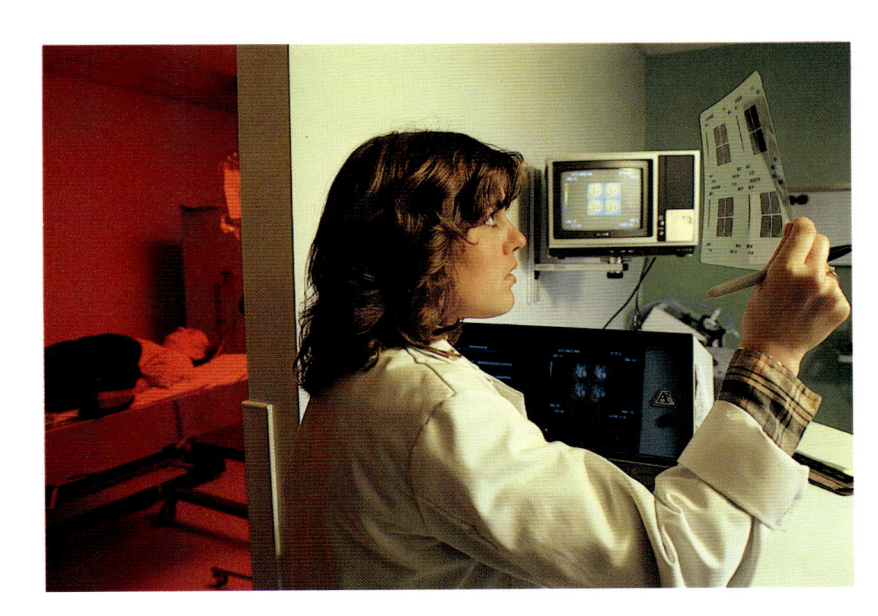

**FAIRY TALES CAN COME TRUE,
IT CAN HAPPEN TO YOU...
OR
IT'S STILL A THR!LL!**

I was a day and a half late on a 2-day project. I had just returned from a "half-day" photo shoot that had turned into an "all-day" ordeal. There were 5 messages on my desk—all from talent reps —marked "Please return call!" One of our efficient traffic coordinators was camped out at my door waiting for estimates on the Christmas project, and behind her was a keyliner who couldn't wrap an abundance of type around an illustration as I had hoped. I realized at that moment that once again I'd be working late. Late enough to miss my dance class (taken in hopes of relieving job-stress). Too late to meet anyone for dinner.

Is it worth it?

It's a dream come true!

Because during that whole process I managed to live an art school dream.

A dream that in art school was a flip remark—"I think I'll get one of those East Coast illustrators to pull this one out for me!" or how about, "Look, I can't join you for lunch, I've got to work on this presentation for the Olympics tie-in." and "Wait 'till the folks in Kalamazoo see this one on TV!" It was almost too much to hope for, that my future would bring projects involving my art school talent idols, men and women that I'd seen in CA, American Showcase, and other impressive art annuals. Men and women that I could learn a lot from.

Most of us can tell horror stories of low-wage first jobs, late-night hours, massive client re-do's. But what we forget in these moments of frustration (I'm going to quit this and sell hot-dogs from a riverboat on the Mississippi) is the fact that we have realized our earlier dreams. We have actually seen our imagined concepts come to life, seen them achieve a goal for our client's product and bring a smile to his face.

It's that appreciation of where we have come from and what we've been through, that gives us a thrill; that makes our hearts stop for a moment when we work a project to the best it can be.

It is the anticipation of that thrill that lets us listen to the writer's or illustrator's or photographer's vision and weave it with ours.

And that weaving gives us more than just an illustrator's or writer's or art director's sample—it gives us a solution that everyone involved can be proud of. One that, after seeing the final cut or press ok, we won't say, "Why didn't I think to try just one more thing?" A solution that used to be an art school dream!

Tomorrow, I'll still initiate each job with an art student's idealism and let my professional expertise overcome the hard realities, because for me—it's still a thrill!

**Vicki Joyce
Senior Art Director
Frankel and Company
Chicago**

# SOUTHEAST

| | |
|---|---|
| **Kohanim, Parish** Atlanta | 248,249 |
| **Chapple, Ron** Charlotte NC | 250 |
| **Kearney, Mitchell** Charlotte NC | 251 |
| **Smith, Richard W.** Greensboro NC | 252 |
| **Jamison, Chipp** Atlanta | 253 |
| **Katz, Arni** Atlanta | 254 |
| **Hood, Robin** Franklin TN | 255 |
| **Abel, Wilton** Charlotte NC | 256 |
| **Barley, Bill** Columbia SC | 257 |
| **Bilby, Glade II** New Orleans LA | 258 |
| **Carriker, Ronald C.** Winston-Salem NC | 259 |
| **Chapple, Ron** Charlotte NC | 250 |
| **De Vault, Jim** Nashville TN | 260,261 |
| **Gleasner, Bill** Denver NC | 262 |
| **Gupton, Lee** Cary NC | 263 |
| **Henderson, Chip** Raleigh NC | 264 |
| **Hood, Robin** Franklin TN | 255 |
| **Jamison, Chip** Atlanta | 253 |
| **Johns, Douglas** St. Petersburg FL | 265 |
| **Katz, Arni** Atlanta | 254 |
| **Kearney, Mitchell** Charlotte NC | 251 |
| **Kohanim, Parish** Atlanta | 248,249 |
| **Miller, Randy** Miami | 266,267 |
| **Murray, Steve** Raleigh, NC | 268 |
| **Petrey, John** Winter Park FL | 269 |
| **Sherman, Ron** Atlanta | 271 |
| **Smith, Richard W.** Greensboro NC | 252 |
| **Vance, David** Miami | 272,273 |

Alabama
Florida
Georgia
Kentucky
Louisiana
Mississippi
North Carolina
South Carolina
Tennessee

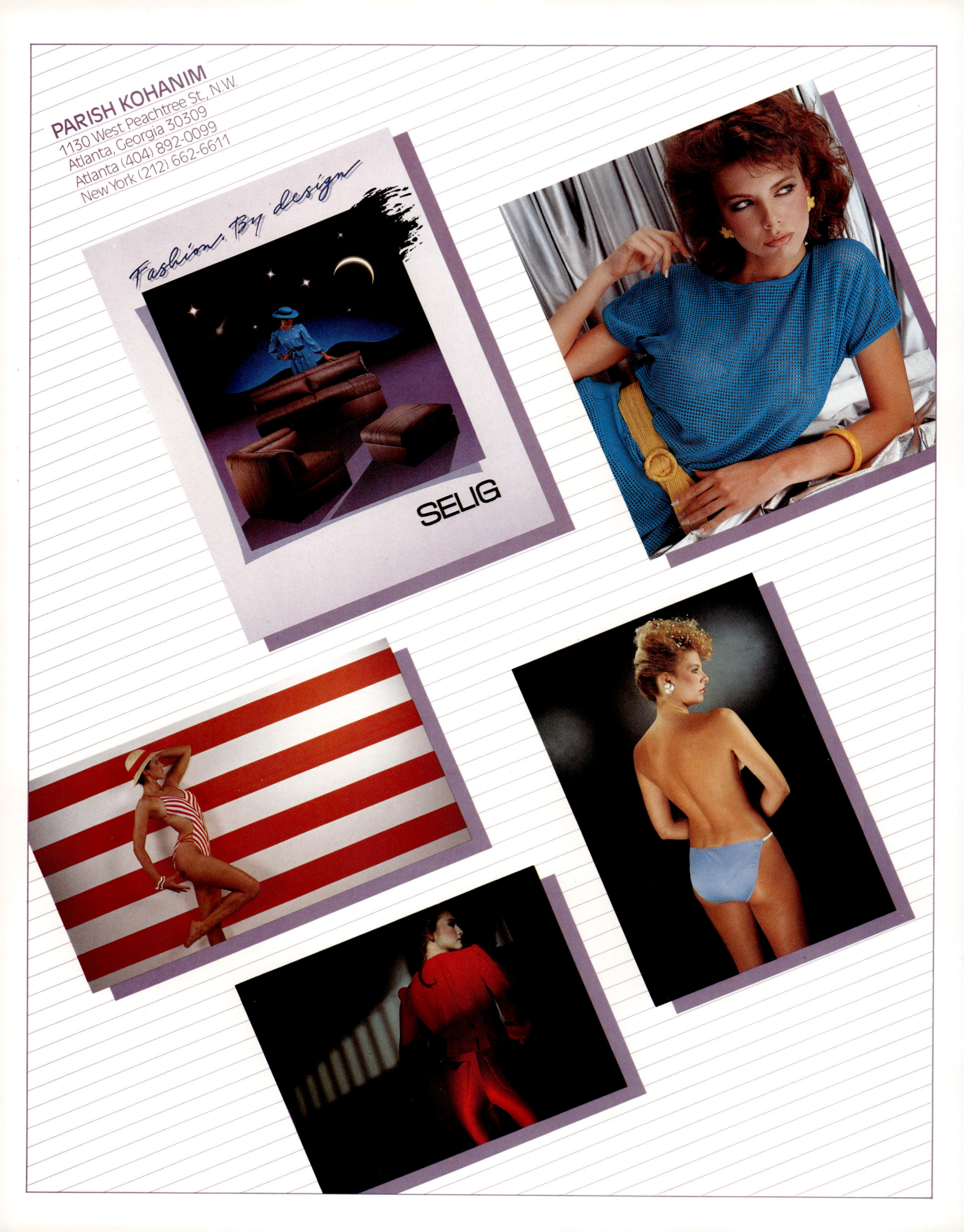

**PARISH KOHANIM**
1130 West Peachtree St., N.W.
Atlanta, Georgia 30309
Atlanta (404) 892-0099
New York (212) 662-6611

Fashion By design

SELIG

**PARISH KOHANIM**
1130 West Peachtree St., N.W.
Atlanta, Georgia 30309
Atlanta (404) 892-0099
New York (212) 662-6611

Fashion. By design

SELIG

# RON CHAPPLE

**RON CHAPPLE & ASSOCIATES, 437 SOUTH TRYON STREET, CHARLOTTE, NORTH CAROLINA 28202**

REPRESENTED BY DUNCAN FICK, (704) 377-4217.

# MITCHELL KEARNEY

**RON CHAPPLE & ASSOCIATES, 437 SOUTH TRYON STREET, CHARLOTTE, NORTH CAROLINA 28202**

REPRESENTED BY DUNCAN FICK, (704) 377-4217.

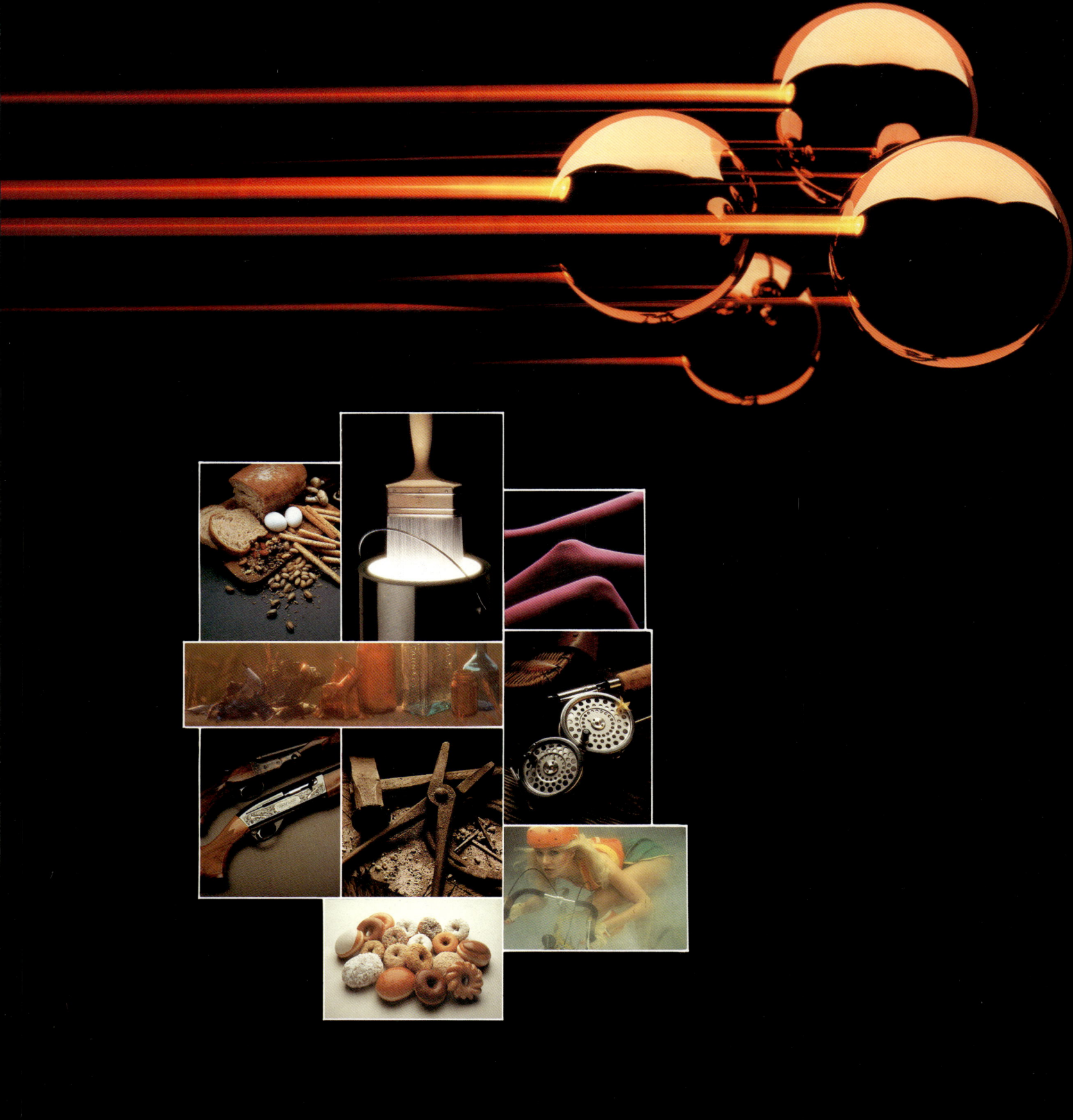

RICHARD W. SMITH • PHOTOGRAPHIC ILLUSTRATIONS • 1007 B NORWALK ST. GREENSBORO, NORTH CAROLINA 27407 • 919 292-1190 • ASMP

# CHIPP JAMISON

EARTHWORK STUDIO
ATLANTA

(404) 873-3636
2131 LIDDELL DRIVE, NE
ATLANTA, GEORGIA 30324

ASSIGNMENT PHOTOGRAPHY
STUDIO AND LOCATION:
ADVERTISING ILLUSTRATION
ANNUAL REPORTS
ARCHITECTURE
INDUSTRY/CORPORATE
NATURE/ENVIRONMENT
PEOPLE
TECHNOLOGY
TRAVEL

EXTENSIVE STOCK FILE
PORTFOLIO ON REQUEST

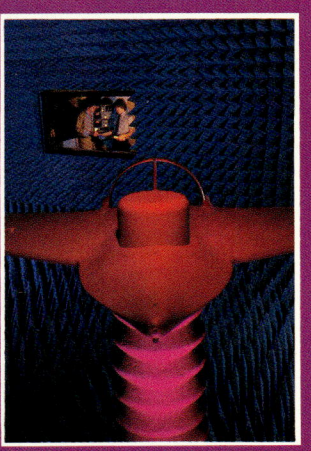

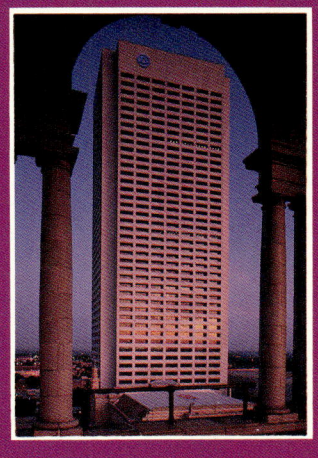

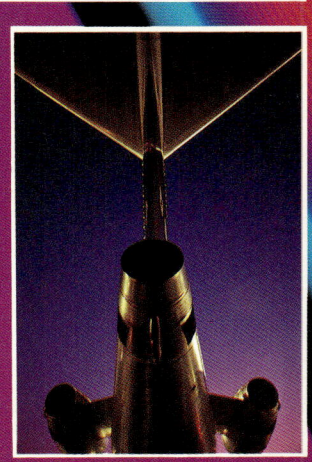

PARTIAL CLIENT LIST:

AMF
AT&T
AVON
COCA-COLA
CONTROL DATA CORPORATION
CSX CORPORATION
DELTA AIRLINES
DuPONT
EASTERN AIRLINES
ETHYL CORPORATION
FANNIE MAE
KNIGHT-RIDDER NEWSPAPERS
MAGNAVOX
MOBIL CHEMICAL
POLO
RAYTHEON COMPANY
SEARS
SHERATON HOTELS
SIEMENS-ALLIS
ST. REGIS PAPER
THE SOUTHERN COMPANY
WANG LABORATORIES
WRANGLER

MEMBER/ASMP
© CHIPP JAMISON 1984

BACKGROUND
PHOTOGRAPH:
WESTERN ELECTRIC
PREFORM LIGHT
GUIDE INSPECTION

# ARNI KATZ STUDIO

PRODUCTS, PLACES, FOOD AND SPECIAL EFFECTS. 35MM TO 8 X 10 STOCK AVAILABLE. P.O. BOX 724507, ATLANTA, GEORGIA 30339  404-953-1168

*Robin Hood*

PULITZER PRIZE WINNING PHOTOGRAPHER ROBIN HOOD PHOTOGRAPHS AMERICA

1101 W. Main St. Franklin, Tennessee 37064 (615) 794-9507
Represented By DYE, VAN MOL, LAWRENCE & ERICSON 1132 Eighth Ave. S. Nashville, Tennessee 37203 (615) 244-1818

**WILTON ABEL**
2609 Commonwealth Avenue
Charlotte, North Carolina 28205
(704) 372-6354

35mm, 120, 4x5, 8x10 formats
Specializing in photography for architectural, industrial, and corporate clients.

(Fluent in German as "second language".)

Member ASMP

Photos © Wilton Abel 1983

See current edition of CORPORATE SHOWCASE also.

**BILL BARLEY**
Bill Barley & Associates, Inc.
P.O. Box 2388
Columbia, South Carolina 29202
(803) 755-1554

Columbia is a nice place to be from. Which is what I usually am, because my work takes me all over the country.

More precisely, my Grumman Tiger takes me all over the country. I not only pilot it, I take pictures out of it. Getting back down to earth, I also take pictures on the ground. And over the past 18 years I've gotten pretty good at both.

So, if you need location photography in just about any location, Columbia is a good location to start from.

Corporate, industrial, advertising and aerial photography.

Stock photography:
Shostal Associates, Inc.,
New York City
(212) 686-8850

© Bill Barley, 1983

Member ASMP

**GLADE BILBY II**
1715 Burgundy
New Orleans, Louisiana 70116
(504) 949-6700

Representative: Martha Torres
(504) 895-6570

People, food & still life. Both in the studio & on location.

Recently completed a cookbook *The Restaurants of New Orleans,* with Roy F. Guste, Jr. of Antoine's.

Clients: Cox Cable; Frey Foods; Kenneth Gordon, Ltd.; Hilton Hotels; J.C. Nellissen, Inc.; Oscar de la Renta; Ramada Hotels; Resilio Sportswear; Sheraton International; TrustHouse Forte; Wembley Industries.

© 1984 Glade Bilby II

*THE RESTAURANTS OF NEW ORLEANS,* A COOKBOOK BY ROY F. GUSTE, JR.

**RONALD C. CARRIKER**
565 Alpine Road
Winston-Salem,
North Carolina 27104
(919) 765-3852

Location Specialist for Corporate, Industrial, and Agency Advertising and Editorial markets.

Duplicate transparencies and retouching by A Printers Film Service, Greensboro, North Carolina.

**JIM DeVAULT**
2400 Sunset Place
Nashville, Tennessee 37212
(615) 269-4538

I specialize in not specializing. Help me.
I enjoy meeting new people. Help me.
I'm a visual artist; I'm a marketing tool. Help me help you.

© Jim DeVault, 1983

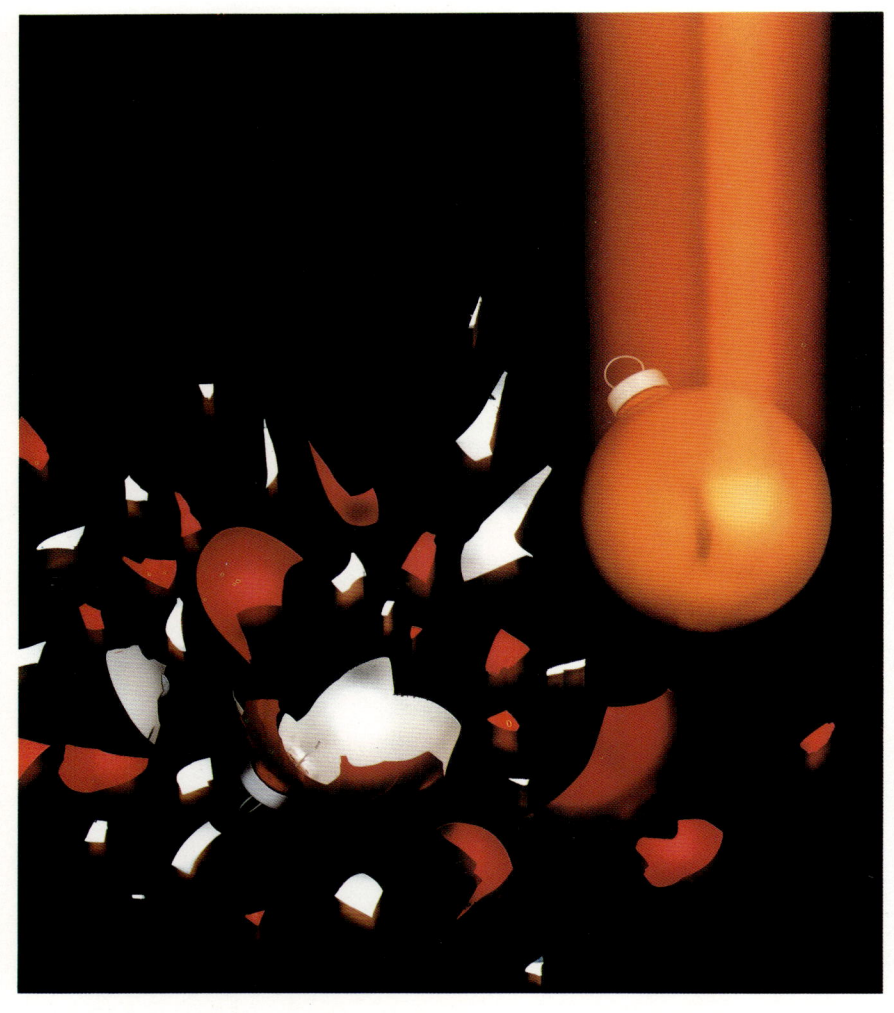

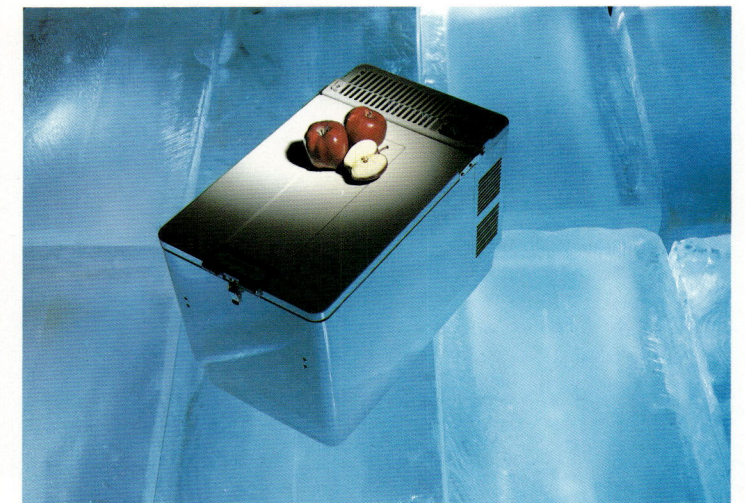

260

**JIM DeVAULT**
2400 Sunset Place
Nashville, Tennessee 37212
(615) 269-4538

Clients include: Genesco Inc., Washington Manufacturing, Standard Candy Co., Northern Telecom, Inc., Samsonite Corp., Southwestern, Hydra-Sports, Camping World, Aladdin Industries, Studer Revox America, Harrison Systems, The Benson Co., Excaliber Energy, Gibson Guitar, Southern Hospitality Corp., Campbell Hausfeld, Commerce Union Bank, Ingram Industries, Bostonian Shoes, B.F. Goodrich, Purity Dairies.

© Jim DeVault, 1983

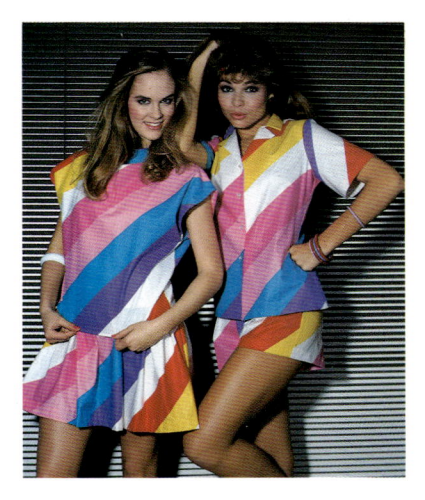

261

**BILL GLEASNER**
132 Holly Court
Denver, North Carolina 28037
(704) 483-9301

Location Specialist
Resorts/Travel
Advertising
Annual Reports

Member: Society of Travel Writers-SATW
American Society of Magazine Photographers

Stock: From around the world. 100,000
transparencies on file. Direct or through:

The Stock Market
New York, NY 10001
(212) 684-7878

Photo Bank
Charlotte, NC 28203
(704) 527-4303

Imperial Press
Tokyo, Japan
81-585-2562

**LEE GUPTON**
P.O. Box 1112
Cary, North Carolina 27511
(919) 469-3025

Advertising Editorial Illustration Annual Reports
Specialist in Location Photography

263

**CHIP HENDERSON PHOTOGRAPHY**
5700 New Chapel Hill Road
Raleigh, North Carolina 27606
(919) 851-0458

Stock Representation through Woodfin Camp & Associates
(212) 750-1020 New York - (202) 638-5705 Washington

Clients include: IBM; Mead CompuChem; Ajinomoto, USA; Union Carbide; Philip Morris, USA; Mallinckrodt; Southern Bell; Wachovia Bank & Trust Company, NA; U.S. Air; North Carolina Division of Travel and Tourism; Bald Head Island Corporation; *The New York Times Magazine* and Time-Life Books.

Advertising
Business Publications/Annual Reports
Corporate/Industrial
Travel/Personalities

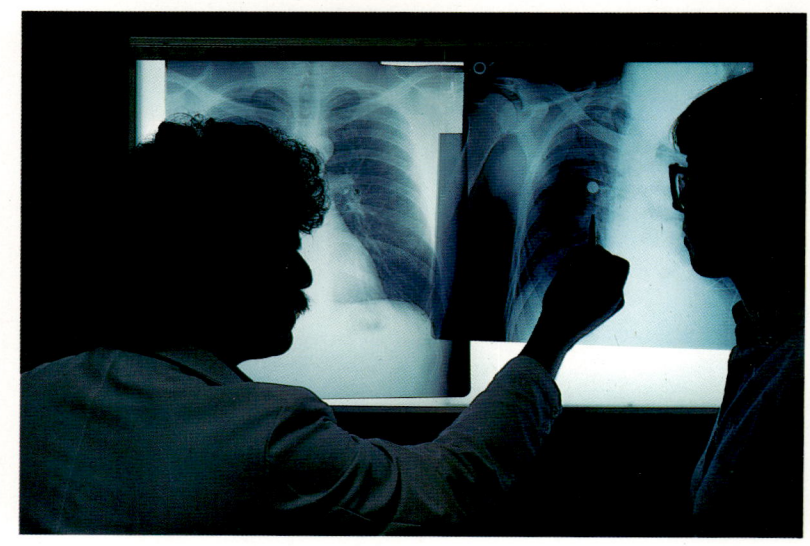

264

**DOUGLAS JOHNS STUDIO**
2535-25th Avenue North
St. Petersburg, Florida 33713
(813) 321-7235

Photographic Design

Member ASMP
© Douglas Johns 1983

*JOHNS*

**RANDY MILLER**
6666 Southwest 96th Street
Miami, Florida 33156
(305) 667-5765

People, smiles, sunny skies, Come to Miami this year and share its delights.
My staff and I will make your next assignment the best ever.

General Accounts:
Smirnoff Vodka, American Express, Bank of America, Kodak, Coke.

Cruise Lines:
Royal Caribbean, Sitmar, Homelines, Norwegian Caribbean.

Hotel and Travel:
Westin Hotels, Omni Hotels, Marriott, Arvida, Eastern Airlines, State of Florida.

266

**RANDY MILLER**
6666 Southwest 96th Street
Miami, Florida 33156
(305) 667-5765

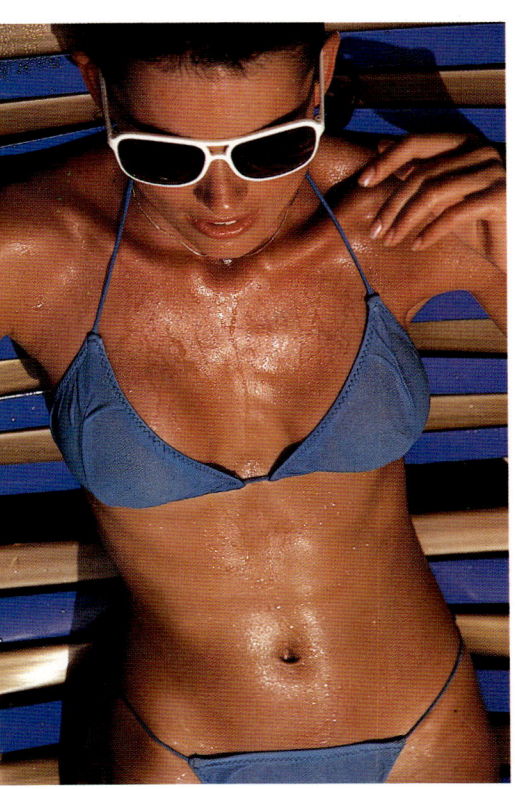

**STEVE MURRAY**
Murray & Associates
1330 Mordecai Drive
Raleigh, North Carolina 27604
(919) 828-0653

Stock
Travel
Corporate
Industrial
Advertising
Annual Report

Represented by:

South: Carol Fantelli
(919) 828-0653

Photos © Steve Murray 1983

Clients:
Aerotron
Almay Cosmetics
Baker-Perkins
Barnett Bank
Borden Brick
Brown & Williamson
Ciba-Giegy
Cooper Group
Diamond Shamrock
*Forbes*
General Electric
GTE
General Mills
Hardee's
IBM
Indigo Resorts
J.P. Stevens
Mallinckrodt
Morrison-Knudsen
McDonald's
Mid-State Tile
N.C. Ports
*New York Times*
NCNB
*Newsweek*
Northern Telecom
Peden Steel
Pfizer
Piedmont Airlines
R.J. Reynolds
Standard Oil of Ohio
State of North Carolina
Tesdata Systems
*Time*
Troxler Electronics
Union Carbide
W. R. Grace

ASMP

**JOHN PETREY—PHOTOGRAPHIC ILLUSTRATOR**
670 Clay Street/P.O. Box 2401
Winter Park, (Orlando) Florida 32790
(305) 645-1718

From the real to the not so real, I create special images of products, people, food, and still lifes for advertising/editorial, catalog and corporate/industrial accounts… in the studio, on location throughout the sunshine state, and on special assignment around the country.

Portfolio on request.

©1983 John Petrey

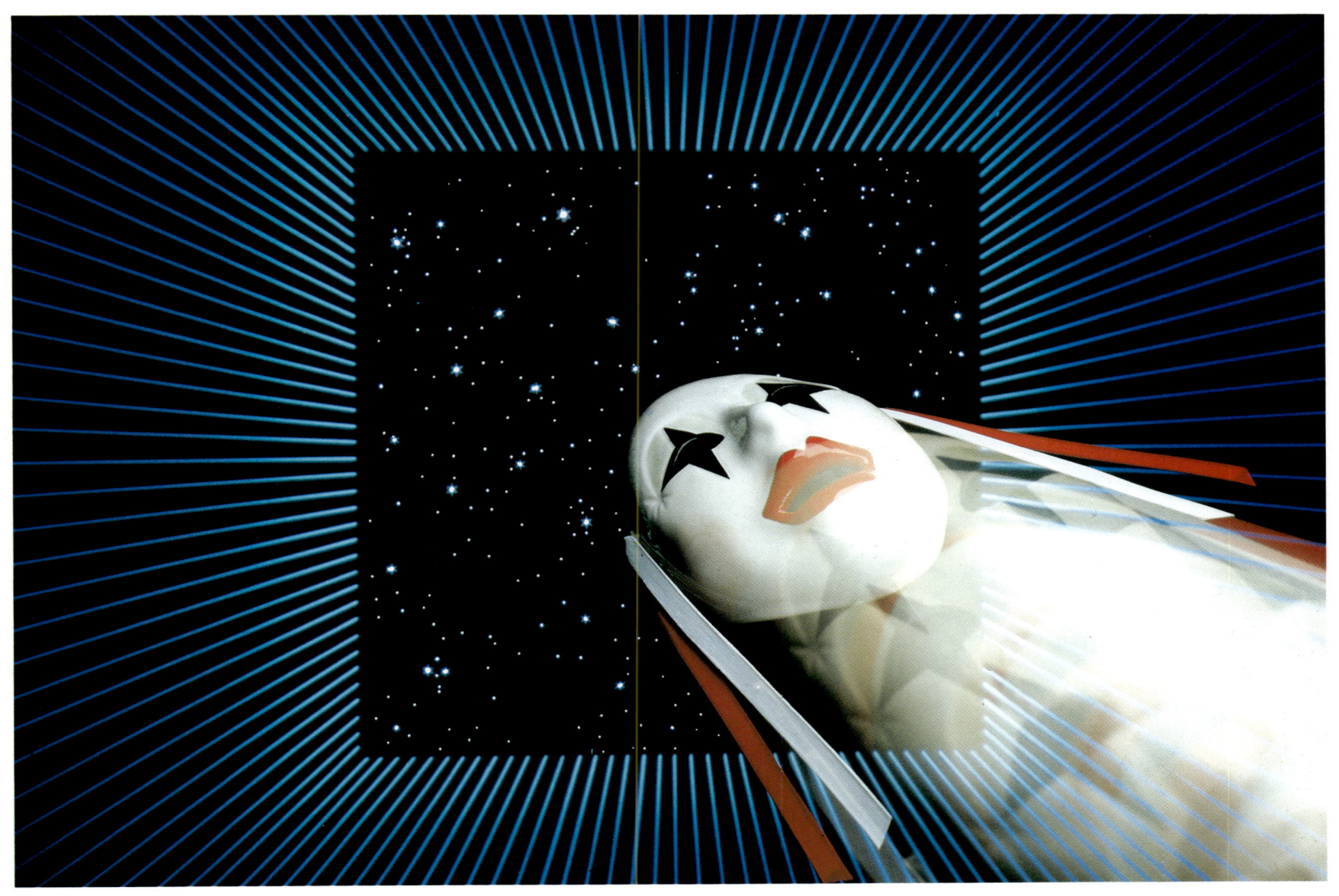

269

## SIMPLIFIED ART BUYING

For some reason, what seems to be a vexing problem elsewhere, is a rewarding experience in Chicago. The process of buying advertising art is so much fun that everyone wants to do it, or at least be a part of it. Recently, sounds of discontent have intruded on the harmony we're used to, so we thought we would mention a few of the reasons it works so well here.

The major reason is that everyone in the business cooperates with us. These professionals know not only their own specialties, but the proper relations with the other specialties which, when assembled, make up advertising.

The knowledgeable people involved in this process include clients, executives, creative people, legal and accounting personnel, suppliers, production and media experts, and staff members, including even the newest members of the agency. Each contributes something which the others don't, and together they make work flow!

But this doesn't just "happen" any more than any other good thing just "happens." It's the result of sincere effort on the part of all. We've found that hard work with good people is a welcome opportunity for personal satisfaction. A "problem" is merely an incompletely prepared work opportunity. When the missing preparation is added, the work becomes fun and the reward is a fuller appreciation of the specialty and the people involved.

True, we all start with a "primer" so we know what everyone else is saying and what the terms mean.

True, we train in the very studios, labs, type and engraving shops with which we later deal. It's easy when you learn from the best!

True, yesterday's best standards become a basis for better work tomorrow. We know that if we aren't reaching we are limiting ourselves. "Same as last time," isn't good enough here.

True, we deal completely in the open with everyone, but the first president of this agency gave us the "Golden Rule" as the best way to serve our clients and ourselves, and to work with all suppliers. In 48 years, the details may have been modified, but not the principles. They work just as well for us today:

*"When you reach for a star, you may not always get one, but you won't come up with a handful of mud, either."*
—Leo Burnett

True, local photographers and artists' agents are associating to foster better business methods and higher standards for their own specialties. We're delighted, because we've led the way in bringing these talents forward in our clients' advertising.

Today, the art buyers are working with computers for billing, accounting, forecasting, and also for technological advances available in engraving, retouching, digital graphic enhancement and other esoteric applications that were only promises yesterday.

The blending of advanced techniques with classic crafts makes the effort all the more rewarding and facilitates even broader communication. Today, with affiliates in all parts of the world to serve our clients' ever growing needs, art buyers here find that what they worked on for Belgium one week helps work in Bangkok the next.

If any reader feels we might be of help, drop us a note. When we have the time (we are busy), we'll be glad to exchange ideas.

**John Long,
Supervisor of Art Buying
and The Art Buying Staff of
Leo Burnett Co.
Chicago**

**RON SHERMAN**
P.O. Box 28656
Atlanta, Georgia 30328
(404) 993-7197

Location photography for annual reports, advertising, corporate, industrial, editorial, travel and sports assignments.

Stock photography available.

Also see ads in American Showcase Volume 5 and Volume 6 and ASMP BOOK 1981 and 1983.

Member ASMP

© 1983 Ron Sherman

Design: Critt Graham & Associates

271

**DAVID VANCE**
13760 Northwest 19th Avenue, #14
Miami, Florida 33054
(305) 685-2433

272

**DAVID VANCE**
13760 Northwest 19th Avenue, #14
Miami, Florida 33054
(305) 685-2433

273

## THE GREATEST THINGS

I've compiled this list from the writings of a very wise man, Earl Nightingale. His thoughts were quite good, so I'd like to pass them along to you.

Here are The Greatest Things: The best day, today. The best play, work. The greatest puzzle, life. The greatest thought, God. The greatest mystery, death. The best work, work you like. The greatest mistake, giving up. The most ridiculous asset, pride. The greatest need, common sense. The most dangerous person, a liar. The best town, where you succeed. The most expensive indulgence, hate. The greatest invention of the devil, war. The most disagreeable person, the complainer. The greatest secret of production, saving waste. The best teacher, one who makes you want to learn. The biggest fool, the man who lies to himself. The worst bankruptcy, the soul who has lost enthusiasm. The cheapest, easiest, and most stupid thing to do, finding fault. The cleverest man, the one who always does what he thinks is right. The greatest bore, one who keeps talking after he has made his point. The greatest comfort, the knowledge that you have done your work well. The most agreeable companion, the one that would not have you any different than you are. The meanest feeling of which any human being is capable, feeling envious of another's success. The greatest sin, fear. The most satisfying experience, doing your duty first. The best action, keeping the mind clear and the judgement good. The greatest blessing, good health. The greatest law of nature, cause and effect. The greatest gamble, substituting hope for facts. The most certain thing in life, change. The greatest joy, being needed. The greatest opportunity, the next one. The greatest victory, victory over yourself. The greatest handicap, egotism. The greatest loss, loss of self-confidence. The greatest waste...all the talent and ability that most of us have but never quite get around to using. The greatest thing, bar none, in the world—love, love for family, home, friends, neighbors...and for the land in which we enjoy our freedom.

Well...there you have it...The Greatest Things defined. Cut this out and save it. It's something we'd all do well to read once in a while. It helps us remember just what's important and what isn't. From time to time, we all need to remind ourselves of what we're after and what we hope to contribute.

**Robert Qually**
**President/Creative Director**
**Qually & Company, Inc.**
**Chicago/Evanston, Illinois**

# CHICAGO

| | |
|---|---|
| **Deahl, David** | 276,277 |
| **Elliott, Peter** | 278,279 |
| **Manarchy, Dennis** | 280,281 |
| **Scott, Denis** | 282 |
| **Keeling, Robert** | 283 |
| **DeBold, Bill** | 284 |
| **Harris, Bart** | 285 |
| **Tucker, Bill** | 286 |
| **Welzenbach, John** | 287 |
| **Rubin, Laurie** | 288 |
| **Click! Chicago** | 289-291 |
| **Cowan, Ralph** | 292 |
| **Deahl, David** | 276,277 |
| **DeBold, Bill** | 284 |
| **Elliott, Peter** | 278,279 |
| **Harris, Bart** | 285 |
| **Hetisimer, Larry** | 293 |
| **Kazu** | 294,295 |
| **Keeling, Robert** | 283 |
| **Manarchy, Dennis** | 280,281 |
| **Rubin, Laurie** | 288 |
| **Scott, Denis** | 282 |
| **Tucker, Bill** | 286 |
| **Warkenthien, Dan** | 296 |
| **Welzenbach, John** | 287 |
| **Zann, Arnold** | 297 |

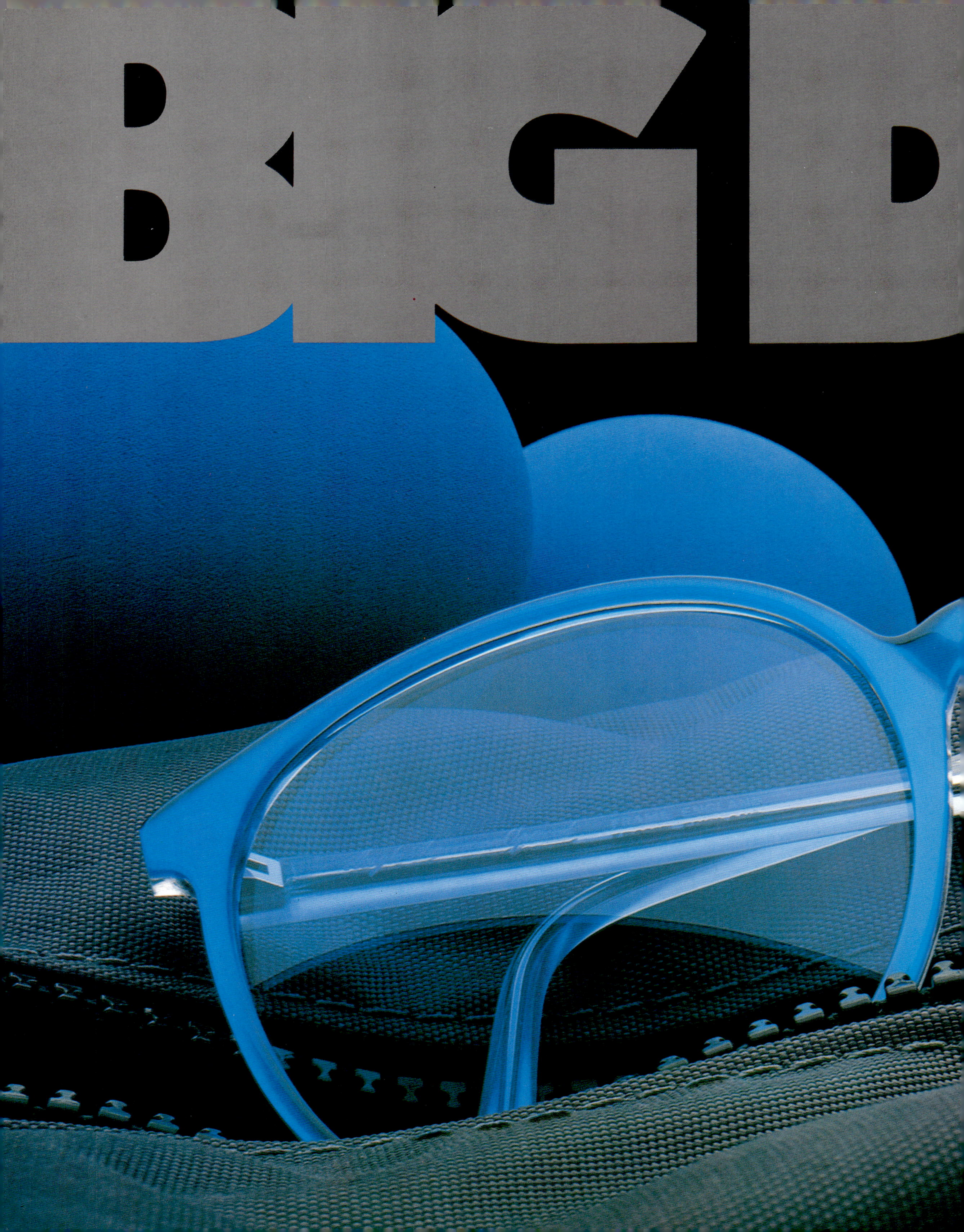

David Deahl Photography, Inc. 312-644-3187

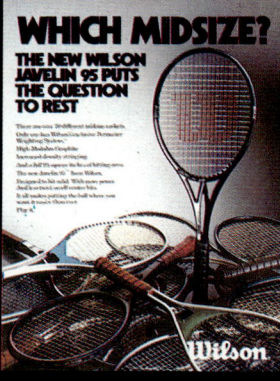

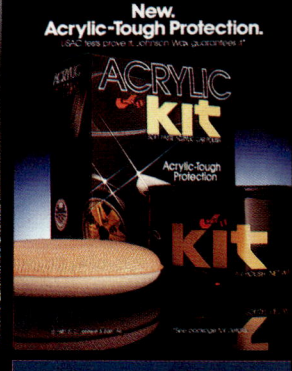

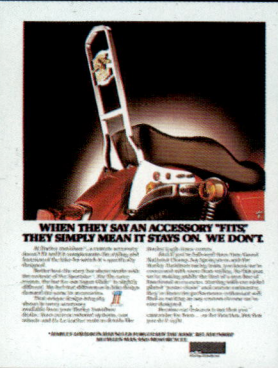

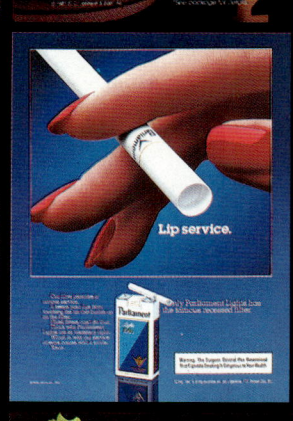

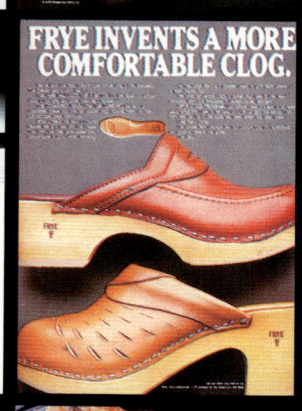

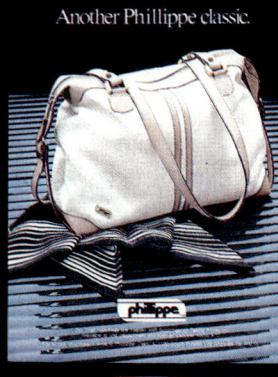

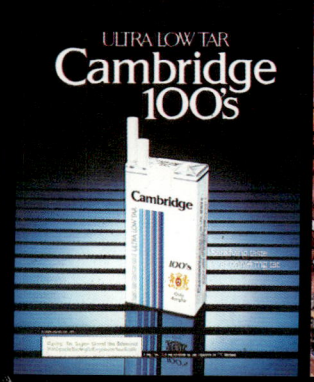

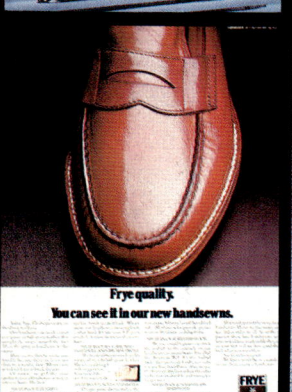

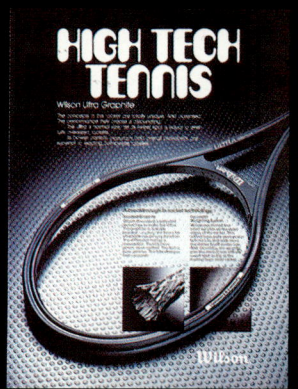

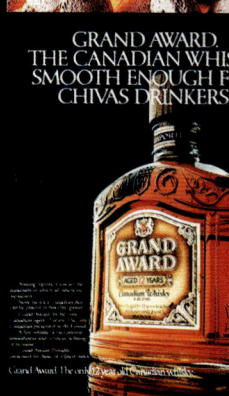

Represented by Joel Harlib  312.329.1370  405 N. Wabash Ave., Chicago 60611

PETER ELLIOTT

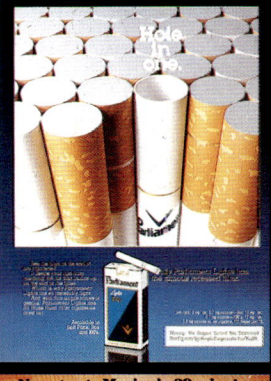

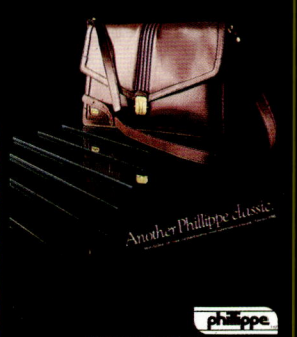

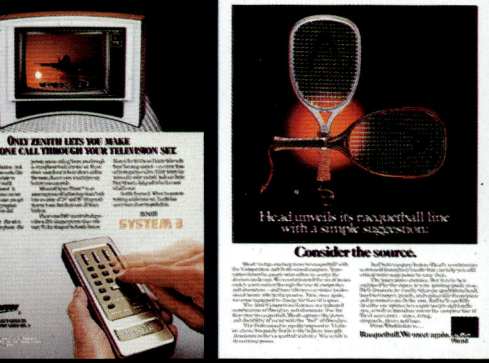

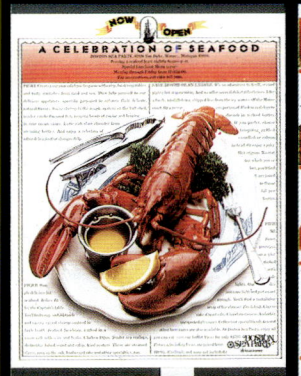

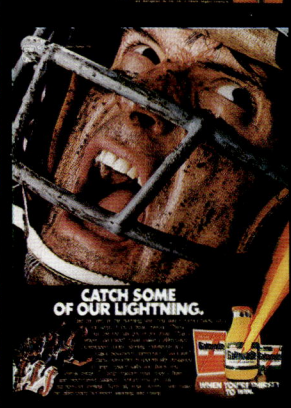

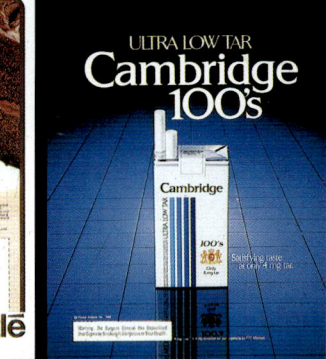

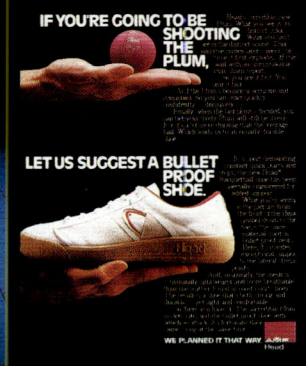

Represented by Joel Harlib 312.329.1370 405 N. Wabash Ave., Chicago 60611

PETER ELLIOTT

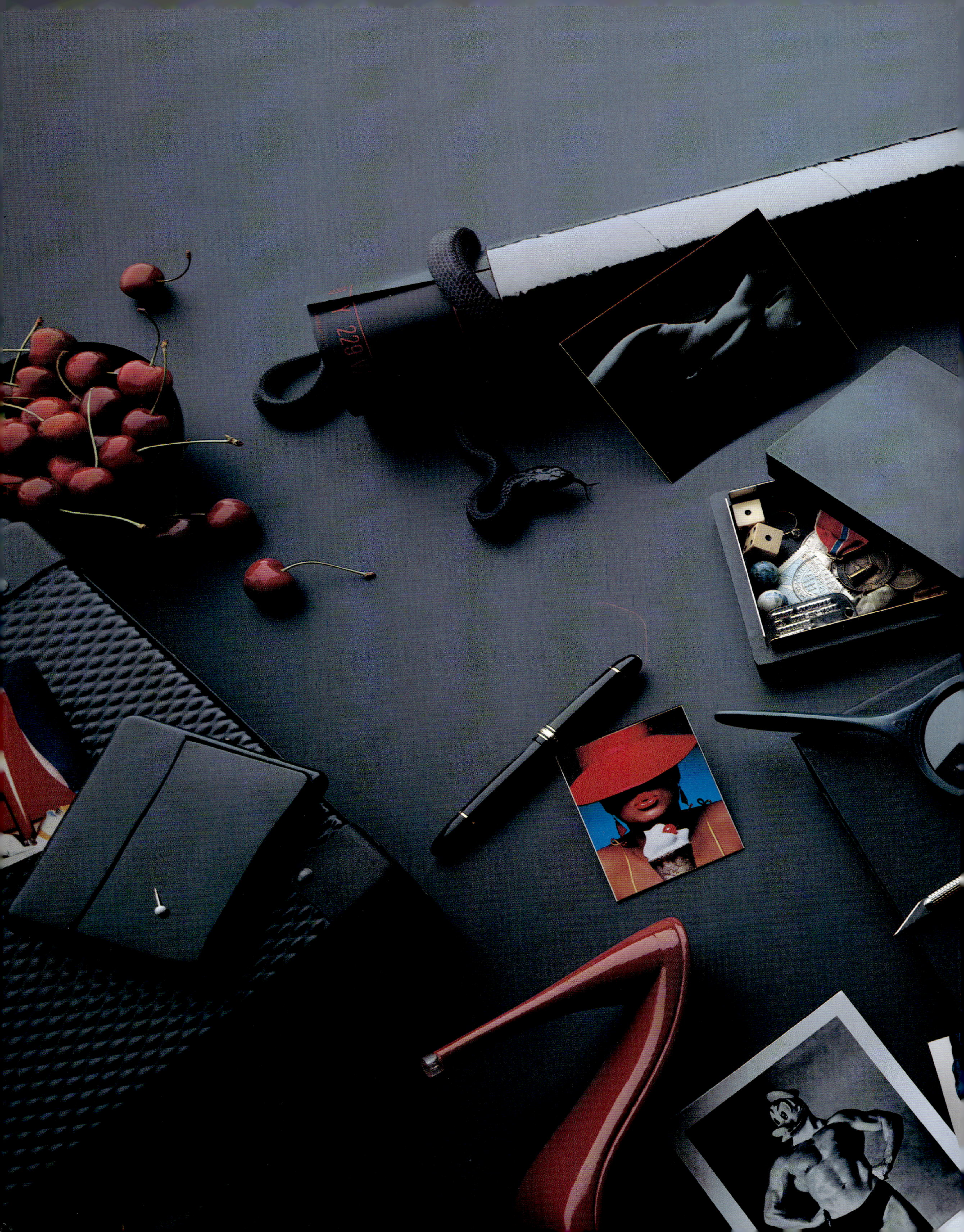

229 West Illinois
Chicago, IL 60610

Represented by   Mary Atois
                 312-828-9117

MANARCHY

Denis Scott
216 West Ohio
Chicago, Illinois 60610
312/467-5663

Represented by
Jim Hanson
312-664-9166

# scott

# KEELING

REPRESENTED BY CONNIE KORALIK   CHICAGO   312 944 5680

COCA-COLA   CONTAINER CORPORATION OF AMERICA   GENERAL MILLS   HART SCHAFFNER MARX   KIMBERLY CLARK   McDONALDS   NESTLES   PROCTER & GAMBLE   QUAKER OATS   R J REYNOLDS   S C JOHNSON   SEARS   TIME-LIFE

Studio 312 | 337-1177

DEBOLD

**BART HARRIS PHOTOGRAPHY, INC.**

**PRINT AND FILM.**

70 W. Hubbard St.
Chicago, Illinois 60610
(312) 751-2977

Call for sample case and reel.

1. S. Cleary/Maxim Coffee
2. R. Volk/Oak Rubber
3. T. Tarrant/Phillip Morris
4. H. Greene/Gatorade
5. D. Tyree/IBC Root Beer
6. H. Cassavant/Nestle Chocolate
7. M. Caulfield & A. Zeleski/Hallmark Greeting Cards
8. G. Reiter/Armour Star Chili
9. H. Smedley/Kelloggs Corn Flakes

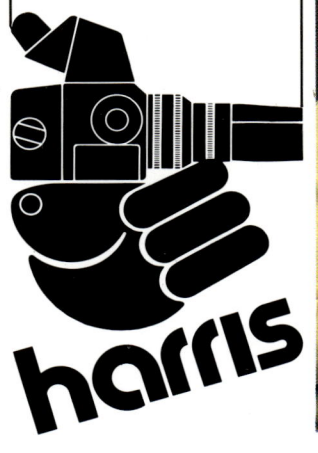

harris

# Bill Tucker Studio, Inc.

114 West Illinois
Chicago, Illinois 60610
312-321-1570
Represented By
Jeanette Mohlman

© 1983 Bill Tucker

# Welzenbach

Welzenbach Photography represented by Joni Tuke Inc.
368 W. Huron · Chicago, Illinois 60610 · 312·787·6826

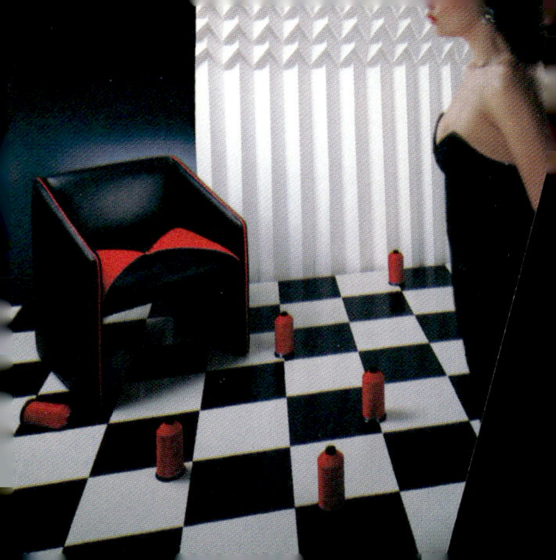

**CLICK! CHICAGO**
213 West Institute Place, Suite 503
Chicago, Illinois 60610
(312) 787-7880

We are the most creative and knowledgeable stock/assignment agency in Chicago.

Our stock files run from Aardvark to Zygophyte, with a host of images in between. If we don't have it we will find or shoot it. We have 40 assignment photographers with a wide range of skills in the USA and in Europe, with the largest number spread throughout the Midwest.

ROBERT FRERCK, ASMP

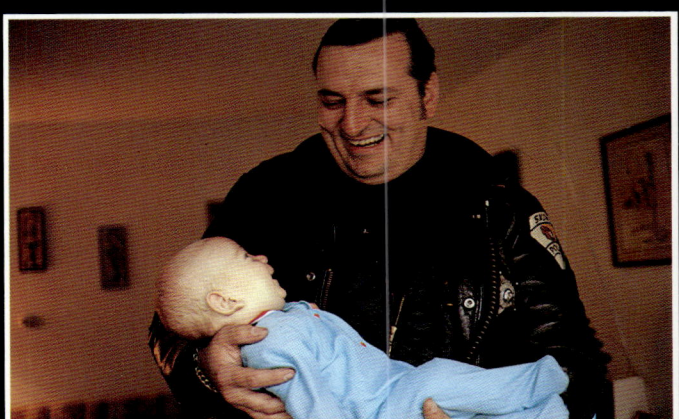

BRIAN SEED, ASMP

DENNIS E. COX, ASMP

STEVE WALL, ASMP

JOHN GARVEY

MICHAEL MAUNEY, ASMP

JAMES P. ROWAN

MARC PoKEMPNER, ASMP

PHILLIP MacMILLAN JAMES, ASMP

FRED LEAVITT, ASMP

DAVID R. PHILLIPS

JOHN SIMS

DON SMETZER, ASMP

**CLICK! CHICAGO**
213 West Institute Place, Suite 503
Chicago, Illinois 60610
(312) 787-7880

Photograph by David R. Phillips, a specialist in the use of panoramic cameras. The image below was made with a camera he developed which has a 25 inch by 70mm format and a 120 degree angle of view. A triple aspheric telephoto lens provides the outstanding sharpness and detail of this "slice of life." For another example of his work see the 180 degree panorama on the previous page.

291

**RALPH COWAN**
452 North Halsted Street
Chicago, Illinois 60622
(312) 243-6696

Ask for Pat Lasko.

Clients include: Abbott Laboratories, Archer Daniels Midland, Boston Consulting Group, Brown & Williamson, Continental Fibre Drum, Eastman Kodak, Kemper Group, Mallinckrodt Chemicals, Meadow Gold, Mister Turkey, Northern Petrochemicals, Pizza Hut, Paine Webber, Pollenex, Ralston Purina, Ryerson Steel, Scott Foresman Books, Sears, Southern Comfort, Southland, Standard Oil, Tampa Maid Seafood, U.S. Navy Recruiting, Wang Laboratories.

The Ad Makers: the account executive.

**LARRY HETISIMER**
1630 5th Avenue
Moline, Illinois 61265
(309) 797-1010

Member ASMP
All Photographs
© Larry Hetisimer 1983

With vision, swiftness, craft, responsibility, enjoyment and care, I will create photography for you.

©Larry Hetisimer 1983

# L.HETISIMER

**KAZU STUDIO**
1211 West Webster
Chicago, Illinois 60614
(312) 348-5393

Represented by:
Connie Koralik
(312) 944-5680

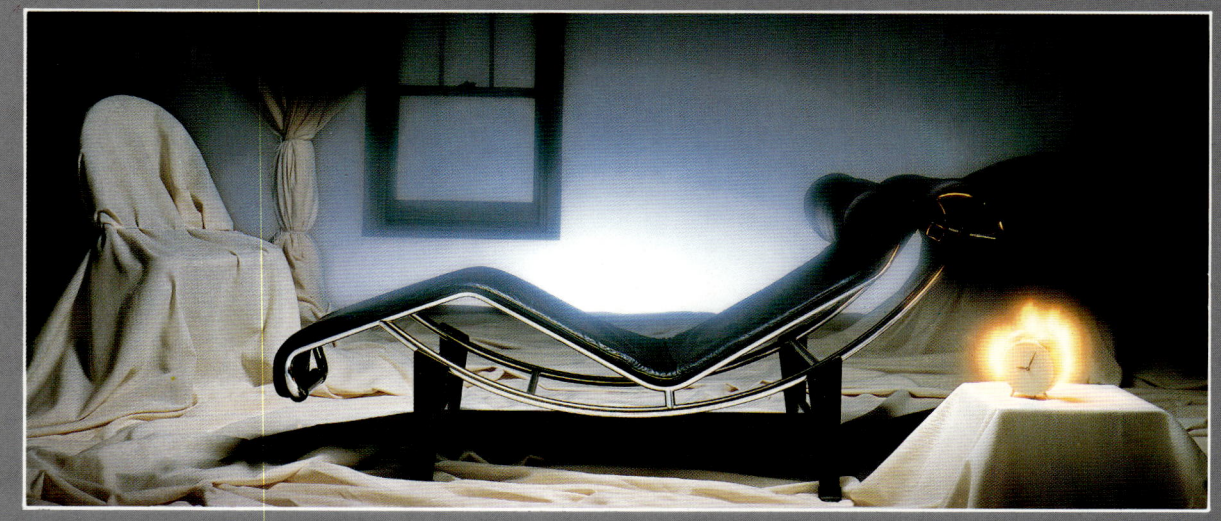

**KAZU**

SERIES/A.D. JIM MOHISER/MARION LABS

A.D. RALPH WOODS/ILLINOIS BELL

A.D. GERRITT BEVERWYK/PANSOPHIC, INC.

A.D. BILL BOHNHOFF/SHAW WALKER

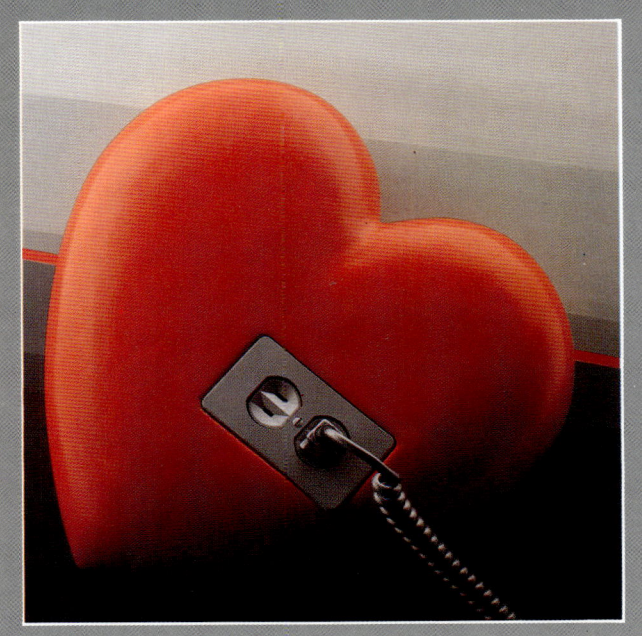

A.D. JERRI JOHNSON/BESNIER AMERICA, INC.

**DAN WARKENTHIEN**
900 North Franklin Suite 3N
Chicago, Illinois 60610
(312) 951-5225

Dan has been a photographer in Chicago for the past 18 years. His new studio located just north of the loop has 4000 square feet of shooting space and a full kitchen. Some of his clients are as follows:

Client List:

Centel
GTE
Wilson Sporting Goods
Gibson Guitars
Slingerland Drums
CIBA-Geigy
Abbott Labs
Burger King
Pieroth Wines
Vaughan's Seed Co
Nor-Am Agricultural Products
Sears
Carte Blanche
Jockey
Kenner
Bell & Howell
Brunswick
ACCO International
Sherwin Williams
International Harvester
White Farm Equipment
Fiat Allis
Elgin Street Sweepers

# WARKENTHIEN
## PHOTOGRAPHY

VAUGHAN'S SEED CO/RHEA & KAISER ADV

GIBSON/MARTIN—DAYLOR ADV

NOR-AM AGRICULTURAL PRODUCTS/RHEA & KAISER ADV

**ARNOLD ZANN**
502 North Grove
Oak Park, Illinois 60302

Chicago Representative:
Sheila Zann (312) 386-2864

New York Representatives:
Black Star (212) 679-3288
Ben Chapnick
Sal Catalano

Location photography for advertising and annual reports.

Additional work can be seen in Showcase V, VI and Corporate Showcase I, II.

© 1983 Arnold Zann

297

# GRAPHIC ARTS ORGANIZATIONS

### Arizona:

**Phoenix Society of Visual Arts**
P.O. Box 469
Phoenix, AZ 85001

### California:

**Advertising Club of Los Angeles**
514 Shatto Pl., Rm. 328
Los Angeles, CA 90020
(213) 382-1228

**Art Directors and Artists Club**
2791 24th St.
Sacramento, CA 95818
(916) 731-8802

**Book Club of California**
312 Sutter St., Ste. 510
San Francisco, CA 94108
(415) 781-7532

**Graphic Artists Guild of Los Angeles**
1258 N. Highland, Ste. 102
Los Angeles, CA 90038
(213) 469-9409

**Institute of Business Designers**
c/o Gensler & Associates
550 Kearney St.
San Francisco, CA 94108
(415) 433-3700

**Los Angeles Advertising Women**
2410 Beverly Blvd.
Los Angeles, CA 90057
(213) 387-7432

**San Francisco Society of Communicating Arts**
445 Bryant St.
San Francisco, CA 94107
(415) 777-5287

**Society of Illustrators of Los Angeles**
1258 N. Highland Ave.
Los Angeles, CA 90038
(213) 469-8465

**Society of Motion Picture & TV Art Directors**
7715 Sunset Blvd., Ste. 224
Hollywood, CA 90046
(213) 876-4330

**Western Art Directors Club**
P.O. Box 996
Palo Alto, CA 94302
(415) 321-4196

**Women in Design**
P.O. Box 2607
San Francisco, CA 94126
(415) 397-1748

**Women's Graphic Center**
The Woman's Building
1727 N. Spring St.
Los Angeles, CA 90012
(213) 222-2477

### Colorado:

**International Aspen Design Conference**
P.O. Box 664
Aspen, CO 81612
(303) 925-2257

### Connecticut:

**Connecticut Art Directors Club**
P.O. Box 1974
New Haven, CT 06521

### District of Columbia:

**American Advertising Federation**
1225 Connecticut Avenue, N.W., Ste. 401
Washington, DC 20036
(202) 659-1800

**American Institute of Architects**
1735 New York Avenue, N.W.
Washington, DC 20006
(202) 626-7300

**Art Directors Club of Washington, DC**
1523 22nd St., N.W.
Washington, DC 20037
(202) 293-3134

**Federal Design Council**
P.O. Box 7537
Washington, DC 20044

**International Copyright Information Center, A.A.D.**
1707 L Street, N.W.
Washington, DC 20036

**NEA: Design Arts Program**
1100 Pennsylvania Ave., N.W.
Washington, DC 20506
(202) 682-5400

### Georgia:

**Atlanta Art Papers, Inc.**
P.O. Box 77348
Atlanta, GA 30357
(404) 885-1273

**Graphics Artists Guild**
3158 Maple Drive, N.E., Ste. 46
Atlanta, GA 30305
(404) 237-6390

### Illinois:

**Institute of Business Designers**
National
1155 Merchandise Mart
Chicago, IL 60654
(312) 467-1950

**Society of Environmental Graphics Designers**
228 N. LaSalle St., Ste. 1205
Chicago, IL 60601

**STA**
233 East Ontario St.
Chicago, IL 60611
(312) 787-2018

**Women in Design**
400 West Madison, Ste. 2400
Chicago, IL 60606
(312) 648-1874

### Kansas:

**Wichita Art Directors Club**
P.O. Box 562
Wichita, KS 67202

### Maryland:

**Council of Communications Societies**
P.O. Box 1074
Silver Springs, MD 20910

### Massachusetts:

**Art Directors Club of Boston**
214 Beacon St.
Boston, MA 02116
(617) 536-8999

**Center for Design of Industrial Schedules**
50 Staniford St., Ste. 800
Boston, MA 02114
(617) 523-6048

**Graphic Artists Guild**
P.O. Box 1454–GMF
Boston, MA 02205
(617) 451-5362

### Michigan:

**Creative Advertising Club of Detroit**
c/o Rhoda Parkin,
30400 Van Dyke
Warren, MI 48093

### Minnesota:

**Minnesota Graphic Designers Association**
P.O. Box 24272
Minneapolis, MN 55424

### Missouri:

**Advertising Club of Greater St. Louis**
410 Mansion House Center
St. Louis, MO 63102
(314) 231-4185

**Advertising Club of Kansas City**
1 Ward Parkway, Ste. 102
Kansas City, MO 64112
(816) 753-4088

### New Jersey:

**Point-of-Purchase Advertising Institute**
2 Executive Dr.
Fort Lee, NJ 07024
(201) 585-8400

### New York:

**The Advertising Club of New York**
Roosevelt Hotel, Rm. 310
New York, NY
(212) 697-0877

**The Advertising Council, Inc.**
825 Third Ave.
New York, NY 10022
(212) 758-0400

**Advertising Typographers Association of America, Inc.**
5 Penn Plaza, 12th Fl.
New York, NY 10001
(212) 594-0685

**Advertising Women of New York Foundation, Inc.**
153 E. 57th St.
New York, NY 10022
(212) 593-1950

**American Association of Advertising Agencies**
666 Third Ave.
New York, NY 10017
(212) 682-2500

**American Booksellers Association, Inc.**
122 E. 42nd St.
New York, NY 10168
(212) 867-9060

**American Council for the Arts**
570 Seventh Ave.
New York, NY 10018
(212) 354-6655

**The American Institute of Graphic Arts**
1059 Third Ave.
New York, NY 10021
(212) 752-0813

continued on page 300

# MIDWEST

| | |
|---|---|
| **Bartz, Carl** St. Louis | 301 |
| **Brimacombe, Gerald** Minneapolis | 302,303 |
| **Hix, Steve** Kansas City MO | 304 |
| **Pitzner, Al** Wichita KS | 305 |
| **Rohman, Jim** Toledo OH | 306 |
| **Sanderson, Glenn** Green Bay WI | 307 |
| **Schridde, Charles** Madison Hts. MI | 308 |
| **Smith, R. Hamilton** St. Paul MN | 309 |
| **Westerman, Charlie** Louisville KY | 310,311 |
| **Kahn, Dick** Waukesha WI | Back Cover |

**Illinois**
**Indiana**
**Iowa**
**Kansas**
**Michigan**
**Minnesota**
**Missouri**
**Nebraska**
**North Dakota**
**Ohio**
**South Dakota**
**Wisconsin**

**American Society of Interior Designers**
National Headquarters
1430 Broadway
New York, NY 10018
(212) 944-9220

New York Chapter
950 Third Ave.
New York, NY 10022
(212) 421-8765

**American Society of Magazine Photographers**
205 Lexington Ave.
New York, NY 10016
(212) 889-9144

**Art Directors Club of New York**
488 Madison Ave.
New York, NY 10022
(212) 838-8140

**Association of American Publishers, Inc.**
1 Park Ave.
New York, NY 10016
(212) 689-8920

**Cartoonists Guild**
156 W. 72nd St.
New York, NY 10023
(212) 861-6377

**Center for Arts Information**
625 Broadway
New York, NY 10012
(212) 677-7548

**The Children's Book Council, Inc.**
67 Irving Place
New York, NY 10003
(212) 254-2666

**CLIO**
336 E. 59th St.
New York, NY 10022
(212) 593-1900

**Foundation for the Community of Artists**
280 Broadway, Ste. 412
New York, NY 10007
(212) 227-3770

**Graphic Artists Guild**
30 E. 20th St., Rm. 405
New York, NY 10003
(212) 777-7353

**Guild of Bookworkers**
663 Fifth Ave.
New York, NY 10022
(212) 757-6454

**Institute of Outdoor Advertising**
342 Madison Ave.
New York, NY 10017
(212) 986-5920

**International Advertising Association, Inc.**
475 Fifth Ave.
New York, NY 10017
(212) 684-1583

**The One Club**
251 E. 50th St.
New York, NY 10022
(212) 935-0121

**Printing Industries of Metropolitan New York, Inc.**
5 Penn Plaza
New York, NY 10001
(212) 279-2100

**The Public Relations Society of America, Inc.**
845 Third Ave.
New York, NY 10022
(212) 826-1750
N.Y. Chapter: (212) 826-1756

**Society of Illustrators**
128 E. 63rd St.
New York, NY 10021
(212) 838-2560

**Society of Photographers and Artists Representatives**
1123 Broadway
New York, NY 10010
(212) 924-6023

**Society of Publication Designers**
25 W. 43rd St., Ste. 711
New York, NY
(212) 354-8585

**Television Bureau of Advertising**
485 Lexington Ave.
New York, NY 10017
(212) 661-8440

**Type Directors Club of New York**
545 W. 45th St.
New York, NY 10036
(212) 245-6300

**U.S. Trademark Association**
6 E. 45th St.
New York, NY 10017
(212) 986-5880

**Volunteer Lawyers for the Arts**
1560 Broadway, Ste. 711
New York, NY 10036
(212) 575-1150

**Women in the Arts**
325 Spring St.
New York, NY 10013
(212) 691-0988

**Women in Design**
P.O. Box 5315
FDR Station
New York, NY 10022

## Ohio:

**Advertising Club of Cincinnati**
385 West Main St.
Batavia, OH 45103
(513) 732-9422

**AIGA Cleveland Chapter**
1021 Euclid Ave.
Cleveland, OH 44115
(216) 781-2400

**Cleveland Society of Communicating Arts**
812 Huron Rd.
Cleveland, OH 44115
(216) 621-5139

**Columbus Society of Communicating Arts**
c/o Salvato & Coe
2015 West Fifth Ave.
Columbus, OH 43221
(614) 488-3131

**Design Collective**
D.F. Cooke
55 Long St.
Columbus, OH 43215
(614) 464-4567

**Society of Communicating Arts**
c/o Tailford Assoc.
1300 Indian Wood Circle
Maumee, OH 43537
(419) 891-0888

## Pennsylvania:

**Art Directors Club of Philadelphia**
2017 Walnut St.
Philadelphia, PA 19103
(215) 569-3650

## Tennessee:

**Engraved Stationery Manufacturers Association**
c/o Printing Industries Association of the South
1000 17th Ave. South
Nashville, TN 37212
(615) 327-4444

## Texas:

**Advertising Artists of Fort Worth**
3424 Falcon Dr.
Fort Worth, TX 76119

**Art Directors Club of Houston**
2135 Bissonet
Houston, TX 77005
(713) 523-1019

**Dallas Society of Visual Communication**
3530 High Mesa Dr.
Dallas, TX 75234
(214) 241-2017

## Virginia:

**Industrial Designers Society of America**
6802 Poplar Pl., Ste. 303
McLean, VA 22101
(703) 556-0919

**Tidewater Society of Communicating Arts**
P.O. Box 153
Norfolk, VA 23501

## Washington:

**Puget Sound Ad Federation**
c/o Sylvia Fruichantie
Kraft Smith Advertising
200 1st West St.
Seattle, WA 98119
(206) 285-2222

**Seattle Design Association**
P.O. Box 1097
Main Office Station
Seattle, WA 98111
(206) 322-2777
(Formerly Seattle Women in Design)

**Seattle Women in Advertising**
801 E. Harrison, Ste. 105
Seattle, WA 98102
(206) 322-2777

**Society of Professional Graphic Artists**
c/o Nancy Gellos, Pres.
1331 Third Ave., Ste. 504
Seattle, WA 98115
(206) 623-4163

## Wisconsin:

**The Advertising Club**
407 E. Michigan St.
Milwaukee, WI 53202
(414) 271-7351

**Illustrators & Designers of Milwaukee**
c/o Don Berg
207 E. Michigan
Milwaukee, WI 53202
(414) 276-7828

**CARL BARTZ**
Bartz Studio, Inc.
321 North 22nd Street
St. Louis, Missouri 63103
(314) 231-8690

Represented by: Vicki Jolliff

Clients include: Adam's Mark, Anheuser-Busch, American Optometric Association, The Brown Group, Budweiser, Centerre Bank, Eagle Brand Snacks, Elanco, Famous Barr, Ferry-Morse, Honey Bran, Intertherm, Jack Daniels, Mallinckrodt Chemical, Moog Industries, Natural Lite, Ozark Airlines, Peter Paul Cadbury, Petrolite, Puppy Chow, Ralston Purina, Rykrisp, Sheraton Hotels, Stix, Baer & Fuller

# Bartz photographs.

**GERALD BRIMACOMBE**
7112 Mark Terrace Drive
Minneapolis, Minnesota 55435
(612) 941-5860

Representatives:
Chicago: Clay Timon (312) 527-1114
New York: Sam Brody (212) 758-0640

Stock photography: The Image Bank, New York

Specializing in location advertising photography worldwide.

Partial list of clients: Land O' Lakes, Philip Morris, Eastman Kodak (Kodak Colorama), Ray O Vac, Budweiser, DuPont, R.C. Cola, 3M Company, Uniroyal, General Mills, Northwest Orient Airlines, FMC Corp., Ford, Burlington-Northern Railroad, Honeywell, Olympia Brewing, Pentax, Green Giant, Pan American World Airways, American Can, *Life, Fortune, Sports Illustrated,* Time-Life Books, AT&T, Andersen Windows, United Airlines, Zero King, Pfizer, Clark Equipment, American Hoist, Control Data Corp., Dayton-Hudson Corp., TWA, International Multifoods, Grain Terminal Assn., *Smithsonian.*

302

**JIM ROHMAN**
Toledo, Ohio
(419) 865-0234

In studio set photography.
See also American Showcase
Volume 6

Photography © 1983 Jim Rohman

306

HOLY TOLEDO!

**AL PITZNER**

**WICHITA STUDIO...**
231 Ohio, Wichita, Kansas 67214
(316) 265-9488

**KANSAS CITY STUDIO...**
300 West 19th Terrace
Kansas City, Missouri 64108
(816) 474-8927

**CHICAGO...**
Represented by
Karen Platzer Associates
(312) 467-1981

**SOME OF THE CLIENTS HE HAS SERVED:**
H.D. Lee
Pfizer Drugs
Dart Trucks
Shepler's Western Stores
Greyhound Hall of Fame
Shangri-La Resort
Hesco Furniture
Capitol Records
The Fuller Brush Co.
Raytheon Corp.
Pratt & Whitney
Coop Farmland Industries
Hesston Farm Equipment
The Broadmoor Hotel
Payless Cashways
Butler Manufacturing
Rival Foods
Twentieth Century-Fox Pictures
Hallmark Cards
The Coleman Co.
Phillips 66
Mead Papers
Rainbird of California
Taco Tico
Cessna Aircraft Co.
Pizza Hut, Inc.
Beech Aircraft Co.
Gates Lear Jet

**AWARDS**
Gold Medals, Best of Show awards in Kansas City, Tulsa, St. Louis Art Directors Show
Silver medal in Denver Art Directors Show
Five Bronze medals in Tulsa and Kansas City Art Directors Shows
Three Special Awards of Excellence
Over 100 Excellence, Honor and Merit awards
The Best Advertising Picture of the Year in Exhibition One Show in Los Angeles
The Best Editorial Picture of the Year in Exhibition One Show in Los Angeles

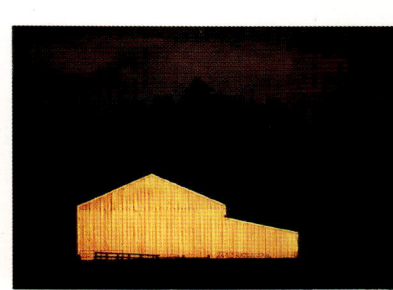

**STEVE HIX PHOTOGRAPHY**
306 West 8th Street
Kansas City, Missouri 64105
(816) 221-2456

Studio and location work for advertising, industrial and corporate clients. Experience ranges from fashion in Peru to computers in Baltimore to a banana split in the studio. Annual reports and image books are very strong.

Clients include: AT&T, Anaconda, DeLaval, Olin Chemical, Kansas City Southern Railroad, Presto Foods, United Telecommunications, Hallmark Cards, Penta Int., Eagle Claw Fishing Tackle, Ranger Boats, Labconco, KC Power & Light, Peruvian Connection, Broadway Collection, and Wire Rope Corp. of America.

**GERALD BRIMACOMBE**
7112 Mark Terrace Drive
Minneapolis, Minnesota 55435
(612) 941-5860

Representative:
Chicago: Clay Timon (312) 527-1114

Stock photography: The Image Bank, New York

Photo assignments for major advertising agencies and corporations have taken Jerry Brimacombe throughout most of the world. Keenly aware of prime shooting locations, he knows how to cope successfully with the fast changing, unplanned conditions inherent to location photography. Send for special free poster packet.

**GLENN SANDERSON**
Sanderson Photography
2936 Gross Street
Green Bay, Wisconsin 54304
(414) 336-6500

Forceful, eye-grabbing photography that evokes the right response and effectively communicates your message.

Commercial • Industrial • Fashion • Corporate Communication

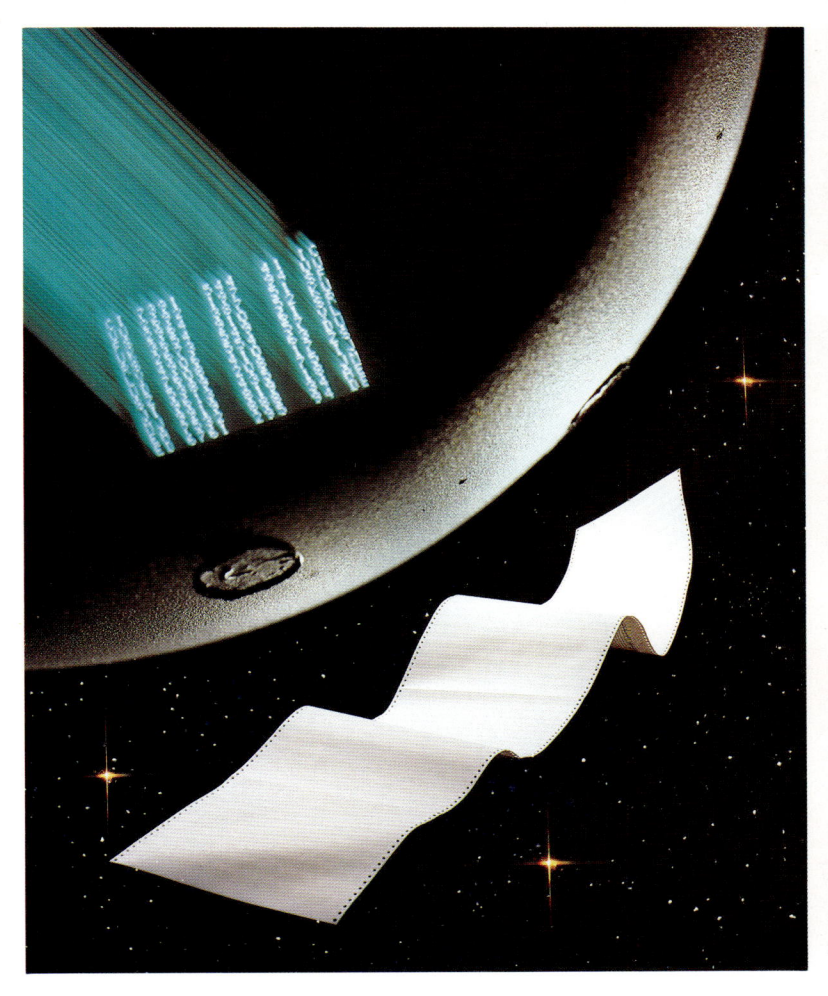

**CHARLES SCHRIDDE**
600 Ajax Drive
Madison Heights (Detroit), Michigan 48071
(313) 589-0111

One
Charlie Schridde
is worth a
thousand words.
Unfortunately, we haven't got room for a thousand words. So we can only give highlights of the Charlie Schridde Legend. His childhood abduction by a crazed film salesman. His lifelong fear of sanity. His successful fight to have his name changed (to Schridde). And above all, his great eye (it's four inches across).

But his pictures say it all. See? They speak of light and mood and tight deadlines. They speak of everything from movie stars to sexy cars. And they whisper TRUTH. Listen. Closely. There!

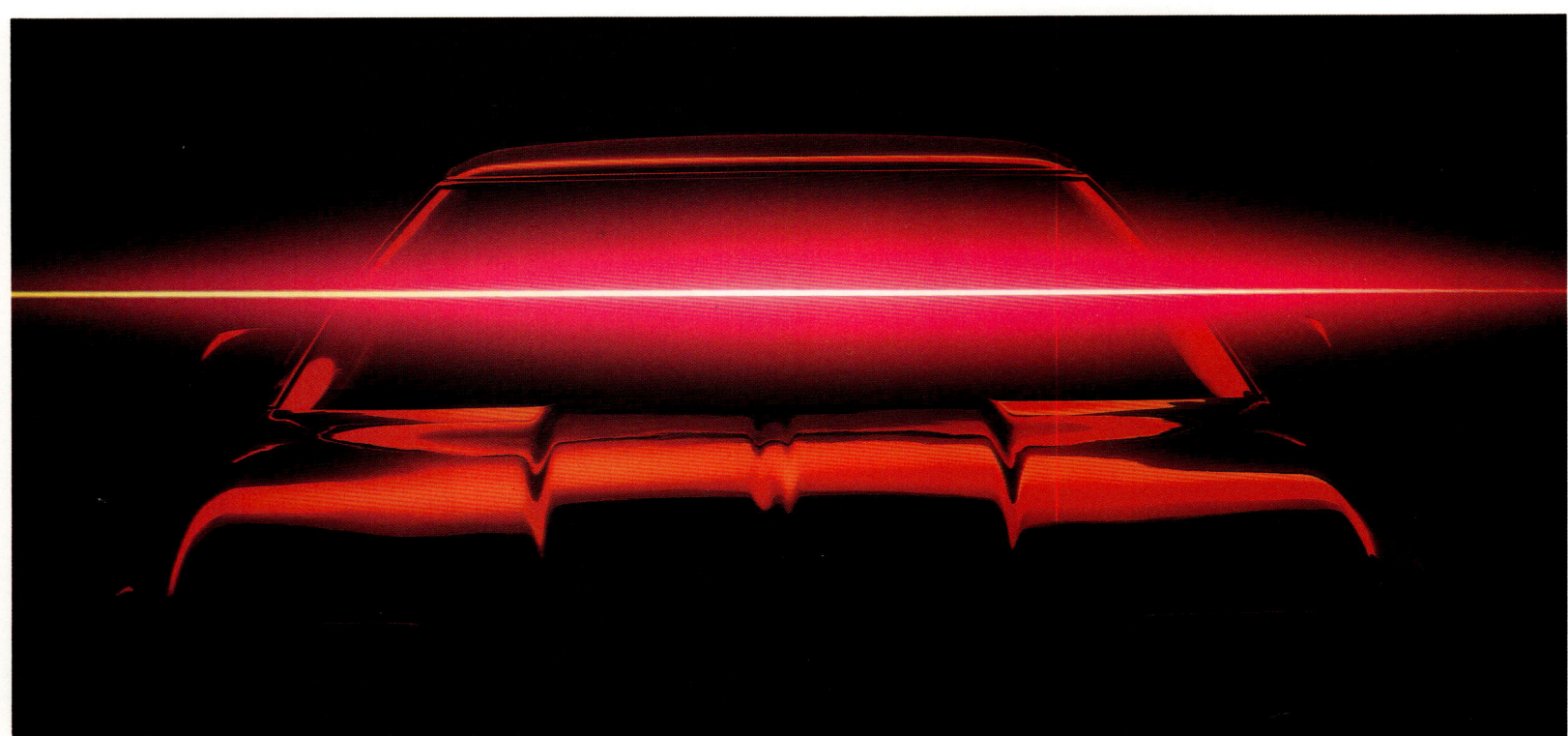

GENE BUTERA/CORVETTE

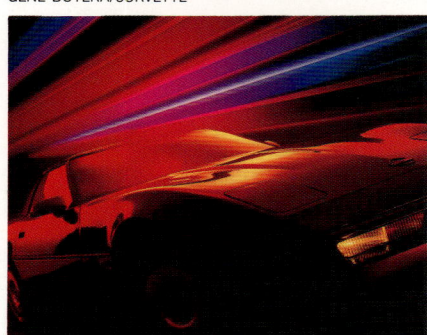

GENE BUTERA/CORVETTE

TOM RICKEY/OLDSMOBILE

K. KOHLBECKER/JACOBS

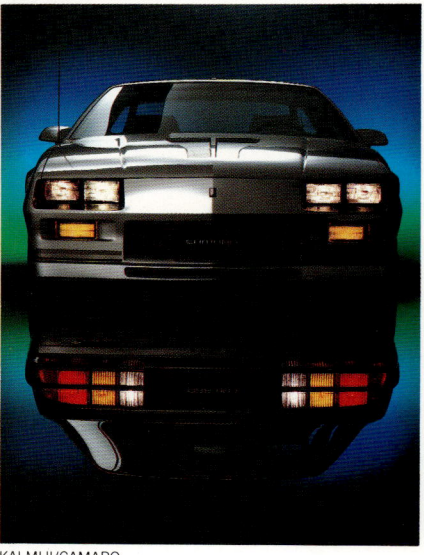

KAI MUI/CAMARO

308

**R. HAMILTON (RICHARD) SMITH**
584 East Rose Avenue
St. Paul, Minnesota 55101
(612) 778-1408

Sensitive and distinctive location photography for advertising, corporate/industrial, agricultural, design and editorial clients.

309

© R. Hamilton Smith

STOCK

KENRICK ADVERTISING

GRAPHIC ARTS CENTER

GRAPHIC ARTS CENTER

CARGILL

FARM JOURNAL

**CHARLIE WESTERMAN**
405 North Wabash
Chicago, Illinois 60611
(312) 565-2589

1310 South Third Street
Ferguson Mansion Carriage House
Louisville, Kentucky 40208
(502) 637-8414

Chicago Representative: Vicki Peterson
(312) 467-0780

A location photographer with offices in Chicago and Louisville, Charlie approaches a wide variety of assignments with an open mind.

Charlie owns and pilots a Cessna 414, a pressurized twin-engine aircraft. This makes commuting between his offices and your location assignments both efficient and convenient. You no longer have to worry that the equipment won't make the connection or that the shooting might have to be rushed to accommodate the airlines schedule. This plane definitely won't leave until Charlie does.

**CHARLIE WESTERMAN**
405 North Wabash
Chicago, Illinois 60611
(312) 565-2589

1310 South Third Street
Ferguson Mansion Carriage House
Louisville, Kentucky 40208
(502) 637-8414

Chicago Representative: Vicki Peterson
(312) 467-0780

Clients over the last few years include:
American National Bank and Trust Company, Anaconda Aluminum Co., BATUS, Inc., Beatrice Foods Co., Bethlehem Steel Corp., Borg-Warner Corp., Clark Equipment Co., General Electric Co., Glenmore Distilleries Co., Humana Inc., Ingersoll-Rand Co., International Harvester Co., Jim Beam Distilling Co., Maker's Mark Distillery Inc., Mazda Motor Co., McDonald's Corp., Meidinger Inc., Merrill Lynch Pierce Fenner and Smith Inc., Pizza Hut, Republic Steel Corp., Searle Pharmaceutical Inc., Stone Container Corp., The Balcor Co., Union Underwear Co., White Farm Equipment Co.

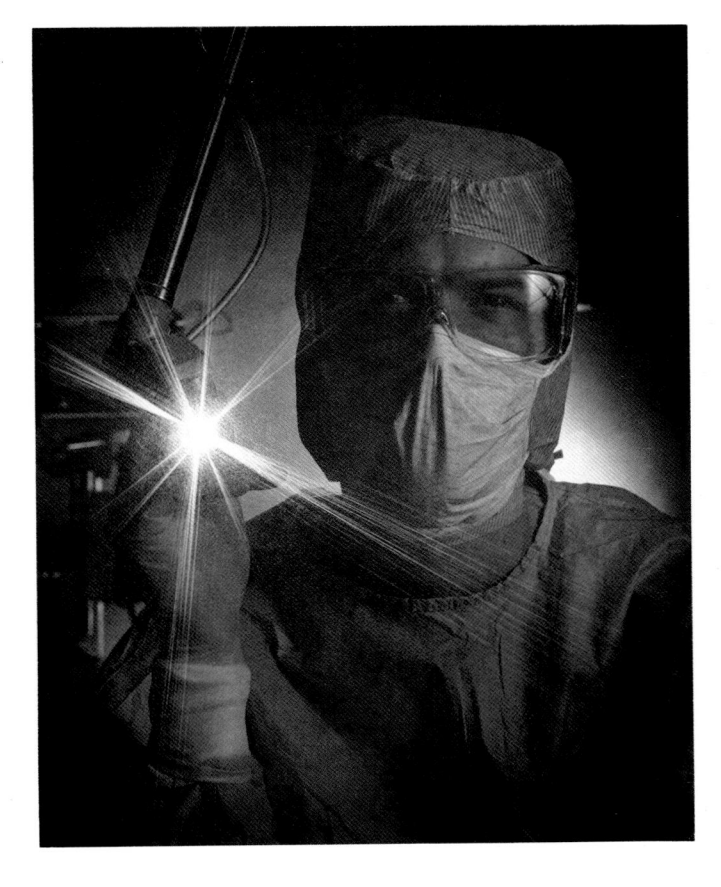

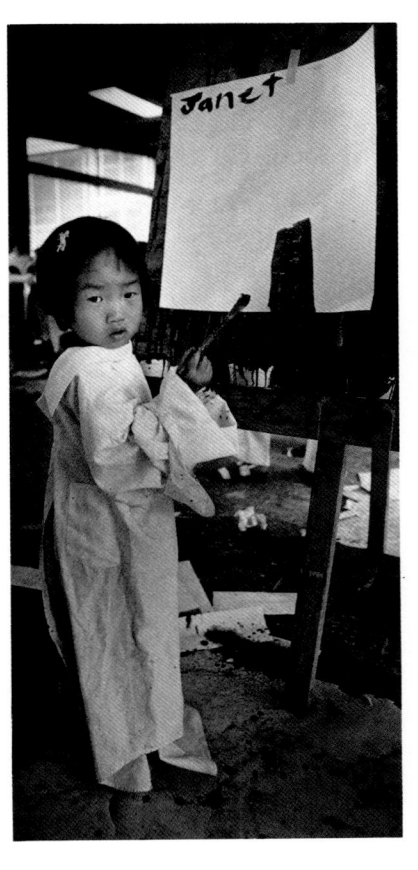

## EDUCATION BY EMULATION

It was 1958.

It was Wichita, Kansas.

It was my first job.

And it was the first time I had ever looked at an award-show book, which happened to be the 37th Annual New York Art Directors Annual.

This turned out to be the first textbook in my postgraduate education in advertising. It provided me with the education, the inspiration and the challenge that I could get nowhere else in Wichita, Kansas.

It was education by emulation.

I learned to do Helmut Krone layouts with Ron-Rosenfeld-like headlines and Howard-Zieff-type photos. When I specified type I chose Herb Lubalin's favorite type. I became so proficient that if I didn't have a budget for Jerome Snyder, I did Jerome Snyder myself.

I had become the consummate copier.

In time, I realized that the ads I was creating were simply facades—a camouflage of sameness. Irrelevant graphics with contrived headlines.

While I had achieved the Doyle Dane look, I had missed the point. The heart. The idea.

It began to dawn on me that no matter how brilliant the execution, the ad is nothing without the underpinnings of sound strategy. The clear expression of a consumer benefit. The presentation of an idea.

I also discovered that part of what makes an ad unique is that it addresses a specific problem for a specific client at a specific point in time.

Today, the young practitioners of advertising have a bigger library. Yes, there's still the New York Art Directors Annual, the 63rd. But there is also a rich collection of inspiration that wasn't around 25 years ago. The CA Annual. The One Show. The Andy. Print Casebooks. Even important reference like D&AD from London.

New shows. New annuals. New heroes.

A lot of great work to study, and a lot to learn from emulation—as long as we keep in mind what Benjamin Franklin once said: "There is much difference between imitating a good man, and counterfeiting him."

**Ron Anderson**
**Executive Creative Director-Midwest**
**Bozell & Jacobs, Inc.**
**Minneapolis**

# SOUTHWEST

| | |
|---|---|
| **Duran, Mark** Phoenix AZ | 314 |
| **Kaluzny, Zigy** Austin TX | 315 |
| **Peterson, Bruce** Phoenix AZ | 316 |
| **Bagshaw, Cradoc** Albuquerque NM | 317 |
| **Baker, Kipp** Fort Worth TX | 318 |
| **Clintsman, Dick** Dallas | 319 |
| **Digital Transparencies, Inc.** Houston | 320 |
| **Duran, Mark** Phoenix AZ | 314 |
| **Faustino** Houston | 321 |
| **Gayle, Rick** Phoenix AZ | 322 |
| **Gerczynski, Tom** Phoenix AZ | 323 |
| **Glentzer, Don** Houston | 324 |
| **Hamilton, Jeffrey Muir** Tucson AZ | 325 |
| **Jones, Jerry** Houston | 326 |
| **Kaluzny, Zigy** Austin TX | 315 |
| **Marshall, Jim** Carefree AZ | 327 |
| **Meyler, Dennis** Houston | 328 |
| **Peterson, Bruce** Phoenix AZ | 316 |

**Arizona**
**Arkansas**
**New Mexico**
**Oklahoma**
**Texas**

# MARK DURAN

**PHOTOGRAPHER**

66 East Vernon • Phoenix, Arizona 85004 • (602) 279-1141

**Zigy Kaluzny**

4700 Strass Drive
Austin, TX 78731
512-452-4463

**Corporate and Editorial
Photography—On Location**

Clients:
    Exxon
    IBM
    Mellon Enterprises
    Robert Webster, Inc.
    *Newsweek*
    *Time*
    *People*
    *GEO*
    *The Atlantic Monthly*
    *Stern Magazine*
    *The New York Times*

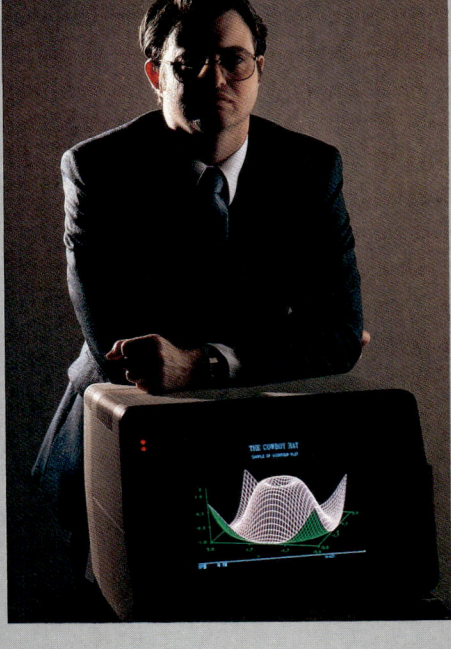

# BRUCE PETERSON

## PHOTOGRAPHY

1222 EAST EDGEMONT • PHOENIX, ARIZONA 85006
602·265·6505

**CRADOC BAGSHAW**
Assignment and Stock Photography
603 High Street Northeast
Albuquerque, New Mexico 87102
(505) 243-1096

Editorial and Corporate Photography

Editorial clients include: *Time, Business Week, Financial World, Woman's Day, LA Times, Home Magazine,* ABC Good Morning America. Corporate clients include: Gulf Oil, Polaroid, J.C. Penney, Thermo Electron, Container Corp. of America, Nissan of America.

Computerized stock file. Write for a subject list.

Los Angeles stock representative, After Image.

317

**KIPP BAKER**
Southern Lights Studio, Inc.
3000 Cullen—A
Fort Worth, Texas 76107
(817) 654-3210 (metro)

Additional work may be found in American Showcase, Volume 6.

Member ASMP

5000 Sq. ft. studio with access for large equipment

Photographs © Kipp Baker, 1983.

318

A.D. TOM DAWSON/ADOBE OIL

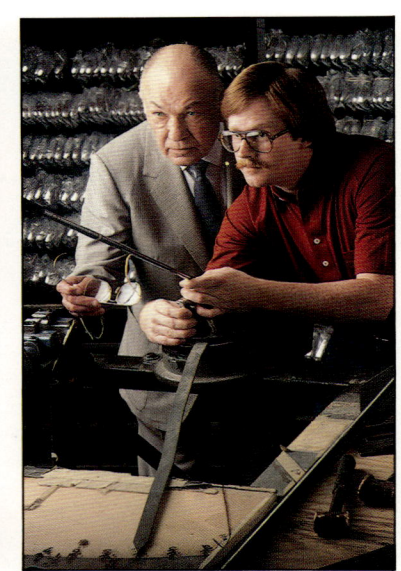

A.D. STEVE TURNER/AMF BEN HOGAN CO.

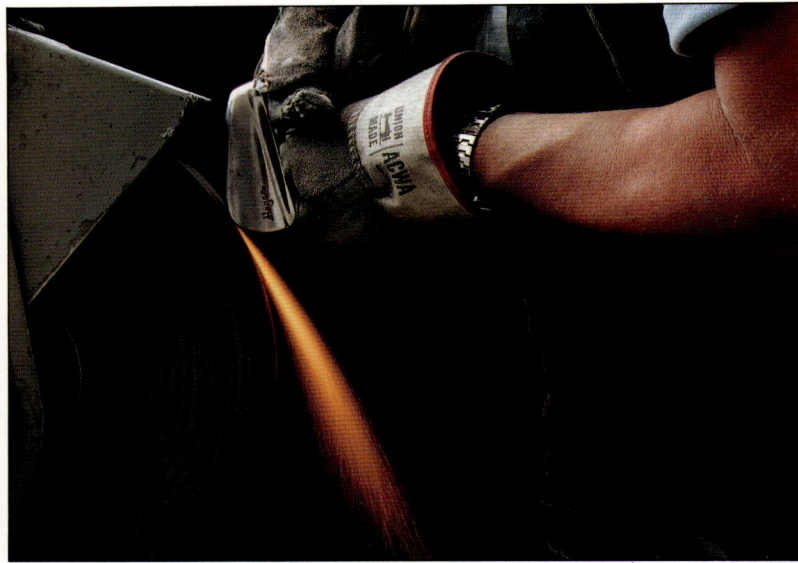

A.D. BOB WALTER/AMF BEN HOGAN CO.

PERSONAL STOCK

A.D. BOB HILL/McSTAY-REGIAN & ASSOC.

A.D. DEE HINKLE/CATALOGUE ASSOC.

A.D. LINC ANGELIUS/PIER ONE, INC.

A.D. LARRY FELDER/McSTAY-REGIAN & ASSOC.

**DICK CLINTSMAN**
Photographix Inc.
2201 North Lamar Street
Dallas, Texas 75202
(214) 651-1081

Advertising/Annual Reports/Editorial/Fashion

© 1982 Dick Clintsman

ASMP Member

Posters Available Upon Request

319

**DIGITAL TRANSPARENCIES, INC.**
**CONTACT RAPHAELE**
616 Hawthorne
Houston, Texas 77006
(713) 524-2211

# DIGITAL TRANSPARENCIES, INC.

## MULTIPLE IMAGE COMPOSITION

Our artists and technicians created this complex image using a sophisticated computer and laser scanning system. With this process, traditional creative limitations disappear. Elements within a photograph or series of photographs can be isolated, then manipulated or moved at will. The result is a unique photo-composition on a high resolution 8 x 10 or 11 x 14 E-6 transparency. Our system provides the ultimate in retouching flexibility and artistic control. To take you wherever your imagination wants to go.

**Contact Raphaële/Digital Transparencies, Inc.**
**616 Hawthorne Houston, Texas 77006 713-524-2211**

# FAUSTINO

Houston
Post Office Box 771234
Houston, Texas 77215
(713) 496-6543

Worldwide Rep.
The Image Bank

Experienced in location photography and cinematography around the world

Advertising, travel/resort, fashion

Stock available

New York
150 West 55th Street
New York, New York 10019
(212) 757-8987
Noel Becker

Advertising: Beechcraft; CBS Records; Fortunoff; *GEOSOURCE;* Johnson & Johnson; Seagram; Shulton-Colombia; Texas Instruments; Vanguard Oil.

Travel: American Express; Palm Beach Polo Club; Paradise Island; Sheraton, Hilton, Holiday Inn Hotels; Japan, Lan-Chile, Pan Am Airlines; Waldorf-Astoria Hotel.

Fashion: Denim Jeans; Fabricato Textiles; Levi Strauss; Leonisa; Monsanto Textile Company.

Colombia: Jorge Vieira
(574) 32-55-54

Work has appeared editorially in:
Eastern Review;
Glamour Magazine;
Review of Food & Wine; Signature;
Travel & Leisure.

Member ASMP

THE IMAGE BANK

**RICK GAYLE STUDIO**
3464 West Earll Drive, Suite D
Phoenix, Arizona 85017
(602) 269-7707

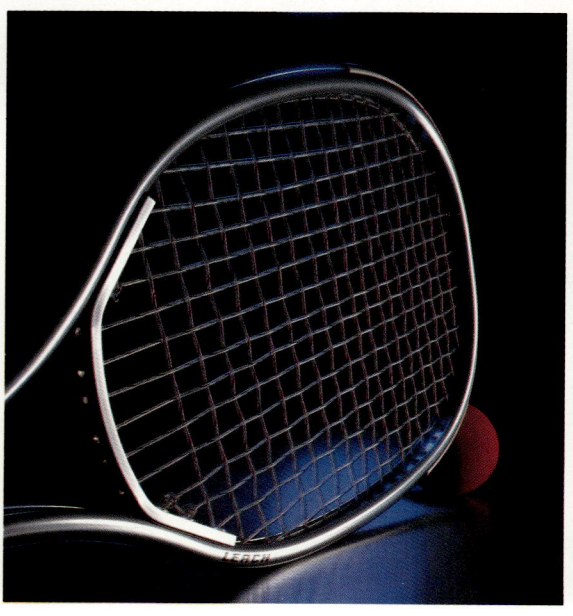

322

**TOM GERCZYNSKI**
Gerczynski Photographs
2211 North 7th Avenue
Phoenix, Arizona 85007
(602) 252-9229

The phone rings.

Wheat fields in Arizona?

*Cosmo, Arizona, just north of Gila Bend on Dion Latham's farm, the only place in the country still cutting spring wheat.*

So, I called the local PCA (Pest Control Agent) for directions and got the helicopter shot of the combines cutting wheat in the desert.

It was exactly what the AD wanted. And I enjoyed doing it. I'm a location photographer because it's what I do best. From gas station signs in Monument Valley to Mitsubishi jets in the Carefree Desert, I do it all. Miles of experience with the weather, the light, the land and man-made objects that seem surreal in the vast natural beauty.

Call me. Let me do it for you. You'll enjoy it, too.

Represented by: Joe Callahan
(602) 248-0777

Stock photography:
Blue Chip Stock
(212) 254-4070

Member ASMP

©Copyright 1983
Gerczynski Photographs

ASMP

**DON GLENTZER PHOTOGRAPHY**
3814 South Shepherd
Houston, Texas 77098
(713) 529-9686

© 1983 Don Glentzer Photography

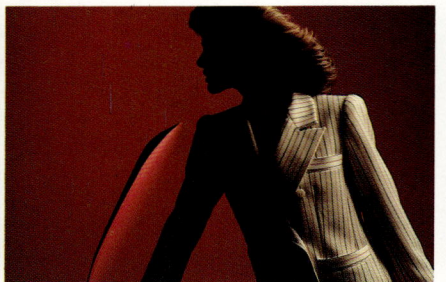

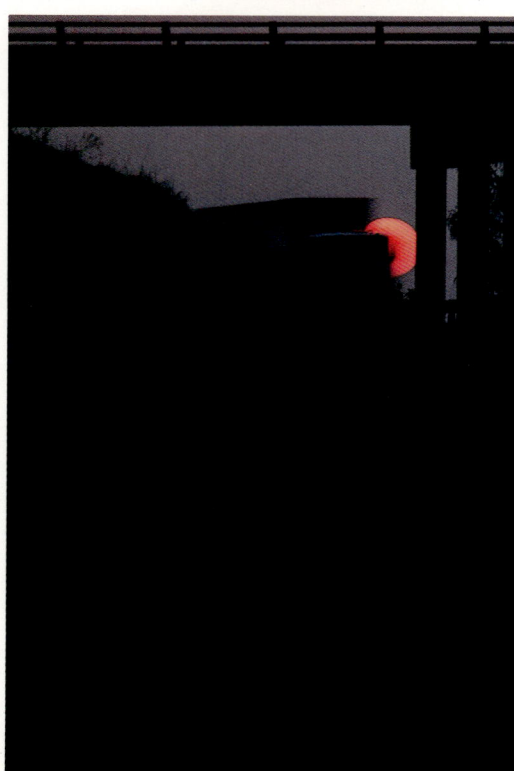

324

**JEFFREY MUIR HAMILTON**
6719 Quartzite Canyon Place
Tucson, Arizona 85718
(602) 299-3624

Assignments
Stock Photography

© Jeffrey Muir Hamilton 1983

325

**JERRY JONES**
6207 Edloe
Houston, Texas 77005
(713) 668-4328

Advertising
Annual Reports
Corporate/Industrial
Travel
Editorial

In studio or on location.

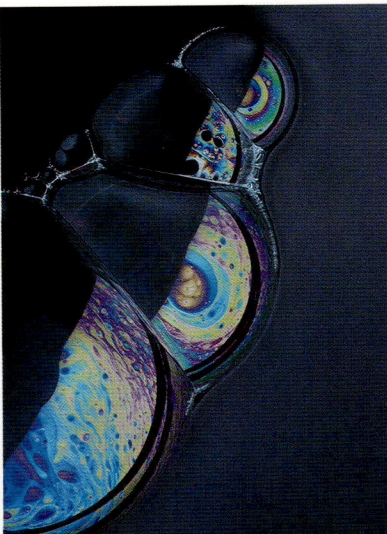

326

**JIM MARSHALL**
Post Office Box 2421
Carefree, Arizona 85377
(602) 488-3373

Advertising, Corporate, Editorial, and Landscape photography.

Clients include: United Airlines, Clipper Cruise Lines, Ticketmaster, Ramada Inn, Best Western Hotels, Arizona Convention Bureau, Hurst Corporation, Casados Farms, SHR Communication & Design, Desert Highlands Development Co.

All Photographs © Jim Marshall 1983/82

Member ASMP

**DENNIS MEYLER**
1903 Portsmouth, No. 25
Houston, Texas 77098
(713) 528-6564

Advertising/Corporate/Annual Reports/Editorial/Illustration

328

# WEST

| | |
|---|---|
| **Zak, Ed** SF | 330,331 |
| **Becker Bishop Studios, Inc** SF | 332,333 |
| **Blakeley, Jim** SF | 334,335 |
| **Heffernan, Terry** SF | 336,337 |
| **Werts Studios, Inc.** LA | 338,339 |
| **Springmann, Christopher** Point Reyes CA | 340 |
| **O'Brien, Tom** LA | 341 |
| **Dunbar, Clark** Mountain View CA | 342 |
| **Young, Ed** SF | 343 |
| **Abraham, Russell** SF | 344 |
| **Ambrose, Paul** Sunnyvale CA | 345 |
| **Bator, Joe** Golden CO | 347 |
| **Becker Bishop Studios, Inc** SF | 332,333 |
| **Blakeley, Jim** SF | 334,335 |
| **Blaustein, John** Berkeley CA | 348,349 |
| **Browne, Warren** SF | 350 |
| **Buchanan, Craig** SF | 351 |
| **Carroon, Chip** Mill Valley CA | 352 |
| **Cassidy Photographic Design** Santa Clara CA | 353 |
| **Chaney, Brad** SF | 354,355 |
| **Cook, Kathleen Norris** Laguna Hills CA | 356 |
| **Dahlstrom Photography, Inc.** Portland OR | 357 |
| **Davidson, Jerry** LA | 358,359 |
| **de Gennaro, George** LA | 360,361 |
| **De Sciose, Nicholas** Denver | 362 |
| **Dunbar, Clark** Mountain View CA | 342 |
| **Fader, Bob** Denver | 363 |
| **Ferro, Daniel J.** La Jolla CA | 364 |
| **Gardner, Robert** LA | 365 |
| **Gottlieb, Mark** Palo Alto CA | 367 |
| **Harrington, Marshall** San Diego CA | 368,369 |
| **Heffernan, Terry** SF | 336,337 |
| **Keenan, Larry** SF | 370 |
| **Lee, Larry** North Hollywood CA | 371 |
| **Livzey, John** Hollywood CA | 372,373 |
| **Masterson, Ed** San Diego CA | 375 |
| **McAllister, Bruce** Denver | 376,377 |
| **Melgar Photographers, Inc.** Santa Clara CA | 378 |
| **Mishler, Clark** Anchorage AK | 379 |
| **O'Brien, Tom** LA | 341 |
| **Percey, Roland** LA | 380 |
| **Peregrine, Paul** Denver | 381 |
| **Perry, David** Seattle | 382 |
| **Photographic Communications** Santa Clara CA | 383 |
| **Ressmeyer, Roger** SF | 384 |
| **Sadlon, Jim** SF | 385 |
| **Schoenfeld, Michael** Salt Lake City UT | 386 |
| **Smith, Charles J.** San Diego CA | 387 |
| **Solomon, Marc** LA | 388,389 |
| **Springmann, Christopher** Point Reyes CA | 340 |
| **Steinberg, Bruce** SF | 391 |
| **Swarthout, Walter** SF | 392,393 |
| **Werts Studios, Inc.** LA | 338,339 |
| **Wood, James B.** LA | 394 |
| **Wortham, Robert** LA | 395 |
| **Young, Ed** SF | 343 |
| **Zak, Ed** SF | 330,331 |

**Alaska**
**California**
**Colorado**
**Hawaii**
**Idaho**
**Montana**
**Nevada**
**Oregon**
**Utah**
**Washington**
**Wyoming**

AL FESSLER/ART DIRECTOR

Additional photography can be seen in Creative Black Books, 1974-75-76-78-79-80-81-82-83 and 84 plus American Showcase Vol. 4 and 5. A portfolio of this work is available upon request.

# ZAK IN THE WEST.

ED ZAK PHOTO INC, 80 TEHAMA STREET, SAN FRANCISCO, CALIF. 94105, (415) 781-1611.

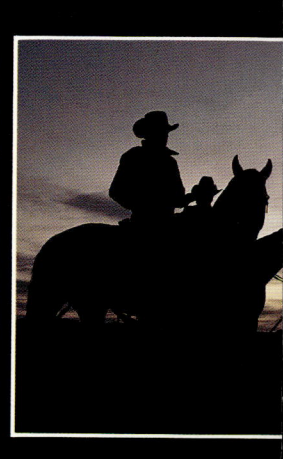

**BECKER BISHOP**

© 1983 Becker Bishop Studios, Inc. 1000 17th St., San Francisco, CA 94100

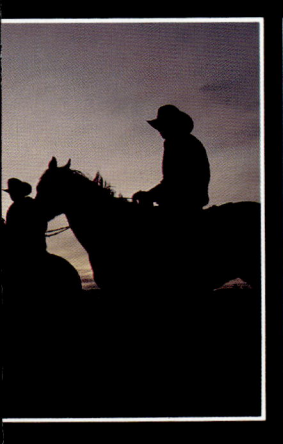

# SAN FRANCISCO

(415) 552-4254  Additional photography in Creative Black Book 1980, 1984

# jim blakeley

"In choosing a photographer you need more than technical proficiency. You need someone who will bring something to the job creatively... actually build on the concept... improving the image indicated on the layout.

But for a shoot to be successful it takes more than creativity—it takes organization, attention to detail. Bringing together the right people, places and props. On time and on budget. All the boring, grunge work nobody wants to do but a good photographer will always do.

And finally its finding someone you want to work with. Someone who can make even the most difficult job exciting and enjoyable. You want to be able to put all your energies into the shoot, not into dealing with problematic personalities.

If you're looking for this composition of ability, performance and attitude you might want to take a closer look at Jim Blakeley."

Al W. Fessler,
Sr. Art Director
Ogilvy & Mather (S.F.)

Printed in Japan. © 1984 American Showcase, Inc.

jim blakeley
Photography, Inc.
1061 Folsom Street
San Francisco 94103
(415) 558-9300

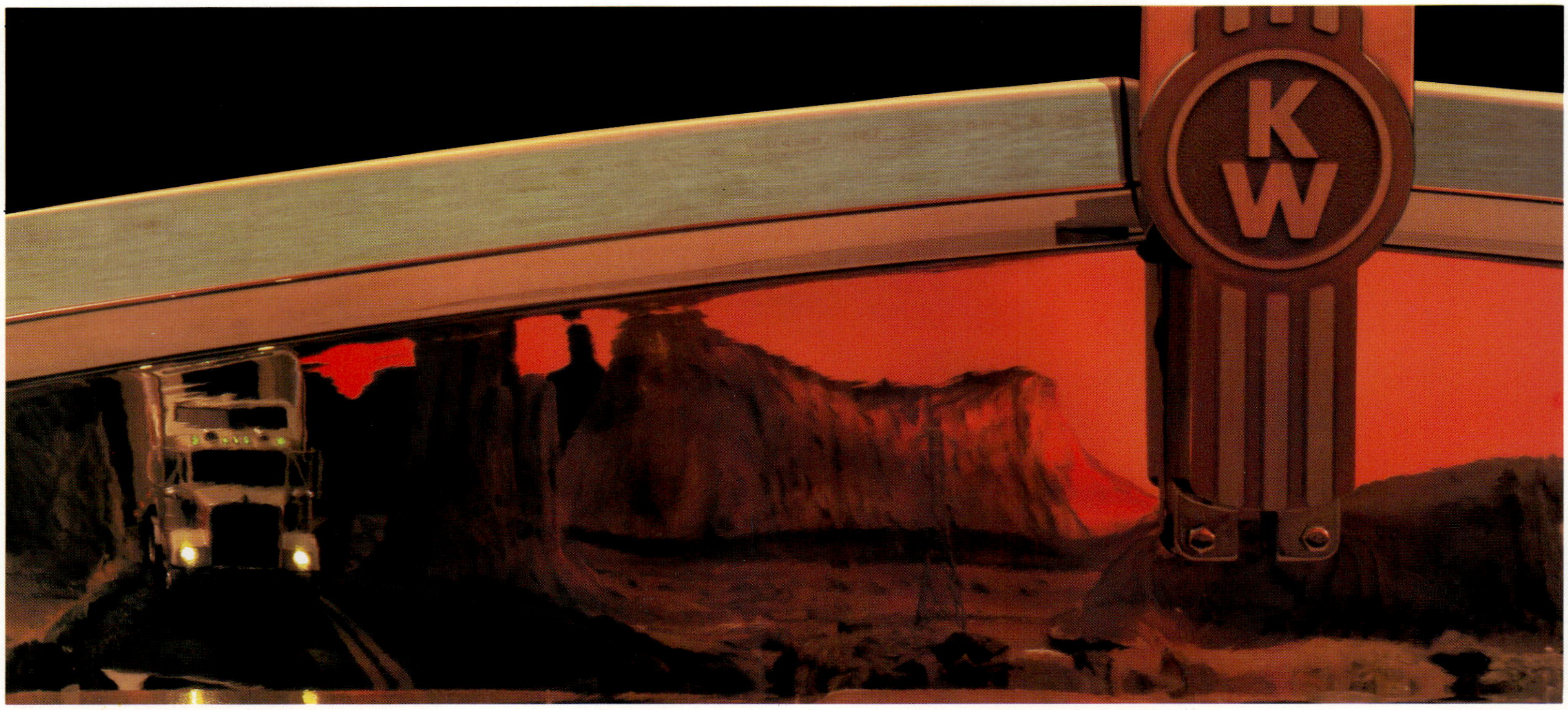
KW

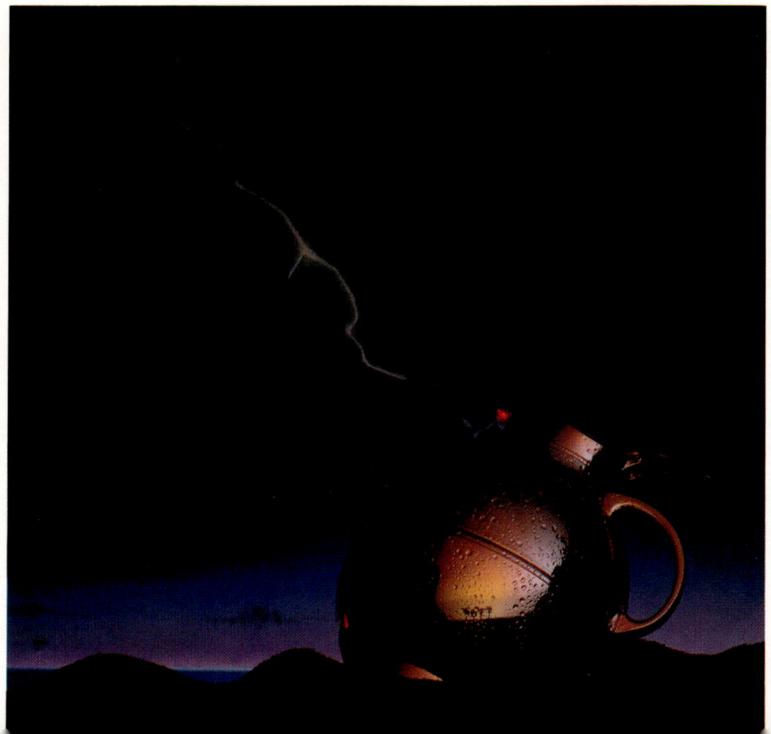

**Terry Heffernan**/Light Language

352 Sixth Street
San Francisco, CA
94103

415/626-1999

**Videotape portfolio presentation
available upon request.**

**Representatives**

Los Angeles/Valerie London
213/277-8090

Chicago/Myrna Hogan
312/372-1616

Seattle/Spencer Church
206/324-1199

# WERTS

Picky. Picky. Pic...

Werts Studios Inc. 732 North Highland Avenue, Los Angeles, CA 90038
Represented by Dianne Brown (213) 464-2775

**Christopher Springmann**
**Photographer, Inc.**
San Francisco
P.O. Box 745
Pt. Reyes, CA
9 4 9 5 6
415 663 8428

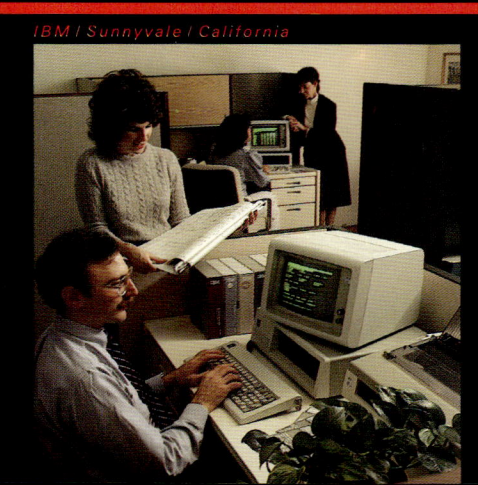

*Geosource / Odessa / Texas*

*AT&T / Apache Junction / Arizona*

*St. Regis / Phoenix / Arizona*

*AT&T / San Francisco / California*

*IBM / Sunnyvale / California*

Design by Lucy H. McCargar

# Tom O'Brien

(213) 938-2008 • 450 SOUTH LA BREA, LOS ANGELES, CALIFORNIA 90036

REPRESENTED IN LOS ANGELES BY BARBARA (213) 935-6668

ASK TO SEE OUR REEL.

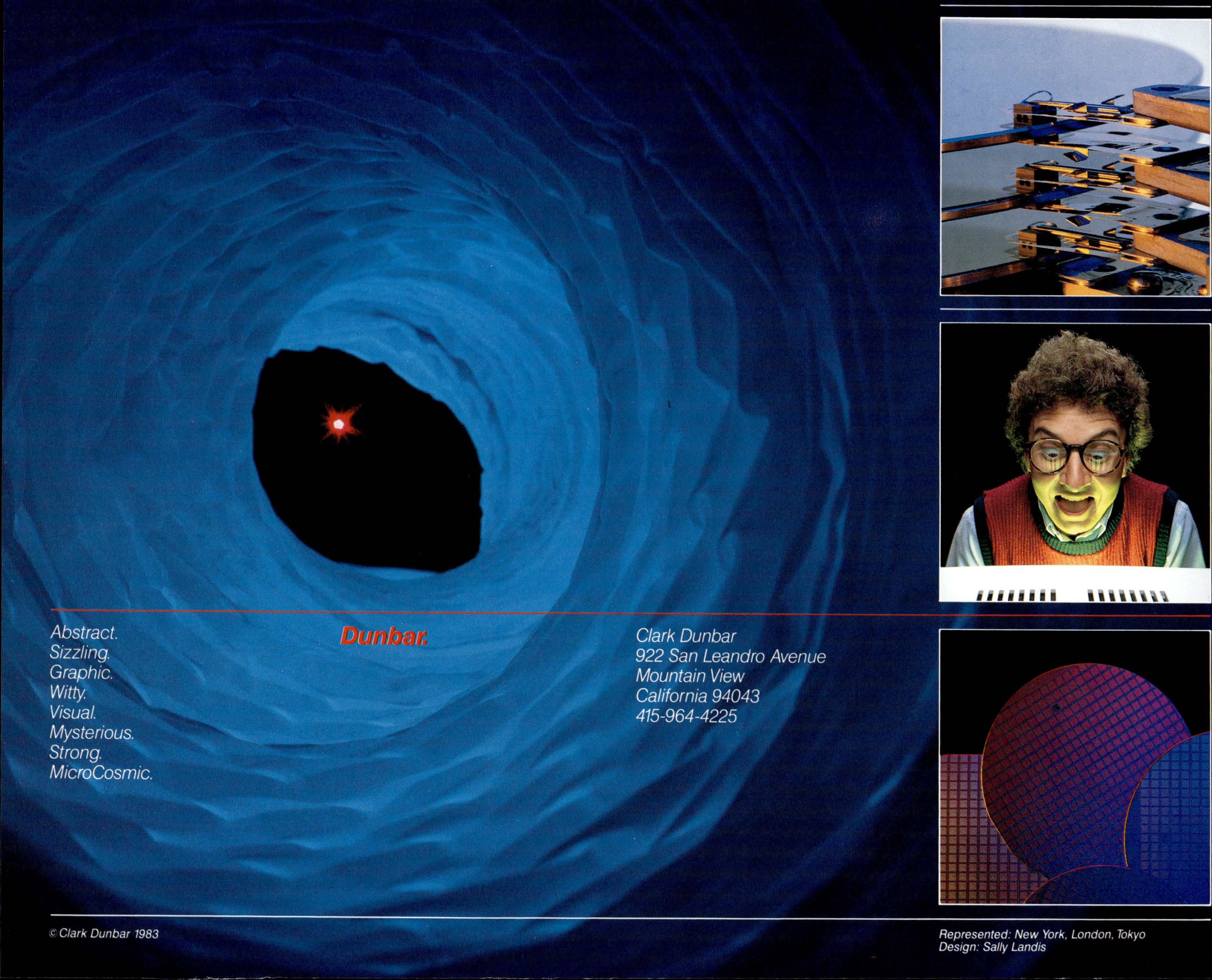

Abstract.
Sizzling.
Graphic.
Witty.
Visual.
Mysterious.
Strong.
MicroCosmic.

**Dunbar.**

Clark Dunbar
922 San Leandro Avenue
Mountain View
California 94043
415-964-4225

© Clark Dunbar 1983

*Represented:* New York, London, Tokyo
*Design:* Sally Landis

# ED YOUNG

415-864-2448
New York Rep:
Joan Kramer
212-224-1758

**E**dward Young, Photography
Advertising, Corporate, Travel,
Multi-image, and Stock

9 Decatur Street
San Francisco, CA 94103

▶ **S**hell Oil
▶ **B**ank of the West

**D**esign: Hartung & Associates, Ltd. 415-838-0602

**RUSSELL ABRAHAM**
17 Brosnan Street
San Francisco, California 94103
(415) 558-9100

Architecture, interiors, furniture, building products. Editorial and advertising assignments. Studio space available.

Representative clients:

*Architectural Record*
Edwin Bronstein Associates
*Designers West Magazine*
Environetics International
Fitschen/Sambucetti Associates
Gensler & Associates
Hallenbeck, Chamorro & Associates
Integrated Ceilings
*Interiors Magazine*
*Interior Design Magazine*
Kaplan, McLaughlin, Diaz
Kenneth Parker & Associates
Kurtzman & Kodama
Levolor
Marquis Associates
Ron Nunn & Associates
William Pereira & Associates
ROMA
*Restaurant & Hotel Design Magazine*
Saga Corp.
Swatt & Stein
Skidmore, Owings & Merrill
Tardy & Associates
Westinghouse

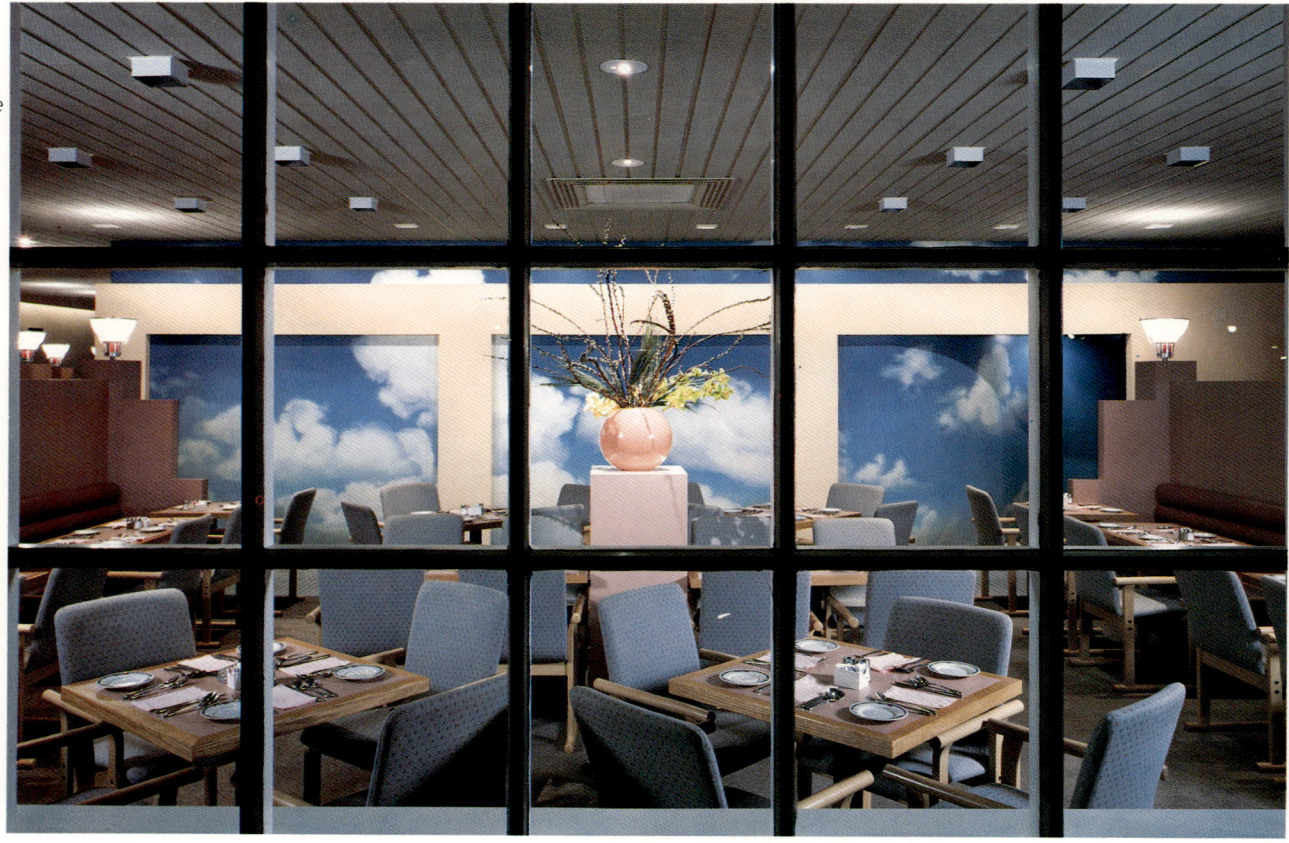

**PAUL AMBROSE STUDIOS**
1231 Alderwood Avenue
Sunnyvale, California 94089
(408) 734-3211

Located in the heart of Silicon Valley, Paul Ambrose Studios specializes in conceptual illustration for high technology industries. The photographs shown here were developed as part of an 8-ad campaign based on the theme "Creating new horizons in Microelectronics."

© Paul Ambrose Studios, 1984

## IRA

When I receive the paper in the morning I always go first to the Sports pages to see how my Dodgers are doing. I am a Dodger fan living in San Francisco, so I can't hear them on the radio. Then, because I'm mostly Irish, I automatically turn to the Obituary page.

Last month the paper dedicated a lengthy tribute to "Ira Gershwin." He was, without a doubt, an incredibly creative man who, without the help of research management, focus groups, etc., created the most memorable lyrics in the past 40 years. If you leave out the Beatles, Gershwin created almost all of them. Call it instinct, creative genius, talent or whatever, he knew how to appeal to people, to "reach out and touch someone," as a wonderful advertising campaign is saying today.

Appealing to people, really touching them, is the key to success in our business. But unlike Gershwin, we live in a world of research, layers of management and focus groups. So the challenge becomes how to create fresh, human, surprising advertising in spite of these potential obstacles. After all, our ads ultimately have to appeal to human emotions as well as satisfy corporate objectives.

In order to create ads that appeal to people, I always try to remember a principle first articulated by the late George Gribbin, creative guru and fourth president of Young & Rubicam.

"I make it a point," Gribbin said, "to compare ads to people. I say to myself, 'would I like a man or woman to act the way this ad does? Are they being boastful? Loud? Informative? Likable? Friendly? Someone I wouldn't mind meeting, or meeting again? Would I choose this ad—if it were a person—for a friend?' If the answer is 'yes', I figure the ad is on the right track."

He went on to compare good ads with friends who are honest with us, who are interested in us, who say things freshly, and—above all—are individuals.

Another principle I like to use is "resist the usual." Creative work that looks or sounds familiar to other work doesn't have much of a chance to be remembered. Really unusual ideas are so fresh to the consumer, they become instantly familiar at the slightest hint of recognition. An example is the fast-talking man for Federal Express. Another example: three or four words of an Ira Gershwin lyric and you can remember most of the song.

Ending with Mr. Gershwin: Along with the amazing list of lyrical credits in the paper were photos of Mr. Gershwin, which told me another thing: "If you're really good, you don't have to look groovy."

I feel sort of pleased that I never invested in gold chains for my neck, but instead kept all my neckties. They look better with my sport coat or suit anyway.

**Tom Sexton**
**Creative Director**
**Young & Rubicam**
**San Francisco**

**JOE BATOR**
2011 Washington Avenue
Golden, Colorado 80401
(303) 279-4163

Stock through: The Stock Market
(212) 684-7878

347

**JOHN BLAUSTEIN**
665 Alvarado Road
Berkeley, California 94705
(415) 845-2525

Stock representative: Woodfin Camp & Associates (212) 750-1020

Representative in San Francisco: Mary Vandamme (415) 433-1292

Also see: American Showcase Volume 5 & 6; Corporate Showcase Volume 1 & 2; ASMP BOOK 1981; ASMP BOOK 2.

348

**JOHN BLAUSTEIN**
(415) 845-2525

**WARREN BROWNE**
1003 Fell Street
Suite "A"
San Francisco, California 94117
(415) 431-7601

Color portfolio available on request.

© 1983 Warren Browne

**CRAIG BUCHANAN**
1026 Folsom Street
San Francisco, California 94103
(415) 861-5566

Architectural, Corporate, Editorial

Hotels, Restaurants, Offices, Residences, People in their work spaces, people at leisure. Interiors and Exteriors for brochures, publication, competitions, advertising/promotion.

**CHIP CARROON**
Post Office Box 5545
Mill Valley, California 94942
(415) 331-0343

World-wide location photography for corporate/industrial advertising and annual reports.

Diverse stock photography available.

Complete underwater photographic capability.

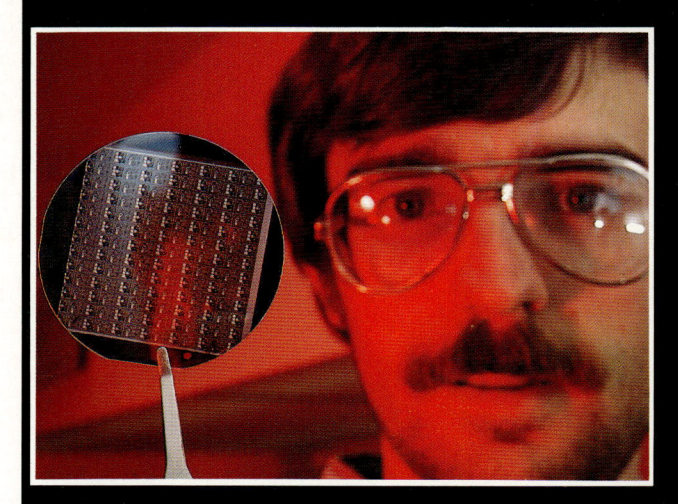

**CASSIDY PHOTOGRAPHIC DESIGN**
3279 Kifer Road
Santa Clara, California 95051
(408) 735-8443

Director of Photography: Peter Buhrman

"We can illustrate your idea...or we can create the idea for you..."

Cassidy Photographic Design is not simply a photographic studio; we are visual communication professionals. To insure greater creative control, we have incorporated in-house design, typography, slide production, and processing. If you have a problem communicating your story or message visually, from the simplest creative assignment to the most complex special effects, we can solve it.

- Advertising/illustration
- Editorial
- Corporate
- Multi camera techniques
- Location and studio

Member of the Advertising Photographers of America, the Peninsula Advertising Photographers Association, and the Western Art Directors Club.

353

**BRAD CHANEY**
Swarthout & Associates, Inc.
370 Fourth Street
San Francisco, California 94107
(415) 543-2525

Representative: Ron Sweet
(415) 433-1222

People; food; still life; high tech.
Studio and location.

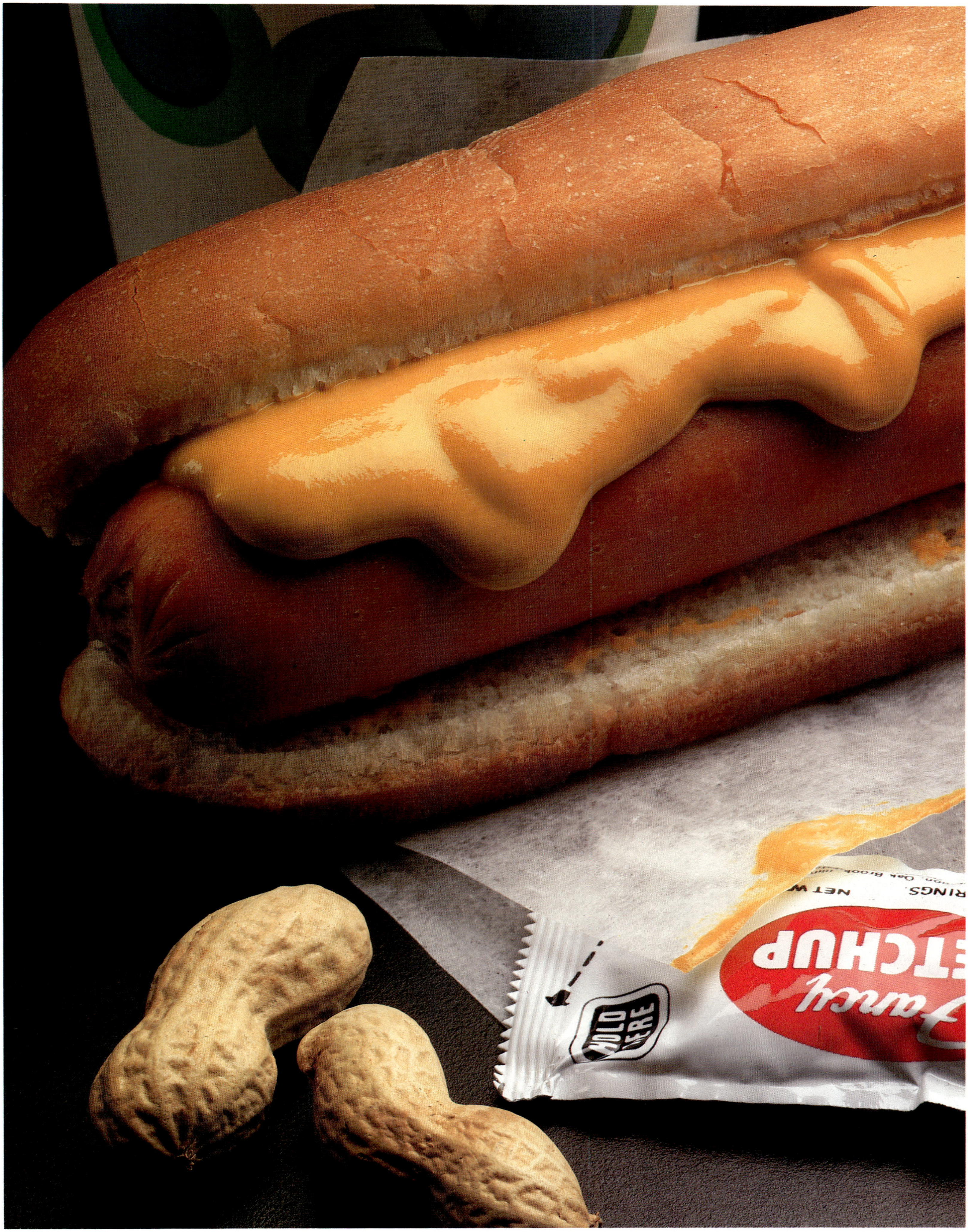

**KATHLEEN NORRIS COOK**
Post Office Box 2159
Laguna Hills, California 92653
(714) 770-4619

Represented by Warren Cook
(714) 770-4619
(213) 857-0981

In the Mountains: The Seldom Inn (303) 325-4193

Photographs © Kathleen Norris Cook 1983

Member ASMP

Additional Images: The Image Bank

Partial Client Listing—American Airlines, American General Insurance, Amfac, Caesar's Tahoe, Consolidated Freightways, Continental Airlines, Control Data Corp., Datsun/Nissan Motors, Eastman Kodak, Epcot Center/Disneyworld, Horizon Corp., Pan American Airlines, Pratt & Lambert, PSA Airlines, S.D. Warren, Stewart, Tabori & Chang, Publishers, Sunkist, Suzuki Motors, Toyota, Visa USA, Western Cities Broadcasting, Word, Inc., Arizona Highways, Sierra Club Books, Westways.

356

**DAHLSTROM PHOTOGRAPHY INC.**
2312 NW Savier
Portland, Oregon 97210
(503) 222-4910

Our Clients and Friends include:

Tektronix Inc.
Electro Scientific Industries
Vidicraft
Videx
Intel Corp.
Floating Point Systems
Orbanco
Meier & Frank
Stretch & Sew
Goldsmith's
Oregon, Washington
   California Pear Board
Ness Foods
Esco Corp.
Subaru N.W.
Precision Castparts Corp.
Mentor Graphics
Northwest Instrument Systems
Gould-Godart
Cummins Diesel

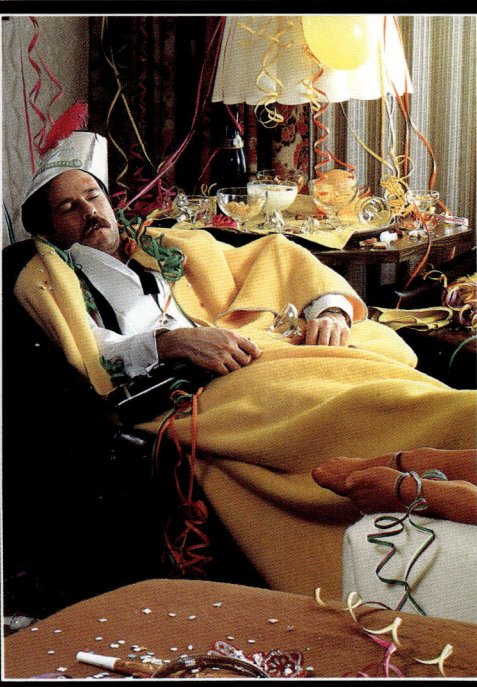

**JERRY DAVIDSON**
3923 West Jefferson Blvd.
Los Angeles, California 90016
(213) 735-1552

Partial Client List:
Datsun
Computer Sciences Corporation
Luckys
Gemco
First Interstate Bank of California
Vidal Sassoon
Toro
Plus Products
National O Ring/Federal-Mogul
Carnation
Brentwood Publishing Corporation
Sentry Safes
U.S. Amada Ltd
Litton Industries
Brentwood Financial Corporation
Hali-Spechts
Silver-Reed Corporation
University of Singapore
Ocean Dynamics
Tiffany's
R&B Enterprises/Oakwood Gardens
RTR Security Products

All Photographs © 1983 Jerry Davidson

358

**JERRY DAVIDSON**
3923 West Jefferson Blvd.
Los Angeles, California 90016
(213) 735-1552

Partial Client List:
Datsun
Computer Sciences Corporation
Luckys
Gemco
First Interstate Bank of California
Vidal Sassoon
Toro
Plus Products
National O Ring/Federal-Mogul
Carnation
Brentwood Publishing Corporation
Sentry Safes
U.S. Amada Ltd
Litton Industries
Brentwood Financial Corporation
Hali-Spechts
Silver-Reed Corporation
University of Singapore
Ocean Dynamics
Tiffany's
R&B Enterprises/Oakwood Gardens
RTR Security Products

All Photographs © 1983 Jerry Davidson

359

**GEORGE de GENNARO STUDIOS**
902 South Norton Avenue
Los Angeles, California 90019
(213) 935-5179

Over 25 years experience specializing in food and still life photography for America's top advertising agencies, corporations, publishers, and design firms.

©George de Gennaro

360

PRINCESS CRUISES/GREY ADVERTISING

HP BOOKS

ARMOUR/YOUNG & RUBICAM

**GEORGE de GENNARO STUDIOS**
902 South Norton Avenue
Los Angeles, California 90019
(213) 935-5179

361

MEREDITH CORPORATION

BON APPETIT

HOUSE BEAUTIFUL

TACO BELL/GREY ADVERTISING

**NICHOLAS DESCIOSE**
2700 Arapahoe Street
Studio No. 2
Denver, Colorado 80205
(303) 455-6315

Chicago Representative:
Vincent J. Kamin Associates
42 East Superior Street
Chicago, Illinois 60611
(312) 787-8834

New York City Answering Service:
663 Fifth Avenue
New York, New York 10022
(212) 757-6454

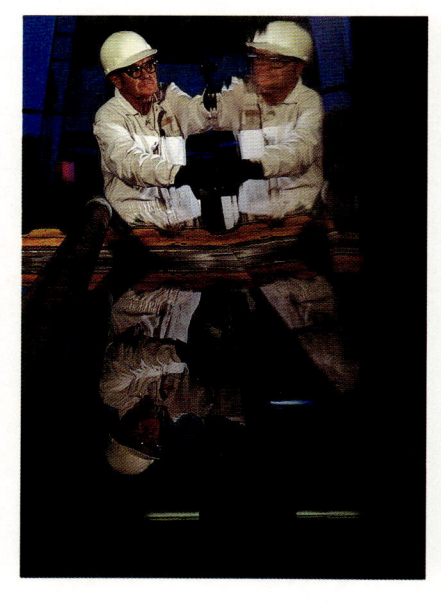

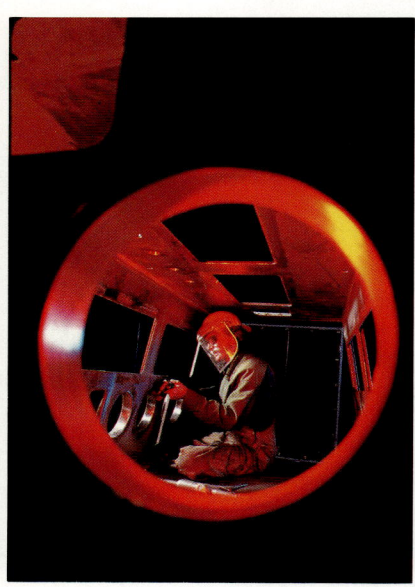

**BOB FADER**
14 Pearl Street
Denver, Colorado 80203
(303) 744-0711

Corporate
Architecture
Industrial

**DANIEL J. FERRO**
8022 El Paseo Grande
La Jolla, California 92037
(619) 456-2213

Clients include: American Assoc for the Advancement of Science, Hansen Ski Boots, Harper & Row Publishers, Ivac Corporation, Mattel Electronics, National Injury Prevention Foundation, Scripps Clinic and Research Foundation, Stelling Banjo Works, Ltd., Sutter Biomedical Inc., Taylor Guitars, Woodhaven Developers, Inc.

© Daniel J. Ferro

**ROBERT GARDNER STUDIO, INC.**
800 South Citrus Avenue
Los Angeles, California 90036
(213) 931-1108

Client Listing: American Express, *Sports Illustrated,* De Beers, Cole of California, Tokina Optical Corp., Barco of California, Avon, Chanel, Clairol, Helena Rubenstein, Jean Naté, Revlon, Vidal Sassoon, Viviane Woodward, Rolex, Benson & Hedges, Continental Airlines, Volkswagen, *Esquire, Modern Bride, Bazaar,* Seagram, Canadian Lord Calvert, Pepsi Cola, Coca-Cola, Shasta, Vassarette, Rogers, Maidenform, Marantz, Clarion, 20th Century Fox, General Foods, Nestea, Carnation, Silverwoods, Harris, J.C. Penney, Bullock's, du Pont Qiana, Montgomery Ward, Broadway, Neiman-Marcus, Glenoit, IBM, Norris Industries, Continental, TWA, Baskin-Robbins, Maude Adams, Jeff Bridges, Christy Brinkley, James Caan, Joan Crawford, Lou Ferigno, Sally Fields, Veronica Hammell, Kay Lenz, Ali MacGraw, Johnny Mathis, Bob Newhart, Rudolf Nureyev, Suzanne Pleshette, Vidal Sassoon, George C. Scott, Arnold Schwarzenegger, Richard Simmons, Cheryl Tiegs, Goldwater's, Harris & Frank, Armstrong, and Del Monte.

Stock photography available through:
After-Image (213) 467-6033

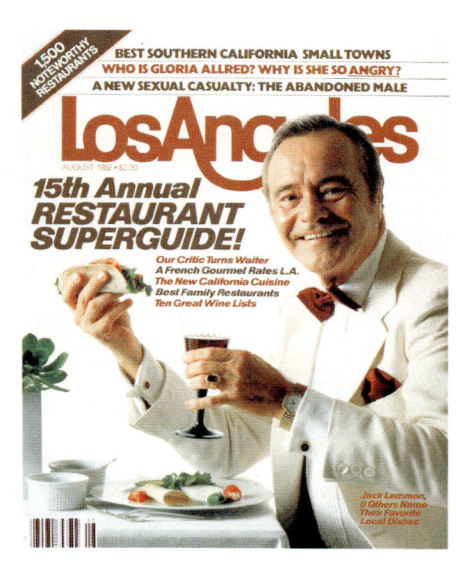

## STRATEGIZING, PHILOSOPHIZING AND OTHER WAYS A CREATIVE DIRECTOR CAN AVOID WORK

Certain things stick. I remember a particular creative director who was absolutely spellbinding when it came to talking about the work. He talked a great ad. He'd even learned how to be conversant in "initialese" and "marketing-speak" (M.B.A.'s loved him). The only problem was the work. It stunk.

When I think of that creative director, I also think of another, a different breed, who, a few years back, gave me some simple advice, "Your philosophy is shown in your work, not your words." (I have, perhaps, made his quote more colorful than it was. Nonetheless, that is the essence of what he said.)

I have tried to always remember that.

It is easy, and certainly tempting, for a creative director to become a marketing/positioning/strategizing/philosophizing junkie. Especially when one considers that advertising is not immune to the "publish or perish" aspect of academia. And that creative directors, like account people and product managers, are sometimes judged on their ability to intellectualize about the work. This may be due to the fact that priorities have occasionally gotten confused in the past few years. Strategy, for instance, has too often become an end product in and of itself, completely independent from the work that will supposedly spring from it.

Naturally, I'm not saying the intellectual part isn't important. Or that it isn't stimulating. Or that it won't make management feel good. Or that it won't make you feel good. I'm saying if you let it, it can get in the way of doing good work.

Philosophizing about doing good work is its own drug. If you're not careful, your head and the heads of all those around you can become so filled with your pontifications that there isn't room for even the smallest idea to hatch.

On the other hand, discovering a good idea, as opposed to writing, talking, or thinking about that idea, remains similar to being able to cut back against the grain and break for the 80-yard touchdown.

You either got it, or you ain't.

If you are a creative director, then chances are you have it.

But the more you burden yourself and others with philosophical pronouncements, the less chance any of you will have of using "it" to break for the long yardage.

The great joy of our business is the work. It is tangible. People can put their hands on it and be affected by it.

Conversely, talking about how to do good work, is sort of like a cool wind on a hot day: it feels great when it's passing through, but once it's gone, you're still left sitting right where you were, all in a sweat.

Therefore, I will write no more on this subject—it's already put me way behind in my work.

**Robert Black**
**Senior Vice-President**
**Group Creative Director**
**Foote, Cone, Belding/Honig**
**San Francisco**

**MARK GOTTLIEB**
378 Cambridge Avenue
Palo Alto, California 94306
(415) 321-8761

Advertising, industrial and corporate photography. Studio and location.

Clients include: Intel, Searle Ultrasound, Zilog, Raychem, Fairchild Instrument, Varian, Hewlett-Packard, National Semiconductor, Intersil Systems, Measurex, Bank of America, Crocker Bank, *Inc. Magazine,* Cromemco, Osborne Computer, Versatec, Onyx Systems, Monoclonal Antibodies, Rolm Corp., Ekoline, Atari, Micronix, AMI.

Member ASMP

© 1982, 1983 Mark Gottlieb

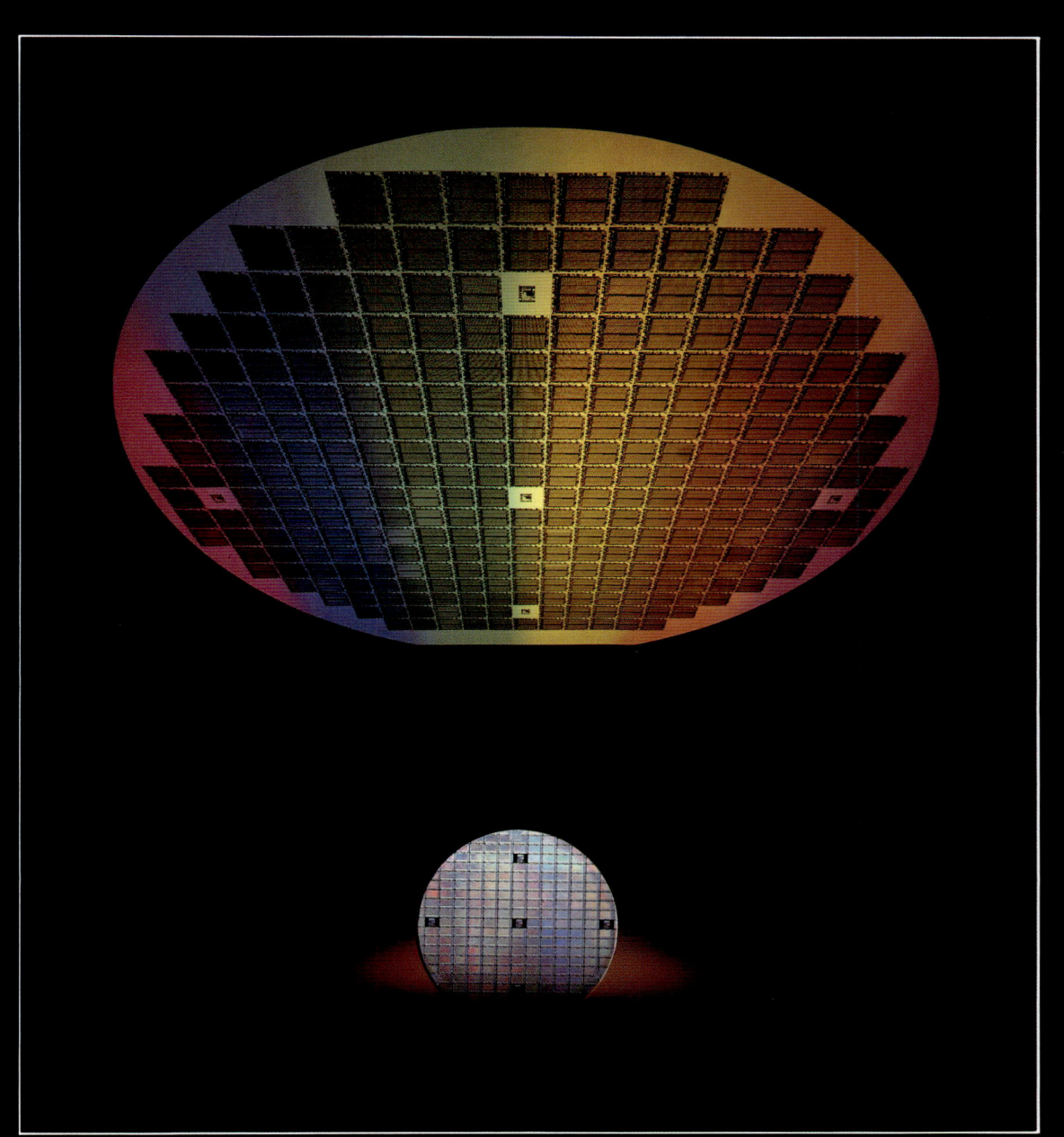

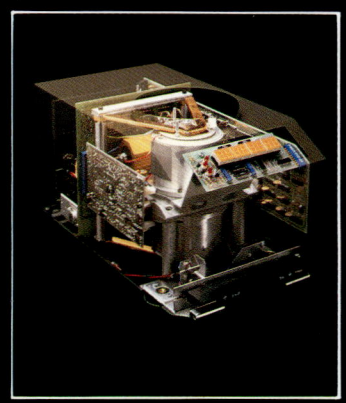

INTEL CORPORATION

ARBOR LABS

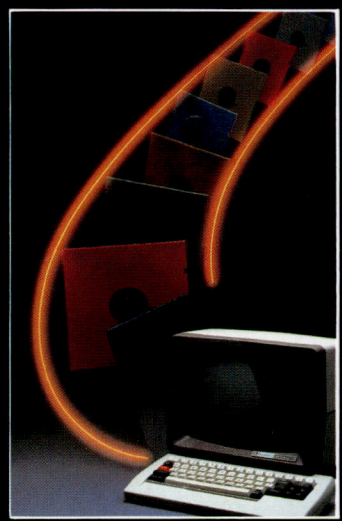

CROMEMCO

BR COMMUNICATIONS

**MARSHALL HARRINGTON**
2775 Kurtz Street, Suite 2
San Diego, California 92110
(619) 291-2775

Photographic image-making
that solves problems.
For advertising, editorial,
and corporate
communications.

© Copyright by
Marshall Harrington, 1984.
All rights reserved.

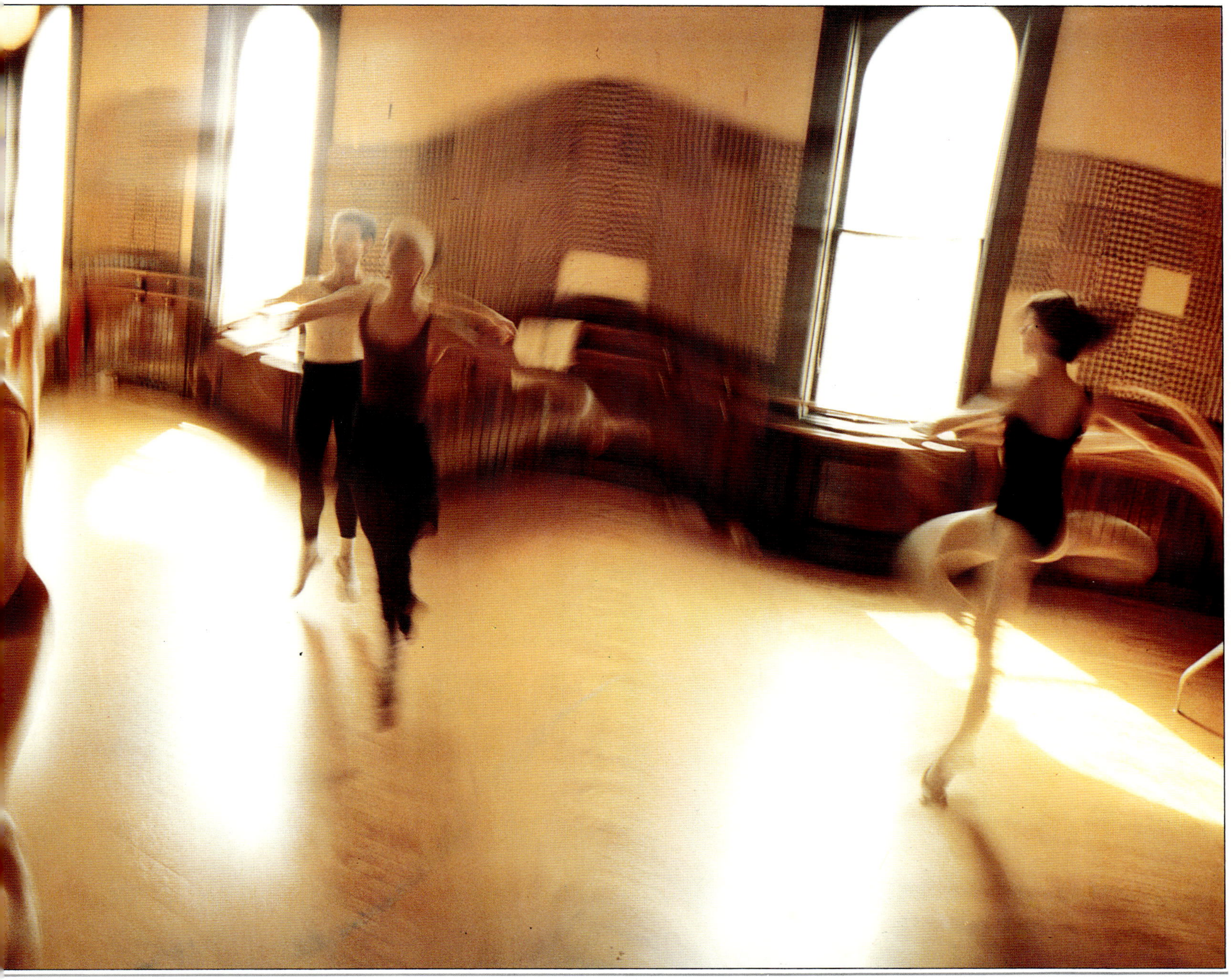

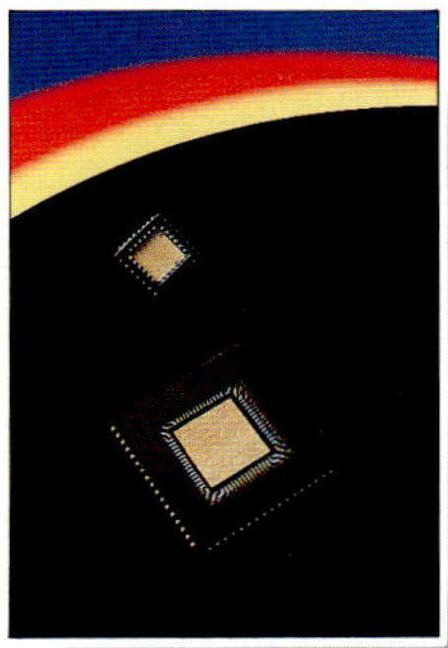

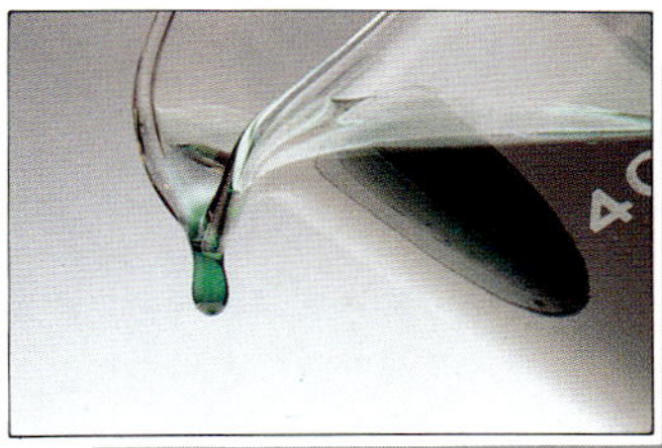

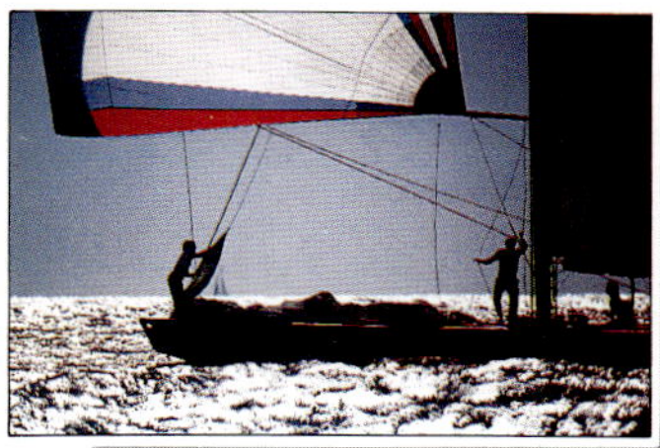

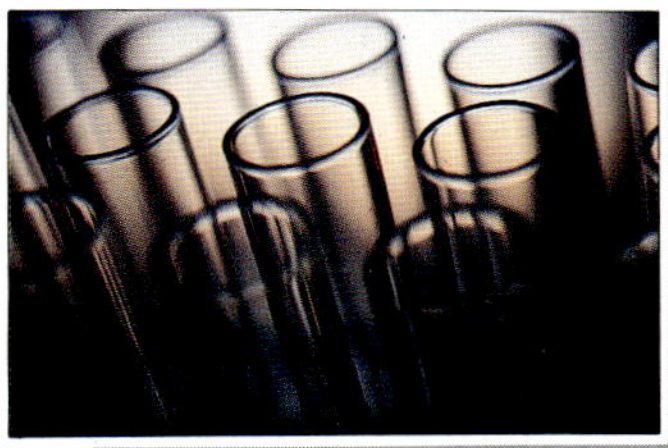

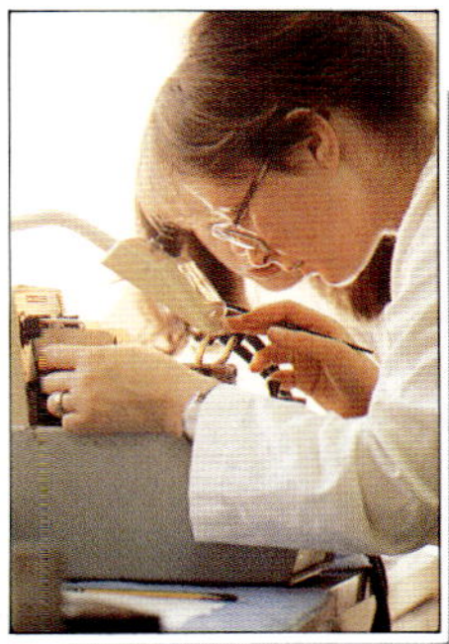

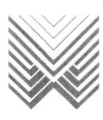

**LARRY KEENAN**
421 Bryant Street
San Francisco, California 94107
(415) 495-6474

Advertising, annual reports, corporate/industrial, travel, conceptual and special effects photography. International experience, numerous awards. Stock photography library. Member: APA.

Clients: Apple, Bank of America, Blue Cross, Clorox, Coherent, Crocker Bank, Electronic Arts, Genentech, General Instruments, Hewlett-Packard, Kaiser Foundation, Levi Strauss, Lorimar Productions, Pacific Telephone, Saga Corporation, Syntex Labs, Tandem Computers, Transamerica, Triad Systems, Xidex Corporation.

Publicité, Rapports annuels, Commercial/Industriel, Reportages, Abstrait/Effets spéciaux, Une expérience internationale, Nombreux prix reçus, Photothèque très complète, Membre APA.

Fotografe für Werbung, Jahresberichte, Reise und Tourismus, Wirtschaft und Industrie. Konzeption und Special Effects Fotografie. Foto Archiev. Internationale Erfahrung, Mitglied: APA.

宣伝広告，決算報告書，会社案内書，観光案内，特殊撮影等最も効果的なイメージにてご希望に応じます。世界各国での仕事経験あります。フィルムライブラリー有ります。ニューヨーク国際広告賞他多数受賞致しました。ASMP会員。

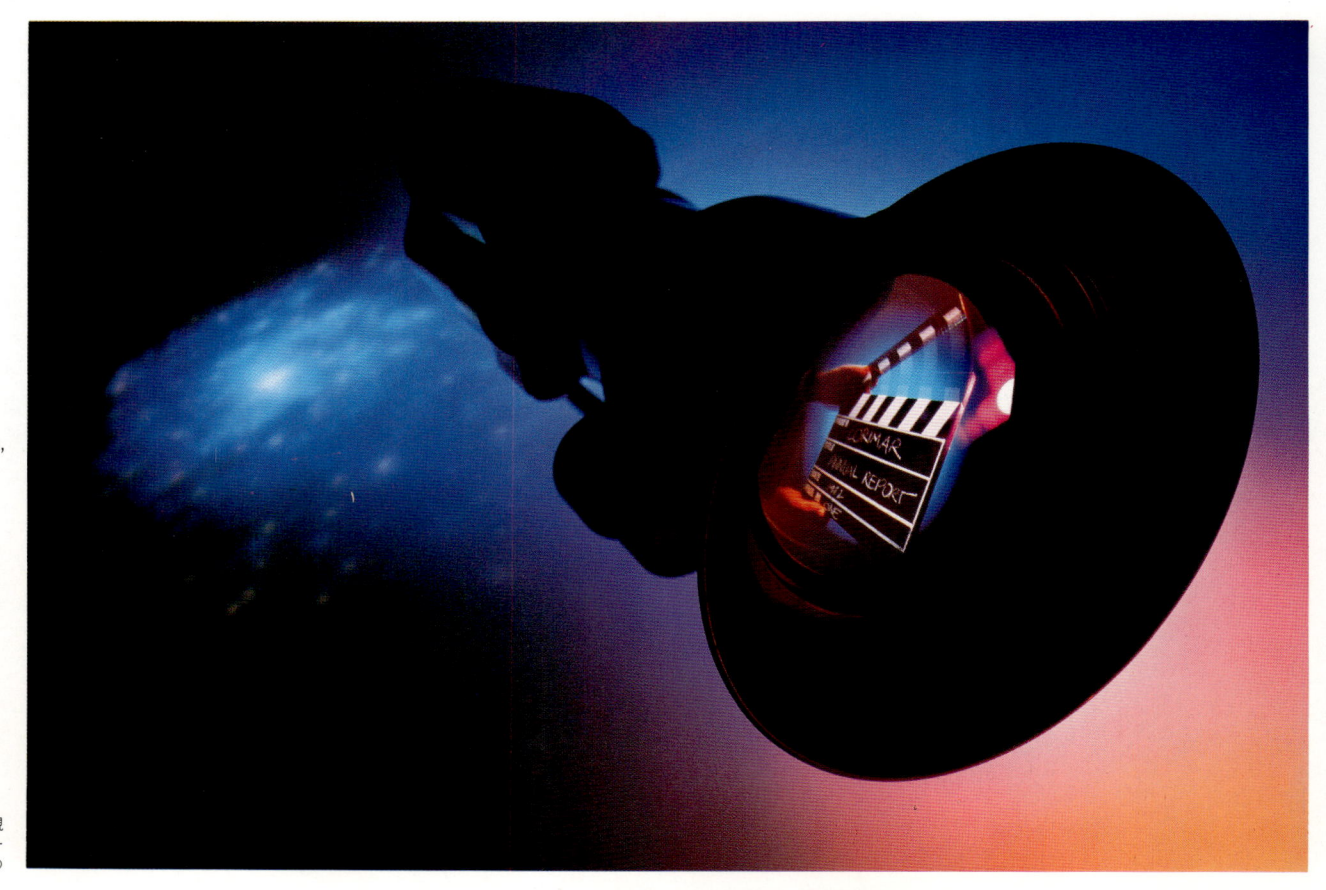

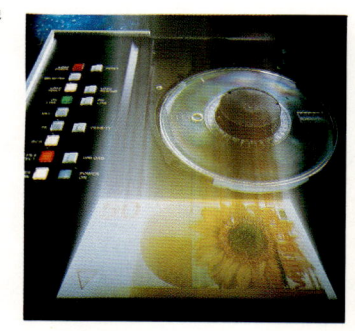

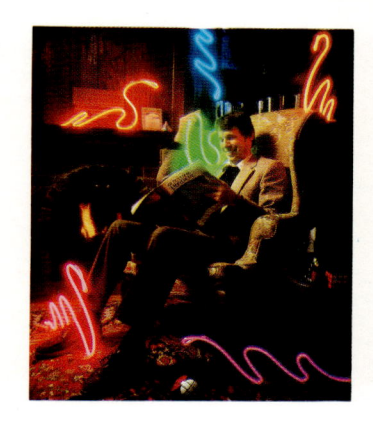

**LARRY LEE**
Post Office Box 4688
North Hollywood, California 91607
(818) 766-2677
   (24 Hour Recorder)
(805) 259-1226
   (Studio and Home)

Industrial photography specializing in petroleum, energy and environmental subjects. Sharing travel expenses among many clients keeps national and international assignment costs to a minimum. Stock photos available. Portfolio by mail on request.

**JOHN LIVZEY**
1510 North Las Palmas Avenue
Hollywood, California 90028
(213) 469-2992

Worldwide assignment, stock & corporate photography.

Stock representation:

Pacific Press Service
Tokyo, Japan
(03) 264-3821

After-Image
Los Angeles, California
(213) 467-6033

Client list: AT&T, CBS Records International, Oberheim Electronics, Warner Brothers Records, Saul Bass/Herb Yager & Associates, Fluor Corporation, Norwegian Caribbean Lines

372

**JOHN LIVZEY**
1510 North Las Palmas Avenue
Hollywood, California 90028
(213) 469-2992

Worldwide assignment, stock & corporate photography.

Stock representation:

Pacific Press Service
Tokyo, Japan
(03) 264-3821

After-Image
Los Angeles, California
(213) 467-6033

Client list: AT&T, CBS Records International, Oberheim Electronics, Warner Brothers Records, Saul Bass/Herb Yager & Associates, Fluor Corporation, Norwegian Caribbean Lines

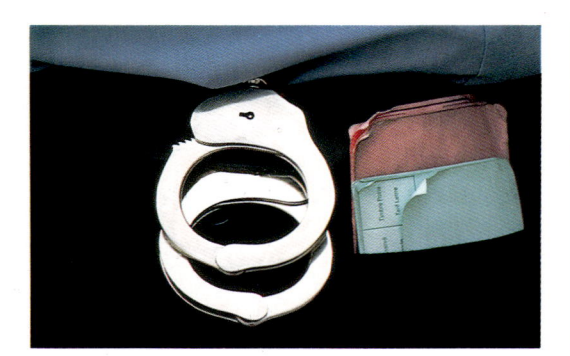

373

## HOW TO AVOID DOING BAD ADVERTISING

Some of the perks you get after you've been around long enough include invitations to speak at some fairly exotic places. The International Creative Conference at Ibiza, Spain was one I found impossible to turn down. Even if it did conflict with the 4A's convention at the Greenbrier.

Ed McCabe had represented the U.S. the previous year. I phoned him to find out some details—and what some of the problems of addressing a non-English-speaking audience might be. In irrepressible McCabe style he said, "Do 10 minutes, ask if there are any questions and go to Majorca for the weekend."

Naturally when I arrived and was given the program I quickly noticed I had been slotted for two hours. Stretching 10 minutes of notes into a two-hour segment was achieved only because of the length of the Spanish translation.

I had asked for a subject to talk about. It's always easier to put a speech together after they've told you what the audience might be interested in hearing. In this case my instructions were simple. "Tell them how you do your work." Have you ever tried to actually figure out how you work? Not an easy task. But from it came the actual title of my talk, "How to Avoid Doing Bad Advertising."

With apologies to David Ogilvy, here are the Chiat/Day rules:

1. Realize early that your agency cannot work for everyone.

2. Recognize there are no shortcuts. It's hard work to do great advertising.

3. Hire only those you believe can do the job better than you can. It not only makes the work brighter, it makes you work brighter.

4. Fire quickly and decisively those who do not measure up. They contaminate the agency by making good people question their judgment.

5. Recognize that all your people have creative capabilities and demand creativity from all departments.

6. Make sure your account-management people are smart marketers. It takes brilliant marketing support to quiet client nervousness.

7. Never stop at the first creative solution. Explore alternatives.

8. Dig for the facts. Interview relentlessly. Your research must be unquestioned.

9. Know your target better than you know yourself.

10. Make sure there is a clear, concise creative brief written for every ad. Yes, every ad.

11. Treat all advertising equal. The trade is as important as the TV commercial. Perhaps more so.

12. Do not permit closet accounts. If the work is not good enough to show new-business prospects, the account is not good enough to keep.

13. Spend time training. Do not assume that people automatically understand what is expected of them.

14. Promote from within when possible. But do not hesitate to seek expertise elsewhere if it is lacking at the agency.

15. Treat everyone with the same level of dignity you expect yourself.

16. Perhaps most important, try to relax and have some fun.

**Jay Chiat**
**President**
**Chiat/Day, Inc.**
**New York City**

Reprinted from
ADWEEK JUNE 20, 1983

**ED MASTERSON**
11211 Sorrento Valley Road
Suite S
San Diego, California
(619) 457-3251

Creative photography in studio or location.

Partial clients list: U.S. Navy, Ralston Purina, Vector Automotive, Holiday Inns, Jantzen, Jeans West, G.E., 3-M, Premex, Dunfey Hotels, Cipher Data, Handyman, Imperial Aire.

©COPYRIGHT '83 ED MASTERSON.

**MCALLISTER OF DENVER**
701 Marion Street
Denver, Colorado 80218

Bruce McAllister
(303) 832-7496

East Coast Representatives
Deborah Wolfe
(215) 928-0918

Gamma Liaison, New York (editorial assignments)
(212) 888-7278

Partial Client List:
ARCO, Getty Oil, IBM, 3M, St. Regis Paper, Texas Gulf, Chevrolet Motor Division, Price Waterhouse, B J Hughes Tool Company, Texaco, Shell Oil, Marathon Oil, *Forbes, People, Business Week.*

Special Equipment & Capabilities

Owner/operator Cessna T210 Aircraft for short notice/remote location assignments. Full complement of 35mm equipment for magazine work, Pentax 6X7, Sinar 4X5, Toyo/Grandagon 8X10 for high resolution specifications, Dynalite 2002 heavy strobes and Honda Generator for location work.

376

**MCALLISTER OF DENVER**
701 Marion Street
Denver, Colorado 80218

Bruce McAllister
(303) 832-7496

Member ASMP since 1963

East Coast Representatives
Deborah Wolfe
(215) 928-0918

Gamma Liaison, New York (editorial assignments)
(212) 888-7278

A craftsman serving sophisticated and demanding clients must also capture moods and fleeting nuances that transform photographic images into profound statements.

Bruce McAllister of Denver creates these statements for some of America's largest corporations' annual reports and magazines.

While McAllister is based in the Rockies, his assignments span the globe. Recently his work has taken him to Alaska's North Slope oil exploration activities in mid-winter, corporate recognition events in Phoenix and Miami, an 80 kilometer survival trek on snowshoes in Canyonlands, Utah with the US Olympic Volleyball Team, and corporate magazine assignments in Indonesia, Singapore, Thailand, and Japan.

While his assignments vary, his work has one common denominator: artistic sensitivity and careful attention to the many technical details that separate a powerful creative statement from an everyday photographic image.

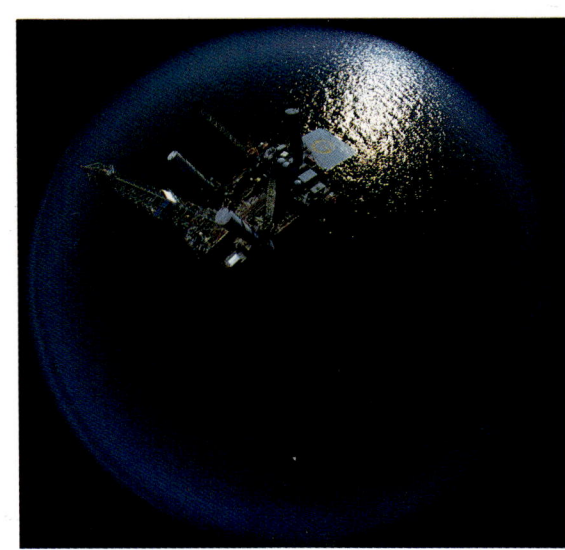

**MELGAR PHOTOGRAPHERS, INC.**
2971 Corvin Drive
Santa Clara, California 95051
(408) 733-4500

Advertising
Commercial
Industrial
Photo-Micrography

Melgar Photographers, Inc., specialists in the field of photomicrography and high-tech studio photography, have been serving our clients for nearly forty years.

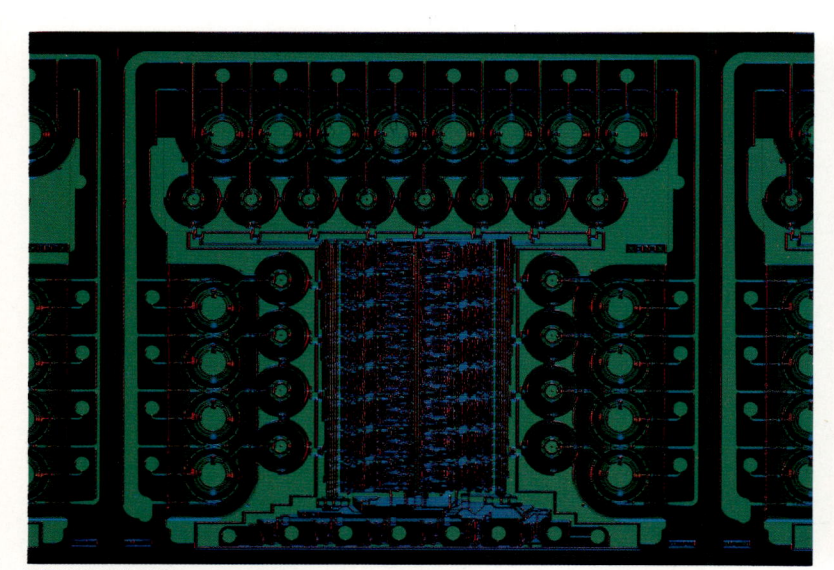

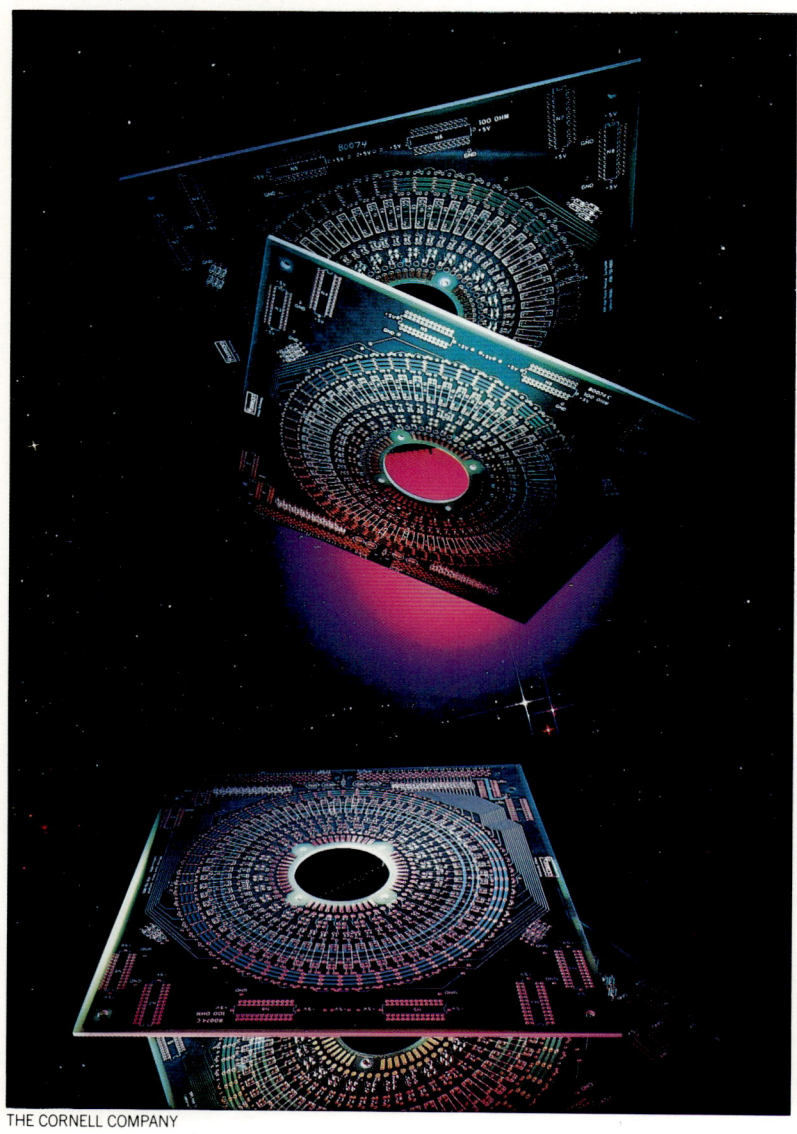

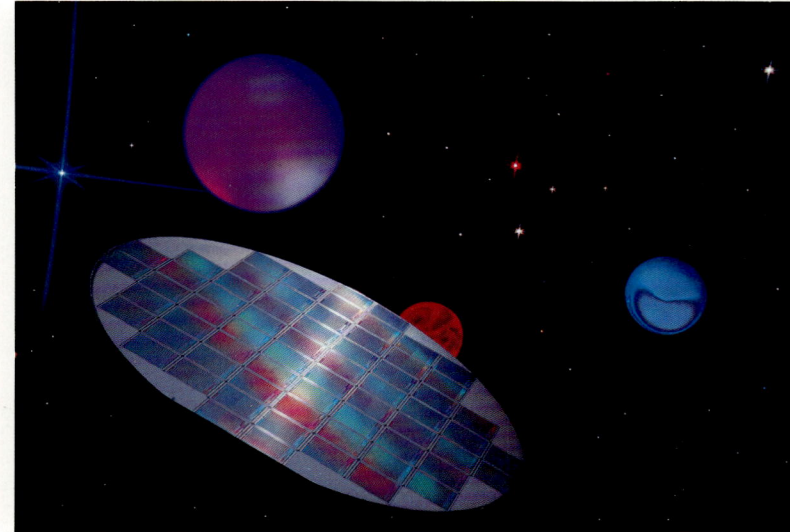

XEROX CORPORATION

LSI LOGIC

THE CORNELL COMPANY

DIME AT 10X

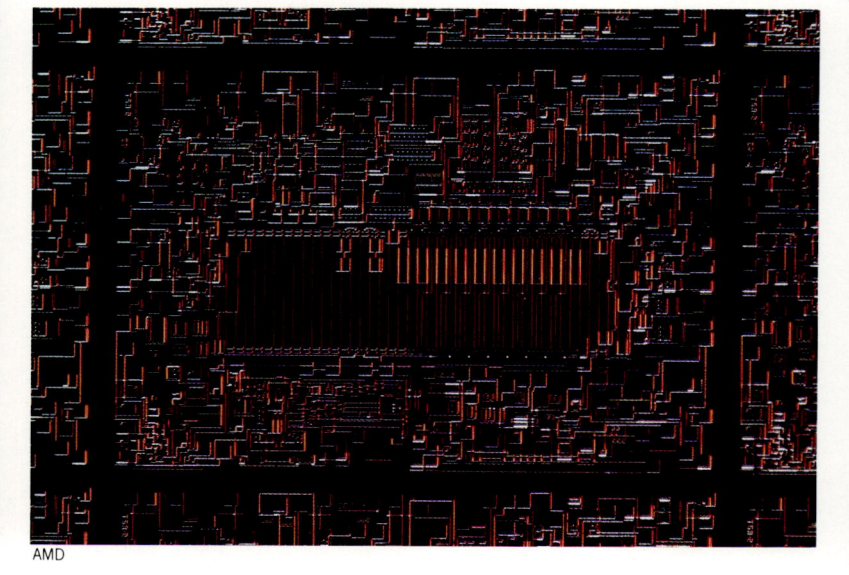

AMD

**CLARK MISHLER**
1238 G Street
Anchorage, Alaska 99501
(907) 279-8847

Annual Reports, Corporate, Industrial, Travel and Editorial Photography.

Member ASMP

Clients/Published Photographs have included: *Alaska Magazine,* The Alaska Railroad, Alyeska Pipeline Service Company, Atlantic Richfield Company, British Petroleum, *Communication Arts Magazine,* NANA/Caminco-Alaska, *National Geographic Magazine,* National Geographic *World* Magazine, Sealand Industries, SOHIO, State of Alaska Division of Tourism, Tesoro Alaska, Wien Air Alaska.

Stock: Aperture PhotoBank
(206) 282-8116

Alaska!

**ROLAND PERCEY**
626 North Hoover Street
Los Angeles, California 90004
(213) 660-7305

380

ADVERTISING, INDUSTRIAL, EDITORIAL work shot in our spacious studio which includes professional black and white processing/finishing facilities and a designer quality kitchen. Strawberries or computers. People or high tech. CORPORATE work on location. Distinctive and dynamic.

A partial list of our clients: Ampereff Computers, Armstrong Floors, Arthur Young & Co., Frito-Lay, Mattel Toys, Maybelline Cosmetics, Pioneer Take-Out Corp., Roberts Consolidated/Weldwood Products.

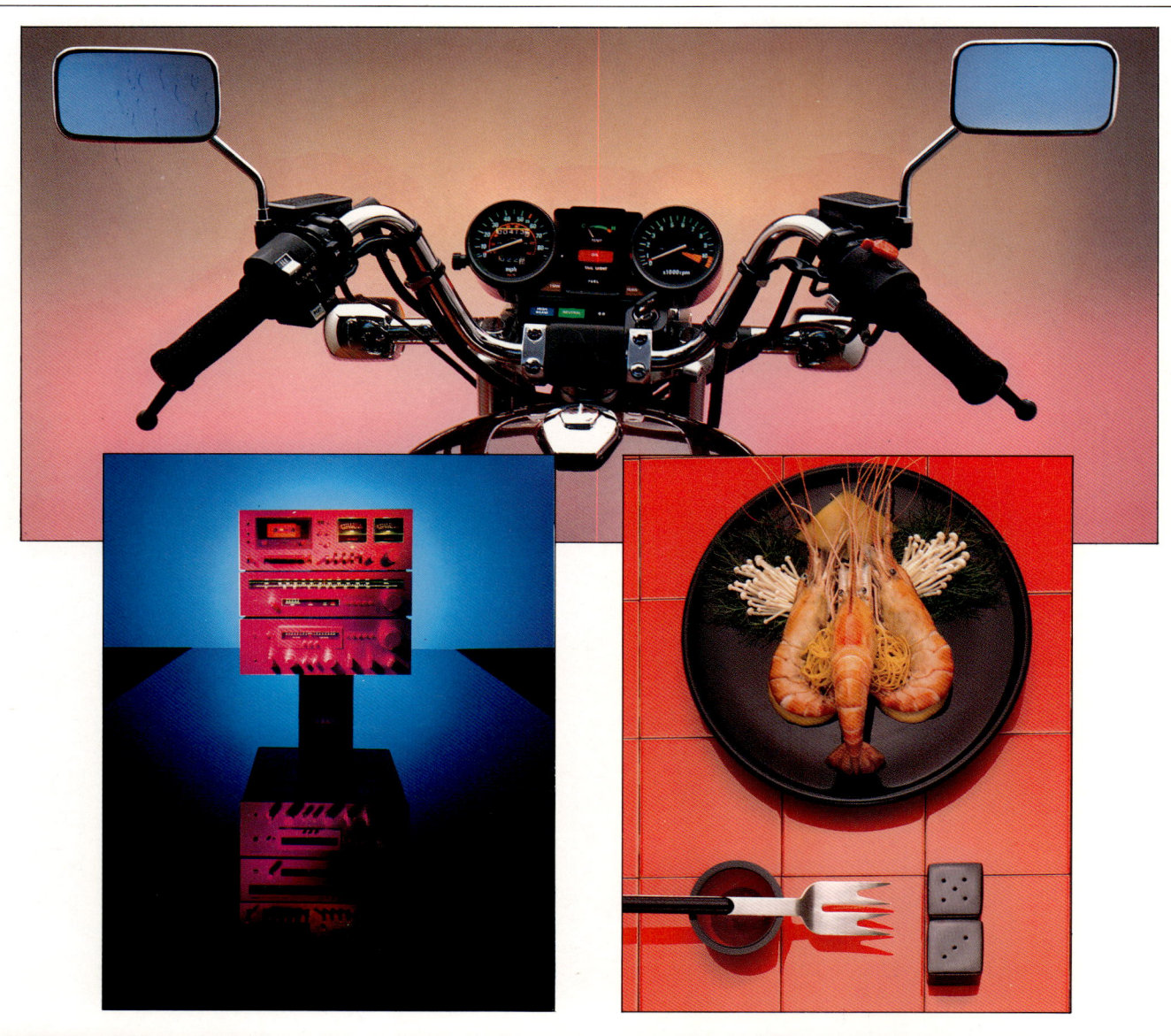

**PAUL PEREGRINE**
Peregrine Studios
1541 Platte Street
Denver, Colorado 80202
(303) 455-6944

381

Advertising and still life photographic productions large and small, on location or in the studio, because a picture is worth...well you know.

Member ASMP

Samples shown are unretouched photographs.

Clients include: Pentax, Samsonite, Quaker Oats, Coors, Phillip Morris, Water-Pik, Mountain Bell, ARCO, Conoco, AMAX, Marker Bindings, Technica, Donnay, Norwegian Ski Council, Celestial Seasonings, Manville Corporation, Honeywell, Bayly Corporation, Hewlett-Packard, Wilfley Corporation, A.O. Smith, W.P. Carey, Mr. Steak Restaurants, Zimmer U.S.A., Aspen Labs, Cederroth, Computer Dialysis Systems, Hemotech, Cobe Laboratories, Tomahawk Oil, Gill Industries, United Banks of Colorado, Colorado National Banks, Foto-Tek, Woolrich, Timberland Shoes, Kenneth Gordon, Stream Designs, Forrest Mountaineering, United Cable, Colorado Lottery, U.S. Meat Council, Lowrey's Beef Jerky, Stephanies Candies, 1984 Olympics.

© 1983 Peregrine Studios

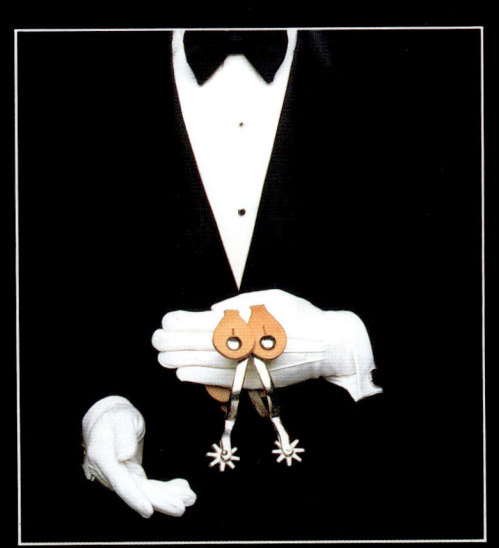

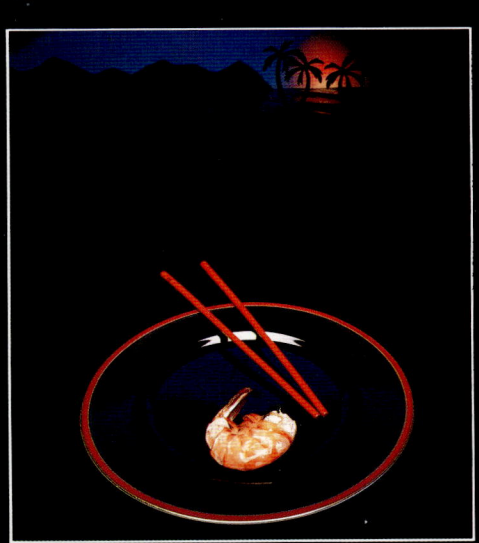

**DAVID PERRY**
4006 California Avenue Southwest
P.O. Box 4165
Seattle, Washington 98104
(206) 932-6614

Special awareness of:
Dramatic natural light.
Interpretations and point of view.
Health care marketing.

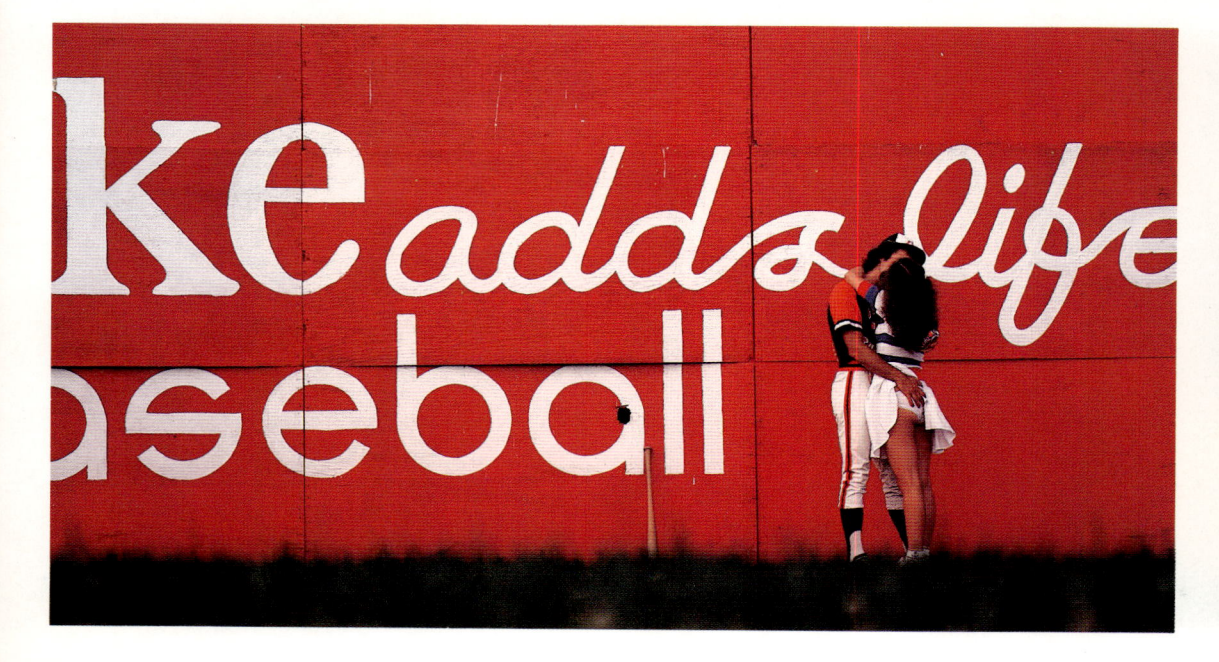

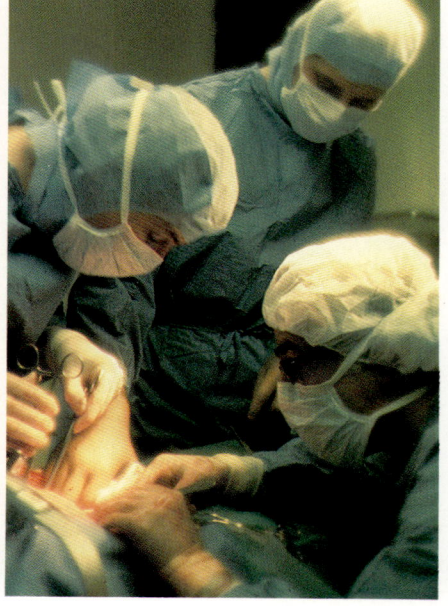

DAVID PERRY
PHOTOGRAPHER

382

**PHOTOGRAPHIC COMMUNICATIONS**
3400-R De La Cruz Boulevard
Santa Clara, California 95050
(408) 727-2233

Represented by Tim Tabke
(408) 727-2348

Our 3600 square foot studio includes three shooting areas with complete set construction capabilities. Our five member staff has the capability of fabricating large studio sets, complex location sets and tabletop sets, including any necessary propping, styling or casting.

As "high tech" specialists, we have developed a range of styles from classic clean shots to exotic, complex special techniques. Our special effects work is designed for single chrome delivery by way of multiple camera techniques or optical printing/cel animation. Thus the need for time consuming and costly airbrushing or stripping is eliminated.

We have our own in-house lab and can turn-around E-6 chromes in one hour to meet last minute deadlines. Our portfolio is available upon request.

All photos are copyrighted 1983 by Photographic Communications.

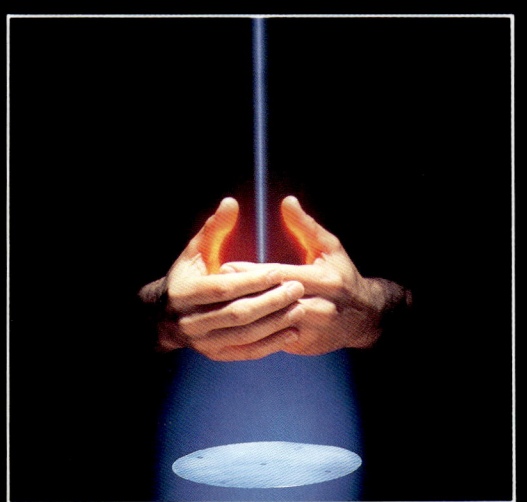

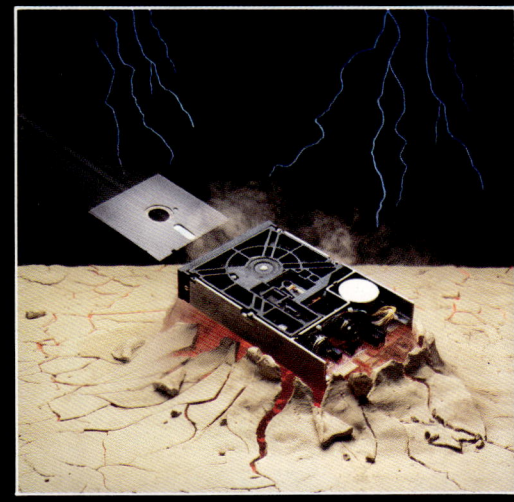

**ROGER RESSMEYER, INC.
STARLIGHT PHOTO AGENCY**
1230 Grant Avenue #574
San Francisco, California 94133
(415) 921-1675

Location and studio photography for advertising, corporate/industrial, and editorial.

Specialties: Celebrities, people, high technology, aerospace, astronomy, special effects.

Clients: *Time, Newsweek, Science Digest, Fortune, Money, Discover, New York Times Magazine, People,* Bantam Books, Dell Publishing, RCA, CBS, Androbot Inc., Catalyst Technologies.

© 1981-1984, Roger Ressmeyer—Starlight

HOME ROBOTS

SHIRLEY MACLAINE

SPACE SHUTTLE COLUMBIA

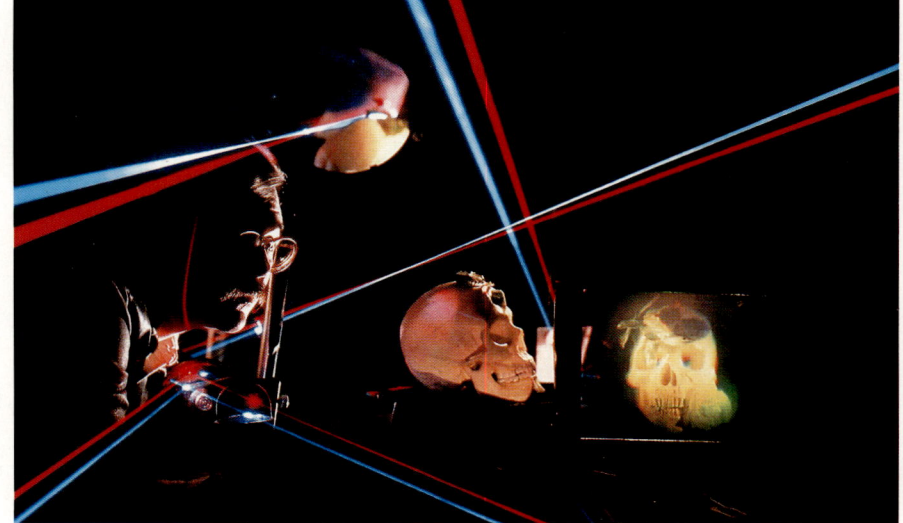

WHITE LIGHT TRANSMISSION HOLOGRAPHY

LINUS PAULING

**ROGER RESSMEYER ★ INC.**

**JIM SADLON
LIGHT LANGUAGE**
352 Sixth Street
San Francisco, California 94103
(415) 626-1900

# MICHAEL SCHOENFELD

Utah:
Design Center
734 West 800 South
Salt Lake City, Utah 84104
(801) 532-6174

Advertising and Corporate Photography

Some of my clients last year included ABC, Abbott Laboratories, American Arms, Barnes Ammunition, Baker Mining International, Bonneville International, Coca-Cola, DeLorean, Denver Post, McNeil Mehew Group, Mormon Church, Snowbird Resort, Surety Life, Utah Arts Council, Utah Shakespearean Festival.

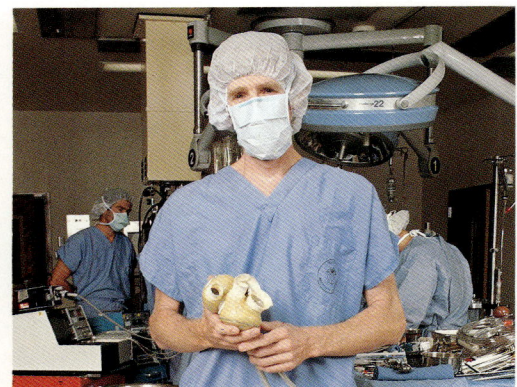

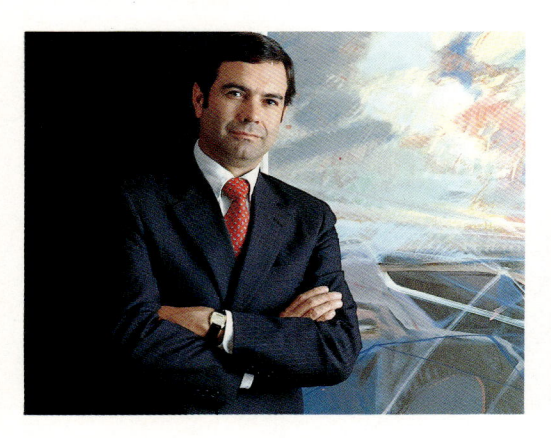

**CHARLES J. SMITH PHOTOGRAPHY**
7163 Construction Court
San Diego, California 92121
(619) 271-6525

Ajax, Corda Diversified, California First Bank, Carver Tripp, Calbiochem-Behring, Cobra Golf, Datagraphix, Digidyne, Digiorgio Corp., Ektelon, Fenwick, Hilton, Hybritech, Hydro Curve, Ivac, KCBQ, KCST, Koll Company, Kyocera, Kunnan, La Jolla Bank, Microtech, Olympian, Paradyne, Pacific Southwest Airlines, Rancho Santa Fe National Bank, San Diego Symphony, Sandoz, The Signal Companies, Speedo, Super Set, Topaz, TRW, Trade Services, Underwater Kinetics, Vacuum General, Wavetek.

© 1983 Charles J. Smith Photography
All effects created by Charles J. Smith

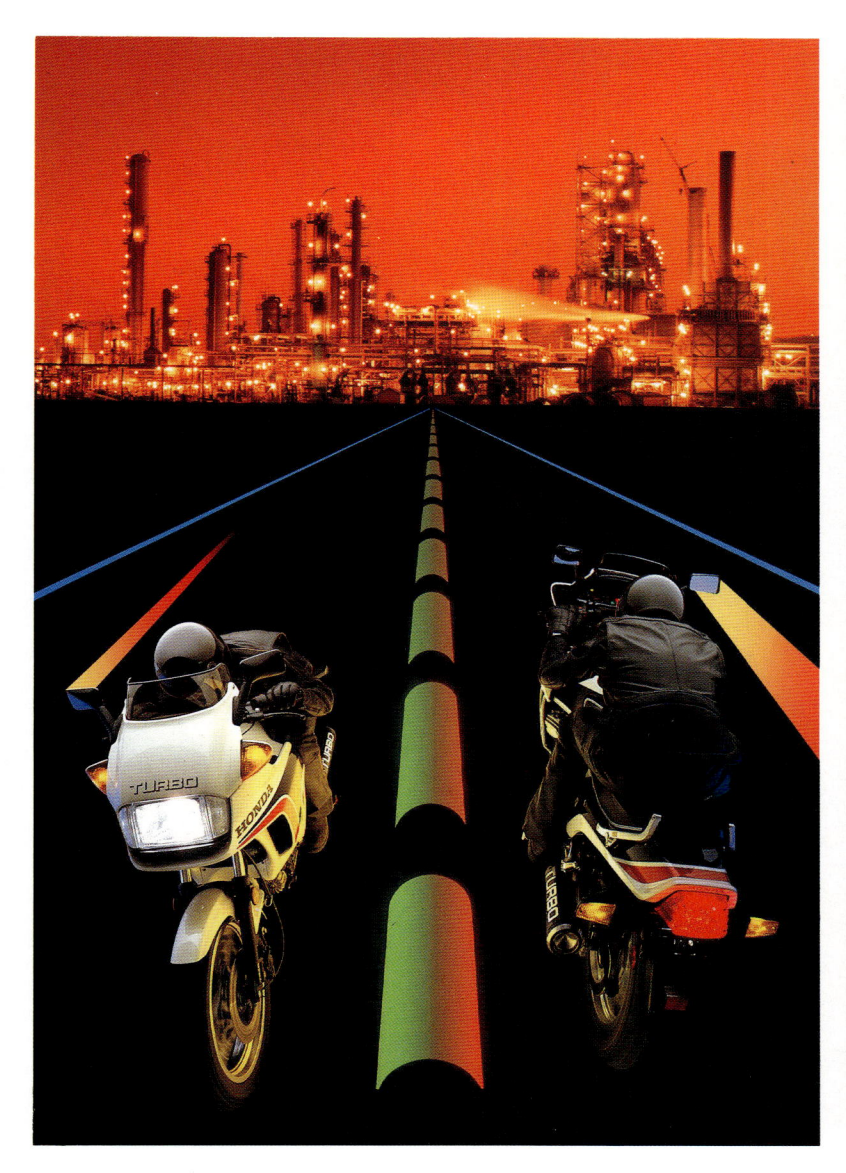

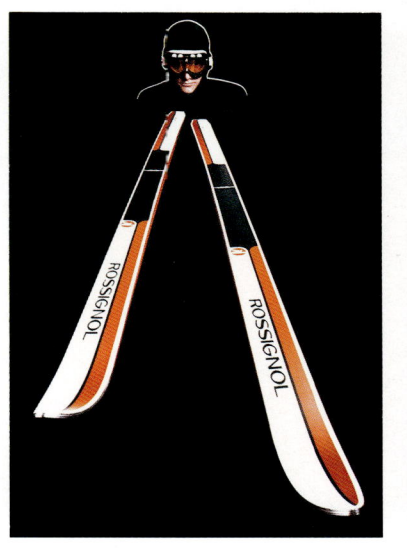

387

**MARC SOLOMON**
Post Office Box 480574
Los Angeles, California 90048
(213) 935-1771

Creative solutions to your location problems. Advertising, Travel, Editorial, Industrial, Agricultural, Corporate.

Assignments have been completed and stock photography sold to: Addison Wesley; Alexander and Alexander; Amphoto; Amtrak; APCOA; Argo Petroleum; Bendix; Celanese; Connecticut Mutual; East/West Network; Fleetwood; Garret Air Research; GATX; Guest Informant; Holt, Rinehart and Winston; *Home Magazine; Money Magazine; NME;* Northrop University; Port of Los Angeles; Potlatch; Security Pacific Corporation; Signal Corporation; Southern California Edison; TRW; Wells Fargo Leasing; Westinghouse; Winnebago...

Portfolio sent upon request. Stock photography available direct or select images through The Image Bank.

388

389

## SILENCE, PLEASE

Dave stopped by to deliver his illustration for the upcoming issue of Legal Considerations in Dentistry, a publication with a title that speaks for itself.

As expected, Dave's keen sense of humor drills straight to the point of the articles.

He waited in the office while I circulated the art among editors and the account team, seeking approval. When I returned, I found him looking through an issue of American Showcase. He said he was considering buying a page in it, but wondered if it would really be worth it. They're sure getting big money for those pages.

He mentioned that he had just returned from New York, where he met with several publishers to review his book.

The telephone rang as he pulled out a new promotion piece to leave behind.

Oh yes, it was early Monday morning and this was the first of many calls to come from reps wanting to set appointments for the week.

Our creative department still does not have a secretary to spare us from the onslaught of calls. I told the caller I was still too busy to see anyone. Maybe in a couple of weeks. So, they call back in a week, and I tell them....

Hey, reps are fine. They're needed. I want to see them all—it's to my benefit. But, lately, the work load is mounting up. There's just no time.

I took another look at Dave's promotion piece, thanked him, and spun around to deposit it in the taboret.

Some art directors plaster their walls with posters. I used to. Now, I keep them in my taboret drawers. THREE AND A HALF DRAWERS FULL. And, still growing.

Now, I want you to know I always look forward, with great enthusiasm, to getting into those drawers, searching for the perfect executionist for my idea.

But, I also have a couple of shelves stacked high with back issues of American Showcase and other reference sources I will not go into at this writing.

When the pressure is on to get a client package out (why is it always under pressure?), you don't have a lot of time to find that sample photograph to send along with the layout. So, I look to the shelf first. For the book. It's a lot faster than going through those drawers.

And, when I think about it, the book is just nice because it doesn't call me every Monday or Tuesday...

Good job, Showcase.

Thanks for the moment of silence.

**Dudley Maddox**
**Art Director**
**Sieber & McIntyre, Inc.**
**Chicago, Illinois**

**BRUCE STEINBERG**
2128 18th Street
San Francisco, California 94107
(415) 864-0739

PUT IT WHERE YOU WANT IT

Some pictures are made, not born. An inaccessible freeway location needs an imaginary signpost. A base-stealing Rickey Henderson needs a new base path. A remote, vacant cabin needs a warm picture window with people in it.

Guitars gotta swim. Eggs gotta fly. And another day of livin' on the fault line goes by. But anything is possible if we team up and engineer your grand illusion right from the beginning.

Make just one call—to this troubleshooting designer/photographer who understands an A/D's problems firsthand.

One whose solid photo-illustrations routinely solve those problems (and show up in the CA Annual, the Art Annual, The One Show, the Print Casebooks and the Andys) because they *work*—conceived, shot and produced with a consistent technical and artistic overview from roughs through press check.

Let's move on up from reality together at the *start* of your next impossible dream. If you can imagine it, you can have it.

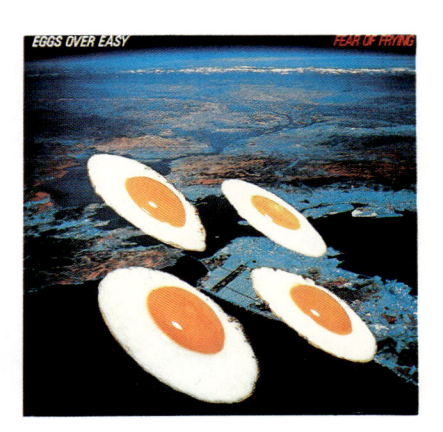

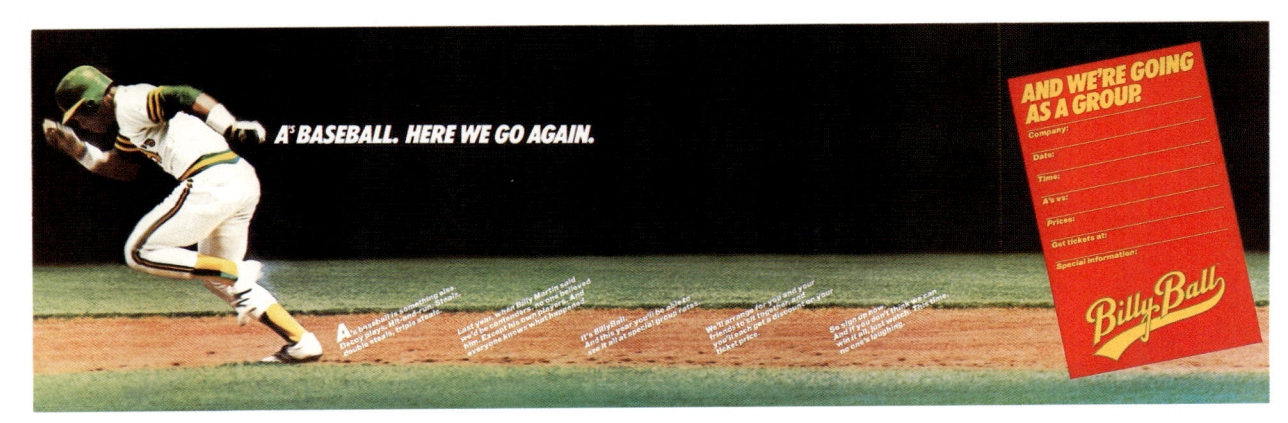

**WALTER SWARTHOUT**
Swarthout & Associates, Inc.
370 Fourth Street
San Francisco, California 94107
(415) 543-2525

Representative: Ron Sweet
(415) 433-1222

Still life; food; women.
Studio and location.

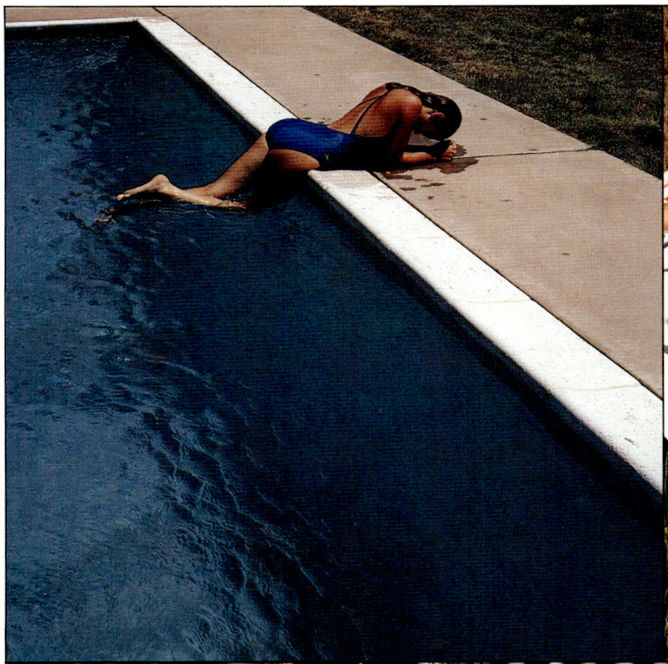

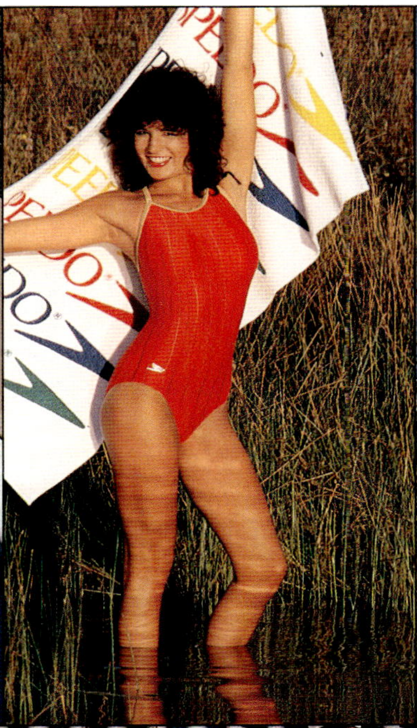

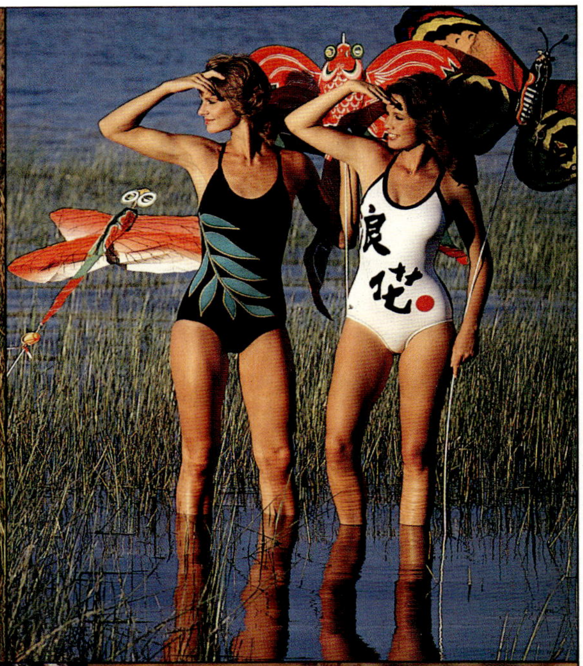
浪花

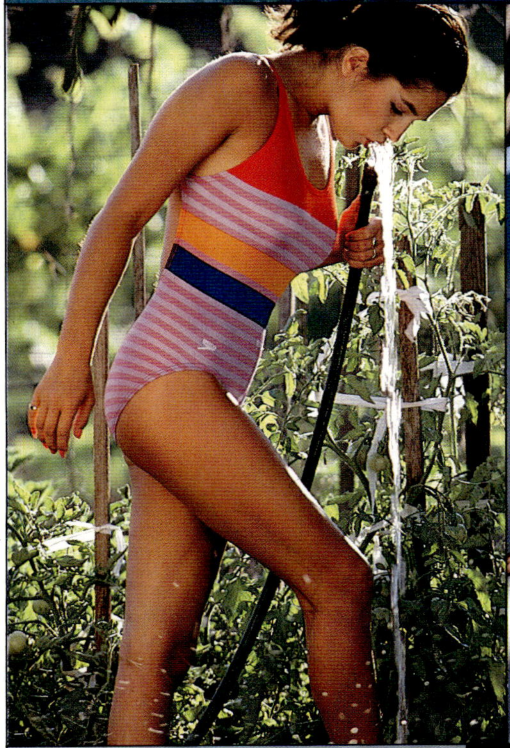

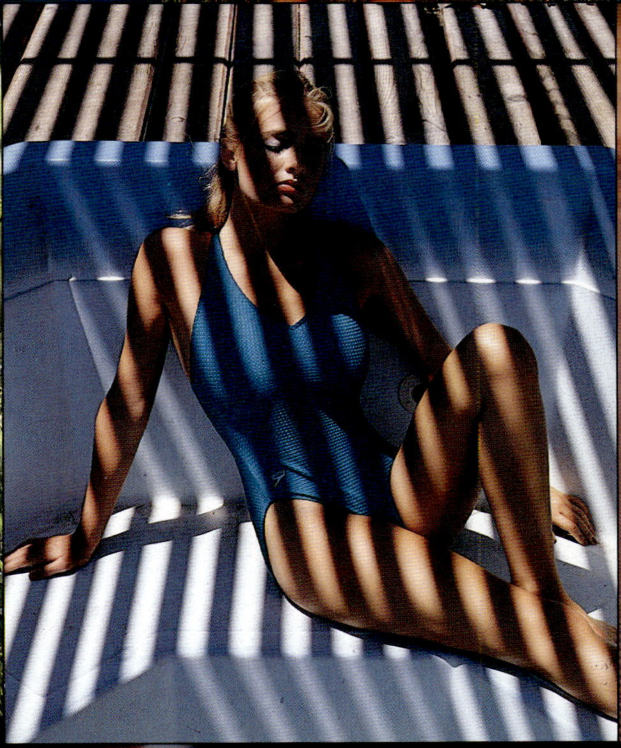

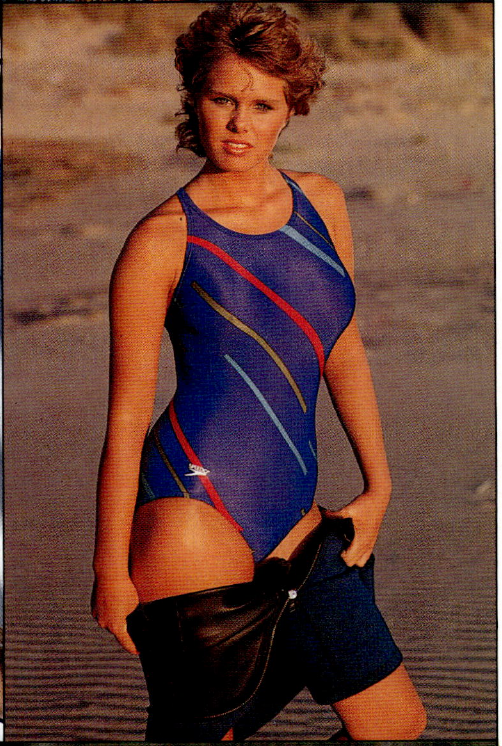

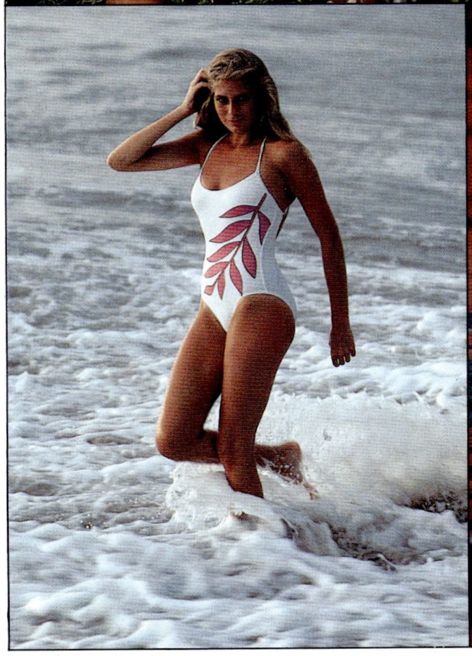

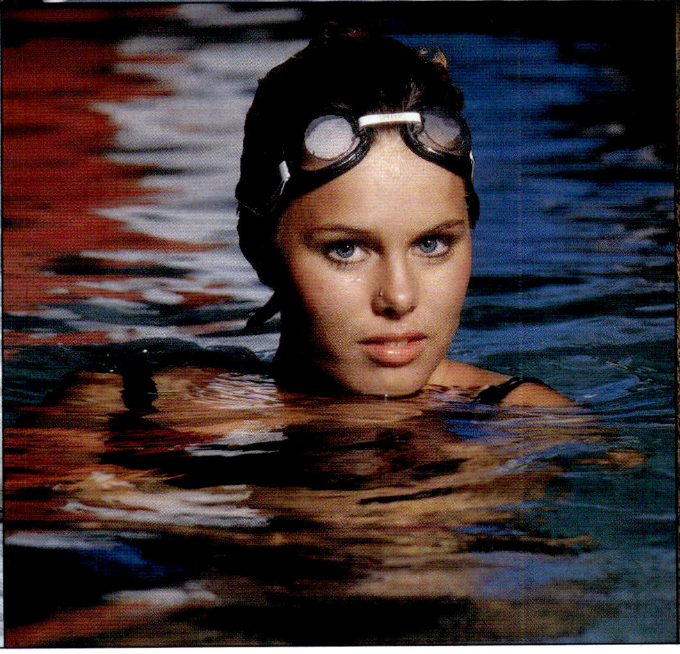

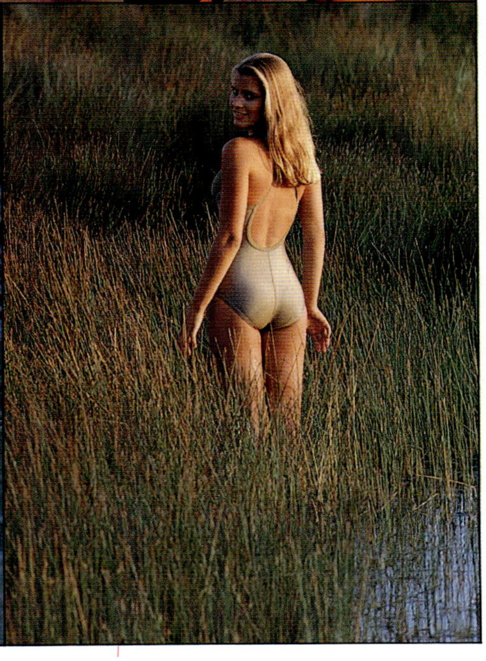

**JAMES B. WOOD PHOTOGRAPHY**

394

6315 Santa Monica Boulevard
Los Angeles, California 90038
(213) 461-3861

Represented in Chicago by:
Toni McNaughton
(312) 782-8586

Represented in Dallas/Atlanta/S.W.:
Liz McCann
(214) 742-3138

Represented in Japan by:
Yoko Tao
03-938-6089

Represented in Los Angeles by:
Joan Wood
(213) 463-7717

Represented in San Francisco by:
Ron Sweet
(415) 433-1222

APA

**ROBERT WORTHAM**
964 North Vermont Avenue
Los Angeles, California 90029
(213) 666-8899

I learn something new everyday in photography. Today I learned not to ask others' opinions of what to say on my Showcase page.

My mother said, "Tell them you're a real nice boy…"
My lady said, "Tell them you're a fox…"
My bookkeeper said, "Tell them to pay their bills…"
My assistant's suggestion was, "No barbell or anvil clients!"

Maybe I'll just leave the space blank.

Clients include: Gucci Watches, 7-Up Bottling Company, Ampex, Lanvin, Marcy Fitness, KTLA.

# AMERICAN SHOWCASE VOLUME 7

## THIS BOOK WAS PRINTED BOUND AND SEPARATED BY DAI NIPPON SINCE VOLUME 3

## DAI NIPPON PRINTING CO., LTD.

| | | |
|---|---|---|
| New York | International Sales Division | London |
| Dusseldorf | 1-12 Ichigaya Kagacho, Shinjuku-ku, | Sydney |
| Hong Kong | Tokyo, Japan Telephone: 03-266-3301 | Jakarta |
| San Francisco | Telex: J22737 DNPRINT TOKYO | Singapore |

| | |
|---|---|
| **Arnold, Peter** NYC | 398,399 |
| **Heilman, Grant** Lititz PA | 400 |
| **La Ferla, Sandro** NYC | 401 |
| **Long, James L.** Fort Lauderdale FL | 402 |
| **Southern Stock Photos** Miami | 403 |
| **Sports Illustrated Pictures** NYC | 404 |
| **Stock Imagery** Denver | 405 |
| **The Stock Market** Denver | 406 |

# PHOTO & PHOTO SERVICES

**PETER ARNOLD, INC.**
The International Photo Agency
1466 Broadway
New York, New York 10036
(212) 840-6928

Cable: Arnoldfoto, New York
Telex: Arnold 428281

The world at our feet as seen through the lens of Hans Pfletschinger's camera:

Stock photography of amphibians, insects and other invertebrates, reptiles, plants and nature studies

Life cycles, sequences and complete stories

All photographs on this page © Hans Pfletschinger

LADYBUG

HONEYBEE

EUROPEAN TOAD, CELL DIVISION

RINGED SNAKE

ORB SPIDER

PRAYING MANTIS

HORNET

DAMSELFLY

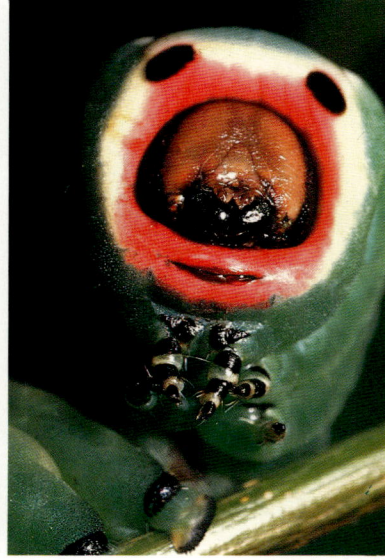

PUSS MOTH LARVA

**PETER ARNOLD, INC.**
The International Photo Agency
1466 Broadway
New York, New York 10036
(212) 840-6928

Cable: Arnoldfoto, New York
Telex: Arnold 428281

Stock Photography for the demanding art director:

Abstracts, Adventure, Family and Children, Industry, Nature and Wildlife, People, Photomicrography (Biomedical, Botany, Chemistry, Computer Science, Geology), Scanning Electron Micrography, Science and Technology, Special Effects, Sports, Surrealism, Travel and Foreign Cultures...

...in color and black and white — Call for a complete stock list.

© ERIKA STONE

© MALCOLM S. KIRK

© JOHN ZOINER

© JAMES H. KARALES

© Y. ARTHUS-BERTRAND

© LIONEL ATWILL

© MICHEL VIARD

© HANSON CARROLL

**GRANT HEILMAN PHOTOGRAPHY**
Box 317
Lititz, Pennsylvania 17543
(717) 626-0296

400

What's a stock photo agency doing in Lititz, Pennsylvania?

Plenty!

No city slickers here. Just a group of dedicated professionals going about the business of providing photographs that fulfill your creative concept and satisfy the technical requirements of your fussiest clients.

Whether you need agricultural images, scientific images or simply beautiful pictures, call the stock photo agency out in the country. We're always ready to go the extra mile for our clients.

Photos by Grant Heilman except where noted. Bread and pasta (Barry L. Runk); beef calf on Missouri pasture; barley field in Washington; harvesting grain in North Dakota's Red River Valley; sunflower field in Texas; sheep in Nevada corral (Linda Dufurrena) Kansas prairie.

Brochures available upon request.

© 1983 Grant Heilman Photography.

P.S. Lititz is on the map! It's a small town in northern Lancaster County, one of the richest agricultural areas of the nation.

**SANDRO LA FERLA BACKDROPS**
135 West 14th Street
New York, New York 10011
(212) 620-0693

Reproduce natural settings or depart from nature with painted backdrops: Choose from architecturally detailed interiors, vividly realistic outdoor scenes, romantic 'soft focus' effects and a variety of abstract, interpretative styles.

Suspend the setting sun over a Jamaican beach and bring it indoors for as many hours as your shoot demands. Backdrops free you from the limitations of ordinary time and distance.

Most important, aside from the practical advantage of substituting for locations, backdrops offer a new range of aesthetic choices when you are first planning your concept.

As easily rolled as seamless paper, drops are available in sizes from a standard 9' high x 12' wide, to a sweep 12' wide x 24' long, or according to your project's requirements.

Photo credits, clockwise from left: Jean Pagliuso, Barry Rosenthal, Bernard Vidal, Richard Blinkoff, Richard Blinkoff.

**JAMES L. LONG ASSOCIATES, INC.**
2631 East Oakland Park Boulevard
Suite 204
Fort Lauderdale, Florida 33306
(305) 563-8033

JAMES L. LONG ASSOCIATES, INC. is a stock photo agency which specializes in serving the aerospace community. Included in the assets of the Company are more than 100,000 frames from all fields in the industry. A staff of award-winning photographers are on call to handle any assignments.

Company credits include covers on *Newsweek, Aviation Week & Space Technology, Technology Illustrated, Microcomputing* and *Satellite Communications* magazines. Major photo essays have appeared in *Omni Magazine.*

Among our many clients are *Geo Magazine* (U.S., Germany and France), *Time, U.S. News & World Report, National Geographic* and *Stern*. Corporate work has included RCA, SBS, Rockwell, Martin Marietta and GTE.

Being specialists in the field gives the agency a greater understanding of the subject matter. This expertise extends to both the civilian and military sectors of the industry.

1ST SPACE SHUTTLE LAUNCH

MANUFACTURING OF ORBITER TILES

SHUTTLE MAIN ENGINE TEST

B-1 BOMBER

## SOUTHERN STOCK PHOTOS

6289 West Sunrise Boulevard
Suite 203
Sunrise, Florida 33313
Miami (305) 949-5191
Fort Lauderdale (305) 791-2772

We specialize in existing photography of the southeastern United States, the Sunbelt, Caribbean, underwater, southern lifestyles, family and romantic couples, sunsets, beaches, fishing, boating, outdoor sports and activities.

Our files also include exciting images from major cities throughout the United States, Asia, Europe, and the Middle East.

Southern Stock Photos represents over 100 of the nation's leading photographers. We can supply creative images for your next stock assignment need.

Contact us for further information.

403

© RICK BOSTICK 1982

© JIM PICKERELL 1983

© STEVEN LUCAS 1983

© EDWARD SLATER 1980

© WERNER BERTSCH 1983

© BARRY KINSELLA 1983

© TONY ARRUZA 1983

© WENDELL METZEN 1983

**SPORTS ILLUSTRATED PICTURES**
Sales Office–19th Floor
Time & Life Building
New York, New York 10020
(212) 841-3663
(212) 841-2803

The best sports photographers in the world shoot for SPORTS ILLUSTRATED. Maybe one of them has already captured just what you're looking for. We have a full range of shots for your editorial, advertising and related promotional needs. Give us a call.

404

**STOCK IMAGERY**
711 Kalamath
Denver, Colorado 80204
(303) 592-1091

Come journey through our files and experience
the Spectacular Rocky Mountain West.

The rugged face of the frontier—
dazzling heights and challenges,
the peace and serenity.

The West, a world in itself—
captured by the best western artists
available for your use
from our international collection.

**stock imagery™**

**stock imagery™** Experience the West as We See It
through the Eyes of the Frontier Spirit.

**THE STOCK MARKET**
740 South Emerson Street
Denver, Colorado 80209
(303) 698-1734

406

We have stock photos from around the world for corporate, editorial, and advertising clients. Our photographers are available for assignments also.

Photo credits (left to right): Bruce Benedict, James Cook, Keith Brofsky, Jeff Cook, Steve Ramsey, Rod Walker, David Goetze, Ron Coppock, Nicholas DeSciose.

Copyright 1983, The Stock Market

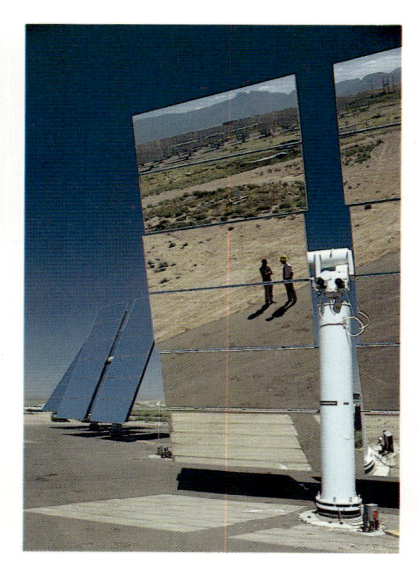

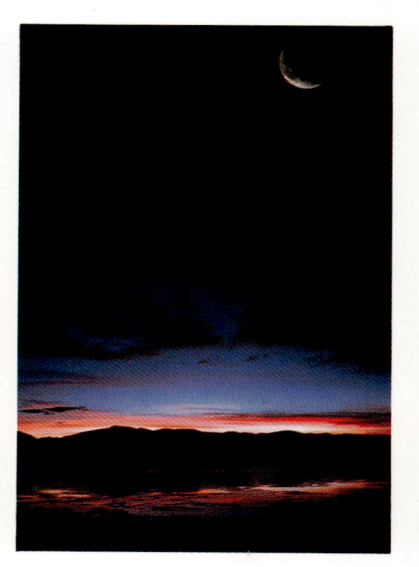

# INDEX

## A

| | |
|---|---|
| Abel, Wilton | 256 |
| Abraham, Russell | 344 |
| Alexander, Jules | 47 |
| Allen, Jim | 48 |
| Alt, Howard | 49 |
| Ambrose, Paul | 345 |
| Arnold, Peter | 398,399 |
| Aubry, Daniel | 38 |

## B

| | |
|---|---|
| brt Photographic Illustrations | 206,207 |
| Bagshaw, Cradoc | 317 |
| Baker, Joe | 50 |
| Baker, Kipp | 318 |
| Barley, Bill | 257 |
| Barrow, Scott | 51 |
| Bartone, Laurence | 33 |
| Bartz, Carl | 301 |
| Bator, Joe | 347 |
| Beaudin, Ted | 52 |
| Becker Bishop Studios, Inc. | 332,333 |
| Bedford Photo-graphic | 208 |
| Benn, Nathan | 240 |
| Berkun, Phil | 53 |
| Bevilacqua | 54 |
| Bezushko | 55 |
| Bilby, Glade II | 258 |
| Blakeley, Jim | 334,335 |
| Blaustein, John | 348,349 |
| Brimacombe, Gerald | 302,303 |
| Browne, Warren | 350 |
| Buchanan, Craig | 351 |
| Byers, Bruce | 56 |

## C

| | |
|---|---|
| Cadge, Bill | 57 |
| Cannon, Gregory | 58 |
| Cantor, Phil | 59 |
| Carriker, Ronald C. | 259 |
| Carroll, Don | 60,61 |
| Carroon, Chip | 352 |
| Cassidy Photographic Design | 353 |
| Certo, Rosemarie | 63 |
| Chaney, Brad | 354,355 |
| Chapple, Ron | 250 |
| Click! Chicago | 289-291 |
| Clifford, Geoffrey C. | 64,65 |
| Clintsman, Dick | 319 |
| Clough, Terry | 66,67 |
| Collins, Fred | 209 |
| Cook, Irvin | 68 |
| Cook, Kathleen Norris | 356 |
| Cowan, Ralph | 292 |
| Crane, Tom | 69 |

## D

| | |
|---|---|
| Dahlstrom Photography, Inc. | 357 |
| Davidson, Jerry | 358,359 |
| Deahl, David | 276,277 |
| DeBold, Bill | 284 |
| de Gennaro, George | 360,361 |
| De Lessio, Len | 70 |
| De Sciose, Nicholas | 362 |
| De Vault, Jim | 260,261 |
| Digital Transparencies, Inc. | 320 |
| D'Innocenzo, Paul | 71 |
| Dreyer, Peter | 210 |
| Dunbar, Clark | 342 |
| Dunn, Phoebe | 72 |
| Dunoff, Rich | 73 |
| Duran, Mark | 314 |
| Dwiggins, Gene | 211 |

## E

| | |
|---|---|
| Elkins, Joel | 34 |
| Elliott, Peter | 278,279 |
| Elmore, Steve | 75 |

## F

| | |
|---|---|
| Fader, Bob | 363 |
| Faustino | 321 |
| Ferro, Daniel J. | 364 |
| Fishbein, Chuck | 76,77 |
| Fishman, Chuck | 78 |
| Flatow, Carl | 79 |
| Forelli, Chip | 81 |
| Foster, Frank | 213 |
| Francekevich, Al | 82,83 |
| Fraser, Douglas | 85 |
| Funk, Mitchell | 86,87 |
| Furman, Michael | 88,89 |

## G

| | |
|---|---|
| Gardner, Robert | 365 |
| Gayle, Rick | 322 |
| Gerczynski, Tom | 323 |
| Giese, Al | 91 |
| Gladstone, Gary | 92,93 |
| Gleasner, Bill | 262 |
| Glentzer, Don | 324 |
| Gordon, Joel | 95 |
| Gottlieb, Mark | 367 |
| Green-Armytage, Stephen | 96,97 |
| Greenberg, David | 98 |
| Gscheidle, Gerhard | 99 |
| Gupton, Lee | 263 |

## H

| | |
|---|---|
| Hamilton, Jeffrey Muir | 325 |
| Hansen, Steve | 214,215 |
| Harrington, Marshall | 368,369 |
| Harrington, Phillip A. | 100 |
| Harris, Bart | 285 |
| Harris, Brownie | 101 |
| Hashi | 102,103 |
| Haviland, Brian | 104 |
| Hedrich, David | 35 |
| Heffernan, Terry | 336,337 |
| Heilman, Grant | 400 |
| Henderson, Chip | 264 |
| Hetisimer, Larry | 293 |
| Hix, Steve | 304 |
| Hood, Robin | 255 |
| Horowitz, Ryszard | 105 |

## J

| | |
|---|---|
| Jamison, Chipp | 253 |
| Joachim, Bruno | 198,199 |
| Joern, James | 106 |
| Johansky, Peter | 107 |
| Johns, Douglas | 265 |
| Jones, Jerry | 326 |
| Jones, Lou | 217 |

## K

| | |
|---|---|
| Kahn, Dick | Back Cover |
| Kalfus, Lonny | 108 |
| Kaluzny, Zigy | 315 |
| Kaplan, Peter B. | 109 |
| Katz, Arni | 254 |
| Kazu | 294,295 |
| Kawalerski, Ted | 218,219 |
| Kearney, Mitchell | 251 |
| Keeling, Robert | 283 |
| Keenan, Larry | 370 |
| Kent, Karen | 110 |
| King, Ralph | 200,201 |
| Kohanim, Parish | 248,249 |
| Korsh, Ken | 111 |

## L

| | |
|---|---|
| La Ferla, Sandro | 401 |
| Landsman, Gary D. | 112,113 |
| Lane, Whitney | 114 |
| La Riche, Michael | 220,221 |
| Lee, Larry | 371 |
| Leeds, Karen | 115 |
| Leighton, Thomas | 116,117 |
| Lerner, Richard | 104 |
| Leung, Jook | 118 |
| Livzey, John | 372,373 |
| Long, James L. | 402 |
| Luria, Dick | 119 |

continued on page 408

# INDEX

continued from page 407

## M

| | |
|---|---|
| Manarchy, Dennis | 280,281 |
| Marchese, Jim | 120,121 |
| Maresca, Frank | 122,123 |
| Marshall, Jim | 327 |
| Marshall, Lee | 124 |
| Martin, Butch | 125 |
| Martin, Marilyn | 222 |
| Masterson, Ed | 375 |
| McAllister, Bruce | 376,377 |
| McCoy, Dan | 223 |
| McGrail, John | 126 |
| McKean, Tom | 224 |
| Melgar Photographers | 378 |
| Mellor, D.W. | 127 |
| Meola, Eric | 128-133 |
| Mervar, Louis | 36,37 |
| Meyler, Dennis | 328 |
| Miller, Donald L. | 134,135 |
| Miller, Randy | 266,267 |
| Mishler, Clark | 379 |
| Morgan, Frank | 241 |
| Mulligan, Joseph | 32 |
| Munson, Russell | 136 |
| Murray, Steve | 268 |
| Musto, Tom | 137 |
| Myers Studio, Inc. | 138 |

## N

| | |
|---|---|
| Nadelson, Jay | 139 |
| Nathan, Simon | 141 |
| Noble, Inc. | 238,239 |
| Northlight Group | 203 |

## O

| | |
|---|---|
| Obremski, George | 142,143 |
| O'Brien, Tom | 341 |
| Ochi | 46 |
| Orenstein, Ronn | 144 |

## P

| | |
|---|---|
| Palmer, Gabe | 145 |
| Parik, Jan | 146 |
| Peacock, Christian | 147 |
| Pease, Greg | 242,243 |
| Peltz, Stuart | 148 |
| Percey, Roland | 380 |
| Peregrine, Paul | 381 |
| Perry, David | 382 |
| Peterson, Bruce | 316 |
| Petrey, John | 269 |
| Photofile International, Ltd. | 44,45 |
| Photographic Communications | 383 |
| Photography Associates | 225 |
| Photoscope | 149 |
| Pitzner, Al | 305 |
| Pohuski, Michael | 237 |
| Pottle, Jock | 150 |
| Powers, Guy | 151-156 |
| Pribula, Barry | 157 |

## R

| | |
|---|---|
| Ressmeyer, Roger | 384 |
| Rezny, Aaron | 159 |
| Rizzo, Alberto | 160 |
| Robinson, George A. | 226 |
| Rockhill, Morgan | 205 |
| Rohman, Jim | 306 |
| Rosner, Eric H. | 161 |
| Roth, Peter | 162 |
| Rotman, Jeffrey L. | 227 |
| Rubin, Laurie | 288 |
| Rusing, Rick | 40,41 |
| Rysinski, Edward | 163 |

## S

| | |
|---|---|
| Sadlon, Jim | 385 |
| Sanderson, Glenn | 307 |
| Sandone, A.J. | 164 |
| Sauter, Ron | 228 |
| Schleipman, Russ | 229 |
| Schoenfeld, Michael | 386 |
| Schoon, Tim | 244 |
| Schridde, Charles | 308 |
| Scott, Denis | 282 |
| Sherman, Ron | 271 |
| Shore, Stephen | 165 |
| Simmons, Erik Leigh | 230 |
| Simpson, Jerry | 166 |
| Skalski, Ken | 167 |
| Smith, Charles J. | 387 |
| Smith, Gordon E. | 168 |
| Smith, R. Hamilton | 309 |
| Smith, Richard W. | 252 |
| Smith, William Edward | 169 |
| Smyth, T. Kevin | 170 |
| Sochurek, Howard | 171 |
| Solomon, Marc | 388,389 |
| Sööt, Olaf | 173 |
| Southern Stock Photos | 403 |
| Sports Illustrated Pictures | 404 |
| Springmann, Christopher | 340 |
| Standart, Joe | 39 |
| Steinberg, Bruce | 391 |
| Steiner, Peter | 231 |
| Stock Imagery | 405 |
| The Stock Market | 406 |
| Stratos, Jim | 174,175 |
| Strongin, Jeanne | 176 |
| Stuart, John | 177 |
| Stuart, Stephen | 179 |
| The Studio Inc. | 202 |
| Swarthout, Walter | 392,393 |

## T

| | |
|---|---|
| Tcherevkoff, Michel | 180,181 |
| Togashi | 183 |
| Touchton, Ken | 245 |
| Tucker, Bill | 286 |

## V

| | |
|---|---|
| Vance, David | 272,273 |
| Vaughan, Ted | 232,233 |

## W

| | |
|---|---|
| Waine, Michael | 184,185 |
| Warkenthien, Dan | 296 |
| Watson, H. Ross | 187 |
| Weidman, H. Mark | 188,189 |
| Weigand, Tom | 190 |
| Weinberg, Michael | 191 |
| Weitz, Allan | 192 |
| Welzenbach, John | 287 |
| Werts Studios, Inc. | 338,339 |
| West, Charles | 193 |
| Westerman, Charlie | 310,311 |
| Wick, Walter | 194,195 |
| Wilcox, Shorty | 42,43 |
| Wood, James B. | 394 |
| Wortham, Robert | 395 |

## Y

| | |
|---|---|
| Yablon, Ron | 234 |
| Young, Ed | 343 |

## Z

| | |
|---|---|
| Zak, Ed | 330,331 |
| Zann, Arnold | 297 |
| Zenreich, Alan | 196 |

# PHONE LISTINGS & ADDRESSES OF VISUAL ARTISTS & SUPPLIERS

REPRESENTATIVES
PHOTOGRAPHERS
STOCK PHOTOGRAPHY
GRAPHIC DESIGNERS
PHOTO/FILM SERVICES
    LABS & RETOUCHERS
    LIGHTING
    STUDIO RENTALS
    ANIMATORS
    MODELS & TALENT
    CASTING
    ANIMALS
    HAIR & MAKE-UP
    HAIR
    MAKE-UP
    STYLISTS
    COSTUMES
    PROPS
    LOCATIONS
    SETS

# REPRESENTATIVES

A = Animator, AV = Audio Visual, C = Cartoonist, D = Director, F = Film, G = Graphic Designer, H & MU = Hair & Make-up, I = Illustrator, L = Lettering, M = Music, P = Photographer, R = Retoucher, TV = Television

## NEW YORK CITY

### A

Abbey, Ken & Assoc/421 Seventh Ave, New York, NY    212-758-5259
    David Greenberg, (P), Alan Kaplan, (P), Hal Oringer, (P)
Adams, Kristine/62 W 45th St, New York, NY    212-869-4170
Adams, Ray/105 E 29th St, New York, NY    212-986-5453
American Artists/353 W 53rd St #1W, New York, NY    212-682-2462
    Don Almquist, (I), Michael Davis, (I), Gabe Defiore, (I), Jan Esteves, (I), George Gaadt, (I), Jackie Geyer, (I), Rainbow Grinder, (I), Todd Kat, (I), Gregory King, (I), Richard Krieger, (I), Ed Lindlof, (I), Don Mahoney, (I), Ray Paleastra, (I), Bob Radigan, (I), Mike Ruland, (I), Jan Sawka, (I), Joe Scrofani, (I), Arthur Shilstone, (I), Jim Trusilo, (I), Ron Wolin, (I), Andy Zito, (I)
Anderson, Michael/125 Fifth Ave, New York, NY    212-620-4075
    Frank Siciliano, (P)
Anton, Jerry/107 E 38th St #5A, New York, NY    212-679-4562
    Bobby Cochran, (I), Abe Echevarria, (I), Norman Green, (I), Bob Ziering, (I)
Arnold, Peter Inc/1466 Broadway, #1405, New York, NY    212-840-6928
    Fred Bavendam, (P), Bob Evans, (P), Jacques Jangoux, (P), Manfred Kage, (P), Stephen Krasemann, (P), Hans Pfletschinger, (P), David Scharf, (P), Bruno Zehnder, (P)
Artists Associates/211 E 51st St, New York, NY    212-755-1365
    Don Braupigam, (I), Michael Deas, (I), Alex Gnidziejko, (I), Robert Heindel, (I), Steve Karchin, (I), Dick Krepel, (I), Rick McCollum, (I), Fred Otnes, (I), Hodges Soileau, (I)
Arton Associates/342 Madison Ave, New York, NY    212-661-0850
    Paul Giovanopoulos, (I), Laurent Hubert, (I), Dan Sneberger, (I), Katrina Taylor, (I)
Ash, Michael/5 W 19th St, New York, NY    212-741-0015

### B

Backer, Vic/30 W 26th St, New York, NY    212-620-0944
    Norman Nishimura, (P)
Badin, Andy/333 E 49th St, #7H, New York, NY    212-980-3578
    Jeff Feinen, (I), Vera, (I), Brad Guice, (P), Alan Neider, (I)
**BAHM, DARWIN/6 JANE ST, NEW YORK, NY (P 133)**    **212-989-7074**
    Joan Landis, (I), Rick Meyerowitz, (I), Don Ivan Punchatz, (I), Arno Sternglass, (I), Robert Weaver, (I)
Barclay, R Francis/5 W 19th St, New York, NY    212-255-3440
    Michele Barclay, (P), Art Cashin, (P), Jim Martone, (P)
Basile, Ron/381 Fifth Ave, New York, NY    212-986-6710
Becker, Noel/150 W 55th St, New York, NY    212-757-8987
    Howard Tangye, (P), Sy Vinopoll, (P), Faustino, (P)
Beilin, Frank/405 E 56th St, New York, NY    212-751-3074
Benedict, Brinker/6 W 20th St, New York, NY    212-675-8067

    Nancy Brown, (P)
**BERNSTEIN & ANDRIULLI/60 E 42ND ST, NEW YORK, NY (P 11-21)**    **212-682-1490**
    Airstream, (I), Garie Blackwell, (I), Tony Antonios, (I), Everett Davidson, (I), Catherin Deeter, (I), Joe Genova, (I), Griesbach/Martucci, (I), Veronika Hart, (I), Catherine Huerta, (I), Kid Kane, (I), Mary Ann Lasher, (I), Bette Levine, (I), Frank Mascotti, (P), Simpson/Flint, (P), Pamela Noftsinger, (I), Chuck Slack, (I), Murray Tinkelman, (I), Chuck Wilkinson, (I)
Berthezen, Cyndie/372 Fifth Ave., New York, NY    212-685-0488
Bishop, Lynn/134 E 24th St, New York, NY    212-254-5737
    Irene Stern, (P)
Black, Joel P/29 E 32nd St, New York, NY    212-685-1555
    Norm Bendell, (I), B Lynne Foster, (I)
Blair, Robin/400 E 78th St, New York, NY    212-249-3138
    Lyons/Stevens, (R)
Bloncourt, Nelson/308 W 30th St, New York, NY    212-594-3679
Blum, Felice S/79 W 12th St, New York, NY    212-929-2166
Boghosian, Marty/7 E 35th St #2B, New York, NY    212-685-8939
    Stephen McCoy, (I), James Salzano, (P)
Bohmark Ltd/404 Park Ave S, New York, NY    212-889-9670
Booth, Tom Inc/435 W 23rd St, New York, NY    212-243-2750
    Mike Datoli, (P), Mats Gustavson, (I), Jon Mathews, (I), Co Rentmeester, (P), Mike VanHorn, (I)
Brackman, Henrietta/415 E 52nd St, New York, NY    212-753-6483
Brackman, Selma/251 Park Ave S, New York, NY    212-777-4210
Brennan, Dan/27 E. 37th St., New York, NY    212-889-6555
Brindle, Carolyn/203 E 89th St #3D, New York, NY    212-249-8883
**BRODY, ANNE/55 BETHUNE ST, NEW YORK, NY (P 37-39)**    **212-242-1407**
    Randy Jones, (I), Claude Martinot, (I), Ann Neumann, (I), Rich Timperio, (I), Debora Whitehouse, (I)
Brody, Sam/141 E 44th St #907, New York, NY    212-758-0640
    Linda Clenney, (I), Peter B. Kaplan, (P), Ed Kasper, (I), Chuck Kuhn, (P), Alan Lieberman, (P), Rudi Tesa, (P)
Brown, Doug/400 Madison Ave, New York, NY    212-980-4971
    Andrew Unangst, (P)
Browne, Pema Ltd/185 E 85th St, New York, NY    212-369-1925
    Joe Burleson, (I), Peter Catalanotto, (I), Ted Enik, (I), Ron Jones, (I), Glee LoScalzo, (I), David Plourde, (I), Paul Reott, (I), John Rush, (I)
Bruck, J.S/157 W 57th St, New York, NY    212-247-1130
    Joseph Cellini, (I), Michael Dudash, (I), Tom Freeman, (I), Donald Hedin, (I), Jim Mathewuse, (I), John Mello, (I), Richard Newton, (I), Victoria Vebell, (I), Sally Jo Vitsky, (I), Gary Watson, (I)
Bruml, Kathy/262 West End Ave, New York, NY    212-874-5659

# REPRESENTATIVES CONT'D.

Please send us your additions and updates.

| | |
|---|---|
| Bush, Nan/56 E 58th St, New York, NY | 212-751-0996 |
|    *Bruce Weber, (P)* | |
| Byrnes, Charles/5 E 19th St, New York, NY | 212-982-9480 |
|    *Steve Steigman, (P)* | |

**C**

| | |
|---|---|
| Cafiano, Charles/140 Fifth Ave, New York, NY | 212-777-2616 |
|    *Stan Fellerman, (P), Kenro Izu, (P)* | |
| Cahill, Joe/135 E 50th St, New York, NY | 212-751-0529 |
|    *Brad Miller, (P), Howard Sochurek, (P)* | |
| Camera 5/6 W 20th St, New York, NY | 212-989-2004 |
|    *Bob Bishop, (P), Peter Calvin, (P), Christopher Casler, (P), Karin Epstein, (P), John Giordano, (P), Curt Gunther, (P), Ralph Lewin, (P), Joe McNally, (P), Ralph Pabst, (P), Neal Preston, (P), Ken Regan, (P), Bob Sherman, (P), Ben Weaver, (P), Bob Wiley, (P)* | |
| Camp, Woodfin & Assoc/415 Madison Ave, New York, NY | 212-750-1020 |
| Carmel/69 Mercer St, New York, NY | 212-925-6216 |
| Carp, Stanley/11 E 48th St, New York, NY | 212-759-8880 |
|    *Allen Vogel, (P)* | |
| Caruso, Frank/523 E 9th St, Brooklyn, NY | 212-854-8346 |
| Casey, Judy/201 W 16th St #12D, New York, NY | 212-929-0537 |
|    *Michael Doster, (I), G Paul Haynes, (I), Giles Tapie, (P)* | |
| Casey, Marge/245 E. 63rd St., New York, NY | 212-486-9575 |
| **CHALEK, RICK/9 E 32ND ST, NEW YORK, NY (P 58)** | **212-688-1080** |
| Chapnick, Ben/450 Park Ave S, New York, NY | 212-679-3288 |
| Chie/15 E 11th St #3M, New York, NY | 212-685-6854 |
| **CHISLOVSKY, CAROL/420 MADISON AVE #401, NEW YORK, NY (P 40-43)** | **212-980-3510** |
|    *Russell Cobane, (I), Robert Cooper, (I), John Gray, (I), Alan Henderson, (I), Tim Herman, (I), William Hosner, (I), Jim Hunt, (I), Joe Lapinski, (I), Felix Marich, (I), Joe Ovies, (I), Vincent Petragnani, (I), Chuck Schmidt, (I), Danny Smythe, (I), Bob Thomas, (I)* | |
| Clarfeld, Suzy/PO Box 455 Murray Hill Station, New York, NY | 212-889-3920 |
| **COLLIGNON, DANIELE/200 W 15TH ST, NEW YORK, NY (P 45)** | **212-243-4209** |
|    *Bob Aiese, (I), David Gambale, (I), Fran Oelbaum, (I), Christine Rodin, (I), Barbara Sandler, (I), Varlet-Martinelli, (I)* | |
| Collins, Chuck/545 W 45th St, New York, NY | 212-765-8812 |
| Conroy, Chris/124 E. 24th St, New York, NY | 212-598-9766 |
| The Corporate Picture/231 E. 76th St, New York, NY | 212-861-0489 |
|    *Dan Lenore, (P), Steve Niedorf, (P), Christopher Springmann, (P)* | |
| Crabb, Wendy/320 E 50th St, #5A, New York, NY | 212-355-0013 |
|    *Linda Crockett-Henzel, (A), Sandra Shap, (I), Norman Walker, (A)* | |
| Creative Freelancers/62 W 45th St, New York, NY | 212-398-9540 |
|    *Harold Brooks, (I), Howard Darden, (I), Claudia Fouse, (I), Arie Hass, (I), Rosanne Percivalle, (I), Alex Tiari, (I)* | |
| Cullom, Ellen/55 E 9th St, New York, NY | 212-777-1749 |
| Czapnik, Tobie/12 W 27th St, New York, NY | 212-354-4916 |

**D**

| | |
|---|---|
| **DPI-ALFRED FORSYTH/521 MADISON AVE, NEW YORK, NY (P 42,43)** | **212-752-3930** |
|    *Robert Panuska, (P), Shorty Wilcox, (P)* | |
| Davies, Nora/370 E 76th St, New York, NY | 212-628-6657 |
| DeBacker, Clo/29 E 19th St, New York, NY | 212-420-1276 |
|    *Bob Kiss, (P)* | |
| Dedell, Jacqueline/58 W 15th St, New York, NY | 212-741-2539 |
|    *Ivan Chermayeff, (I), Teresa Fasolino, (I), Kip Lott, (I), Ivan Powell, (I), Tommy Soloski, (I), Richard Williams, (I), Henry Wolf, (P)* | |
| **DELLACROCE, JULIA/226 E 53RD ST #3C, NEW YORK, NY (P 100,101)** | **212-580-1321** |
|    *Shig Ikeda, (P), Winslow Pinney Pels, (P), Michael Sell, (I)* | |
| Delvecchio, Lorraine/3156 Baisley, Bronx, NY | 212-829-5194 |
| Des Verges, Diana/73 Fifth Ave, New York, NY | 212-691-8674 |
| Deverin, Daniele/226 E 53rd St, New York, NY | 212-755-4945 |
|    *Kenneth Dewey, (I), Mort Drucker, (I), Lazlo Kubinyi, (I), Stan Mack, (I), Charles Shields, (I), Don Weller, (I)* | |
| DeVito, Kitty/43 E 30th St, New York, NY | 212-889-9670 |
| DeWan, Michael/154 W 77th St, New York, NY | 212-362-0043 |
|    *Nancy Bundt, (P), Ted Kaufman, (P), Don Sparks, (P)* | |
| Dewey, Frank & Assoc/420 Lexington Ave, New York, NY | 212-986-1249 |
| Di Como, Charles & Assoc Inc/12 W 27th St, New York, NY | 212-689-8670 |
| DiBartolo, Joseph/270 Madison Ave, New York, NY | 212-532-0018 |
|    *Larry Robins, (P)* | |
| DiCarlo, Barbara/500 E 85th St, New York, NY | 212-734-2509 |
|    *John Gregory, (P)* | |
| Dickinson, Alexis/42 E 23rd St, New York, NY | 212-473-8020 |
|    *Gianni Cargasacchi, (P), Richard Dunkley, (P), Doug Hopkins, (P)* | |
| DiMartino, Joseph/200 E 58th St, New York, NY | 212-935-9522 |
|    *Graphicsgroup, (I), Whistl'n-Dixie, (I)* | |
| Dorman, Paul/419 E 57th St, New York, NY | 212-826-6737 |
|    *Studio DGM, (I)* | |
| Drexler, Sharon/New York, NY | 212-284-4779 |
| Du Bane, Jean-Jacques/130 W 17th St, New York, NY | 212-697-6860 |
|    *Bruce Plotkin, (P), Carmen Schiavone, (P)* | |
| Dubner, Logan/342 Madison Ave, New York, NY | 212-883-0242 |
|    *Charles Kemper, (P), Siorenzo Niccoli, (P)* | |
| Dunkel, Elizabeth/231 E 76th St, New York, NY | 212-861-0489 |
|    *Dan Lenore, (P), Steve Niedorf, (P), Christopher Springmann, (P)* | |

**E F**

| | |
|---|---|
| East Village Enterprises/231 29th St #807, New York, NY | 212-563-5722 |
|    *Gordon Harris, (I), David Jehn, (G), Carlos Torres, (I)* | |
| Edlitz, Ann/230 E 79th St #14F, New York, NY | 212-744-7945 |
| Eng, Barbara/110 E 23rd St, New York, NY | 212-254-8334 |
| Erlacher, Bill/211 E 51st St, New York, NY | 212-755-1365 |
| Feldman, Robert/358 W 18th St, New York, NY | 212-741-7254 |
|    *Alen MacWeeney, (P), Terry Niefield, (P)* | |
| Ficalora, Michael/28 E 29th St, New York, NY | 212-679-7700 |
| Fischer, Bob/135 E 54th St, New York, NY | 212-755-2131 |
|    *Bill Siliano, (P)* | |
| Flood, Phyllis Rich/67 Irving Pl, New York, NY | 212-674-8080 |
|    *Christopher Blumrich, (I), Seymour Chwast, (I), Vivienne Flesher, (I), Kallan Kallan, (I), Sarah Moon, (P), Elwood H Smith, (I), Stanislaw Zagorski, (I)* | |
| Foster, Peter/870 United Nations Plaza, New York, NY | 212-593-0793 |
|    *Charles Tracey, (P)* | |
| Friscia, Salmon/20 W 10th St, New York, NY | 212-228-4134 |
| Furst, Franz/420 E 55th St, New York, NY | 212-753-3148 |

**G**

| | |
|---|---|
| Gamma-Liason/150 E 58th St, New York, NY | 212-888-7272 |
| Garten, Jan And Jack/50 Riverside Dr, New York, NY | 212-787-8910 |
|    *Drovetto, (I)* | |
| Gebbia, Doreen/156 Fifth Ave., New York, NY | 212-807-0588 |
| Gelb, Elizabeth/330 W 28th St, New York, NY | 212-222-1215 |
| Ginsburg, Michael/Furer, Douglas/145 E 27th St, #7L, New York, NY | 212-628-2379 |
| Giraldi, Tina/160 W 46th St, New York, NY | 212-840-8225 |
| Goldman, David/18 E 17th St, New York, NY | 212-807-6627 |
| Goldstein, Michael L/107 W 69th St, New York, NY | 212-874-6933 |
|    *Sandra Cheiten, (P), Fred Schulze, (P)* | |
| Goodman, Barbara L/435 E 79th St, New York, NY | 212-288-3076 |
|    *Pat Hill, (P), Bryan King, (P), Bill Margerine, (P)* | |
| Goodwin, Phyllis A/10 E 81st St, New York, NY | 212-570-6021 |
|    *Art Kane, (P), Neil Rice, (P)* | |
| **GORDON, BARBARA ASSOC/165 E 32ND ST, NYC, NY (P 46,47)** | **212-686-3514** |
|    *Ron Barry, (I), Higgins Bond, (I), Bob Clarke, (I), Keita Colton, (I), Bob Dacey, (I), James Dietz, (I), Emily Dubowski, (I), Victor Gadino, (I), Glenn Harrington, (I), Nenad Jaksevic, (I), Jackie Jasper, (I), Dick Kramer, (I), Sonja Lamut, (I), Dick Lubey, (I), Cliff Miller, (I), David Myers, (I), Sharleen Pederson, (I), Judith York, (I),* | |
| Grayson, Jay/230 Park Ave, New York, NY | 212-490-6490 |
|    *Paul Barton, (I), Bob Gomel, (I), David Hendrich, (I), James B Wood, (P), Ed Zak, (P)* | |
| **GREEN, ANITA/160 E 26TH ST, NEW YORK, NY (P 148)** | **212-532-5083** |
|    *Nick Mellillo, (P), Stuart Peltz, (P)* | |
| Greenblatt, Eunice N/370 E 76th St, New York, NY | 212-772-1776 |
| Grey, Barbara L/1519 50th St, Brooklyn, NY | 212-851-0332 |

# REPRESENTATIVES CONT'D.

Please send us your additions and updates.

**GRIEN, ANITA/155 E 38TH ST, NEW YORK, NY (P 162,165)**    212-697-6170
    *Dolores Bego, (I), Bruce Cayard, (I), Hal Just, (I), Jerry McDaniel, (I), Don Morrison, (I), Marina Neyman-Levikova, (I), Alan Reingold, (I), Ellen Rixford, (I), Bill Wilkinson, (I)*
Griffith, Valerie/10 Sheridan Square, New York, NY    212-675-2089
Groves, Michael/113 E 37th St, New York, NY    212-532-2074

## H
Handwerker, Elise/2752 Whitman Dr, Brooklyn, NY    212-251-9404
**HANKINS & TEGENBORG LTD/310 MADISON AVE #1225, NEW YORK, NY (P 22-27)**    212-867-8092
    *Ralph Brillhart, (I), David Cook, (I), Robert Crofut, (I), John Dawson, (I), John Dismukes, (I), John Ennis, (I), David Gaadt, (I), Paul Gleason, (I), James Griffin, (I), Edward Herder, (I), Michael Herring, (I), Uldis Klavins, (I), Wendell Minor, (I), Charles Moll, (I), Greg Moraes, (I), Greg Olanoff, (I), Walter Rane, (I), Kirk Reinert, (I), Robert Savin, (I), Harry Schaar, (I), Bill Schmidt, (I), Mario Stasolla, (I), Frank Steiner, (I), Robert Travers, (I), Victor Valla, (I)*
Hanson, Wendy/126 Madison Ave, New York, NY    212-684-7139
Hare, Fran/126 W 23rd St, New York, NY    212-794-0043
    *Peter B Kaplan, (P)*
Harmon, Rod/130 W 57th St, New York, NY    212-582-1501
Henry, John/237 E 31st St, New York, NY    212-686-6883
    *David W Hamilton, (P), Iain Lowrie, (P), Walter Putrez, (P)*
**HEYL, FRAN/230 PARK AVE, STE 2525, NEW YORK, NY (P 100)**    212-687-8930
Hoeye, Michael/120 W 70th St, New York, NY    212-362-9546
    *Richie Williamson, (I)*
Hollyman, Audrey/300 E 40th St 19R, New York, NY    212-867-2383
    *Ted Horowitz, (P)*
Holt, Rita/280 Madison Ave, New York, NY    212-683-2002
Hovde, Nob/829 Park Ave, New York, NY    212-753-0462
    *Malcolm Kirk, (I), J Frederick Smith, (P), Michel Tcherevkoff, (P)*
Hurewitz, Gary/5 E 19th St, New York, NY    212-982-9480
    *Steve Steigman, (P)*
Husak, John/444 E 82nd St, #12-C, New York, NY    212-988-6267
    *Frank Marchese, (G), William Sloan, (I)*
Hyde, Pamela/532 E 83rd St, New York, NY    212-734-9456

## J
Jacobsen, Vi/333 Park Ave S, New York, NY    212-677-3770
Jedell, Joan/370 E 76th St, New York, NY    212-861-7861
Johnson, Evelyne Assoc/201 E 28th St, New York, NY    212-532-0928
Johnson, Janice/340 E 93rd St, NY, NY    212-722-4964
    *Fred Winkowski, (I)*
Judge, Marie/1 W 64th St, New York, NY    212-874-4200
Jupena, Nancy/310 Madison Ave., New York, NY    212-883-8977
    *West Fraser, (I), David Gadt, (I), Paul Gleason, (I), Perico Pastor, (I), Joe Saffold, (I), Victor Valla, (I)*

## K
Kahn, Harvey/50 E 50th St, New York, NY    212-752-8490
    *Nicholas Gaetano, (I), Gerald Gersten, (I), Hal Herrman, (I), Wilson McLean, (I), Bob Peak, (I), Robert Peak, (P), Isadore Seltzer, (I), Kirsten Soderlind, (I)*
Kammler, Fred/225 E 67th St, New York, NY    212-249-4446
    *Joe Long, (P)*
Kane, Barney Inc/120 E 32nd St, New York, NY    212-689-3233
    *Alan Daniels, (I), Michael Farina, (I), William Harrison, (I), Steve Hochman, (I), Peter Lloyd, (I), Ted Lodigensky, (I), Rich Mahon, (I), Robert Melendez, (I), Larry Winborg, (I)*
Keating, Peggy/30 Horatio St, New York, NY    212-691-4654
    *Georgan Damore, (I), June Grammer, (I), Gerri Kerr, (I), Bob Parker, (I), Frank Paulin, (I), Fritz Varady, (I), Carol Vennell, (I)*
Keaton, Liz/40 W 27th St, New York, NY    212-532-2580
Kenney, John/12 W 32nd St, New York, NY    212-594-1543
    *James McLoughlin, (P)*
Kestner, VG/427 E 77th St #4C, New York, NY    212-535-4144
Kim/209 E 25th St, New York, NY    212-679-5628
**KIMCHE, TANIA/470 W 23RD ST, NEW YORK, NY (P 48,49)**    212-242-6367
    *Michael Hostovich, (I), Rafal Olbinski, (I), Miriam Schottland, (I), E T Steadman, (I)*

Kirchmeier, Susan/c/o N Lee Lacy, 160 E 61st St, New York, NY    212-758-4242
Kirchoff-Wohlberg Inc./866 UN Plaza #4014, New York, NY    212-644-2020
    *Angela Adams, (I), Bob Barner, (I), Bradley Clark, (I), Brian Cody, (I), Gwen Connelly, (I), Betsy Day, (I), Alice D'Onofrio, (I), Arlene Dubanevich, (I), Lois Ehlert, (I), Al Fiorentino, (I), Frank Fretz, (I), Jon Friedman, (I), Jon Goodell, (I), Jeremy Guitar, (I), Konrad Hack, (I), Pamela Higgins, (I), Ron Himler, (I), Rosekrans Hoffman, (I), Gerry Hoover, (I), Mark Kelley, (I), Christa Kieffer, (I), Dora Leder, (I), Tom Leonard, (I), Susan Lexa, (I), Ron Logan, (I), Don Madden, (I), Lyle Miller, (I), Carol Nicklaus, (I), Ed Parker, (I), Charles Robinson, (I), Sue Rother, (I), Trudi Smith, (I), Robert Steele, (I), Arvis Stewart, (I), Jas Szygiel, (I), Phero Thomas, (I), Pat Traub, (I), Lou Vaccaro, (I), Joe Veno, (I), John Wallner, (I), Alexandra Wallner, (I), Arieh Zeldich, (I)*
Klein, Leslie D/130 E 37th St, New York, NY    212-683-5454
    *Eric Meola, (P)*
**KLIMT, BILL & MAURINE/15 W 72ND ST, NYC, NY (P 50,51)**    212-799-2231
    *Jeffrey Adams, (I), Ted Detoy, (P), David FeBland, (I), Ken Joudrey, (I), Michael Kane, (I), Frank Morris, (I), Joseph Nettis, (P), Greg Pheakston, (I), Pino, (I), Michael Rodericks, (I), Sharon Spiak, (I), Steven Stroud, (I), Ben Swedowsky, (P)*
Kooyker, Valerie/201 E 12th St, New York, NY    212-673-4333
Kopel, Shelly & Assoc/342 Madison Ave #261, New York, NY    212-986-3282
Kotin, Rory/1414 Ave. of the Americas, New York, NY    212-832-2343
Kramer, Joan & Assoc/720 Fifth Ave, New York, NY    212-224-1758
    *Ron Botier, (P), John Brooks, (P), David Cornwell, (P), Tom DeSanto, (P), Clark Dunbar, (P), John Lawlor, (P), Tom Leighton, (P), Frank Moscati, (P), Jeff Perkell, (P), John Russell, (P), Ken Whitmore, (P), Bill Wilkinson, (P)*
Kreis, Ursula G/63 Adrian Ave, Bronx, NY    212-562-8931
    *Stephen Green-Armytage, (P), Bruce Pendleton, (P)*
Krongard, Paula/1 Riverview Dr W, Upper Montclair, NJ    201-783-6155
    *Skip Hine, (P)*

## L
Lada, Joe./330 E 19th St, New York, NY    212-254-0253
    *George Hausman, (P)*
Lafayette-Nelson & Assoc/64 W 15th St, New York, NY    212-989-7059
Lakin, Gaye/345 E 81st St, New York, NY    212-861-1892
Lamont, Mary/200 W 20th St, New York, NY    212-242-1087
**LANDER, JANE ASSOC/333 E 30TH ST, NEW YORK, NY (P 52,53)**    212-679-1358
    *Francois Cloteaux, (I), Patrick Couratin, (I), Phil Franke, (I), Mel Furukawa, (I), Helen Guetary, (I), Cathy Culp Heck, (I), Saul Lambert, (I), Dan Long, (I), Jack Pardue, (I), Frank Riley, (I)*
Lane Talent Inc/104 Fifth Ave, New York, NY    212-861-7225
Larkin, Mary/503 E 72nd St, New York, NY    212-861-1188
Lavaty, Frank & Jeff/50 E 50th St #5, New York, NY    212-355-0910
    *John Berkey, (I), Tom Blackshear, (I), Jim Butcher, (I), R Crosthwaite, (I), Don Dally, (I), Bernie D'Andrea, (I), Domenick D'Andrea, (I), Roland Descombes, (I), Christine Duke, (I), Gervasio Gallardo, (I), Martin Hoffman, (I), Stan Hunter, (I), Chet Jezierski, (I), David McCall Johnston, (I), Mart Kunstler, (I), Lemuel Line, (I), Robert LoGrippo, (I), Don Maitz, (I), Mara McAfee, (I), Darrell Millsap, (I), Carlos Ochagavia, (I)*
Lee, Alan/33 E 22nd St, NY, NY    212-673-2484
    *David Haggerty, (P), Werner Kappes, (I)*
Lee, Barbara/307 W 82nd St, New York, NY    212-724-6176
    *Russell Kirk, (P)*
**LEFF, JERRY/342 MADISON AVE #949, NEW YORK, NY (P 54,55)**    212-697-8525
    *Franco Accornero, (I), James Barkley, (I), Ken Barr, (I), Tom Beecham, (I), Mel Crair, (I), Ron DiCianne, (I), Bryant Eastman, (I), Charles Gehm, (I), Penelope Gottlieb, (I), Steve Gross, (I), Gary Lang, (I), Jeff Leedy, (I), Ron Lesser, (I), Dennis Magdich, (I), Saul Mandel, (I), Michael Nicastre, (I), John Parsons, (I), Bill Selby, (I), Marie Tobre, (I), Jon Townley, (I), James Woodend, (I)*

## REPRESENTATIVES CONT'D.

Please send us your additions and updates.

| | |
|---|---|
| Legrand, Jean Yves & Assoc/41 W. 84th St., New York, NY | 212-724-5981 |
|    *Robert Farber, (P), Peter Sato, (I)* | |
| Leonian, Edith/220 E 23rd St, New York, NY | 212-989-7670 |
| Lerman, Gary/40 E 34th St #203, New York, NY | 212-683-5777 |
|    *John Bechtold, (P)* | |
| Levy, Leila/4523 Broadway #7G, New York, NY | 212-942-8185 |
| Lichtman, Cathy/5 E 17th St 8th flr, New York, NY | 212-736-2639 |
| Lingren, Patricia/194 Third Ave, New York, NY | 212-475-0440 |
| Locke, John Studios Inc/15 E 76th St, New York, NY | 212-288-8010 |
|    *Ernst Aebi, (I), Walter Allner, (I), John Cayea, (I), John Clift, (I), Laura Cornell, (I), Oscar DeMejo, (I), Jean-Pierre Desclozeaux, (I), Blair Drawson, (I), James Endicott, (I), Richard Erdoes, (I), Jean Michel Folon, (I), Michael Foreman, (I), Andre Francois, (I), George Giusti, (I), Edward Gorey, (I), Peter Lippman, (I), Sam Maitin, (I), Richard Oden, (I), William Bryan Park, (I), David Passalacqua, (I), Colette Portal, (I), Robert Pryor, (I), Fernando Puigrosado, (I), Hans-Georg Rauch, (I), Ronald Searle, (I), Tim, (I), Roland Topor, (I)* | |
| Loshe, Diane/10 W 18th St, New York, NY | 212-691-9920 |
| Lott, George/60 E 42nd St #411, New York, NY | 212-687-4185 |
|    *Ted Chambers, (I), Tony Cove, (I), Jim Dickerson, (I), David Halpern, (I), Ed Kurtzman, (I), Marie Peppard, (I), Steen Svensson, (P)* | |
| Lundgren/45 W 60th St, New York, NY | 212-399-0005 |
| Lurman, Gary/117 E 31 St, New York, NY | 212-533-1422 |

### M

| | |
|---|---|
| Mace, Zelda/1133 Broadway, New York, NY | 212-929-7017 |
| Madris, Stephen/445 E 77th St, New York, NY | 212-744-6668 |
|    *Gary Perweiler, (P)* | |
| Mandel, Bette/265 E 66th St, New York, NY | 212-737-5062 |
| Mann, Ken/313 W 54th St, New York, NY | 212-245-3192 |
| Mann, William Thompson/219 W 71st St, New York, NY | 212-228-0900 |
| Marchesano, Frank/Cosimo Studio/35 W 36th St, New York, NY | 212-563-2730 |
| Marino, Frank/35 W 36th St, New York, NY | 212-563-2730 |
| Mariucci, Marie A/c/o R&V Studio 32 W 39th St, New York, NY | 212-944-9590 |
| Marks, Don/50 W 17th St, New York, NY | 212-807-0457 |
| Mars, Sallie/30 E. 38th St., New York, NY | 212-684-2828 |
|    *Don Hamerman, (P), Layman/Newman, (P), Nobu, (P), Peter Ross, (G), Don Hamerman, (P), Layman/Newman, (P), Nobu, (P), Peter Ross, (G)* | |
| Marshall, Mel/40 W 77th St, New York, NY | 212-877-3921 |
| Marshall, Winifred/2350 Broadway #625, New York, NY | 212-674-1270 |
|    *Richard Dunkley, (P), Doug Hopkins, (P), James A Spilman, (I)* | |
| Mason, Kathy/101 W 18th St 4th Fl., New York, NY | 212-675-3809 |
| Masucci, Myrna/Image Bank/633 Third Ave., New York, NY | 212-953-0303 |
| Mathias, Cindy/7 E 14th St, New York, NY | 212-741-3191 |
| **MATTELSON, JUDY/88 LEXINGTON AVE, NEW YORK, NY (P 83,130,148)** | **212-684-2974** |
|    *Karen Klugein, (I), Marvin Mattelson, (I), Gary Viskupic, (I)* | |
| Mautner, Jane/85 Fourth Ave, New York, NY | 212-777-9024 |
| McVey, Meg/54 W 84th St #2F, New York, NY | 212-362-3739 |
|    *Barbra Walz, (P)* | |
| Media Management Corp/12 W 27th St, New York, NY | 212-696-0880 |
| Melsky, Barney/157 E 35th St, New York, NY | 212-532-3311 |
| Mendelsohn, Richard/353 W 53rd St #1W, New York, NY | 212-682-2462 |
| **MENDOLA, JOSEPH/420 LEXINGTON AVE, NEW YORK, NY (P 30-33)** | **212-986-5680** |
|    *Paul Alexander, (I), Robert Berrar, (I), Dan Brown, (I), Jim Campbell, (I), Carl Cassler, (I), Joe Csatari, (I), Jim Dye, (I), John Eggert, (I), Peter Fiore, (I), Antonio Gabriele, (I), Tom Gala, (I), Hector Garrido, (I), Mark Gerber, (I), Ted Giavis, (I), Dale Gustavson, (I), Chuck Hamrick, (I), Richard Harvey, (I), Dave Henderson, (I), John Holmes, (I), Mitchell Hooks, (I), Joel Iskowitz, (I), Bob Jones, (I), Stuart Kaufman, (I), Michael Koester, (I), Richard Leech, (I), Dennis Lyall, (I), Jeffery Mangiat, (I), Goeffrey McCormack, (I), Ann Meisel, (I), Ted Michner, (I), Mike Mikos, (I), Jonathon Milne, (I), Wally Neibart, (I), Tom Newsome, (I), Mike Noome, (I), Chris Notarile, (I), Kukalis Romas, (I), Mort Rosenfeld, (I), Greg Rudd, (I), Rob Sauber, (I), David Schleinkofer, (I), Mike Smollin, (I), Kip Soldwedel, (I), John Solie, (I), George Sottung, (I), Joel Spector, (I), Cliff Spohn, (I), Jeffrey Terreson, (I), Mark Watts, (I), Allen Welkis, (I), Ben Wohlberg, (I), Ray Yeldman, (I)* | |
| Michalski, Ben/118 E 28th St, New York, NY | 212-683-4025 |
| Miller, Marcia/60 E 42nd St #648, New York, NY | 212-682-2555 |
|    *Monica Incisa, (I), Donald Kahn, (I), Yourcorporatelook, (G), Johanna Sherman, (I)* | |
| **MINTZ, LES/111 WOOSTER ST, #PHC, NEW YORK, NY (P 34,35)** | **212-925-0491** |
|    *Robert Burger, (I), Hovik Dilakian, (I), Amy Hill, (I), Susannah Kelly, (I), George Masi, (I), Tina Mercie, (I), Kirsten Soderlind, (I), Dennis Ziemienski, (I),* | |
| Mohan, Jim/160 W 46th St, New York, NY | 212-247-2777 |
|    *Ben Fernandez, (P), Frank Giraldi, (P), Hedi Tahar, (P)* | |
| Moretz, Eileen P/141 Wooster St, New York, NY | 212-254-3766 |
| **MORGAN, VICKI/194 THIRD AVE, NEW YORK, NY (P 97,120, 139,146,151,167,173,184,185,190 )** | **212-475-0440** |
|    *Joe Heiner, (I), Kathy Heiner, (I), Tim Lewis, (I), Wayne McLoughlin, (I), Emanuel Schongut, (I), Nancy Stahl, (I), Williardson/White, (I), Brian Zick, (I)* | |
| Morse, Lauren/78 Fifth Ave., New York, NY | 212-807-1551 |
|    *Alan Zenreich, (P)* | |
| Mosel, Sue/310 E 46th St, New York, NY | 212-599-1806 |
|    *Bill Connors, (P), Mark Platt, (P)* | |
| Moskowitz, Marion/315 E 68th St, New York, NY | 212-472-9474 |
|    *Diane Teske Harris, (I), Arnie Levin, (I), Geoffrey Moss, (I), Marty Norman, (I), Gary Ruddell, (I)* | |
| **MOSS, EILEEN/333 W 49TH ST #3J, NEW YORK, NY (P 56,57)** | **212-980-8061** |
|    *Kari Brayman, (I), Mike Davies, (I), Scott Pollack, (I), Phillip Salaverry, (P), Norm Siegel, (I),* | |
| Moss, Susan/29 W 38th St, New York, NY | 212-354-8024 |
| Mulvey Associates/1457 Broadway #1001, New York, NY | 212-840-8223 |
|    *Dick Amundsen, (I), Gil Cohen, (I), Olivia Cole, (I), Bill Colrus, (I), Art Cumings, (I), Lou Cunette, (I), Ric DelRossi, (I), John Dyess, (I), Len Epstein, (I), Ethel Gold, (I), Leigh Grant, (I), Les Gray, (I), Meryl Henderson, (I), Phil Jones, (I), John Killgrew, (I), Bob Kray, (I), Ken Longtemps, (I), Rebecca Merrilees, (I), John Murphy, (I), Tom Noonan, (I), Michael O'Reilly, (I), Taylor Oughton, (I), Tom Powers, (I), Don Pulver, (I), Herb Reed, (I), Jose Reyes, (I), Diane Shapiro, (I), Kyuzo Tsugami, (I), Ron Wing, (I), Jim Woodend, (I)* | |

### N O

| | |
|---|---|
| Newborn, Milton/135 E 54th St, New York, NY | 212-421-0050 |
|    *Stephen Alcorn, (I), Braldt Bralds, (I), Mark English, (I), Robert Giusti, (I), Dick Hess, (I), Mark Hess, (I), Edward Sorel, (I), Simms Taback, (I), David Wilcox, (I)* | |
| **OPTICALUSIONS/9 E 32ND ST, NEW YORK, NY (P 58)** | **212-688-1080** |
|    *Stephen Durke, (I), George Kanelous, (I), Rudy Laslo, (I), Kenvin Lyman, (I), Roger Metcalf, (I), George I Parish, (I), Penelope, (I), Mike Robins, (I), Terry Ryan, (I), Ed Scarisbrick, (I), Bruce Young, (I)* | |
| O'Rourke, Gene/200 E 62nd St, New York, NY | 212-935-5027 |
|    *Warren Flagler, (P), Sam Haskins, (P), Douglas Kirkland, (P), Robert Kligge, (P), James Long, (P), Smith-Garner, (P), William Sumner, (P), John Thornton, (P), Alexis Urba, (P), Rob VanPetten, (P), Balfour Walker, (P), John Zimmerman, (P)* | |

### P Q

| | |
|---|---|
| Palevitz, Bob/333 E 30th St, New York, NY | 212-684-6026 |
| Palmer-Smith, Glenn Assoc/160 Fifth Ave, New York, NY | 212-807-1855 |
|    *Claude Mougin, (P), John Stember, (P)* | |
| **PENNY & STERMER GROUP/114 E 32ND ST, NEW YORK, NY (P 59-65)** | **212-685-2770** |
|    *Bob Alcorn, (I), Manos Angelakis, (I), Deborah Bazzel, (I), Ron Becker, (I), Julian Graddon, (I), Rich Grote, (I), Michael Kanarek, (I), Andy Lackow, (I), Alan Lynch, (I), Steve Shub, (I), Page Wood, (I),* | |
| Peretti, Linda/420 Lexington Ave., New York, NY | 212-687-7392 |
| Peters, Barbara/280 Madison Ave, Rm 1103, New York, NY | 212-683-2830 |

# REPRESENTATIVES CONT'D.

Please send us your additions and updates.

Leslie Harris, (P), Thomas Hooper, (P), Studio McLaughlin, (P), Ron Morecraft, (P), Leonard Nones, (P), Bradley Olman, (P)
Plessner International/95 Madison Ave, New York, NY — 212-686-2444
Powers, Elizabeth/1414 Ave. of the Americas, New York, NY — 212-832-2342
Quercia, Mat/78 Irving Pl, New York, NY — 212-477-4491
The Quinlan Artwork Co/330 E 49th St, New York, NY — 212-867-0930

## R
**RAPP, GERALD & CULLEN INC/108 E. 35TH ST #1, NEW YORK, NY (P 10)** — 212-889-3337
Ray, Marlys/350 Central Pk W, New York, NY — 212-222-7680
Reese, Kay Assoc/156 Fifth Ave #1107, New York, NY — 212-924-5151
  Jonathan Atkin, (P), Lee Balterman, (P), Lev Borodulin, (P), Richard Checani, (P), Gerry Cranham, (P), Scott C Dine, (P), Claudio Edinger, (P), Ashvin Gatha, (P), Peter Gullers, (P), Arno Hammacher, (P), Jay Leviton, (P), George Long, (P), George Love, (P), Lynn Pelham, (P), Richard Saunders, (P), T Tanuma, (P), Mark Wexler, (P)
Reid, Pamela/420 E 64th St, New York, NY — 212-832-7589
  Sandy Hill, (S), Bert Stern, (P), Sandy Hill, (S), Bert Stern, (P)
Renard, Madeline/501 Fifth Ave #1407, New York, NY — 212-490-2450
  Chas Wm Bush, (P), John Collier, (I), Etienne Delessert, (I), Tim Girvin, (I), Kunio Hagio, (I), Lamb-Hall, (P), Rudy Legname, (P), Al Pisano, (I), Robert Rodriguez, (I), Michael Schwab, (I), Jozef Sumichrast, (I), Kim Whitesides, (I)
Rhodes, Lela/327 West 89 St, New York, NY — 212-787-3885
Riley, Catherine/12 E 37th St, New York, NY — 212-532-8326
Riley, Ted/215 E 31st St, New York, NY — 212-684-3448
  Zevi Blum, (I), William Bramhall, (I), David Gothard, (I), James Grashow, (I), Paul Hogarth, (I), Edward Koren, (I), Pierre Le-Tan, (I), Joseph Mathieu, (I), Roy McKie, (I), Robert Parker, (I), Cheryl Peterson, (I), J J Sempe, (I), Patricia Wynne, (I)
Rivelli, Cynthia/303 Park Ave S, New York, NY — 212-254-0990
Rosenberg, Arlene/200 E 16th St, New York, NY — 212-289-7701
Rothenberg, Judith A/123 E 75th St, New York, NY — 212-861-7745
Rubin, Elaine R/301 E 38th St #14E, New York, NY — 212-725-8313
Rudoff, Stan/271 Madison Ave, New York, NY — 212-679-8780

## S
S. I. Artists/43 E. 19th St, New York, NY — 212-254-4996
SPAR/PO Box 845, FDR Sta, New York, NY — 212-490-5895
Sacramone & Valentine/302 W 12th St, New York, NY — 212-929-0487
  Stephen Ladner, (P), Tohru Nakamura, (P), John Pilgreen, (P), Robin Saidman, (P), Gianni Spinazzola, (P)
Salomon, Allyn/271 Madison Ave #207, New York, NY — 212-684-5586
Samuels, Rosemary/39 E 12th St, New York, NY — 212-477-3567
Sander, Vicki/48 Gramercy Park North #3B, New York, NY — 212-674-8161
Savello, Denise/381 Park Ave S, New York, NY — 212-730-1188
Sawyer/Nagakura & Assoc Inc/36 W 35th St, New York, NY — 212-563-1982
Schecter Group, Ron Long/430 Park Ave, New York, NY — 212-752-4400
Schickler, Paul/135 E 50th St, New York, NY — 212-355-1044
Schon, Herb/1240 Lexington Ave, New York, NY — 212-249-3236
Schub, Peter & Robert Bear/37 Beekman Pl, New York, NY — 212-246-0679
  Peter Hill Beard, (P), Robert Freson, (P), Alexander Lieberman, (P), Gordon Parks, (P), Irving Penn, (P), Rico Puhlmann, (P), Snowdon, (P), Albert Watson, (P)
**SEIGEL, FRAN/515 MADISON AVE, NEW YORK, NY (P 66-68)** — 212-486-9644
  Leslie Cabarga, (I), Cheryl Cooper, (I), Kinuko Craft, (I), Peter Cross, (I), Earl Keleny, (I)
Shamilzadeh, Sol/1155 Broadway 3rd Fl, New York, NY — 212-532-1977
  The Strobe Studio, (P)
Shapiro, Elaine c/o Doyle Reporting/369 Lexington Ave, New York, NY — 212-867-8220
Sheer, Doug/29 John St, New York, NY — 212-732-4216
Shepherd, Judith/186 E 64th St, New York, NY — 212-838-3214
  Barry Seidman, (P)
Shostal Assoc/60 E 42nd St, New York, NY — 212-687-0696
Sigman, Joan/336 E 54th St, New York, NY — 212-832-7980
  Robert Goldstrom, (I), John H Howard, (I), Jeff Seaver, (I)
Simon, Debra/527 Madison Ave #310, New York, NY — 212-421-5703
Sims, Jennifer/1150 Fifth Ave, New York, NY — 212-860-3005

Chris Collins, (P), Shorty Wilcox, (P)
Slocum, Linda/15 W. 24th St. 11th fl., New York, NY — 212-243-0649
Slome, Nancy/125 Cedar St, New York, NY — 212-227-4854
  Joe Morello, (P)
Smith, Emily/30 E 21st St, New York, NY — 212-674-8383
Smith, Karen/202 E 42nd St, New York, NY — 212-490-0355
  Didier Dorot, (P)
Smith, Rose/400 E 56th St, #19D, New York, NY — 212-758-8711
  Peter Sagara, (P)
Solomon, Richard/121 Madison Ave, New York, NY — 212-683-1362
  Stanislaw Fernandes, (I), Vivienne Flesher, (I), Mark Edward McCandlish, (I), Lev Nisnevich, (P), Shelly Thornton, (I)
Spencer, Carlene/462 W 23rd St, New York, NY — 212-924-2498
Steiner, Susan/130 E. 18th St., New York, NY — 212-673-4704
Stermer, Carol Lee/114 E 32nd St, New York, NY — 212-685-2770
Stevens, Norma/1075 Park Ave, New York, NY — 212-427-7235
  Hiro, (P)
Stockland, Bill/7 W 16th St, New York, NY — 212-242-7693
  Laurence Bartone, (P)
Susse, Ed/40 E 20th St, New York, NY — 212-477-0674

## T
Therese, Jane/6 W 20th St, New York, NY — 212-675-8067
  Nancy Brown, (P)
Thomas, Brenda & Assoc/127 W 79th St, New York, NY — 212-873-7236
Tise, Katherine/200 E 78th St, New York, NY — 212-570-9069
  Raphael Boguslav, (I), John Burgoyne, (I), Bunny Carter, (I), Cheryl Roberts, (I)
Tralono, Katrin/144 W 27th St, New York, NY — 212-255-1976

## UV
Umlas, Barbara/131 E 93rd St, New York, NY — 212-534-4008
  Hunter Freeman, (P)
Van Arnam, Lewis/154 W 57th St, New York, NY — 212-541-4787
  Paul Amato, (P), Mike Reinhardt, (P)
Van Orden, Yvonne/119 W 57th St, New York, NY — 212-265-1223
Vollbracht, Michelle/225 E 11th St, New York, NY — 212-475-8718

## WYZ
Wainscott, Barbara/321 E 54th St, New York, NY — 212-753-1249
Walker, Eleanora/120 E 30th St, New York, NY — 212-689-4431
Walker, Nancy/160 E 65th St #18C, New York, NY — 212-744-3608
Wasserman, Ted/331 Madison Ave #1007, New York, NY — 212-867-5360
Watterson, Libby/350 E 30th St, New York, NY — 212-696-1461
  Lee Balterman, (P)
Wein, Gita/320 E 58th St, New York, NY — 212-759-2763
Weissberg, Elyse/299 Pearl St, New York, NY — 212-406-2566
West, Beatrix/485 Fifth Ave. #407, New York, NY — 212-986-2110
Wheeler, Paul/50 W 29th St, #11W, New York, NY — 212-696-9832
  Enrico Fercrelli, (P), John McGrail, (P), Michael Melford, (P), Bill Pierce, (P), Steven Smith, (P), Peter Tenzer, (P)
Williamson, Jack/1414 Ave. of the Americas, New York, NY — 212-832-2343
Yellen, Bert & Assoc/838 Ave of Americas, New York, NY — 212-889-4701
  Gordon Munro, (P)
Zanetti, Lucy/139 Fifth Ave, New York, NY — 212-473-4999

# NORTHEAST

## AB
Ackermann, Marjorie/2112 Goodwin Lane, North Wales, PA — 215-646-1745
Bancroft, Carol & Friends/185 Goodhill Rd., Weston, CT — 203-226-7674
  Judith Cheng, (I), Bernie Colonna, (I), Jim Cummins, (I), Alan Daniel, (I), Kees DeKiefte, (I), Andrea Eberbach, (I), Fuka, (I), Jackie Geyer, (I), Fred Harsh, (I), Dennis Hockerman, (I), Ann Iosa, (I), Doug Jamieson, (I), Laurie Jordan, (I), Mila Lazarevich, (I), Karin Lidbeck, (I), Suen Lindman, (I), Karen Loccisano, (I), Al Lorenz, (I), Bob Masheris, (I), Yoshi Miyake, (I), Daryl Moore, (I), Nancy Munger, (I), Rodney Pate, (I), Larry Raymond, (I), Jenny Rutherford, (I), Judy Sakaguchi, (I), Monica Santa, (I), Miriam Schottland, (I), Blanche Sims, (I), Sally Springer, (I), Clifford Timm, (I), Linda Boehm Weller, (I), Debby Young, (I)
Birenbaum, Molly/7 Williamsburg Dr, Cheshire, CT — 203-272-9253
Bloch, Peggy J/464 George Rd #5A, Cliffside Park, NJ — 201-943-9435
Brown, Jill/911 State St, Lancaster, PA — 717-393-0918

# REPRESENTATIVES CONT'D.
Please send us your additions and updates.

## CD
Callahan, Jim/A & M Resources/US Rte 202, Peterborough, NH — 603-924-6168
**CAMP, WOODFIN INC/925 1/2 F ST NW, WASHINGTON, DC (P 240)** — **202-638-5705**
Chandoha, Sam/RD 1 PO Box 287, Annandale, NJ — 201-782-3666
Crandall, Robert/Saunders, Marvin Assoc/516 West Boston Post Rd, Mamaroneck, NY — 914-381-4400
Curtin, Susan/323 Newbury St, Boston, MA — 617-536-6600
D'Aquino, Connie/Rt 22, PO Box 64, Bedford Village, NY — 914-234-3123
Donaldson, Selina/118 Lowell St, Arlington, MA — 617-646-1687
Dunn, Tris/20 Silvermine Rd, New Canaan, CT — 203-966-9791

## GHI
Gidley, Fenton/43 Tokeneke Rd, Darien, CT — 212-772-0846
  Mark Segal, (P)
Glover, Cynthia/103 E Read St, Baltimore, MD — 301-385-1716
Gruder, Jean/90 Park Ave, Verona, NJ — 201-239-7088
Haas, Ken/717 N Fifth St, Reading, PA — 215-374-4431
Hopkins, Nanette/18 North New St, Westchester, PA — 215-431-3240
Hubbell, Marian/99 East Elm St, Greenwich, CT — 203-629-9629
Imlay, Kathy/41 Upton St, Boston, MA — 617-262-5388

## KL
Kell & Associates/1110 Fidler Ln, #710, Silver Spring, MD — 202-585-0700
**KENNEY, ELLA/229 BERKELEY #52, BOSTON, MA (P 28,29)** — **617-266-3858**
  Bente Adler, (I), Wilbur Bullock, (I), Anna Davidian, (I), Eaton & Iwen, (R), Ralph King, (P)
Kessler, Linda/PO Box 1352, Princeton, NJ — 609-466-3718
Lubbe, Francis/PO Box 215, Stevenson, MD — 301-583-9147

## MN
McNamara, Paula B/182 Broad St, Wethersfield, CT — 203-563-6159
  Jack McConnell, (P)
Metzger, Rick/186 South St, Boston, MA — 617-426-2290
Morgan, Wendy/5 Logan Hill Rd, Northport, NY — 516-757-5609
  Fred Schrier, (I), Mary Selfridge, (I), Art Szabo, (P), Wozniaks, (I)
Nealy, Jesse/Conant Valley Rd, Pound Ridge, NY — 914-764-5981
  Bob Baxter, (I), Jon & Tony Gentile, (I), Barney Plotkin, (I), Benjamin Stahl, (I), Herb Tauss, (I)
Nichols, Eva/1241 University Ave, Rochester, NY — 716-275-9666

## OPR
Olsen, James A/c/o Smith, Tower Dr, Darien, CT — 203-655-2899
Photo-Graphic Agency/58 Pine St, Malden, MA — 617-944-3166
Photogroup/5161 River Rd, Washington, DC — 301-652-1303
  Steve Little, (P), Lenny Rizzi, (P), Paul Eric Smith, (P), Barry Soorenko, (P)
Picture That, Inc/880 Briarwood, Newtown Square, PA — 215-353-8833
Radxevich Standke/15 Intervale Terr, Reading, MA — 617-944-3166
Ricci, Ron/201 King St, Chappaqua, NY — 914-238-4221

## ST
Schooley & Associates/10 Highland Ave, Rumson, NJ — 201-530-1480
  Lorraine Dey, (I), Kevin Dougherty, (I), Geoffrey Gove, (I), William Laird, (I), Gary Smith, (I)
Schoon, Deborah/838 Columbia Ave, Lancaster, PA — 717-626-0296
Smith, Wayne R./The Penthouse, 145 South St, Boston, MA — 617-426-7262
Stevens, Rick/925 Penn Ave, #404, Pittsburgh, PA — 412-765-3565
Ternay, Louise/119 Birch Ave, Bala Cynwyd, PA — 215-664-3761
  Bruce Blank, (P), Len Epstein, (I), Don Everhart, (I), Geri Grienke, (I), Peter Sasten, (G), Bill Ternay, (I), Kate Ziegler, (I)
Troussoff, Gail/925 1/2 F St NW, Washington, DC — 202-393-2658

## UV
Unicorn Enterprises, Jean Gruder/90 Park Ave, Verona, NJ — 201-239-7088
Valen Assocs/PO Box 8, Westport, CT — 203-227-7806
  George Booth, (C), Whitney Darrow, (C), Elvin Dedini, (C), Joe Farris, (C), William Hamilton, (C), Bud Handelsman, (C), Stan Hunt, (C), Anatol Kovarsky, (C), Lee Lorenz, (C), Henry Martin, (C), Warren Miller, (I), Frank Modell, (C), George Price, (C), Mischa Richter, (C), Charles Saxon, (C), Jim Stevenson, (C), Henry Syverson, (C), Bob Weber, (C), Gahan Wilson, (C), Rowland Wilson, (I), Bill Woodman, (C), Bill Ziegler, (I)

## W
Waldron, Diana/1411 Hollins St, Baltimore, MD — 301-566-1222
Wolf, Deborah/731 N 24th St, Philadelphia, PA — 215-928-0918
  John Collier, (I), Paul Dodge, (I), Dan Forer, (P), Robert Halalski, (P), Ron Lehew, (I), Bill Margerin, (I), Bruce McAllister, (P), Fran Orlando, (P), Bob Schenker, (I), Jim Sharpe, (I), Charles Weckler, (P), Frank Williams, (I), Liz Wuillerman, (P)
Worral, Dave/125 S 18th St, Philadelphia, PA — 215-567-2881

# SOUTHEAST

## ABCF
Aldridge, Donna/1154 #2 Briarcliff NE, Atlanta, GA — 404-872-7980
  Trevor Irwin, (I)
Ayres, Beverly/PO Box 11531, Atlanta, GA — 404-262-2740
Beck, Susanne/2721 Cherokee Rd, Birmingham, AL — 205-871-6632
Burnett, Yolanda/559 Dutch Vall Rd, Atlanta, GA — 404-873-5858
  Charlie Latham, (P)
Couch, Tom/1164 Briarcliff Rd, NE #2, Atlanta, GA — 404-872-5774
  Richard Hoflich, (P), Warren Weber, (I)
Fink, Duncan/437 S Tryon St, Charlotte, NC — 704-377-4217

## JLM
Jourdan, Carolyn/4222 Inverrary Blvd, Lauderhill, Fl — 305-350-5596
Linden, Tamara/One Park Place #120 1900 E, Atlanta, GA — 404-355-0729
  Joseph M Ovies, (I), Charles Passarelli, (I), Larry Tople, (I)
McGee, Linda/1816 Briarwood Industrial Ct, Atlanta, GA — 404-633-1286
McLean Represents/401 W Peachtree St NW #3050, Atlanta, GA — 404-221-0700
  Jack Jones, (I), Martin Pate, (I), Steve Spetzeris, (I), Warren Weber, (I)

## PQ
The Phelps Agency/32 Peachtree St NW #201, Atlanta, GA — 404-524-1234
  Tom McCarthy, (P), Tommy Thompson, (P), Bill Weems, (P)
Poland, Kiki/848 Greenwood Ave NE, Atlanta, GA — 404-875-1363
Quinlan, Kelly/6053 Tammy Dr, Alexandria, VA — 703-971-2584
  Jamie Phillips, (P)

## ST
Silva, Naomi/100 Colony Square (n) 200, Atlanta, GA — 404-892-8314
  Joe DiNicola, (I), Rob Horn, (G), Christy Sheets Mull, (I), Gary Penca, (I), Don Sparks, (P)
Tamara Inc/One Park Place #120, Atlanta, GA — 404-355-0729
  Tom Fleck, (I), Joseph M Ovies, (I)
Torres, Martha/1715 Burgundy, New Orleans, LA — 504-895-6570

## W
Watson, Beth/1925 College Ave, Atlanta, GA — 404-371-8086
Wells, Susan/51434 Timber Trails, Atlanta, GA — 404-255-1430
Wexler, Marsha Brown/6108 Franklin Park Rd, McLean, VA — 703-241-1776
Williams, Phillip/1106 W Peachtree St, #201, Atlanta, GA — 404-873-2287
  Jamie Cook, (I), Stan Hobbs, (I), Rick Lovell, (I), Bill Mayer, (I), David McKelvey, (I), John Robinette, (I)
Wooden Reps/503 Ansley Villa Dr, Atlanta, GA — 404-892-6303
  Ian Greathead, (I), Mike Lester, (I), Chris Lewis, (I), Ted Rodgers, (P), Joe Saffold, (P), Bruce Young, (I), Cooper-Copeland, (I)

# MIDWEST

## AB
Appleman, Norm/679 E Mandoline, Madison Hts, MI — 313-589-0066
  Art Hansen, (P), Jerry Kolesar, (P), Larry Melkus, (P), Glenn Schoenbach, (P)
Asad, Susan/420 W Huron, Chicago, IL — 312-266-7540
Ball, John/203 N Wabash, Chicago, IL — 312-332-6041
  Christy Sheets Mull, (I), Joe Saffold, (I), Janie Wright, (I)
Berk, Ida/1350 N La Salle, Chicago, IL — 312-944-1339
Berntsen, Jim/520 N Michigan Ave, Chicago, IL — 312-822-0560
  Jim Conahan, (I), Denis Johnson, (I), Diana Magnuson, (I), Simeon Marshall, (P), Leonard Morgan, (P), Sam Thiewes, (I), Jim Turgon, (P)
Blanchette, Dan/645 N Michigan Ave, Chicago, IL — 312-280-1077

# REPRESENTATIVES CONT'D.

Please send us your additions and updates.

| | |
|---|---|
| Brenner, Harriet/660 W Grand Ave, Chicago, IL | 312-243-2730 |
| Buermann, Jeri/321 N 22nd St, St Louis, MO | 314-231-8690 |

## C
| | |
|---|---|
| Chauncey, Michelle/1029 N Wichita #13 & 15, Wichita, KS | 316-262-6733 |
| Christell, Jim & Assoc/307 N Michigan Ave, Chicago, IL | 312-236-2396 |

*Michel Ditlove, (P), Ron Harris, (P), Sinnott/Assoc, (F),*
*Michel Ditlove, (P), Ron Harris, (P), Sinnott/Assoc, (F)*

| | |
|---|---|
| Clausen, Bo/643 W Arlington Pl, Chicago, IL | 312-871-1242 |
| Cohen, Janice/117 North Jefferson, Chicago, IL | 312-454-0680 |
| Coleman, Woody/1034 Main Ave, Cleveland, OH | 216-621-1771 |
| Conahan-Berntsen/520 N Michigan Ave, Chicago, IL | 312-822-0560 |

*Jim Conahan, (I), Denis Joanson, (I), Diana L Magnuson, (I), Josef Sumichrast, (I), Sam Thiewes, (I), Jim Turgeon, (I)*

## EF
| | |
|---|---|
| Emerich Studios/300 W 19th Terr, Kansas City, MO | 816-474-8888 |
| Erdos, Kitty/210 W Chicago, Chicago, IL | 312-787-4976 |
| Fiat, Randy/208 W Kinzie, Chicago, IL | 312-467-1430 |
| Fleming, Laird Tyler/1 Memorial Dr., St. Louis, MO | 314-982-1700 |

*John Bilecky, (P), Willardson & White, (P)*

| | |
|---|---|
| Frost, Brent/4037 Queen Ave S, Minneapolis, MN | 612-920-3864 |

## H
| | |
|---|---|
| Hanson, Jim/6959 N Hamilton, Chicago, IL | 312-338-4344 |
| Harlib, Joel/405 N Wabash #3203, Chicago, IL | 312-329-1370 |

*Bob August, (I), John Casado, (I), Peter Elliott, (P), Ignacio Gomez, (I), Barbara Higgins-Bond, (I), Richard Leech, (I), Tim Lewis, (I), Peter Lloyd, (I), David McMacken, (I), Midocean, (F), Claude Mougin, (I), Dennis Mukai, (I), Joe Ovies, (I), Tony Petrocelli, (P), Todd Shorr, (I), Kim Whitesides, (I), Bruce Wolfe, (I), Bob Ziering, (I)*

| | |
|---|---|
| Hartig, Michael/3620 Pacific, Omaha, NB | 402-345-2164 |
| Harwood, Tim/646 N Michigan, Chicago, IL | 312-828-9117 |
| Hedrich-Blessing/11 W Illinois, Chicago, IL | 312-321-1151 |
| Higgens Hegner Genovese Inc/510 N Dearborn St, Chicago, IL | 312-644-1882 |
| Horton, Nancy/939 Sanborn, Palatine, IL | 312-934-8966 |
| Hull, Scott/2154 Willowgrove Ave, Dayton, OH | 513-298-0566 |

*Tracy Britt, (I), Andy Buttram, (I), Richard Cohen, (I), David Groff, (I), John Maggard, (I), Ernest Norcia, (I), Mark Riedy, (I), Don Vanderbeck, (I)*

## KL
| | |
|---|---|
| Kamin, Vince/42 E Superior, Chicago, IL | 312-787-8834 |

*Jan Cobb, (P), Nicholas DeSciose, (P), Lee Duggin, (I), Dick Durrance, (P), Dennis Gray, (P), Hans Hoffman, (P), Dave Jordano, (P), Dan Morrill, (P), Michael Pruzan, (P), Steve Steigman, (P), Roy Volkman, (P)*

| | |
|---|---|
| Kapes, Jack/218 E Ontario, Chicago, IL | 312-664-8282 |

*Jerry Friedman, (P), Carl Furuta, (P), Klaus Lucka, (P), Dan Romano, (I), Nicolas Sidjakov, (G)*

| | |
|---|---|
| Kezelis, Elena/215 W Illinois, Chicago, IL | 312-644-7108 |
| Klemp, O.J./311 Good Ave., Des Plaines, IL | 312-297-5447 |
| Koralik, Connie/26 E Huron, Chicago, IL | 312-944-5680 |

*Robert Keeling, (P)*

| | |
|---|---|
| Lakehomer & Assoc/307 N Michigan Ave, Chicago, IL | 312-236-7885 |

*Tom Petroff, (P), Fredric Stein, (P)*

| | |
|---|---|
| Lasko, Pat/452 N Halsted, Chicago, IL | 312-243-6696 |
| Linzer, Jeff/4001 Forest Rd, Minneapolis, MN | 612-926-4390 |

## M
| | |
|---|---|
| McManus, Mike/3423 Devon Rd, Royal Oak, MI | 313-549-8196 |
| McMasters, Deborah/157 W Ontario, Chicago, IL | 312-943-9007 |
| McNamara Associates/1250 Stephenson Hwy, Troy, MI | 313-583-9200 |

*Max Alterruse, (I), Gary Ciccarelli, (I), Garry Colby, (I), Hank Kolodziej, (I), Chuck Passarelli, (I), Tony Randazzo, (I), Gary Richardson, (I), Dick Scullin, (I), Don Wieland, (I)*

| | |
|---|---|
| McNaughton, Toni/230 N Michigan, Chicago, IL | 312-782-8586 |

*Pam Haller, (P), Rodica Prato, (I), James B. Wood, (P)*

| | |
|---|---|
| Melkus, Larry/679 Mandoline, Madison Hts, MI | 313-589-0066 |

*Bob Hughes, (P), Jerry Kolesar, (P), Glenn Schoenbach, (P)*

| | |
|---|---|
| Miller, Richard/743 N Dearborn, Chicago, IL | 312-280-2288 |
| Moore, Connie/1540 North Park, Chicago, IL | 312-787-4422 |

*Richard Shirley, (F), Richard Shirley, (F)*

| | |
|---|---|
| **MOSHIER & MALONEY/535 N MICHIGAN, CHICAGO, IL (P 102,189)** | **312-943-1668** |

*Nicolette Anastas, (I), Kenneth Call, (P), Steve Carr, (P),*
*Dan Clyne, (I), Dan Coha, (P), Joyce Culkin, (I), Ron DiCianni, (I), Pat Dypold, (I), David Gaadt, (I), John Hamagami, (I), Rick Johnson, (I), Bill Kastan, (I), Roy Moody, (I), Colleen Quinn, (I), Paul Ristau, (I), Stephen Rybka, (I), Skidmore-Sahratian, (I), Ray Smith, (I), Kathy Spalding, (I), Al Stine, (I), Jim Trusilo, (I), George Welch, (I), John Youssi, (I)*

| | |
|---|---|
| Murphy, Sally/70 W Hubbard, Chicago, IL | 312-751-2977 |
| Myrna Hogan & Assoc/333 N Michigan, Chicago, IL | 312-372-1616 |

## NO
| | |
|---|---|
| Nagan, Rita/1514 NE Jefferson St, Minneapolis, MN | 612-788-7923 |
| Newman, Richard/1866 N Burling, Chicago, IL | 312-266-2513 |
| Nicholson, Richard B/2310 Denison Ave, Cleveland, OH | 216-398-1494 |

*J David Wilder, (P)*

| | |
|---|---|
| O'Farrel, Eileen/311 Good Ave, Des Plaines, IL | 312-297-5447 |
| Osler, Spike/2616 Industrial Row, Troy, MI | 313-280-0640 |

*Madison Ford, (P), Rob Gage, (P), Rick Kasmier, (P), Jim Secreto, (P)*

## P
| | |
|---|---|
| Parker, Tom/1750 N Clark, Chicago, IL | 312-266-2891 |
| Perne, Tom/9124 W Terrace Pl, Des Plaines, IL | 312-635-0864 |
| Photographic Services Owens-Corning/Fiberglass Towers, Toledo, OH | 419-248-8041 |

*Jay Langlois, (P), Joe Sharp, (P)*

| | |
|---|---|
| Pike, Cindy/510 N Dearborn, Chicago, IL | 312-644-1882 |
| Platzer, Karen & Assoc/535 N Michigan Ave, Chicago, IL | 312-467-1981 |

*Michael Caporale, (P), Steve Clay, (I), Don Getsug, (P), Jan Halt, (P), Dion Hitchings, (I), Robert Sacco, (P), Peter James Samerjan, (P)*

| | |
|---|---|
| **POTTS, CAROLYN/2350 N CLEVELAND, CHICAGO, IL (P 94,95,171,187,286)** | **312-935-1707** |

*John Craig, (I), Gregory King, (I), Gregory Murphey, (P), Raymond Smith, (I), Bill Tucker, (P), Leslie Wolf, (I)*

| | |
|---|---|
| Potts, Vicki/139 N. Wabash, Chicago, IL | 312-726-5678 |

*Tom Perne, (P), Bob Randall, (P), Kenneth Short, (P)*

## R
| | |
|---|---|
| Rabin, Bill & Assoc/666 N Lake Shore Dr, Chicago, IL | 312-944-6655 |

*Joel Baldwin, (P), Guy Billout, (I), Fred Brodersen, (P), Robert Giusti, (I), Lamb&Hall, (P), Joe Heiner, (I), Kathy Heiner, (I), Mark Hess, (I), Richard Hess, (I), Lynn St John, (P), Art Kane, (P), Rudy Legname, (P), Jay Maisel, (P), Eric Meola, (P), Richard Noble, (P), Robert Rodriguez, (I), John Thompson, (I), Pete Turner, (P), David Wilcox, (I), John Zimmerman, (P)*

| | |
|---|---|
| Ray, Rodney/405 N Wabash #3106, Chicago, IL | 312-472-6550 |

## S
| | |
|---|---|
| Scarff, Signe/22 W Erie, Chicago, IL | 312-266-8352 |
| Schuck, John/614 Fifth Ave S, Minneapolis, MN | 612-338-7829 |
| Sell, Dan/233 E Wacker, Chicago, IL | 312-332-5168 |

*Alvin Blick, (I), Wayne Carey, (I), Dick Flood, (I), Bill Harrison, (I), Gregory Manchess, (I), Bill Mayer, (I), Tim Raglin, (I), Theo Rudnak, (I), Mark Schuler, (I), R J Shay, (I), Phil Wendy, (I), Gene Wilkes, (I), John Zielinski, (I)*

| | |
|---|---|
| Sharrard, Chuck/1546 N Orleans, Chicago, IL | 312-751-1470 |
| Shulman, Salo/215 W Ohio, Chicago, IL | 312-337-3245 |
| Siegel, Gerald & Assoc/118 W Ohio, Chicago, IL | 312-266-2323 |

*Bruce Rosmis, (P)*

| | |
|---|---|
| Skillicorn, Roy/233 E Wacker #29031, Chicago, IL | 312-856-1626 |

*Tom Curry, (I), David Scanlon, (I)*

| | |
|---|---|
| Stephenson & Taylor/19 N Erie St, Toledo, OH | 419-242-9170 |

*Tony Duda, (I), Richard Reed, (I)*

| | |
|---|---|
| Strickland, Joann/405 N Wabash #1003, Chicago, IL | 312-467-1890 |
| Strohmeyer, Pamela/929 Argyle St, Chicago, IL | 312-271-6110 |

## T
| | |
|---|---|
| Timon, Clay & Assoc Inc/405 N Wabash, Chicago, IL | 312-527-1114 |

*Bob Bender, (P), Michael Fletcher, (P), Larry Dale Gordon, (P), Don Klumpp, (P), Chuck Kuhn, (P), Barry O'Rourke, (P), Ron Pomerantz, (P), Al Satterwhite, (P), Michael Slaughter, (P)*

| | |
|---|---|
| Trinko, Genny/126 W Kinzie St, Chicago, IL | 312-222-9242 |
| Tuke, Joni/368 W Huron, Chicago, IL | 312-787-6826 |

*Bill DeBold, (P), Ken Goldammer, (I), Dennis Magdich, (I),*

# REPRESENTATIVES CONT'D.

Please send us your additions and updates.

*John Welzenbach, (P)*

## WYZ
Walsh, Richard/1118 W Armytage, Chicago, IL — 312-944-4477
Wilde, Nancy/2033 N Orleans, Chicago, IL — 312-642-4426
Witmer, Bob c/o Norris McNamara/411 North LaSalle, Chicago, IL — 312-944-4477
Yunker, Kit/3224 N Racine, Chicago, IL — 312-975-8116
Zann, Shelia/502 N Grove, Oak Park, IL — 312-386-2864

# SOUTHWEST

## ABC
Art Rep Inc/3511 Cedar Springs #4a, Dallas, TX — 214-521-5156
Assid, Carol/122 Parkhouse, Dallas, TX — 214-748-3765
Booster, Barbara/4001 Byrn Maur, Dallas, Tx — 214-373-4284
Callahan, Joe/224 N Fifth Ave, Phoenix, AZ — 602-248-0777
*Kateri Dufault, (I), Tom Gerczynski, (P), Mike Gushock, (I), Mike Karbelnikoff, (P), Jon Kleber, (I), Marlowe Minnich, (I), Howard Post, (I), Dick Varney, (I), Balfour Walker, (P)*
Campbell, Patty/1222 Manufacturing St, Dallas, TX — 214-330-0304
Corcoran, Arlene/224 N 5th Ave, Phoenix, AZ — 602-257-9509
Crowder, Bob/3603 Parry Ave, Dallas, TX — 214-823-9000
*Mark Johnson, (P), Barry Kaplan, (P), Moses Olmoz, (P), Al Rubin, (P)*

## DFH
DiOrio, Diana/4146 Amherst St, Houston, TX — 713-669-0362
*JoAnn Collier, (I), Ray Mel Cornelius, (I), Regan Dunnick, (I), Richard High, (I), Larry Keith, (I), Dennis Mukai, (I), Patrick Nagel, (I), Thom Ricks, (I), Randy Rogers, (I), Peter Stallard, (I), James Stevens, (I)*
Fuller, Alyson/5610 Maple Ave, Dallas, TX — 214-688-1855
Hamilton, Chris/3900 Lemmon, Dallas, TX — 214-526-2050
Harris Management Technology/2900 N Loop West #700, Houston, TX — 713-680-1888

## LMP
Laurance Lynch/Repertoire/3317 Montrose #1130, Houston, TX — 713-520-9938
*Robert Lattorre, (P)*
McCann/3000 Carlisle #202, Dallas, TX — 214-742-3138
*Michael Doret, (I)*
Production Services/1711 Hazard, Houston, TX — 713-529-7916
*George Craig, (P), C Bryan Jones, (P), Thaine Manske, (P)*

## SVW
Smith, Linda/3511 Cedar Springs #4a, Dallas, TX — 214-521-5156
Vidal, Jessica/155 Pittsburg, Dallas, TX — 214-747-7766
*Jerry Segrest, (P)*
WILLARD, PAUL ASSOC/313 E THOMAS RD #205, PHOENIX, AZ (P 69) — 602-279-0119
*Rick Kirkman, (I), Kevin MacPherson, (I), Nancy Pendleton, (I), Bob Peters, (I), Rick Rusing, (P), Wayne Watford, (I)*

# WEST

## A
After Image Inc/6855 Santa Monica Blvd, Los Angeles, CA — 213-467-6033
Albertine, Dotti/202 A Westminster Ave, Venice, CA — 213-392-4877
Aline, France & Marsha Fox/4121 Wilshire Blvd, Los Angeles, CA — 213-933-2500
*Lou Beach, (I), Guy Billout, (I), Thomas Blackshear, (I), Ed Curvin, (I), Guy Fery, (I), Randy Glass, (I), Bret Lopez, (P), Steve Miller, (I), Bill Rieser, (I), Carl Savlicek, (I), Dave Scanlon, (I), Joe Spencer, (I), Joe Spencer, (A), Steve Sulen, (I), Ezra Tucker, (I), Kim Whitesides, (I), Bruce Wolfe, (I), James Wood, (P), Bob Zoell, (A)*
Annika/8301 W Third St, Los Angeles, CA — 213-655-3527

## B
Bob Morris/JCA/14019-A Paramount Ave., Los Angeles, CA — 213-633-4429
Bonar, Ellen/1925 S Beverly Glenn, Los Angeles, CA — 213-474-7911
*Chuck Schmidt, (I)*
Bowler, Ashley & Assoc/2194 Ponet Dr, Los Angeles, CA — 213-467-8200
Brady, Dana/125 N Doheny Dr, Los Angeles, CA — 213-275-4455
Bright & Agate Inc/8322 Beverly Rd, Los Angeles, CA — 213-658-8844
Brooks/6628 Santa Monica Blvd, Los Angeles, CA — 213-463-5678
*Paul Gersten, (P), Bill Robbins, (P)*
Brown, Dianne/732 N Highland, Los Angeles, CA — 213-464-2775
Burlingham, Tricia/8275 Beverly Blvd, Los Angeles, CA — 213-651-3212

## C
Carroll, J J/Los Angeles, CA — 213-545-3583
*Christine Nasser, (I), Studio Swarthout, (P)*
Church, Spencer/515 Lake Washington Blvd., Seattle, WA — 206-324-1199
*John Fretz, (I), Mits Katayama, (I), Light Language, (P), Ann Marra, (G), Scott McDougall, (I), Dale Nordell, (I), Marilyn Noudell, (I), Rusty Platz, (I), Ted Rand, (I), Diane Solvang-Angell, (I), Dugald Stermer, (I), West Stock, (S), Craig Walden, (I), Dale Windham, (P)*
Collier, Jan/1535 Mission St, San Francisco, CA — 415-552-4252
Conroy, Marie-Anais/603 Kings Rd, Newport Beach, CA — 714-646-8604
*Greg Fulton, (P), Dean Gerrie, (I), Walter Urie, (I), Roger Vega, (I)*
Consolidated Artists/22561 Claude Cir, El Toro, CA — 714-770-9738
*Art Banuelos, (I), Mark K Brown, (I), Randy Chewning, (I), Kevin Davidson, (I), Kernie Erickson, (I), Bob Hord, (I), Joe Kennedy, (I), Larry McAdams, (I), Kenton Nelson, (I), Mike Rill, (I), Robert Woodcox, (I)*
Cook, Warren/PO Box 2159, Laguna Hills, CA — 714-770-4619
Copeland, Stephanie M/11836 San Vicente Blvd #20, Los Angeles, CA — 213-826-3591
*Ralph B Pleasant, (P)*
Cormany, Paul/11607 Clover Ave, Los Angeles, CA — 213-828-9653
*Jim Endicott, (I), Bob Gleason, (I), Jim Heimann, (I), Bob Krogle, (I), Lamb/Hall, (P), Gary Norman, (I), Ed Scarisbrick, (I), Stan Watts, (I), Dick Wilson, (I), Andy Zito, (I)*
Cornell, Kathleen/90 Corona #508, Denver, CO — 303-778-6016
*Nancy Duell, (I), Miles Hardiman, (I), Masami, (I), Daniel McGowan, (I), Jan Oswald, (P), David Spira, (I), Bonnie Timmons, (I)*
Costello/Daley/1317 Maltman St, Los Angeles, CA — 213-667-2959
Courie, Jill/8322 Beverly Blvd., Los Angeles, CA — 213-658-8844
Courtney, Mary Ellen/1808 Diamond, So Pasadena, CA — 213-256-4655
Creative Assoc/5233 Bakman Ave, North Hollywood, CA — 213-985-1224
Creative Associates/5233 Bakman Ave, N. Hollywood, CA — 213-985-1224
*Chris Dellorco, (I), Don Dixon, (I), Derrick Gross, (I), Phillip Howe, (I), Davin Mann, (I), Pat Ortega, (I), Scott Ross, (I), Paul Stinson, (I)*
Cross, Anne/10642 Vanora Dr, Sunland, CA — 213-792-9163

## DEF
Denkensohn, Dale/520 N Western Ave, Los Angeles, CA — 213-467-2135
Design Pool/11936 Darlington Ave, #303, Los Angeles, CA — 213-826-1551
Diskin, Donnell/143 Edgemont, Los Angeles, CA — 213-383-9157
Drayton, Sheryl/5018 Dumont Pl, Woodland Hills, CA — 213-347-2227
Drexler, Steve/2256 Pinecrest, Altadena, CA — 213-684-7902
*Teri Sandison, (I)*
Du Bow & Hutkin/7461 Beverly Blvd, Los Angeles, CA — 213-938-5177
DuBow & Hutkin/7461 Beverly Blvd, Los Angeles, CA — 213-938-5177
Eisenrauch, Carol & Assoc/1105 Alta Loma #3, Los Angeles, CA — 213-652-4183
Ericson, William/1714 N Wilton Pl, Hollywood, CA — 213-461-4969
Fleming, Laird Tyler/407 1/2 Shirley Pl, Beverly Hills, CA — 213-552-4626
*John Bilecky, (P), Willardson & White, (P)*

## G
George, Nancy/360 1/2 N Mansfield Ave, Los Angeles, CA — 213-935-4696
*Brent Bear, (P), Justin Carroll, (I), Randy Chewning, (I), Bruce Dean, (I), Hank Hinton, (I), Gary Hoover, (I), Andy Hoyos, (I), Richard Kriegler, (I), Larry Lake, (I), Gary Lund, (I), Rob Sprattler, (I)*
Geovani, Harry/947 La Cienaga, Los Angeles, CA — 213-652-7011
Gilbert, Sam/410 Sheridan, Palo Alto, CA — 415-325-2102
Gilson, Janet/820 N LaBrea Ave, Los Angeles, CA — 213-466-5404
Globe Photos/8400 W Sunset Blvd, Los Angeles, CA — 213-654-3350
Gonter, Richard/1765 N. Highland Ave., #40, Los Angeles, CA — 213-874-1122
*Roger Marshutz, (P)*
Gray, Connie/248 Alhambra, San Francisco, CA — 415-922-4304
*Debbie Cotter, (I), Alan Daniels, (I), Don Evenson, (I), Ernie Friedlander, (P), Max Gisko, (I), Bob Gleason, (I), Fred*

# REPRESENTATIVES CONT'D.

Please send us your additions and updates.

Nelson, (I), David Oshiro, (GD), Suzanne Phister, (I), Randy South, (I), Michael Utterbock, (P), Raul Vega, (P), Will Westin, (I), Barry Wetmore, (I)
Greenwald, Kim/1115 5th St #202, Santa Monica, CA — 213-394-6502
Grossman, Neal/Los Angeles, CA — 213-462-7935
   Tom Zimberoff, (P)
Group West/5455 Wilshire Blvd #1212, Los Angeles, CA — 213-937-4472

## H
Hackett, Pat/2030 1st Ave, #201, Seattle, WA — 206-623-9459
   Larry Duke, (I), Bill Evans, (I), Randy Grochoske, (D), Rudi Legname, (P), Louise Lewis, (I), Bill Mayer, (I), Booker McDraw, (I), Mike Schumacher, (I), Gretchen Siege, (G), John C Smith, (I), John Terence Turner, (P)
Haigh, Nancy/90 Natoma St, San Francisco, CA — 415-391-1646
Hallowell, Wayne/11046 Mccormick, North Hollywood, CA — 213-769-5694
   Alden Butcher, (AV), Emerson/Johnson/MacKay, (I), Ed Masterson, (P), Bill McCormick, (G), Louis McMurray, (I), Pro/Stock, (P), Diana Robbins, (I)
Hamik/Marechal/PO Box 1677, Sausalito, CA — 415-332-8100
Hamilton Productions, Dan Wilcox/1484 Hamilton Ave, Palo Alto, CA — 415-321-6837
Happe, Michele L/1183 N Michigan, Pasadena, CA — 213-684-3037
   Tom Engler, (P), Rich Mahon, (I), Linda Medina, (I)
Harris, Amy/536 Westbourne, Los Angeles, CA — 213-659-7466
Harte, Vikki/409 Bryant St, San Francisco, CA — 415-495-4278
Hauser, Barbara/7041 Hemlock St., Oakland, CA — 415-339-1885
Hawke, Sindy/22612 Leaflock Rd - Lake Fores, El Toro, CA — 714-837-7138
Hedge, Joanne/1838 El Cerrito Pl #3, Hollywood, CA — 213-874-1661
   Delana Bettoli, (I), John Harmon, (I), Bo Hylen, (P), Jeff Leedy, (I), Kenvin Lyman, (I), Scott Miller, (I), Dennis Mukai, (I)
Hillman, Betsy/65 Cervantes Blvd #2, San Francisco, CA — 415-563-2243
   Tim Boxell, (I), Graham Henman, (P), Hiro Kimura, (I), Michael Koester, (I), John Marriott, (P), J T Morrow, (I), Joe Spencer, (I), Jeremy Thornton, (I), Jackson Vereen, (P)
Homan, Beth, Group West, Inc./5455 Wilshire Blvd., #1212, Los Angeles, CA — 213-937-4472
Hunt, Lou/Los Angeles, CA — 213-462-6565
Hyatt, Nadine/P O Box 2455, San Francisco, CA — 415-543-8944
   Jeanette Adams, (I), Ted Betz, (P), Ellen Blonder, (I), Charles Bush, (P), Frank Cowan, (P), Duck-Soup, (A), Marty Evans, (P), Gerry Gersten, (I), John Hyatt, (I), Bret Lopez, (P), Tom McClure, (I), Jan Schockner, (L), Liz Wheaton, (I)

## JK
Jones, B.C./229 S Kenmore Ave, Los Angeles, CA — 213-389-5196
Kerz, Valerie/P.O. Box 480678, Los Angeles, CA — 213-876-6232
   Brian Leatart, (P), Ken Nahoun, (P), Jane O'Neill, (P), Matthew Rosen, (P)
Kirsch, Melanie/2643 S Fairfax Ave, Culver City, CA — 213-559-0059
Knable, Ellen/717 N La Cienega, Los Angeles, CA — 213-855-8855
   Bryant Eastman, (I), Marc Feldman, (P), Joe Heiner, (I), Kathy Heiner, (I), Rudy Legname, (P), Dave McMacken, (I), Richard Noble, (P), Vigon/Nahas/Vigon, (I), Brian Zick, (I)

## L
Laycock, Louise/8800 Venice Blvd, Los Angeles, CA — 213-870-6565
   Mike Barry, (I), Ben Bensen, (I), Ray Cadd, (I), Bob Drake, (I), Rod Dryden, (I), Ken Hoff, (I), Dick Laycock, (I), Nancy Moyna, (I), Ben Nay, (I), Ken Siefried, (I), Shari Wickstrom, (I)
Lee & Lou/618 S Western Ave #202, Los Angeles, CA — 213-388-9465
   Rob Gage, (P), Bob Grige, (P), Richard Leech, (I)
Lerwill, Phyllis/6635 Leland Way, Los Angeles, CA — 213-461-5540
Lilie, Jim/1801 Franklin St #404, San Francisco, CA — 415-441-4384
   Lou Beach, (I), Sid Evans, (I), Nancy Freeman, (I), Steve Fukuda, (P), Sharon Harker, (I), Jen-Ann Kirchmeier, (I), Jeff Leedy, (I), Jeff McCaslin, (I), Masami Miyamoto, (I), Mike Murphy, (I), Dennis Ziemienski, (I)
Lippert, Tom/1100 Glendon Ave, Los Angeles, CA — 213-279-1539
London, Valerie Eve/820 N Fairfax Ave, Los Angeles, CA — 213-655-4214
   Robert Stein, (P)
Luna, Tony/45 E Walnut, Pasadena, CA — 213-681-3130

## MN
Marie, Rita/6443 Lindenhurst Ave., Los Angeles, CA — 213-247-0135
Marlene/7801 Beverly Blvd, Los Angeles, CA — 213-934-5817
Martha Productions/1830 S. Robertson Blvd, Los Angeles, CA — 213-204-1771
   Ken Lee Chung, (P), Jacques Devand, (I), Stan Evenson, (I), John Hamagami, (I), Catherine Leary, (I), Manuel Nunez, (I), Rudy Obrero, (I)
Maslansky, Marsha/7927 Hillside Ave., Los Angeles, CA — 213-851-0210
McBride, Elizabeth/70 Broadway, San Francisco, CA — 415-986-2733
   Keith Criss, (I), Robert Holmes, (P), Patricia Pearson, (I), Bill Sanchez, (I), Earl Thollander, (I), Tom Vano, (P)
McCullough, Gavin/638 S Van Ness, Los Angeles, CA — 213-382-6281
McKenzie, Dianne/839 Emerson St, Palo Alto, CA — 415-322-8036
   Victor Budnik, (P)
Media Services/Gloria Peterson/10 Aladdin Terr, San Francisco, CA — 415-928-3033
Merschel, Sylvia/1341 Ocean Ave, Santa Monica, CA — 213-826-9155
   Elizabeth Brady, (I), Kevin Burke, (P), Bob Drake, (I), David Gaines, (I), John Megowan, (I), Curtis Mishiyama, (I), Janice O'Meara, (I), Robert Ruff, (P)
Michaels, Martha/3279 Kifer Rd, Santa Clara, CA — 408-735-8443
Millsap, Darrel/1744 6th Ave, San Diego, CA — 619-232-4519
Minter, John/911 Western #510, Seattle, WA — 206-292-9931
Morgan, Michele/22561 Claude, El Toro, CA — 714-770-9738
Morico, Mike/638 S Van Ness, Los Angeles, CA — 213-382-6281
   Chuck Coppock, (I), Carl Crietz, (I), George Francuch, (I), Bill Franks, (G), Jill Garnett, (I), Duane Gordon, (G), Elgas Grim, (I), Chuck Coppock, (I), Carl Crietz, (I), George Francuch, (I), Bill Franks, (G), Jill Garnett, (I), Duane Gordon, (G), Elgas Grim, (I)
Morris, Bob Jr/JCA/14019-A Paramount Ave, Paramount, CA — 213-633-4429
Morris, Leslie/1062 Rengstorff Ave, Mountain View, CA — 415-966-8301
   Paul Olsen, (I)
Murray, Natalia/Impact Photo/San Vincente, Los Angeles, CA — 213-852-0481
   Brent Bear, (P), Roy Bishop, (P), Jim Cornfield, (P), Arthur Montes DeOca, (P), Tom Engler, (P), Doug Kennedy, (P), Steve Smith, (P), Steve Strickland, (P), Ken Whitmore, (P)
Noyd, Jim/6412 Hollywood Blvd, Los Angeles, CA — 213-469-9924

## OPQ
Ogden, Robin/412 N Doheny Dr, Los Angeles, CA — 213-858-0946
   Bob Commander, (I), Paul Kiesow, (I), Marilyn Shinokochi, (I), Bob Simmons, (I), Bob Towner, (I), Jeannie Winston-Davis, (I), The Wizard Works, (AV)
Parsons, Ralph/1232 Folsom St, San Francisco, CA — 415-339-1885
Pate, Randy/The Source/5029 Westpark Dr, North Hollywood, CA — 213-985-8181
Patterson, Lore L/3281 Oakshire Dr., Los Angeles, CA — 213-851-3284
Pepper, Don/638 S Van Ness, Los Angeles, CA — 213-382-6281
   Chuck Coppock, (I), Carl Crietz, (I), George Francuch, (I), Bill Franks, (G), Jill Garnett, (I), Duane Gordon, (G), Elgas Grim, (I), Chuck Coppock, (I), Carl Crietz, (I), George Francuch, (I), Bill Franks, (G), Jill Garnett, (I), Duane Gordon, (G), Elgas Grim, (I)
Pierceall, Kelly/25260 Piuma Rd, Malibu, CA — 213-559-4327
Piscopo, Maria Representatives/2038 Calvert Ave, Costa Mesa, CA — 714-556-8133
Prapas, Christine/3757 Wilshire Blvd #205, Los Angeles, CA — 213-385-1743
Pre-Production West/6429 W 6th St, Los Angeles, CA — 213-655-1263
Quon, Milton/3900 Somerset Dr, Los Angeles, CA — 213-293-0706

## R
Robbins, Leslie/68 Cumberland St, San Francisco, CA — 415-826-8741
   Jim Korte, (I), James LaMarche, (I), Scott Miller, (I), Vida Pavesich, (I), Julie Peterson, (I), David Tise, (P), Tom Wyatt, (P)
Rosenthal, Elise/3336 Tilden Ave, Los Angeles, CA — 213-204-3230
   Alan Daniels, (I), Myron Grossman, (I), Alan Hashimoto, (I), James Henry, (I), Tim Huhn, (I), Robert Hunt, (I), Mark Edward McCandlish, (I), Tom Pansini, (I), Kim Passey, (I), Ward Shumacker, (I), Will Weston, (I), Larry Winborg, (I)

## S
Salisbury, Sharon/185 Berry St, San Francisco, CA — 415-495-4665
   Stewart Danials, (I), Jim Endicott, (I), Jim Evans, (I), Bob

# REPRESENTATIVES CONT'D.

Please send us your additions and updates.

Graham, (I), Dennis Gray, (P), Dave McMacken, (I), Norman Seef, (P), John VanHammersveld, (G)
Salzman, Richard W/1352 Honrblend St, San Diego, CA — 619-272-8147
Scroggy, David/2124 Froude St, San Diego, CA — 619-222-2476
  Chris Miller, (I), John Pound, (I)
Slobodian, Barbara/745 N Atta Vista Blvd, Hollywood, CA — 213-935-6668
  David Graves, (I), Bob Greisen, (I), Tom O'Brien, (P), Scott Slobodian, (P), Gary Watson, (I)
Sobol, Lynne/4302 Melrose Ave, Los Angeles, CA — 213-665-5141
  Frank Marquez, (I)
The Source/5029 Westpark Dr, North Hollywood, CA — 213-985-8181
  Mario Cassilli, (P), Steve Chorny, (I), Studio Pacifica, (L), Pencil Pushers,Inc, (D), Drew Struzan, (I)
Spraulding, David/2019 Pontiuf Ave, Los Angeles, CA — 213-475-7794
Steinberg, John/10434 Corfu Lane, Los Angeles, CA — 213-279-1775
  John Alvin, (I), Roger Bergendorf, (I), Phil Davis, (I), Penelope Gottlieb, (I), Hank Hinton, (I), David Kimble, (I), Reid Miles, (P), Larry Noble, (I), Chuck O'Rear, (P), Frank Page, (I), Carol Shields, (I), Bob Tanenbaum, (I)
Stern, Gregg/23870 Madison St, Torrence, CA — 213-373-6789
Sullivan, Diane/10 Hawthorne St, San Francisco, CA — 415-543-8777
Sweeney, Barbara/1720 Whiteley Ave, Hollywood, CA — 213-462-2143
Sweet, Ron/716 Montgomery St, San Francisco, CA — 415-433-1222
  Charles East, (D), John Hamagami, (I), Bob Haydock, (I), Richard Leech, (I), Walter Swarthout, (P), Don Weller, (I), Bruce Wolfe, (I), James B Wood, (P)

**T**
Taggard, Jim/PO 4064 Pioneer Square Station, Seattle, WA — 206-935-5524
  Sjef's-Photographie, (P)
Terry, Gloria/511 Wyoming St, Pasadena, CA — 213-681-4115
Todd, Deborah/259 Clara St, San Francisco, CA — 415-495-3556
Torrey/11201 Valley Spring Lane, Studio City, CA — 213-277-8086
  Stewart Daniels, (I), Jim Evans, (I), Bob Hickson, (I), Peter Lloyd, (I), Jim Miller, (P), Michael Schwab, (I), Jackson Vereen, (P), Barry Wetmore, (C), Dick Zimmerman, (P), Lumeni-Productions, (A)
Tos, Debbie/119 N La Brea, Los Angeles, CA — 213-932-1291
  Art Pasquali, (P)
**TRIMPE, SUSAN/2717 WESTERN AVE, SEATTLE, WA (P 107,159)** — **206-382-1100**

**V**
Vandamme, Mary/1165 Francisco #5, San Francisco, CA — 415-433-1292
  John Collier, (I), Robert Giusti, (I), Joe and Kathy Heiner, (I), Alan Krosnick, (P), Kenvin Lyman, (I), Dennis Mukai, (I), Pat Nagel, (I), Bill Rieser, (I), Ed Scarisbrick, (I), Michael Schwab, (I), Joseph Sellers, (I), Charles Shields, (I), Rick Strauss, (P), Carol Wald, (I), Kim Whitesides, (I)
Varie, Chris/2210 Wilshire Blvd, Santa Monica, CA — 213-395-9337

**W**
Wagoner, Jae/200-A Westminster Ave, Venice, CA — 213-392-4877
  Michael Backus, (I), Roger Beerworth, (I), Stephen Durke, (I), Bruce Miller, (I), Tom Nickosev, (I), Gregg Rowe, (I), Randy Scott, (I), Alice Simpson, (I), Robert Tanenbaum, (I), Don Weller, (I)
Wallach, Terri/1039 S Fairfax, Los Angeles, CA — 213-931-1169
Walsh, Sam/PO Box 5298, University Statio, Seattle, WA — 206-522-0154
West End Studios/1100 Glendon #732, Los Angeles, CA — 213-279-1539
West Light/1526 Pontius Ave, Los Angeles, CA — 213-473-3736
  Chuck O'Rear, (P)
Wiegand, Chris/7106 Waring Ave, Los Angeles, CA — 213-931-5942
Wilcox, Dan/1484 Hamilton Ave, Palo Alto, CA — 413-321-6837
  Sally Landis, (G)
Williams, Gavin/638 S Van Ness, Los Angeles, CA — 213-382-6281
Williams, George A/638 S Van Ness, Los Angeles, CA — 213-382-6281
Wood, Joan/141 N St Andrews Pl, Los Angeles, CA — 213-463-7717

**YZ**
Youmans, Jill/830, Los Angeles, CA — 213-469-8624
  Carole Etow, (I), Jeff George, (I), Roger Gordon, (I), Brian Leng, (P), Russ Simmons, (I)
Young, Jill/Compendium Inc/945 Front St #201, San Francisco, CA — 415-392-0542
  Richard Clark, (P), Judy Clifford, (I), Celeste Ericsson, (I), Marilee Heyer, (I), Bonnie Matza, (G), Barbara Mulhauser, (G), Donna Mae Shaver, (P), Sarn Suvityasin, (I), Ed Taber, (I)
Young, RW/9445 Amboy Ave, Pacoima, CA — 213-767-1945
Youno, Max/7207 Melrose Ave, Los Angeles, CA — 213-937-2255
Zimmerman, Delores H/9135 Hazen Dr., Beverly Hills, CA — 213-273-2642

# PHOTOGRAPHERS

## NEW YORK CITY

### A
| | |
|---|---|
| Abramowitz, Jerry/680 Broadway | 212-420-9500 |
| Abramson, Michael/84 University Pl | 212-691-2601 |
| Adams, George G./15 W 38th St | 212-391-1345 |
| Aerographics/514 W 24th St | 212-362-9546 |
| Aich, Clara/218 E 25th St | 212-686-4220 |
| Akis, Emanuel/6 W 18th St, #803 | 212-620-0299 |
| Albarello/Pettinato/156 Fifth Ave #200 | 212-929-6016 |
| Albert, Jade/9 E 68th St | 212-288-9653 |
| Alcorn, Richard/160 W 95th St, #7A | 212-866-1161 |
| **ALEXANDER, JULES/333 PARK AVE S (P 47)** | **212-533-3150** |
| Alexanders, John W/308 E 73rd St | 212-734-9166 |
| **ALLEN, JIM/21 E 22ND ST (P 48)** | **212-473-8020** |
| Allison, David/42 E 23 St | 212-460-9056 |
| **ALT, HOWARD/24 W 31ST ST (P 49)** | **212-594-3300** |
| Ambrose, Ken/44 E 23rd St | 212-260-4848 |
| Amplo, Nick/271 1/2 W 10th St | 212-741-2799 |
| Amrine, Jamie/900 Broadway | 212-254-4108 |
| Anderson, Jim/317 E 9th St, #1 | 212-473-4690 |
| Arakawa, Nobu/40 E 21st St | 212-475-0206 |
| Aranita, Jeffrey/310 Madison Ave Ste 1915 | 212-625-7672 |
| Arky and Barrett/40 E 20 St, 7th Fl | 212-777-7309 |
| Arma, Tom/38 W 26th St | 212-243-7904 |
| Ashe, Bill/534 W 35th St | 212-695-6473 |
| Atkin, Jonathan/23 E 17th St | 212-242-5218 |
| **AUBREY, DANIEL L/365 FIRST AVE (P 38)** | **212-598-4191** |
| Augustine, Pauline/825 West End Ave | 212-749-8285 |
| Avedis/381 Park Ave S | 212-685-5888 |
| Avedon, Richard/407 E 75th St | 212-879-6325 |
| Azzi, Robert/415 Madison Ave | 212-750-1020 |

### B
| | |
|---|---|
| Baasch, Diane/41 W 72nd St #11F | 212-724-2123 |
| Babushkin, Mark/110 W 31st St | 212-239-6630 |
| Bahrt, Irv/303 E 46th St | 212-759-1750 |
| Baillie, Allan & Gus Francisco/220 E 23rd St 11th fl | 212-683-0418 |
| **BAKER, JOE/156 FIFTH AVE, STUDIO 925 (P 50)** | **212-924-3440** |
| Baldwin, Joel/20 E 20th St | 212-533-7470 |
| Barba, Dan/201 E 16th St | 212-533-6385 |
| Barboza, Ken/108 E 16th St | 212-674-5759 |
| Barboza, Tony/108 E 16th St | 212-674-5759 |
| Barclay, Bob Studios/5 W 19th St | 212-255-3440 |
| Barkentin, George/45 W 18th St | 212-243-2174 |
| Barnell, Joe/60 E 42nd St | 212-687-0696 |
| Barnett, Peggy/26 E 22nd St | 212-673-0500 |
| Barns, Larry/200 E 53rd St | 212-355-1371 |
| Barr, Neal/222 Central Park South | 212-765-5760 |
| Barrett, John E/40 E 20th St | 212-777-7309 |
| **BARROW, SCOTT/214 W 30TH ST (P 51)** | **212-736-4567** |
| Barrows, Wendy/172 Lexington Ave | 212-685-0799 |
| Barton, Paul/101 W 18th St | 212-533-1422 |
| Bartone, Lawrence/20 E 20th St | 212-254-6430 |
| **BARTONE, LAURENCE/20 E 20TH ST (P 33)** | **212-254-6430** |
| Batlin, Lee/37 E 28th St | 212-685-9492 |
| Baumel, Ken/119 W 23rd St | 212-929-7550 |
| Bean, John/5 W l9th St | 212-242-8106 |
| Beauchamp, Jacques/42 E 23rd St 6th fl | 212-475-7787 |
| **BEAUDIN, TED/6 W 37TH ST (P 52)** | **212-683-5480** |
| Bechtold, John/117 E 31st St | 212-679-7630 |
| Beck, Arthur/119 W 22nd St | 212-691-8331 |
| Beebe, Morton/220 Central Park South #13 | 212-247-3772 |
| Belinsky, Jon/119 E 17th St | 212-254-5238 |
| Beller, Janet/228 W 72nd St | 212-799-1126 |
| Belott/Wolfson Photography Inc/156 Fifth Ave, #327 | 212-924-1510 |
| Benedict, William/5 Tudor City | 212-697-4460 |
| Bennett, Philip/1181 Broadway | 212-683-3906 |
| Benson, Richard/156 Fifth Ave #410 | 212-242-3126 |
| Bergman, Beth/150 West End Ave | 212-724-1867 |
| **BERKUN, PHIL/179 COLUMBIA HEIGHTS (P 53)** | **212-596-0294** |
| Berman, Brad/365 Washington Ave | 212-638-7942 |
| Bernstein, Alan/365 First Ave, 2nd Fl | 212-254-1355 |
| Bernstein, Bill/59 Thompson St | 212-925-6853 |
| Bester, Roger/119 Fifth Ave | 212-254-0108 |
| Betts, Glynne/116 E 63rd St | 212-688-4591 |
| Betz, Charles/50 W 17th St | 212-807-0457 |
| **BEVILACQUA/202 E 42ND ST (P 54)** | **212-490-0355** |
| Bijur, Hilda/190 E 72nd St | 212-737-4458 |
| Bisbee, Terry/290 W 12th St | 212-242-4762 |
| Bishop, David/251 W 19th St | 212-929-4355 |
| Blackman, Barry/115 E 23rd St | 212-473-3100 |
| Blake, Rebecca/35 W 36th St | 212-695-6438 |
| Bleiweiss, Herb/959 Eighth Ave | 212-262-3603 |
| Blinkoff, Richard/147 W 15th St, 3rd Fl | 212-620-7883 |
| Bodi Studios/340 W 39th St | 212-947-7883 |
| Bodick, Gay/11 E 80th St | 212-772-8584 |
| Bolesta, Alan/11 Riverside Dr, 13 SE | 212-873-1932 |
| Bolster, Mark/1736 2nd Ave | 212-348-0965 |
| Bordnick, Barbara/39 E 19th St | 212-533-1180 |
| Bosch, Peter/477 Broome St | 212-925-0707 |
| Bough, Martin/78 Fifth Ave | 212-989-5871 |
| Bracco, Bob/43 E 19th St | 212-228-0230 |
| Brady, Mathew B/31 W 27th St | 212-683-6060 |
| Brandt, Peter/73 Fifth Ave #6B | 212-242-4289 |
| Braverman, Alan M/485 Fifth Ave | 212-682-1794 |
| Breitenbach, Josef/165 W 66th St | 212-799-3019 |
| Brenner, Jay/18 E 17th St | 212-741-2244 |
| Breskin/Imberling/324 Lafayette | 212-925-2271 |
| Brewster, Don/235 West End Ave | 212-874-0548 |
| Britton, Peter/315 E 68th St | 212-737-1664 |
| Brizzi, Andrea/175 Washington Park | 212-522-0836 |
| Brody, Bob/5 W 19th | 212-741-0013 |
| Bronstein, Steve/5 E 19th St | 212-982-9480 |
| Brosan, Roberto/873 Broadway | 212-473-1471 |
| Brown, David/6 W 20th St | 212-675-8067 |
| Brown, Ed/146 W 29th St | 212-563-2084 |
| Brown, Nancy/6 W 20th St | 212-675-8067 |
| Bruderer, Rolf/443 Park Ave S | 212-684-4890 |
| Bryce, Sherman E/201 Eastern Pkwy | 212-783-3237 |
| Bryson, John/12 E 62nd St | 212-755-1321 |
| Buceta, Jaime/300 Park Ave S 1406 | 212-254-2160 |
| Buck, Bruce/171 1st Ave | 212-777-8309 |
| Buckler, Susanne/325 W 37th St | 212-279-0043 |
| Buckley, Peter/140 E 83rd St, #10 | 212-744-0658 |
| Bud Cannarella Inc/156 Fifth Ave | 212-691-1750 |
| Bullaty, Sonja/336 Central Park West | 212-663-2122 |
| Burjoski, David/448 W 37th St | 212-736-0298 |
| Burklin, Bruno/873 Broadway | 212-420-0208 |
| Burrell, Fred/16 W 22nd St | 212-691-0808 |
| **BYERS, BRUCE/11 W 20TH ST (P 56)** | **212-242-5846** |

### C
| | |
|---|---|
| **CADGE, WILLIAM F/15 W 28TH ST (P 57)** | **212-685-2435** |
| Cahill, Bill/37 E 28th St | 212-725-8178 |
| Cailor/Resnick/237 W 54th St | 212-977-4300 |
| Cal, Mario/140 W 57th St | 212-582-3142 |
| Camera Communications/39 W 38th St | 212-391-1373 |
| Camp, E J/101 W 18th St | 212-362-9546 |
| Canady, Philip/1411 Second Ave | 212-737-3855 |
| **CANNON, GREGORY/44 W 17TH ST (P 58)** | **212-243-2798** |
| Canton, Brian/205 E 42nd St | 212-221-7318 |
| **CANTOR, PHIL/75 NINTH AVE (P 59)** | **212-243-1143** |
| Cardacino, Michael/310 E 49th St | 212-308-3287 |
| Carrino, John/160 Fifth Ave | 212-243-3623 |
| **CARROLL, DON/188 GRAND ST (P 60,61)** | **212-371-3648** |
| Carron, Les/15 W 24th St, 2nd Fl | 212-255-8250 |
| Carter, Bill/39 E 12th | 212-505-6088 |
| Carter, Dwight/120 W 97th St | 212-662-8116 |
| Cashin, Art/5 W 19th St | 212-255-3440 |
| Casper, Mike/70 Wooster St | 212-219-1257 |
| Castagneto, Stephen/4465 Douglas Ave | 212-752-0099 |
| Caulfield, Patricia/115 W 86th St, #2E | 212-799-8068 |
| Cearley, Guy/156 Fifth Ave, Rm 600 | 212-243-6629 |
| Chalk, David/825 President St | 212-638-2816 |
| Chalkin, Dennis/91 Fifth Ave | 212-929-1036 |

# PHOTOGRAPHERS CONT'D.

Please send us your additions and updates.

| | |
|---|---|
| Chaney, Scott/150 W 26th St, #503 | 212-741-3254 |
| Chanteau, Pierre/209 W 38th St | 212-221-5860 |
| Charles, Bill/265 W 37th St | 212-719-9156 |
| Checani, Richard/31 E 32nd St | 212-889-2049 |
| Chen, Paul Inc/133 Fifth Ave | 212-674-4100 |
| Chernin, Bruce/330 W 86th St | 212-496-0266 |
| Cheser, Vickie/211 E 70th St #17C | 212-570-6876 |
| Choroszewski, Walter J/4515 Auberndale La | 212-463-5439 |
| Christensen, Paul H/286 Fifth Ave | 212-279-2838 |
| Chu, H L/39 W 29 St | 212-889-4818 |
| Cirone, Bettina/57 W 58th St | 212-888-7649 |
| Clarke, Kevin/900 Broadway | 212-460-9360 |
| Clayman, Andrew/334 Bowery #6F | 212-674-4906 |
| Clayton, Tom/1591 Second Ave | 212-744-1415 |
| **CLOUGH, TERRY/147 W 25TH ST (P 66,67)** | **212-255-3040** |
| Cobb, Jan/381 Park Ave S, #922 | 212-889-2257 |
| Cochran, George/381 Park Ave S | 212-689-9054 |
| Coggin, Roy/64 W 21st St | 212-929-6262 |
| Cohen, Mark David/5 W 19th | 212-741-0015 |
| Cohn, Ric/156 Fifth Ave | 212-924-6749 |
| Colby, Ron/140 E 28th St | 212-684-3084 |
| Coleman, Gene/250 W 27th St | 212-691-4752 |
| Collins, Chris/381 Park Ave S | 212-725-0237 |
| Collins, Sheldon/27 W 24th St | 212-242-0076 |
| Colton, Robert/1700 York Ave | 212-831-3953 |
| Connelly, Hank/6 W 37th St | 212-563-9109 |
| Connors, William/310 E 46th St | 212-490-3801 |
| **COOK, IRVIN/69 MERCER ST (P 68)** | **212-925-6216** |
| Cook, Rod/108 W 25th St | 212-242-4463 |
| Cooke, Colin/380 Lafayette St | 212-254-5090 |
| Cooke, Jerry/161 E 82nd St | 212-288-2045 |
| Cooper, Martha/310 Riverside Dr #805 | 212-222-5146 |
| Cooper, Steve/5 W 31st St | 212-279-4543 |
| Corman, Bert/5 Union Sq | 212-924-8774 |
| Cornicello, John/245 W 29th St | 212-564-0874 |
| Corporate Photographers Inc/45 John St | 212-964-6515 |
| Corporate Studios Inc/78 Fifth Ave | 212-989-5871 |
| Cosimo/35 W 36th St | 212-563-2730 |
| Couzens, Larry/16 E 17th St | 212-620-9790 |
| Cowan, Frank/5 E 16th St | 212-675-5960 |
| Crampton, Nancy/35 W 9th St | 212-254-1135 |
| Croner, Ted/15 W 28th St | 212-685-3944 |
| Cserna, George/148 W 57th St | 212-477-3472 |
| Cunningham, Peter/214 Sullivan St | 212-475-4866 |
| Curatola, Tony/18 E 17th St | 212-243-5478 |
| Czaplinski, Czeslaw/90 Dupont St | 212-389-9606 |

**D**

| | |
|---|---|
| Dantuono, Paul/433 Park Ave So | 212-683-5778 |
| Dantzic, Jerry/910 President St | 212-789-7478 |
| Dauman, Henri/136 E 76th St | 212-737-1434 |
| Davidson, Darwin K/32 Bank Street | 212-242-0095 |
| Davis, Dick/400 E 59th St | 212-751-3276 |
| Davis, Hal/220 E 23rd St | 212-689-7787 |
| Davis, Richard/17 E 16th St 9th Fl | 212-675-2428 |
| Day, Bob/29 E 19th St | 212-475-7387 |
| Day, Olita/29 E 19th St | 212-475-7387 |
| **DELESSIO, LEN/49 W 27TH ST (P 70)** | **212-683-3522** |
| DeMelo, Antonio/524 W 23rd St | 212-929-0507 |
| DeMenil, Adelaide/222 Central Park South | 212-541-8265 |
| DeMilt, Ronald/873 Broadway | 212-228-5321 |
| Denner, Manuel/249 W 29th St | 212-947-6220 |
| DePra, Nancy/15 W 24th St | 212-242-0252 |
| Derex, David/247 W 35th St | 212-947-9302 |
| DeRosa, Peter/117 W 95th St | 212-864-3007 |
| Derr, Steve/418 W 46th St, #4B | 212-246-5920 |
| DeSanto, Thomas/134 Fifth Ave, 2nd Fl | 212-989-5622 |
| Detay, Ted/15 W 72nd St | 212-799-2231 |
| DeToy, Ted/205 W 19th St | 212-675-6744 |
| DeVito, Bart/43 E 30th St, 14th Fl | 212-889-9670 |
| DeVoe, Marcus E/34 E 81st St | 212-737-9073 |
| Di Martini, Sally/201 W 16th St | 212-989-8369 |
| Diamond, Joseph/43 W 29th St | 212-807-0138 |
| Dibue, Robert/245 E 40th St, #23C | 212-490-0486 |
| Dicran Studio/100 Fifth Ave 15th Fl | 212-242-0055 |
| DiFranza-Williamson Inc/1414 Ave of Americas | 212-832-2343 |
| **D'INNOCENZO, PAUL/13 E 16TH ST (P 71)** | **212-620-0610** |
| Dixon, Mel/29 E 19th St | 212-677-5450 |
| Dockery, Larry/378 Third Ave | 212-684-4432 |
| Dolce Steven,/135 Fifth Ave | 212-777-3350 |
| Dominis, John/Time Life Bldg #2020 | 212-841-2340 |
| Dorf, Myron Jay/205 W 19th St, 3rd Fl | 212-255-2020 |
| Dorin, Jay/220 Cabrini Blvd | 212-781-7378 |
| Doubilet, David/1040 Park Ave, #6J | 212-348-5011 |
| Drew, Rue Faris/177 E 77th St | 212-794-8994 |
| Duke, Dana/329 W 87th St | 212-362-5605 |
| Dunand, Frank/18 W 27th St | 212-686-3478 |
| Duncan, Kenn/853 Seventh Ave | 212-582-7080 |
| Dunning, Hank/50 W 22nd St | 212-675-6040 |
| Dunning, Robert and Diane/57 W 58th St | 212-688-0788 |
| Durrance, Dick/50 Vanderbilt Ave | 207-236-3990 |

**E**

| | |
|---|---|
| Eagan, Timothy/10 W 74th St | 212-874-0055 |
| Eager, Sean/15 W 18th St | 212-826-6107 |
| Eagle, Stephen/599 West End Ave | 212-362-4205 |
| Eastep, Wayne/443 Park Ave South #1006 | 212-686-8404 |
| Eberstadt, Fred/791 Park Ave | 212-794-9471 |
| Eckstein, Ed/234 Fifth Ave, #31 E | 212-685-9342 |
| Edahl, Edward/100 Fifth Ave | 212-929-2002 |
| Edgeworth, Anthony/333 Fifth Ave | 212-679-6031 |
| Edwards, Gregory/30 East End Ave | 212-879-4339 |
| Ehrenpreis, Dave/156 Fifth Ave | 212-242-1976 |
| Ehrlich, George/PO Box 186 | 914-355-1757 |
| Eisenberg, Steve/448 W 37th St | 212-228-8616 |
| Elbers, Johan/18 E 18th St | 212-929-5783 |
| Elgort, Arthur/300 Central Park West | 212-724-6557 |
| Elio Productions, Inc/220 E 23rd St | 212-684-7440 |
| Elkin, Irving/12 E 37th St | 212-686-2980 |
| **ELKINS, JOEL/5 E 16TH ST (P 34)** | **212-989-4500** |
| Ellis, Ray/176 Westminster Rd | 212-282-6449 |
| Elmer, Jo/200 E 87th St | 212-369-7077 |
| **ELMORE, STEVE/1640 YORK AVE, #3B (P 75)** | **212-472-2463** |
| Elness, Jack/61 W 23rd St | 212-242-5045 |
| Emil, Pamela/327 Central Park West | 212-662-4821 |
| Endress, John Paul/254 W 31st St | 212-736-7800 |
| Englander, Maury/41 Union Square W | 212-982-2800 |
| Enko Phtographics/40-53 243rd St | 212-423-2662 |
| Epstein, S Karin/233 E 70th St | 212-472-0771 |
| Erwin, David/600 W 111 St #11D | 212-865-4325 |
| Essel, Robert/39 W 71st St | 212-877-5228 |
| Estrada, Sigrid/902 Broadway | 212-673-4300 |
| Everett, Michael/15 W 28th St | 212-683-6223 |
| Excalibur Photo Graphics/Bruce Kaplan/444 Madison Ave | 212-759-8280 |

**F**

| | |
|---|---|
| Farber, Robert/35 W 31st St | 212-564-0031 |
| Farrell, John/611 Broadway #905 | 212-460-9001 |
| Fay, Joyce/1275 Third Ave | 212-988-8361 |
| Fay, Stephen Studios/154 W 57th St | 212-757-3717 |
| Feinstein, Gary/19 E 17th St | 212-242-3373 |
| Fell, John/160 W 71st St | 212-580-8327 |
| Fellerman, Stan/152 W 25th St | 212-243-0027 |
| Ferguson, Phoebe/260 W 71st St | 212-595-9572 |
| Ferorelli, Enrico/50 W 29th St | 212-685-8181 |
| Fetter, Frank/400 E 78th St | 212-249-3138 |
| Field, Pat/16 E 23rd St | 212-477-9016 |
| Fields, Bruce/71 Greene St | 212-431-8852 |
| Finlay, Alastair/38 E 21st St, 9th Fl | 212-260-4297 |
| Firman, John/434 E 75th St | 212-794-2794 |
| **FISCHER, CARL/121 E 83RD ST (P 12,13)** | **212-794-0400** |
| **FISHBEIN, CHUCK/49 W 27TH ST (P 76,77)** | **212-532-4452** |
| **FISHMAN, CHUCK/69 1/2 MORTON ST (P 78)** | **212-242-3987** |
| Fiur, Lola Troy/360 E 65th St | 212-861-1911 |
| Flagler, Warren/200 E 62nd St | 212-935-5027 |
| Fland, Peter/423 W 55th St | 212-586-7918 |
| **FLATOW, CARL/20 E 30TH ST (P 79)** | **212-683-8688** |

# PHOTOGRAPHERS CONT'D.

Please send us your additions and updates.

| | |
|---|---|
| Floret, Evelyn/3 E 80 St | 212-472-3179 |
| Flynn, Richard/306 W 4th St | 212-243-0834 |
| Forastieri, Marili/156 Fifth Ave, Rm 1301 | 212-924-9412 |
| Ford, Carol/20 W 84th St, #2C | 212-580-1187 |
| **FORELLI, CHIP/316 FIFTH AVE (P 81)** | **212-564-1835** |
| Forrest, Bob/273 Fifth Ave | 212-288-4458 |
| Forte, Brian/421 Hudson St, #311 | 212-620-5676 |
| Forte, John/162 W 21 St | 212-620-0584 |
| Fox, Jeffrey/6 W 20th St | 212-620-0147 |
| **FRANCEKEVICH, AL/73 FIFTH AVE (P 82,83)** | **212-691-7456** |
| Francisco, Gus/220 E 23rd St | 212-683-0418 |
| Frank, Dick/11 W 25th St | 212-242-4648 |
| Frank, Richard/162 Eighth Ave | 212-636-0022 |
| Frankel, Tracy/41 Union Sq | 212-243-5687 |
| **FRASER, DOUGLAS/9 E 19TH ST (P 85)** | **212-777-8404** |
| Frazier, David/254 W 51st St | 212-582-1501 |
| Freas, John/353 W 53rd St #1W | 212-682-2462 |
| Freed, Leonard/251 Park Ave S | 212-475-7600 |
| Freedman, Lionel/325 E 73rd St | 212-737-8540 |
| Freson, Robert/37 Beekman Pl | 212-246-0679 |
| Fried, Richard/430 W 14th St | 212-929-1052 |
| Friedman, Benno/26 W 20th St | 212-255-6038 |
| Friedman, Jerry/873 Broadway | 212-533-1960 |
| Friedman, Steve/545 W 111th St | 212-864-2662 |
| Friedman, Walter/58 W 68th St | 212-874-5287 |
| **FUNK, MITCHELL/500 E 77TH ST (P 86,87)** | **212-988-2886** |
| Funt, David W/220 E 23rd St | 212-686-4111 |
| Furones, Claude Emile/40 Waterside Plaza | 212-683-0622 |
| Fusco, Paul/251 Park Ave S | 212-475-7600 |
| Gairy, John/11 W 17th St, 2nd Fl | 212-242-5805 |
| Galante, Dennis/9 W 31st St | 212-239-0412 |
| Gallucci, Ed/381 Park Ave S | 212-532-2720 |
| Galton, Beth/91 5th Ave | 212-242-2266 |
| Gans, Hank/40 Waterside Plaza | 212-683-0622 |
| Garbin Photography/208 Fifth Ave #3E | 212-683-9188 |
| Garetti, John/140 W 22nd St | 212-242-1154 |
| Garlanda, Gino/300 E 33rd St | 212-685-0358 |
| Gartel, Larry/85 E 10th St | 212-228-1281 |
| Gee, Elizabeth/280 Madison | 212-683-6924 |
| Geer, Garry/77 Bleecker St, #823 | 212-533-8467 |
| Georges, Sammy/256 Fifth Ave | 212-683-6353 |
| Gescheidt, Alfred/175 Lexington Ave | 212-889-4023 |
| Gibson, Sam/139 E 30th St, #3C | 212-689-8071 |
| Gidion Inc/119 Fifth Ave | 212-677-8600 |
| **GIESE, AL/156 FIFTH AVE (P 91)** | **212-675-2727** |
| Gigli, Ormond/327 E 58th St | 212-758-2860 |
| Gillardin, Andre/6 W 20th St | 212-675-2950 |
| Gilmour, James/377 Park Ave S | 212-532-8288 |
| Giovanni, Rae Anne/32 Union Sq E #613 | 212-254-6406 |
| Giraldi, Frank/54 W 39th St | 212-840-8225 |
| **GLADSTONE, GARY/237 E 20TH ST (P 92,93)** | **212-777-7772** |
| Glancz, Jeff/38 W 21st St 12th Fl | 212-741-2504 |
| Glassman, Carl/80 N Moore St, #37G | 212-732-2458 |
| Glaviano, Marco/40 W 27th St #9 Flr | 212-683-8680 |
| Glinn, Burt/41 Central Park W | 212-877-2210 |
| Globe Photos/275 7th Ave | 212-689-1340 |
| Globus Brothers/1 Union Square W | 212-243-1008 |
| Gneiting, Robin/444 E 86th St | 212-239-1423 |
| Goff, Lee/32 E 64th St | 212-759-5194 |
| Gold, Bernie/873 Broadway, #301 | 212-677-0311 |
| Gold, Charles/170 Fifth Ave | 212-242-2600 |
| Goldberg, Ken/141 Fifth Ave | 212-807-8244 |
| Goldfarb, Ed/428 E 84th St | 212-543-6183 |
| Goldman, A Bruce/440 Riverside Dr | 212-666-9143 |
| Goldman, Richard/36 W 20th St | 212-675-3021 |
| Goldsmith, Gary/201 E 66th St | 212-288-4851 |
| Goldsmith, Lynn/15 E 61st St | 212-593-2677 |
| Goldstein, Arthur/253 W 28th St | 212-695-7246 |
| Golob, Stanford/40 Waterside Plaza | 212-532-7166 |
| Gonzalez, Luis/85 Livingston St | 212-834-0426 |
| Gonzalez, Manuel/119 Fifth Ave | 212-254-2200 |
| Gordon, Brad/200 Riverside Dr | 212-222-3707 |
| **GORDON, JOEL/5 E 16TH ST (P 95)** | **212-989-9207** |
| Gorin, Bart/1160 Broadway | 212-683-3743 |
| Gorodnitzki, Diane/160 W 71st St | 212-724-6259 |
| Gotfryd, Bernard/46 Wendover Rd | 212-350-2505 |
| Gottheil, Philip/249 W 29th St | 212564-0971 |
| Gould, Peter L/7 E 17th St | 212-675-3707 |
| Gove, Geoffrey/117 Waverly Pl | 212-260-6051 |
| Grant, Robert/91 Fifth Ave | 212-255-2323 |
| Gray, Bernard/225 E 67th St | 212-249-4446 |
| Gray, Dudley/118 E 25th St | 212-473-7584 |
| Gray, Mitchell/169 E 86th St | 212-427-2287 |
| Green, Allen/1601 Third Ave | 212-534-1718 |
| Green, Gary/200 W 95th St | 212-678-0763 |
| **GREEN-ARMYTAGE, STEPHEN/171 W 57TH ST (P 96,97)** | **212-247-6314** |
| **GREENBERG, DAVID/54 KING ST (P 98)** | **212-243-7351** |
| Greene, Joshua/156 Fifth Ave | 212-741-2232 |
| Gregory, John/105 Fifth Ave 9C | 212-691-1797 |
| Griffiths, Philip Jones/251 Park Ave S | 212-475-7600 |
| Grill, Tom/32 E 31st St | 212-989-0500 |
| Griner/Cuesta & Assoc/720 Fifth Ave | 212-246-7600 |
| Grodman, Robert Photography/18 E 18th St | 212-929-0424 |
| Gross, Cy/59 W 19th St | 212-243-2556 |
| Gross, Garry/907 Broadway | 212-260-5597 |
| Grossman, Henry/37 Riverside Dr | 212-580-7751 |
| Group Four/225 E 67th St | 212-249-4446 |
| Gruen, John/20 W 22nd ST | 212-248415 |
| Gruszczynski/821 Broadway | 212-673-1243 |
| **GSCHEIDLE, GERHARD E/381 PARK AVE S (P 99)** | **212-532-1374** |
| Gudnason, Torkil/58 W 15th St | 212-929-6680 |
| Gulardo, John/110 W 31st St | 212-736-2172 |
| Gurovitz, Judy/207 E 74th St | 212-988-8685 |
| Guyaux, Jean-Marie/29 E 19th St | 212-677-1224 |
| Haak, Ken/122 E 30th St | 212-679-6284 |
| Haar, Thomas/463 West St | 212-929-9054 |
| Haas, David/330 W 86th St | 212-877-5003 |
| **HAAS, ERNST/853 SEVENTH AVE (P 14,15)** | **212-247-4543** |
| Haas, Ken/15 Sheridan Square | 212-255-0707 |
| Hagen, Boyd/680 Broadway #1 | 212-473-2008 |
| Hagg, Ahmad W/156 Fifth Ave #308 | 212-691-1750 |
| Haggerty, David/17 E 67th St | 212-989-0600 |
| Haling, George/231 W 29th St #302 | 212-683-2558 |
| Hall, Clayton/247 W 35th St | 212-947-8160 |
| Hamilton, David W/47 Walker St, #2B | 212-226-1271 |
| Hamilton, Keith/749 FDR Dr. | 212-982-3375 |
| Hammond, Maury/9 E 19th St | 212-460-9990 |
| Hanlon, Gary Inc/12 W 32nd St | 212-594-1543 |
| Hanson, Kent/344 W 17th St #40 | 212-691-7910 |
| Harbutt, Charles/1 Fifth Ave | 212-475-1489 |
| Hardin, Ted/156 Fifth Ave | 212-242-2958 |
| Harrington, Grace/300 W 49th St | 212-246-1749 |
| **HARRINGTON, PHILLIP/230 PARK AVE (P 100)** | **212-284-0212** |
| **HARRIS, BROWNIE/459 W 21ST ST (P 101)** | **212-929-1796** |
| Harris, Michael/18 W 21st St | 212-255-3377 |
| Harris, Ronald G/119 W 22nd St | 212-255-2330 |
| Hartman, Harry/61 W 23rd St | 212-675-5454 |
| Hartmann, Erich/251 Park Ave S | 212-475-7600 |
| Harty, Mary/117 W 95th St | 212-864-3007 |
| **HASHI STUDIO/49 W 23RD ST, 3RD FL (P 102,103)** | **212-675-6902** |
| Haskins, Sam/200 E 62nd St | 212-935-5027 |
| Hausman, George/1181 Broadway | 212-686-4810 |
| **HAVILAND, BRIAN/34 E 23RD ST (P 104)** | **212-598-0070** |
| Hayes, Kerry/156 Fifth Ave | 212-442-4804 |
| Hayward, Bill/215 Park Ave S | 212-228-6206 |
| **HEDRICH, DAVID/7 E 17TH ST (P 35)** | **212-924-3324** |
| Hege, Laszlo/13 E 30th St | 212-679-8220 |
| Heir, Stuart/20 W 20th St | 212-620-0754 |
| Heisler, Gregory/611 Broadway | 212-777-8100 |
| Helms, Bill/1175 York Ave | 212-759-2079 |
| Henze, Don Studio/126 Fifth Ave, 7th Fl | 212-989-3576 |
| Heron, Michal/28 W 71st St | 212-787-1272 |

# PHOTOGRAPHERS CONT'D.

Please send us your additions and updates.

| | |
|---|---|
| Herr, H Buff/56 W 82nd St | 212-595-4783 |
| Herr, Jim/433 E 51st St | 212-371-0076 |
| Hess, Brad/485 Fifth Ave | 212-599-1500 |
| Hill, Pat/118 E 28th ST | 212-679-0884 |
| Hilliard, Mary/120 E 85 St | 212-879-7839 |
| Hine, Skip/34 W 17th St | 212-691-5903 |
| Hiro/50 Central Park West | 212-580-8000 |
| Hirst, Michael/300 E 33rd St | 212-982-4062 |
| Hoban, Tana/105 E 16th St | 212-477-6071 |
| Hochman, Allen Studio/9-11 E 19 St | 212-777-8404 |
| Hofer, Evelyn/55 Bethune St | 212-691-0084 |
| Holbrooke, Andrew/50 W 29th St | 212-679-2477 |
| Hollyman, Tom/300 E 40th St | 212-867-2383 |
| Holt, Katheryn/45 Riverside Dr | 212-874-2345 |
| Holtzman Photography/41 Union Sq #425 | 212-242-7985 |
| Hooper, Thomas/126 Fifth Ave | 212-691-0122 |
| Hopkins, Douglas/636 Sixth Ave | 212-243-1774 |
| Hopkins, Stephen/475 Carlton Ave | 212-783-6461 |
| Hopson, Gareth/61 W 23rd St | 212-535-3800 |
| Horowitz, Leonard/645 Broadway | 212-673-4212 |
| **HOROWITZ, RYSZARD/103 FIFTH AVE (P 105)** | **212-243-6440** |
| Horowitz, Ted/465 West End Ave | 212-595-0040 |
| Horst/166 E 63rd St | 212-751-4937 |
| Horvath, Jim/306 E 38th St | 212-679-7384 |
| Houghton, Jim/106 E 31st St | 212-889-3920 |
| Houser, Robt/75-19 184th St | 212-454-0757 |
| Howard, David/42 W 39th St, 7th Fl | 212-719-5888 |
| Howard, Ken/130 W 17th St, 9th Fl | 212-691-3445 |
| Howard, Rosemary/902 Broadway | 212-473-5552 |
| Hugelmeyer, John/6 E 39th St | 212-889-1189 |
| Huntzinger, Bob/514 W 37th St | 212-947-4177 |
| Huszar/156 Fifth Ave | 212-929-2593 |
| Hutchings, Richard/174 Rochelle St | 212-885-0846 |
| Hyatt, Morton/352 Park Ave S 2nd Fl | 212-889-2955 |
| **I** Ihara/5 Union Sq W | 212-243-4862 |
| Ikeda, Shig/636 Sixth Ave | 212-924-4744 |
| Illography/49 Crosby St | 212-219-0244 |
| The Image Bank/633 Third Ave | 212-953-0303 |
| Image Makers/310 E 23rd St, #9F | 212-533-4498 |
| Images/7 E 17th St | 212-675-3707 |
| Ing, Francis/112 W 31st St | 212-279-5022 |
| Ioss, Walter/344 W 72nd St | 212-787-8984 |
| Irish, Len/11 W 17th St | 212-242-2237 |
| Ishimuro, Eisuke/170 Fifth Ave | 212-255-9198 |
| **J** Jacobs, Eric Stephen/230 Central Park W | 212-877-8444 |
| Jacobs, Marty/34 E 23rd St | 212-475-1160 |
| Jacobsen, Paul/150 Fifth Ave | 212-243-4732 |
| Jacobson, Alan/1466 Broadway | 212-221-0464 |
| Janeart Ltd/154 W 57th St, #810 | 212-765-1121 |
| Jawitz, Louis H/13 E 17th St #PH | 212-929-0008 |
| Jeffery, Richard/119 W 22nd St | 212-255-2330 |
| Jeffrey, Lance/30 E 21st St | 212-674-0595 |
| Jeffry, Alix/71 W 10th St | 212-982-1835 |
| Jenkinson, Mark/142 Bleeker St #6 | 212-982-8567 |
| Jensen, Peter M/22 E 31st St | 212-689-5026 |
| Joel, Seth Photography/440 Park Ave S | 212-685-3179 |
| **JOERN, JAMES/125 FIFTH AVE (P 106)** | **212-260-8025** |
| **JOHANSKY, PETER/108 E 16TH ST 6TH FL (P 107)** | **212-260-4301** |
| Jones, Chris/220 Park Ave So #6B | 212-777-5361 |
| Jones, Wesley/114 E 25th St | 212-580-2872 |
| Joseph, Meryl/158 E 82nd St | 212-861-5057 |
| Juliano, Vincent T/P O Box 404 | 212-777-2980 |
| Jurado, Lewis/119 Fifth Ave, #607 | 212-677-3100 |
| **K** Kachaturian, Armen/10 E 23rd St | 2-533-3550 |
| Kahn, R T/156 E 79th St | 212-988-1423 |
| Kalan, Mark R/922 S President St | 212-857-3677 |
| Kaltman, Len/500 Park Ave | 212-750-1386 |
| Kamsler, Leonard/140 Seventh Ave | 212-242-4678 |
| Kane, Art/1181 Broadway | 212-679-2016 |
| Kane, Peter T/342 Madison Ave | 212-687-5848 |
| Kaplan, Alan/7 E 20th St | 212-982-9500 |
| Kaplan, Barry/323 Park Ave S | 212-254-8461 |
| Kaplan, Bruce/Excalibur Photographics/444 Madison Ave | 212-759-8280 |
| **KAPLAN, PETER B/126 W 23RD ST (P 109)** | **212-206-1362** |
| Kaplan, Peter J/924 West End Ave | 212-222-1193 |
| Karales, James H/147 W 79th St | 212-799-2483 |
| Karia, Bhupendra/9 E 96th St #15 B | 212-860-5479 |
| Karlin, Lynn/241 Ascot Ave | 212-667-1839 |
| Kassabian Photography/127 E 59th St | 212-268-6480 |
| Katz, Paul/381 Park Ave S | 212-684-4395 |
| Kaufman, Curt/320 E 58th St | 212-759-2763 |
| Kaufman, Micky/144 W 27th St | 212-255-1976 |
| Kaufman, Ted/121 Madison Ave, #4E | 212-685-0349 |
| Keaveny, Francis/260 Fifth Ave | 212-683-1033 |
| Keegan, Marcia/140 E 46th St | 212-953-9023 |
| Keller, Tom/440 E 78th St | 212-472-3667 |
| Kellner, Jeff/16 Waverly Pl | 212-475-3719 |
| Kelly, Bill/140 Seventh Ave, #1N | 212-989-2794 |
| Kemper, Charles/97 Perry St | 212-807-0323 |
| Kennedy, David Michael/10 W 18th St | 212-255-9212 |
| Kennedy, Donald J/400 West End Ave | 212-877-4583 |
| Kennedy, William/1 W 64th St | 212-874-4200 |
| **KENT, KAREN/29 JOHN ST** | **212-962-6793** |
| Kerr, Justin and Barbara/14 W 17th St | 212-741-1731 |
| Khornak, Lucille/425 E 58th St | 212-593-0933 |
| Kiehl, Stuart/365 First Ave | 212-260-5466 |
| King, Bill/100 Fifth Ave | 212-675-7575 |
| Kingsford, Michael Studio/874 Broadway | 212-475-0553 |
| Kirk, Barbara E/447 E 65th St | 212-734-3233 |
| Kirk, Charles/333 Park Ave S | 212-677-3770 |
| Kirk, Malcolm/12 E 72nd St | 212-744-3642 |
| Kirk, Russell/13 E 16th St | 212-691-0014 |
| Kiss, Bob/29 E 19th St | 212-505-6650 |
| Kittle, Kit/511 E 20th St | 212-673-0596 |
| Klein, Matthew/15 W 18th St | 212-255-6400 |
| Kligge, Robert/5 W 30th St | 212-736-0119 |
| Kluetmeier, Heinz/54 W 84th St #2F | 212-362-3739 |
| Knowles, Robert/24 Fifth Ave, #219 | 212-677-7396 |
| Koenig, Phil/49 Market | 212-964-1590 |
| Komar, Greg/30 Waterside Sq #18a | 212-685-0275 |
| Koner, Marvin/345 E 56th St | 212-751-7734 |
| Kopelow, Paul/135 Madison Ave | 212-689-0685 |
| **KORSH, KEN/118 E 28TH ST (P 111)** | **212-685-8864** |
| Kosoff/Butensky Photography/40 W 24th St | 212-243-4880 |
| Kouirinis, Bill/381 Park Ave South c/o Matus P | 212-696-5674 |
| Kozan, Dan Productions/89 Fifth Ave | 212-691-2288 |
| Kozlowski, Mark/39 W 28th St | 212-684-7487 |
| Kramer, Daniel/110 W 86th St | 212-873-7777 |
| Krementz, Jill/228 E 48th St | 212-688-0480 |
| Kresch, Jerry/175 W 76th St | 212-787-7396 |
| Krieger, Harold/225 E 31st St | 212-686-1690 |
| Krongard, Steve/212A E 26th St | 212-689-5634 |
| Kuentz, Mike/66 W 38th St #205 | 212-840-7475 |
| Kuhn, Ann/1155 Broadway | 212-685-1774 |
| **L** Lambray, Maureen/52 E 81st St | 212-879-3960 |
| LaMonica Chuck/16 W 22nd St | 212-243-4400 |
| Langerman, Steve/16 W 22nd St | 212-691-9322 |
| Langley, David/536 W 50th St | 212-581-3930 |
| Langley, J Alex/212 E 16th St | 212-673-6640 |
| Langley, Kelly/212 E 16th St | 212-777-1853 |
| Lapinski, Keith/45 W 27th St | 212-686-5534 |
| Larrain, Gilles/95 Grand St | 212-925-8494 |
| Laser Light/451 W Broadway | 212-237-2126 |
| Laszlo Studio/28 W 39th St | 212-575-0314 |
| Lategan, Barry/502 Laguardia Pl | 212-228-6850 |
| Laurance, Bruce Studio/253 W 28th St | 212-947-3451 |
| Laure, Jason/8 W 13th St | 212-691-7466 |
| Laurence, Mary/PO Box 1763 | 212-903-4025 |
| Lax, Ken/239 Park Ave So | 212-228-6191 |
| Layman/Newman/133 W 19th St | 212-989-5845 |

# PHOTOGRAPHERS CONT'D.

Please send us your additions and updates.

| | |
|---|---|
| LeBaube, Guy/310 E 46th St | 212-986-6981 |
| Lecca, Dumitru Dan/378 Third Ave | 212-684-4432 |
| Leduc, Lyle/320 E 42nd St #1014 | 212-697-9216 |
| Lee, Vincent/5 Union Sq West | 212-620-7080 |
| **LEEDS, KAREN/119 W 23RD ST (P 115)** | **212-243-4546** |
| Legrand, Michel/152 W 25th St | 212-807-9754 |
| **LEIGHTON, THOMAS/321 E 43RD ST C/O PH 12 (P 116,117)** | **212-370-1835** |
| Leiter, Saul/156 Fifth Ave | 212-475-6034 |
| Lenore, Dan/15 W 17th St | 212-924-1675 |
| Leo, Donato/170 Fifth Ave | 212-989-4200 |
| Leonian, Phillip/220 E 23rd St | 212-989-7670 |
| Lerman, Peter M/37 E 28th St #506 | 212-685-0053 |
| **LERNER, RICHARD/34 E 23D ST (P 104)** | **212-598-0070** |
| Let There Be Neon/451 W Broadway | 212-226-7747 |
| **LEUNG, JOOK/110 E 23RD ST (P 118)** | **212-254-8334** |
| Levine, Jonathan/11 W 9th St | 212-673-4698 |
| LeVine, Nancy/60 E 9th St #330 | 212-473-0015 |
| Levitin, Nicholas/44 W 96th St | 212-662-6027 |
| Levy, Peter/119 W 22nd St | 212-691-6600 |
| Levy, Richard/5 W 19th St | 212-243-4220 |
| Levy, Yoav/4523 Broadway | 212-942-8185 |
| Lewis, Ross/460 W 24th St | 212-691-6878 |
| Lieberman, Allen/5 Union Square W, 4th Floor | 212-255-4646 |
| Liebman, Phil/315 Hudson | 212-269-7777 |
| Liebowitz, Eric/245 E 19th St | 212-477-2899 |
| Liftin, Joan/1 Fifth Ave | 212-475-1489 |
| Lim/6 W 37th St | 212-736-4143 |
| Lindner, Steven/18 W 27th St | 212-683-1317 |
| Lipton, Trina/60 E 8th St | 212-533-3148 |
| Little, Christopher/4 W 22nd St | 212-691-1024 |
| Lockhart, George/210 E 63rd St | 212-355-1313 |
| Lokmer, John/873 Broadway | 212-678-4343 |
| Lombardi, Frederick/180 Pinehurst Ave | 212-568-0740 |
| Londener, Hank/18 W 38th St | 212-354-0293 |
| Long, Joe/225 E 67th St | 212-249-4446 |
| Lonsdale, William J/35 Orange St | 212-834-8281 |
| Lorenz, Robert/373 Broadway | 212-505-8483 |
| Love, Robin/333 W 19th St | 212-243-7339 |
| Lubianitsky, Leonid/1674 Broadway | 212-541-6611 |
| Lucka, Klaus/35 W 31st St | 212-594-5910 |
| Ludders, Leora/61 W 23rd St | 212-929-1462 |
| Luftig, Allan/873 Broadway | 212-533-4113 |
| **LURIA, DICK/5 E 16TH ST (P 119)** | **212-929-7575** |
| Lusk, Frank/25 E 37th St | 212-679-1441 |
| Lustica, Tee/156 Fifth Ave, #925 | 212-924-3440 |

## M

| | |
|---|---|
| Mac Weeney, Alen/171 First Ave | 212-473-2500 |
| MacGreggor, Helen/60 E 11th St | 212-505-7561 |
| MacLaren, Mark/430 E 20th St | 212-674-8615 |
| Mace, Mort/1133 Broadway | 212-929-7017 |
| Macedonia, Carmine/6 W 20th St | 212-255-7910 |
| Mack, Donald/69 W 55th | 212-246-6086 |
| Madere, John/306 W 80th St | 212-724-3424 |
| Magnum Photos/251 Park Ave S | 212-475-7600 |
| **MAISEL, JAY/190 THE BOWERY (P 16,17)** | **212-431-5013** |
| Malignon, Jacques/34 W 28th St | 212-532-7727 |
| Malone, Lyn/200 East End Ave | 212-534-5827 |
| Manna, Lou/20 E 30th St | 212-683-8689 |
| Manno, John/20 W 22nd St #802 | 212-243-7353 |
| Manos, Constantine/251 Park Ave S | 212-475-7600 |
| **MARCHESE, JIM/200 W 20TH ST (P 120,121)** | **212-242-1087** |
| **MARCO, PHIL/104 FIFTH AVE #4 FLR (P 18,19)** | **212-929-8082** |
| Marcus, Helen/120 E 75th St | 212-879-6903 |
| **MARESCA, FRANK/236 W 26TH ST (P 122,123)** | **212-620-0955** |
| Margerin, William D/251 Park Ave S | 212-473-7945 |
| Mark, Mary Ellen/251 Park Ave S | 212-431-1610 |
| Marmaras, John/22 W 21st St | 212-741-0212 |
| **MARSHALL, LEE/201 W 89TH ST (P 124)** | **212-799-9717** |
| **MARTIN, BUTCH/344 W 38TH ST #10E (P 125)** | **212-370-4959** |
| Martin, Dennis/11 W 25th St | 212-929-2221 |
| Martin, Miguel/5 W 31st St | 212-564-3677 |
| Marvullo, Joseph E/404 Park Ave S | 212-532-2773 |
| Marx, Richard/8 W 19th St | 212-929-8880 |
| Masca/109 W 26th St | 212-929-4818 |
| Mason, Donald Studio/101 W 18th St, 4th Fl. | 212-675-3809 |
| Masser, Randy/6 W 18th St, 7th Fl | 212-807-7271 |
| Mathews, Barbara Lynn/16 Jane St | 212-691-0823 |
| Matsumoto, Tosh/30 E 23rd St | 212-989-5663 |
| Matsuo, Toshi/135 Fifth Ave | 212-260-2556 |
| Matthews, Cynthia/200 E 78th St | 212-288-7349 |
| Maucher, Arnold/527 3rd St | 212-788-3616 |
| Maynard, Chris/297 Church St | 212-966-0558 |
| Mazzurco, Phil/150 Fifth Ave #319 | 212-989-1220 |
| McCabe, David/39 W 67th St, #1403 | 212-874-7480 |
| McCabe, Robert/117 E 24th St | 212-677-1910 |
| McCarthy, Margaret/31 E 31st St | 212-696-5971 |
| McCartney, Susan/902 Broadway #1608 | 212-533-0660 |
| McClean, Cyril H/119 W 25th St | 212-989-7880 |
| McCurdy, John Chang/156 Fifth Ave | 212-243-6949 |
| McFarland, Lowell/115 W 27th St | 212-691-2600 |
| McGlynn, David/18-23 Astoria Blvd | 212-626-9427 |
| **MCGRAIL, JOHN/522 E 20TH ST (P 126)** | **212-475-4927** |
| McGrath, Norman/164 W 79th St | 212-799-6422 |
| McKiernan, Scott/129 Front St | 212-825-0073 |
| McLaughlin-Gill, Frances/49 E 86th St | 212-534-5596 |
| McLoughlin, James/12 W 32nd St | 212-244-1595 |
| McNally, Joe/56 W 65th St | 212-873-2638 |
| McQueen, Hamilton/126 Fifth Ave | 212-924-1393 |
| Mead, Chris/215 Park Ave S | 212-475-7600 |
| Media Management Corp/12 W 27th St | 212-696-0880 |
| Media Photo Group, Inc/745 Seventh Ave | 212-582-6880 |
| Meiselas, Susan/251 Park Ave S | 212-475-7600 |
| Meiselas, Susan/251 Park Ave S | 212-475-7600 |
| Melford, Michael/32 E 22nd St | 212-473-3095 |
| Melillo, Nick/118 W 27th St, #3r | 212-691-7612 |
| Mellon/69 Perry St | 212-691-4166 |
| Memo Studio/39 W 67th St, #1402 | 212-787-1658 |
| Menashe, Abraham/900 West End Ave | 212-254-2754 |
| Menken Studios/119 W 22nd St | 212-924-4240 |
| **MEOLA, ERIC/535 GREENWICH ST (P 128-133)** | **212-255-5150** |
| Merle, Michael G/5 Union Square West | 212-741-3801 |
| Merrim, Lewis J/31 E 28th St | 212-889-3124 |
| **MERVAR, LOUIS/29 W 38TH ST, 16TH FL (P 36,37)** | **212-354-8024** |
| Meyer, Paul/340 6th Ave | 212-499-9372 |
| **MEYEROWITZ, JOEL/151 W 19TH ST (P 20,21)** | **212-666-6505** |
| Michals, Duane/109 E 19th | 212-473-1563 |
| Mike Yamaoka Studio/146 W 29th St | 212-736-8292 |
| Milbauer, Dennis/330 W 52nd St | 212-245-2121 |
| Miles, Ian/313 E 61st St | 212-688-1360 |
| Miljakovich, He en/114 Seventh Ave, #3C | 212-242-0646 |
| Miller, Bert/30 Dongan Pl | 212-567-7947 |
| **MILLER, DONALD/485 FIFTH AVE (P 134,135)** | **212-986-9783** |
| Miller, Eileen/28 W 38th St | 212-944-1507 |
| Miller, Myron/23 E 17th St | 212-242-3780 |
| Miller, Peter M/80 East End Ave | 212-879-3443 |
| Miller, Wayne F./251 Park Ave S | 212-475-7600 |
| Miller, Bill/36 E 20th St | 212-674-8026 |
| Minh Studio/200 Park Ave S, #1507 | 212-477-0649 |
| Mitchell, Benn/103 Fifth Ave | 212-255-8686 |
| Mitchell, Jack/356 E. 74th St | 212-737-8940 |
| Molofsky, Rica/243 West End Ave | 212-362-3592 |
| Moon, Sarah/67 Irving Pl | 212-674-8080 |
| Moore, Jimmy/38 E 19th St | 212-674-7150 |
| Moore, Truman/873 Broadway, 4th Fl. | 212-533-3655 |
| Morecraft, Ron/920 Broadway | 212-475-6101 |
| Morello, Joe/40 W 28th St | 212-684-2340 |
| Moretz, Charles/141 Wooster St | 212-254-3766 |
| Morgan, Jeff/5 W 19th St | 212-741-0015 |
| Morris, Bill/81 Irving Place | 212-473-2296 |
| Morris, Leonard/200 Park Ave S | 212-473-8485 |
| Morrison, Ted/286 Fifth Ave | 212-279-2838 |
| Morsch, Roy J/1200 Broadway | 212-679-5537 |
| Moscati, Frank/139 Fifth Ave | 212-228-4000 |
| Mougin, Claude/138 W 17th St | 212-691-7895 |

# PHOTOGRAPHERS CONT'D.

Please send us your additions and updates.

| | |
|---|---|
| Muller, Rudy/318 E 39th St | 212-679-8124 |
| Mulvehill, Larry/30 Lincoln Plz | 212-582-7475 |
| Munro, Gordon/381 Park Ave S | 212-889-1610 |
| **MUNSON, RUSSELL/6 E 39TH ST (P 136)** | **212-689-7672** |
| Muresan, John/42 W 96th St | 212-222-6643 |
| Murphy, Art/675 West End Ave | 212-222-5751 |
| Murray, Robert/149 Franklin St | 212-226-6860 |
| Murro, A & Assoc Inc/152 W 25th St | 212-691-4220 |
| Myers, Robert J/407 E 69th St | 212-249-8085 |

### N
| | |
|---|---|
| Naar, John/230 E 50th St | 212-752-4625 |
| **NADELSON, JAY/116 MERCER ST (P 139)** | **212-226-4266** |
| Nakamura, Tohru/112 Greene St | 212-334-8011 |
| Nakano, George/119 W 22nd St | 212-228-9370 |
| Namuth, Hans/157 W 54th St | 212-245-2811 |
| Nardelli, Will/114 E 32nd St | 212-683-6930 |
| **NATHAN, SIMON/275 W 96TH ST (P 141)** | **212-873-5560** |
| National Imagemakers/1250 Broadway | 212-563-5000 |
| Nealy, Keith/12 E 22nd St | 212-673-9870 |
| Needham, Steven/159 Madison Ave #4A | 212-696-4973 |
| Nelken, Dan/43 W 27th St | 212-532-7471 |
| Nelsena, Burt/360 W 21 St | 212-683-4900 |
| Nelson, Michael/7 E 17th St, 5th Fl | 212-924-2892 |
| Nemeth Studio/220 E 23rd St | 212-686-3272 |
| Newman, Allan/133 W 19th St | 212-989-5845 |
| Newman, Arnold/39 W 67th St | 212-877-4510 |
| Newman, Irving/900 Broadway | 212-228-2760 |
| Newman, Marvin E/227 Central Park West | 212-362-2044 |
| Niccolini, Dianora/356 E 78th St | 212-288-1698 |
| Nichols, Peter/25 W 39th St | 212-354-4681 |
| Nicholson, Nick/121 W 72nd St #2E | 212-362-8418 |
| Nicolaysen, Ron/130 W 57th St | 212-947-5167 |
| Niefield, Terry/210 Fifth Ave | 212-686-8722 |
| Nikas, Basil W/710 Park Ave | 212-750-3736 |
| Nisnevich, Lev/164 Madison Ave | 212-725-5810 |
| Nivelle, Serge/36 Gramercy Pk East | 212-473-2802 |
| Niwa-Ogrudek Ltd/30 E 23rd St | 212-982-7120 |
| Nobart NY, Inc/33 E 18th St | 212-475-5522 |
| Nons, Leonard/5 Union Sq West | 212-741-3990 |
| Norstein, Marshall/248 6th Ave | 212-768-0786 |

### O
| | |
|---|---|
| **OBREMSKI, GEORGE/1200 BROADWAY (P 142,143)** | **212-684-2933** |
| **OCHI/636 6TH AVE (P 46)** | **212-807-7711** |
| Ogrudek, Robert/36-19 167th St | 212-939-5193 |
| Ohara, Hiro/5 Union Sq W | 212-243-4862 |
| Ohringer, Frederick/130 E 18th St | 212-473-6701 |
| Ohta Studio/15 E 11th St | 212-243-2353 |
| Oliphant, Sarah/38 Cooper Square | 212-741-1233 |
| Olivo, John/545 W 45th St | 212-765-8812 |
| Olman, Bradley/15 W 24th St | 212-243-0649 |
| Olson, John/135 W 27th St | 212-243-5800 |
| **O'NEILL, MICHAEL/134 TENTH AVE (P 22,23)** | **212-807-8777** |
| Oppersdorff, Mathias/1220 Park Ave | 212-860-4778 |
| **ORENSTEIN, RONN/55 W 26TH ST (P 144)** | **212-685-0563** |
| Oringer, Hal/32 W 31st St | 212-564-7544 |
| Orkin, Ruth/65 Central Park West | 212-362-1658 |
| Orling, Alan S/53 E 10th St | 212-473-8363 |
| O'Rourke, J. Barry/1181 Broadway | 212-686-4224 |
| Ort, Samuel/3323 Kings Hghwy | 212-377-1218 |
| Ortner, Jon/64 W 87th St | 212-873-1950 |
| Osonitsch, Robert/112 Fourth Ave | 212-533-1920 |
| Otsuki, Toshi/241 W 36th St | 212-594-1939 |
| Oudi/325 Bowery | 212-777-0847 |
| Owen Brown Studio/134 W 29th St | 212-947-9470 |
| Owens, Sigrid/221 E 31st St | 212-686-5190 |
| Ozgen, Nebil/6 W 20th St 5th Fl | 212-924-1719 |

### P Q
| | |
|---|---|
| Paccione/73 Fifth Ave | 212-691-8674 |
| Pagliuso, Jean/315 CPW | 212-873-6594 |
| Pagnano, Patrick/217 Thompson St | 212-475-2566 |
| Panuska, Robert/521 Madison Ave | 212-752-3930 |
| Papadopolous, Peter/78 Fifth Ave | 212-675-8830 |
| Pappas, Tony/110 W 31st | 212-868-2032 |
| Paras, Michael N/236 Elizabeth St | 212-278-6768 |
| **PARIK, JAN/165 E 32ND ST (P 146)** | **212-686-3514** |
| Parks, Claudia/310 E 23rd St | 212-533-4498 |
| Pastner, Robert L/166 E 63rd St | 212-838-8335 |
| Pateman, Michael/155 E 35th St | 212-685-6584 |
| Paul, Kenneth/342 Flushing Ave | 212-624-8157 |
| Paz, Peter/Box 596 219 E 70th St | 212-672-7790 |
| **PEACOCK, CHRISTIAN/28 W 86TH ST, #2F (P 147)** | **212-580-1422** |
| Peden, John/168 Fifth Ave | 212-255-2674 |
| Pederson/Erwin/924 Broadway | 212-677-0044 |
| **PELTZ, STUART/6 W 18TH ST, (P 148)** | **212-929-4600** |
| Pemberton, John/37 E 28th St | 212-532-9285 |
| Pendleton, Bruce/485 Fifth Ave | 212-986-7381 |
| Penn, Irving/37 Beekman Pl | 212-245-7913 |
| Peppi, John David Studio/1220 Broadway | 212-594-9221 |
| Peress, Gilles/251 Park Ave S | 212-475-7600 |
| Perkell, Jeff/141 Fifth Ave | 212-684-3988 |
| Perricone, Paul/ | 212-581-6470 |
| Perron, Robert/104 E 40th St | 212-661-8796 |
| Perweiler, Gary/873 Broadway | 212-254-7247 |
| Pfeffer, Barbara/40 W 86th St | 212-877-9913 |
| Pfizenmaier, Edward/42 E 23rd | 212-475-0910 |
| Phillips, Robert/101 W 57th St | 212-757-5190 |
| **PHOTOFILE INTL LTD/32 E 31ST (P 44-45)** | **212-989-0500** |
| **PHOTOSCOPE INC/12 W 27TH ST (P 149)** | **212-696-0880** |
| Pilgreen, John/91 Fifth Ave #300 | 212-243-7516 |
| Pinney, Doris/555 Third Ave | 212-683-0637 |
| Pippin, Wilbor/106 Fifth Ave | 212-675-5514 |
| Pite, Schwartz, White/115 W 29th St 10th Fl | 212-564-0875 |
| Plotkin, Bruce/3 W 18th, 7th Fl | 212-691-6185 |
| Pobiner, Ted/381 Park Ave S | 212-679-5911 |
| Pollard, Kirsty/5 Union Sq West | 212-255-4646 |
| Polsky, Herb/1024 Sixth Ave | 212-730-0508 |
| Porta, Art/29 E 32nd St | 212-685-1555 |
| Porter, Alan/213 E 25th St | 212-689-5894 |
| Poster Studio/210 Fifth Ave Suite 402 | 212-349-3720 |
| **POTTLE, JOCK/301 W 89TH ST #15 (P 150)** | **212-874-0216** |
| **POWERS, GUY/69 MERCER ST (P 151-156)** | **212-925-6216** |
| Pozarik, James/43-19 168th | 212-539-7836 |
| Pressman, Herb/118 E 28th St #908 | 212-686-5055 |
| Prezant, Steve Studios/1181 Broadway, 9th Fl | 212-684-0822 |
| **PRIBULA, BARRY/62 SECOND AVE (P 157)** | **212-777-7612** |
| Price, Clayton J/50 W 17th St | 212-929-7721 |
| Price, David/4 E 78th St | 212-794-9040 |
| Priggen, Leslie/144 W 27th St | 212-243-4800 |
| Probst, Kenneth/251 W 19 St | 212-929-2031 |
| Prochnow, Bob/9 E 32nd St | 212-689-4133 |
| Proctor, Keith/78 Fifth Ave | 212-807-1044 |
| Pruitt, David/156 5th Ave | 212-807-0767 |
| Pruzan, Michael/1181 Broadway | 212-686-5505 |
| Puhlmann, Rico/419 E 50th St | 212-246-0679 |
| Quat, Dan/156 Fifth Ave | 212-807-0588 |

### R
| | |
|---|---|
| Raab, Michael/831 Broadway | 212-533-0030 |
| Rahl Studio/17 W 45th St | 212-840-8516 |
| Rajs, Jake/36 W 20th St | 212-242-2321 |
| Rapa-Nui Studio/139 E 57th St | 212-888-6732 |
| Raso, Peter/1940 Mayflower Ave | 212-829-4992 |
| Ratkai, George/404 Park Ave S | 212-725-2505 |
| Ratzkin, Lawrence/392 Fifth Ave | 212-279-1314 |
| Ray, Bill/350 Central Park West | 212-222-7680 |
| Rea, Jimmy/165-20 Northern Blvd | 212-961-6217 |
| Reed, Edward/124 Thompson St | 212-677-7480 |
| Reinhardt, Mike/154 W 57th St | 212-541-4787 |
| Reinmiller, Mary Ann/163 W 17th St | 212-243-4302 |
| Rentmeester, Co/4479 Douglas Ave | 212-757-4796 |
| **REZNY, AARON/119 W 23RD ST (P 159)** | **212-691-1894** |
| Rezny, Abe/28 Cadman Plaza West | 212-237-2126 |
| Rice, Neil/91 Fifth Ave | 212-924-6096 |
| Ries, Henry/204 E 35th St | 212-689-3794 |
| Ries, Stan/48-52 Great Jones St | 212-533-1852 |

# PHOTOGRAPHERS CONT'D.

Please send us your additions and updates.

| | |
|---|---|
| Riley, David-Carin/152 W 25th St | 212-741-3662 |
| Riley, Jon/12 E 37th St | 212-532-8326 |
| Ritter, Frank/127 E 90th St | 212-427-0965 |
| Rivelli, William/303 Park Ave S #204 | 212-254-0990 |
| Rizende, Sidney/64-48 Booth St. | 212-896-0660 |
| **RIZZO, ALBERTO/220 E 23RD ST (P 160)** | **212-684-7440** |
| Roberts, Stefan K/155 E 47th St | 212-688-9798 |
| Robins, Lawrence/5 E 19th St | 212-677-6310 |
| Robison, Chuck/21 Stuyvesant Oval | 212-777-4894 |
| Rodriguez, Maria/617 54th St | 212-851-2770 |
| Rose, Uli/527 Madison Ave | 212-741-1741 |
| Rosen, David/238 E 24th St | 212-684-5193 |
| Rosenblatt, George/11 E 68th St | 212-288-0250 |
| Rosenfeld, Stanley Z/175 Riverside Dr #8K | 212-787-6653 |
| Rosenthal, Barry/1155 Broadway 3rd Fl | 212-889-5840 |
| Ross, Ben/488 Clinton St | 212-858-4067 |
| Ross, Mark/345 E 80th St | 212-744-7258 |
| Ross, Steve/10 Montgomery Pl | 212-783-6451 |
| Rossum, Cheryl/310 E 75th St | 212-628-3173 |
| **ROTH, PETER/8 W 19TH ST (P 162)** | **212-242-4853** |
| Rothaus, Ede/34 Morton St | 212-989-8277 |
| Rotkin, Charles E/850 Seventh Ave | 212-757-9255 |
| Rubenstein, Raeanne/8 Thomas St | 212-964-8426 |
| Rubin, Al/250 Mercer St #1501 | 212-674-4535 |
| Rubin, Daniel/1032 Sixth Ave | 212-989-2400 |
| Rubin, Darleen/159 Christopher St | 212-243-6973 |
| Rubinstein, Eva/145 W 27th St | 212-243-4115 |
| Rudolph, Nancy/35 W 11th St | 212-989-0392 |
| Rugen-Kory/150 E 18th St | 212-777-3889 |
| Rummler, Tom/213 E 38th St | 212-683-8250 |
| Russell, Ted/37 E 28th | 212-532-4150 |
| Russell, Tom/636 Ave of the Americas | 212-989-9755 |
| Ryan, Will/16 E 17th St | 212-242-6270 |
| **RYSINSKI, EDWARD/636 AVE OF THE AMERICAS (P 163)** | **212-807-7301** |

## S

| | |
|---|---|
| S and J Studio/40 W 27th St | 212-807-7866 |
| Sahula, Peter/45 E 19th St | 212-982-4340 |
| Sakas, Peter/400 Lafayette St | 212-254-6096 |
| Salaff, Fred/225 W 57th St | 212-246-3996 |
| Salmieri, Steve/325 Broome St | 212-431-7606 |
| Salvati, Jerry/206 E 26th | 212-696-0454 |
| Salzano, Jim/91 Fifth Ave | 212-242-4820 |
| Samardge, Nick/220 E 23rd St | 212-679-2526 |
| Sanchez, Alfredo/14-23 30th Dr | 212-726-0182 |
| Sand/Stephen Anderson/641 Lexington Ave | 212-421-6249 |
| **SANDONE, A J/91 FIFTH AVE (P 164)** | **212-807-6472** |
| Sandone, AJ/91 Fifth Ave #501 | 212-807-6472 |
| Sanford, Tobey/888 Eighth Ave | 212-245-2736 |
| Sarapochiello Studio/106 Fifth Ave | 212-242-0413 |
| Satterwhite, Al/515 Broadway #2B | 212-219-0808 |
| Scarlett, Nora/100 Fifth Ave | 212-741-2620 |
| **SCAVULLO, FRANCESCO/212 E 63RD ST (P 24,25)** | **212-838-2450** |
| Schenk, Fred/112 Fourth Ave | 212-677-1250 |
| Schiff, Nancy Rica/24 W 30th St | 212-679-9444 |
| Schiller, Leif/244 Fifth Ave | 212-532-7272 |
| Schinz, Marina/222 Central Park South | 212-246-0457 |
| Schlachter, Trudy/160 Fifth Ave | 212-741-3128 |
| Schneider, Josef/119 W 57th St | 212-265-1223 |
| Schneider, Peter/902 Broadway | 212-982-9040 |
| Schneider, Roy/116 Lexington Ave | 212-686-5814 |
| Schreck, Bruno/873 Broadway, #304 | 212-254-3078 |
| Schulze, Fred/38 W 21st St | 212-242-0930 |
| Schwartz, Marvin/223 W 10th St | 212-929-8916 |
| Schwartz, Sing-Si/39 W 38th St | 212-228-4466 |
| Schweitzer, Andrew/333 Park Ave So | 212-533-7982 |
| Schwerin, Ron/889 Broadway | 212-228-0340 |
| Sclight, Greg/146 W 29th St | 212-736-2957 |
| Scocozza, Victor/117 E 30th St | 212-686-9440 |
| Seaton, Tom/91 Fifth Ave | 212-989-3550 |
| Secunda, Sheldon/112 Fourth Ave | 212-477-0241 |
| Seghers, Carroll/441 Park Ave S | 212-679-4582 |
| Seidman, Barry/119 Fifth Ave | 212-477-6600 |
| Seitz, Sepp/381 Park Ave S | 212-683-5588 |
| Selby, Richard/113 Greene St | 212-431-1719 |
| Seligman, Paul/163 W 17th St | 212-242-5688 |
| Seltzer, Abe/524 W 23d St | 212-807-0660 |
| Seltzer, Kathleen/25 E 4th St | 212-475-0314 |
| Shaefer, Richard/20 E 35 St #14 | 212-684-7252 |
| Shaffer, Stan/2211 Broadway | 212-807-7700 |
| Sharko, Greg/103-56 103 St | 212-738-9694 |
| Sherman, Guy/108 E 16th St | 212-675-4983 |
| Shiansky, Harry Studio/118 E 28th St | 212-889-5489 |
| Shiraishi, Carl/137 E 25th St 11th Fl | 212-679-5628 |
| Shung, Ken/220 E 49th St #1B | 212-759-5317 |
| Si Drabkin Studios, Inc/25 W 39th St | 212-398-0050 |
| Siciliano, Frank/125 Fifth Ave | 212-620-4075 |
| Silano, Bill/138 E 27th St | 212-889-0505 |
| Silver, Larry/236 W 26th St | 212-807-9560 |
| Simon, Peter Angelo/504 La Guardia Pl | 212-473-8340 |
| **SIMPSON, JERRY/28 W 27TH ST (P 166)** | **212-696-9738** |
| Simpson/Flint/156 5th Ave, #1214 | 212-741-3104 |
| Singer, Michelle/251 W 19th St #5C | 212-675-3431 |
| Sirdofsky, Arthur/112 W 31st St | 212-279-7557 |
| **SKALSKI, KEN/866 BROADWAY (P 167)** | **212-777-6207** |
| The Sketch Pad Studio/6 Jane St | 212-989-7074 |
| Skogsbergh, Ulf/100 Fifth Ave #800 | 212-255-7536 |
| Skolnik, Lew/135 W 29th St | 212-239-1455 |
| Skott, Michael/244 Fifth Ave Penthouse | 212-686-4807 |
| Slade, Chuck/70 Irving Pl | 212-673-3516 |
| Slavin, Neal/62 Greene St | 212-925-8167 |
| Sloan-White, Barbara/209 E 56th St, #1E | 212-903-4343 |
| Slovak, Kenneth/144-22 22nd Ave | 212-762-4369 |
| Smilow, Stanford/5 Union Sq W | 212-255-0310 |
| Smith, Bill/498 WestEnd Ave | 212-877-8456 |
| Smith, E Gordon/36 W 25th St, 4th Fl | 212-807-7840 |
| **SMITH, GORDON E/TOWER DR (P 168)** | **212-807-7840** |
| Smith, J Frederick/400 E 52nd St | 212-838-9797 |
| Smith, Jeff/30 E 21st St | 212-674-8383 |
| **SMITH, WILLIAM E/498 WEST END AVE (P 169)** | **212-877-8456** |
| Smolan, Rick/237 Lafayette St, #6N | 212-431-4239 |
| Snedeker, Katherine/16 E 30th St | 212-684-0788 |
| Snider, Ed/106 E 19th St | 212-673-3652 |
| Snyder, Norman/514 Broadway #3H | 212-219-0094 |
| So Studio/34 E 23rd St | 212-475-0090 |
| **SOCHUREK, HOWARD/680 FIFTH AVE (P 171)** | **212-582-1860** |
| Solo, Jules/313 W 77th St #1R | 212-877-0574 |
| Solomon, Chuck/622 Greenwich St | 212-243-4036 |
| Solowinski, Ray/154 W 57th | 212-757-7940 |
| Soluri, Michael/490 Second Ave, #9A | 212-683-1982 |
| **SOOT, OLAF/419 PARK AVE S (P 173)** | **212-686-4565** |
| Sorce, Wayne/20 Henry St, #5G | 212-237-0497 |
| Sorensen, Chris/PO Box 1760 | 212-684-0551 |
| Spahn, David/381 Park Ave S, #915 | 212-689-6120 |
| Spatz, Eugene/264 Sixth Ave | 212-777-6793 |
| Speier, Leonard/190 Riverside Dr | 212-595-5480 |
| Spindel, David M/18 E 17th St | 212-989-4984 |
| Spinelli, Frank/119 W. 23rd St | 212-243-8318 |
| Spiro, Edward/82-01 Britten | 212-424-7162 |
| St John, Lynn/308 E 59th St | 212-308-7744 |
| Stahman, Robert/1200 Broadway | 212-679-1484 |
| Stan Goldberg Assoc/235 W 76th St | 212-799-5991 |
| **STANDART, JOE/5 W 19TH ST (P 39)** | **212-605-0555** |
| Stanton, William/160 W 95th St, #9D | 212-662-3571 |
| States, Randy/406 Sackett St | 212-852-8674 |
| Steadler, Lance/154 W 27th St | 212-243-0935 |
| Steedman, Richard/214 E 26th St | 212-679-6684 |
| Steigman, Steve/5 E 19th St | 212-473-3366 |
| Stein, Larry/5 W 30th St | 212-239-7264 |
| Steiner, Charles/61 Second Ave | 212-777-0813 |
| Steiner, Christian/300 Central Park West | 212-799-4522 |
| Steiner, Karel/22 E 21st St | 212-460-8254 |
| Steiph/133 Fifth Ave | 212-533-8627 |
| Stember, John/154 W 57th St | 212-757-0067 |
| **STERN, BERT C/O PAM REID/420 E 64TH ST (P 26,27)** | **212-832-7539** |

# PHOTOGRAPHERS CONT'D.

Please send us your additions and updates.

| | |
|---|---|
| Stern, Bob/12 W 27th St | 212-889-0860 |
| Stern, Irene/117 E 24th St | 212-475-7464 |
| Stern, Laszlo/157 W 54th St | 212-757-5098 |
| Stettner, Bill/118 E 25th St | 212-684-4058 |
| Stevens, Roy/1349 Lexington Ave | 212-831-3495 |
| Stock, Dennis/251 Park Ave S | 212-475-7600 |
| Stokes, Stephanie/40 E 68th St | 212-744-0655 |
| Stoltman, Adam/207 E 85th St, #458 | 212-724-2800 |
| Stone, Bob/104 Fifth Ave | 212-807-2457 |
| Stone, Erika/327 E 82nd St | 212-737-6435 |
| **STRATOS, JIM/176 MADISON AVE (P 174,175)** | **212-696-1133** |
| Straus, Steve/43 W 39th St | 212-354-7828 |
| The Strobe Studio/91 Fifth Ave | 212-532-1977 |
| **STRONGIN, JEANNE/61 IRVING PL (P 176)** | **212-473-3718** |
| **STUART, JOHN/80 VARICK ST #4B (P 177)** | **212-966-6783** |
| Studio Nishio/874 Broadway #1003 | 212-475-6613 |
| Studio North/135 W 26th St #11 Flr | 212-255-8128 |
| Stupakoff, Otto/80 Varik St | 212-334-8032 |
| Sussman, David/115 E 23rd St | 212-744-1556 |
| Sutton, Humphrey/18 E 18th St | 212-989-9128 |
| Svensson, Steen/52 Grove St | 212-242-7272 |
| Swedowsky, Ben/381 Park Ave S | 212-684-1454 |
| Szasz, Suzanne/15 W 46th St | 212-832-9387 |
| Szkodzinsky, Wasyl/350 Manhattan Ave | 212-383-2407 |

## TU

| | |
|---|---|
| Taiman Photos Inc/595 Madison Ave | 212-751-6516 |
| Tamaccio, Larry/243 WestEnd Ave | 212-362-3592 |
| Tamin Productions/595 Madison Ave, #1527 | 212-807-6691 |
| Tanaka, Victor/156 Fifth Ave | 212-675-3445 |
| Tannenbaum, Ken/16 W 21st St | 212-675-2345 |
| Taylor, Jonathan/5 W 20th St | 212-741-2805 |
| **TCHEREVKOFF, MICHEL/873 BROADWAY (P 180,181)** | **212-228-0540** |
| Tenison, John/119 W 22nd St | 212-243-3418 |
| Terk, Harold/198 E 58th St | 212-838-1922 |
| Tervanski, Steve/125 E 39th St | 212-986-2237 |
| Tesa, Rudi/119 W 23rd St | 212-620-4514 |
| Thomas, Mark/501 E 82nd St 4W | 212-562-6892 |
| Thorton, John/200 E 62nd St | 212-935-5027 |
| Tillman, Denny/39 E 20th St | 212-674-7160 |
| Today's Photos Inc/17 E 28th St | 212-686-0071 |
| **TOGASHI/36 W 20TH ST (P 183)** | **212-929-2290** |
| Tomono, Yuji/112 Fourth Ave | 212-982-2392 |
| Tornberg, Ralph/6 E 39th St | 212-685-7333 |
| The Total Picture/902 Broadway | 212-982-9040 |
| Toto, Joe/23 E 21st St | 212-260-3377 |
| Townsend, Wendy/301 E 78th St | 212-744-5753 |
| Tucker, Toba/476 Broome St | 212-925-1478 |
| Tully, Roger/215 E 24th St | 212-947-3961 |
| Tur, Stefan/30 E 20th St | 212-475-1699 |
| **TURBEVILLE, DEBORAH/160 FIFTH AVE #600 (P 28,29)** | **212-924-6760** |
| Turner, Pete/154 W 57th St | 212-765-1733 |
| Tweedy-Holmes, Karen/180 Claremont Ave, #51 | 212-866-2289 |
| Tyler, Mark/233 Broadway Rm 3712 | 212-962-3690 |
| Umans, Marty/110 W 25th St | 212-242-4463 |
| Unangst, Andrew/381 Park Ave S | 212-889-4888 |
| Underhill, Les/10 W 18th St | 212-691-9920 |
| Ursillo, Catherine/1040 Park Ave | 212-722-9297 |

## V

| | |
|---|---|
| Vaeth, Peter/295 Madison Ave | 212-685-4700 |
| Valentin, Augusto/202 E 29th St, 6th Fl | 212-532-7480 |
| Vallini Productions/43 E 20th St, 2nd Fl. | 212-674-6581 |
| Varnedoe, S./12 W 27th St | 212-679-1230 |
| Varon, Malcolm/125 Fifth Ave | 212-473-5957 |
| Vartoogian, Jack/262 W 107th St #6A | 212-663-1341 |
| Veldenzer, Alan/78 Fifth Ave | 212-242-3263 |
| Vendikos, Tasso/20 E 20th St | 212-260-3750 |
| Vest, Michael/343 E 65th St #4RE | 212-734-9122 |
| Vicari, Jim/8 E 12th St | 212-675-3745 |
| Vickers, Camille/200 W 79th St, Penthouse | 212-580-8649 |
| Victor, Thomas/131 Fifth Ave | 212-777-6004 |
| Vidal, Bernard/853 Seventh Ave | 212-582-3284 |
| Vidol, John/37 W 26th St | 212-889-0065 |
| Vine, David/873 Broadway, 2nd Fl | 212-691-7433 |
| Vinopoll, Sy/39 W 38th St | 212-840-6590 |
| Vishniac, Roman/219 W 81st St | 212-787-0997 |
| Vogel, Allen/126 Fifth Ave | 212-675-7550 |
| Vos, Gene/440 Park Ave S | 212-685-8384 |

## W

| | |
|---|---|
| Wagner, David/156 Fifth Ave | 212-741-1171 |
| **WAINE, MICHAEL/873 BROADWAY (P 184,185)** | **212-533-4200** |
| Wallace, Randall/43 W 13th St | 212-242-2930 |
| Wallen, Jonathan/149 Franklin St | 212-966-7531 |
| Walsh, Bob/231 E 29th St | 212-684-3015 |
| Waltzer, Bill/110 Greene St #96 | 212-925-1242 |
| Waltzer, Carl/873 Broadway, #412 | 212-475-8748 |
| Walz, Barbra/143 W 20th St | 212-242-7175 |
| Wang, John Studio Inc/30 E 20th St | 212-982-2765 |
| Warchol, Paul/298 Garfield Pl | 212-788-5224 |
| Warsaw Photographic Assocs/36 E 31st St | 212-725-1888 |
| Warwick, Ben/100 Fifth Ave | 212-243-1806 |
| Watanabe, Nana/31 Union Sq W | 212-741-3248 |
| Watson, Albert M/237 E 77th St | 212-628-7886 |
| Watts, Cliff/304 E 20th St Penthse E | 212-807-7703 |
| Webb, Alex/251 Park Ave S | 212-475-7600 |
| Weber, Alan/156 Fifth Ave #701 | 212-255-4317 |
| Weidlein, Peter/122 W 26th St | 212-989-5498 |
| Weihs, Tom/121 E 24th St | 212-673-7767 |
| **WEINBERG, MICHAEL/5 E 16TH ST (P 191)** | **212-691-0713** |
| Weiner, Steve/37 W 26th St | 212-679-8373 |
| Weinstein, Todd/47 Irving Pl | 212-254-7526 |
| Weiss, Allen/228 E 85th St | 212-737-7172 |
| Weiss, Michael/10 W 18th St #2nd Flr | 212-929-4073 |
| **WEITZ, ALLAN/373 PARK AVE SO (P 192)** | **212-725-8041** |
| West, Bonnie/156 Fifth Ave | 212-929-3338 |
| **WEST, CHARLES/304 HENRY ST (P 193)** | **212-624-5920** |
| Wexler, Mark/137 W 80th St | 212-595-2153 |
| Wheeler, Paul/50 W 29th St | 212-696-9832 |
| White, Anne B/170 E 88th St | 212-860-1776 |
| White, Frank/Time Life Building Rm 2850 | 212-581-8338 |
| White, John/138 W 17th St | 212-691-1133 |
| Whitely Presentations/60 E 42nd St | 212-490-3111 |
| **WICK, WALTER/119 W 23RD ST #201 (P 194,195)** | **212-243-3448** |
| Wier, Terry/378 Third Ave | 212-684-4432 |
| Wiesehahn, Charles/200 E 37th St | 212-679-8342 |
| **WILCOX, SHORTY/DPI/521 MADISON AVE (P 42,43)** | **212-246-6367** |
| Wilkes, Stephen/48 E 13th St | 212-925-1939 |
| Williams, Larry/43 W 29th St | 212-684-1317 |
| Wilson, Mike/516 E 86th St 4C | 212-683-3557 |
| Wilson, Steve/12 W 21st St 9th flr | 212-807-7866 |
| Wing Studio/30 W 26th St | 212-620-0944 |
| Wolf, Bernard/214 E 87th St | 212-427-0220 |
| Wolf, Henry/167 E 73rd St | 212-472-2500 |
| Wolfe, Bruce/123 W 28th St | 212-695-8042 |
| Wolff, Brian R/131 E 23rd #7B | 212-598-4619 |
| Wolfson, Steve and Jeff/12 W 21st St #9 Flr | 212-807-7866 |
| Wolgast, Russ/114 W 27th St | 212-206-0494 |
| Wong, Leslie/43 W 69th St | 212-595-0434 |
| Wong, Victor/200 E 26th St | 212-878-8710 |
| Wood, Susan/641 Fifth Ave | 212-371-0679 |
| Woodson, LeRoy Jr/347 W 39th St | 212-535-4797 |
| Woodward, Herbert/555 3rd Ave | 212-685-4385 |
| Wormser, Richard L/800 Riverside Dr | 212-928-0056 |
| Wrenn, Bill/661 W 187th St | 212-923-6619 |
| Wynn, Dan/170 E 73rd St | 212-535-1551 |

## YZ

| | |
|---|---|
| Yamashiro, Tad/224 E 12th St | 212-473-7177 |
| Yee, Tom/30 W 26th St | 212-242-0301 |
| Yenachem/35 W 31st ST | 212-736-2254 |
| Young, Jim/110 W 25th St | 212-924-5444 |
| Zager, Howard/430 W 31 | 212-239-8082 |
| Zakarian, Aram/25 E 20th St | 212-674-3680 |
| Zanetti, Gerry/139 Fifth Ave | 212-473-4999 |
| Zappa, Tony/28 E 29th St | 212-532-3476 |
| Zehnder, Bruno/PO Box 5996; Grand Central Sta | 212-840-1234 |

# PHOTOGRAPHERS CONT'D.

Please send us your additions and updates.

| | |
|---|---|
| ZENREICH, ALAN/78 FIFTH AVE 3RD FL (P 196) | 212-807-1551 |
| Zens, Michael/15 W 29th St | 212-683-7258 |
| Zingler, Joseph/18 Desbrosses St | 212-226-3867 |
| Zoiner, John/12 W 44th St | 212-972-0357 |
| Zuretti, Charles Jr/156 Fifth Ave Rm 1301 | 212-924-9412 |
| Zwiebel, Michael/42 E 23 St | 212-477-5629 |

## NORTHEAST

### A

| | |
|---|---|
| Aaron, Peter/222 Valley Pl, Mamaroneck, NY | 914-698-4060 |
| Abadie, Frank Jr/596 Willis St, South Hempstead, NY | 516-489-4447 |
| Abarno, Richard/515 Spring St, Newport, RI | 401-846-5820 |
| Adams Studio Inc/1523 22nd St NW Courtyard, Washington, DC | 202-785-2188 |
| Adams, Molly/Kennedy Rd, Mendham, NJ | 201-543-4521 |
| Aks, Lee R/3 Parkway Rd, Briarcliff Manor, NY | 914-941-3833 |
| Alexander, Jules/9 Belmont Ave, Rye, NY | 914-967-8985 |
| Alexanian, Nubar/1 Thompson Sq., Charlestown, MA | 617-242-4312 |
| Alonso, Manuel/425 Fairfield Ave, Stamford, CT | 203-359-2838 |
| Ancona, George/Crickettown Rd, Stony Point, NY | 914-786-3043 |
| Anderson, Richard/2523 N Calvert St, Baltimore, MD | 301-889-0585 |
| Anderson, Susanne/Box 6, Waterford, VA | 703-882-3244 |
| Ansin Mikki/2 Ellery Sq, Cambridge, MA | 617-661-1640 |
| Anyon, Benjamin/206 Spring Run La, Downington, PA | 215-363-0744 |
| Anzalone, Joseph/PO Box 1802, S Hackensack, NJ | 201-440-6845 |
| Appleton, Hal/Kingston, Doug/52 Pickering St Box 404, Needham, MA | 617-449-1484 |
| Arbor Studios/56 Arbor St, Hartford, CT | 203-232-6543 |
| Armstrong, James/127 Mill St, Springfield, MA | 413-532-9406 |
| Auerbach, Scott/32 Country Rd, Mamaroneck, NY | 914-698-9073 |
| Avis, Paul/Rd 9 Woodhill Rd, Boscawen, NH | 603-224-2860 |

### B

| | |
|---|---|
| Baese/Randall/2229 N. Charles St, Baltimore, MD | 301-235-2226 |
| Bain, Christopher/11 Orchard Farm Rd, Port Washington, NY | 516-883-2163 |
| Baker, Bill/1045 Pebble Hill Rd RD3, Doylestown, PA | 215-348-9743 |
| Ballantyne, Thomas C/270 Westford Rd, Concord, MA | 617-369-7599 |
| Barlow, Kurt/P O Box 8863, Washington, DC | 202-543-5506 |
| Barlow, Len/392 Boylston, Boston, MA | 617-266-4030 |
| Bartlett, Linda/3316 Runnymede Pl NW, Washington, DC | 202-362-4777 |
| Baskin, Gerry/12 Union Pk St, Boston, MA | 617-482-3316 |
| Bates, Ray/West St, Newlane, VT | 802-365-7770 |
| Beaudin, Ted/56 Arbor St, Hartford, CT | 203-232-6198 |
| BEDFORD PHOTO-GRAPHIC STUDIO/PO BOX 64 RT 22, BEDFORD VILLAGE, NY (P 208) | 914-234-3123 |
| Bell, Chuck/818 Liberty Ave, Pittsburgh, PA | 412-261-2022 |
| Bender, Frank/2215 South St, Philadelphia, PA | 215-985-4664 |
| Bender, Michael/29 Arista Dr, Dix Hills, NY | 516-549-9158 |
| BENN, NATHAN/925 1/2 F ST NW, WASHINGTON, DC (P 240) | 202-638-5705 |
| Bergman, LV & Assoc/E Mountain Rd, S, Cold Spring, NY | 914-265-3656 |
| Berman, Malcolm/253 N 3rd St, Philadelphia, PA | 215-928-1061 |
| Bernstein, Daniel/7 Fuller St, Waltham, MA | 617-894-0473 |
| BEZUSHKO, BOB/1311 IRVING ST, PHILADELPHIA, PA (P 55) | 215-735-7771 |
| Bibikow, Walter/76 Batterymarch St, Boston, MA | 617-451-3464 |
| Bindas Studio/205 A St, Boston, MA | 617-268-3050 |
| Binzen, Bill/Indian Mountain Rd, Lakeville, CT | 203-435-2485 |
| Bishop, Edward/100 Clarendon St, Boston, MA | 617-542-0707 |
| Bishop, Jennifer/924 N Calvert St, Baltimore, MD | 301-539-4121 |
| Blake, Mike/107 South Street, Boston, MA | 617-451-0660 |
| Blank, Bruce/202 Ross Rd, King of Prussia, PA | 215-265-0828 |
| Blevins, Burgess/103 E Read St, Baltimore, MD | 301-685-0740 |
| Bomzer, Barry/66 Canal St, Boston, MA | 617-227-5151 |
| Bookbinder, Sigmund/Box 833, Southbury, CT | 203-264-5137 |
| Bossart, Bob/PO Box 734/Cathedral St, Boston, MA | 617-423-2323 |
| Boswell, Theodore/575 Kearney Ave, Cliffside Park, NJ | 201-941-4205 |
| Boulton, Alexander O/35 Kingston St, Boston, MA | 617-426-0938 |
| Bowman, Jo/1102 Manning St, Philadelphia, PA | 215-625-0200 |
| Boxer,Jeff Photography/14 Newbury St, Boston, MA | 617-266-4037 |
| Bragstad, Jeremiah O/72 German Cross Rd, Ithaca, NY | 607-273-4039 |
| Braverman, Ed/344 Boylston St, Boston, MA | 617-266-1616 |
| Brignolo, Joseph B/Oxford Springs Rd, Chester, NY | 914-496-4453 |
| Broderick, Jim/241 Wilson St, Saddlebrook, NJ | 914-351-2725 |
| Brown, Jim/286 Summer St, Boston, MA | 617-423-6484 |
| Brown, Martin/Cathance Lake, Grove Post Office, ME | 207-454-7708 |
| Brown, Stephen/1901 Columbia Rd NW, Washington, DC | 202-667-1965 |
| Brownell, David/Box 97, Hamilton, MA | 617-468-4284 |
| Brownell, W D Photography/48 Mayfair Rd, Nesconset, NY | 516-360-0007 |
| BRT PHOTOGRAPHIC ILLUSTRATIONS/911 STATE ST, LANCASTER, PA (P 206,207) | 717-393-0918 |
| Bukevicz, Wayne Photography/655 Georges Rd, North Brunswick, NJ | 201-545-7861 |
| Burak, Jonathan/50 Woodward, Quincy, MA | 617-770-3380 |
| Burke, John Hamilton/31 Stanhope St, Boston, MA | 617-536-4912 |
| Burns, George/3909 State St, Schenectady, NY | 518-393-3633 |
| Burns, Terry/8409 Germantown Ave, Philadelphia, PA | 215-242-9022 |
| Burwell, John/5 Normandy Dr, Silver Spring, MD | 301-565-0207 |
| Buschner, Ken/77 Saginaw Dr., Rochester, NY | 716-473-0010 |

### C

| | |
|---|---|
| Callaghan, Charles/129 S 18th St, Philadelphia, PA | 215-568-9869 |
| Carbone, Fred/140 Ramblewood Rd, Moorestown, NJ | 609-428-9047 |
| Carroll, Hanson/11 New Boston Rd, Norwich, VT | 802-649-1094 |
| Carstens, Don/19 E 22nd St, Baltimore, MD | 301-385-3049 |
| Carter, Philip/Seventeen Sunset Dr, Bedford Hills, NY | 914-241-4901 |
| CERTO, ROSEMARIE/2519 PARRISH ST, PHILADELPHIA, PA (P 63) | 215-232-2814 |
| Chadman, Bob/595-603 Newbury St, Boston, MA | 617-426-4926 |
| Chandoha, Walter/RD 1, P O Box 287, Annandale, NJ | 201-782-3666 |
| Cherin, Alan/955 Liberty Ave, Pittsburgh, PA | 412-261-2717 |
| Cisek, Darla/725 Liberty Ave, Pittsburgh, PA | 412-765-1666 |
| Cleff, Bernie Studio/715 Pine St, Philadelphia, PA | 215-922-4246 |
| Clemens, Clint/346 Newbury St, Boston, MA | 617-437-1309 |
| CLIFFORD, GEOFFREY/CRAGGLE RIDGE RD, READING, VT (P 64,65) | 802-484-5047 |
| Cmiejko Associates/Box 126, Freeland, PA | 717-636-2304 |
| Cole, Helen/60 Taylors Mill Rd, Englishtown, NJ | 201-446-4726 |
| Coleman, Alix/PO Box 23, Bryn Mawr, PA | 215-525-3828 |
| Collette, Roger/39 Pinehurst Rd, East Providence, RI | 401-433-2143 |
| COLLINS, FRED/186 SOUTH ST, BOSTON, MA (P 209) | 617-426-5731 |
| Conboy, John/1225 State St, Schenectady, NY | 518-346-2346 |
| Conklin, Paul S/3900 Tunlaw Rd N W, Washington, DC | 202-387-5133 |
| Conte, Margot/165 Old Mamaroneck Rd, White Plains, NY | 914-997-1322 |
| Coulson, Cotton/745 10th St SE, Washington, DC | 202-289-4174 |
| CRANE, TOM/113 CUMBERLAND PL, BRYN MAWR, PA (P 69) | 215-525-2444 |
| Cunningham, Chris/9 East St, Boston, MA | 617-542-4640 |
| Curtis, Bruce/70 Belmont Dr, Roslyn Heights, NY | 516-484-2570 |
| Curtis, Jackie/Alewives Rd, Norwalk, CT | 203-866-9198 |
| Curtis, John/50 Melcher St, Boston, MA | 617-451-9117 |
| Cushner, Susie/241 Crescent St, Waltham, MA | 617-647-0294 |

### D

| | |
|---|---|
| Dapkiewicz, Steve/211 A St, Boston, MA | 617-268-3764 |
| Davidson, Cameron/2311 Calvert St NW, Washington, DC | 202-328-3344 |
| Davis, Howard/2108 St Paul St, Baltimore, MD | 301-243-7089 |
| Degast, Robert/Harborton, VA | 804-442-2438 |
| DeGrado, Drew/PO Box 445, Elmwood Pk, NJ | 201-797-2890 |
| Delbert, Christian/19 Linell Circle, Billerica, MA | 617-663-2568 |
| DeWaele, John/14 Almy St, Lincoln, RI | 401-726-0084 |
| Di Maggio, Joe/512 Adams St, Centerport, NY | 516-271-6133 |
| Diamond, Herb/8 Mayflower Rd, Framingham, MA | 617-877-2752 |
| Dickstein, Bob/101 Hillturn Lane, Roslyn Heights, NY | 516-621-2413 |
| Diebold, George/416 Bloomfield Ave, Montclair, NJ | 201-744-5789 |
| Dietz, Donald/Box 177, Dorchester, MA | 617-265-3436 |
| DiGiacomo, Melchior/32 Norma Rd, Harrington Park, NJ | 201-767-0870 |
| DiMarco, Salvatore C Jr/1002 Cobbs St, Drexel Hill, PA | 215-789-3239 |
| DiMarzo, Bob/109 Broad St, Boston, MA | 617-482-0328 |
| Dolin, Penny/107 Briar Brae, Stamford, CT | 203-322-7499 |
| Dormeyer, Don/464 Dutchess Turnpike, Rt. 44, Poughkeepsie, NY | 714-593-1420 |
| Douglas Associates/ #3 Cove of Cork Lane, Annapolis, MD | 301-266-5060 |
| DREYER, PETER H/166 BURGESS AVE, WESTWOOD, MA (P 210) | 617-762-8550 |
| Duke, Christine/R D #1, Millbrook, NY | 914-677-9510 |

# PHOTOGRAPHERS CONT'D.

Please send us your additions and updates.

| | |
|---|---|
| Dunn, Paul/239 A St, Boston, MA | 617-542-9554 |
| **DUNN, PHOEBE/20 SILVERMINE RD, NEW CANAAN, CT (P 72)** | **203-966-9791** |
| **DUNOFF, RICHARD/407 BOWMAN AVE, MERION STATION, PA (P 73)** | **215-627-3690** |
| Dunwell, Steve/Box 390 Back Bay Annex, Boston, MA | 617-423-4916 |
| **DWIGGINS, GENE/204 WESTMINSTER MALL, PROVIDENCE, RI (P 211)** | **401-421-6466** |

### E
| | |
|---|---|
| Earle, John/76 Lexington Ave, Somerville, MA | 617-628-1454 |
| Edson, Steven/210 Amory St, Boston, MA | 617-522-8903 |
| Egan, Jim/Visualizations/220 W Exchange St, Providence, RI | 401-521-7052 |
| Emmott, Bob/624 S Front, Philadelphia, PA | 215-925-2773 |
| Envision Corp/270 Congress, Boston, MA | 617-482-3444 |
| Epstein, Alan Photography/694 Center St, Chicopee, MA | 413-736-8532 |
| Evans, John C/507 Liberty Ave, Pittsburgh, PA | 412-391-4400 |
| Everett Studios/22 Barker Ave, White Plains, NY | 914-997-2200 |
| Expressive Photography/544 Chestnut Street, West Reading, PA | 215-376-3461 |
| Eyle, Nicolas/1018 Butternut St, Syracuse, NY | 315-422-6231 |

### F
| | |
|---|---|
| F-90/Kris Franklin/60 Sindle Ave, Little Falls, NJ | 201-785-9090 |
| Faragan, George/1621 Wood St, Philadelphia, PA | 215-564-5711 |
| Farris, Mark/3733 Benton St NW, Washington, DC | 202-965-0075 |
| Faulkner, Douglas/46 Parkview Terr, Summit, NJ | 201-277-2949 |
| Feil, Charles W III/Mulberry Studio/Box 201, Washington Grove, MD | 301-258-8328 |
| Feinberg, Milton/12 Gerald Rd, Boston, MA | 617-254-2360 |
| Fellows & Hone/2130 Arch St, Philadeaphia, PA | 215-568-5434 |
| Fesler, James/11-1 Granada Crescent, White Plains, NY | 914-761-8282 |
| Ficara Studios Ltd/880 Canal St, Stamford, CT | 203-327-4535 |
| Fischer, Al/601 Newbury St, Boston, MA | 617-536-7126 |
| Fish, Dick/40 Center St, Northampton, MA | 413-584-6500 |
| Fitzhugh, Susan/3809 Beech Ave, Baltimore, MD | 301-243-6112 |
| Flanigan, Jim/2302 Lombard St, Philadelphia, PA | 215-546-5545 |
| Focus Photography/2300 Walnut St #421, Philadelphia, PA | 215-567-0187 |
| Foley, Paul/791 Tremont, Boston, MA | 617-266-9336 |
| Foote, Jim/22 Tomac Ave, Old Greenwich, CT | 203-637-3228 |
| **FOSTER, FRANK/323 NEWBURY ST, BOSTON, MA (P 213)** | **617-536-8267** |
| Foster, Nicholas/143 Claremont Rd, Bernardsville, NJ | 201-766-7526 |
| Fox, Peggy/371 Padonia Rd, Cockeysville, MD | 301-252-0003 |
| Francoeur, Norm/2 Grand Ave #6, Nashua, NH | 603-882-7990 |
| Fraser, Renee/1167 Massachusetts Ave, Arlington, MA | 617-646-4296 |
| Freeman, Roland L/117 Ingraham St NW, Washington, DC | 202-882-7764 |
| Freid, Joel Carl/812 Loxford Terr, Silver Spring, MD | 301-681-7211 |
| **FURMAN, MICHAEL/115 ARCH ST, PHILADELPHIA, PA (P 88,89)** | **215-925-4233** |

### G
| | |
|---|---|
| G/Q Studios/1 Roundhill Rd, Kenneth Square, PA | 215-444-5500 |
| Galella, Ron/17 Glover Ave, Yonkers, NY | 914-237-2988 |
| Gallery, Bill/86 South St, Boston, MA | 617-542-0499 |
| Galvin, Kevin/P O Box 30, Hanover, MA | 617-826-4795 |
| Ganson, John/14 Lincoln Rd, Wayland, MA | 617-358-2543 |
| Garber, Ira/23 Peck St, Providence, RI | 401-274-3723 |
| Gardner, Charles/1318 Walnut, Philadelphia, PA | 215-732-1128 |
| Garfield, Peter/3401 K St, NW, Washington, DC | 202-333-1379 |
| Garrett, Kenneth/1703 Seaton St NW, Washington, DC | 202-387-2201 |
| Garrett-Stow, Liliane/18 Tuthill Point Rd, East Moriches, NY | 516-878-8587 |
| **GEER, RICHARD/611 CATHEDRAL ST, BALTIMORE, MD (P 238,239)** | **301-244-0292** |
| Gerbode & Stier/93 Massachusettes Ave, Boston, MA | 617-247-3822 |
| Germer, Michael/839 Beacon St Intramedia, Boston, MA | 617-262-6980 |
| Giandomenico, Bob/13 Fern Ave, Collingswood, NJ | 609-854-2222 |
| Giglio, Harry/925 Penn Ave, #305, Pittsburgh, PA | 412-261-3338 |
| Gillette, Guy/133 Mountainadale Rd, Yonkers, NY | 914-779-4684 |
| Goell, Jonathan J/109 Broad St, Boston, MA | 617-423-2057 |
| Goembl, Ponder/617 S 10th St, Philadelphia, PA | 215-928-1797 |
| Goldberg, Rich/52 Chestnut St, Cambridge, MA | 617-876-7360 |
| Goldblatt, Steven/32 S Strawberry St, Philadelphia, PA | 215-925-3825 |
| Goldenberg, Barry/1 Baltimore Ave - 70 Jackson D, Cranford, NJ | 201-276-1510 |
| Goldman, Mel/329 Newbury St, Boston, MA | 617-536-0539 |
| Goldstein, Robert/P O Box 310, New Milford, NJ | 201-262-5959 |
| Good, Richard/5226 Osage Ave, Philadelphia, PA | 215-472-7659 |
| Goodman, John/337 Summer St, Boston, MA | 617-482-8061 |
| Goodman, John D/5 Indian Creek, Colchester, VT | 802-878-2904 |
| Goodman, Lou/322 Summer St, Boston, MA | 617-542-8254 |
| Goodwin, John C/28 Meadow St, Demarest, NJ | 201-768-0777 |
| Gorchev & Gorchev/11 Cabot Rd, Woburn, MA | 617-933-8090 |
| Gordon, Lee/725 Boylston St, Boston, MA | 617-267-3006 |
| Goro, Fritz/324 N Bedford Rd, Chappaqua, NY | 914-238-8788 |
| Gorrill, Robert B/P O Box 206, North Quincy, MA | 617-328-4012 |
| Grace, Arthur/1928 35th Pl NW, Washington, DC | 202-333-6568 |
| Graphic Accent/446 Main St PO Box 243, Wilmington, MA | 617-658-7602 |
| Graphics Plus Corp/198 Ferry St, St Malden, MA | 617-321-7500 |
| Grehan, Farrell/245 W 51 St, #306, New York, NY | 914-359-0404 |
| Greniers' Commercial Photography/127 Mill St, Springfield, MA | 413-532-9406 |
| Griebsch, John/183 St Paul St, Rochester, NY | 716-546-1303 |
| Griffing, Fred/Ferris Lane, Upper Grandview, NY | 914-353-0619 |
| Grohe, Stephen F/186 South St, Boston, MA | 617-523-6655 |

### H
| | |
|---|---|
| Hagerman, Ron/51 Clearview Ave, Somerset, MA | 617-676-9017 |
| Hahn, Bob/2405 Exeter Ct, Bethlehem, PA | 215-868-0339 |
| Hakalski, Robert/731 N 24th St, Philadelphia, PA | 215-928-0918 |
| Hamlin, Elizabeth/Box 177, Dorchester, MA | 617-265-3436 |
| Hammell, Craig/6 Skyline Dr, North Caldwell, NJ | 201-228-4994 |
| **HANSEN, STEVE/40 WINCHESTER ST, BOSTON, MA (P 214,215)** | **617-426-6858** |
| Hanstein, George/389 Belmont Ave, Haledon, NJ | 201-790-0505 |
| Harris, Bill/286 Summer St, Boston, MA | 617-426-0989 |
| Hart, Bob/15 2nd St, Dravosburg, PA | 412-466-3037 |
| Hauptchein, Michael/6304 Dahlonega Rd, Bethesda, MD | 301-320-4706 |
| Heath, Mark/4338 Roland Springs Dr, Baltimore, MD | 301-366-4633 |
| Heayn, Mark/17 W 24th St, Baltimore, MD | 301-235-1608 |
| **HEILMAN, GRANT/BOX 317, LITITZ, PA (P 400)** | **717-626-0296** |
| Heist, Scott/616 Walnut St, Emmaus, PA | 215-965-5479 |
| Helmar, Dennis/134 Beach St, Boston, MA | 617-451-1496 |
| Henis, Marshall C/P O Box 1088, Great Neck, NY | 516-466-9098 |
| Herko, Robert/PO Box 961, Piscataway, NJ | 201-356-2880 |
| Hess, Bob/375 Sylvan Ave, Englewood Cliffs, NJ | 201-567-8585 |
| Hines, Harry/PO Box 10061, Newark, NJ | 201-242-0214 |
| Hirshfeld, Max/P.O. Box 50814, Washington, DC | 202-638-3131 |
| Hobson, Mark/180 St Paul St, Rochester, NY | 716-232-6064 |
| Holland, James R/208 Commonwealth Ave, Boston, MA | 617-321-3638 |
| Holniker, Barry/400 E. 25th St, Baltimore, MD | 301-889-1919 |
| Holt, Amina/Philip/145 Ipswich St, Boston, MA | 617-262-2359 |
| Holt, John/145 South St, Boston, MA | 617-426-7262 |
| Hoops, Jay/Peconic Rd, Southampton, NY | 516-728-4017 |
| Hornick/368 Congress, Boston, MA | 617-482-8614 |
| Horowitz, Abby/922 Chestnut, Philadelphia, PA | 215-925-3600 |
| Howard, Carl/27 Huckleberry La, Ballston Lake, NY | 518-877-7615 |
| Howard, Richard/Box 1022, Marblehead, MA | 617-631-8260 |
| Hoyt, Wolfgang/222 Valley Pl, Mamaroneck, NY | 914-698-4060 |
| Hubbell, William/57 Wood Rd, Bedford Hills, NY | 914-666-5792 |
| Huehnegarth, John/196 Snowden Lane, Princeton, NJ | 609-921-3211 |
| Hunsberger, Douglas/115 W Fern Rd, Wildwood Crest, NJ | 609-522-6849 |
| Hutchinson, Gardiner/280 Friend St, Boston, MA | 617-523-5180 |
| Hyde, Dana/Box 1302, South Hampton, NY | 516-283-1001 |

### IJ
| | |
|---|---|
| Ickow, Marvin/1824 35th St NW, Washington, DC | 202-342-0250 |
| Iglarsh, Gary/2229 N Charles St, Baltimore, MD | 301-235-3385 |
| The Image Factory/2229 N Charles St, Baltimore, MD | 301-235-2226 |
| In Slide Out/1701 Eben St, Pittsburgh, PA | 412-343-2112 |
| Jackson, Don/933 Cuthbert St, Philadelphia, PA | 215-923-7450 |
| Jackson, Reggie/135 Sheldon Terr, New Haven, CT | 203-787-5191 |
| Jaramillo, Alain/PO Box 25, Riderwood, MD | 301-583-7410 |
| **JOACHIM, BRUNO/326 A STREET, BOSTON, MA (P 198,199)** | **617-451-6156** |
| Joel, Yale/Woodybrook Ln, Croton-On-Hudson, NY | 914-271-8172 |
| Jones, G P - Stock/45 Newbury St, Boston, MA | 617-267-6450 |
| **JONES, LOU/22 RANDOLPH ST, BOSTON, MA (P 217)** | **617-426-6335** |
| Jones, Peter/139 Main St, Cambridge, MA | 617-492-3545 |
| Joseph, George E/19 Barnum Rd, Larchmont, NY | 914-834-5687 |

# PHOTOGRAPHERS CONT'D.

Please send us your additions and updates.

## K

| | |
|---|---|
| **KALFUS, LONNY/36 MYRTLE AVE, EDGEWATER, NJ (P 108)** | **201-886-0776** |
| Kalish, Joanne/512 Adams St, Centerport, NY | 516-271-6133 |
| Kamper, George/180 St Paul St, Rochester, NY | 716-454-7006 |
| Kan, Dennis/3845 Beecher St NW, Washington, DC | 202-965-2935 |
| Kaplan, Carol/20 Beacon St, Boston, MA | 617-720-4400 |
| Katz, Dan/36 Aspen Rd, W Orange, NJ | 201-731-8956 |
| Kaufman, Eliot/255 W 90th St, New York, NY | 212-922-2864 |
| **KAWALERSKI, TED/52 SAN GABRIEL DR, ROCHESTER, NY (P 218,219)** | **716-244-4656** |
| Keller, Mike/Studio 15 15 S Grand Ave, Baldwin, NY | 516-889-2934 |
| Kelly/Mooney Photography/87 Willow Ave, North Plainfield, NJ | 201-757-1746 |
| Kernan, Sean/576 Leetes Island Rd, Stoney Creek, CT | 203-865-4100 |
| **KING, RALPH/103 BROAD ST, BOSTON, MA (P 200,201)** | **617-426-3565** |
| Kligman, Fred/4733 Elm St, Bethesda, MD | 301-652-6333 |
| Knapp, Stephen/74 Commodore Rd, Worcester, MA | 617-757-2507 |
| Kobrin, Harold/822 Commonwealth, Newton, MA | 617-332-8152 |
| Krist, Bob/538 Undercliff Ave, Edgewater, NJ | 201-943-8874 |
| Krockman, Arnold F/241 Cliff St, Woodridge, NJ | 201-438-7815 |
| Kron, Dan/134 North 13th St, Philadelphia, PA | 215-567-6506 |
| Kruper, Alexander Jr/518 Miner Terr., Linden, NJ | 201-272-8880 |
| Kuhn, Werner J/3 Davos Rd, Woodbridge, NY | 716-321-6254 |

## L

| | |
|---|---|
| **LANDSMAN, GARY D/12011 NEBEL ST, ROCKVILLE, MD (P 112,113)** | **301-468-2588** |
| **LANE, WHITNEY/109 SOMERSTOWN RD, OSSINING, NY (P 114)** | **914-762-5335** |
| LaPete, William/259 A St, Boston, MA | 617-482-3456 |
| **LARICHE, MICHAEL/30 S BANK ST, PHILADELPHIA, PA (P 220,221)** | **215-922-0447** |
| Lautman, Robert C/4906 41 St NW, Washington, DC | 202-966-2800 |
| Lawfer, Larry/107 South St, Boston, MA | 617-451-0628 |
| Lazzini, Gary/725 Liberty Ave, Pittsburgh, PA | 412-765-1666 |
| Leaman, Chris/105 Plant Ave, Wayne, PA | 215-688-3290 |
| Lee, Carol/214 Beacon St, Boston, MA | 617-523-5930 |
| Lefcourt, Victoria/1733 Baton St, Baltimore, MD | 301-225-0405 |
| Leney, Julia/Box 434, Wayland, MA | 617-358-7229 |
| Levart, Herb/566 Secor Rd, Hartsdale, NY | 914-946-2060 |
| Leveille, David/27-31 St Bridget's Dr, Rochester, NY | 716-381-5341 |
| Lidington, John/2 C St, Hull, St | 617-246-0300 |
| Lieberman Photography/2426 Linden La, Silver Spring, MD | 301-565-0644 |
| Liebman, Larry/45 F Dunes La, Port Washington, NY | 212-354-8737 |
| Lilley, Weaver/125 S 18th St, Philadelphia, PA | 215-567-2881 |
| Lillibridge, David/Rt 4 Box 1172, Burlington, CT | 203-673-9786 |
| Limont, Alexander/137 W Harvey St, Philadelphia, PA | 215-438-7259 |
| Linck, Tony/2100 Linwood Ave, Fort Lee, NJ | 201-944-5454 |
| Lisanti, Vincent/330 Clinton Ave, Dobbs Ferry, NY | 914-693-9228 |
| Little, Steve/5161 River Rd, Bethesda, MD | 301-652-1303 |
| Littlewood, John/Box 141, Woodville, MA | 617-435-4262 |
| Lockwood, Lee/27 Howland Rd, West Newton, MA | 617-965-6343 |
| Lokmer, John/925 Penn Ave #404, Pittsburgh, PA | 412-765-3565 |
| Long Shots/4421 East West Hwy, Bethesda, MD | 301-654-0279 |

## M

| | |
|---|---|
| Mackenzie, Maxwell/2321 37th St NW, Washington, DC | 202-342-8266 |
| Maclean, Alex/77 Conant Rd, Lincoln, MA | 617-259-8310 |
| Magnet, Jeff/628B-1620 Worchester Rd, Framingham, MA | 617-875-4227 |
| Malitsky, Ed/337 Summer St, Boston, MA | 617-451-0655 |
| Malyszko, Michael/90 South St, Boston, MA | 617-426-9111 |
| Manheim, Michael Philip/P O Box 35, Marblehead, MA | 617-631-3560 |
| Manop Photography/30 Olive St, Greenfield, MA | 413-774-5752 |
| Marchese, Frank/56 Arbor St, Hartford, CT | 203-232-4417 |
| Marinelli, Jack/673 Willow Rd, Waterbury, CT | 203-756-3273 |
| Maroon, Fred J/2725 P St NW, Washington, DC | 202-337-0337 |
| Marshall, John/344 Boylston St, Boston, MA | 617-536-2988 |
| Martin Paul, Ltd./247 Newbury St, Boston, MA | 617-536-1644 |
| **MARTIN, MARILYN/560 HARRISON AVE, BOSTON, MA (P 222)** | **617-426-0064** |
| Massar, Ivan/296 Bedford St, Concord, MA | 617-369-4090 |
| Matt, Philip/P O Box 3910, Rochester, NY | 716-461-5977 |
| McCormick & Nelson, Inc/34 Piave St, Stamford, CT | 203-348-5062 |
| **MCCOY, DAN/ BOX 573, HOUSATONIC, MA (P 223)** | **413-274-6211** |
| **MCKEAN, THOMAS R/742 CHERRY CI, WYNNEW'D, PA (P 224)** | **215-642-0966** |
| McLaren, Lynn/42 W Cedar, Boston, MA | 617-227-7448 |
| McQueen, Ann/791 Tremont St, # W 401, Boston, MA | 617-267-6258 |
| Media Concepts/14 Newbury St, Boston, MA | 617-437-1382 |
| Mednick, Seymour/316 S Camac, Philadelphia, PA | 215-735-6100 |
| Meek, Richard/8 Skyline Dr, Huntington, NY | 516-271-0072 |
| Meiller, Henry Studios/1026 Wood St, Philadelphia, PA | 215-922-1525 |
| **MELLOR, D W /DARBY & MARPLE RDS, HAVERFORD, PA (P 127)** | **215-649-6087** |
| Melton, Janice Munnings/5 Franklin Gardens, Boston, MA | 617-298-1443 |
| Mendelsohn, David/Sky Farm Rd, Northwood, NH | 603-942-7622 |
| Mercer, Ralph/369 W Union, East Bridgewater, MA | 617-378-7512 |
| Meyers Studio/21 Princeton St, Orchard Park, NY | 716-662-6002 |
| Miller, Bruce Photography/9 Tall Oaks Dr, East Brunswick, NJ | 201-257-0211 |
| Miller, Gary Photography/15 Overhill Rd, Scarsdale, NY | 914-232-8279 |
| Miller, Roger/1411 Hollins St Union Sq, Baltimore, MD | 301-566-1222 |
| Millman, Lester Jay/23 Court St, White Plains, NY | 914-946-2093 |
| Mindell, Doug/132 Newbury St, Boston, MA | 617-262-3968 |
| Minohr, Martha/912 N Madison St, Wilmington, DE | 302-654-9990 |
| Mitchell, Mike/930 F St #712, Washington, DC | 202-347-3223 |
| Moerder, Dan/2115 Wallace St, Philadelphia, PA | 215-978-7414 |
| Molinaro, Neil R/46 Lindsley Ave, Irvington, NJ | 201-399-7735 |
| Monroe, Robert/Cuddebackville, NY | 914-754-8329 |
| Mopsik, Eugene/419 S Perth St, Philadelphia, PA | 215-922-3489 |
| Morgan, Bruce/55 S Grand St, Baldwin, NY | 516-546-3554 |
| Morley, Bob/129 South St, Boston, MA | 617-482-7279 |
| Morrow, Christopher W/163 Pleasant St, Arlington, MA | 617-648-6770 |
| Moyer, Robin/304 Windsor Pl, Brooklyn, NY | 212-499-4330 |
| Mozo, Carlos/74 Oakland St, Stratford, CT | 203-377-0500 |
| **MULLIGAN, JOSEPH/ 239 CHESTNUT ST, PHILADELPHIA, PA (P 32)** | **215-592-1359** |
| Mungin, Carol/642 South Fifth Ave, Mount Vernon, NY | 914-668-2803 |
| Munster, Joseph/Old Rt 28, Phoenicia, NY | 914-688-5347 |
| **MUSTO, TOM/225 S MAIN ST, WILKES-BARRE, PA (P 137)** | **717-822-5798** |
| Mydans, Carl/212 Hommocks Rd, Larchmont, NY | 914-834-9206 |
| **MYERS STUDIOS INC/21 PRINCETON PLACE, ORCHARD PARK, NY (P 138)** | **716-662-6002** |
| Myriad Communications, Inc/357 Robin Rd, Englewood, NJ | 201-871-0190 |
| Myron/127 Dorrance St, Providence, RI | 401-421-1946 |

## N

| | |
|---|---|
| Nagler, Lanny/56 Arbor St, Hartford, CT | 203-233-4040 |
| Nasca, Rosalyn/19361 Keymar Way, Gaithersburg, MD | 301-948-4062 |
| Nearney, Dan/137 Rowayton Ave, Rowayton, CT | 203-853-2782 |
| Nelson, Janet/Finney Farm, Croton-On-Hudson, NY | 914-271-5453 |
| Nettis, Joseph/719 Walnut St, Philadelphia, PA | 215-563-5444 |
| New Wave Photo/220 Ferris Ave, White Plains, NY | 914-949-5508 |
| Nichols, Don/1241 University Ave, Rochester, NY | 716-275-9666 |
| **NOBLE INC/611 CATHEDRAL ST, BALTIMORE, MD (P 238,239)** | **301-244-0292** |
| Nochton, Jack/1238 W Broad St, Bethlehem, PA | 215-691-2223 |
| Nordstrom, Matzgh/125 St Paul St, Brookline, MA | 617-739-6795 |
| **NORTHLIGHT/45 ACADEMY ST, NEWARK, NJ (P 203)** | **201-624-3990** |
| Nubar-Alexanian/1 Thompson Sq, Charlestown, MA | 617-242-4312 |

## O

| | |
|---|---|
| O'Donoghue, Ken/8 Union Park St, Boston, MA | 617-542-4898 |
| Oeltjen, John/4853 Cordell Ave, Bethesda, MD | 301-474-3440 |
| Olbrys, Anthony/41 Pepper Ridge Rd, Stamford, CT | 203-322-9422 |
| Olivera, Bob/42 Weybossett St, Providence, RI | 401-272-1170 |
| Olmstead Studio/118 South St, Boston, MA | 617-542-2024 |
| Orel, Mano/PO Box E, Dove Court, Croton-On-Hudson, NY | 914-271-5542 |
| Orlando, Fran/731 N 24th St, Philadelphia, PA | 215-928-0918 |
| Orrico, Charles/72 Barry Ln, Syosset, NY | 516-364-2257 |
| O'Shaughnessy, Bob/50 Melcher, Boston, MA | 617-542-7122 |

## P Q

| | |
|---|---|
| **PALMER, GABE/269 LYONS PLAINS RD, WESTON, CT (P 145)** | **203-227-1477** |
| Pantages, Tom/7 Linden Ave, Gloucester, MA | 617-525-3678 |
| Paradigm Productions/6437 Ridge Ave, Philadelphia, PA | 215-482-8404 |
| Parks, Paul/1355A Washington St #312, Boston, MA | 617-267-3806 |
| Patrey, Dan/3 Cornell Pl, Great Neck, NY | 516-466-4396 |
| **PEASE, GREG/23 E 22ND ST, BALTIMORE, MD (P 242,243)** | **301-332-0583** |
| Penneys, Robert/147 N 12th St, Philadelphia, PA | 215-925-6699 |
| Perez, P R Photographic Prod/143 Hoffman Ave, Lindhurst, NY | 516-226-0846 |

# PHOTOGRAPHERS CONT'D.

Please send us your additions and updates.

| | |
|---|---|
| Pete Silver & Associates/Box 86, Southport, CT | 203-254-1400 |
| Peterson, Brent/15 Davenport Ave #2G, New Rochelle, NY | 212-573-7195 |
| Philiba, Allan A/3408 Bertha Dr, Baldwin, NY | 212-286-0948 |
| Photo Plus/PO Box 221, Nutting Lake, MA | 617-663-8662 |
| Photographic Associates/8 Monmouth St, Red Bank, NJ | 201-747-0269 |
| Photographic Illustration Ltd/7th & Ranstead, Philadelphia, PA | 215-925-7073 |
| **PHOTOGRAPHY ASSOCIATES/140-150 HUYSHOPE AVE BOX 3727, HARTFORD, CT (P 225)** | **203-249-1105** |
| Photography Works/1700 Pine St, Philadelphia, PA | 215-985-9090 |
| Photogroup Inc/5161 River Rd, Bethesda, MD | 301-652-1303 |
| Photohandwerk/Michael D McGuire/51 W Walnut La, Philadelphia, PA | 215-844-0754 |
| Pickerell, Jim H/8104 Cindy Ln, Bethesda, MD | 301-365-1126 |
| Picture Group Inc/9 Steeple St, Providence, RI | 401-273-5473 |
| Plank, David/530-544 Chestnut St, West Reading, PA | 215-376-3461 |
| Poggenpohl, Eric/1816 "S" St. NW, Washington, DC | 202-387-0826 |
| **POHUSKI, MICHAEL/36 SOUTH PACA ST, BALTIMORE, MD (P 237)** | **301-962-5404** |
| Polansky, Allen/1431 Park Ave, Baltimore, MD | 301-383-9021 |
| Policastro, Anthony/117 Isabelle St, Metuchen, NJ | 201-494-2990 |
| Polumbaum, Ted/326 Harvard St, Cambridge, MA | 617-491-4947 |
| Porcella, Phil/109 Broad St, Boston, MA | 617-426-3222 |
| Porter, Charles/Georgetown Square C-4, Poughkeepsie, NY | 914-454-7033 |
| Powell, Bolling/157 Milk St, Boston, MA | 617-426-3996 |
| Pownall, Ron/7 Ellsworth Ave, Cambridge, MA | 617-354-0846 |
| Praus, Edgar/796 South Ave, Rochester, NY | 716-442-4820 |
| Prodian, James/319 A St, Boston, MA | 617-426-1300 |
| Profit, Everett R/533 Massachusetts Ave, Boston, MA | 617-267-5840 |
| Projections/142-7 Hyatt Park, Ijamsville, MD | 301-831-8242 |
| Quality Images/7 River St, Milford, CT | 203-878-5090 |
| Quindry, Richard/200 Loney St, Philadelphia, PA | 215-742-6300 |
| **R** RS Studio Inc/244 Alexander St, Princeton, NJ | 609-921-6830 |
| **RAINBOW/ BOX 573, HOUSATONIC, MA (P 223)** | **413-274-6211** |
| Rawle, Johnathan/PO Box 292, Lexington, MA | 617-862-7100 |
| Raycroft/McCormick/179 South St, Boston, MA | 617-542-7229 |
| Redding, Jim/149 Staniford St, Boston, MA | 617-523-2380 |
| Reeling, Will/12 Witherwood G, Baltimore, MD | 301-321-6141 |
| Renard, Jean/304 Boylston, Boston, MA | 617-266-8673 |
| Renckly, Joe/725 Liberty Ave, Pittsburgh, PA | 412-261-4029 |
| Retallack, John/127 Golden Rod Ln, Rochester, NY | 716-334-1530 |
| Richards, Jim/83 Custer Ave, Williston Park, NY | 516-248-2359 |
| Richards, Toby/RS Studio/244 Alexander St, Princeton, NJ | 609-921-6830 |
| Richman, Mel Inc/15 N Presidential Blvd, Bala-Cynwyd, PA | 215-667-8900 |
| Richmond, Jack/109 Broad St, Boston, MA | 617-482-7158 |
| Riley & Riley/Middle St, PO Box 408, Wiscasset, ME | 207-882-7912 |
| Riley, Laura/Hidden Spring Farm, PO Box 186, Pittstown, NJ | 201-735-7707 |
| Rizzi, Leonard F/5161 River Rd, Bethesda, MD | 301-652-1303 |
| Robins, Susan/2005 Old Cuthbert Rd, Cherry Hill, NJ | 609-795-8386 |
| **ROBINSON, GEORGE A/BOX 377 OLD PUMP RD, JERICHO, VT (P 226)** | **802-899-3703** |
| Robinson, Mike/11 Earlswood Ave, Pittsburgh, PA | 412-431-4102 |
| **ROCKHILL, MORGAN/204 WESTMINSTER MALL, PROVIDENCE, RI (P 205)** | **401-274-3472** |
| Rode, Robert/2670 Arleigh Rd, East Meadow, NY | 516-579-9462 |
| Roseman, Shelly/723 Chestnut, Philadelphia, PA | 215-922-1430 |
| Rosenberg, Arnold/Box 1034, East Hampton, NY | 516-324-1227 |
| Rosenthal, Steve/59 Maple St, Auburndale, MA | 617-244-2986 |
| **ROSNER, ERIC/1133 ARCH ST, PHILADELPHIA, PA (P 161)** | **215-567-2758** |
| **ROTMAN, JEFF/14 COTTAGE AVE, SOMERVILLE, MA (P 227)** | **617-666-0874** |
| Ruggeri, Lawrence/10 Old Post Office Rd, Silver Spring, MD | 301-588-3131 |
| Russ, Clive/34 River St, Boston, MA | 617-720-0979 |
| **S** Sa'Adah, Jonathan/Box 247, Hartford, VT | 802-295-5327 |
| Sagala, Steve/60 Main St, Madison, NJ | 201-377-1418 |
| Sakmanoff, George/179 Massachusetts Ave, Boston, MA | 617-262-7227 |
| Salomone, Frank/296 Brick Blvd, Bricktown, NJ | 201-920-1525 |
| Salsbery, Lee/14 Seventh St, NE, Washington, DC | 202-543-1222 |
| Samuels Studio/8 Waltham St, PO Box 201, Maynard, MA | 617-897-7901 |
| Sanford, Eric/219 Turnpike Rd, Manchester, NH | 603-624-0122 |
| **SAUTER, RON/183 ST PAUL ST, ROCHESTER, NY (P 228)** | **716-232-1361** |
| Schaefer, Dave/48 Grove St, Belmont, MA | 617-484-4010 |
| Scherzi, James/116 Town Line Rd, Syracuse, NY | 315-455-7961 |
| **SCHLEIPMAN, RUSSELL F/ZERO NEAREN ROW, CHARLESTOWN, MA (P 229)** | **617-242-9298** |
| Schlowsky/376 Boylston St, Boston, MA | 617-247-2133 |
| Schlowsky Studios/376 Boylston St, Boston, MA | 617-247-2133 |
| Schmitt, Steve/337 Summer St, Boston, MA | 617-482-5482 |
| **SCHOON, TIM/BOX 7446, LANCASTER, PA (P 244)** | **717-291-9483** |
| Schweikardt, Eric/Box 56, Southport, CT | 203-375-8181 |
| Sculnick, Herb/7 2nd St, Athens, NY | 518-777-3232 |
| Sedik, Joe/342 Perkiomen Ave, Lansdale, PA | 215-368-6832 |
| Segal, Mark/2141 Newport Place, NW, Washington, DC | 202-223-2618 |
| Seger, Toby/4025 Rt 8, Allison Park, PA | 412-487-6474 |
| Serbin, Vincent/19 Primrose Ln, Bricktown, NJ | 201-458-4647 |
| Shafer, Bob/3554 Quebec St N W, Washington, DC | 202-362-0630 |
| Share, Jed/61 Chestnut St, Englewood, NJ | 201-569-7877 |
| Shelton, Sybil/416 Valley View Rd, Englewood, NJ | 201-568-8684 |
| Sherbow, Robert/1607 Colonial Terr, Arlington, VA | 202-522-3644 |
| Sherman, Mark/1508 Scenic Dr., Ewing Township, NJ | 609-896-2228 |
| Sherman, Steve/26 Otis St, Cambridge, MA | 617-492-0241 |
| Sherriffe, Bob/69 Lynn Way, Revere, MA | 617-284-3228 |
| **SHORE, STEPHEN/RD 3 BOX 280, RHINEBECK, NY (P 165)** | **914-876-4450** |
| Siegler, William/PO Box 422, Walden, NY | 914-778-7300 |
| Silk, Georgiana B/190 Godfrey Rd E, Weston, CT | 203-226-0408 |
| **SIMMONS, ERIK LEIGH/295 A ST, BOSTON, MA (P 230)** | **617-482-5325** |
| Simpson/Flint/2133 Maryland Ave, Baltimore, MD | 301-837-9923 |
| Sint, Steven/6 Second Rd, Great Neck, NY | 516-487-4918 |
| Siteman, Frank/136 Pond St, Winchester, MA | 617-729-3747 |
| Skoogford, Leif/1648A Beekman St, Washington, DC | 202-265-5299 |
| Smith, Ellen/Box 3727, Hartford, CT | 203-249-1105 |
| Smith, Hugh R/2515 Burr St, Fairfield, CT | 203-255-1942 |
| Smith, Michael W/14 Woodlawn Ave, S Norwalk, CT | 203-838-8534 |
| Smith, Phillip W/Rt. 31, Pennytown, Pennington, NJ | 609-466-0011 |
| Smith, Stuart/68 Raymond La, Wilton, CT | 203-762-3158 |
| **SMYTH, T. KEVIN/604 MAIN ST, BELMAR, NJ (P 170)** | **201-681-2602** |
| Solomon Assoc/424 E 25th St, Baltimore, MD | 301-366-6118 |
| Soluri, Michael/3181 E River Rd, Rochester, NY | 716-436-0168 |
| Somers, Jo/29 Newbury St, Boston, MA | 617-267-4444 |
| Soorenko, Barry A/5161 River Rd, Bethesda, MD | 301-652-1303 |
| Sorcher, David/431 Beach 69th St, Arverne, NY | 212-474-5807 |
| Sparks, Don/802 3rd St, SW, Washington, DC | 703-734-4977 |
| Sperduto, Stephen/615 Fenimore Rd, Mamaroneck, NY | 914-381-4220 |
| Spiegel, Ted/RD 2 Box 353 A, South Salem, NY | 914-763-3668 |
| Stafford, Rick/26 Wadsworth, Allston, MA | 617-495-2389 |
| Stage, John Lewis/Iron Mountain Rd, New Milford, NY | 914-986-1620 |
| Stecker, Elinor H/16 Kilmer Rd, Larchmont, NY | 914-834-8514 |
| Stein, Geoffrey R/348 Newbury St, Boston, MA | 617-536-8227 |
| Steiner, Lisl/"El Retecho" Trinity Pass, Pound Ridge, NY | 914-764-5538 |
| **STEINER, PETER/183 ST PAUL ST, ROCHESTER, NY (P 231)** | **716-454-1012** |
| Stierer, Dennis/34 Plympton St, Boston, MA | 617-357-9488 |
| Stills/1 Winthrop Sq, Boston, MA | 617-482-0660 |
| Storch, Otto/Box 712, 22 Pondview Ln, East Hampton, NY | 516-324-5031 |
| Stratos, Jim/56 Arbor St, Hartford, CT | 203-233-4636 |
| Strongin, James W/11 Henhawk Ln, Huntington, NY | 516-421-4307 |
| **STUART, STEPHEN/9 LEGION DR, VALHALLA, NY (P 179)** | **914-682-1418** |
| Stuart, Stephen Photography/9 Legion Dr, Valhalla, NY | 914-682-1418 |
| **THE STUDIO INC/818 LIBERTY AVE, PITTSBURGH, PA (P 202)** | **412-261-2022** |
| Susoeff, Bill/1063 Elizabeth Dr, Pittsburgh, PA | 412-941-8606 |
| Sweeney, Dan/337 Summer St, Boston, MA | 617-482-5482 |
| Sweet, Ozzie/Mill Village Hill, Francestown, NH | 603-547-6611 |
| **T** Tadder, Morton/501 St Paul Place, Baltimore, MD | 301-837-7427 |
| Tardi, Joseph/100 Seventh Ave, Troy, NY | 518-783-0770 |
| Tchakirides, Bill/140-150 Huyshope Ave, Hartford, CT | 203-249-1105 |
| Tenin, Barry/PO Box 2660, Westport, CT | 203-226-9396 |
| Tepper, Peter/195 Tunxis Hill Rd, Fairfield, CT | 203-367-6172 |
| **TOLBERT, BRIAN R/911 STATE ST, LANCASTER, PA (P 206,207)** | **717-393-0918** |
| Tornallyay-Weir Assoc/63 Taff Ave, Stamford, CT | 203-357-1777 |
| **TOUCHTON, KEN/PO BOX 9435, WASHINGTON, DC (P 245)** | **703-534-4497** |
| Traub, Willard/Box 276, Lincoln, MA | 617-259-9656 |

# PHOTOGRAPHERS CONT'D.

Please send us your additions and updates.

| | |
|---|---|
| Trefethen, Jim/PO Box 165, Charlestown, MA | 617-242-0064 |
| Tretick, Stanley/4365 Embassy Park Dr, NW, Washington, DC | 202-537-1445 |
| Trola, Bob/112 N 12th St, Philadelphia, PA | 215-925-4322 |
| Trone, Larry P/1131 Ralph Rd, Newark, DE | 302-762-3310 |
| Trottier, Charles/PO Box 581, Burlington, VT | 802-864-9148 |
| Trzoniec, Stanley/58 W Main St, Northboro, MA | 617-842-6721 |
| Tuckerman, John/Box 301, Springhouse, PA | 215-643-6663 |
| Twarog, Richard R/PO Box 355, Essex Sta, Boston, MA | 617-426-1120 |

## U V
| | |
|---|---|
| Uniphoto/1071 Wisconsin Ave, Washington, DC | 202-333-0500 |
| Urban, John/1424 Canton Ave, Milton, MA | 617-333-0343 |
| Urbina, Walt/7208 Thomas Blvd, Pittsburgh, PA | 412-242-5070 |
| Van Arsdale, Nancy/300 Franklin Tpk, Ridgewood, NJ | 201-652-1202 |
| Van Camp, Louis/Rt 110 535 Broad Hollow Rd, Melville, NY | 516-752-1511 |
| Van Petten, Rob/109 Broad St, Boston, MA | 617-426-8641 |
| Van Schalkwyk, John/50 Melcher St, Boston, MA | 617-542-4825 |
| **VAUGHAN, TED/423 DOE RUN RD, MANHEIM, PA (P 232,233)** | **717-665-6942** |
| Visual Media Prod/155 Main St, Peabody, MA | 617-531-5182 |
| Von Hoffmann/2 Green Village Rd, Madison, NJ | 201-377-0317 |
| Voscar The Maine Photographer/P O Box 661, Presque Isle, ME | 207-769-5911 |

## W
| | |
|---|---|
| Wachter, Jerry/1410 Bare Hills Ave, Baltimore, MD | 301-337-2977 |
| Waggaman, John/2746 N 46 St, Philadelphia, PA | 215-473-2827 |
| Walch, Robert/310 W Main St, Kutztown, PA | 215-683-5701 |
| Walther, Michael/Pro Am Photo/4900 Merrick Rd, Massapequa Pk, NY | 516-799-2580 |
| **WATSON, ROSS H/859 LANCASTER AVE, BRYN MAWR, PA (P 187)** | **215-527-1519** |
| Watson, Tom/2172 W Lake Rd, Skaneateles, NY | 315-685-6033 |
| Weckler, Chad/825 Washington St, Hoboken, NJ | 201-656-6006 |
| Weckler, Charles/731 N 24th St, Philadelphia, PA | 215-928-0918 |
| Weems, Bill/2030 Pierce Mill Rd NW, Washington, DC | 202-667-2444 |
| Weems, Samuel/119 College Ave, West Somerville, MA | 617-666-4666 |
| **WEIDMAN, H MARK/2112 GOODWIN LANE, NORTH WALES, PA (P 188,189)** | **215-646-1745** |
| **WEIGAND, TOM/707 N FIFTH ST, READING, PA (P 190)** | **215-374-4431** |
| Weinberg, Abe/1230 Summer St, Philadelphia, PA | 215-567-5454 |
| Weinrebe, Steve/354 Congress St, Boston, MA | 617-423-9130 |
| Wendler, Hans/RD 1 Box 191, Epsom, NH | 603-736-9383 |
| West Pen Products/1701 Cochran Rd, Pittsburgh, PA | 412-687-7500 |
| Westwood Photo Productions/76 Astor Ave, Norwood, MA | 617-769-5410 |
| Wheeler, Edward F/1050 King of Prussia Rd, Radnor, PA | 215-964-9294 |
| White, Sharon/144 Moody St, Waltham, MA | 617-891-6011 |
| Wilkins, Doug/33 Church St, Canton, MA | 617-828-2379 |
| Willard, David/80 Summer St, Boston, MA | 617-542-4802 |
| Williams, Jay/9101 W Chester Pike, Upper Darby, PA | 215-789-3830 |
| Williams, Lawrence S/9101 W Chester Pike, Upper Darby, PA | 215-789-3030 |
| Williams, Ron/1703 Walnut, Philadelphia, PA | 215-563-0880 |
| Wilson, Paul S/1225 Spring St, Philadelphia, PA | 215-564-2772 |
| Wilson, Robert L/PO Box 1742, Clarksburg, WV | 304-623-5368 |
| Wittstein, William H/160 Forest Hill Rd, North Haven, CT | 203-265-5930 |
| Wolley, Jane/130 Chestnut West, Randolph, MA | 617-961-4237 |
| Wornom, Bob/19 E 21st St, Baltimore, MD | 301-539-2624 |
| Wu, Ron/179 St Paul St, Rochester, NY | 716-454-5600 |
| Wuillerman, Liz/731 N 24th St, Philadelphia, PA | 215-928-0918 |
| Wurster, George/22 Hallo St, Edison, NJ | 201-352-2134 |
| Wyman, Ira/14 Crane Ave, West Peabody, MA | 617-535-2880 |

## Y
| | |
|---|---|
| **YABLON, RON/PO BOX 128, EXTON, PA (P 234)** | **215-363-2596** |
| Yamashita, Michael/Roxticus Rd, Mendham, NJ | 201-543-4473 |
| Young, Don/Box 249, Exton, PA | 215-363-2596 |
| Young, Ellan/86 Prospect Dr, Chappaqua, NY | 914-238-4837 |

## Z
| | |
|---|---|
| Zappala, John/Candlewood Echoes, Sherman, CT | 203-354-6420 |
| Zavalishin, Nick/1324 Boston Post Rd, Box 84 Wo, Milford, CT | 203-878-2065 |
| Zmiejko, Tom/PO Box 126, Freeland, PA | 717-636-2304 |

# SOUTHEAST

## A
| | |
|---|---|
| **ABEL, WILTON/2609 COMMONWEALTH AVE, CHARLOTTE, NC (P 256)** | **704-372-6354** |
| Abell, Sam/Route 2, Box 292, Crozet, VA | 804-823-5669 |
| Allard, William Albert/Marsh Run Farm Box 549, Someset, VA | 703-672-5316 |
| Allen, Bob/710 W Lane St, Raleigh, NC | 919-833-5991 |
| Alterman, Jack/285 Meeting St, Charleston, SC | 803-577-0647 |
| Andrea, Michael/225 So Mint St, Cahrlotte, NC | 704-334-3992 |
| Arnold, Harriet/4500 S Ocean Blvd, Palm Beach, FL | 305-582-0606 |
| Arpino, Matthew/502 Armour Circle, NE, Atlanta, GA | 404-881-1213 |
| Ayres, Jim/1824 Briarwood Ind. Ct, Atlanta, GA | 404-262-2740 |

## B
| | |
|---|---|
| Bachmann, Bill/1550 W 84th St, Hialeah, FL | 305-558-7023 |
| Balbuza, Joseph/25 NE 210 St, Miami, FL | 305-652-1728 |
| Ball, Roger/4059 Yancey Rd, Charlotte, NC | 704-525-2306 |
| **BARLEY, BILL/PO BOX 2388, COLUMBIA, SC (P 257)** | **803-755-1554** |
| Barrs, Michael/6303 SW 69th St, Miami, FL | 305-665-2047 |
| Beck, Charles/2721 Cherokee Rd, Birmingham, AL | 205-871-6632 |
| Becker, Art/1881 NW 42nd Terr #F410, Lauderhill, FL | 305-485-7639 |
| Behrens, Bruce/541 W Fairbanks Ave, Winter Park, FL | 305-645-2501 |
| Berger, Erica/9341 NW 57th ST, Tamarack, FL | 305-527-8445 |
| Biannan, R H/PO Box 724001, Atlanta, GA | 404-957-1401 |
| **BILBY, GLADE/1715 BURGUNDY, NEW ORLEANS, LA (P 258)** | **504-949-6700** |
| Bollman, Brooks/1179 Virginia Ave NE, Atlanta, GA | 404-876-2422 |
| Borchelt, Mark/2310 So Columbus St, Arlington, VA | 79-9156 |
| Borum, Michael/625 Fogg St, Nashville, TN | 615-259-9750 |
| Bostick, Rick/1814 Canton St, Orlando, FL | 305-677-5717 |
| Bowden, John/816 N St Asaph St, Alexandria, VA | 703-549-5151 |
| Brack, Dennis/3609 Woodhill Pl, Fairfax, VA | 703-280-2285 |
| Brill, David/Route 4, Box 121-C, Fairbourn, GA | 404-461-5488 |
| Brinson, Rob/2184 Peachtree Rd #4, Atlanta, GA | 404-351-6444 |
| Brooks, John/PO Box 05-459, Fort Myers, FL | 212-224-1758 |
| Brown, Richard/PO Box 1249, Ashville, NC | 704-253-1634 |
| Burns, Jerry/986 Hemphill Ave NW, Atlanta, GA | 404-881-9860 |

## C
| | |
|---|---|
| Camera Graphics/1230 Gateway Rd, Lake Park, FL | 305-844-3399 |
| **CARRIKER, RONALD/565 ALPINE RD, WINSTON SALEM, NC (P 259)** | **919-765-3852** |
| Caudle Harris Studio/1231 A Collier Rd, Atlanta, GA | 404-352-5580 |
| Cerny, Paul/3662 S West Shore Blvd, Tampa, FL | 813-839-7710 |
| Chalfant, Flip/1252 Eastland Rd, Atlanta, GA | 404-627-4451 |
| **CHAPPLE, RON/437 S TRYON ST, CHARLOTTE, NC (P 250,251)** | **704-377-4217** |
| Chapple, Ross/Sundance Farm, Hume, VA | 703-364-1568 |
| Chernush, Kay/3855 N 30th St, Arlington, VA | 703-528-1195 |
| Chimera Productions/PO Box 1742, Clarksburg, WV | 304-623-5368 |
| Choiniere, Gerin/900 Greenleaf Ave, Charlotte, NC | 704-372-0220 |
| Clayton, Al/141 The Prado NE, Atlanta, GA | 404-881-1170 |
| Cody, Dennis/5320 SW 51 Terr, Miami, FL | 305-666-0247 |
| Colbroth, Ron/4421 Airlie Way, Annandale, VA | 703-354-2729 |
| Contorakes, George/PO Box 430901, South Miami, FL | 305-661-0731 |
| Cook, Jamie/653 Ethel St, Atlanta, GA | 404-892-1393 |
| Cooke, Bill/7761 SW 88th St, Miami, FL | 305-596-2454 |
| Copeland, Jim/559 Dutch Vall Rd, Atlanta, GA | 404-873-5858 |
| Cravotta, Jeff/1212 E 10th St, Charlotte, NC | 704-334-5115 |
| Creative Photographers Inc/2214 Hawkins St, Charlotte, NC | 704-376-6475 |
| Cromer, Peggo/1206 Andora Ave, Coral Gables, FL | 305-667-3722 |

## D
| | |
|---|---|
| David, Alan/Chiaroscuro/1186 D N Highland Ave, Atlanta, GA | 404-872-2142 |
| DeAzoulay, Daniel/1237 E Las Olas Blvd, Fort Lauderdale, FL | 305-462-4183 |
| DeCasseres Photography/418 Calhoun St NW, Atlanta, GA | 404-872-2753 |
| **DEVAULT, JIM/2400 SUNSET PL, NASHVILLE, TN (P 260,261)** | **615-269-4538** |
| Diamond, Hindi/7250 SW 126th St Box 1701, Miami, FL | 305-475-5511 |
| Dickinson, Dick/1854 County Line Rd, Sarasota, FL | 813-351-2036 |
| Dinkins, Stephanie/7912 Willow St, New Orleans, LA | 504-866-3337 |
| Dobbs, David/1536 Monroe Dr NE, Atlanta, GA | 404-885-1460 |
| Dryman, Terry/5021 Anderson Ave, Tampa, FL | 813-872-0603 |
| Duer, Deryl/1027 Elm Hill Pike, Nashville, TN | 615-255-1919 |

# PHOTOGRAPHERS CONT'D.

Please send us your additions and updates.

| | |
|---|---|
| Duvall Thurman Studio III/1021 Northside Dr NW, Atlanta, GA | 404-875-0161 |

## E
| | |
|---|---|
| Edwards, Jack/209 N Rocheblave St, New Orleans, LA | 504-822-2111 |
| Elliot, Tom/19756 Bel Aire Dr, Miami, FL | 305-251-4315 |
| Ellis & Ingendaay/1299 Spring St NW, Atlanta, GA | 404-876-4058 |
| Ellis, Bill/406 Edwards Dr, Greensboro, NC | 919-299-5074 |
| English, Melissa Hayes/PO Box 14391, Atlanta, GA | 404-261-7650 |
| Evensen, Bruce M/79-25 4th St N, St Petersburg, FL | 813-577-5626 |

## F
| | |
|---|---|
| Fineman, Michael/7521 SW 57th Terr, Miami, FL | 305-666-1250 |
| Fisher, Ray/10700 SW 72nd Ct, Miami, FL | 305-665-7659 |
| Forer, Dan/1970 NE 149th St, North Miami, FL | 305-949-3131 |
| Fowley, Douglas/103 N Hite Ave, Louisville, KY | 502-897-7222 |
| Frink, Stephen/PO Box 19-A, Key Largo, FL | 305-451-3737 |

## G
| | |
|---|---|
| Gandy, Skip/302 East Davis Blvd, Tampa, FL | 813-253-0340 |
| Gardella Photography & Design/781 Miami Cr NE, Atlanta, GA | 404-231-1316 |
| Gefter, Judith/1725 Clemson Rd, Jacksonville, FL | 904-733-5498 |
| Gelberg, Bob/3200 Ponce De Leon Blvd, Coral Gables, FL | 305-448-8458 |
| Gemigani, Joe/13833 NW 19th Ave, Miami, FL | 305-685-7636 |
| **GLEASNER, BILL/132 HOLLY CT, DENVER, NC (P 262)** | **704-483-9301** |
| Graham, Curtis/648 1st Ave So, St Petersburg, FL | 813-821-0444 |
| Granberry Studios/1211 Spring St, NW, Atlanta, GA | 404-874-2426 |
| Grigg, Roger Allen/PO Box 52851, Atlanta, GA | 404-876-4748 |
| Grimes, Billy/PO Box 19739 N, Atlanta, GA | 404-971-0446 |
| Groendyke, Bill/7320 Fox Chappel Dr, Miami, FL | 305-822-7559 |
| Guerry, Tim/3035 Castleton Way, Marietta, GA | 404-973-5664 |
| Guider, John/302 Hill Ave, Nashville, TN | 615-255-4495 |
| Gupton, Charles/Route 2, Box 206, Wake Forest, NC | 919-556-6511 |
| **GUPTON, LEE/PO BOX 1112, CARY, NC (P 263)** | **919-469-3025** |
| Guravich, Dan/PO Box 891, Greenville, MS | 601-335-2444 |

## H
| | |
|---|---|
| Haggerty, Richard/656 Ward St, High Point, NC | 919-889-7744 |
| Hannau, Michael/13225 NW 42nd Ave, Miami, FL | 305-687-3543 |
| Harbison, Steve/3808-B Woodmont Ln, Nashville, TN | 615-890-5449 |
| Harris, Christopher/3039 Desoto St, New Orleans, LA | 504-586-0209 |
| Havkand, Patrick/3642 Tryclan Dr, Charlotte, NC | 704-527-8795 |
| **HENDERSON, CHIP/5700 NEW CHAPEL HILL RD, RALEIGH, NC (P 264)** | **919-851-0458** |
| Higgins, Neal/1540 Monroe Dr, Atlanta, GA | 404-876-3186 |
| Hill, Jackson/Box 15276, New Orleans, LA | 504-891-4747 |
| Hines, Bill & Susan/6814-F Glenridge Dr NE, Atlanta, GA | 404-394-5939 |
| Hoflich, Richard/1189 Virginia Ave NE, Atlanta, GA | 404-872-3491 |
| Holland, Ralph/3706 Alliance Dr, Greensboro, NC | 919-855-6422 |
| **HOOD, ROBIN/110 W MAIN ST, FRANKLIN, TN (P 255)** | **615-794-9507** |
| Hyman, Bill/689 Antoine St NW, Atlanta, GA | 404-355-8069 |

## I J
| | |
|---|---|
| Isaacs, Lee/807 9th Court South, Birmingham, AL | 205-252-2698 |
| James, Bill/15840 SW 79th Ct, Miami, FL | 305-238-5709 |
| **JAMISON, CHIPP/2131 LIDDELL DR NE, ATLANTA, GA (P 253)** | **404-873-3636** |
| Jimson, Tom/5929 Annunciation, New Orleans, LA | 504-891-8587 |
| **JOHNS, DOUGLAS/2535 25TH AVE N, ST PETERSBURG, FL (P 265)** | **813-321-7235** |
| Jordan/Rudolph Studios/1446 Mayson St NE #5L, Atlanta, GA | 404-874-1829 |
| Joyner, Louis O/3591 Burnt Leaf Ln, Birmingham, AL | 205-877-6000 |
| Jureit, Robert A/9200 S Dadeland Blvd, #506, Miami, FL | 305-667-1346 |

## K
| | |
|---|---|
| Kaplan, Al/PO Box 611373, North Miami, FL | 305-891-7595 |
| **KATZ, ARNI/PO BOX 724507, ATLANTA, GA (P 254)** | **404-953-1168** |
| **KEARNEY, MITCHELL/437 S TRYON ST, CHARLOTTE, NC (P 251)** | **704-377-4217** |
| Kern Photography/1243 N 17th Ave, Lake Worth, FL | 305-582-2487 |
| Kersh, Viron/PO Box 51201, New Orleans, LA | 504-523-1221 |
| King, J Brian/1267 Coral Way, Miami, FL | 305-856-6534 |
| King, Ken/3629 Vacation Ln, Arlington, VA | 703-524-5950 |
| Kinsella, Barry/1010 Andrews Rd, West Palm Beach, FL | 305-832-8736 |
| Kluetmeier, Heinz/1482 NE 63rd Ct, Ft. Lauderdale, FL | 305-771-2824 |
| Knight, Steve/1212 E 10th St, Charlotte, NC | 704-334-5115 |
| **KOHANIM, PARISH/1130 W PEACHTREE ST, ATLANTA, GA (P 248,249)** | **404-892-0099** |
| Kollar, Robert E/1431 Cherokee Trail #52, Knoxville, TN | 615-632-8055 |

| | |
|---|---|
| Kufner, Gary/305 NW 10th Terr, Hallendale, FL | 305-944-7740 |

## L
| | |
|---|---|
| Langone, Peter/516 N East 13th ST, Ft Lauderdale, FL | 305-467-0654 |
| Lathem, Charles/559 Dutch Valley Rd, Atlanta, GA | 404-873-5858 |
| Lau, Glenn H/7665 SW 105th St, Ocala, FL | 904-237-4123 |
| Lavenstein, Lance/4605 Pembroke Lake Cir, Virginia Beach, VA | 804-499-9959 |
| Lawson, Slick/3801 Whitland Ave, Nashville, TN | 615-383-0147 |
| Leviton Atlanta Inc/1271 Roxboro Dr NE, Atlanta, GA | 404-237-7766 |

## M
| | |
|---|---|
| Magruder, Mary and Richard/2156 Snap Finger Rd, Decatur, GA | 404-289-8985 |
| Malles, Ed/807 9th Court S, Birmingham, AL | 205-251-0651 |
| Maratea, Ronn/4338 Virginia Beach Blvd, Virginia Beach, VA | 804-340-6464 |
| Marden, Bruce F Productions/5020 Atlanta Rd, #3, Smyrna, GA | 404-351-8152 |
| McCarthy, Tom/8960 SW 114th St, Miami, FL | 305-233-1703 |
| McCord, Fred/2720 Piedmont Rd NE, Atlanta, GA | 404-262-1538 |
| McCoy, Frank T/131 Donmond Dr, Hendersonville, TN | 615-822-4437 |
| McGee, E Alan/1816 Briarwood Ind Ct, Atlanta, GA | 404-633-1286 |
| McIntyre, William/3746 Yadkinville Rd, Winston-Salem, NC | 919-922-3142 |
| McKee, Lee/1007 Armada Ct, Ocoee, FL | 305-656-9289 |
| McKelvey, Michael/44 12th St NE, Atlanta, GA | 404-892-8223 |
| McNeely, Burton/PO Box 338, Land O'Lakes, FL | 813-996-3025 |
| Medina, Nelson/3211 Bay To Bay Blvd, Tampa, FL | 813-839-6754 |
| Miller, Brad/3645 Stewart, Coconut Grove, FL | 305-666-1617 |
| Miller, Bruce/16 Palm Island, Miami, FL | 305-534-1441 |
| Miller, Frank J/PO Box 1990, Hickory, NC | 704-324-8758 |
| Miller, Frank Lotz/1115 Washington Ave, New Orleans, LA | 504-899-5688 |
| **MILLER, RANDY/6666 SW 96TH ST, MIAMI, FL (P 266,267)** | **305-667-5765** |
| Minardi, Mike/3312 Perry Ave, Tampa, FL | 813-251-6885 |
| **MORGAN, FRANK/2414 ARTIC AVE #5, VIRGINIA BEACH, VA (P 241)** | **804-422-9328** |
| Morgan, Red/970 Hickory Trail, W Palm Beach, FL | 305-793-6085 |
| **MURRAY, STEVE/1330 MORDECAI DR, RALEIGH, NC (P 268)** | **919-828-0653** |
| Myers, Fred/114 Regent Ln, Florence, AL | 205-386-2207 |
| Myhre, Gordon/PO Box 1226, Indian Rocks Beach, FL | 813-584-3717 |
| Mykietyn, Walt/10110 SW 133 St, Miami, FL | 305-235-2342 |

## N
| | |
|---|---|
| Nemeth, Judy/PO Box 37108, Charlotte, NC | 704-375-9292 |
| Neubauer, John/1525 S Arlington Ridge Rd, Arlington, VA | 703-920-5994 |
| Nicholson, Nick/1503 Brooks Ave, Raleigh, NC | 919-787-6076 |
| Norling Studios Inc/PO Box 7004, High Point, NC | 919-434-3151 |
| Norton, Mike/4917 W Nassau, Tampa, FL | 813-876-3390 |
| Olive, Tim/754 Piedmont Ave NE, Atlanta, GA | 404-872-0500 |
| Osborne, Mitchel L/326 Picayune Pl #200, New Orleans, LA | 504-522-1871 |

## P
| | |
|---|---|
| **PETREY, JOHN/670 CLAY ST PO BOX 2401, WINTER PARK, FL (P 269)** | **305-645-1718** |
| The Photographic Center/2909 Baltic Ave, Greensboro, NC | 919-275-7691 |
| Photographic Group/74-07 Chancery Ln, Orlando, FL | 305-855-4306 |
| Photographic Ideas/PO Box 285, Charleston, SC | 803-577-7020 |
| Photography Unlimited/3662 S West Shore Blvd, Tampa, FL | 813-839-7710 |
| Pierce, Nancy J/PO Box 30815, Charlotte, NC | 704-333-4221 |
| Pietersen, Alex Photographics/4411 Sheridan Ave, Miami Beach, FL | 305-538-3180 |

## R
| | |
|---|---|
| Ransom, William/3008 Saratoga Dr, Orlando, FL | 305-898-4749 |
| Rathe, Robert A/9018 Jersey Dr, Fairfax, VA | 703-560-7222 |
| Ratkiewicz, Ken/211 N Howard St #203, Alexandria, VA | 703-751-6843 |
| Riley, Richard/24 N Ft Harrison, Clearwater, FL | 813-446-2626 |
| Rodgers, Ted/503 Ansley Villa Dr, Atlanta, GA | 404-892-6303 |
| Rogers, Chuck/508 Armour Cr, Atlanta, GA | 404-872-0062 |
| Rogers, Ted/1157 W Peachtree, N W, Atlanta, GA | 404-892-0967 |
| Rubio, Manny/1203 Techwood Dr, Atlanta, GA | 404-892-0783 |
| Rudolph, Jordan Studios/1429 Mayson St NE, Atlanta, GA | 404-874-1829 |
| Russell, John/PO Box 2141, High Point, NC | 919-887-1163 |
| Rutledge, Don/1300 Edgetree Ct, Midlothian, VA | 804-353-0151 |

## S
| | |
|---|---|
| Sahuc, Louis/530 Royal St, New Orleans, LA | 504-523-2809 |
| Salmon, George/10325 Delmar Cr, Tampa, FL | 813-961-8687 |

# PHOTOGRAPHERS CONT'D.

Please send us your additions and updates.

| | |
|---|---|
| Saylor, Ted/2312 Farwell Dr, Tampa, FL | 813-879-5636 |
| Schaedler, Tim/PO Box 1081, Safety Harbor, FL | 813-796-0366 |
| Scheff, Joe/2609 Ninth St N, St Petersburg, FL | 813-822-3599 |
| Schenck, Gordon H/PO Box 35203, Charlotte, NC | 704-332-4078 |
| Schiavone, George/355 NE 59th Terr, Miami, FL | 305-758-7334 |
| Schiff, Ken/4406 SW 74th Ave, Miami, FL | 305-262-2022 |
| Schulke, Flip/PO Box 430760, Miami, FL | 305-667-5671 |
| Sharpe, David/816 N St Asaph St, Alexandria, VA | 703-683-3773 |
| Sheldon, Mike/Rt 2, Box 61A, Canton, NC | 704-235-8345 |
| Sherman, Bob/1166 NE 182nd St, North Miami BE, FL | 305-944-2111 |
| **SHERMAN, RON/PO BOX 28656, ATLANTA, GA (P 271)** | **404-993-7197** |
| Shooters Photographic/PO Box 36464, Charlotte, NC | 704-334-7267 |
| Siebenthaler, John/2426 S. Boulevard, New Port Richey, FL | 813-848-2927 |
| Slater, Edward/6289 W Sunrise Blvd #203, Sunrise, Fl | 305-949-5191 |
| **SMITH, RICHARD W/1007-B NORWALK ST, GREENSBORO, NC (P 252)** | **919-292-1190** |
| Smith/Garner Studios/1114 W Peachtree St, Atlanta, GA | 404-875-0086 |
| Sparks, Don/670 11th St NW, Atlanta, GA | 404-876-7354 |
| Stansfield, Ross/4938 D Eisenhower Ave, Alexandria, VA | 703-370-5142 |
| Stewart, Harvey & Co Inc/836 Dorse Rd, Lewisville, NC | 919-945-2101 |
| The Stoppe Photographics Group/13 W Main St, Richmond, VA | 804-644-0266 |
| Strode, William A/1008 Kent Rd, Prospect, KY | 502-228-4446 |
| Studio 5/523 Lupton Dr, Chattanooga, TN | 615-870-9612 |

## T

| | |
|---|---|
| Thomas, J Clark/2305 Elliston Place, Nashville, TN | 615-327-1757 |
| Thompson, Thomas L/32 Peachtree St, NW, Atlanta, GA | 404-524-1234 |
| Tilley, Arthur/1925 College Ave, Atlanta, GA | 404-371-8086 |
| Tribuzio Studio/605 Ward Ave, High Point, NC | 919-883-4171 |
| Tucker, Mark Studio/117 Second Ave N, Nashville, TN | 615-254-5555 |
| Turnau, Jeffrey/10800 SW 68th Ave, Miami, FL | 305-666-5454 |
| Tutino, Aldo/407 N Washington St, Alexandria, VA | 703-549-8014 |

## UV

| | |
|---|---|
| Uzzel, Steve/2505 N Custis Rd, Arlington, VA | 703-522-2320 |
| Van Calsem, Bill/824 Royal St, New Orleans, LA | 504-522-7346 |
| **VANCE, DAVID/13760 NW 19TH AVE #14, MIAMI, FL (P 272,273)** | **305-685-2433** |
| Vaughn, Marc/PO Box 660706, Miami Springs, FL | 305-888-4926 |
| Vern, Ike/10431 Larissa St, Orlando, FL | 305-352-1620 |
| Vullo, Phillip Photography/565 Dutch Valley Rd NE, Atlanta, GA | 404-874-0822 |

## W

| | |
|---|---|
| Walters, Tom/804 Atando, Charlotte, NC | 704-333-6294 |
| Webb, Jon Photography/2023 Kenilworth Ave, Louisville, KY | 502-459-7081 |
| **WESTERMAN, CHARLIE/1310 SOUTH THIRD, LOUISVILLE, KY (P 310,311)** | **502-637-8414** |
| Weston, Ganoff, Marini/5707 NE 27th Ave, Ft Lauderdale, FL | 305-772-0110 |
| Wexler, Ira/6108 Franklin Pk Rd, McLean, VA | 703-241-1776 |
| Wheless, Rob Studio/2239 Faulkner Rd NE, Atlanta, GA | 404-321-3557 |
| Williams, Jimmy/3801 Beryl Rd, Raleigh, NC | 919-832-5971 |
| Williamson, Thomas A Photography Inc/9501 SW 160th St, Miami, FL | 305-255-6400 |
| Wilson, Andrew/3110 Roswell Rd NW, Atlanta, GA | 404-231-4013 |
| Wilt, Greg/PO Box 212, Clearwater, FL | 813-536-1524 |
| Wray, Michael/7210 Red Rd #221 S, Miami, FL | 305-266-8550 |
| The Wright Studio/3708 Cheverly Rd, Richmond, VA | 804-320-3807 |

## YZ

| | |
|---|---|
| Youngblood, David/212 E Broadway, Hopewell, VA | 804-458-0491 |
| Zaruba, Jeff/905 N Columbus St, Alexandria, VA | 703-548-1506 |

# MIDWEST

## A

| | |
|---|---|
| A&B Photography Inc/720 N Franklin, Chicago, IL | 312-337-4741 |
| AGS & R Studios/425 N Michigan Ave, Chicago, IL | 312-836-4500 |
| Abel Photographics/7035 Ashland Dr, Cleveland, OH | 216-526-5732 |
| Abramson-Culbert/246 W Washington #202, Chicago, IL | 312-930-1992 |
| Adams Studio, Inc/1701 S Hanley, Brentwood, MO | 314-781-6676 |
| Adams, Janet L/1233 West Sixth Ave, Columbus, OH | 614-486-4528 |
| Adcock, Gary/PO Box 229, Elkhart, IN | 219-294-2964 |
| Advertisers Photography/114 W Illinois, Chicago, IL | 312-644-5211 |
| Albiez, Scott/4144 N Clarendon, Chicago, IL | 312-327-8999 |
| Albright, Dave/200 S Main, Northville, MI | 313-348-2248 |
| Aleksandrowicz, F J/624 St Clair Ave NW, Cleveland, OH | 216-696-4566 |
| Alexander, Gordon/920 Cherry SE, Suite 340, Grand Rapids, MI | 616-451-0736 |
| Alfa Studio/401 W Superior, Chicago, IL | 312-787-2136 |
| Allan-Knox Studios/1014 N Van Buren St, Milwaukee, WI | 414-272-4999 |
| Alpha Photochrome/Box 2062, St Louis, MO | 314-772-8540 |
| Alternative Design/8232 W Michols, Detroit, MI | 313-342-2000 |
| Anderson, Curt/Box 3213, Minneapolis, MN | 612-332-2008 |
| Anderson-Perlstein Ltd/560 Zenith Ave, Glenview, IL | 312-827-7884 |
| Andre, Bruce/436 N Clark, Chicago, IL | 312-661-1060 |
| Anna Commercial Photography/401 W Superior, Chicago, IL | 312-943-8848 |
| Apolinski Photography/522 N Seminary, Park Ridge, IL | 312-696-3156 |
| Ardisson Photography/436 N Clark, Chicago, IL | 312-951-8393 |
| Arndt & Berthiaume/1008 Nicollet Mall, Minneapolis, MN | 612-338-1984 |
| Arndt, David M/4620 N Winchester, Chicago, IL | 312-334-2841 |
| Arsenault, Bill/570 W Fulton, Chicago, IL | 312-454-0544 |
| Askenas Studio, ULF/409 W Huron, Chicago, IL | 312-944-4630 |
| Atelier Photographics/679 E Mandoline, Madison Heights, MI | 313-589-0066 |
| Atkinson, David/3923 W Pine Blvd, St Louis, MO | 314-535-6484 |
| Atoz Images/333 E Ontario #601B, Chicago, IL | 312-664-8400 |
| Ayala, George & Assoc/70 W Hubbard, Chicago, IL | 312-644-6025 |
| Azuma, Don/1335 N Wells, Chicago, IL | 312-337-2101 |

## B

| | |
|---|---|
| Baer, Gordon/PO Box 2467, Cincinnati, OH | 513-281-2339 |
| Baker, Jim/1905 Main, Kansas City, MO | 816-471-5565 |
| Balosky & Assoc/20 No Tower Rd 1G, Oak Brook, IL | 312-932-0050 |
| Bankhead, Walter Jr/207 E Buffalo St, Milwaukee, WI | 414-273-4864 |
| Banner & Burns Inc/153 W Ohio, Chicago, IL | 312-644-4770 |
| Bardner, Al/7120 Eugene, St Louis, MO | 314-752-5278 |
| Barlow Photography Inc/1125 S Brentwood Blvd, Richmond Hts., MO | 314-721-2385 |
| Barrett, Bob/3733 Pennsylvania, Kansas City, MO | 816-753-3208 |
| Bartholomew, Gary/263 Columbia Ave, Des Plaines, IL | 312-824-8473 |
| **BARTZ, CARL/321 N 22ND ST, ST LOUIS, MO (P 301)** | **314-231-8690** |
| Bass, Alan/126 W Kinzie, Chicago, IL | 312-280-9140 |
| Baver, Perry L/8706 N Drake, Skokie, IL | 312-673-4275 |
| Bayalis, John R/42 E Superior, Chicago, IL | 312-266-9572 |
| Bayles, Dal/4431 N 64th St, Milwaukee, WI | 414-464-8917 |
| Beasley, Michael/1210 W Webster, Chicago, IL | 312-248-5769 |
| Beckett Studios/340 W Huron, Chicago, IL | 312-943-2648 |
| Benda, Tom/20555 LaGrange, Frankfurt, IL | 815-469-3600 |
| Bender, Bob/1 Rockefeller Bldg, Cleveland, OH | 216-861-4338 |
| Bennington, Alan/633 Huron Rd, Cleveland, OH | 216-522-2929 |
| Benoit, Bill/1708 1/2 Washington, Wilmette, IL | 312-251-7634 |
| Bentley, David/208 West Kinzie, Chicago, IL | 312-836-0242 |
| Bentley, Gary/1611 N Sheffield 3rd Fl, Chicago, IL | 312-642-6650 |
| Bergos, Jim Studio/122 W Kinzie St, Chicago, IL | 312-527-1769 |
| Berlin Chic Photo/1120 W Barry St, Chicago, IL | 312-327-2266 |
| Bieber, Tim/405 N Wabash #4705, Chicago, IL | 312-661-1663 |
| Biel Photographic Studios/2289-91 N Moraine Blvd, Dayton, OH | 513-298-6621 |
| Bilisko, Norman Photography/110 W Kinzie, Chicago, IL | 312-222-0949 |
| Bloch, Stuart/1242 W Washington, Chicago, IL | 312-733-3600 |
| Bob Elmore & Assoc/217 W Huron, Chicago, IL | 312-751-2275 |
| Bock, Edward/400 N First Ave 207, Minneapolis, MN | 612-332-8504 |
| Bolber Studio/6706 Northwest Hwy, Chicago, IL | 312-763-5860 |
| Bosek, George/114 W Kinzie, Chicago, IL | 312-828-0988 |
| Bosy, Peter/311 N Desplaines, Chicago, IL | 312-559-0042 |
| Boucher, J/5765 S Melinda St, Milwaukee, WI | 414-281-7653 |
| Bowen, Paul/Box 3375, Wichita, KS | 316-263-5537 |
| Boyer, Dick/401 W Superior, Chicago, IL | 312-337-7211 |
| Braddy, Jim/720 N Wabash, Chicago, IL | 312-337-5664 |
| Braun Photography/3966 W Bath Rd, Akron, OH | 216-666-4540 |
| **BRIMACOMBE, GERALD/7112 MARK TERR DR, MINNEAPOLIS, MN (P 302,303)** | **612-941-5860** |
| Broderson, Fred/215 W Huron, Chicago, IL | 312-787-1241 |
| Brody, Jerry/70 W Hubbard, Chicago, IL | 312-329-0660 |
| Brooks & Van/1230 W Washington Blvd, Chicago, IL | 312-226-4060 |
| Brooks & Vankirk/1230 W Washington, Chicago, IL | 312-226-4060 |
| Brooks, John/116 E 48th St, Indianapolis, IN | 317-283-2281 |
| Brown, Alan J/1151 Halpin Ave, Cincinnati, OH | 513-321-7541 |
| Brown, David/900 Jorie Blvd, # 70, Oakbrook, IL | 312-654-2515 |
| Brown, Steve/107 W Hubbard, Chicago, IL | 312-467-4666 |
| Bruno, Sam/1630 N 23rd, Melrose Park, IL | 312-345-0411 |
| Bruton, Jon/3838 W Pine Blvd, St Louis, MO | 314-533-6665 |

# PHOTOGRAPHERS CONT'D.

Please send us your additions and updates.

| | |
|---|---|
| Buka, Walt/118 Anchor, Michigan City, IN | 219-872-9469 |
| Bundt, Nancy/4001 Forest Rd, Minneapolis, MN | 612-926-4390 |
| Burns Copeland Photography/6651 N Artesian, Chicago, IL | 312-465-3240 |
| Burress, Cliff/343 S Dearborn, Chicago, IL | 312-427-3335 |
| Burris, Zack/230 E Ohio, Chicago, IL | 312-951-0131 |

## C
| | |
|---|---|
| Cabanban, Orlando/410 S Michigan Ave, Chicago, IL | 312-922-1836 |
| Cain, C C/420 N Clark, Chicago, IL | 312-644-2371 |
| Camera Works Inc/1260 Carnegie Ave, Cleveland, OH | 216-687-1788 |
| Camermann International/PO Box 413, Evanston, IL | 312-777-5656 |
| Camlen Studio/3695 A N 126th St, Brookfield, WI | 414-781-9477 |
| Candee & Assoc/216 S Jefferson, Chicago, IL | 312-876-0409 |
| Caporale, Michael/6710 Madison Rd, Cincinnati, OH | 513-561-4011 |
| Carlson Photography/905 Park Ave, Minnneapolis, MN | 612-338-7761 |
| Carlson, David/1321 Birchwood, Chicago, IL | 312-875-5667 |
| Carney, Joann/368 W Huron, Chicago, IL | 312-266-7620 |
| Carr Photography/311 N Des Plaines, Chicago, IL | 312-454-0984 |
| Carr, Steve/535 N Michigan Ave, Chicago, IL | 312-943-1668 |
| Casalini, Tom/10 1/2 N Main St, Zionsville, IN | 317-873-5229 |
| Cascarano, John/657 W Ohio, Chicago, IL | 312-733-1212 |
| Caulfield, James/114 W Kinzie, Chicago, IL | 312-828-0004 |
| Ceolla, George/5700 Ingersoll Ave, Des Moines, IA | 515-279-3508 |
| Chambers, Ron/1546 N Orleans, Chicago, IL | 312-642-8715 |
| Chambers, Tom/153 W Ohio, Chicago, IL | 312-828-9488 |
| Chapman, Cam/126 W Kinzie, Chicago, IL | 312-222-9242 |
| Chare Photography/1045 Northwest Hwy, Park Ridge, IL | 312-696-3188 |
| Charlie Company/1375 Euclid Ave, #326, Cleveland, OH | 216-566-7464 |
| Chartmasters Inc/150 E Huron St, Chicago, IL | 312-787-9040 |
| Chauncey, Paul C/1029 N Wichita #13&15, Wichita, KS | 316-262-6733 |
| Chicago Photographers/58 W Superior, Chicago, IL | 312-944-4828 |
| Chin, Ruth/108 E Jackson, Muncie, IN | 317-284-4582 |
| Chobot, Dennis/2857 E Grand Blvd, Detroit, MI | 313-875-6617 |
| Christell & Assoc/307 N Michigan #1008, Chicago, IL | 312-236-2396 |
| Christian Studios Inc/5408 N Main St, Dayton, OH | 513-275-3775 |
| Clark, Junebug/30419 W Twelve Mile Rd, Farmington Hills, MI | 313-478-3666 |
| **CLICK! CHICAGO/213 W INSTITUTE PL #503, CHICAGO, IL (P 289-291)** | **312-787-7880** |
| Coha, Dan/535 N Michigan, Chicago, IL | 312-943-1668 |
| Compton, Ted/112 N Washington St, Hinsdale, IL | 312-654-8781 |
| Contemporary Illustrations/300 W 19th Terr, Kansas City, MO | 816-474-8888 |
| Corey, Carl/222 S Morgan, Chicago, IL | 312-421-3232 |
| Coster-Mullen, John E/698 Ellis, Fond Du Lac, WI | 414-342-6363 |
| **COWAN, RALPH/452 N HALSTED ST, CHICAGO, IL (P 292)** | **312-243-6696** |
| Cowen, Frank/2350 N Cleveland, Chicago, IL | 312-935-1707 |
| Crane, Arnold/134 N LaSalle, Chicago, IL | 312-346-9152 |
| Creative Photography/3 Saint Lambert Dr, Cahokia, IL | 618-337-5504 |
| Crosby, Paul/1701 E 79th St Ste 17B, Minneapolis, MN | 612-854-3060 |
| Culver/Kuslich & Assoc/115 Washington Ave N #200, Minneapolis, MN | 612-332-2425 |
| Cunningham, Elizabeth/1122 W Lunt Ave, Chicago, IL | 312-761-9323 |
| Curtis, Lucky/1540 N North Park, Chicago, IL | 312-787-4422 |

## D
| | |
|---|---|
| DGM Studios/70 E Long Lake, Bloomfield Hills, MI | 313-645-2222 |
| Damien, Paul/180 N 69th St, Milwaukee, WI | 414-259-1987 |
| **DEAHL, DAVID/70 W HUBBARD, CHICAGO, IL (P 276,277)** | **312-644-3187** |
| **DEBOLD, BILL/1801 N HALSTED, CHICAGO, IL (P 284)** | **312-337-1177** |
| DeFrancesco, Joe/911 Broadway, #300, Kansas City, MO | 816-474-6166 |
| DeMarco Photographers/7145 W Addison, Chicago, IL | 312-282-1422 |
| DeNatale, Joe/215 W Ohio, Chicago, IL | 312-329-0234 |
| DeRussy, Myles/53 W Jackson Blvd, Chicago, IL | 312-559-0232 |
| Deutsch, Owen/1759 N Sedgewick, Chicago, IL | 312-943-7155 |
| Devenny-Wood Ltd/56 W Huron, Chicago, IL | 312-944-7070 |
| Dieringer, Rick/19 West Court St, Cincinnatti, OH | 513-621-2544 |
| Ditlove, Michel/18 W Hubbard, Chicago, IL | 312-644-5233 |
| Ditz, Michael/8138 W 9 Mile Rd, Oak Park, MI | 313-546-1759 |
| Don Marshall Photography/361 W Superior, Chicago, IL | 312-944-0720 |
| Donner, Michael/5534 S Dorchester, Chicago, IL | 312-241-7896 |
| D'Orio, Tony/1147 W Ohio, Chicago, IL | 312-421-5532 |
| Dorrell/Creightney/314 W Institute, Chicago, IL | 312-266-8885 |
| Doyle, Tim/259 E Frank, Birmingham, MI | 313-642-5658 |
| Dreier, David/807 Reba Pl, #2W, Evanston, IL | 312-475-1992 |
| Du Broff, Don/2031 W Cortez, Chicago, IL | 312-252-7390 |
| DuBiel, Dennis/1313 Randolph, #310, Chicago, IL | 312-666-0136 |
| Dublin, Rick/1019 Currie Ave N, Minneapolis, MN | 612-332-8924 |

## E
| | |
|---|---|
| ETM Studios/130 S Morgan, Chicago, IL | 312-666-0660 |
| Eagles/415 W Superior, Chicago, IL | 312-280-1919 |
| Ebel, Bob Photography/415 N Dearborn, Chicago, IL | 312-222-1123 |
| Ebenoh, Tom/3886 Fairview, St Louis, MO | 314-772-1073 |
| Ebert Photography/227 S Marion, Chicago, IL | 312-386-6222 |
| Eiler, Lynthia & Terry/329-D Barker Rd, Rt 2, Athens, OH | 614-592-1280 |
| Eisner, Scott Photography/323 S Franklin, Chicago, IL | 312-670-2217 |
| **ELLIOTT, PETER/405 N WABASH AVE, CHICAGO, IL (P 278,279)** | **312-329-1370** |
| Errera, Jim/5085 N Ottawa, Chicago, IL | 312-774-9355 |
| Evans, Patricia/1153 E 56th St, Chicago, IL | 312-288-2291 |
| Ewert, Steve/17 N Elizabeth, Chicago, IL | 312-733-5762 |

## F
| | |
|---|---|
| Farber, Gerald/10910 Whittier, Detroit, MI | 313-371-4161 |
| Faverty, Richard/340 W Huron, Chicago, IL | 312-943-2648 |
| Feferman, Steve/209 W Illinois, Chicago, IL | 312-541-4754 |
| Fegley, Dick/405 N Wabash, Chicago, IL | 312-527-1114 |
| Feldkamp-Malloy/185 N Wabash, Chicago, IL | 312-263-0633 |
| Feldman, Stephen L/2705 W Agatite, Chicago, IL | 312-539-0300 |
| Firak Photography/11 E Hubbard, Chicago, IL | 312-467-0208 |
| Firestone, Ken/P O Box 14433, Chicago, IL | 312-975-7208 |
| Fischer, Harry/14254 Buck, Taylor, MI | 313-946-9949 |
| Fish Studios/125 W. Hubbard, Chicago, IL | 312-944-1570 |
| Fisher, Mike/35 E Wacker Dr, Chicago, IL | 312-262-0969 |
| Floyd, Bill/215 W Ohio, Chicago, IL | 312-321-1770 |
| Fontayne Studios Ltd/4528 W Oakton, Skokie, IL | 312-676-9872 |
| Ford, Madison/2616 Industrial Row, Troy, MI | 313-280-0640 |
| Forsyte, Alex/1180 Oak Ridge Dr, Glencoe, IL | 312-835-0307 |
| Forth, Ron/316 W 4th St, Cincinnatti, OH | 513-621-0841 |
| Foster, Richard/157 W Ontario St, Chicago, IL | 312-943-9005 |
| Foto-Graphics/2402 N Shadeland Ave, Indianapolis, IN | 317-353-6259 |
| Foto/Ed Sacks/Box 7237, Chicago, IL | 312-871-4700 |
| Fox Commercial Photography/119 W Hubbard, Chicago, IL | 312-664-0162 |
| Frantz, Ken/706 N Dearborn, Chicago, IL | 312-951-1077 |
| Franz, Bill/820 E Wisconsin, Delavan, WI | 414-728-3733 |
| Futran, Eric/4637 N Paulina, Chicago, IL | 312-728-8811 |

## G
| | |
|---|---|
| GSP/156 W Jefferson, Chicago, IL | 312-944-3000 |
| Gabriel, Anthony/160 E Illinois, Chicago, IL | 312-787-2915 |
| Gale, Bill/3041 Aldrich Ave S, Minneapolis, MN | 612-827-5858 |
| Gardner, Al/7120 Eugene, St Louis, MO | 314-752-5278 |
| Gedman, Robert/1968 W Foster, Chicago, IL | 312-878-0260 |
| Gerard, Steve/1785 Northwest Coult #E, Columbus, OH | 614-267-0206 |
| Gerding, Gary/4623 N 93d St, Omaha, NE | 402-571-2515 |
| Giannetti, Joseph/1008 Nicollet Mall, Minneapolis, MN | 612-339-3172 |
| Gillette, Bill/2917 Eisenhower, Ames, IA | 515-294-4340 |
| Gino Photography/721 Rappolo Dr., Elk Grove Village, IL | 312-364-6804 |
| Glenn, Eileen/One Playhouse Sq, Cleveland, OH | 216-621-9288 |
| Goez, Bill/213 W Institute Pl #402, Chicago, IL | 312-787-5854 |
| Gold, Peter N/25 University Ave SE, Minneapolis, MN | 612-379-2517 |
| Goldberg, Lenore/210 Park Ave, Glencoe, IL | 312-835-4226 |
| Goldstein, Steven/14982 Country Ridge, St Louis, MO | 314-532-0660 |
| Goodman, Anne Margaret/411 N LaSalle St, Chicago, IL | 312-670-3660 |
| Gorecki Studio/5011 W Fullerton, Chicago, IL | 312-622-8146 |
| Gould, Christopher/224 W Huron, Chicago, IL | 312-944-5545 |
| Graham-Henry, Diane/2943 N Seminary, Chicago, IL | 312-327-4493 |
| Gray, Walter/215 W Huron, Chicago, IL | 312-733-3800 |
| Grayson, Dan/831 W Cornelia, Chicago, IL | 312-477-8659 |
| Greenblatt, William/20 Nantucket Ln, St Louis, MO | 314-991-2227 |
| Gremmler, Paul/430 W Erie, Chicago, IL | 312-951-6654 |
| Griffith, Sam/154 W Hubbard, Chicago, IL | 312-648-1900 |
| Griffith, Walter/719 S 75th St, Omaha, NB | 402-391-8474 |
| Grignon Studios/1300 W Altgeld Dr, Chicago, IL | 312-975-7200 |
| Grippentrag, Dennis/70 E Long Lake Rd, Bloomfield Hills, MI | 313-645-2222 |
| Groen, John/676 N LaSalle, Chicago, IL | 312-266-2331 |
| Gross, Frank/125 W Hubbard, Chicago, IL | 312-644-5126 |
| Grubman, Steve/442 N Wells, Chicago, IL | 312-787-2272 |
| Gubin, Mark/2893 S Delaware Ave, Milwaukee, WI | 414-482-0640 |
| Guenther, Stephen/1939 Sherman Ave, Evanston, IL | 312-864-5381 |

# PHOTOGRAPHERS CONT'D.

Please send us your additions and updates.

## H
| | |
|---|---|
| Haefner, Jim/1407 B Allen, Troy, MI | 313-583-4747 |
| Hall, Brian/1015 N LaSalle St, Chicago, IL | 312-642-6764 |
| Hall, Brian Photography/514 W Webster, Chicago, IL | 312-477-4628 |
| Haller, Pam/215 W Huron, Chicago, IL | 312-649-0920 |
| Hamilton Smith, R/584 Rose Ave, St Paul, MN | 612-778-1408 |
| Hammarlund, Vern/135 Park St, Troy, MI | 313-588-5533 |
| Handelan-Pedersen/333 N Michigan, Chicago, IL | 312-782-6833 |
| Handley, Robert E/1920 E Croxton, Bloomington, IL | 309-828-4661 |
| Harding Studio/727 Hudson, Chicago, IL | 312-943-4010 |
| Harlan, Bruce/52922 Camellia Dr, South Bend, IN | 219-239-7350 |
| Harney, Sandra/4947 North Leavitt, Chicago, IL | 312-728-0509 |
| Harper, Hugo/7159 Washington Ave, St Louis, MO | 314-727-4735 |
| **HARRIS, BART/70 W HUBBARD ST, CHICAGO, IL (P 285)** | **312-751-2977** |
| Hart, Bob/116 W Illinois, Chicago, IL | 312-644-3636 |
| Hauser, Mark/1810 W Cortland, Chicago, IL | 312-486-4581 |
| Hecht, Frederick/947 Wesley St, Evanston, IL | 312-869-8072 |
| Hedrich-Blessing/11 W Illinois, Chicago, IL | 312-321-1151 |
| Heilbron, Kenneth/1357 N Wells, Chicago, IL | 312-787-1238 |
| Hermann, Dell/676 N LaSalle, Chicago, IL | 312-664-1461 |
| **HETISIMER, LARRY/1630 5TH AVE, MOLINE, IL (P 293)** | **309-797-1010** |
| Hickson Bender Photography/Box 201, #281 Klingel Rd, Waldo, OH | 614-726-2470 |
| Hill, Roger/140 Jefferson SE, Grand Rapids, MI | 517-371-3036 |
| Hirschfeld, Corson/316 W Fourth St, Cincinnati, OH | 513-241-0550 |
| **HIX, STEVE/306 W 8TH ST, KANSAS CITY, MO (P 304)** | **816-221-2456** |
| Hobson, Royden L/436 Swan Blvd, Deerfield, IL | 312-459-9568 |
| Hoffman-Wilber Inc/618 W Jackson, Chicago, IL | 312-454-0303 |
| Holcepl, Robert/2044 Euclid Ave, Cleveland, OH | 216-621-3838 |
| Honor, David/1424 W Thorndale, Chicago, IL | 312-751-0974 |
| Hooke Photography/125 W Hubbard, Chicago, IL | 312-222-1261 |
| Hoppe, Ed Photography/401 W Superior, Chicago, IL | 312-787-2136 |
| Howard Marks Studio/3725 W Morse, Lincolnwood, IL | 312-673-0980 |
| Howrani, Armeen/15 E Baltimore St, Detroit, MI | 313-875-3123 |
| Hurling, Robert/225 W Huron, Chicago, IL | 312-944-2022 |
| Hyman, Randy/7709 Carnell Ave, St Louis, MO | 314-721-7489 |

## I
| | |
|---|---|
| Iann-Hutchins/2044 Euclid Ave, Cleveland, OH | 216-579-1570 |
| Imagematrix/2 Garfield Pl, Cincinnati, OH | 513-381-1380 |
| Imagetrix/2 Garfield Pl, Cincinnati, OH | 513-381-1380 |
| Inflight Photo/3114 St Mary's, Omaha, NB | 402-345-2164 |
| International Photo Corp./1035 Wesley, Evanston, IL | 312-475-6400 |
| Irving, Gary/PO Box 38, Wheaton, IL | 312-653-0641 |
| Issacs, Michael/2558 Madison Rd, Cincinnati, OH | 513-241-4622 |
| Itahara, Tets/676 N LaSalle, Chicago, IL | 312-649-0606 |
| Italo, Ed/2161 Thurman, St Louis, MO | 314-664-2895 |
| Izokaitis, Kastytis/441 N Clark, Chicago, IL | 312-321-1388 |
| Izui, Richard/315 W Walton, Chicago, IL | 312-266-8029 |

## J
| | |
|---|---|
| Jack O'Grady Studios Inc/333 N Michigan, Chicago, IL | 312-726-9833 |
| Jackson, Jack/207 E Buffalo, Milwaukee, WI | 414-289-0890 |
| Jacob, David/6412 N Glenwood, Chicago, IL | 312-274-9191 |
| Jacquin Enterprize/1219 Holly Hills, St Louis, MO | 314-832-4221 |
| James, E Michael/10757 S Peoria, Chicago, IL | 312-928-5908 |
| Jilling, Helmut/1759 State Rd, Cuyahoga Falls, OH | 216-928-1330 |
| Jo, Isac/4344 N Wolcott, Chicago, IL | 312-472-1607 |
| Joel, David/1771 W Winnemac, Chicago, IL | 312-271-4789 |
| Johnson, Chaz T/Box 1813, 123 5th St, Fond du Lac, WI | 414-921-6249 |
| Johnson, Donald/1680 Landwehr, Northbrook, IL | 312-480-9336 |
| Johnson, Jim/802 W Evergreen, Chicago, IL | 312-943-8864 |
| Jones, Arvell/8232 W Michols, Detroit, MI | 313-342-2000 |
| Jones, Dawson/44 E Franklin St, Dayton, OH | 513-435-1121 |
| Jones, Dick/325 W Huron St, Chicago, IL | 312-642-0242 |
| Jordano, Dave/1335 N Wells, Chicago, IL | 312-280-8212 |
| Joseph, Mark/1007 N La Salle, Chicago, IL | 312-951-5333 |

## K
| | |
|---|---|
| **KAHN, DICK/21750 DORAL RD, WAUKESHA, WI (P B C)** | **414-784-1994** |
| Kapal Photo Studio/233 Ridge Rd, Munster, IN | 219-836-2176 |
| Kaplan, Dick/1694 First St, Highland Park, IL | 312-432-0632 |
| Karant & Assoc/215 W Ohio St, Chicago, IL | 312-527-1880 |
| Kauck, Jeff/205 W Fourth, Cincinnati, OH | 513-241-5435 |
| Kavola, Ken/19 E Pearson, Chicago, IL | 312-280-9060 |
| **KAZU/1211 W WEBSTER, CHICAGO, IL (P 294,295)** | **312-348-5393** |
| Kean, Christopher/624 W Adams St, Chicago, IL | 312-559-0880 |
| **KEELING, ROBERT/26 E HURON, CHICAGO, IL (P 283)** | **312-944-5680** |
| Kem, Patrick/1832 E 38th St, Minneapolis, MN | 612-729-8989 |
| Kilkelly, James/836 Glenwood Ave, Minneapolis, MN | 612-374-1332 |
| King Studios/1024 W Armitage, Chicago, IL | 312-327-0011 |
| King, Jay/1024 W Armitage, Chicago, IL | 312-327-0011 |
| Kizorex, Bill/1147 W Ohio St, Chicago, IL | 312-369-0410 |
| Klein Photography/952 W Lake, Chicago, IL | 312-226-1878 |
| Kluetmeier, Heinz/PO Box 1647, Milwaukee, WI | 414-258-5063 |
| Kogan, David/1313 W Randolph St, Chicago, IL | 312-243-1929 |
| Kolesar, Jerry Photographics/679 E Mandoline, Madison Hts, MI | 313-589-0066 |
| Kolze, Larry/22 W Erie, Chicago, IL | 312-266-8352 |
| Kondor, Laszlo/430 N Clark St, Chicago, IL | 312-642-7365 |
| Korab, Balthazar/PO Box 895, Troy, MI | 313-641-8881 |
| Kransberger, Jim/2247 Boston SE, Grand Rapids, MI | 616-777-9404 |
| Kranzten Studios/612 S Clinton, Chicago, IL | 312-922-9200 |
| Krejei, Don/1825 Chester Ave, Cleveland, OH | 216-831-0743 |
| Kroeger-Zieminski/225 W Huron, Chicago, IL | 312-751-1711 |
| Krueger, Dick/660 W Grand, Chicago, IL | 312-243-2730 |
| Krupp, Carl/220 S State #1908, Chicago, IL | 312-427-6100 |
| Kulp, Curtis/222 W Ontario, Chicago, IL | 312-266-0477 |

## L
| | |
|---|---|
| Lacopo, John C/6320 Meridian Woods Blvd, Indianapolis, IN | 317-783-4096 |
| Landau, Allan/613 W Arlington Pl, Chicago, IL | 312-472-2437 |
| Lane, Jack/5 W Grand, Chicago, IL | 312-337-2326 |
| Laroche, Andre/32470 Dequiendre, Warren, MI | 313-978-8932 |
| LaTona, Tony/1317 E 5th, Kansas City, MO | 816-474-3119 |
| Lawson, James/220 S State #1908, Chicago, IL | 312-337-8100 |
| Leavitt, Fred/316 Carmen, Chicago, IL | 312-784-2344 |
| Lee, Terry/4420 N Paulina, Chicago, IL | 312-561-1153 |
| LeGrand, Peter/413 Sandburg, Park Forest, IL | 312-747-4923 |
| Lehn, John/1900 Lasalle Ave, Carriage Hou, Minneapolis, MN | 612-871-2577 |
| Leick, Jim/1312 Washington, St Louis, MO | 314-241-2354 |
| Leifer, John/410 Archibold, Suite 100, Kansas City, MO | 816-756-2244 |
| Levey, Don/15 W Delaware Pl, Chicago, IL | 312-329-9040 |
| Lewis, John R/Rte 3 Farrell Rd, Kaukauna, WI | 414-766-4281 |
| Lieberman, Archie/1135 Asbury, Evanston, IL | 312-475-8508 |
| Lightfoot, Robert/311 Good Ave, Des Plaines, IL | 312-297-5447 |
| Lindblade, George R/PO Box 1342, Sioux City, IA | 712-255-4346 |
| Lipschis, Helmut Photography/903 W Armitage, Chicago, IL | 312-871-2003 |
| Liss, Leroy/6243 N Ridgeway Ave, Chicago, IL | 312-539-4540 |
| Little, Scott/1515 Linden, Des Moines, IA | 515-243-4428 |
| Lowenthal, Jeff/c/o Newsweek 200 E Randolph Dr, Chicago, IL | 312-861-1180 |
| Ludwigs, David/3600 Troost St, Kansas City, MO | 816-531-1363 |

## M
| | |
|---|---|
| Maas, Curt/7000 Pioneer Pkwy, Johnston, IA | 515-270-3436 |
| MacDonald, Al/32 Martin Lane, Elk Grove, IL | 312-437-8850 |
| Mack, Richard/900 N Franklin Ste 3N, Chicago, IL | 312-642-2724 |
| Maenza, David/1030 North State St, Chicago, IL | 312-645-0611 |
| Maguire, Jim/144 Lownsdale, Akron, OH | 216-836-6984 |
| Malinowski, Stan/1221 N Astor, Chicago, IL | 312-280-5353 |
| Mally Assoc/3427 W Schubert, Chicago, IL | 312-227-3837 |
| Maloney, Michael/57 W Third St, Cincinnati, OH | 513-721-2384 |
| **MANARCHY, DENNIS/229 W ILLINOIS, CHICAGO, IL (P 280,281)** | **312-828-9117** |
| Mann, Milton & Joan/P O Box 413, Evanston, IL | 312-777-5656 |
| Marguaradt, Walter/8044 N Tripp Ave, Skokie, IL | 312-675-4234 |
| Marogol, Mike/903 W Armitage, Chicago, IL | 312-871-2003 |
| Marovitz, Bob/3450 N Lake Shore Dr, Chicago, IL | 312-975-1265 |
| Marshall, Paul/117 N Jefferson St #304, Chicago, IL | 312-559-1270 |
| Marshall, Simeon/617 W Fulton, Chicago, IL | 312-454-0419 |
| Marvy Advertising Photography/41 12th Ave N, Minneapolis, MN | 612-935-0307 |
| Maselli Studios/139 W Wabash, Chicago, IL | 312-726-5678 |
| Masheris, R Assoc Inc/1338 Hazel Ave, Deerfield, IL | 312-945-2055 |
| Matusik, Jim/3714 N Racine, Chicago, IL | 312-327-5615 |
| Matz, Fred/225 W Hubbard, Chicago, IL | 312-828-9216 |
| McCann, Larry/125 W Hubbard, Chicago, IL | 312-329-0370 |
| McCay, Larry Inc/1162 E Altgeld, South Bend, IN | 219-259-1414 |
| McClelan, Thompson/206 S First St, Champaign, IL | 217-356-2767 |
| McDonough, Ted/RR 3, Box W-30, Coon Rapids, IA | 712-684-5449 |

# PHOTOGRAPHERS CONT'D.

Please send us your additions and updates.

| | |
|---|---|
| McHale Studios Inc/2349 Victory Pkwy, Cincinnati, OH | 513-961-1454 |
| McMahon, Franklin/1352 Elmwood Ave, Wilmette, IL | 312-256-5528 |
| McNichol, Greg/1638 Greenleaf Ave, Chicago, IL | 312-973-1032 |
| Meineke, David/703 E Golf Rd, Schaumburg, IL | 312-884-6006 |
| Merle Morris Photographers/614 Fifth Ave S, Minneapolis, MN | 612-338-7829 |
| Merrill, Frank/2939 West Touhy, Chicago, IL | 312-764-1672 |
| Meyer, Robert E Photographer/208 W Kinzie St, Chicago, IL | 312-467-1430 |
| Mignard Associates/1950R S Glenstone, Springfield, MO | 417-881-7422 |
| Mihalevich, Mike/9235 Somerset Dr, Overland Park, KN | 913-642-6466 |
| Miller, Buck/8132 N 37th St, Milwaukee, WI | 414-354-9260 |
| Miller, Daniel D/2025 W North Ave, Chicago, IL | 312-944-7192 |
| Miller, Frank/6016 Blue Circle Dr, Minnetonka, MN | 612-935-8888 |
| Mitchell, John Sr/2617 Greenleaf, Elk Grove, IL | 312-956-8230 |
| Mitchell, Rick/652 W Grand, Chicago, IL | 312-829-1700 |
| Mohlenkamp, Steve/632 West Pleasant, Freeport, IL | 815-235-1918 |
| Morgan, Roger/3315 W Pershing Rd, Lincoln, NE | 402-423-5646 |
| Morrill, Dan/1811 N Sedgewick, Chicago, IL | 312-787-5095 |
| Moss, Jean/222 W Ontario, Chicago, IL | 312-787-0260 |
| Mottel, Ray/ Studio 400/400 N Michigan, Chicago, IL | 312-467-5460 |
| Murphey, Gregory/2109 N Kenmore, Chicago, IL | 312-327-4856 |
| Mutrux, John L/6250A Marty Ln, Sha Mission, KS | 913-722-4343 |

## N
| | |
|---|---|
| Nano, Ed/3413 Rocky River Rd, Cleveland, OH | 216-941-3373 |
| Nardi, Bob/1015 N Halsted Ave, Chicago, IL | 312-454-0286 |
| Nawrocki, William S/11401 S Lothair, Chicago, IL | 312-445-8920 |
| Neumann, Robert/4595 Webber St, Saginaw, MI | 517-753-7907 |
| Newcomer, David New-Graphics/2209 Middlefield Rd, Cleveland, OH | 216-932-5439 |
| Nick Faitage Photography/1910 W North Ave, Chicago, IL | 312-276-9321 |
| Niedorf, Steve/700 N Washington, Minneapolis, MN | 612-332-7124 |
| Nielsen, Ron/1313 W Randolf, Chicago, IL | 312-226-2661 |
| Norris, James/2301 N Lowell, Chicago, IL | 312-342-1050 |
| Northlight Studio/1231 Superior Ave, Cleveland, OH | 216-621-3111 |
| Novak, Sam/230 W Huron, Chicago, IL | 312-664-6733 |

## O P
| | |
|---|---|
| Olsson, Russ/215 W Illinois, Chicago, IL | 312-329-9358 |
| Ontiveros, Don/5516 N Kenmore Ave, Chicago, IL | 312-878-9009 |
| O'Rourke, John/P O Box 52, Wilmington, OH | 513-382-3782 |
| Oxendorf, Eric/3825 W. Center St./PO Box 1030, Milwaukee, WI | 414-871-5958 |
| Palmisano, Vito/436 W Clark, Chicago, IL | 312-565-0524 |
| Panich, Wil/20 W Hubbard, Chicago, IL | 312-828-0742 |
| Parks, Jim/210 W Chicago, Chicago, IL | 312-321-1193 |
| Paternite, David/2300 Payne Ave, Cleveland, OH | 216-771-7696 |
| Patterson, Dan/3005 Salem Ave, Dayton, OH | 513-278-0323 |
| Payne/430 W Erie, Chicago, IL | 312-280-8414 |
| Payne, Scott/611 Lunt Unit B, Schaumburg, IL | 312-980-3337 |
| Pazovski, Kazik/2340 Laredo Ave, Cincinnati, OH | 513-281-0030 |
| Pearson, Stuart C/1005 Campbell, Joliet, IL | 815-726-5128 |
| Peretzky, Drew/2300 Payne Ave, Cleveland, OH | 216-771-7682 |
| Perkins, Ray/5111 N Milwaukee, Chicago, IL | 312-282-6450 |
| Perraud, Gene/535 N Michigan #2601, Chicago, IL | 312-467-4000 |
| Perspective Inc/23-22 Pennsylvania St, Fort Wayne, IN | 219-426-8461 |
| Peterson, Chester N Jr/PO Box 71, Lindsborg, KS | 913-227-3880 |
| Peterson, Garrick Photography/213 W Institute Pl, Chicago, IL | 312-266-8986 |
| Petroff, Tom/59 W Hubbard, Chicago, IL | 312-836-0411 |
| Phillips, David R/1230 W Washington Blvd, Chicago, IL | 312-733-3277 |
| Photo Design/145 W 4th ST, Cincinnati, OH | 513-421-5588 |
| The Photo Place/4737 Butterfield, Hillside, IL | 312-544-1222 |
| Photo-Image/4958 W Oakton, Skokie, IL | 312-674-0864 |
| Photographers Associated/719 S 75th St, Omaha, NB | 402-391-8474 |
| Photographic Illustrators, Inc/405 1/2 E Main, Muncie, IN | 317-288-1454 |
| Photographic Stimuli/2407 W Main St, Kalamazoo, MI | 616-349-6805 |
| Photographics/10837 Midwest Industrial Blvd, St Louis, MO | 314-423-8383 |
| Photography Inc/685 Pallister, Detroit, MI | 313-874-1155 |
| The Picture Place/689 Craig Rd, St Louis, MO | 314-872-7506 |
| Pintozzi, Peter/42 E Chicago, Chicago, IL | 312-266-7775 |
| **PITZNER, AL/424 WESTPORT RD, KANSAS CITY, MO. (P 305)** | **816-561-7641** |
| Plowden, David/609 Cherry, Winnetka, IL | 312-446-2793 |
| Pohlman Studios, Inc/527 N 27th St, Milwaukee, WI | 414-342-6363 |
| Pokempner, Marc/1453 W Addison, Chicago, IL | 312-525-4567 |
| Polaski, James/215 W Superior, Chicago, IL | 312-751-2526 |
| Poli, Frank/158 W Huron, Chicago, IL | 312-944-3924 |
| Polin, Jack Photography/7306 Crawford, Lincolnwod, IL | 312-676-4312 |
| Pomerantz, Ron/325 W Huron #406, Chicago, IL | 312-787-6407 |
| Portnoy, Lewis/No 5 Carole La, St Louis, MO | 314-567-5700 |
| Powell, Jim/326 W Kalamazoo, Kalamazoo, MI | 616-381-2302 |
| Preis, Donna/2102 N Sheffield, Chicago, IL | 312-472-6708 |
| Progressive Visuals/2550 Northridge Ave, Arlington Heights, IL | 312-577-0255 |
| Pruitt, Brett/164 Willow, Elk Grove, IL | 312-944-0720 |
| Puffer, David/420 W Huron, Chicago, IL | 312-266-7540 |
| Pulse Productions Inc/110 N Van Buren Ave, St Louis, MO | 314-822-0511 |
| Puza, Greg/PO Box 1986, Milwaukee, WI | 414-444-9882 |

## Q R
| | |
|---|---|
| Quist, Bruce/1370 N Milwaukee, Chicago, IL | 312-252-3921 |
| Rack, Ron/205 W Fourth St, Cincinnati, OH | 513-421-6267 |
| Raczynski, Walter/117 North Jefferson, Chicago, IL | 312-454-0680 |
| Radlund & Associates/331 Coyier Ln, Madison, WI | 608-274-0344 |
| Randall, Bob/325 W Huron, Chicago, IL | 312-664-7008 |
| Rawson, Jon/42 E Superior, Chicago, IL | 312-787-8834 |
| Ray Reiss Photography/2144 N Leavitt, Chicgo, IL | 312-384-3245 |
| Raynor, Dorka/1063 Ash St, Winnetka, IL | 312-446-1187 |
| Reed, Dick/1330 Coolidge, Troy, MI | 313-280-0090 |
| Reffner, Wayne/4178 Dayton-Xenia Rd, Dayton, OH | 513-429-2392 |
| Renerts, Peter Studio/633 Huron Rd, Cleveland, OH | 216-781-2440 |
| Ricco, Ron/207 E Buffalo #514, Milwaukee, WI | 414-271-4360 |
| Rich, Larry/29731 Everett, Southfield, MI | 313-557-7676 |
| Rick Gould Studios/217 N 10th St, St Louis, MO | 314-241-4862 |
| Robinson, David/215 W Ohio, Chicago, IL | 312-266-9050 |
| Rogers, Bill Arthur/846 Wesley Ave, Oak Park, IL | 312-848-3900 |
| Rogowski, Tom/214 E 8th St, Cincinnati, OH | 513-621-3826 |
| **ROHMAN, JIM/2254 MARENGO, TOLEDO, OH (P 306)** | **419-865-0234** |
| Ron Coil Studio/15 W Hubbard St, Chicago, IL | 312-321-0155 |
| Rosmis, Bruce/118 W Ohio, Chicago, IL | 312-787-9046 |
| Ross, Allan/1123 W Armitage, Chicago, IL | 312-975-5657 |
| Ross, Doug/1009 W Webster, Chicago, IL | 312-327-7878 |
| Rottinger, Ed/2518 N Southport, Chicago, IL | 312-262-5135 |
| Rowley, Joe/368 W Huron, Chicago, IL | 312-266-7620 |
| **RUBIN, LAURIE/719 W WILLOW ST, CHICAGO, IL (P 288)** | **312-784-2343** |
| Rutt, Don/8743 Sky Lane, Traverse City, MI | 616-946-2727 |
| Ryan, Gary/23245 Woodward, Ferndale, MI | 313-542-6006 |

## S
| | |
|---|---|
| S T Studio/325 W Huron #711, Chicago, IL | 312-943-2565 |
| Sacco, Robert T/730 Franklin, Chicago, IL | 312-943-5757 |
| Sacks, Andrew/RR2, Chelsea, MI | 313-475-2310 |
| Sadin/Karant Photography, Inc/215 W Ohio St, Chicago, IL | 312-527-1696 |
| **SANDERSON, GLENN/2936 GROSS ST, GREEN BAY, WI (P 307)** | **414-336-6500** |
| Sandoz Studios/415 W Huron, Chicago, IL | 312-440-0004 |
| Schewe, Jeff/624 West Willow, Chicago, IL | 312-951-6334 |
| Schnaible, Gerry/1888 Jamestown Cle, Hoffman Estates, IL | 312-490-1191 |
| Schoenbach, Glenn/679 E Mandoline, Madison Hts., MI | 313-546-1927 |
| Schrempp, Erich/120 W Kinzie, Chicago, IL | 312-321-0768 |
| **SCHRIDDE, CHARLES/600 AJAX DR, MADISON HTS., MI (P 308)** | **313-589-0111** |
| Schuemann, Bill/1591 S Belvoir Blvd, South Euclid, OH | 216-382-4409 |
| Schultz, Tim/2000 N Clifton, Chicago, IL | 312-871-4488 |
| Schwartz, Linda/72 E Oak, #3E, Chicago, IL | 312-266-7868 |
| Scott, Bob/25 E Cedar, Chicago, IL | 312-337-4240 |
| **SCOTT, DENIS/216 W OHIO ST, CHICAGO, IL (P 282)** | **312-467-5663** |
| Secreto, Jim/2626 Industrial Row, Troy, MI | 313-280-0640 |
| Seed, Brian/7432 Lamon Ave, Skokie, IL | 312-787-7880 |
| Seed, Suzanne/175 E Delaware, Chicago, IL | 312-266-0621 |
| Seymour, Ronald/314 W Superior, Chicago, IL | 312-642-4030 |
| Shaffer, Mac/526 E Dunedin Rd, Columbus, OH | 614-268-2249 |
| Shambroom, Paul/529 S 7th St Ste 537, Minneapolis, MN | 612-340-9179 |
| Shapiro, Terry/314 W Superior, Chicago, IL | 312-664-0620 |
| Sharp, Joe/Owens Corning Fiberglass Tower, Toledo, OH | 419-248-8041 |
| Shay, Arthur/618 Indian Hill Rd, Deerfield, IL | 312-945-4636 |
| Shigeta-Wright Assoc/1546 N Orleans St, Chicago, IL | 312-642-8715 |
| Shoots, Jim Weiner/230 E Ohio, #402, Chicago, IL | 312-337-0220 |
| Shotwell, Chuck/2111 N Clifton, Chicago, IL | 312-929-0168 |
| Shoulders, Terry/676 N LaSalle, Chicago, IL | 312-644-0616 |
| Shulte, Lisa/7711 Carondelet, St Louis, MO | 314-726-6020 |

# PHOTOGRAPHERS CONT'D.

Please send us your additions and updates.

| | |
|---|---|
| Siede, George/2102 N Sheffield, Chicago, IL | 312-472-6708 |
| Sieracki, John/676 N LaSalle, Chicago, IL | 312-664-7824 |
| Silker, Glenn/5249-A W 73rd St, Edina, MN | 612-835-1811 |
| Sills, Casey/411 N Lasalle, Chicago, IL | 312-670-3660 |
| Simmons Photography, Inc/326 W Chicago Ave, Chicago, IL | 312-944-0326 |
| Skalak, Carl/47-46 Grayton Rd, Cleveland, OH | 216-676-6508 |
| Skrebneski, Victor/1350 N LaSalle St, Chicago, IL | 312-944-1339 |
| Skritski, Steve/2117 Gratiot, Detroit, MI | 313-962-0877 |
| Sladcik, William/215 W Illinois, Chicago, IL | 312-644-7108 |
| Smetzer, Donald/2534 N Burling St, Chicago, IL | 312-327-1716 |
| **SMITH, R. HAMILTON/584 ROSE AVE E, ST PAUL, MN (P 309)** | **612-778-1408** |
| Snook, J J/118 W Ohio, Chicago, IL | 312-664-0371 |
| Snyder, John/368 W Huron, Chicago, IL | 312-440-1053 |
| Solis Studio/4161 S Archer, Chicago, IL | 312-890-0555 |
| Soluri, Tony/1147 W Ohio, Chicago, IL | 312-243-6580 |
| Soren Larsen, Kim/228 W Kinzie 5th Fl, Chicago, IL | 312-329-0377 |
| Spadaro, Boller Coates/742 N Wells St, Chicago, IL | 312-787-2783 |
| Spingola, Laurel/6225 N Forest Glen, Chicago, IL | 312-685-8593 |
| Stansfield, Stan/215 W Ohio, Chicago, IL | 312-337-3245 |
| Stein, Frederic/229 W Illinois, Chicago, IL | 312-222-1133 |
| Stenberg, Pete Photography/225 W Hubbard, Chicago, IL | 312-644-6137 |
| Sterling, Joseph/2216 N Cleveland Ave, Chicago, IL | 312-348-4333 |
| Stoz Images/333 E Ontario #601B, Chicago, IL | 312-664-8400 |
| Stratford Studios Inc/2857 E Grand Blvd, Detroit, MI | 313-875-6617 |
| Straus, Jerry/247 E Ontario, Chicago, IL | 312-787-2628 |
| Struse, Perry L, Jr/232 Sixth St, Des Moines, IA | 515-279-9761 |
| The Studio/3926 N Fir Rd, Bay 12, Mishawaka, IN | 219-259-1414 |
| Studio 400/400 N Michigan, Chicago, IL | 312-467-5460 |
| Studios Assoc/2204 Prudential Plaza, Chicago, IL | 312-372-4013 |
| Summers Studio/153 W Ohio, Chicago, IL | 312-527-0908 |

## T
| | |
|---|---|
| TPS Studio/4016 S California, Chicago, IL | 312-847-1221 |
| Taber, Gary/229 W Illinois, Chicago, IL | 312-329-1038 |
| Taxel, Barney & Co/4614 Prospect Ave, Cleveland, OH | 216-431-2400 |
| Thien, Alex/2754 N Prospect Ave, Milwaukee, WI | 414-964-2711 |
| Thomas, Bill/Rt 4, Box 387, Nashville, IN | 812-988-7865 |
| Thomas, Jim Photography/2958 N Lotus, Chicago, IL | 312-777-7775 |
| Thomas, Tony/676 N Lasalle St, Chicago, IL | 312-337-2274 |
| Thompson, McClelan/206 South First St, Champaign, IL | 217-356-2767 |
| Thumbtac Studio/213 E 7th, Wellington, KS | 316-326-8631 |
| Tomlinson, Michael D/8110 Paragon Rd, Centerville, OH | 513-433-9865 |
| **TUCKER, BILL/114 W ILLINOIS, CHICAGO, IL (P 286)** | **312-321-1570** |
| Tucker, Paul/2518 Marigold Dr, Dayton, OH | 513-435-9866 |
| Tunison, Richard/5511 E Lake Dr, Lisle, IL | 312-944-1188 |

## U V
| | |
|---|---|
| Umland, Steve/6156 Olson Hwy, Golden Valley, MN | 612-546-6768 |
| Upitis, Alvis/620 Morgan Ave S, Minneapolis, MN | 612-374-9375 |
| Urba, Alexis/148 W Illinois, Chicago, IL | 312-644-4466 |
| Valterman, Lee/910 N Lake Shore Dr, Chicago, IL | 312-642-9040 |
| Van Marter, Robert/1209 Alstoff Dr S, Howell, MI | 517-546-1923 |
| Vander Veen, David/5151 N 35th ST, Milwaukee, WI | 414-527-0450 |
| VanderLende, Craig/214 Fulton East, Grand Rapids, MI | 616-459-2880 |
| Variakojis, Danguole/5743 S Campbell, Chicago, IL | 312-776-4668 |
| Vaughan, Jim/321 S Jefferson, Chicago, IL | 312-663-0369 |
| Vedros, Nick/215 W 19th St, Kansas City, MO | 816-471-5488 |
| Villa, Armando/544 N Wells, Chicago, IL | 312-828-0096 |
| Visual Data Systems Inc./5617 W 63rd Pl, Chicago, IL | 312-585-3060 |
| Vizanko Advertising Photo/11511 K Tel Dr., Minnetonka, MN | 612-933-1314 |
| Vogue-Wright/3201 Randolf, Bellwood, IL | 312-547-1300 |
| Vollan, Michael/222 W Huron, Chicago, IL | 312-644-1792 |
| Von Photography/715 N Franklin, Chicago, IL | 312-787-9408 |
| Voyles, Dick & Assoc/2822 Breckenridge Ind Ctr, St. Louis, MO | 314-968-3851 |

## W
| | |
|---|---|
| Wahlberg, Salomon & Friends/9 W Hubbard, Chicago, IL | 312-467-1048 |
| Waite, Tim/717 S Sixth St, Milwaukee, WI | 414-643-1500 |
| Walker, Jessie Assoc/241 Fairview, Glencoe, IL | 312-835-0522 |
| Wans, Glen/325 W 40th, Kansas City, MO | 816-931-8905 |
| **WARKENTHIEN, DAN/900 N FRANKLIN #3N, CHICAGO, IL (P 296)** | **312-951-5225** |
| Warren, Lennie/40 W Superior, Chicago, IL | 312-664-5392 |
| Weiner, Jim Shoots/230 E Ohio, # 402, Chicago, IL | 312-337-0220 |
| Weinstein, John/3119 N Seminary Ave, Chicago, IL | 312-327-8184 |
| **WELZENBACH, JOHN/368 W HURON ST, CHICAGO, IL (P 287)** | **312-787-6826** |
| Wenkus/Nugent/1100 Northwest Hwy, Des Plaines, IL | 312-694-4151 |
| West, Stu/430-1st Ave, #210, Minneapolis, MN | 612-871-0333 |
| **WESTERMAN, CHARLIE/405 N WABASH, CHICAGO, IL (P 310,311)** | **312-565-2589** |
| Whitehead, Jack/2117 Gratiot, Detroit, MI | 313-962-0877 |
| Wilder, Dave/2300 Payne Ave, Cleveland, OH | 216-771-7687 |
| Willett, Mike/221 W Walton, Chicago, IL | 312-527-2360 |
| Willette, Brady T/2720 W 43rd St, Minneapolis, MN | 612-926-4261 |
| Williams, Alfred G/5230 S Blackstone Ave #306, Chicago, IL | 312-947-0991 |
| Wilson/Lund/1533 Seventh Ave, Moline, IL | 309-762-7366 |
| Witkin, Louise Photography/11 E Hubbard, Chicago, IL | 312-661-1099 |
| Witte, Scott J/2534 N Prospect Ave, Milwaukee, WI | 414-963-0232 |
| Wittner, Dale/PO Box 11086, Chicago, IL | 312-787-6445 |
| Woehrle, Mark/83-22 Olive Blvd, St Louis, MO | |
| Wolf, Bobbe/440 W Oakdale, Chicago, IL | 212-472-9503 |
| Wolf, Don/300 W 19th Terrace, Kansas City, MO | 800-821-5623 |
| Wolfe, Crowther/2210 Superior Viaduct West, Cleveland, OH | 216-566-8066 |
| Woodcock, Richard/1735 Chase Dr, Fenton, MO | 314-343-5805 |
| Woodward, Greg/401 W Superior, Chicago, IL | 312-337-5838 |

## Y Z
| | |
|---|---|
| Yapp, Charles/510 N Dearborn 12th Fl, Chicago, IL | 312-644-1882 |
| Yuichi, Idaka/4100 W Irving Park Rd, Chicago, IL | 312-282-7155 |
| Zamiar, Thomas/210 W Chicago, Chicago, IL | 312-787-4976 |
| **ZANN, ARNOLD/502 N GROVE AVE, OAK PARK, IL (P 297)** | **312-386-2864** |
| Zehrt, Jack/4211 Flora Pl, St Louis, MO | 314-458-3600 |
| Zukas, R/311 N Desplaines #500, Chicago, IL | 312-648-0100 |

# SOUTHWEST

## A B
| | |
|---|---|
| Aker, Joe/710 Main, Gulf Bldg Lobby, Houston, TX | 713-228-8348 |
| Alford, Jess/1800 Lear St #3, Dallas, TX | 214-421-3107 |
| Ashe, Gil/Box 686, Bellaire, TX | 713-668-8766 |
| Ashley, Constance/2024 Farrington, Dallas, TX | 214-747-2501 |
| Assid, Al/122 Parkhouse, Dallas, TX | 214-748-3765 |
| **BAGSHAW, CRADOC/603 HIGH ST NE, ALBUQUERQUE, NM (P 317)** | **505-243-1096** |
| **BAKER, KIPP/3000 CULLEN-A, FORT WORTH, TX (P 318)** | **817-654-3210** |
| Baldwin/Watriss Assoc/1405 Branard St, Houston, TX | 713-524-9199 |
| Baraban, Joe/2426 Bartlett #2, Houston, TX | 713-526-0317 |
| Bealmear, Brad/PO Box 521, Santa Fe, NM | 505-471-2518 |
| Beebower Brothers/9995 Monroe, #209, Dallas, TX | 214-358-1219 |
| Bell, David/406 West 2nd, Roswell, NM | 505-624-0445 |
| Bennett, Sue/PO Box 1574, Flagstaff, AZ | 602-282-3899 |
| Black, Randy/12215 Coit Rd #258, Dallas, TX | 214-239-8119 |
| Booth, Greg/1322 Round Table, Dallas, TX | 214-688-1855 |
| Bouche, Len/PO Box 5188, Sante Fe, NM | 505-471-2044 |
| Braden, Bruce E/4235 Rawlins #2, Dallas, TX | 214-528-8249 |
| Bradshaw, Regan/PO Box 12457, Austin, TX | 512-458-6101 |
| Brady, Steve Photography/2426 Bartlett #2, Houston, TX | 713-524-0527 |
| Branner, Phil/2700 Commerce St, Dallas, TX | 214-698-1881 |
| Brousseau, Jay/2408 Farrington, Dallas, TX | 214-638-1248 |
| Buffington, David/2772 El Tivoli, Dallas, TX | 214-943-4721 |
| Bullard, Tony/702 Jackson Hill, Houston, TX | 713-223-8184 |
| Burwell, William Inc/1177 W Loop S #1450, Houston, TX | 713-957-4889 |

## C
| | |
|---|---|
| Cabluck, Jerry/Box 9601, Fort Worth, TX | 817-336-1431 |
| Caldwell, Jim/2422 Quenby, Houston, TX | 713-527-9121 |
| Campbell, Tom/1815 Indian School Rd, Phoenix, AZ | 602-264-1151 |
| Carr, Fred/8303 Westglen Dr, Houston, TX | 713-266-2872 |
| Carter Studios Inc/3603 Parry Ave, Dallas, TX | 214-823-9000 |
| Chenn, Steven/9511 Windswept, Houston, TX | 713-974-2879 |
| Chisholm, Rich & Assoc/3233 Marquart, Houston, TX | 713-623-8790 |
| Clemens, Frank H/9707 Richmond #65, Houston, TX | 713-784-3188 |
| **CLINTSMAN, DICK/2201 N LAMAR, DALLAS, TX (P 319)** | **214-651-1081** |
| Connolly, Danny F/PO Box 1290, Houston, TX | 713-862-8146 |
| Cotter, Austin/1350 Manufacturing #211, Dallas, TX | 214-742-3633 |
| Cove Lake Photography/Rt 1 Box 312, Paris, AR | 501-963-6429 |
| Craig, George/2405 Sage Rd, Houston, TX | 713-871-9329 |

# PHOTOGRAPHERS CONT'D.

Please send us your additions and updates.

| | |
|---|---|
| Crane, Christopher/1821 W Alabama, Houston, TX | 713-520-1993 |

## D
| | |
|---|---|
| Dark, Daphne/2712 Meadowstone, Carrolton, TX | 214-242-0140 |
| Davis, Dave/5715 N 13th St, Phoenix, AZ | 602-266-9851 |
| Dayton, Ted/2406 Converse St, Dallas, TX | 214-631-5514 |
| Derrevere, Mark/2421 Westcreek Lane #76H, Houston, TX | 713-629-9918 |
| **DIGITAL TRANSPARENCIES INC/616 HAWTHORNE, HOUSTON, TX (P 320)** | **713-524-2211** |
| Doering, Douglas/2823 W Davis St, Dallas, TX | 214-330-0304 |
| **DURAN, MARK/66 EAST VERNON, PHOENIX, AZ (P 314)** | **602-279-1141** |

## E F
| | |
|---|---|
| Edens, Swain/104 Heiman, San Antonio, TX | 512-226-2210 |
| **FAUSTINO/PO BOX 771234, HOUSTON, TX (P 321)** | **713-496-6543** |
| Fluitt, Michael/7315 Ashcroft, Houston, TX | 713-774-5800 |
| Fodera, Tony/1302 Redwood La, Dallas, TX | 214-421-2540 |
| Francisco & Booth Inc./5610 Maple Ave, Dallas, TX | 214-688-1855 |
| Freeman, Charlie/333 Elm, #A, Dallas, TX | 214-742-1446 |
| Fuelner, Cliff/4848 N Woodmere Fairway #1, Scottsdale, AZ | 602-946-6069 |
| Fuller, Timothy/135 1/2 S Sixth Ave, Tucson, AZ | 602-622-3900 |

## G
| | |
|---|---|
| Galloway, Jim/2201 N Lamar, Dallas, TX | 214-651-1081 |
| **GAYLE, RICK/3464 W EARLL STE D, PHOENIX, AZ (P 322)** | **602-269-7707** |
| **GERCZYNSKI, TOM/2211 N 7TH AVE, PHOENIX, AZ (P 323)** | **602-252-9229** |
| **GLENTZER, DON PHOTOGRAPHY/3814 S SHEPHERD DR, HOUSTON, TX (P 324)** | **713-529-9686** |
| Goldman, Richard/5310 Beverly Hill Lane #14, Houston, TX | 713-961-9243 |
| Gomel, Bob/5755 Bonhomme Rd #408, Houston, TX | 713-977-6390 |
| Grass, John/1345 Chemical St, Dallas, TX | 214-634-1455 |
| The Great Shooting Gallery Inc/1000 Munger, Dallas, TX | 214-742-1668 |
| Green Jeremy/2700 Commerce St, Dallas, TX | 214-698-1881 |
| Grossman, John/1752-B Branard St, Houston, TX | 713-523-2316 |

## H
| | |
|---|---|
| Hale, Butch/2041 Farrington, Dallas, TX | 214-741-3987 |
| Halpern, David/4153 S 87 E Ave, Tulsa, OK | 918-252-4973 |
| Hamburger, Jay/1817 State St, Houston, TX | 713-869-0869 |
| **HAMILTON, JEFFREY MUIR/6719 QUARTZITE CANYON PL, TUCSON, AZ (P 325)** | **602-299-3624** |
| Handel, Doug/3016 Selma, Dallas, TX | 214-241-1549 |
| Harris, Ron/PO Box 56446, Houston, TX | 713-680-1888 |
| Hart, Michael/7320 Ashcroft #105, Houston, TX | 713-271-8250 |
| Hartman, Gary/911 S St Mary's St, San Antonio, TX | 512-225-2404 |
| Hatcok, Tom/PO Box 588, Deer Park, TX | 713-479-2603 |
| Haynes, Mike/2700 Commerce St, Dallas, TX | 214-698-1881 |
| Haynsworth, John/86 1/2 Highland Park Villag, Dallas, TX | 214-559-3700 |
| Hazen, Ryne/325 E 2550 North #82, Ogden, UT | 801-782-3943 |
| Heinsohn, Bill/5455 Dashwood #300, Houston, TX | 713-666-6515 |
| Hendrickson, Michael/9317 County View Rd, Dallas, TX | 214-298-9236 |
| Henry, Steve/7403 Pierreport, Houston, TX | 713-937-4514 |
| Hight, George C/1404 Linda Dr Box 327, Gallup, NM | 505-863-3222 |
| Hollenbeck, Phil/PO Box 224034, Dallas, TX | 214-631-6845 |
| Housel, James F/1308 Welch St, Houston, TX | 713-523-2624 |
| Hulsey, Jim/803 Northbrook Ave, Edmond, OK | 405-348-1156 |
| Hulsey, Jim Photography/500 E Britton Rd, Oklahoma City, OK | 405-478-1212 |
| Hunt, John Photography/7575 Cambridge #1001, Houston, TX | 713-797-0133 |
| Hurd, Paul/2812 Lakeside, Carrollton, TX | 214-245-6058 |

## I J
| | |
|---|---|
| Ives, Tom/2250 El Moraga, Tucson, AZ | 602-743-0750 |
| Jackson, Duane/3403 41st St, Lubbock, TX | 806-796-0354 |
| Jew, Kim/4013 Central NE, Albuquerque, NM | 505-255-6424 |
| Jones, C. Bryan/PO Box 66691, Houston, TX | 713-524-5594 |
| Jones, Harrison/847 N 1st Ave, Phoenix, AZ | 602-254-0847 |
| **JONES, JERRY/6207 EDLOE, HOUSTON, TX (P 326)** | **713-668-4328** |

## K L
| | |
|---|---|
| **KALUZNY, ZIGY/4700 STRASS DR, AUSTIN, TX (P 315)** | **512-452-4463** |
| Kenny, Gill/3515 N Camino De Vista, Tucson, AZ | 602-743-0963 |
| King Douglas Studios/1319 Conant St, Dallas, TX | 214-630-4700 |
| King, Sandy/2014 Waugh Dr, Houston, TX | 713-524-6432 |
| Kirkley Photography/1345 Conant St, Dallas, TX | 214-630-0051 |
| Klumpp, Don Productions/804 Colguitt, Houston, TX | 713-521-2090 |
| Knudson, Kent/PO Box 26481, Phoenix, AZ | 602-251-0481 |
| Kretchmar, Phil Photography/3333 Elm, Dallas, TX | 214-744-2039 |
| Laccoy, Gary/2700 Commerce St, Dallas, TX | 214-698-1881 |
| Lallo/6737 S Peoria #216A, Tulsa, OK | 918-492-2888 |
| Latorre, Robert/101 Howell St, Dallas, TX | 214-651-7516 |
| Lindstrom, Eric/2408 Farrington, Dallas, TX | 214-638-1247 |
| Luker, Tom/Route 2, Box 127-16A, Coweta, OK | 918-486-5264 |

## M
| | |
|---|---|
| Manske, Thaine/7313 Ashcroft, #216, Houston, TX | 713-771-2220 |
| Manstein, Ralph/5353 Institute La, Houston, TX | 713-523-2500 |
| Markow, Paul & Assoc/2222 E McDowell Rd, Phoenix, AZ | 602-273-7985 |
| **MARSHALL, JIM/PO BOX 2421, CAREFREE, AZ (P 327)** | **602-488-3373** |
| McKee, Crane/9113 Sovereign Rd, Dallas, TX | 214-638-1498 |
| McLaughlin, Herb and Dorothy/2344 W Holly St, Phoenix, AZ | 602-258-6551 |
| McMichael, Garry D/RT 1 Box 312, Paris, AR | 501-963-6429 |
| Meyerson, Arthur/4215 Bellaire Blvd, Houston, TX | 713-660-0405 |
| **MEYLER, DENNIS/1903 PORTSMOUTH #25, HOUSTON, TX (P 328)** | **713-523-2731** |
| Mills, Jack R./PO Box 32583, Oklahoma City, OK | 405-787-7271 |
| Moore, Terrence/PO Box 41536, Tucson, AZ | 602-623-9381 |
| Morris, Mike/Air Cargo Bay K, Lovefield Ter, Dallas, TX | 214-352-2892 |
| Murphy, Dennis/101 Howell St, Dallas, TX | 214-651-7516 |

## N P
| | |
|---|---|
| Nance, David/8202 Fenbrook La, Houston, TX | 713-469-4757 |
| Noble, Davis/324 W Third St, Tyler, TX | 214-592-3736 |
| Pantin, Tomas/PO Box 1146, Austin, TX | 512-474-9968 |
| Parsons, Bill/722 Boyle Bldg, Little Rock, AR | 501-372-5892 |
| Patrick, Richard/401 Lavaca, Austin, TX | 512-472-9092 |
| Payne, Al/830 N 4th Ave, Phoenix, AZ | 602-258-3506 |
| **PETERSON, BRUCE/1222 E EDGEMONT, PHOENIX, AZ (P 316)** | **602-265-6505** |
| Photocom Inc/155 Pittsburg, Dallas, TX | 214-747-7766 |
| The Photographers/2121 Regency Dr, Irving, TX | 214-438-4114 |
| The Photographers Inc/2121 Regency Dr, Irving, TX | 214-438-4114 |
| **PHOTOGRAPHIX OF DALLAS/2201 N LAMAR ST, DALLAS, TX (P 318)** | **214-651-1081** |
| Prosen, Phil/2200 N Griffin St, Dallas, TX | 214-651-9408 |

## Q R
| | |
|---|---|
| The Quest Group/3007 Paseo, Oklahoma City, OK | 405-525-6591 |
| Raphaele, Inc/616 Hawthorne, Houston, TX | 713-524-2211 |
| Reisch, Jim/Studio 2025 Levee St, Dallas, TX | 214-748-0456 |
| Rich, Wilburn/3233 Marquart, Houston, TX | 713-626-7199 |
| Running, John/PO Box 1237, Flagstaff, AZ | 602-774-2923 |
| **RUSING, RICK/22 E 15TH ST, TEMPE, AZ (P 40,41)** | **602-967-1864** |
| Russell, Gail/Box 241, Taos, NM | 505-776-8474 |
| Russell, Nicholas/2014 Waugh Dr, Houston, TX | 713-524-6432 |
| Ryan, Tom/1821 Levee, Dallas, TX | 214-651-7085 |
| Ryuzo/1222 Manufacturing St, Dallas, TX | 214-741-9190 |

## S
| | |
|---|---|
| Salas, Michael/1109 Whitehall Dr, Plano, TX | 214-423-4396 |
| Savant, Joseph/2312 Grand Ave, Dallas, TX | 214-428-7223 |
| Schlesinger, Terrence/PO Box 32877, Phoenix, AZ | 602-957-7474 |
| Schrengohst, Mike/5930 Arapaho, #2131, Dallas, TX | 214-386-0227 |
| Schuster, Ellen/3719 Gilbert, Dallas, TX | 214-526-6712 |
| Scott, Ron/1000 Jackson Blvd, Houston, TX | 713-529-5868 |
| Scruggs, Jim/2410 Taft, Houston, TX | 713-523-1217 |
| Segrest, Jerry Photography/1319 Conant, Dallas, TX | 214-630-7766 |
| Shaw, Robert/1723 Kelly Ave, Dallas, TX | 214-428-1757 |
| Siegel, David Martin/224 N 5th Ave, Phoenix, AZ | 602-257-9509 |
| Sieve, Jerry/PO Box 1777, Cave Creek, AZ | 602-488-9561 |
| Smothers, Brian/843 W 43rd St, Houston, TX | 713-695-0873 |
| Smusz, Ben/7313 Ashcroft Ste 216, Houston, TX | 713-772-5026 |
| Sorlie, Michael/PO Box 12604, Dallas, TX | 214-669-0984 |
| **SOUTHERN LIGHTS STUDIO/3000 CULLEN-A, FORT WORTH, TX (P 317)** | **817-654-3210** |
| St Gil & Associates/2230 Ashford Hollow Ln, Houston, TX | 713-870-9458 |
| Stewart, Ed/5950 Westward Ave, , TX | 713-988-0775 |
| Stibbens, Steve/Photoworks/104 Cole St, Dallas, TX | 214-651-8224 |
| Stroud, Dan/1350 Manufacturing, #211, Dallas, TX | 214-745-1933 |
| Sumner, Bill/122 Parkhouse, Dallas, TX | 214-748-3766 |
| Swenson, John/102 W San Francisco 16, Santa Fe, NM | 505-988-9520 |

## T
| | |
|---|---|
| Thompson, Michael/1921 1/2 Greenville Ave, Dallas, TX | 214-823-6677 |
| Tomlinson, Doug/5651 East Side Ave, Dallas, TX | 214-821-1192 |
| True, Redd/1000 Munger, Dallas, TX | 214-638-0602 |

# PHOTOGRAPHERS CONT'D.

Please send us your additions and updates.

| | |
|---|---|
| Turner, Rick/1117 Welch, Houston, TX | 713-524-2576 |
| Turtle Creek Studio/1405 B Turtle Creek Blvd, Dallas, TX | 214-742-1045 |

## UVW

| | |
|---|---|
| Untersee, Chuck/2747 Seelcco, Dallas, TX | 214-358-2306 |
| Viewpoint Photographers/217 McKinley, Phoenix, AZ | 602-245-0013 |
| Von Helms, Michael/4212 San Felipe, Houston, TX | 713-666-1212 |
| Walker, Balfour/150 Avenida De Palmas, Tucson, AZ | 602-881-3373 |
| Wanbaugh Photo Studio/847 N First Ave, Phoenix, AZ | 602-252-8313 |
| Watkins, JC/2329 Thomas Blvd, Port Arthur, TX | 713-982-3666 |
| Wells, Craig/537 W Granada, Phoenix, AZ | 602-252-8166 |
| Wheeler, Don/4928 E 26th Pl, Tulsa, OK | 918-744-8902 |
| Williams, Oscar/8535 Fairhaven, San Antonio, TX | 512-690-8888 |
| Wilson, Jennifer/8303 Westglen Dr, Houston, TX | 713-266-2872 |
| Wilson, Michael/3016 Selma La, Dallas, TX | 214-241-1549 |
| Witt, Lou/5531 Timber Creek Dr, Houston, TX | 713-944-1603 |
| Wolfhagen, Vilhelm/4916 Kelvin, Houston, TX | 713-522-2787 |
| Wollam, Les/5215 Goodwin Ave, Dallas, TX | 214-760-7721 |
| Wristen, Don/2025 Levee St, Dallas, TX | 214-748-5317 |

## WEST

### A

| | |
|---|---|
| Abecassis, Andree L/429 Berkeley Park Blvd, Berkeley, CA | 415-644-2988 |
| **ABRAHAM, RUSSELL/17 BROSNAN ST, SAN FRANCISCO, CA (P 344)** | **415-558-9100** |
| Ackroyd, Hugh S/Box 10101, Portland, OR | 503-227-5694 |
| Adler, Allan S/PO Box 2251, VAn Nuys, CA | 213-769-6880 |
| Adler, Gale/3740 Veteran Ave #1, Los Angeles, CA | 213-837-9224 |
| Agrimage, Phil Rudy/411 E Olive, Fresno, CA | 209-266-0305 |
| Ahlberg, Holly/1117 N Wilcox Pl, Los Angeles, CA | 213-462-0731 |
| Ahrend, Jay/5047 W Pico Blvd, Los Angeles, CA | 213-934-9596 |
| Aiuppy, Larry/Box 26, Livingston, MT | 406-222-7308 |
| Albert, Betty/519 Mount St, Richmond, CA | 415-235-2856 |
| Alex and Smith/7163 Construction Ct, San Diego, CA | 619-271-6525 |
| Alexander, David/1545 N Wilcox #202, Hollywood, CA | 213-464-8690 |
| Alexander, Michael/1717 Mason, San Francisco, CA | 415-441-6700 |
| Allan, Larry/PO Box 99585, San Diego, CA | 619-270-9549 |
| Allen, Judson Photo/654 Gilman, Palo Alto, CA | 415-324-8177 |
| Allison, Glen/PO Box 1833, Santa Monica, CA | 213-392-1388 |
| **AMBROSE, PAUL STUDIOS/1231 ALDERWOOD AVE, SUNNYVALE, CA (P 345)** | **408-734-3211** |
| Amer, Tommy/1858 Westerly Terr, Los Angeles, CA | 213-664-7624 |
| Andersen, Welden/2643 S Fairfax Ave, Culver City, CA | 213-559-0059 |
| Anderson & Carry Studio/2224 Old Middlefield Way, Mountain View, CA | 415-967-8470 |
| Anderson, Borge/231 Edison St, Salt Lake City, UT | 801-359-7703 |
| Anderson, Karen/833 N Las Palmas Ave, Los Angeles, CA | 213-461-1420 |
| Antal, Hicks & Assoc/1500 Wyatt Dr #4, Santa Clara, CA | 408-748-8595 |
| Aperture Photo Bank/1530 Westlake Ave N, Seattle, WA | 206-447-9446 |
| Appleton, Roger/3043 W Pikes Peak, Colorado Springs, CO | 303-635-0393 |
| Apton, Bill/577 Howard St, San Francisco, CA | 415-543-6313 |
| Armas, Richard/6913 Melrose Ave, Los Angeles, CA | 213-931-7889 |
| Arnold, Robert/1379 Natoma, San Francisco, CA | 415-621-6161 |
| Arnone, Ken/4071 Hawk St, San Diego, CA | 619-234-5202 |
| Arrindell, Richard/415 Molino St, Los Aneles, CA | 213-202-0670 |
| Art Zone, The/404 Piikoi St, Honolulu, HI | 808-537-6647 |
| Ashley, Chuck/237 Clara St, San Francisco, CA | 415-974-5645 |
| Ashley, Theodore/5371 Wilshire Blvd #207, Los Angeles, CA | 213-939-1666 |
| Attebery, Barton L/8406 Linden Ave, North Seattle, WA | 206-783-0321 |
| Aurness, Craig/1526 Pontius Ave, Los Angeles, CA | 213-473-3736 |
| Avery, Franklin/PO Box 8444, Santa Cruz, CA | 415 986-3701 |
| Avery, Ron/820 N La Brea, Los Angeles, CA | 213-465-7193 |
| Avery, Sid/820 N LaBrea, Los Angeles, CA | 213-465-7193 |
| Ayres, Robert Bruce/521 Calle Baranda, San Clemente, CA | 714-661-6898 |
| Ayres, Robert Bruce/5635 Melrose Ave, Los Angeles, CA | |

### B

| | |
|---|---|
| Baasch, Diane/1015 N Cahuenga Blvd, Hollywood, CA | 213-467-0266 |
| Baasch, Diane/13455 Ventura Blvd, Sherman Oaks, CA | 213-762-7680 |
| Baasch, Diane/1003 Fell St, San Francisco, CA | 415-431-7601 |
| Babincszk, Bob/451/2 Ozone St, Venice, CA | 213-392-3885 |
| Baehr, Sarah/2202 California St, San Francisco, CA | 415-346-1366 |
| Baer, Morley/PO Box 2228, Monterey, CA | 408-624-3530 |
| Bagley, John/730 Clemintina, San Francisco, CA | 415-861-1062 |
| Bailey, Brent P/759 W 19th St, Costa Mesa, CA | 619-548-9683 |
| Bair, Royce/409 West 400 South, Salt Lake City, UT | 801-328-9808 |
| Baker, Bill/265 29th St, Oakland, CA | 415-832-7685 |
| Baker, Jack/3108 Marburger Pl, Belmont, CA | 415-592-0292 |
| Baldwin, Doug/10518-2 Sunland Blvd, Sunland, CA | 213-353-7270 |
| Banko, Phil/1249 First Ave S, Seattle, WA | 206-621-7008 |
| Barkentin, Pamela/1218 N LaCienega, Los Angeles, CA | 213-654-6003 |
| Barnes, David/500 NE 70th St, #306, Seattle, WA | 206-525-1965 |
| Bartholomeu, Bart/419 Ocean Ave, Santa Monica, CA | 213-394-7449 |
| Bartone, Tom/7403 W Sunset Blvd, Los Angeles, CA | 213-469-4585 |
| Bartruff, Dave/Box 800, San Anselmo, CA | 415-457-1482 |
| Batista Moon Studio/444 Pearl B-1, Monterey, CA | 408-373-1947 |
| **BATOR, JOE/2011 WASHINGTON AVE, GOLDEN, CO (P 347)** | **303-279-4163** |
| Bauer, Erwin A/Box 543, Teton Village, WY | 307-733-4023 |
| Bauer, Karel M/141 10th St, Mill Valley, CA | 415-863-5155 |
| Bayalis, John/583 Kamolku #2703, Honolulu, HI | 808-943-0333 |
| Bear, Brent/8566 W Pico Blvd, Los Angeles, CA | 213-652-1156 |
| Bear, Royce/409 West & 400 South, Salt Lake City, UT | 801-328-9808 |
| Becker Bishop Studios/1535 Mission, San Francisco, CA | 415-552-4254 |
| **BECKER BISHOP /1830 17TH ST, SAN FRANCISCO, CA (P 332,333)** | **415-552-4254** |
| Beebe, Morton P/409 Bryant St #207, San Francisco, CA | 415-362-3530 |
| Behrman, C H/8036 Kentwood, Los Angeles, CA | 213-645-8892 |
| Belcher, Richard/3435 Army St #217, San Francisco, CA | 415-641-8912 |
| Belknap, Bill/PO Box 365, Boulder City, NV | 702-293-1406 |
| Ben Gersten, Paul/428 1/2 San Vicente Blvd S, Los Angeles, CA | 213-652-6111 |
| Bencze, Louis/1025 SE 17th Ave, Portland, OR | 503-236-3328 |
| Benson, John/1261 Howard, San Francisco, CA | 415-621-5247 |
| Bergman, Alan/8241 W 4th St, Los Angeles, CA | 213-852-1408 |
| Berman, Ellen/5425 Senford Ave, Los Angeles, CA | 213-641-2783 |
| Berman, Steve/7955 W 3rd, Los Angeles, CA | 213-933-9185 |
| Bernstein, Cal/722 N Seward St, Los Angeles, CA | 213-461-3737 |
| Bernstein, Gary/8735 Washington Blvd, Culver City, | 213-550-6891 |
| Best Image Studio/8148 Ronson Rd, San Diego, CA | 619-292-5258 |
| Betz, Ted R/531 Howard St, San Francisco, CA | 415-433-0470 |
| Bez, Frank/1880 Santa Barbara Ave, San Luis Obispo, CA | 805-541-2878 |
| Bfrenneis, Jon/311 Wells Fargo, Berkeley, CA | 415-845-3377 |
| Bielenberg, Paul/2447 Lanterman Terr, Los Angeles, CA | 213-669-1085 |
| Biggs, Ken/1147 N Hudson Ave, Los Angeles, CA | 213-462-2739 |
| Bilechy, John/2865 W 7th St, Los Angeles, CA | 213-384-0738 |
| Birnbach, Allen/3600 Tejon St, Denver, CO | 303-455-7800 |
| Bischoff & Assoc/1201 1st Ave S #1227-B, Seattle, WA | 206-292-9931 |
| Bishop, David/PO Box 2309, San Francisco, CA | 415-441-5611 |
| **BLAKELEY, JIM/1061 FOLSOM ST, SAN FRANCISCO, CA (P 334,335)** | **415-558-9300** |
| Blakeman, Bob/2032 Stoner Ave, West Los Angeles, CA | 213-479-4327 |
| Blattel, David/4132 Hood Ave, Burbank, CA | 213-937-0366 |
| Blau, Barry/1750 Westwood Blvd, Los Angeles, CA | 213-474-5705 |
| **BLAUSTEIN, JOHN/665 ALVARADO RD, BERKELEY, CA (P 348,349)** | **415-845-2525** |
| Blumensaadt, Mike/1261 Howard St, San Francisco, CA | 415-864-4172 |
| Bodnar, Joe/2817 Selby, Los Angeles, CA | 213-838-6587 |
| Boulger & Kanuit/503 S Catalina, Redondo Beach, CA | 213-540-6300 |
| Boyer, Neil/1416 Analeon Blvd, Redondo Beach, CA | 213-374-0443 |
| Braasch, Gary/PO Box 1465, Portland, OR | 206-695-3844 |
| Brabant, Patricia/2325 3rd St, #201, San Francisco, CA | 415-864-0591 |
| Bracke, Vic/560 S Main St, Los Angeles, CA | 213-623-6522 |
| Bradley, Leverett/Box 1793, Santa Monica, CA | 213-394-0908 |
| Bragstad, Jeremiah O/1041 Folsom St, San Francisco, CA | 415-776-2740 |
| Brantley, Robert/1414 S 7th West, Salt Lake City, UT | 801-972-8293 |
| Braun, Ernest/PO Box 627, San Anselmo, CA | 415-454-2791 |
| Brawer, Sid/10625 Magnolia Blvd, N Hollywood, CA | 213-278-6821 |
| Brian, Rick/555 S Alexandria Ave, Los Angeles, CA | 213-387-3017 |
| Britt, Jim/140 N LaBrea, Los Angeles, CA | 213-936-3131 |
| Brod, Garry/6502 Santa Monica Blvd, Hollywood, CA | 213-463-7887 |
| Bronson, Bob/3517 N Verdugo Rd, Glendale, CA | 213-249-5864 |
| Browne, Rick/145 Shake Tree La., Scotts Valley, CA | 408-438-3919 |
| **BROWNE, WARREN/1003 FELL ST STE A, SAN FRANCISCO, CA (P 350)** | **415-431-7601** |
| Bryan, J Y/3594 Ramona Dr, Riverside, CA | 619-684-8266 |

# PHOTOGRAPHERS CONT'D.

Please send us your additions and updates.

| | |
|---|---|
| **BUCHANAN, CRAIG/1026 FOLSOM #207,** | |
| **SAN FRANCISCO, CA (P 351)** | **415-861-5566** |
| Buckley, Robin/13455 Ventura Blvd #231, Sherman Oaks, CA | 213-906-2670 |
| Buckner, Ken/5636 Melrose Ave, Hollywood, CA | 213-464-4003 |
| Budnik, Victor Photography/839 Emerson St, Palo Alto, CA | 415-322-8036 |
| Buhrman, Peter/3279 Kifer Rd, Santa Clara, CA | 408-735-8443 |
| Burke, Kevin/1015 N Cahuenga, Hollywood, CA | 213-467-0266 |
| Burke, Leslie/947 La Cienaga, Los Angeles, CA | 213-652-7011 |
| Burkhart Photography/231 Olive #10, Inglewood, CA | 213-671-2283 |
| Burr, Bruce/2867 1/2 W 7th St, Los Angeles, CA | 213-388-3361 |
| Burr, Larry/1115 Sir Francis Drake Blvd ((, Kentfield, CA | 415-456-9158 |
| Burroughs, Robert/6713 Bardonia St, San Diego, CA | 619-469-6922 |
| Burry, D L Commercial Photography/2 N Santa Cruz Ave, Los Gatos, CA | 408-354-1922 |
| Burt, Pat/1412 SE Stark, Portland, OR | 503-284-9989 |
| Bush, Chan/PO Box 819, Montrose, CA | 213-242-7381 |
| Bush, Charles/7623 Beverly Blvd, Los Angeles, CA | 213-937-8248 |
| Busher, Dick/7042 20th Place NE, Seattle, WA | 206-523-1426 |
| Bussey, Bill/7915 Via Stefano, Burbank, CA | 213-767-5078 |
| Bybee, Gerald/925 SW Temple, Salt Lake City, UT | 801-363-1061 |

## C

| | |
|---|---|
| CAG Graphics/11602 KNOTT ST, GARDEN GROVE, CA | 714-898-0719 |
| CBS Special Effects/PO BOX 5545, MILL VALLEY, CA | 415 331-0343 |
| CBS Special Effects/60 FEDERAL ST, SAN FRANCISCO, CA | 415-543-4883 |
| CPC Assoc Inc/1910 WEEPAH WAY, LOS ANGELES, CA | 213-656-7449 |
| CPC Assoc Inc/2106 S GRAND, SANTA ANA, CA | 714-545-6466 |
| Cable, Ron/11602 Knott St, Garden Grove, Ca | 714-898-0719 |
| Caccavo, James/4317 W 2nd St, Los Angeles, CA | 213-385-6858 |
| Cacitti, Stanley R/589 Howard, San Francisco, CA | 415-974-5668 |
| Cahoon, John/613 S LaBrea Ave, Los Angeles, CA | 213-930-1144 |
| Camera Hawaii/206 Koula St, Honolulu, HI | 808-536-2302 |
| Cameras Unlimited/1258-170th Ave NE, Bellevue, WA | 206-643-1638 |
| Cameron, Robert/235 Montgomery, San Francisco, CA | 415-981-1135 |
| Cannon, Bill/516 Yale Ave, Seattle, WA | 206-682-7031 |
| Caplan, Stan/7014 Santa Monica, Los Angeles, CA | 213-462-1271 |
| Cappel, Gerry/1164 S La Brea, Los Angeles, CA | 213-466-1612 |
| Capps, Alan/137 S La Peer Dr, Los Angeles, CA | 213-276-3724 |
| Caputo, Tony/6636 Santa Monica Blvd, Hollywood, CA | 213-464-4400 |
| **CARROON, CHIP/PO BOX 5545, MILL VALLEY, CA (P 352)** | **415-331-0343** |
| Carey, Ed/60 Federal St, San Francisco, CA | 415-543-4883 |
| Carofano, Ray/1011 1/4 W 190th St, Gardena, CA | 213-515-0310 |
| Carpenter, Mert/2020 Granada Wy, Los Gatos, CA | 408-370-1663 |
| Carroll, Bruce/517 Dexter Ave N, Seattle, WA | 206-623-2119 |
| Carroll, Tom/28 Ensueno E, Irvine, CA | 714-731-7740 |
| Carroon, Chip/PO Box 5545, Mill Valley, CA | 415-331-0343 |
| Carruth, Kerry/7153 Helmsdale Circle, Canoga Park, CA | 213-704-6570 |
| Carry, Mark/2354 Walsh AVe, Santa Clara, CA | 408-727-2580 |
| **CASSIDY PHOTOGRAPHIC DESIGN/3279 KIFER RD,** | |
| **SANTA CLARA, CA (P 353)** | **408-735-8443** |
| Cassidy/Advertising Design/3279 Kifer Rd, Santa Clara, CA | 408-735-8443 |
| Cato, Eric/1314 N Hayworth, Los Angeles, CA | 213-851-5606 |
| Caulfield, Andy/PO Box 41131, Los Angeles, CA | 213-258-3070 |
| **CHANEY, BRAD/370 4TH ST,** | |
| **SAN FRANCISCO, CA (P 354,355)** | **415-543-2525** |
| Chartmasters Inc/639 Howard, San Francisco, CA | 415-421-6591 |
| Chen, James/1917 Anacapa St, Santa Barbara, CA | 805-569-1849 |
| Chernus, Ken/9531 Washington Blvd, Culver City, CA | 213-838-3116 |
| Chesley, Paul/Box 94, Aspen, CO | 303-925-1148 |
| Chesser, Mike/6628 Santa Monica Blvd, Los Angeles, CA | 213-463-4988 |
| Chester, Mark/PO Box 99501, San Francisco, CA | 415-922-7512 |
| Childers, Michael Studio/637 Westborne, #A, Los Angeles, CA | 213-937-3821 |
| Chin, K P/835 Kapaakea La 404, Honolulu, HI | 808-944-3946 |
| Chmielewfki, Mike/14120 E Temple Dr #410, Aurora, CO | 303-693-1116 |
| Chromosohm/Joe Sohm/PO Box 48184, Los Angeles, CA | 213-203-9438 |
| Chun, Mike/35 Russia - Studio A, San Francisco, CA | 415-469-7220 |
| Chung, Ken-Jei/5216 Venice Blvd, Los Angeles, CA | 213-938-9117 |
| Ciskowski, Jim/413 S La Brea, Los Angeles, CA | 213-937-0413 |
| Clark, Gordon/1687 3rd St, Livermore, CA | 415-443-4281 |
| Clark, Richard/334 S LaBrea, Los Angeles, CA | 213-933-7407 |
| Clark, William F/515 S Flower, #1663, Los Angeles, CA | 213-486-2564 |
| Classon, Norm/Box 4230, Aspen, CO | 303-925-4418 |
| Claxton, William/1368 Angelo Dr, Beverly Hills, CA | 213-276-4228 |
| Cobb, Bruce/1537-A 4th St #102, San Raphael, CA | 415-454-0619 |
| Cogan, Bill/582 Market, San Francisco, CA | 415-391-1350 |
| Coit, Jim/635 State St, San Diego, CA | 619-234-1677 |
| Coleman, Arthur Photography/505 N Palm Canyon Dr, Palm Springs, CA | 619-325-7015 |
| Collison, James/3737 Weslin Ave, Sherman Oaks, CA | 213-872-2717 |
| Coluzzi, Tony Photography/897 Independence Ave, Mountain View, CA | 415-969-2955 |
| Constantine, Lois/19108 Ingomar St, Reseda, CA | 213-993-1031 |
| **COOK, KATHLEEN NORRIS/PO BOX 2159,** | |
| **LAGUNA HILLS, CA (P 356)** | **714-770-4619** |
| Coopersmith, Peter/5936 W Linderhurst, Los Angeles, CA | 213-849-6321 |
| Coppos, Mark/1248 S Fairfax Ave, Los Angeles, CA | 213-938-2481 |
| Cormany, George/115 East Alton, Santa Ana, CA | 714-549-4101 |
| Cosman, Wayne Photographics/227 E Chapman Ave, Orange, CA | 714-538-5080 |
| Courbat, Gordon A/331 E Ojai Ave, Ojai, CA | 805-646-1616 |
| Cowin, Morgin/252 Caselli Ave, San Francisco, CA | 415-431-0203 |
| Crane, Wally/PO Box 81, Los Altos, CA | 415-960-1990 |
| Crawford, Dick/PO Box 747, Sanger, CA | 209-875-3800 |
| Crowley, Eliot/706 W Pico Blvd, Los Angeles, CA | 213-742-0367 |
| Cruickshank/505 C Street, Lewiston, ID | 208-743-9411 |
| Cruver, Dick/1016 First Ave S, Seattle, WA | 206-621-8434 |
| Cummins, Jim/1527 13th Ave, Seattle, WA | 206-322-4944 |
| Cupp, David/2520 Albion St, Denver, CO | 303-321-3581 |

## D

| | |
|---|---|
| DJM Films/512 N Sycamore Ave, Los Angeles, CA | 213-934-3602 |
| **DAHLSTROM PHOTOGRAPHY INC/2312 NW SAVIER,** | |
| **PORTLAND, OR (P 357)** | **503-222-4910** |
| Dain, Martin/16-B Ford Rd, Carmel Valley, CA | 408-625-1110 |
| Daly, Michael Kevin/Box 5002, Eugene, OR | 503-683-1496 |
| Daniels, Josephus/PO Box 7418, Carmel, CA | 408-625-3316 |
| Davey, Robert/PO Box 69291, Los Angeles, CA | 213-659-3542 |
| David/Gayle Photography/911 Western Ave, #510, Seattle, WA | 206-624-5207 |
| Davidson, Dave/25003 S Beeson Rd, Beavercreek, OR | 503-632-7650 |
| **DAVIDSON, JERRY/3923 W JEFFERSON BLVD,** | |
| **LOS ANGELES, CA (P 358,359)** | **213-735-1552** |
| Dean, Bill/Route 1, Morgan, UT | 801-876-2711 |
| DeCastro, Mike/2415 De La Cruz, Santa Clara, CA | 408-988-8696 |
| DeCruyenaere, Howard/1825 E Albion Ave, Santa Ana, CA | 714-997-4446 |
| **DEGENNARO, GEORGE/902 SOUTH NORTON AVE,** | |
| **LOS ANGELES, CA (P 360,361)** | **213-935-5179** |
| DeLancie-Mayer Photographics/1129 Folsom St, San Francisco, CA | 415-864-2220 |
| DeLespinasse, Hank/PO Box 14061, Las Vegas, NV | 702-798-6693 |
| Della Grotta, Vivienne/PO Box 927, Carpinteria, CA | 805-684-1339 |
| DeMont, Debbi/3825 E 7th St, Long Beach, CA | 213-433-1087 |
| Denman, Frank B/131 15th Ave E, Seattle, WA | 206-325-9260 |
| Dennison, Bob/6412 Hollywood Blvd, Hollywood, CA | 213-469-9924 |
| Denny, Michael/2631 Ariane Dr, San Diego, CA | 619-272-0909 |
| Der, Rick Photography/1125 Grant Ave, San Francisco, CA | 415-433-2055 |
| **DESCIOSE, NICK/2700 ARAPAHOE ST #2,** | |
| **DENVER, CO (P 362)** | **303-455-6315** |
| Devine, W L Studios/PO Box 67, Maple Falls, WA | 206-599-2927 |
| DeVore, Nicholas III/PO Box 812, Aspen, CO | 303-925-2317 |
| DeWilde, Roc/139 Noriega, San Francisco, CA | 415-681-4612 |
| Diaz, Armando/19 S Park, San Francisco, CA | 415-495-3552 |
| Dickson, Don/512 N Sycamore Ave, Los Angeles, CA | 213-934-3602 |
| Dolgins, Alan/1640 S La Cienega Blvd, Los Angeles, CA | 213-273-5794 |
| Dominick/7311 Melrose Ave, Los Angeles, CA | 213-934-3033 |
| Dondero, Donald/270 Mountain View Dr, Reno, NV | 702-825-7348 |
| Doran, Dennis/PO Box 4033 Pioneer Sq Sta, Seattle, WA | 206-621-8840 |
| Dow, Larry/1537 W 8th St, Los Angeles, CA | 213-483-7970 |
| Downs, Jerry/1315 Oak Ct, Boulder, CO | 303-444-8910 |
| Dreiwitz, Herb/145 N Edgemont St, Los Angeles, CA | 213-383-1746 |
| Drenick, David R./1215 Ashland Ave, Santa Monica, CA | 213-396-1932 |
| Driver, Wallace/2510 Clairemont Dr #113, San Diego, CA | 619-275-3159 |
| Drumbor, David C/1330 Idaho St, San Jose, CA | 408-246-2230 |
| Dudley, Hardin & Yang/3839 Stoneway Ave N, Seattle, WA | 206-632-3001 |
| Duff, Rodney/4901 Morena Blvd #323, San Diego, CA | 619-270-4082 |
| Dull, Ed/1745 NW Marshall, Portland, OR | 503-224-3754 |

# PHOTOGRAPHERS CONT'D.

Please send us your additions and updates.

| | |
|---|---|
| Dumentz, Barbara/452 S LaBrea Ave, Los Angeles, Ca | 213-938-7189 |
| **DUNBAR, CLARK/922 SAN LEANDRO AVE #C, MOUNTAIN VIEW, CA (P 342)** | **415-964-4225** |
| Dunmire, Larry/PO Box 338, Balboa Island, CA | 714-673-4058 |

### E
| | |
|---|---|
| Eastabrook, William R/3281 Oakshire Dr, Los Angeles, CA | 213-851-3281 |
| Edwards, Grant P./3083 Trinity Dr, Costa Mesa, CA | 714-966-1160 |
| Edwin Hopper/Photography, Los Altos, CA | 415-941-9000 |
| Elder, Jim/PO Box 1600, Jackson Hole, WY | 307-733-3555 |
| Elias, Robert Studio/8301 W Third St, Los Angeles, CA | 213-655-3527 |
| Elich, George/PO Box 255016, Sacramento, CA | 916-481-5021 |
| Elk, John III/583 Weldon, Oakland, CA | 415-834-3024 |
| Emanuel, Manny/2257 Hollyridge Dr, Hollywood, CA | 213-465-0259 |
| Emberly, Gordon/1479 Folsom, San Francisco, CA | 415-621-9714 |
| England, Jim/602 Parkman Ave, Los Angeles, CA | 213-413-2575 |
| Enkelis, Liane/764 Sutter Ave, Palo Alto, CA | 415-326-3253 |
| Epstein, Mike/P O Box 6753, Bend, OR | 503-382-7370 |
| Errico, Sam/3435 Army St #327, San Francisco, CA | 415-641-1999 |
| Estel, Suzanne/2325 3rd St, San Francisco, CA | 415-543-1494 |
| Evans, Marty/6644 Santa Monica Blvd, Los Angeles, CA | 213-466-7279 |

### F
| | |
|---|---|
| FDC Planning & Design Corp/14 PEARL ST, DENVER, CO | 303-744-0711 |
| **FADER, BOB/14 PEARL ST, DENVER, CO (P 363)** | **303-744-0711** |
| Falk, Randolph Photo/123 16th Ave, San Francisco, CA | 415-751-8800 |
| Feldman, Marc/6442 Santa Monica Blvd, Hollywood, CA | 213-463-4829 |
| Felker, Richard/504 Central, Alameda, CA | 415-521-4458 |
| Felt, Jim/1316 SE 12th Ave, Portland, OR | 503-238-1748 |
| Felzman, Joe/421 NW Fourth Ave, Portland, OR | 503-224-7983 |
| Fenton, Reed/922 N Formosa, Los Angeles, CA | 213-651-4646 |
| **FERRO, DANIEL J/8022 EL PASEO GRANDE, LA JOLLA, CA (P 364)** | **619-456-2213** |
| Finn, Dennis/PO Box 5638, Santa Monica, CA | 213-463-9700 |
| Finnegan, Kristin/P O Box 8404, Portland, OR | 503-241-2701 |
| Firebaugh, Steve/3107 S Dearborn, Seattle, WA | 206-325-4044 |
| Fischer, Curt/51 Stillman, San Francisco, CA | 415-974-5568 |
| Fischer, David/340 Harriet, San Francisco, CA | 415-495-4585 |
| Fish, Richard/16642 Oldham St, Encino, CA | 213-986-5190 |
| Fisher, Arthur Vining/271 Missouri St, San Francisco, CA | 415-626-5483 |
| Flavin, Frank/PO Box 8-9172, Anchorage, AK | 907-561-1606 |
| Flood, Alan/206 14th Ave, San Mateo, CA | 415-572-0439 |
| Fogg, Don/1641 El Camino Real, Palo Alto, CA | 415-321-3113 |
| Foothorap, Robert/426 Bryant St, San Francisco, CA | 415-957-1447 |
| Ford Photography/906 1/2 S Robertson Blvd, Los Angeles, CA | 213-655-7655 |
| Forsman, John/5437 W Sixth St, Los Angeles, CA | 213-933-9339 |
| Forster, Bruce/431 NW Flanders, Portland, OR | 503-222-5222 |
| Fortson, Ed/Shoshana/434 S Plymouth Bl, Los Angeles, CA | 213-934-6368 |
| Fouler, Brad/9053 3/4 Lanewood Ave, Hollywood, CA | 213-464-2242 |
| Fowler, Bradford/7053 3/4 Lanewood Ave, Los Angeles, CA | 213-464-5708 |
| Fox, Paul/71256 Cypress La, Rancho Mirage, CA | 619-328-4587 |
| Frank, Jim/508 N San Vincente, Los Angeles, CA | 213-657-5551 |
| Freed, Jack/749 N La Brea, Los Angeles, CA | 213-931-1015 |
| Freeman, Hunter/852 Santa Fe Dr, Denver, CO | 303-893-5730 |
| Freis, Jay/416 Richardson St, Sausalito, CA | 415-332-6709 |
| Freppel, Denis/2865 W 7th St, Los Angeles, CA | 213-387-9028 |
| Friedlander, Ernie/82 Ringold Alley, San Francisco, CA | 415-626-6111 |
| Friedman, Todd/PO Box 3737, Beverly Hills, CA | 213-390-3401 |
| Friend, Dave/2631 Ariane Dr, San Diego, CA | 619-272-9090 |
| Fries, Janet/2017 Tiffin Rd, Oakland, CA | 415-482-5158 |
| Frisella, Josef/7065 Lexington Ave, Hollywood, CA | 213-462-2593 |
| Fritz, Steve/1023 S Santa Fe Ave, Los Angeles, CA | 213-629-8052 |
| Fronk, Peter/203 Indian Way, Novato, CA | 415-883-5253 |
| Fruchtman, Jerry/8735 Washington Blvd, Culver City, CA | 213-839-7891 |
| Fry III, George B/PO Box 2465, Menlo Park, CA | 415-323-7663 |
| Fugate, Randy/7811 Alabama #14, Canoga Park, CA | 213-883-7870 |
| Fujioka, Robert/1915 University Ave, Palo Alto, CA | 415-323-1336 |
| Fukuda, Curtis/897 Independence Ave #3C, Mountain View, CA | 415-962-9131 |
| Fukuda, Steve/2215 Filbert St, San Francisco, CA | 415-567-1325 |
| Fukuhara, Richard Yutaka/3267 Grant St, Signal Hill, CA | 213-597-4497 |
| Fulton, Greg/2800 So Main, Ste 1, Santa Ana, CA | 714-646-8604 |
| Furuta, Carl/7360 Melrose, Los Angeles, CA | 213-655-1911 |
| Fusco, Paul/7 Melody Ln, Mill Valley, CA | 415-388-8940 |

### G
| | |
|---|---|
| GKD/5739 3/4 Tujunga Ave, N Hollywood, CA | 213-762-3659 |
| GSP/11102 Blix St, N Hollywood, CA | 213-760-1236 |
| Gage, Rob/789 Pearl St, Laguna Beach, CA | 714-494-7265 |
| **GARDNER, ROBERT/800 S CITRUS AVE, LOS ANGELES, CA (P 365)** | **213-931-1108** |
| Garretson, James/135 Redwood Ave, Corte Madera, CA | 415-668-3235 |
| Garrison, Ron/San Diego Zoo Box 551, San Diego, CA | 619-231-1515 |
| Gary Wincott Photography/1087 Robbia Dr, Sunnyvale, CA | 408-245-9559 |
| Gascon, Enrique Jr/143 S. Edgemont, Los Angeles, CA | 213-383-9157 |
| Geissler, Rick/1729 Vista Del Valle, El Cajon, CA | 619-440-5594 |
| Gelineau, Val/1041 N McCadden Pl, Los Angeles, CA | 213-465-6149 |
| George, Martin/5739 3/4 Tujunga Ave, N Hollywood, CA | 213-762-3659 |
| Gerba, Peter/50 Ringold St, San Francisco, CA | 415-864-5474 |
| Gerretsen, Charles/8983 Hollywood Hills Rd, Los Angeles, CA | 213-656-7407 |
| Gersten, Paul/1021 1/2 N La Brea, Los Angeles, CA | 213-652-6111 |
| Gibson, Mark/PO Box 14542, San Francisco, CA | 415-431-5411 |
| Gnass, Jeff/PO Box 2196, Oroville, CA | 916-533-6788 |
| Going, Michael/1117 N Wilcox Pl, Los Angeles, CA | 213-465-6853 |
| Goldstein, Edward/1920 Main St #6, Santa Monica, CA | 213-396-1726 |
| Goodman, Jamison/1001 E 1st St, Los Angeles, CA | 213-617-1900 |
| Gordon, Charles M/19226 35th Pl NE, Seattle, WA | 206-365-2132 |
| Gordon, Jon/2052 Los Feliz Rd, Thousand Oaks, CA | 805-496-1485 |
| Gordon, Larry Dale/2047 Castilian Dr., Los Angeles, CA | 213-874-6318 |
| **GOTTLIEB, MARK/378 CAMBRIDGE AVE, PALO ALTO, CA (P 367)** | **415-321-8761** |
| Graham, Don/426 S Norton Ste 304, Los Angeles, CA | 213-386-7441 |
| Graham, Ellen/614 N Hillcrest Rd, Beverly Hills, CA | 213-275-6195 |
| Gray, Dennis/250 Newhall St, San Francisco, CA | 415-641-4009 |
| Gray, Todd/4359 W Third St, Los Angeles, CA | 213-380-1939 |
| Greenleigh, John/434 9th St, San Francisco, CA | 415-864-4147 |
| Greg Newman Photography/Los Angeles, CA | 213-257-6247 |
| Grimm, Tom/PO Box 83, Laguna Beach, CA | 714-494-1336 |
| Gross, Hoppy/RAW Studios, Box 99001, Denver, CO | 303-371-3609 |
| Gross, Richard/133 Putnam, San Francisco, CA | 415-558-8075 |
| Gullette, William/3410 Villa Terr, San Diego, CA | 619-692-3801 |

### H
| | |
|---|---|
| Hagopian, Jim/915 N Mansfield Ave, Hollywood, CA | 213-856-0018 |
| Hagyard, Dave/1205 E Pike, Seattle, WA | 206-322-8419 |
| Hailey, Jason/6700 W 5th, Los Angeles, CA | 213-653-7710 |
| Hall, George/82 Macondray Ln, San Francisco, CA | 415-775-7373 |
| Hampton, Ralph/PO Box 480057, Los Angeles, CA | 213-934-5781 |
| Hanauer, Mark/1717 N Vine, #12, Hollywood, CA | 213-462-2421 |
| Harding, C B/660 N Thompson St, Portland, OR | 503-281-9907 |
| Harlem, Jason/2534 W 7th St, Los Angeles, CA | 213-383-2774 |
| Harlow, Bruce/314 E Denny Way, Seattle, WA | 206-323-1771 |
| **HARRINGTON, MARSHALL PHOTOGRAPHY/2775 KURTZ ST #2, SAN DIEGO, CA (P 368,369)** | **619-291-2775** |
| Harris, Kay/212 S Second, Apt. 25, El Cajon, CA | 619-447-0786 |
| Hartman, Raiko/6916 Melrose, Los Angeles, CA | 213-278-4700 |
| Hartung Assoc Ltd/12919 Alcosta Blvd #4, San Ramon, CA | 415-838-0608 |
| Harvey, Stephen/7801 W Beverly Blvd, Los Angeles, CA | 213-934-5817 |
| Hawke, Sindy/22612 Leaflock Rd, Lake Forest, El Toro, CA | 714-837-7138 |
| **HEFFERNAN, TERRY/352 6TH ST, SAN FRANCISCO, CA (P 336,337)** | **415-626-1999** |
| Henderson Assoc/473 Sapenar Ct 5, Santa Clara, CA | 408-727-7906 |
| Henson-Hathaway/173 Bluxome, San Francisco, CA | 415-495-3473 |
| Herbeck, William/5739 3/4 Tujunga Ave, N Hollywood, CA | 213-464-5678 |
| Herridge, Brent/1201 E 2100 S, Salt Lake City, UT | 801-467-9752 |
| Herron, Matt/PO Box 1860, Sausalito, CA | 415-332-7388 |
| Hewett, Richard/5725 Buena Vista Terr, Los Angeles, CA | 213-254-4577 |
| Hicks, Alan/333 N W Park, Portland, OR | 503-226-6741 |
| Hicks, John and Regina/PO Box 5162, Carmel, CA | 408-624-7573 |
| Higgins, Donald/201 San Vincente Blvd, #14, Santa Monica, CA | 213-393-8858 |
| Hildreta, James/225 Jersey St, San Francisco, CA | 415-821-7398 |
| Hill, Dennis/994 North Altadena, Pasadena, CA | 213-795-2589 |
| Hirshew, Lloyd/758 Natoma, San Francisco, CA | 415-861-3902 |
| Hiser, David C/Box 113, Aspen, CO | 303-925-2317 |
| Hishi, James/612 S Victory Blvd, Burbank, CA | 213-849-4871 |
| Hixson, Richard/1261 Howard St, San Francisco, CA | 415-621-0246 |
| Hodge, Nettie/9687 Adams Ave, Huntington Beach, CA | 714-964-3166 |

# PHOTOGRAPHERS CONT'D.

Please send us your additions and updates.

| | |
|---|---|
| Hodges, Walter/4106 32nd St, SW, Seattle, WA | 206-935-5649 |
| Hoffman, Davy/1923 Colorado Ave, Santa Monica, CA | 213-829-5158 |
| Hoffman, Paul/4500 19th St, San Francisco, CA | 415-663-3575 |
| Hogg, Peter/1221 S La Brea, Los Angeles, CA | 213-937-0642 |
| Holdman, Floyd/1908 N Main, Orem, UT | 801-224-9966 |
| Hollenbeck, Cliff/Box 4247, Pioneer Square, Seattle, WA | 206-682-6300 |
| Holz, William/7630 W Norton Ave, Los Angeles, CA | 213-656-4061 |
| Hooper, H Lee/30708 Monte Lado Dr, Malibu, CA | 213-457-2897 |
| Hooper, Robert Scott/4330 W Desert Inn Rd, Las Vegas, NV | 702-873-5823 |
| Hopkins, Chris/1133 15th St #4, Santa Monica, CA | 213-394-4130 |
| Hopkins, Stew/345 5th Ave, Venice, CA | 213-396-8649 |
| Hough, John David/591 Mission, San Francisco, CA | 415-495-5769 |
| Hughes, John/PO Box 1470, Durango, CO | 303-247-1166 |
| Hulen, Steve/1640 S La Cienega Blvd, Los Angeles, CA | 213-271-6543 |
| Hungerford, Lauren/1000 N Bundy Dr, Los Angeles, CA | 213-476-1108 |
| Hunt, Phil Photography/3435 Army St #308, San Francisco, CA | 415-821-9879 |
| Hunt, Steven/PO Box 9393, Salt Lake City, UT | 801-485-9140 |
| Hutson, Larry/219 1/2 S Washington, Seattle, WA | 206-622-7197 |
| Hylen, Bo/1640 S LaCienega, Los Angeles, CA | 213-271-6543 |
| Imagery/PO Box 338, Balboa Island, CA | 714-673-4058 |
| Images/Tom Juell/11316 NE Stutz Rd, Vancouver, WA | 206-573-6203 |
| Inahara, Sharon/178 N Mansfield, Los Angeles, CA | 213-931-3664 |
| Iri, Carl/929 S Hampshire Ave, Los Angeles, CA | 213-388-5737 |
| Isaacs, Robert/1646 Mary Ave, Sunnyvale, CA | 408-245-1690 |
| Ito, Brad/2442 Harding Ave, Menlo Park, CA | 415-366-7815 |
| Jacobs, Michael/7466 Beverly Blvd, Los Angeles, CA | 213-934-7863 |
| James, Dick/23870 Madison St, Torrance, CA | 213-373-6789 |
| Jameson, Bob Assoc Inc/24 S Market St, Wailuku, HI | 808-244-9092 |
| Jay, Michael/1 Zeno Pl, San Francisco, CA | 415-543-7101 |
| Jensen, John/449 Bryant St, San Francisco, CA | 415-957-9449 |
| Johns, Rob/1895 Bluff St, Boulder, CO | 303-449-9192 |
| Johnson, Charles/Box 1686, Vail, CO | 303-393-0990 |
| Johnson, Payne B/4650 Harvey Rd, San Diego, CA | 619-299-4567 |
| Jones, Aaron/107 NW Fifth Ave, Portland, OR | 503-241-3648 |
| Jones, Bill/2171 India St Ste B, San Diego, CA | 619-235-8892 |
| Jones, DeWitte/Box 116, Bolinas, CA | 415-868-0674 |
| Jones, Dewitt/Box 116, Bolinas, CA | 415-868-0675 |
| Jones, Douglas/906 Lombard Ct, Costa Mesa, CA | 714-557-2300 |
| Jones, Rodney/22381/2 Purdue, Los Angeles, CA | 213-208-1404 |
| Josefsberg, Henry/975 Worcester Ave, Pasadena, CA | 213-791-4135 |
| Kaestner, Reed/1867 Montgomery Ave, Cardiff, CA | 619-942-0042 |
| Kahana, Yoram/1909 N Curson Pl, Hollywood, CA | 213-876-8208 |
| Kaplan, Marty/5637 Columbus Ave, Van Nuys, CA | 213-994-6987 |
| Kappes, Nicholas Wm/PO Box 927, San Pedro, CA | 213-547-0477 |
| Karageorge, Jim/418 Precita Ave, San Francisco, CA | 415-648-3444 |
| Katano, Nicole/36 Clyde St, San Francisco, CA | 415-495-6549 |
| Katzenberger, George/857 Joann St, Costa Mesa, CA | 714-631-5139 |
| Katzencompany/857 Joann St, Costa Mesa, CA | 714-631-5139 |
| Kauffman, Helen/9017 Rangeley Ave, Los Angeles, CA | 213-275-3569 |
| Kaufman, Robert/819 Stonegate Dr, So San Francisco, CA | 415-588-6385 |
| Keenan, Elaine Faris/90 Natoma St, San Francisco, CA | 415-546-9246 |
| **KEENAN, LARRY PHOTOGRAPHY/421 BRYANT ST, SAN FRANCISCO, CA (P 370)** | **415-495-6474** |
| Kehl, Robert/769 22nd St, Oakland, CA | 415-452-0501 |
| Kehrwald, Richard J/32 S Main, Sheridan, WY | 307-674-4679 |
| Keller, Greg/769 22nd St, Oakland, CA | 415-452-0501 |
| Kelley, Tom/8525 Santa Monica Blvd, Los Angeles, CA | 213-657-1780 |
| Kiesow, Paul Studio/549 1/2 N Fairfax Ave, Los Angeles, CA | 213-655-1897 |
| Kilberg, James/3371 Cahuenga Blvd W, Los Angeles, CA | 213-874-9514 |
| King, Heather/2029 Tierce St, San Francisco, CA | 415-563-1613 |
| Kious, Gary/9841 Airport Blvd Ste1414, Los Angeles, CA | 213-536-4880 |
| Kirkland, Douglas/9060 Wonderland Park Ave, Los Angeles, CA | 213-656-8511 |
| Koga, Dean/20219 S.W. Birch St., Santa Ana Hts., CA | 714-545-6043 |
| Kohler, Heinz/163 W Colorado Blvd, Pasadena, CA | 213-681-9195 |
| Kolsky, Rose/651 N Russell, Portland, OR | 503-249-5864 |
| Kopp, Pierre/2304 Rutgers Ave, Long Beach, CA | 213-597-5933 |
| Koropp, Robert/901 E 17 Ave, Denver, CO | 303-830-6000 |
| Kredenser, Peter/2551 Angelo Dr, Los Angeles, CA | 213-278-6356 |
| Kreher, Mark/6636 Santa Monica Blvd, Hollywood, CA | 213-464-4400 |
| Krosnick, Alan/215 Second St, San Francisco, CA | 415-957-1520 |
| Krueger, Gary/PO Box 543, Montrose, CA | 213-249-1051 |
| Krupp, Carl/PO Box 256, Merlin, OR | 503-479-6699 |
| Kuhn, Chuck/206 Third Ave S, Seattle, WA | 206-624-4706 |
| Kuhn, Robert/550 N Larchmont Blvd, Los Angeles, CA | 213-461-3656 |
| Kupersmith, Dan/1615 N Cahuenga, Los Angeles, CA | 213-980-5878 |
| Kurihara, Ted/680 Beach St #484, San Francisco, CA | 415-771-5100 |
| Kurisu/819 1/2 N Fairfax, Los Angeles, CA | 213-655-7287 |
| Kwong, Sam & Khoo, Henry Studio/741 S LaBrea Ave, Los Angeles, CA | 213-931-9393 |
| LA Uniform Exchange/55 ANCHORAGE RD, SAUSALITO, CA | 415-332-3725 |
| Lamb & Hall/7318 Melrose, Los Angeles, CA | 213-828-9653 |
| Lamotte, Michael Studios/828 Mission St, San Francisco, CA | 415-777-1443 |
| Landecker, Tom/1028 Folsom St, San Francisco, CA | 415-864-8888 |
| Langdon, Harry/8275 Beverly Blvd, Los Angeles, CA | 213-651-3212 |
| Lange, Erwin G/814 Robinson Rd, Topanga, CA | 213-455-1000 |
| LaRocca, Jerry/3840 NW Yeon Ave, Portland, OR | 503-223-0300 |
| Larson, Dean/7668 Hollywood Blvd, Los Angeles, CA | 213-876-1033 |
| LaTona, Kevin/159 Western Ave W #454, Seattle, WA | 206-285-5779 |
| Laughmiller, Allen/3923 W Jefferson Blvd, Los Angeles, CA | 213-735-1551 |
| Lawder, John/2672 S Grand, Santa Ana, CA | 714-557-3657 |
| Lawlor, John/325 Toyopa Dr, Pacific Palisades, CA | 213-458-1029 |
| Lawrence, Buzz/6422 Lankershim Blvd, N Hollywood, CA | 213-980-5725 |
| Laxer, Jack/16952 Dulce Ynez Ln, Pacific Palisades, CA | 213-459-1213 |
| Lea, Tom/185 Alpine, San Francisco, CA | 415-864-5941 |
| Leach, David/7408 Beverly Blvd, Los Angeles, CA | 213-932-1234 |
| Leatart, Brian/520 N Western, Los Angeles, CA | 213-386-3003 |
| Lee, C. Robert/PO Box 897, Idyllwild, CA | 619-659-3325 |
| **LEE, LARRY/PO BOX 4688, NORTH HOLLYWOOD, CA (P 371)** | **818-766-2677** |
| Legname, Rudy/389 Clementina St, San Francisco, CA | 415-777-9569 |
| LeGoy, James M/PO Box 6446, Reno, NV | 702-322-0116 |
| Lehman, Danny/6643 W 6th St, Los Angeles, CA | 213-652-1930 |
| Leng, Brian/1021 1/2 N LaBrea, Los Angeles, CA | 213-469-8624 |
| Leon Lecash Studio/1736 Hollyvista Ave, Los Angeles, CA | 213-934-9819 |
| Leonard, Joseph/610 22nd St, San Francisco, CA | 415-552-4090 |
| Lesinski, Martin/144 S Catalina, Pasadena, CA | 213-792-7659 |
| Lesley-Hille Inc/144 So Catalina, Pasadena, CA | 213-792-7659 |
| Levasheff, Michael/821 N La Brea, Los Angeles, CA | 213-932-0807 |
| Levy, Paul/2867 1/2 W 7th, Los Angeles, CA | 213-385-9046 |
| Lewin, Elyse/820 N Fairfax, Los Angeles, CA | 213-655-4214 |
| Lewine, Rob/8929 Holly Pl, Los Angeles, CA | 213-654-0830 |
| Lewis, Don/2350 Stanley Hills Dr, Los Angeles, CA | 213-656-2138 |
| Lichter, Michael/3300 14th St, Boulder, CO | 303-443-9198 |
| Lichtner, Marvin/715 Shotwell St, San Francisco, CA | 415-824-7167 |
| **LIGHT LANGUAGE/352 6TH ST, SAN FRANCISCO, CA (P 336,337)** | **415-863-9300** |
| Liles, Harry/1060 N Lillian Way, Hollywood, CA | 213-466-1612 |
| Linden, Seymour/794 Montecito Dr, Los Angeles, CA | 213-286-5896 |
| Lindstrom, Eric/2320 First Ave, Seattle, WA | 206-583-0601 |
| Lissy, David/Box 11122, Aspen, CO | 303-963-1410 |
| **LIVZEY, JOHN/1510 N LAS PALMAS, HOLLYWOOD, CA (P 372,373)** | **213-469-2992** |
| Lockwood, Scott/317 Willow, Los Angeles, CA | 714-551-6102 |
| Loeser, Peter/1431 Ocean Ave #819, Santa Monica, CA | 213-393-5576 |
| Long, John/1231 Alderwood Ave, Sunnyvale, CA | 408-734-3211 |
| Lopez, Bret/4121 Wilshire Blvd #406, Los Angeles, CA | 213-744-0494 |
| Lopez, Joel Alien/2865 W 7th St, Los Angeles, CA | 213-384-1016 |
| Lorenzo/4654 El Cajon Blvd, San Diego, CA | 619-280-6010 |
| Lowry, Alexander/PO Box 1500, Santa Cruz, CA | 408-425-8081 |
| Lund, John M/860 Second St, San Francisco, CA | 415-957-1775 |
| Lyon, Fred/237 Clara St, San Francisco, CA | 415-974-5645 |
| Lyons, Marv/2865 W 7th St, Los Angeles, CA | 213-384-0732 |
| MIAD Photography/115 E Alton Ave, Santa Ana, CA | 714-549-4101 |
| Madden, Daniel J/PO Box 965, Los Alamitos, CA | 213-429-3621 |
| Maddocks, J H/4766 Melrose Ave, Los Angeles, CA | 213-660-1321 |
| Madison, David/2284 Old Middlefield #8, Mountain View, CA | 415-961-6297 |
| Mahieu, Ted/PO Box 42578, San Francisco, CA | 415-641-4747 |
| Mallen, Edward J/12502 E Whitley St, Whittier, CA | 213-692-1455 |
| Malphettes, Benoit/816 S Grand St, Los Angeles, CA | 213-629-9054 |

# PHOTOGRAPHERS CONT'D.

Please send us your additions and updates.

|  |  |
|---|---|
| Mangold Productions/PO Box 1001, Palo Alto, CA | 415-469-9897 |
| Manning, Lawrence/15507 Doty Ave, Lawndale, CA | 213-679-4774 |
| Mar, Tim/P O Box 3488, Seattle, WA | 206-583-0093 |
| Marchack Productions/1041 N Mansfield Ave Ste 208, Hollywood, CA | 213-461-3200 |
| Marcus, Ken/6916 Melrose Ave, Los Angeles, CA | 213-937-7214 |
| Mareschal, Tom/129 First Ave W, Seattle, WA | 206-282-9478 |
| Margolies, Paul/2695 Greenwich St, San Francisco, CA | 415-346-4845 |
| Margolis, Paul/480 Potrero, San Francisco, CA | 415-621-3306 |
| Marley, Stephen/1062 N Rengstorff Ave, Mountain View, CA | 415-966-8301 |
| Marriott, John F./1271 California St, #6, San Francisco, CA | 415-673-7159 |
| Marshall, Jim/1831 Union St, San Francisco, CA | 415-931-4555 |
| Marshutz, Roger/1649 S La Cienega Blvd, Los Angeles, CA | 213-273-1610 |
| Martin Photography/1053 Blossom Dr, Santa Clara, CA | 408-985-9378 |
| Martinelli Photography/608 So Railroad Ave, San Mateo, CA | 415-347-3589 |
| **MASTERSON, ED/11211 SORRENTO VALLEY RD, SAN DIEGO, CA (P 375)** | **619-457-3251** |
| May, Ron/PO Box 7308, Menlo Park, CA | 415-854-4103 |
| Mc Hugh, Jim/218 Maberry, Santa Monica, CA | 213-454-2519 |
| McAfee, Lynn/11159 1/4 Acama St, North Hollywood, CA | 213-761-1317 |
| McAfee, Tom/971 Howard, San Francisco, CA | 415-777-1736 |
| **MCALLISTER, BRUCE/701 MARION ST, DENVER, CO (P 376,377)** | **303-832-7496** |
| McBride, Ritch/1033 Battery St, San Francisco, CA | 415-392-2971 |
| McCluskey, Holloway/134 NE 9th, Hillsboro, OR | 503-640-6980 |
| McCrary, Jim/211 S LaBrea Ave, Los Angeles, CA | 213-936-5115 |
| McDermott, John/3836A Sacramento St, San Francisco, CA | 415-668-5622 |
| McDowell, Pat/PO Box 283, Park City, UT | 801-649-3403 |
| McMahon, Steve/1164 S LaBrea, Los Angeles, CA | 213-937-3345 |
| Mehlman, Elwyn/31141/2 Sherwood Ave, Alhambra, CA | 213-289-5826 |
| **MELGAR PHOTOGRAPHERS INC/2971 CORVIN DR, SANTA CLARA, CA (P 378)** | **408-733-4500** |
| Melick, Jordan/1250 W Cedar St, Denver, CO | 303-744-1414 |
| Melley, Peter Read/PO Box 24363, Los Angeles, CA | 213-359-9414 |
| Menzel Peter J/136 N Deer Run Lane, Napa, CA | 707-255-3528 |
| Menzie, W Gordon/2311 Kettner Blvd, San Diego, CA | 619-234-4431 |
| Messineo, John/PO Box 1636, Fort Collins, CO | 303-482-9349 |
| Micoine, Christian/4208 Santa monica Blvd, Los Angeles, CA | |
| Mike Muckley Photography Inc/3731 6th Ave, San Diego, CA | 619-297-0271 |
| Miles, Reid/1136 N Las Palmas, Hollywood, CA | 213-462-6106 |
| Milkie, Fred/127 Boylston E, Seattle, WA | 206-324-3000 |
| Miller, Bill/7611 Melrose Ave, Los Angeles, CA | 213-651-5630 |
| Miller, Bruce/202 A Westminster Ave, Venice, CA | 213-392-4877 |
| Miller, Donald/2032 Stoner Ave, Los Angeles, CA | 213-477-2491 |
| Miller, Ed/705 32nd Ave, San Francisco, CA | 415-221-5687 |
| Miller, Jim/1122 N Citrus Ave, Los Angeles, CA | 213-466-9515 |
| Miller, Jordan/506 S San Vicente Blvd, Los Angeles, CA | 213-655-0408 |
| Miller, Peter Read/PO Box 24363, Los Angeles, CA | 213-474-5887 |
| Miller, Randy/PO Box 24363, Los Angeles, CA | 213-474-5887 |
| Miller, Ray/PO Box 450, Balboa, CA | 714-673-7295 |
| Miller, Scott/1836 El Cerrito Pl, Los Angeles, CA | 213-874-3868 |
| Miller, Wynn/4083 Glencoe Ave, Marina Del Ray, CA | 213-821-4948 |
| Milmoe, James O/14900 Cactus Cr, Denver, CO | 303-279-4364 |
| Milne, Robbie/2717 Western, Seattle, WA | 206-682-6828 |
| **MISHLER, CLARK/1238 G ST, ANCHORAGE, AK (P 379)** | **907-279-8847** |
| Mississippi State Film Commission/1238 G St, Anchorage, AK | 907-279-8847 |
| Mitchell, David Paul/564 Deodar Ln, Bradbury, CA | 213-358-3328 |
| Mitchell, Josh Photography/706 W Pico Blvd, Los Angeles, CA | 213-742-0368 |
| Mitchell, Margaretta K/280 Hillcrest Rd, Berkeley, CA | 415-655-4950 |
| Mitchell, Tommy/6410 A Sunset Blvd, Los Angeles, CA | 213-933-7201 |
| Moldvay, Albert/1380 Morningside Way, Venice, CA | 213-392-6537 |
| Monkton, Robert/430 Hill St, Laguna Beach, CA | 714-494-8473 |
| Montes de Oca, Arthur/4302 Melrose Ave, Los Angeles, CA | 213-665-5141 |
| Moore, Charles/PO Box 1876, Columbia, CA | 209-532-2645 |
| Moore, Gary/1125 E Orange Ave, Monrovia, CA | 213-359-9414 |
| Morfit, Mason Inc/897 Independent Ave #5D, Mountain View, CA | 415-969-2209 |
| Morgan, David Scott/502 Plaza Rubio, Santa Barbara, CA | 805-569-1412 |
| Moulin, Gabriel/465 Green St, San Francisco, CA | 415-986-4224 |
| Moyer, Robin/465 Green St, San Francisco, CA | 415-986-4224 |
| Mudford, Grant/5619 W 4th St #2, Los Angeles, CA | 213-936-9145 |
| Muench, David/PO Box 30500, Santa Barbara, CA | 805-967-4488 |
| Muench, Josef/839 Mission Canyon Rd, Santa Barbara, CA | 805-682-4333 |
| Mulligan, Frank/7898 Ostrow #G, San Diego, CA | 619-569-8391 |
| Muna, R J/63 Encina Ave, Palo Alto, CA | 415-328-1131 |
| Munroe, Joe/100 Estates Dr Box 308, Orinda, CA | 415-254-5112 |
| Murphy, Suzanne/2442 Third St, Santa Monica, CA | 213-399-6652 |
| Murphy, William/7771 Melrose Ave, Los Angeles, CA | 213-651-4800 |
| Murray 111, Wm J/1507 Belmont Ave, Seattle, WA | 206-322-3377 |
| Murray, Mike/1622 Moulton Pkwy, Tustin, CA | 714-730-5793 |
| Murray, Tom/1896 Rising Glen Rd, Los Angeles, CA | 213-654-0364 |
| Myer, Eric/4536 Marvin St, Pasadena, CA | 213-790-9698 |
| Myers, Jeffry W Photography/Joseph Vance Bldg #414, Seattle, WA | 206-621-7609 |
| Myers, Tom/1737 Markham Way, Sacramento, CA | 916-443-8886 |
| **N** Nadel, Leonard/2121 Alcyona Dr, Hollywood, CA | 213-465-7405 |
| Nadler, Jeff/520 N Western Ave, Los Angeles, CA | 213-467-2135 |
| Nagler, Bernard/27730 Sequoia Glen Dr, Valencia, CA | 805-255-9114 |
| Nahoum, Ken/6609 Orange St, Los Angeles, CA | 213-559-3244 |
| Narciso, Mike/505 S Market, San Jose, CA | 408-298-7688 |
| Nardelli, Will/505 S Market, San Jose, CA | 408-298-7688 |
| Nebbia, Thomas/911 9th St, #302, Santa Monica, CA | 213-395-5679 |
| Neihouse, Jim/1870 Camino De Vida, Santa Barbara, CA | 805-964-5970 |
| Noble, Richard/7618 Melrose Ave, , CA | 213-655-4711 |
| Normark, Don/1622 Taylor Ave N, Seattle, WA | 206-284-9393 |
| Norwood, David/4040 Del Rey Ave, Marina Del Rey, CA | 213-827-2020 |
| Nuding, Peter/3181 Melendy Dr, San Carlos, CA | 415-591-1953 |
| Nunzi Productions/3181 Melendy Dr, San Carlos, CA | 415-591-1953 |
| Nyerges, Suzanne/413 S Fairfax, Los Angeles, CA | 213-938-0151 |
| **O** Obrien, George/1515 Merced St, Fresno, CA | 209-226-4000 |
| **O'BRIEN, TOM/450 S LA BREA, LOS ANGELES, CA (P 341)** | **213-938-2008** |
| Ogilvie, Peter/90 Natoma, San Francisco, CA | 415-391-1646 |
| Ogle, Douglas/3839 Stoneway Ave N, Seattle, WA | 206-632-3001 |
| O'Hara, Yoshi/6341 Yucca St, Hollywood, CA | 213-466-8031 |
| Oppenheimer, Kent/1344 Devlin Dr, Los Angeles, CA | 213-652-3923 |
| O'Rear, Chuck/PO Box 361, St Helena, CA | 707-963-2663 |
| Osbourne, Jan/460 NE 70th St, Seattle, WA | 206-524-5220 |
| Oswald, Jan/90 Corona St #508, Denver, CO | 303-778-6016 |
| Otto, Glenn/7188 Sunset Blvd, Los Angeles, CA | 213-851-3046 |
| Outland, Joe/Box 6202 Point Loma Station, San Diego, CA | 619-222-4558 |
| **P** PSI Film Lab Inc/916 Rodney Dr, San Leandro, CA | 415-483-3683 |
| Pacheco, Robert/11152 3/4 Morrison, No Hollywood, CA | 213-761-1320 |
| Padys, Diane/PO Box 77307, San Francisco, CA | 415-285-6443 |
| Pagenhart, Alan/PO Box 1230, La Jolla, CA | 619-456-0881 |
| Painter, Charles/2513 Devri Ct, Mountain View, CA | 415-968-7467 |
| Pasquali, Art/1061 Sunset Blvd, Los Angeles, CA | 213-250-0134 |
| Patterson, Marion/1745 Croner Ave, Menlo Park, CA | 209-379-2838 |
| Patterson, Robert/915 N Mansfield Ave, Hollywood, CA | 213-462-4401 |
| Paulus, Bill Photography/P O Box 432, Pacific Grove, CA | 408-649-1624 |
| Pavloff, Nick/PO Box 2339, San Francisco, CA | 415-989-2664 |
| Peais, Larry/165 Jessie, San Francisco, CA | 415-957-1366 |
| Pearson, Charles R/PO Box 350, Leavenworth, WA | 509-548-7983 |
| Pearson, John/1343 Sacramento, Berkeley, CA | 415-525-7553 |
| Pedrick, Frank/P O Box 411, Point Richmond, CA | 415-237-7259 |
| Peebles, Douglas Photography/1100 Alakea St, #221, Honolulu, HI | 808-533-6686 |
| **PERCEY, ROLAND/626 N HOOVER, LOS ANGELES, CA (P 380)** | **213-660-7305** |
| **PEREGRINE STUDIO/1541 PLATTE ST, DENVER, CO (P 381)** | **303-455-6944** |
| Perkins, Robert/49-305 Highway 74 #21, Palm Desert, CA | 619-568-3871 |
| Perla, Dario/628 W Bourne Dr #3, Los Angeles, CA | 213-854-3921 |
| **PERRY, DAVID/4006 CALIFORNIA AVE SW, SEATTLE, WA (P 382)** | **206-932-6614** |
| Pesin, Harry/PO Box 350, Rancho Santa Fe, CA | 619-756-2101 |
| Peterman, Joan & Herbert/1118 Fifth St #7, Santa Monica, CA | 213-395-7668 |
| Petermann, Herbert/1118 Fifth St, Santa Monica, CA | 213-395-7668 |
| Petersen, Ragnar M/1467 Laurelwood Rd, Santa Clara, CA | 408-748-9049 |
| Peterson, Darrell/747 Belmont Pl E, Seattle, WA | 206-324-0307 |
| Peterson, Robert/915 Yale Ave N, Seattle, WA | 206-329-2299 |
| Pett, Laurence J/5907 Cahill Ave, Tarzana, CA | 213-344-9453 |
| Pettce, Jack/1501 Mission St, S Pasadena, CA | 213-682-1121 |

# PHOTOGRAPHERS CONT'D.

Please send us your additions and updates.

| | |
|---|---|
| Pfleger, Michael/Box 22457, San Francisco, CA | 415-355-1772 |
| **PHOTOGRAPHIC COMMUNICATIONS/3400-R DE LA CRUZ BLVD, SANTA CLARA, CA (P 383)** | **408-727-2233** |
| Photography Northwest/1415 Elliot Ave W, Seattle, WA | 206-285-5249 |
| Photopia Image/PO Box 2309, San Francisco, CA | 415-441-5611 |
| Pildas, Ave/1231 Ozeta Terr, Los Angeles, CA | 213-275-2353 |
| Pinckney, Jim/PO Box 1149, Carmel Valley, CA | 408-375-3534 |
| Piper, Jim/922 SE Ankeny, Portland, OR | 503-231-9622 |
| Place, Chuck/612 W Arrellaga St, Santa Barbara, CA | 805-965-7621 |
| Planning & Design Corp/14 Pearl St, Denver, CO | 303-744-0711 |
| Pleasant, Ralph B/814 Seward St, Hollywood, CA | 213-467-3588 |
| Porter, James/3955 Birch St, #F, Newport Beach, CA | 714-751-7231 |
| Poucel, William/123 La Vereda Rd, Santa Barbara, CA | 805-969-9382 |
| Powers, David/17 Brosnan, San Francisco, CA | 415-864-7974 |
| Powers, Lisa/2073 Outpost Dr, Los Angeles, CA | 213-874-5877 |
| Preuss, Karen/369 Eleventh Ave, San Francisco, CA | 415-752-7545 |
| Prince, Norman/3340-B 22nd St, San Francisco, CA | 415-647-0278 |
| Pritchett, Bill/PO Box 756, Coronado, CA | 619-421-6005 |
| Proehl, Steve/916 Rodney Dr, San Leandro, CA | 415-483-3683 |
| **R** | |
| RFT Productions Ltd/306 Grand Blvd, Los Angeles, CA | 213-822-5663 |
| Raabe, Dan/5923 W Pico Blvd, Los Angeles, CA | 213-934-8447 |
| Rafkind, Andrew/200 N 3rd St, #2, Boise, ID | 208-344-9918 |
| Rahn, Stephen/259 Clara St, San Francisco, CA | 415-495-3556 |
| Rakebrandt, John/118 King St, San Francisco, CA | 415-543-6232 |
| Rakowsky Steiner, Glenn/9 Decatur St, San Francisco, CA | 415-861-4118 |
| Ralph Chandler Studio Inc/1111 N Tamarind, Los Angeles, CA | 213-469-6205 |
| Ramsey, Steve/4800 E Washington St, Denver, CO | 303-295-2135 |
| Randlett, Mary/Box 10536, Bainbridge Island, WA | 206-842-3935 |
| Rapoport, Aaron/3119 Beverly Blvd, Los Angeles, CA | 213-738-7277 |
| Rawcliffe, David/7609 Beverly Blvd, Los Angeles, CA | 213-938-6287 |
| Reed, Bob/1816 N Vermont Ave, Los Angeles, CA | 213-662-9703 |
| Reiff, Robert/306 Grand Blvd, Los Angeles, CA | 213-822-5663 |
| **RESSMEYER, ROGER/1230 GRANT AVE, SAN FRANCISCO, CA (P 384)** | **415-921-1675** |
| Reynolds, Roger/3310 S Knox Ct, Englewood, CO | 303-789-4307 |
| Richard Blair & Associates/450-24th St, Oakland, CA | 415-893-2840 |
| Richard, Armas/1110 N Hudson Ave, #B, Los Angeles, CA | 213-464-5016 |
| Riss, Owen/27532 Velador Rd, Mission Viejo, CA | 714-770-6451 |
| Ritts, Herb/7927 Hillside Ave, Los Angeles, CA | 213-876-6366 |
| Rixson, Mike/13558 Moor Pk #7, Sherman Oaks, CA | 213-783-5276 |
| Robbins, Bill/7016 Santa Monica Blvd, Los Angeles, CA | 213-550-7075 |
| Roberge, Earl/764 Bryant, Walla Walla, WA | 509-525-7385 |
| Robinson, Dave/911 Western Ave, #510, Seattle, WA | 206-624-5207 |
| Rodal, Arney A/395 Winslow Way E, Bainbridge Island, WA | 206-842-4989 |
| Rogers, Kenneth/PO Box 3187, Beverly Hills, CA | 213-553-5532 |
| Rokeach, Barrie/32 Windsor, Kensington, CA | 415-527-5376 |
| Roland, Charles/1837 S Clovedale Ave, Los Angeles, CA | 213-464-0300 |
| Rorke, Lorraine/146 Shrader St, San Francisco, CA | 415-386-2121 |
| Rosenberg, Allan/963 North Point St, San Francisco, CA | 415-775-4272 |
| Rosenberg, David/16 W 13th Ave, Denver, CO | 303-893-0893 |
| Roslan, Thom Studios/7073 Vineland Ave, Van Nuys, CA | 213-901-0250 |
| Ross, Alan C/202 Culper Ct, Hermosa Beach, CA | 213-379-2015 |
| Ross, Bill/22920 Lanark St, Canoga Park, CA | 213-884-1083 |
| Ross, James Studio/1261 Howard St, San Francisco, CA | 415-861-1093 |
| Rothman, Michael/1816 N Vermont Ave, Los Angeles, CA | 213-662-9703 |
| Rowan, Bob/939 Janet La, Lafayette, CA | 415-930-8687 |
| Rozsa, Nick/6620 Melrose, Los Angeles, CA | 213-939-4888 |
| Rubins, Richard/3757 Wilshire Blvd, Los Angeles, CA | 213-387-9989 |
| Russell, John/Box 4739, Aspen, CO | 303-920-1431 |
| Rychetnik, Joseph S/184 Palm Ave #106, Marina | 415-563-0851 |
| **S** | |
| **SADLON, JIM/352 6TH ST, SAN FRANCISCO, CA (P 385)** | **415-626-1900** |
| Saehlenou, Kevin/1633 York St, Denver, CO | 303-322-6601 |
| Safron, Marshal/1816 N Vermont Ave, Los Angeles, CA | 213-663-2418 |
| Sagara, Peter/736 N LaBrea, Los Angeles, CA | 213-933-7531 |
| Saitta, Joseph/1525 Gordon St, Redwood City, CA | 415-494-1684 |
| Salazar, Tony/2019 A P S, Santa Barbara, CA | 805-569-2490 |
| Salskou, Rocky/3839 Stoneway Ave N., Seattle, WA | 206-632-3001 |
| Salutos, Pete/4083 Glencoe Ave, Marina Del Ray, CA | 213-821-4948 |
| Samerjan, Peter/743 N Fairfax, Los Angeles, CA | 213-653-2940 |
| Sandison, Teri/1545 N Wilcox, #102, Hollywood, CA | 213-461-3529 |
| Sato, Garry/645 N Martel Ave, Los Angeles, CA | 213-658-8645 |
| Scharf, David/2100 Loma Vista Pl, Los Angeles, CA | 213-666-8657 |
| Scherl, Ron/218 Union St, San Francisco, CA | 415-421-1160 |
| Schiff, Darryll/8153 W Blackburn Ave, Los Angeles, CA | 213-658-6179 |
| Schiller, Lawrence Productions/PO Box 5345, Beverly Hills, CA | 213-906-0926 |
| Schmiett, Skip/740 W 1700 S #10, Salt Lake City, UT | 801-973-0642 |
| Schneider, Charles/72 Half Moon Bend, Coronado, CA | 619-429-3987 |
| **SCHOENFELD, MICHAEL/734 W 800 ST SOUTH, SALT LAKE CITY, UT (P 386)** | **801-532-6122** |
| Schroeder, Roxanne/1665 Maurice Ln, San Jose, CA | 408-257-1940 |
| Schubert, John/5959 W Third, Los Angeles, CA | 213-935-6044 |
| Schwartz, George J/PO Box 413, Bend, OR | 503-389-4062 |
| Schwartz, Monserrate/PO Box 413, Bend, OR | 503-389-4062 |
| Scorza, Salvatore/PO Box 1072, Burbank, CA | 213-997-3542 |
| Selig, Jonathan/3112 Barrington Ave, Los Angeles, CA | 213-827-4911 |
| Selland, George/461 Bryant St, San Francisco, CA | 415-495-3633 |
| Selland, Stuart D./461 Bryant St, San Francisco, CA | 415-495-3633 |
| Sexton, Richard/1261 Howard St, San Francisco, CA | 415-864-4172 |
| Shaffer, Bob/1250 Folsom, San Francisco, CA | 415-552-4884 |
| Sharpe, Dick/2475 Park Oak Dr., Los Angeles, CA | 213-462-4597 |
| Shipps, Raymond/1325 A Morena Blvd, San Diego, CA | 619-276-1690 |
| Sholik, Stan/15455 Red Hill Ave, Tustin, CA | 714-731-7826 |
| Short, Glenn/14641 La Maida, Sherman Oaks, CA | 213-990-5599 |
| Shorten, Chris/60 Federal St, SanFrancisco, CA | 415-543-4883 |
| Shupe, John R/4090 Edgehill Dr, Ogden, UT | 801-392-2523 |
| Shuper, Kay/6084 W Pico Blvd, Los Angeles, CA | 213-852-0075 |
| Shuper, Phil/6084 W Pico Blvd, Los Angeles, CA | 213-852-0075 |
| Sievert, John/2421 Cabrillo St, San Francisco, CA | 415-751-2369 |
| Silk, Gary Photography/6546 Hollywood Blvd, #215, Hollywood, CA | 213-466-1785 |
| Silverek, Don/914 Ripley St, Santa Rosa, CA | 707-525-1155 |
| Silverman, Jay/1039 S Fairfax Ave, Los Angeles, CA | 213-931-1169 |
| Simpson, Stephen/PO Box 2888, La Jolla, CA | 619-454-2949 |
| Sinick, Gary/3246 Ettie, Oakland, CA | 415-655-4538 |
| Sinklier, Scott/286 Banner Ave, Ventura, CA | 805-647-1792 |
| Sjef's Fotographie/2311 NW Johnson St, Portland, OR | 503-223-1089 |
| Skarsten & Dunn Studios/1062 N Rengstorff #E, Mountain View, CA | 415-969-5759 |
| Slatery, Chad/11627 Ayres Ave, Los Angeles, CA | 213-477-0734 |
| Slaughter, Michael/2867 1/2 W 7th St, #A, Los Angeles, CA | 213-388-3361 |
| Slenzak, Ron/7106 Waring Ave, Los Angeles, CA | 213-934-9088 |
| Slobodian, Scott/6630 Santa Monica Blvd, Los Angeles, CA | 213-464-2341 |
| Sloneker, Sam/490 Tigertail Rd, Los Angeles, CA | 213-472-5100 |
| Smith, Bradley/5858 Desert View Dr, La Jolla, CA | 619-454-4321 |
| **SMITH, CHARLES J/7163 CONSTRUCTION CRT, SAN DIEGO, CA (P 387)** | **619-271-6525** |
| Smith, Elliott Varner/Box 5268, Berkeley, CA | 415-654-9235 |
| Smith, Gil/2865 W 7th St, Los Angeles, CA | 213-384-1016 |
| Smith, Kerby/8033 Sunset Blvd, Hollywood, CA | 213-463-7474 |
| Smith, Mike/8030 Owensmouth #1, Canoga Park, CA | 213-340-0908 |
| Smith, Steve/228 Main St E, Venice, CA | 213-392-4982 |
| Smith, Todd/2643 S Fairfax, Culver City, CA | 213-559-0059 |
| Snyder Photographic/2415 3rd St Ste 265, San Francisco, CA | 415-861-7514 |
| Sokol, Howard/3006 Zuni St, Denver, CO | 303-433-3353 |
| Sollecito, Tony/1120B W Evelyn Ave, Sunnyvale, CA | 408-773-8118 |
| Solo, Jules/1120B W Evelyn Ave., Sunnyvale, CA | 408-773-8118 |
| **SOLOMON, MARC/PO BOX 480574, LOS ANGELES, CA (P 388,389)** | **213-935-1771** |
| Specific Image/3052 Clairemont Dr, San Diego, CA | 619-276-2475 |
| Spitz, Harry Photography/6153 Carpenter Ave, North Hollywood, CA | 213-761-9828 |
| Sporkin, Lee/135 S Detroit, Los Angeles, CA | 213-934-6737 |
| Spradling, David/2515 Patricia Ave, Los Angeles, CA | 213-202-1627 |
| **SPRINGMANN, CHRISTOPHER/PO BOX 745, POINT REYES, CA (P 340)** | **415-663-8428** |
| St Arnold, Walt/615 W Dryden #4, Glendale, CA | 213-242-3828 |
| St Jivago Desanges/413 S Fairfax, Los Angeles, CA | 213-938-0151 |
| **STARLIGHT PHOTO AGENCY/1230 GRANT AVE #574, SAN FRANCISCO, CA (P 384)** | **415-921-1675** |
| Stearns, Doug/901 East 17th Ave, Denver, CO | 303-830-6633 |
| Stefan Merken Studio/900 N Citrus, Los Angeles, CA | 213-466-4533 |
| Stein, Robert/319 1/2 S Robertson Blvd, Beverly Hills, CA | 213-652-2030 |

# PHOTOGRAPHERS CONT'D.

Please send us your additions and updates.

| | |
|---|---|
| **STEINBERG, BRUCE/2128 18TH ST,** | |
| **SAN FRANCISCO, CA (P 391)** | **415-864-0739** |
| Steinberg, Claire/10434 Corfu Ln, Los Angeles, CA | 213-279-1775 |
| Steinberg, Mike/715 S Coast Hwy, Laguna Beach, CA | 714-494-2888 |
| Steiner, Glenn/9 Decatur St, San Francisco, CA | 415-861-4118 |
| Steinheimer, Richard/897 Independence Ave, # 3-, Mountain View, CA | 415-968-8436 |
| Stevens, Bob/9048 Santa Monica Blvd, Los Angeles, CA | 213-271-8123 |
| Stewart, Stephen/939 N Alfred #7, West Hollywood, CA | 213-656-2270 |
| Stewart, Tom/Studio 3/1316 SE 12th Ave, Portland, OR | 503-238-1748 |
| Stone, Pete/1410 NW Johnson, Portland, OR | 503-224-7125 |
| Stott, Barry/Stott Shot Box 1550, Vail, CO | 303-476-3334 |
| Strauss, Andrew/6442 Santa Monica Blvd, Los Angeles, CA | 213-464-5394 |
| Strauss, Rick/1319 Harvard St, Santa Monica, CA | 213-453-2879 |
| Streano, Vince/PO Box 662, Laguna Beach, CA | 714-497-1908 |
| Streshinsky, Ted/PO Box 674, Berkeley, CA | 415-526-1976 |
| Strickland, Steve/Box 3486, San Bernardino, CA | 619-883-4792 |
| Stryker, Ray/12518 80th Ave S, Seattle, WA | 206-772-3310 |
| Studio 3 Photography/3246 Ettie St, Oakland, CA | 415-655-4538 |
| Studio 3, Inc./1316 S.E. 12th Ave, Portland, OR | 503-238-1748 |
| Studio AV/1227 First Ave S, Seattle, WA | 206-223-1007 |
| Studio E/D. Sweitzer/4800 N Washington, Denver, CO | 303-295-0703 |
| **STUDIOS INC/1830 17TH ST,** | |
| **SAN FRANCISCO, CA (P 332,333)** | **415-552-4254** |
| Su, Andrew/5733 Benner St, Los Angeles, CA | 213-256-0598 |
| Sugasawara, George/411 S Fairfax, Los Angeles, CA | 213-934-3850 |
| Sullivan, Jeremiah S/1105 Sunset Cliffs Blvd, San Diego, CA | 619-224-0070 |
| Sullivan, Michael/2247 Boundary St, San Diego, CA | 619-282-5001 |
| Sund, Harald/PO Box 16466, Seattle, WA | 206-932-1120 |
| Super, Rob/933 Hilldale Ave, Berkeley, CA | 415-525-4855 |
| Surber, Bruce/13622 NE 20th, #D, Bellevue, WA | 206-641-6003 |
| Sutton, David/11502 Dona Teresa Dr, Studio City, CA | 213-654-7979 |
| **SWARTHOUT, WALTER/370 FOURTH ST,** | |
| **SAN FRANCISCO, CA (P 392,393)** | **415-543-2525** |
| Swartz, Fred/135 S LaBrea, Los Angeles, CA | 213-939-2789 |
| Symmes, Joel/1112 N Beachwood, Los Angeles, CA | 213-462-0712 |
| **T** TOPS Talent Agency/404 Piikoi St, Honolulu, HI | 808-537-6647 |
| Tachibana, Kenji/1067 26th Ave East, Seattle, WA | 206-325-2121 |
| Taggart, Fritz/1117 N Wilcox Pl, Los Angeles, CA | 213-469-8227 |
| Tahoe Photographic Workshop/PO Box 3060, Truckee, CA | 916-587-4500 |
| Tanous, Dorothy/1041 N McCadden Pl, Los Angeles, CA | 213-465-6149 |
| Tatem, Mike/6256 S Albion Way, Denver, CO | 303-770-6080 |
| Tauber, Richard/4221 24th ST, San Francisco, CA | 415-824-6837 |
| Team Production Co Inc/10616 Moorpark St, North Hollywood, CA | 213-506-5700 |
| Teke/4338 Shady Glade Ave, Studio City, CA | 213-985-9066 |
| Teschl, Josef/31 Brock Ave, Toronto, On | 416-532-3495 |
| Thomas, Greg/2238 1/2 Purdue Ave, Los Angeles, CA | 213-479-8477 |
| Thomas, Mort Photography/359 W El Camino Real, Mountain View, CA | 415-960-3626 |
| Thompson, Michael/7811 Alabama Ave, #14, Canoga Park, CA | 213-883-7870 |
| Thompson, Mike/1032 NW 14th St, Portland, OR | 503-224-6555 |
| Thompson, Wesley/3316 53rd St, San Diego, CA | 619-582-0812 |
| Thompson, William/PO Box 5298 University Sta, Seattle, WA | 206-621-9069 |
| Thornton, Tyler/4706 Oakwood Ave, Los Angeles, CA | 213-465-0425 |
| Tilger, Stewart/71 Columbia #206, Seattle, WA | 206-682-7818 |
| Tise, David/975 Folsom St, San Francisco, CA | 415-777-0669 |
| Tolbert, Richard/127 W Broadway Ste 148, Anaheim, CA | 714-536-1392 |
| Tracy, Tom/1155 Harrison, San Francisco, CA | 415-861-2822 |
| Trafficanda, Gerald/1514 N Gardner, Los Angeles, CA | 213-876-0444 |
| Trailer, Martin/1514 N Gardner, Los Angeles, CA | 213-769-0373 |
| Trainor, Ted/1600 Broadway Ste 540, Denver, CO | 303-831-1113 |
| Trank, Steven/6801 E Gage Ave, Los Angeles, CA | 213-927-1459 |
| Tregeagle, Steve/2994 S Richards St, #C, Salt Lake City, UT | 801-484-1673 |
| Trexler, Pete/5888 Smiley Dr Studio B, Culver City, CA | 213-558-8226 |
| Trindl, Gene/3950 Vantage Ave, Studio City, CA | 213-877-4848 |
| Trout Studios/505 S Market St, San Jose, CA | 408-298-7688 |
| Tucker, Kim/2428 Canyon Dr., Los Angeles, CA | 213-465-9233 |
| Tucker, Tom/846 Micheltorena St, Los Angeles, CA | 213-663-7656 |
| Turner, John Terence/173 37th Ave E, Seattle, WA | 206-325-9073 |
| Turner, Philip/545 Sutter St, #202, San Francisco, CA | 415-956-2146 |
| Turner, Richard P/PO Box 64205, Rancho Pk Statio, Los Angeles, CA | 213-279-2127 |
| Turner, Ronald/2134 Old Middlefield, Mountain View, CA | 415-967-7418 |
| Tuschman, Mark/300 Santa Monica, Menlo Park, CA | 415-322-4157 |
| Tuttle, Tom/205 W Carrillo #B, Santa Barbara, CA | 805-966-0963 |
| **UV** Ueda, Richard/1816 South Flower, Los Angeles, CA | 213-747-7259 |
| Uniack/8933 National Blvd, Los Angeles, CA | 213-938-0287 |
| Urie, Walter Photography/1810 E Carnegie, Santa Ana, CA | 714-556-0334 |
| Vanderpoel, Fred/1547 Mission, San Francisco, CA | 415-621-4405 |
| Vano Photography/Pier 17 Embarcadero, San Francisco, CA | 415-421-8612 |
| Varie, Bill/2210 Wilshire Blvd, Santa Monica, CA | 213-395-9337 |
| Vaughan, Jim/3246 Ettie, Oakland, CA | 415-655-4538 |
| Vega, Raul/3511 W 6th Tower Suite, Los Angeles, CA | 213-387-2058 |
| Vendenberg, Greg/1901 E 47th Ave, Denver, CO | 303-295-2525 |
| Vendikos, Tasso/1901 E 47 Ave, Denver, CO | 303-295-2525 |
| Vereen, Jackson/301 Eighth St, San Francisco, CA | 415-552-7546 |
| Viggio Studio/2400 Central Ave, Boulder, CO | 303-444-3342 |
| Vignes, Michelle/654 28th St, San Francisco, CA | 415-550-8039 |
| Visioneering/2565 Third St, #339, , Sa | 415-282-6630 |
| Vollick, Tom/415 28th St, Hermosa Beach, CA | 213-374-2786 |
| Von Dem Bussche, Wolf/7144 Norfolk Rd, Berkeley, CA | 415-845-2448 |
| **W** Wade, Bill/5608 E 2nd St, Long Beach, CA | 213-439-6826 |
| Wahlstrom, Richard/650 Alabama St, San Francsico, CA | 415-550-1400 |
| Wallace, Marlene/7801 Beverly Blvd, Los Angeles, CA | 213-826-1027 |
| Wallick, Philip/PO Box 3096, Chico, CA | 916-893-8464 |
| Ward, David/4901 Morena Blvd #323, San Diego, CA | 619-295-7516 |
| Warren Aerial Photography/PO Box 4155, Pasadena, CA | 213-681-1006 |
| Warren E Williams & Assoc/PO Box 4155, Pasadena, CA | 213-681-1006 |
| Warren, Cameron A/Box 10588, Reno, NV | 702-323-7446 |
| Warren, William James/509 S Gramercy Pl, Los Angeles, CA | 213-383-0500 |
| Watamura, Ed Photography/130 McCormick Ave, Costa Mesa, CA | 714-540-3978 |
| Watanabe, David/13217 NE 97th Ave, Kirkland, WA | 206-823-0692 |
| Watson, Allen/635 State St, San Diego, CA | 714-239-5555 |
| Wayda, Steve/1201 E 2100 S, Salt Lake City, UT | 801-467-9752 |
| Waz, Tony/1115 S Trotwood Ave, San Pedro, CA | 213-548-3758 |
| Weir, Tom/PO Box 403, Inverness, CA | 415-669-1178 |
| Weiss & Mahoney Inc/PO Box 403, Inverness, CA | 415-669-1178 |
| Weissman, Jeff/3025 Jordan Rd, Oakland, CA | 415-482-3891 |
| Werner, Jeffrey/14002 Palawan Way, Marina Del Rey, CA | 213-821-2384 |
| **WERTS STUDIOS INC./732 N HIGHLAND,** | |
| **LOS ANGELES, CA (P 338,339)** | **213-464-2775** |
| West, Andrew/527 17th St, Santa Monica, CA | 213-394-7076 |
| Wexler, Glen/1041 N McCadden Pl, Los Angeles, CA | 213-465-0268 |
| Wheeler, Jeoffery Photography/1827 Pearl St, Boulder, CO | 303-449-2137 |
| Wheeler, Nik/7444 Woodrow Wilson Dr, Los Angeles, CA | 213-850-0234 |
| Whetstone, Wayne/117 E Second Ave, Vancouver, BC | 604-873-4914 |
| White, Charles William/11543 Hesby St, North Hollywood, CA | 213-985-3539 |
| Whitmore, Ken/PO Box 49373, Los Angeles, CA | 213-472-4337 |
| Whittaker, Steve/111 Glenn Way #8, Belmont, CA | 415-595-4242 |
| Wiener, Leigh/2600 Carman Crest Dr, Los Angeles, CA | 213-876-0990 |
| Wietstock, Wilfried/877 Valencia St, San Francisco, CA | 415-285-4221 |
| Wilcox, Jed/P.O. Box 4091, Palm Springs, CA | 213-467-6033 |
| Wilde, Edward/2865 W 7th St, Los Angeles, CA | 213-384-1016 |
| Wilder, Mani/3105 Nichols Canyon Rd, Los Angeles, CA | 213-874-2824 |
| Willett, Larry/2424 West 7th, Los Angeles, CA | 213-739-8425 |
| William Arbogast Studios/1915 University Ave, Palo Alto, CA | 415-323-1336 |
| Williams, David Jordan/645 S Dunsmuir #3, Los Angeles, CA | 213-936-3170 |
| Williams, Harold/705 Bayswater Ave, Burlingame, CA | 415-340-7017 |
| Williams, Sandra/PO Box 16130, San Diego, CA | 619-563-8313 |
| Williams, Steven Burr/8306 Wilshire Blvd #444, Beverly Hills, CA | 213-469-5749 |
| Wilson, Bruce/1022 1st Ave South, Seattle, WA | 206-621-9182 |
| Wilson, Burton/3110 Argonne Ct, Santa Barbara, CA | 805-687-4408 |
| Wilson, Douglas M/10133 NE 113th Pl, Kirkland, WA | 206-822-8604 |
| Wimpey, Christopher/627 Eighth Ave, San Diego, CA | 619-232-3222 |
| Windham, Dale/1249 First Ave S, Seattle, WA | 206-587-6522 |
| Wolf, Marvin J/1819 Alsuna Ln, Huntington Beach, CA | 714-536-0435 |
| Wolfe, Dan E/45 E Walnut, Pasadena, CA | 213-681-3130 |
| Wolman, Baron/P O Box 1000, Mill Valley, CA | 415-388-0181 |

# PHOTOGRAPHERS CONT'D.

Please send us your additions and updates.

| | |
|---|---|
| Wood, Harold/314 NW Glisan, Portland, OR | 503-248-0534 |
| **WOOD, JAMES/6315 SANTA MONICA BLVD, LOS ANGELES, CA (P 394)** | **213-461-3861** |
| Woody, Steve/1258 170th Ave NE, Bellevue, WA | 206-643-1638 |
| Woolf, Billy/1258 170th Ave NE, Bellevue, WA | 206-643-1638 |
| Wordal, Eric Photography/P O Box 595, Helena, MT | 406-443-1530 |
| **WORTHAM, ROBERT/964 N VERMONT AVE, LOS ANGELES, CA (P 395)** | **213-666-8899** |
| Wyatt, Tom Photography/215 Second St, San Francisco, CA | 415-543-2813 |

## YZ

| | |
|---|---|
| Yamaguchi, Kenneth/5636 Melrose Ave, Los Angeles, CA | 213-464-6202 |
| **YOUNG, EDWARD/9 DECATUR ST, SAN FRANCISCO, CA (P 343)** | **415-864-2448** |
| Young, Ellan/9 Deactur St, San Francisco, CA | 415-864-2448 |
| Youngblood, Lee/2538 Alvin St, Mountain View, CA | 415-329-1085 |
| Zajack, Greg/441 E Columbine, Santa Ana, CA | 714-545-4022 |
| **ZAK, ED/80 TEHAMA ST, SAN FRANCISCO, CA (P 330,331)** | **415-781-1611** |
| Zephyr Picture Agency/725 Neptune Ave, Leucadia, CA | 619-436-7614 |
| Zimberoff, Tom/PO Box 5212, Beverly Hills, CA | 213-271-5900 |
| Zimmerman, Dick/8743 W Washington Blvd, Los Angeles, CA | 213-204-2911 |
| Zimmerman, John/9135 Hazen Dr, Beverly Hills, CA | 213-273-2642 |
| Zippel, Arthur/2100 E Mcfadden #D, Santa Ana, CA | 714-835-8400 |
| Zlozower, Neil/6341 Yucca, Los Angeles, CA | 213-935-0606 |
| Zurek, Nikolay/276 Shipley St, San Francisco, CA | 415-777-9210 |
| Zwart, Jeffrey R/3031 Croyden Bay, Costa Mesa, CA | 619-557-8166 |

# STOCK PHOTOGRAPHY

## NEW YORK CITY

| | |
|---|---|
| Alpha Photo Assoc/251 Park Ave S | 212-777-4216 |
| Animals Animals/203 W 81st St | 212-580-9595 |
| **ARNOLD, PETER/1466 BROADWAY (P 398,399)** | **212-840-6928** |
| Bernsens Intern Press Srvc Ltd/15 E 40th St | 212-685-0464 |
| Black Star Publishing Co/450 Park Ave S | 212-679-3288 |
| Blackstone-Shelburne NY Inc/42 W 48th St | 212-736-9100 |
| Blue Chip Stock Photography/500 Park Ave | 212-750-1386 |
| Camera 5/6 W 20th St | 212-989-2004 |
| Camp, Woodfin & Assoc/415 Madison Ave | 212-750-1020 |
| Coleman, Bruce Inc/381 Fifth Ave | 212-683-5227 |
| College Newsphoto Alliance/342 Madison Ave | 212-697-1136 |
| Consolidated Poster Service/341 W 44th St | 212-581-3105 |
| Culver Pictures Inc/660 First Ave | 212-684-5054 |
| Design Photographers Intl Inc/521 Madison Ave | 212-752-3930 |
| DeWys, Leo/200 Madison Ave, #2225 | 212-986-3190 |
| Editorial Photocolor Archives/342 Madison Ave | 212-697-1136 |
| European Art Color Slides/120 W 70th St | 212-877-9654 |
| Ewing Galloway/1466 Broadway | 212-719-4720 |
| Fairchild Publications, Inc/7 E 12th St | 212-741-4000 |
| Flying Camera, Inc/140 Pearl St | 212-619-0808 |
| Focus on Sports/222 E 46th St | 212-661-6860 |
| Ford Foundation Photo Library/320 E 43rd St | 212-573-5000 |
| Four by Five Inc/485 Madison Ave | 212-355-2323 |
| Gamma-Liaison Photo Agency/150 E 58th St | 212-888-7272 |
| Globe Photos Inc/404 Park Ave S | 212-689-1340 |
| **GORDON, JOEL/5 E 16TH ST (P 95)** | **212-989-9207** |
| Group 4/225 E 67th St | 212-249-4446 |
| Hamilton, Alexander/946 Atlantic Ave | 212-748-8329 |
| Hamilton, Bryan J/946 Atlantic Ave | 212-622-7001 |
| Harold M Lambert Studios/15 W 38th St | 212-921-2850 |
| Hayes, Kerry Photography/156 Fifth Ave | 212-242-2012 |
| Heyman, Ken/3 E 76th St | 212-879-8377 |
| Heyman, Ken/3 E 76th St | 212-879-8377 |
| Image Bank/633 Third Ave | 212-953-0303 |
| Index/Stock Photography/126 Fifth Ave | 212-929-4644 |
| International Stock Photos/113 E 31st St #1A | 212-696-4666 |
| Keystone Press Agency Inc/202 E 42nd St | 212-924-8123 |
| Kramer, Joan & Assoc/720 Fifth Ave | 212-224-1758 |
| Lewis, Frederic/15 W 38th St | 212-921-2850 |
| Life Picture Service/Rm 25-58, Time & Life Bldg, Ro | 212-841-4800 |
| Magnum Photos Inc/251 Park Ave S | 212-475-7600 |
| **MAISEL, JAY/190 BOWERY (P 16,17)** | **212-431-5013** |
| Medichrome/279 E 44th St | 212-679-8480 |
| Memory Shop Inc/109 E 12th St | 212-473-2404 |
| Mercier, Louis/342 Madison Ave | 212-972-1701 |
| Monkmeyer Press Photo Agency/15 E 48th St | 212-755-1715 |
| Movie Star News/212 E 14th St | 212-982-8364 |
| Museum of the City of New York/Fifth Ave & 103rd St | 212-534-1672 |
| Penguin Photo/663 Fifth Ave | 212-758-7328 |
| Peter Arnold Inc/1466 Broadway | 212-840-6928 |
| Photo Researchers Inc/60 E 56th St | 212-758-3420 |
| Photo Trends/1328 Broadway | 212-279-2130 |
| Photo World Inc/251 Park Ave S | 212-777-4214 |
| **PHOTOFILE INTERNATIONAL LTD/32 E 31ST ST (P 44,45)** | **212-989-0500** |
| Phototake/4523 Broadway #76 | 212-942-8185 |
| Photounique/381 Fifth Ave | 212-244-5511 |
| Plessner Int'l/95 Madison Ave | 212-686-2444 |
| Reese, Kay & Assoc/156 Fifth Ave #1106 | 212-924-5151 |
| SO Studio Inc/34 E 23rd St | 212-475-0090 |
| Scala Fine Arts Publishers/342 Madison Ave | 212-354-9646 |
| Shostal Assoc/60 E 42nd St | 212-687-0696 |
| Spano/Roccanova/16 W 46th St | 212-840-7450 |
| **SPORTS ILLUSTRATED PICTURES/TIME & LIFE BLDG (P 404)** | **212-841-2803** |
| Stock Photos Unlimited Inc/275 7th Ave | 212-421-8980 |
| Stock Shop/279 E 44th St | 212-679-8480 |
| Stockmarket, The/1181 Broadway | 212-684-7878 |
| Tamin Stock Photos/595 Madison Ave #1537 | 212-751-6516 |
| Taurus Photos/118 E 28th St | 212-683-4025 |
| United Press Int'l News Pictures/220 E 42nd St | 212-850-8639 |
| Wheeler Pictures/50 W 29th St | 212-696-9832 |
| Wide World Photos Inc/50 Rockefeller Plaza | 212-621-1930 |
| **THE WILCOX COLLECTION/CO DPI,521 MADISON (P 42,43)** | **212-752-3930** |

## NORTHEAST

| | |
|---|---|
| Blizzard, William C/PO Box 1696, Beckley, WV | 304-252-4652 |
| Boston Stock Photographs/36 Gloucester St, Boston, MA | 617-266-2573 |
| Camerique Stock Photography/PO Box 175, Bluebell (Philadelphia), PA | 215-272-7649 |
| Chandoha, Walter/Rd 1 Box 287, Annandale, NJ | 201-782-3666 |
| Esto Photographics, Inc/222 Valley Pl, Mamaroneck, NY | 914-698-4060 |
| Global Focus/9 Poplar Road, Cambridge, MA | 617-491-7124 |
| Globe Photos/9 Poplar Road, Cambridge, MA | 617-491-7124 |
| **HEILMAN, GRANT/BOX 317, LITITZ, PA (P 400)** | **717-626-0296** |
| Kramer, Erwin/5 N Clover Dr, Great Neck, NY | 516-466-5582 |
| Light Wave/1430 Massachusetts Ave, Cambridge, MA | 617-566-0364 |
| Lightfoot, Robert/1430 Massachusetts Ave, Cambridge, MA | 617-566-0364 |
| Lumiere/512 Adams St, Centerport, NY | 516-271-6133 |
| Pete Silver & Assoc/Box 86, Southport, CT | 203-254-1400 |
| Philiba, Alan A/3408 Bertha Dr, Baldwin, NY | 516-623-7841 |
| The Picture Cube/89 State St, Boston, MA | 617-367-1532 |
| The Picture Place/89 State St, Boston, MA | |
| Picture Research/6307 Bannockburn Dr, Bethesda, MD | 301-229-6722 |
| **RAINBOW/BOX 573, HOUSATONIC, MA (P 223)** | **413-274-6211** |
| Roberts, H. Armstrong/4203 Locust St, Philadelphia, PA | 215-386-6300 |
| Siquis Stock Photography/PO Box 215, Stevenson, MD | 301-583-9177 |
| Siracusa, Catherine/PO Box 215, Stevenson, MD | |
| Unicorn/Photographic Images Div/90 Park Ave, Verona, NJ | 201-239-7088 |
| Uniphoto Picture Agency/1071 Wisonsin Ave, Washington, DC | 202-333-0500 |
| Wide World Photos Inc/260 Summer, Boston, MA | 617-337-8104 |
| **WOODFIN CAMP INC./925 1/2 F ST NW, WASHINGTON, DC (P 240)** | **202-638-5750** |

## SOUTHEAST

| | |
|---|---|
| **LONG, JAMES L/2631 E OAKLAND PARK BLVD, FT LAUDERDALE, FL (P 402)** | **305-563-8033** |
| McCarthy, Tom/8960 SW 114th St, Miami, FL | 305-233-1703 |
| The Phelps Agency/32 Peachtree St NW, Atlanta, GA | 404-524-1234 |
| Photo Options/3313 CastleCrest Dr, Birmingham, AL | 205-979-8412 |
| Photri-Photo Research Intl./505 W Windsor/PO Box 971, Alexandria, VA | 703-836-4439 |
| **SHERMAN, RON/PO BOX 28656, ATLANTA, GA (P 271)** | **404-993-7197** |
| **SOUTHERN STOCK PHOTO/6289 W SUNRISE BLVD #203, SUNRISE, FL (P 403)** | **305-791-2772** |

## MIDWEST

| | |
|---|---|
| A- Stock Photo Finder & Photographers/1030 N State St, Chicago, IL | 312-645-0611 |
| A-Stock Photo Finder/1030 North State St, Chicago, Il | 312-645-0611 |
| Artstreet/25 E Delaware, Chicago, IL | 312-664-3049 |
| Atoz Images/333 E Ontario #601B, Chicago, IL | 312-664-8400 |
| Brandt & Assoc/Route 2 Box 148, Barrington Hills, IL | 312-428-6363 |
| Cameramann International/PO Box 413, Evanston, IL | 312-777-5657 |
| Charlton Photos/8330 N Teutonia Ave, Milwaukee, WI | 414-354-6170 |
| Collectors Series/161 W Harrison, Chicago, IL | 312-427-5311 |
| Design Marks Corp/1462 W Irving Park, Chicago, IL | 312-327-3669 |
| Gartman, Marilyn/5549 N Clark St, Chicago, IL | 312-561-5504 |
| Gress-Rupert/251 E Grand, Chicago, IL | 312-642-1188 |
| Hedrich-Blessing/11 W Illinois St, Chicago, IL | 312-321-1151 |
| Ibid Inc/125 W Hubbard, Chicago, IL | 312-644-0515 |
| Image Bank/510 Dearborn, Chicago, IL | 312-329-1817 |
| Johnson, Chaz T/225 N Park Ave Box 1813, Fond du Lac, WI | 414-923-4494 |
| Milt & Joan Mann Photojournalism/PO Box 413, Evanston, IL | 312-777-5657 |
| Photosearch International/Pine Lake Farm, Osceola, WI | 715-248-3800 |
| TRW/23555 Euclid Ave, Cleveland, OH | 216-383-2121 |
| Webb Photos/1999 Shepherd Rd, St Paul, MN | 612-690-7200 |
| Zehrt, Jack/4211 Flora Pl, St Louis, MO | 314-458-3600 |

## SOUTHWEST

| | |
|---|---|
| Arizona Photographic Assoc Inc/2344 West Holly, Phoenix, AZ | 602-258-6551 |

# STOCK PHOTOGRAPHY CONT'D.

Please send us your additions and updates.

| | |
|---|---|
| Campbell, Tom Photo/1815 Indian Schod Rd, Phoenix, AZ | 602-264-1151 |
| Ives, Tom/2250 El Moraga, Tuscon, AZ | 602-743-0750 |
| McLaughlin, Herb & Dorothy/2344 W Holly, Phoenix, AZ | 602-258-6551 |
| Photoworks/Uniphoto International/215 Asbury, Houston, TX | 713-864-3638 |
| Running Productions/PO Box 1237, Flagstaff, AZ | 602-774-2923 |
| Victures/2039 Farrington, Dallas, TX | 214-748-4221 |

## WEST

| | |
|---|---|
| After Image/6855 Santa Monica Blvd, Los Angeles, CA | 213-467-6033 |
| Alaskaphoto/1530 Westlake Ave N, Seattle, WA | 206-282-8116 |
| American Stock Photos/6842 Sunset Blvd, Los Angeles, CA | 213-469-3908 |
| Aperture Photo Bank/1530 Westlake Ave N, Seattle, WA | 206-282-8116 |
| Beebe, Morton & Assoc/409 Bryant St, San Francisco, CA | 415-362-3530 |
| Burkhart Photography, Howard Burkhart/231 Olive #10, Inglewood, CA | 212-671-2283 |
| Camerique Stock Photography/6842 Sunset Blvd, Los Angeles, CA | 213-469-3908 |
| Cornwell, David/1311 Kalakava Ave, Honolulu, HA | 808-949-7000 |
| DMR/2800 DeLa Cruz Blvd, Santa Clara, CA | 408-496-5012 |
| Daly, Michael Kevin/Box 5002, Eugene, OR | 503-683-1496 |
| FirstVision/4020 Birch St #201, Newport Beach, CA | 714-553-9333 |
| Focus West/5158 Edgeware Road, San Diego, CA | 619-280-3595 |
| Focus on Sports/5158 Edgeware Rd, San Diego, CA | 619-280-3595 |
| Grubb, TD/11102 Blix St, N Hollywood, CA | 213-760-1236 |
| Image Bank West/151 Union St, San Francisco, CA | 415-398-2242 |
| Impact Photos/8566 W Pico Blvds, Los Angeles, CA | 213-852-0481 |
| Peebles, Douglas Photography/1100 Alakea St, #435, Honolulu, HI | 808-533-6686 |
| Photofile/Pier 17 Embarcadero, San Francisco, CA | 415-397-3040 |
| Photographsanstuff/730 Clemintina, San Francisco, CA | 415-861-1062 |
| Photophile/2311 Kettner Blvd, San Diego, CA | 619-234-4431 |
| Prince, Norman/3340-B 22nd St, San Francisco, CA | 415-647-0278 |
| Ross, Bill/22920 Lanark St, Canoga Park, CA | 213-703-7605 |
| Shooting Star Inc/1909 N Curson Pl, Hollywood, CA | 213-876-8208 |
| **STOCK IMAGERY/711 KALAMATH ST, DENVER, CO (P 405)** | **303-592-1091** |
| **STOCK MARKET/740 S EMERSON, DENVER, CO (P 406)** | **303-698-1734** |
| Stock Photography Outdoor Studio/740 S. Emerson, Denver, CO | 303-698-1734 |
| Stock, Richard Photography/1767 N Orchid Ave, #312, Los Angeles, CA | 213-876-7436 |
| TRW/9841 Airport Blvd, #1414, Los Angeles, CA | 213-536-4880 |
| Visual Media Inc/2661 Vassar St, Reno, NV | 702-322-8868 |
| West Light/1526 Pontius Ave, Los Angeles, CA | 213-473-3736 |
| West Stock/157 Yesler Way, #600, Seattle, WA | 206-621-1611 |
| Westside Productions Stock/504 Central, Alameda, CA | 415-521-4458 |

# GRAPHIC DESIGNERS

## NEW YORK CITY

### A
| | |
|---|---|
| AKM Associates | 212-687-7636 |
| Abramson, Michael R Studio | 212-683-1271 |
| Adams, Gaylord Design | 212-684-4625 |
| Album Graphics Inc | 212-489-0793 |
| Allied Graphic Arts | 212-730-1414 |
| American Express Publishing Co | 212-399-2500 |
| Anagraphics Inc | 212-279-2370 |
| Ancona Design Atelier | 212-947-8287 |
| Anspach Grossman Portugal | 212-692-9000 |
| Antler & Baldwin Graphics | 212-751-2031 |
| Antupit and Others Inc | 212-686-2552 |
| Appelbaum & Curtis | 212-752-0679 |
| Apple Design | 212-752-1710 |
| Appletree Ad Agencey | 212-697-8746 |
| Apteryx Ltd | 212-838-9483 |
| Art Department | 212-391-1826 |
| The Art Farm Inc | 212-688-4555 |
| Art Plus Studio | 212-564-8258 |
| Associated Industrial Design Inc | 212-765-7693 |

### B
| | |
|---|---|
| BN Associates | 212-684-7210 |
| Bain, S Milo | 212-947-1427 |
| Balasas, Cora | 212-633-7753 |
| Balin & Veres Inc | 212-684-7450 |
| Bantam Books Inc | 212-765-6500 |
| Barmache, Leon Design Assoc Inc | 212-752-6780 |
| Barnett Design Group | 212-677-8830 |
| Barry Douglas Designs Ltd | 212-734-4137 |
| Barry, Jim | 212-873-6787 |
| Beau Gardner Assoc. | 212-832-2426 |
| Becker, Richard | 212-475-1756 |
| Bell, James Graphic Design Inc | 212-929-8855 |
| Berger, Barry David | 212-734-4137 |
| Besalel, Ely | 212-759-7820 |
| Bessen & Tully, Inc | 212-838-6406 |
| Betty Binns Graphic Design | 212-679-9200 |
| Biondo, Charles Design Assoc | 212-867-0760 |
| Birch, Colin Assoc Inc | 212-223-0499 |
| Bloch, Graulich & Whelan, Inc | 212-687-8375 |
| Boker Group | 212-686-1132 |
| Bonnell Design Associates Inc | 212-921-5390 |
| Bordnick & Assoc | 212-777-1860 |
| Botero, Samuel Assoc | 212-935-5155 |
| Bradford, Peter | 212-982-2090 |
| Branin, Max | 212-254-9608 |
| Braswell, Lynn | 212-222-8761 |
| Brier, David Design Works | 212-362-7786 |
| Brochure People | 212-580-9177 |
| Brodsky Graphics | 212-684-2600 |
| Brown, Alastair Assoc | 212-221-3166 |
| Buckley Designs Inc. | 212-861-0626 |
| Burdick, Joshua Assoc Inc | 212-696-4440 |
| Burns, Tom Assoc Inc | 212-888-1855 |
| By Design | 212-684-0388 |
| The Byrne Group | 212-354-3996 |

### C
| | |
|---|---|
| C L Mauro Assoc Inc | 212-391-1990 |
| CCI Art Inc | 212-687-1552 |
| Cain, David | 212-691-5783 |
| Cannan, Bill & Co Inc | 212-580-1700 |
| Caravello Studios | 212-661-5540 |
| Carnase, Inc | 212-679-9880 |
| Cetta, Al | 212-989-9696 |
| Chajet Design Group Inc | 212-684-3669 |
| Chang, Ivan | 212-777-6102 |
| Charles W North Studio | 212-686-5740 |
| Charles, Irene Assoc | 212-765-8000 |
| Chermayeff & Geismar Assoc. | 212-759-9433 |
| Clarke, John | 212-730-7026 |
| Composto, Mario Assoc | 212-922-1058 |
| Condon, J & M Assoc | 212-242-7811 |
| Corchia Woliner | 212-977-9778 |
| Corpographics, Inc. | 212-483-9065 |
| Corporate Annual Reports Inc. | 212-889-2450 |
| Corporate Graphics Inc | 212-599-1820 |
| Corporate Images | 212-686-5221 |
| Cosgrove Assoc Inc | 212-889-7202 |
| Cotler, Sheldon Inc | 212-719-9590 |
| Cousins, Morison S & Assoc | 212-751-3390 |
| Crane, Susan Inc | 212-260-0580 |
| Csoka/Benato/Fleurant Inc | 212-686-6741 |
| Cuevas, Robert | 212-661-7149 |
| Curtis Design Inc. | 212-685-0670 |

### D
| | |
|---|---|
| DMCD | 212-682-9044 |
| Daniel Design | 212-889-0071 |
| Danne & Blackburn Inc. | 212-371-3250 |
| Davis-Delaney-Arrow Inc | 212-686-2500 |
| DeCamps, Craig | 212-564-2691 |
| DeHarak, Rudolph | 212-929-5445 |
| Delphan Company | 212-371-6700 |
| Design Alliance | 212-689-3503 |
| Design Derivatives Inc | 212-751-7650 |
| Design Group Inc | 212-475-2822 |
| Design Influence Inc | 212-840-2155 |
| The Design Organization | 212-661-1070 |
| Designers 3 Inc. | 212-986-5454 |
| Designframe | 212-924-2426 |
| The Designing Women | 212-864-0909 |
| Diamond Art Studio Ltd. | 212-355-5444 |
| Dick Lopez Inc | 212-599-2327 |
| DiComo, Charles & Assoc | 212-689-8670 |
| DiFranza-Williamson Inc | 212-832-2343 |
| Displaycraft | 212-784-8186 |
| Domino, Bob | 212-935-0139 |
| Donovan & Green Inc | 212-755-0477 |
| **DORET, MICHAEL (P 106)** | **212-889-0490** |
| Draper Shreeve Design | 212-675-7534 |
| Dreyfuss, Henry Assoc | 212-957-8600 |
| Dubins, Milt Designer Inc | 212-691-0232 |
| Dubrow, Oscar Assoc | 212-688-0698 |
| Duffy, William R | 212-682-6755 |
| Dwyer, Tom | 212-986-7108 |

### E
| | |
|---|---|
| E M Mitchell Inc | 212-986-5595 |
| Edelman Studios Inc | 212-255-7250 |
| Edge, Dennis Design | 212-679-0927 |
| Edward C Kozlowski Design Inc | 212-988-9761 |
| Eichinger, Inc | 212-421-0544 |
| Eisenman and Enock | 212-431-1000 |
| Ellies, Dave Industrial Design Inc | 212-679-9305 |
| Emerson, Wajdowicz | 212-807-8144 |
| Environetics Inc | 212-759-3830 |
| Environment Planning Inc | 212-661-3744 |
| Erikson Assoc. | 212-688-0048 |
| Eskil Ohlsson Assoc Inc | 212-758-4412 |
| Etheridge, Palombo, Sedewitz | 212-944-2530 |
| Eucalyptus Tree Studio | 212-226-0331 |

### F
| | |
|---|---|
| FDC Planning & Design Corp | 212-355-7200 |
| Failing, Kendrick G Design | 212-677-5764 |
| Falkins, Richard Design | 212-840-3045 |
| Farmlett Barsanti Inc | 212-691-9398 |
| Farrell, Bill | 212-562-8931 |
| Feucht, Fred Design Group Inc | 212-682-0040 |
| Filicori, Mauro Visual Communications | 212-677-0065 |
| Fineberg Associates | 212-734-1220 |
| Florville, Patrick Design Research | 212-271-3723 |
| Flying Eye Graphics | 212-725-0658 |
| Foyster, Gerry | 212-674-0259 |
| Freelancenter Inc | 212-683-6969 |

# GRAPHIC DESIGNERS CONT'D.

Please send us your additions and updates.

| | |
|---|---|
| Freeman, Irving | 212-674-6705 |
| Friday Saturday Sunday Inc | 212-260-8479 |
| Friedlander, Ira | 212-580-9800 |
| Froma/Graphics | 212-391-8399 |
| Fulgoni, Louis | 212-243-2959 |
| Fulton & Partners | 212-695-1625 |

## G
| | |
|---|---|
| GL & C Advertising Design Inc. | 212-683-5811 |
| **GALE, CYNTHIA (P 113)** | **212-860-5429** |
| Gale, Robert A Inc | 212-535-4791 |
| Gardner, Beau Assoc | 212-832-2426 |
| Gatter Inc | 212-687-4821 |
| Geismar, Tom | 212-759-9433 |
| Gentile Studio | 212-986-7743 |
| George, Hershell | 212-925-2505 |
| Gerstman & Meyers Inc. | 212-586-2535 |
| Gianninoto Assoc, Inc. | 212-759-5757 |
| Giovanni Design Assoc. | 212-725-8536 |
| Gips & Balkind & Assoc | 212-421-5940 |
| Gladstein, Renee | 212-873-0257 |
| Gladych, Marianne | 212-925-9712 |
| Glaser, Milton | 212-889-3161 |
| Glusker Group | 212-757-4438 |
| Goetz Graphics | 212-679-4250 |
| Goldman, Neal Assoc | 212-687-5058 |
| **GORDON, JOEL (P 95)** | **212-989-9207** |
| Gorman, W Chris Assoc | 212-696-9377 |
| The Graphic Expression Inc. | 212-759-7788 |
| Graphic Workshop | 212-759-4524 |
| Graphics 60 Inc. | 212-687-1292 |
| Graphics Institute | 212-887-8670 |
| Graphics by Nostradamus | 212-581-1362 |
| Graphics for Industry | 212-889-6202 |
| Graphics to Go | 212-889-9337 |
| Gray, George | 212-873-3607 |
| Gregory & Clyburne | 212-686-3338 |
| Griffler Designs | 212-794-2625 |
| Grossberg, Manuel | 212-532-3335 |
| Grunfeld Graphics, Ltd | 212-431-8700 |
| Gucciardo & Shapokas | 212-683-9378 |
| Guy Marino Graphic Design | 212-935-1141 |

## H
| | |
|---|---|
| H.G. Assoc, Inc. | 212-221-3070 |
| H.L. Chu & Company Ltd. | 212-889-4818 |
| HBO Studio Productions Inc | 212-889-4818 |
| Haas, Arie | 212-382-1677 |
| Haines, John Design | 212-254-2326 |
| Halversen, Everett | 212-438-4200 |
| Hamid, Helen | 212-752-2546 |
| Handler Group Inc | 212-391-0951 |
| Harris-Gorbaty Assoc Inc | 212-689-4295 |
| Harry Moshier & Assoc | 212-873-6130 |
| Harvey Offenhartz Inc | 212-421-2242 |
| Haydee Design Studio | 212-242-3110 |
| Hecker, Mark Studio | 212-620-9050 |
| Heiney, John & Assoc | 212-686-1121 |
| Helio Design | 212-532-3340 |
| Heston, Charles Assoc | 212-889-6400 |
| Hnath, John | 212-684-0388 |
| Holzsager, Mel Assoc Inc | 212-741-7373 |
| Holzsager, Mel Assoc Inc | 212-741-7373 |
| Hooper, Ray Design | 212-924-5480 |
| Hopkins, Will | 212-580-9800 |
| Horvath & Assoc Studios Ltd | 212-741-0300 |
| Howard Mont Assoc Inc | 212-683-4360 |
| Hub Graphics | 212-421-5807 |
| Huerta, Gerard | 212-753-2895 |
| Human Factors/Industrial Design Inc | 212-730-8010 |

## I
| | |
|---|---|
| ISD Inc. | 212-751-0800 |
| Image Communications Inc | 212-838-0713 |
| Infield & D'Astolfo | 212-924-9206 |
| Inner Thoughts | 212-674-1277 |
| Intersight Design Inc | 212-696-0700 |
| Irving D Miller Inc. | 212-755-4040 |
| Isip Rey Design Assoc. | 212-475-2822 |

## J
| | |
|---|---|
| J P Maggio Design Assoc Inc | 212-725-9660 |
| Jaffe Communications, Inc | 212-697-4310 |
| Jarrin Design Inc | 212-879-3767 |
| Jass, Milton Assoc | 212-874-0418 |
| Johnson, Dwight | 212-834-8529 |
| Johnston, Shaun & Susan | 212-663-4686 |
| Jonson Pedersen Hinrichs & Shakery | 212-889-9611 |

## K
| | |
|---|---|
| KLN Publishing Services Inc | 212-686-8200 |
| Kacik Design | 212-753-0031 |
| Kaeser & Wilson Design | 212-563-2400 |
| Kahn, Al Group | 212-580-3517 |
| Kahn, Al Group | 212-580-3517 |
| Kallir Phillips Ross Inc. | 212-878-3700 |
| Katz, Marjorie L Design | 212-751-3028 |
| Kaye Graphics | 212-889-8240 |
| Keithley & Assoc | 212-679-5317 |
| Kleb Associates | 212-246-2847 |
| Ko Noda and Assoc International | 212-759-4044 |
| Kollman, Joady | 212-586-3416 |
| Koons, Irv Assoc | 212-752-4130 |
| Koons, Irv Assoc | 212-752-4130 |
| Kozlowski, Edward C Design Inc | 212-988-9761 |

## L
| | |
|---|---|
| LCL Design Assoc Inc | 212-758-2604 |
| The Lamplight Group | 212-682-6270 |
| Landi-Handler Design Inc | 212-661-3630 |
| Lassen, Robert | 212-929-0017 |
| Lee & Young Communications | 212-689-4000 |
| Lefkowith Inc. | 212-758-8550 |
| Legaspi Designs Inc | 212-255-0015 |
| Leo Art Studio | 212-736-8785 |
| Lesley-Hille Inc | 212-421-2421 |
| Lester & Butler | 212-889-0578 |
| Levine, Gerald | 212-751-3645 |
| Levine, William V & Assoc | 212-683-7177 |
| Lichtenberg, Al Graphic Art | 212-679-5350 |
| **LIEBERMAN, RON (P 140)** | **212-947-0653** |
| Liebert Studios Inc | 212-686-4520 |
| Lika Association | 212-490-3660 |
| Lind Brothers Inc. | 212-924-9280 |
| Lippincott & Margulies Inc | 212-832-3000 |
| Lopez, Dick Inc | 212-599-2327 |
| Loscalzo/Michaelson & Assoc | 516-482-7677 |
| Loukin, Serge Inc | 212-685-6473 |
| Lowel-Light | 212-947-0950 |
| Lubliner/Saltz | 212-679-9810 |
| Luckett Slover & Partners | 212-620-9770 |
| Luth & Katz Inc | 212-644-5777 |

## M
| | |
|---|---|
| M & Co A Design Group Inc | 212-582-7050 |
| Maddalone, John | 212-807-6087 |
| Maggio, Ben Assoc Inc | 212-697-8600 |
| Maggio, Ben Assoc Inc | 212-697-8600 |
| Maggio, J P Design Assoc Inc | 212-725-9660 |
| Maleter, Mari | 212-726-7124 |
| Marchese, Frank | 212-988-6267 |
| Marciuliano Inc. | 212-697-0740 |
| Marino, Guy Graphic Design | 212-935-1141 |
| Mauro, Frank Assoc | 212-391-1990 |
| Mayo-Infurna Design | 212-757-3136 |
| McDonald, B & Assoc | 212-869-9717 |
| McFarlane, John | 212-935-4676 |
| McGhie Assoc. Inc. | 212-661-2990 |
| McGovern & Pivoda | 212-840-2912 |
| Media Design Group | 212-758-1116 |
| Meier Adv | 212-355-6460 |

# GRAPHIC DESIGNERS CONT'D.

Please send us your additions and updates.

| | |
|---|---|
| Mentkin, Robert | 212-534-5101 |
| Merrill, Abby Studio Inc | 212-753-7565 |
| Messling, Jack A | 212-724-6445 |
| The Midnight Oil | 212-582-9071 |
| Millenium Design | 212-986-4540 |
| The Miller Organization Inc | 212-685-7700 |
| Miller, David | 212-274-4335 |
| Milton Kass Assoc Inc | 212-874-0418 |
| Mirenburg, Barry | 212-885-0835 |
| Mitchell, E M Inc | 212-986-5595 |
| Mizerek Design | 212-986-5702 |
| Modular Marketing Inc. | 212-581-4690 |
| Mont, Howard Assoc Inc | 212-683-4360 |
| Montoya, Juan Design Corp | 212-242-3622 |
| Morning, John Design | 212-689-0088 |
| Morris, Dean | 212-533-5039 |
| **MOSELEY, RICHIE (P 142)** | **212-499-7045** |
| Moshier, Harry & Assoc | 212-873-6130 |
| Moskof & Assoc. | 212-765-4810 |
| Mossberg, Stuart Design Assoc | 212-873-6130 |
| Muir, Cornelius, Moore | 212-687-4055 |
| Murro, A & Assoc Inc | 212-691-4220 |
| Murtha Desola Finsilver Fiore | 212-832-4770 |

## N

| | |
|---|---|
| N B Assoc Inc | 212-684-8074 |
| National Imagemakers Inc | 212-563-5000 |
| National Photo Service | 212-563-5000 |
| Neal Goldman Assoc | 212-687-5058 |
| Nelson, George & Assoc | 212-777-4300 |
| Nelson, George & Co | 212-777-4300 |
| Nemser & Howard, Inc | 212-832-9595 |
| New American Graphics | 212-661-6820 |
| Newman, Harvey Assoc | 212-391-8060 |
| Newport, R L & Co | 212-935-3920 |
| Newport, R L & Co | 212-935-3920 |
| Nightingale Gordon | 212-685-9263 |
| Nobart-New York | 212-475-5522 |
| Noneman & Noneman Design | 212-473-4090 |
| Norman Gorbaty Design | 212-684-1665 |
| North, Charles W Studio | 212-686-5740 |
| Notovitz & Perrault Design Inc | 212-686-3300 |

## O

| | |
|---|---|
| Offenhartz, Harvey Inc | 212-421-2242 |
| Ohlsson, Eskil Assoc Inc | 212-4412 |
| On Target | 212-840-0766 |
| Ong & Assoc | 212-355-4343 |
| O'Reilly, Robert Graphic Studio | 212-832-8992 |
| Orlov, Christian | 212-873-2381 |
| Oz Communications Inc | 212-686-8200 |

## PQ

| | |
|---|---|
| Page, Arbitrio, Resen Ltd. | 212-421-8190 |
| Palladino, Tony | 212-751-0068 |
| Paragraphic Inc | 212-421-3970 |
| Parshall, C A Inc | 212-685-6370 |
| Parsons School of Design | 212-741-8900 |
| Patel, Harish Design Assoc | 212-686-7425 |
| Pellegrini & Assoc | 212-686-4481 |
| Pellegrini & Assoc | 212-686-4481 |
| Pellegrini & Assoc | 212-686-4481 |
| Pencils Portfolio Inc | 212-683-3732 |
| Penpoint Studio Inc. | 212-243-5435 |
| Penraat Jaap Assoc | 212-873-4541 |
| Performing Dogs | 212-260-1880 |
| Perlman, Richard Design | 212-599-2380 |
| Peters, Stan Assoc Inc | 212-684-0315 |
| Peterson & Blyth Assoc Inc | 212-421-1769 |
| Pettis, Valerie | 212-683-7382 |
| Pierre Dinand Inc | 212-751-3086 |
| Planning & Design Corp | 212-355-7200 |
| Plumb Design Group Inc | 212-673-3490 |
| Podob, Al | 212-486-0024 |
| Prendergast, J W & Assoc Inc | 212-972-9000 |
| Primary Design Group | 212-977-5700 |
| Profile Press Inc | 212-675-4188 |
| Progressive Designers | 212-532-3693 |
| Projection Systems International | 212-682-0995 |
| Push Pin Lubalin Pecolick | 212-674-8080 |
| Quon, Mike Graphic Design | 212-226-6024 |

## R

| | |
|---|---|
| RC Graphics | 212-755-1383 |
| RD Graphics | 212-682-6734 |
| Rafkin Rubin Inc | 212-869-2540 |
| Rapecis Assoc. Inc. | 212-697-1760 |
| Ratzkin, Lawrence | 212-279-1314 |
| Ray Hooper Design | 212-924-5480 |
| Regn-Califano Inc | 212-239-0380 |
| Richard Rogers Inc. | 212-685-3666 |
| Rosebud Studio | 212-752-1144 |
| Rosenthal, Herb & Assoc Inc | 212-685-1814 |
| Ross/Pento Inc. | 212-757-5604 |
| Royce Graphics | 212-239-1990 |
| Russell, Anthony Inc | 2120255-0650 |

## S

| | |
|---|---|
| SCR Design Organization | 212-752-8496 |
| Saiki Design | 212-679-3523 |
| Saks, Arnold | 212-861-4300 |
| Salisbury & Salisbury Inc. | 212-575-0770 |
| Salpeter, Paganucci, Inc | 212-683-3310 |
| The Mike Saltzman Group, Inc | 212-929-4655 |
| Sandgren Associates Inc | 212-687-5060 |
| Sant'Andrea, Jim | 212-974-5400 |
| Saunier, Fredric | 212-307-5244 |
| Saville Design | 212-759-7002 |
| Saxton Communications Group | 212-953-1300 |
| Say It In Neon | 212-691-7977 |
| Schaefer-Cassety Inc | 212-840-0175 |
| SchaefferBoehm, Ltd | 212-947-4345 |
| Schechter Group Inc. | 212-752-4400 |
| Schecterson, Jack Assoc Inc | 212-889-3950 |
| Schumach, Michael P | 212-445-1587 |
| Schwartz, Robert & Assoc | 212-689-6482 |
| Scott, Louis Assoc | 212-674-0215 |
| Serge Loukin Inc. | 212-685-6473 |
| Shapiro, Ellen Graphic Design | 212-221-2625 |
| Shareholders Reports | 212-686-9099 |
| Sherin & Matejka Inc | 212-661-3232 |
| Siegel & Gale Inc. | 212-759-5246 |
| Silberlicht, Ira | 212-595-6252 |
| Silverman, Bob Design | 212-371-6472 |
| Sloan, William | 212-988-6267 |
| Sobel, Phillip | 212-476-3841 |
| Sochynsky, Ilona | 212-686-1275 |
| Solay/Hunt | 212-840-3313 |
| Sorvino, Skip | 212-580-9638 |
| St Vincent Milone & McConnells | 212-921-1414 |
| Stonehill Studio | 212-689-7074 |
| Stuart Mossberg Design Assoc. | 212-873-6130 |
| Stuart, Gunn & Furuta | 212-695-7770 |
| Stuart, Neil | 212-751-9275 |
| Studio 42 | 212-354-7298 |
| Styrowicz, Tom | 212-582-2978 |
| Systems Collaborative Inc | 212-483-0585 |

## T

| | |
|---|---|
| THe Sukon Group, Inc | 212-986-2290 |
| Tapa Graphics | 212-243-0176 |
| Tauss, Jack George | 212-279-1658 |
| Taylor & Ives | 212-244-0750 |
| Taylor, Stan | 212-685-4741 |
| Teague, Walter Dorwin Assoc | 212-557-0920 |
| Tercovich, Douglas Assoc Inc | 212-838-4800 |
| Theoharides Inc. | 212-838-7760 |
| Thompson Communications | 212-986-3570 |
| Three | 212-988-6267 |
| Tobias, William | 212-741-1712 |

# GRAPHIC DESIGNERS CONT'D.

Please send us your additions and updates.

| | |
|---|---|
| Tower Graphics Arts Corp | 212-421-0850 |
| Tribich, Jay Design Assoc | 212-679-6016 |
| Tschantre, J Graphic Svcs Ltd | 212-279-4040 |
| Tscherny, George Design | 212-734-3277 |
| Tunstull Studio | 212-834-8529 |
| Turner/Miller | 212-371-3035 |
| Tusa, Philip Design Inc | 212-753-2810 |
| Type Trends | 212-986-1783 |

## U V
| | |
|---|---|
| Ultra Arts Inc | 212-679-7493 |
| Viewpoint Graphics | 212-685-0560 |
| Vignelli Assoc. | 212-593-1416 |
| Visible Studio Inc | 212-683-8530 |
| Visual Accents Corp | 212-777-7766 |
| Visual Communications | 212-677-0065 |
| Visual Development Corp | 212-532-3202 |

## W
| | |
|---|---|
| W Chris Gorman Assoc. | 212-696-9377 |
| Wajdowicz, Jurek | 212-807-8144 |
| Waldman, Veronica | 212-260-3552 |
| Wallace Church Assoc. | 212-755-2903 |
| Wardell-Berger Design | 212-398-9355 |
| Warren A Kass Graphics Inc. | 212-868-3133 |
| Waters, John Assoc Inc | 212-807-0717 |
| Waters, Pamela Studio Inc | 212-677-2966 |
| Webster, Robert Inc | 212-677-2966 |
| Weed, Eunice Assoc Inc | 212-725-4933 |
| Weeks & Toomey | 212-564-8260 |
| What have You Done For Me Lately Co | 212-757-9210 |
| Whelan Design Office | 212-691-4404 |
| The Whole Works | 212-575-0765 |
| Wijtvliet, Ine | 212-684-4575 |
| Wilke, Jerry | 212-679-1318 |
| Wilke/Davis Assoc Inc | 212-532-5500 |
| William V Levine & Assoc. | 212-683-7177 |
| Withers, Bruce Graphic Design | 212-599-2388 |
| Wizard Graphics Inc | 212-686-8200 |
| Wjdowiecz, Jurek | 212-371-0699 |
| Wolf, Henry Production Inc | 212-472-2500 |
| Wolff, Rudi Inc | 212-873-5800 |
| Wood, Alan | 212-889-5195 |
| Works | 212-696-1666 |

## Y Z
| | |
|---|---|
| Yale Forman Designs Inc | 212-799-1665 |
| Yasumura & Assoc | 212-953-2000 |
| Yoshimura-Fisher Graphic Design | 212-431-4776 |
| Young Goldman Young Inc | 212-697-7820 |
| Zeitsoff, Elaine | 212-580-1282 |
| Zimmerman & Foyster | 212-674-0259 |

# NORTHEAST

## A
| | |
|---|---|
| Advertising Design Assoc Inc/Baltimore, MD | 301-752-2181 |
| Alber Associates/Philadelphia, PA | 215-969-4293 |
| Another Color Inc/Washington, DC | 202-547-3430 |
| Aries Graphics/Manchester, NH | 603-668-0811 |
| Art Service Assoc Inc/Pittsburgh, PA | 412-391-0902 |
| Art Services Inc/Washington, DC | 202-526-5607 |
| Art Staff & Co/Potomac, MD | 301-983-0531 |
| The Artery/Baltimore, MD | 301-752-2979 |
| Arts and Words/Washington, DC | 202-463-4880 |
| Artstyles Inc/Pittsburgh, PA | 412-261-1601 |
| Artwork Unlimited Inc/Washington, DC | 202-638-6352 |
| Ashley, Ellen Smith/Danbury, CT | |
| Autograph/Rockville, MD | 301-770-0360 |
| The Avit Corp/Fort Lee, NJ | 201-886-1100 |

## B
| | |
|---|---|
| Baldwin Design/Salem, MA | 617-745-6250 |
| Bally Design Inc/Carnegie, PA | 412-276-5454 |
| Banks & Co/Boston, MA | 617-262-0020 |
| Bartlett, Morton & Associates/Boston, MA | 617-536-8421 |
| Barton-Gillet/Baltimore, MD | 301-685-3626 |
| Baskin & Assoc/Washington, DC | 202-331-1098 |
| **BEDFORD PHOTO-GRAPHIC STUDIO/BEDFORD, NY (P 208)** | **914-234-3123** |
| Bellows, Amelia/Bethesda, MD | 202-337-0412 |
| Belser, Burkey/Washington, DC | 202-462-1482 |
| Bennardo, Churik Design Inc/Pittsburgh, PA | 412-366-3362 |
| Berns & Kay Ltd/Washington DC, | 202-387-7032 |
| Beveridge and Associates, Inc/Washington, DC | 202-223-4010 |
| Blum, William Assoc/Boston, MA | 617-232-1166 |
| Bogus, Sidney A & Assoc/Melrose, MA | 617-662-6660 |
| Bookmakers/Westport, CT | 203-226-4293 |
| Boscobel Advertising, Inc/Laurel, MD | 301-953-7294 |
| Boulanger Associates Inc/Armonk, NY | 914-273-5571 |
| Bradick Design & Methods Inc/Guys Mills, PA | 814-967-2332 |
| Brady, John Design Consultants/Pittsburgh, PA | 412-288-9300 |
| Bressler, Peter Design Assoc/Philadelphia, PA | 215-925-7100 |
| Bridy, Dan/Pittsburgh, PA | 412-288-9362 |
| Brown Design Comm/Bethesda, MD | 301-986-8872 |
| Brown and Craig Inc/Baltimore, MD | 301-837-2727 |
| Brown, Michael David Inc/Rockville, MD | 301-762-4474 |
| Buckett, Bill Assoc/Rochester, NY | 716-546-6580 |
| Burke & Michael Inc/Pittsburgh, PA | 412-321-2301 |
| Byrne, Ford/Philadelphia, PA | 215-564-0500 |

## C
| | |
|---|---|
| Cabot, Harold & Co Inc/Boston, MA | 617-426-7600 |
| Cameron Inc/Boston, MA | 617-267-2667 |
| Captain Graphics/Boston, MA | 617-367-1008 |
| Carmel, Abraham/Peekskill, NY | 914-737-1439 |
| Case/Washington, DC | 202-328-5900 |
| Chaparos Productions Limited/Washington, DC | 202-289-4838 |
| Charysyn & Charysyn/Westkill, NY | 518-989-6720 |
| Chase, David O Design Inc/Skaneateles, NY | 315-685-5715 |
| Colopy Dale Inc/Pittsburgh, PA | 412-471-0522 |
| Communications Design/Laurel Springs, NJ | 609-627-6979 |
| Concept Packaging Inc/Ft Lee, NJ | 201-224-5762 |
| Consolidated Visual Center Inc/Tuxedo, MD | 301-772-7300 |
| Cook & Shanosky Assoc/Princeton, NJ | 609-921-0200 |
| Creative Communications Center/Pennsauken, NJ | 609-665-2058 |
| The Creative Dept/Philadelphia, PA | 215-988-0390 |
| The Creative Group/Baltimore, MD | 301-889-1404 |
| Creative Presentations Inc/Washington, DC | 202-737-7152 |
| Curran & Connors Inc/Jericho, NY | 516-433-6600 |

## D
| | |
|---|---|
| D.P.W Inc/Rochester, NY | 716-325-6295 |
| Dakota Design/King of Prussia, PA | 215-265-1255 |
| Daroff Design Inc/Philadelphia, PA | 215-546-3440 |
| D'Art Studio Inc/Boston, MA | 617-482-4442 |
| Dawson Designers Associates/Boston, MA | 617-644-2940 |
| DeCesare, John/Darien, CT | 203-655-6057 |
| DeMartin-Marona-Cranstoun-Downes/Wilmington, DE | 302-654-5277 |
| DeMartin-Marona-Cranstoun-Downes/Briarcliff Manor, NY | 914-941-1634 |
| Design Associates/Arlington, VA | 703-243-7717 |
| Design Center Inc/Boston, MA | 617-536-6846 |
| Design Communication Collaboration/Washington, DC | 202-833-9087 |
| Design Group of Boston/Boston, MA | 617-437-1084 |
| Design Plus/Schenectady, NY | 518-377-1327 |
| The Design Solution/Washington, DC | 202-965-6040 |
| Design Technology Corp/Burlington, MA | 617-272-8890 |
| Design for Medicine Inc/Philadelphia, PA | 215-925-7100 |
| Designworks Inc/Cambridge, MA | 617-876-7035 |
| DiFiore Associates/Pittsburgh, PA | 412-471-0608 |
| Dohanos, Steven/Westport, CT | 203-227-3541 |
| Downing, Allan/Needham, MA | 617-449-4784 |
| Drafting and Design Studio/Columbia, MD | 301-730-5596 |
| Duffy, Bill & Assoc/Washington, DC | 202-965-2216 |

## E
| | |
|---|---|
| Edigraph Inc/Katonah, NY | 914-232-3725 |
| Educational Media/Graphics Division/Washington, DC | 202-625-2211 |
| Edwards, Joan & Assoc/Washington, DC | 202-966-3365 |
| Egress Concepts/Katonah, NY | 914-232-8433 |
| Environetics DC Inc/Washington, DC | 202-466-7110 |
| Eucalyptus Tree Studio/Baltimore, MD | 301-243-0211 |

# GRAPHIC DESIGNERS CONT'D.

Please send us your additions and updates.

| | |
|---|---|
| Evans Garber & Paige/Utica, NY | 315-733-2313 |
| Evans, Timothy Graphics/Washington, DC | 202-337-1608 |

## F
| | |
|---|---|
| Fader Jones & Zarkades/Boston, MA | 617-267-7779 |
| Falcone & Assoc/Chatham, NJ | 201-635-2900 |
| Fall, Dorothy Graphic Design/Washington, DC | 202-338-2022 |
| Fannell Studio/Boston, MA | 617-267-0895 |
| Fitzpatrick & Associates/Silver Springs, MD | 301-946-4677 |
| Forum Inc/Fairfield, CT | 203-259-5686 |
| Fossella, Gregory Assoc/Boston, MA | 617-267-4940 |
| Fresh Produce/Lutherville, MD | 301-821-1815 |
| Friday Design Group Inc/Washington, DC | 202-965-9600 |
| Froelich Advertising Service/Mahwah, NJ | 201-529-1737 |

## G
| | |
|---|---|
| Gasser, Gene/Chatham, NJ | 201-635-6020 |
| Gateway Studios/Pittsburgh, PA | 412-471-7224 |
| Gene Galasso Assoc Inc/Washington, DC | 202-223-5680 |
| Geyer, Jackie/Pittsburgh, PA | 412-261-1111 |
| Gilliam Communications Inc/Washington, DC | 202-232-6080 |
| Glickman, Frank Inc/Boston, MA | 617-524-2200 |
| Good, Peter Graphic Design/Chester, CT | 203-526-9597 |
| Graham Associates Inc/Washington, DC | 202-833-9657 |
| Grant Marketing Assoc./Philadelphia, PA | 215-985-9079 |
| The Graphic Suite/Pittsburgh, PA | 412-661-6699 |
| Graphics By Gallo/Washington, DC | 202-234-7700 |
| Graphics, Communications Systems/Silver Spring, MD | 301-587-1505 |
| Graphicus Corp/Baltimore, MD | 301-727-5553 |
| Graphiti/Philadelphia, PA | 215-925-0280 |
| Grear, Malcolm Designers Inc/Providence, RI | 401-331-5656 |
| Groff-Long Associates/Bethesda, MD | 301-654-0279 |
| Group Four Inc/Avon, CT | 203-678-1570 |
| Gunn Associates/Boston, MA | 617-267-0618 |

## H
| | |
|---|---|
| Hain, Robert Assoc/Scotch Plains, NJ | 201-322-1717 |
| Hallock, Robert/Newtown, CT | 203-426-4751 |
| Hammond Design Assoc/Milford, NH | 603-673-5253 |
| Hancock Gross/Philadelphia, PA | 215-567-4000 |
| Harish Patel Design Assoc/Boston, MA | 617-423-3633 |
| Harrington-Jackson/Boston, MA | 617-536-6164 |
| Hegemann Associates/Nyack, NY | 914-358-7348 |
| Herbick & Held/Pittsburgh, PA | 412-321-7400 |
| Herbst Lazar Design Inc/Lancaster, PA | 717-291-9042 |
| Herman & Lees/Cambridge, MA | 617-876-6463 |
| Hiestand Design Associates/Watertown, MA | 617-923-8800 |
| Hillmuth, James/Washington, DC | 202-244-0465 |
| The Hoyt Group/Waldwick, NJ | 201-652-6300 |
| Hrivnak, James/Silver Spring, MD | 301-681-9090 |

## IJ
| | |
|---|---|
| Identitia Incorporated/Newburyport, MA | 617-462-3146 |
| Image Consultants/Burlington, MA | 617-273-1010 |
| Imarc Corporation/Newtown Square, PA | 215-356-2000 |
| Innovations & Development Inc/Ft Lee, NJ | 201-944-9317 |
| Inwil International Inc/Paterson, NJ | 201-684-1024 |
| J H Roth Inc/Peekskill, NY | 914-737-6784 |
| Jack Hough Inc/Stamford, CT | 203-357-7077 |
| Jaeger Design Studio/Washington, DC | 202-785-8434 |
| Jensen, R S/Baltimore, MD | 301-727-3411 |
| Johnson & Simpson Graphic Design/Newark, NJ | 201-624-7788 |
| Johnson, Karl Graphic Design/Acton, MA | 617-263-5345 |
| Jones, Tom & Jane Kearns/Washington, DC | 202-232-1921 |

## K
| | |
|---|---|
| KBH Graphics/Baltimore, MD | 301-539-7916 |
| Kahana Associates/Jenkintown, PA | 215-887-0422 |
| Kaufman, Henry J & Assoc Inc/Washington, DC | 202-333-0700 |
| Keaton Design/Washington, DC | 202-547-4422 |
| Ketchum International/Pittsburgh, PA | 412-456-3693 |
| King-Casey Inc/New Canaan, CT | 203-966-3581 |
| Klim, Matt & Assoc/Avon, CT | 203-678-1222 |
| Knox, Harry & Assoc/Washington, DC | 202-833-2305 |
| Kostanecki, Andrew Inc/New Canaan, CT | 203-966-1681 |
| Kovanen, Erik/Wilton, CT | 203-762-8961 |
| Kramer/Miller/Lomden/Glossman/Philadelphia, PA | 215-545-7077 |
| Krone Graphic Design/Lemoyne, PA | 717-774-7431 |

## L
| | |
|---|---|
| LAM Design Inc/White Plains, NY | 914-948-4777 |
| **LANGDON, JOHN/WENONAH, NJ (P 134)** | **609-468-7868** |
| Lange, Erwin G/Wenonah, NJ | 609-468-7868 |
| Lapham/Miller Assoc/Boston, MA | 617-367-0110 |
| Latham Brefka Associates/Boston, MA | 617-227-3900 |
| Lausch, David Graphics/Baltimore, MD | 301-235-7453 |
| Lebowitz, Mo/N Bellemore, NY | 516-826-3397 |
| Leeds, Judith K Studio/West Caldwell, NJ | 201-226-3552 |
| Leotta Designers Inc/Conshohocken, PA | 215-828-8820 |
| Lester Associates Inc/West Nyack, NY | 914-358-6100 |
| Levinson Zaprauskis Assoc/Philadelphia, PA | 215-248-5242 |
| Lewis, Hal Design/Philadelphia, PA | 215-563-4461 |
| Lion Hill Studio/Baltimore, MD | 301-837-6218 |
| Lizak, Matt/N Smithfield, RI | 401-766-8885 |

## M
| | |
|---|---|
| M&M Graphics/Baltimore, MD | 301-747-4555 |
| MacIntosh, Rob Communication/Boston, MA | 617-267-4912 |
| Macey-Noyes/Ossining, NY | 914-941-7120 |
| Mahoney, Ron/Pittsburgh, PA | 412-261-3824 |
| Major Assoc/Baltimore, MD | 301-752-6174 |
| Malcolm R Mansfield Graphics/Boston, MA | 617-437-1922 |
| Mandala/Philadelphia, PA | 215-923-6020 |
| Marcus, Sarna/Amazing Graphic Design/Washington, DC | 202-234-4592 |
| Mariuzza, Pete/Briarcliff Manor, NY | 914-769-3310 |
| Martucci Studio/Boston, MA | 617-266-6960 |
| Mauro, Joseph & Miller, Ruthea/Wilmington, DE | 302-762-5753 |
| McDade Inc/Morristown, NJ | 201-538-8133 |
| Media Concepts/Boston, MA | 617-437-1382 |
| Media Graphics/Washington, DC | 202-265-9259 |
| Melancon, Joseph Studios/Wilmington, DE | 302-762-5753 |
| Melanson, Donya Assoc/Boston, MA | 617-482-0421 |
| Micolucci, Nicholas Assoc/King of Prussia, PA | 215-265-3320 |
| Miho, J Inc/Redding, CT | 203-938-3214 |
| Milcraft/Annandale, NJ | 201-735-8632 |
| Mitchell & Company/Washington, DC | 202-483-1301 |
| Mitchell & Webb Inc/Boston, MA | 617-262-6980 |
| Morlock Graphics/Tuson, MD | 301-825-5080 |
| Moss, John C/Chevy Chase, MD | 301-320-3912 |
| Mossman Art Studio/Baltimore, MD | 301-243-1963 |
| Mueller & Wister/Philadelphia, PA | 215-568-7260 |
| Muller-Munk, Peter Assoc/Pittsburgh, PA | 412-261-5161 |
| Myers, Gene Assoc/Pittsburgh, PA | 412-661-6314 |
| Myers, Patricia Inc/Chevy Chase, MD | 202-657-2311 |

## NO
| | |
|---|---|
| Nason Design Assoc/Boston, MA | 617-266-7286 |
| Navratil Art Studio/Pittsburgh, PA | 412-471-4322 |
| Nimeck, Fran/South Brunswick, NJ | 201-821-8741 |
| Nolan & Assoc/Washington, DC | 202-363-6553 |
| North Charles Street Design Org./Baltimore, MD | 301-539-4040 |
| Odyssey Design Group, Inc/Washington, DC | 202-783-6240 |
| Ollio Studio/Pittsburgh, PA | 412-281-4483 |
| Omnigraphics/Cambridge, MA | 617-354-7444 |
| One Harvard Sq Design Assoc/Cambridge, MA | 617-876-9673 |

## P
| | |
|---|---|
| Paganucci, Bob/Montvale, NJ | 201-391-1752 |
| Paine, Larry & Associates/Bethesda, MD | 301-493-8445 |
| Paragraphics Inc./White Plains, NY | 914-948-4777 |
| Parks, Franz & Cox, Inc/Washington, DC | 202-797-7568 |
| Pasinski, Irene Assoc/Pittsburgh, PA | 412-683-0585 |
| Patazian Design Inc/Boston, MA | 617-262-7848 |
| Pesanelli, David Assoc/Washington, DC | 202-363-4760 |
| Petco Design/Stamford, CT | 203-348-3734 |
| Phillips Design Assoc/Boston, MA | 617-787-5757 |
| Pilgrim Design Inc/Bloomfield, NJ | 201-429-9449 |
| Planert, Paul Design Assoc/Pittsburgh, PA | 412-621-1275 |
| Plataz, George/Pittsburgh, PA | 412-322-3177 |
| Porter, Al/Graphics Inc/Washington, DC | 202-244-0403 |
| Presentation Associates/Washington, DC | 202-333-0080 |
| Prestige Marking & Coating Co/Stamford, CT | 203-329-0384 |
| Production Studio/Port Washington, NY | 516-944-6688 |

# GRAPHIC DESIGNERS CONT'D.

Please send us your additions and updates.

| | |
|---|---|
| Publication Services Inc/Stamford, CT | 203-348-7351 |

## R
| | |
|---|---|
| RSV/Boston, MA | 617-262-9450 |
| RZA Inc/Westwood, NJ | 201-664-4543 |
| Ralcon Inc/West Chester, PA | 215-692-2840 |
| Rand, Paul Inc/Weston, CT | 203-227-5375 |
| Redtree Associates/Washington, DC | 202-628-2900 |
| Research Planning Assoc/Philadelphia, PA | 215-561-9700 |
| Richard Ritter Design Inc/Berwyn, PA | 215-296-0400 |
| Rieb, Robert/Westport, CT | 203-227-0061 |
| Ringel, Leonard Lee Graphic Design/Kendall Park, NJ | 201-297-9084 |
| Romax Studio/Stamford, CT | 203-324-4260 |
| Ronald R. Miller & Co./Rockaway, NJ | 201-625-9280 |
| Rosborg Inc/Newton, CT | 203-426-3171 |
| Roth, J R/Peekskill, NY | 914-737-6784 |

## S
| | |
|---|---|
| Sanchez/Philadelphia, PA | 215-564-2223 |
| Sanders & Noe Inc/Arlington, VA | 703-524-0544 |
| Schneider Design/Baltimore, MD | 301-467-2611 |
| Schoenfeld, Cal/Parsippany, NJ | 201-334-6257 |
| Schwartz, Adler Graphics Inc/Baltimore, MD | 301-433-4400 |
| Selame Design Associates/Newton Lower Falls, MA | 617-969-6690 |
| Shapiro, Deborah/Jersey City, NJ | 201-432-5198 |
| Simpson Booth Designers/Cambridge, MA | 617-661-2630 |
| Smith, Doug/Larchmont, NY | 914-834-3997 |
| Smith, Gail Hunter III/Barnegat Light, NJ | 609-494-9136 |
| Smith, Tyler Art Direction/Providence, RI | 401-751-1220 |
| Snowden Associates Inc/Washington, DC | 202-362-8944 |
| Sparkman & Bartholomew/Washington, DC | 202-785-2414 |
| Star Design Inc/Moorestown, NJ | 609-235-8150 |
| Steel Art Co Inc/Boston, MA | 617-566-4079 |
| Stettler, Wayne Design/Philadelphia, PA | 215-235-1230 |
| Stockman & Andrews Inc/E Providence, RI | 401-438-0694 |
| Stolt, Jill Design/Rochester, NY | 716-461-2594 |
| Studio Six Design/Springfield, NJ | 201-379-5820 |
| Studio Three/Philadelphia, PA | 215-665-0141 |

## T
| | |
|---|---|
| Takajian, Asdur/N Tarrytown, NY | 914-631-5553 |
| Taylor, Ron V Assoc/Stratford, CT | 203-378-3090 |
| Team One/Pittsburgh, PA | 412-471-1065 |
| Telesis/Baltimore, MD | 301-235-2000 |
| Tetrad Inc/Annapolis, MD | 301-268-8680 |
| Thompson, Bradbury/Riverside, CT | 203-637-3614 |
| Thompson, George L/Reading, MA | 617-944-6256 |
| Torode, Barbara/Philadelphia, PA | 215-732-6792 |
| Totally Board/Boston, MA | 617-437-1914 |
| Town Studios Inc/Pittsburgh, PA | 412-471-5353 |
| Troller, Fred Assoc Inc/Rye, NY | 914-698-1405 |

## V
| | |
|---|---|
| van der Sluys Graphics Inc/Washington, DC | 202-265-3443 |
| VanDine,Horton,McNamara,Manges/Pittsburgh, PA | 412-261-4280 |
| Vance Wright Adams & Assoc/Pittsburgh, PA | 412-322-1800 |
| Victoria Group/Natick, MA | 617-235-2003 |
| Vinick, Bernard Assoc Inc/Hartford, CT | 203-525-4293 |
| Viscom Inc/Baltimore, MD | 301-727-6476 |
| Vista Design Group/Pittsburgh, PA | 412-441-8500 |
| Visual Research & Design Corp/Boston, MA | 617-536-2111 |
| The Visualizers/Pittsburgh, PA | 412-281-9387 |

## W
| | |
|---|---|
| Warkulwiz Design/Philadelphia, PA | 215-546-0880 |
| Wasserman's, Myron Graphic Design Group/Philadelphia, PA | 215-922-4545 |
| Weadock, Rutka/Baltimore, MD | 301-358-3588 |
| Weitzman & Assoc/Bethesda, MD | 301-652-7035 |
| Wetherell, Joseph J Industrial Design/Katonah, NY | 914-232-8227 |
| Weymouth Design/Boston, MA | 617-542-2647 |
| White, E James Co/Alexandria, VA | 703-750-3680 |
| Wickham & Assoc Inc/Washington, DC | 202-296-4860 |
| Wilke, Jerry Design/Croton-On-Hudson, NY | 212-690-2644 |
| Willard, Janet Design Assoc/Pittsburgh, PA | 412-661-9100 |
| William E Young & Co/Neptune, NJ | 201-922-1234 |
| Williams Associates/Lynnfield, MA | 617-599-1818 |
| Wills Group/Philadelphia, PA | 215-985-1377 |
| Wilson-Pirk/Washington, DC | 202-244-5736 |
| Wistrand,John Design/New Canaan, CT | 203-966-9849 |
| World Wide Agency/Baltimore, MD | 301-385-0800 |
| Worseldine Graphics/Washington, DC | 202-965-4325 |
| Wright, Kent M Assoc Inc/Sudbury, MA | 617-443-9909 |

## YZ
| | |
|---|---|
| Yurdin, Carl Industrial Design Inc/Port Washington, NY | 516-944-7811 |
| Zeb Graphics/Washington, DC | 202-293-1687 |
| Zmiejko & Assoc Design Agcy/Freeland, PA | 717-636-2304 |

# SOUTHEAST

## A
| | |
|---|---|
| Ace Art/New Orleans, LA | 504-861-2222 |
| The Alderman Co/High Point, NC | 919-889-6121 |
| Allyn, Richar Studio/N Miami, FL | 305-945-1702 |
| Alphabet Group/Atlanta, GA | 404-892-6500 |
| Amberger, Michael/Miami, FL | 305-531-4932 |
| Archigraphics/Coral Gables, FL | |
| Art Services/Atlanta, GA | 404-892-2105 |
| Arts & Graphics/Annandale, VA | 703-941-2560 |
| Arunski, Joe & Assoc/Miami, FL | 305-253-3337 |
| Asi/Ft Lauderdale, FL | 305-561-0551 |
| The Associates Inc/Arlington, VA | 703-534-3940 |

## B
| | |
|---|---|
| Blair, Inc/Baileys Cross Roads, VA | 703-820-9011 |
| Bodenhamer, William S Inc/Miami, FL | 305-253-9284 |
| Bonner Advertising Art/New Orleans, LA | 504-895-7938 |
| Brimm, Edward & Assoc/Palm Beach, FL | 305-655-1059 |
| Brothers Bogusky/Miami, FL | 305-891-3642 |
| Bugdal Group/Miami, FL | 305-264-1860 |
| Burch, Dan Associates/Louisville, KY | 502-895-4881 |

## C
| | |
|---|---|
| Carlson Design/Gainesville, FL | 904-373-3153 |
| Chartmasters Inc/Atlanta, GA | 404-262-7610 |
| Communications Graphics Inc/Atlanta, GA | 404-231-9039 |
| Corporate Advertising & Graphics/Ft Lauderdale, Fl | 305-776-4060 |
| Creative Design Assoc/Palm Beach Garden, FL | 305-694-2711 |
| Creative Services Inc/New Orleans, LA | 504-943-0842 |
| Creative Services Unlimited/Naples, FL | 813-262-0201 |

## DEF
| | |
|---|---|
| Deltacom/McLean, VA | 703-790-4800 |
| Design Consultants Inc/Falls Church, VA | 703-241-2323 |
| Design Workshop Inc/N Miami, FL | 305-893-2820 |
| Designcomp/Vienna, VA | 202-938-1822 |
| Emig, Paul E/Arlington, VA | 703-522-5926 |
| First Impressions/Tampa, FL | 813-224-0454 |
| Foster, Kim A/Miami, FL | 305-642-1801 |
| From Us Advertising & Design/Atlanta, GA | 404-373-0373 |

## G
| | |
|---|---|
| Garrett Lewis Johnson/Atlanta, GA | 404-221-0700 |
| Garrett, Kenneth/Atlanta, GA | 404-221-0700 |
| Gerbino Advertising Inc/Ft Lauderdale, FL | 305-776-5050 |
| Gestalt Associates, Inc/Alexandria, VA | 703-683-1126 |
| Graphic Arts Inc/Alexandria, VA | 703-683-4303 |
| Graphics 4/Ft Lauderdale, FL | 305-764-1470 |
| Graphics Associates/Atlanta, GA | 404-873-5858 |
| Graphics Group/Atlanta, GA | 404-261-5146 |
| Graphicstudio/N Miami, FL | 305-893-1015 |
| Great Incorporated/Alexandria, VA | 703-836-6020 |
| Gregg, Bill Advertising Design/Miami, FL | 305-854-7657 |

## H
| | |
|---|---|
| Hall Graphics/Miami, FL | 305-856-6536 |
| Hall, Stephen Design Office/Louisville, KY | 502-584-5030 |
| Hannau, Michael Ent. Inc/Hialeah, FL | 305-887-1536 |
| Hansen, James N/Orlando, FL | 305-896-4240 |
| Hauser, Sydney/Sarasota, FL | 813-388-3021 |
| Helms, John Graphic Design/Memphis, TN | 901-363-6589 |

## J
| | |
|---|---|
| Jensen, Rupert & Assoc Inc/Atlanta, GA | 404-892-6658 |
| Johnson Design Group Inc/Arlington, VA | 703-525-0808 |
| Jordan Barrett & Assoc/Miami, FL | 305-667-7051 |

# GRAPHIC DESIGNERS CONT'D.

Please send us your additions and updates.

## K L
| | |
|---|---|
| Kelly & Co Graphic Design Inc/St Petersburg, FL | 813-327-1009 |
| Kjeldsen, Howard Assoc Inc/Atlanta, GA | 404-266-1897 |
| Leisuregraphics Inc/Miami, FL | 305-751-0266 |
| Leonard, Dick Group/St Petersburg, FL | 813-576-6723 |
| Lollis & Turpin/Atlanta, GA | 404-261-0705 |
| Lowell, Shelley Design/Atlanta, GA | 404-636-9149 |

## M
| | |
|---|---|
| Mabrey Design/Sarasota, FL | 813-957-1063 |
| Maxine, J & Martin Advertising/McLean, VA | 703-356-5222 |
| McGurren Weber Ink/Alexandria, VA | 703-548-0003 |
| Michael, Richard S/Knoxville, TN | 615-584-3319 |
| Miller, Hugh K/Orlando, FL | 305-293-8220 |
| Morgan-Burchette Assoc/Alexandria, VA | 703-549-2393 |
| Morris, Robert Assoc Inc/Ft Lauderdale, FL | 305-973-4380 |
| Muhlhausen, John Design Inc/Atlanta, GA | 404-393-0743 |

## P
| | |
|---|---|
| P & W Inc/Louisville, KY | 502-499-9220 |
| PL&P Advertising Studio/Ft Lauderdale, FL | 305-776-6505 |
| PRB Design Studio/Winter Park, FL | 305-671-7992 |
| Parallel Group Inc/Atlanta, GA | 404-261-0988 |
| Pertuit, Jim & Assoc Inc/New Orleans, LA | 504-581-7500 |
| Piatti and Wolk Design Assoc/Coral Gable, FL | 305-445-0553 |
| Platt, Don Advertising Art/Hialeah, FL | 305-888-3296 |
| Point 6/Ft Lauderdale, FL | 305-563-6939 |
| Polizos, Arthur Assoc/Norfolk, VA | 804-622-7033 |
| Positively Main St Graphics/Sarasota, FL | 813-366-4959 |
| Promotion Graphics Inc/N Miami, FL | 305-891-3941 |
| Publications Studio/Arlington, VA | 703-241-1980 |

## R S
| | |
|---|---|
| Rasor & Rasor/Cary, NC | 919-362-7266 |
| Rebeiz, Kathryn Dereki/Vienna, VA | 703-560-7784 |
| Rodriguez, Emilio Jr/Miami, FL | 305-235-4700 |
| Sager Assoc Inc/Sarasota, FL | 813-366-4192 |
| Salmon, Paul/Burke, VA | 703-250-4943 |
| Schulwolf, Frank/Coral Gables, FL | 305-665-2129 |
| Seay, Jack Design Group/Norcross, GA | 404-447-4840 |
| Showcraft Designworks/Clearwater, FL | 813-461-4471 |
| Sirrine, J E/Greenville, SC | 803-298-6000 |
| Supertype/Hialeah, FL | 305-885-6241 |

## T V W
| | |
|---|---|
| Thayer, Dan Industrial Design/Monroe, VA | 804-929-6359 |
| Varisco, Tom Graphic Design Inc/New Orleans, LA | 504-949-2888 |
| Visualgraphics Design/Tampa, FL | 813-877-3804 |
| Wells Squire Assoc Inc/Ft Lauderdale, FL | 305-763-8063 |
| Whitver, Harry K Graphic Design/Nashville, TN | 615-320-1795 |
| Will and Assoc/Atlanta, GA | 404-355-3194 |
| Wilsonwork Graphic Design/Alexandrea, VA | 703-836-8343 |
| Winner, Stewart Inc/Louisville, KY | 502-583-5502 |
| Wood, Tom/Atlanta, GA | 404-262-7424 |
| The Workshop/Atlanta, GA | 404-875-0141 |

# MIDWEST

## A
| | |
|---|---|
| Ades, Leonards Graphic Design/Northbrook, IL | 312-564-8863 |
| Advertising Art Studios Inc/Milwaukee, WI | 414-276-6306 |
| Album Graphics/Melrose Park, IL | 312-344-9100 |
| Allan Aarons Design/Northbrook, IL | 312-291-9800 |
| Allied Design Group/Chicago, IL | 312-743-3330 |
| Alpha Designs Inc/Cincinnati, OH | 513-579-8569 |
| Anderson Studios/Chicago, IL | 312-922-3039 |
| Anderson, I K Studios/Chicago, IL | 312-664-4536 |
| Architectural Signing/Chicago, IL | 312-871-0100 |
| Art Forms Inc/Cleveland, OH | 216-361-3855 |
| Artform/Evanston, IL | 312-864-2994 |
| Arvind Khatkate Design/Chicago, IL | 312-337-1478 |

## B
| | |
|---|---|
| Babcock & Schmid Assoc/Bath, OH | 216-666-8826 |
| Bailey Orner Makstaller Inc/Cincinnati, OH | 513-281-1338 |
| Bal Graphics Inc/Chicago, IL | 312-337-0325 |
| Banka Mango Design Inc/Chicago, IL | 312-467-0059 |
| Beck, Bruce Design Assoc/Evanston, IL | 312-869-7100 |
| Bieger, Walter Assoc/Arden Hills, MN | 612-636-8500 |
| Blake, Hayward & Co/Evanston, IL | 312-864-9800 |
| Blau-Bishop & Assoc/Chicago, IL | 312-321-1420 |
| Boelter Industries Inc/Minneapolis, MN | 612-831-5338 |
| Boller-Coates-Spadero/Chicao, IL | 312-787-2798 |
| Bowlby, Joseph A/Chicago, IL | 312-782-1253 |
| Bradford-Cout Graphic Design/Skokie, IL | 312-539-5557 |
| Bradick Design & Methods Inc/Cleveland, OH | 216-531-1711 |
| Broin, Steven/St Paul, MN | 612-644-7314 |
| Brooks Stevens Assoc Inc/Mequon, WI | 414-241-3800 |
| Burton E Benjamin Assoc/Highland Park, IL | 312-432-8089 |
| Busch, Lonnie/Fenton, MO | 314-343-1330 |

## C
| | |
|---|---|
| CMO Graphics/Chicago, IL | 312-527-0900 |
| Campbell Art Studio/Cinncinati, OH | 513-221-3600 |
| Campbell Creative Group Inc/Milwaukee, WI | 414-351-4150 |
| Carol Naughton & Assoc/Chicago, IL | 312-427-9800 |
| Carter, Don W/ Industrial Design/Kansas City, MO | 816-356-1874 |
| Centaur Studios Inc/St Louis, MO | 314-421-6485 |
| Centermark Corp./Des Moines, IA | 515-288-7000 |
| Chartmaster Inc/Chicago, IL | 312-787-9040 |
| Chestnut House/Chicago, IL | 312-822-9090 |
| Chott & Janah Design, Inc./Chicago, IL | 312-726-4560 |
| Combined Services Inc/Minneapolis, MN | 612-339-7770 |
| Communications Network Sys Inc/Minneapolis, MN | 612-341-2029 |
| Container Corp of America/Chicago, IL | 312-580-5500 |
| Contours Consulting Design Group/Bartlett, IL | 312-837-4100 |
| Coons/Beirise Design Associate/Cincinnati, OH | 513-751-7459 |
| Creative Directions Inc/Milwaukee, WI | 414-466-3910 |
| Creative Environments/Glen Ellyn, IL | 312-858-9222 |

## D
| | |
|---|---|
| David Day/Designer & Assoc/Cincinnati, OH | 513-621-4060 |
| David Doty Design/Chicago, IL | 312-348-1200 |
| DeBrey Design/Minneapolis, MN | 612-935-2292 |
| DeGoede & Others/Chicago, IL | 312-828-0056 |
| Dektas Eger Inc/Cincinnati, OH | 513-621-7070 |
| Design Alliance Inc/Cincinnati, OH | 513-621-9373 |
| Design Consultants/Chicago, IL | 312-372-4670 |
| Design Dynamics Inc/Union, IL | 815-923-2221 |
| Design Factory/Overland Park, KS | 913-383-3085 |
| The Design Group/Madison, WI | 608-274-5393 |
| Design Group Three/Chicago, IL | 312-929-6313 |
| Design House III/Cleveland, OH | 216-621-7777 |
| Design Mark Inc/Indianapolis, IN | 317-872-3000 |
| Design Marks Corp/Chicago, IL | 312-327-3669 |
| Design North Inc/Racine, WI | 414-639-2080 |
| The Design Partnership/Minneapolis, MN | 612-338-8889 |
| Design Planning Group/Chicago, IL | 312-943-8400 |
| Design Programs Inc/Milwaukee, WI | 414-276-6505 |
| Design Train/Cincinnati, OH | 513-761-7099 |
| Design Two Ltd/Chicago, IL | 312-642-9888 |
| Di Cristo & Slagle Design/Milwaukee, WI | 414-273-0980 |
| Dickens Design Group/Chicago, IL | 312-222-1850 |
| Dimensional Communications/Evanston, IL | 312-492-1033 |
| Dimensional Designs Inc/Indianapolis, IN | 317-637-1353 |
| Dresser, John Design/Libertyville, IL | 312-362-4222 |
| Dynamic Graphics/Ted Lane/Peoria, IL | 309-688-8800 |

## E
| | |
|---|---|
| Eaton and Associates/Minneapolis, MN | 612-871-1028 |
| Eberle, Robert A & Assoc Inc/Kansas City, MO | 816-931-2428 |
| Ellies, Dave IndustrialDesign Inc/Columbus, OH | 614-488-7995 |
| Elyria Graphics/Elyria, OH | 216-365-9384 |
| Engelhardt Design/Minneapolis, MN | 612-377-3389 |
| Environmental Graphics Inc/Indianapolis, IN | 317-634-1458 |
| Epstein & Szilagyi/Cleveland, OH | 216-421-1600 |
| Evans, Cecil Jr Interiors/Chicago, IL | 312-943-8974 |

## F
| | |
|---|---|
| Falk, Robert Design Group/St Louis, MO | 314-531-1410 |
| Feldkamp-Malloy/Chicago, IL | 312-263-0633 |
| Ficho & Corley Inc/Chicago, IL | 312-787-1011 |
| Final Draft Graphic Art/Cleveland, OH | 216-861-3735 |

# GRAPHIC DESIGNERS CONT'D.
Please send us your additions and updates.

| | |
|---|---|
| Fleishman-Hillard, Inc/St Louis, MO | 314-982-1700 |
| Flexo Design/Chicago, IL | 312-321-1368 |
| Ford & Earl Design Assoc Inc/Warren, MI | 313-539-2280 |
| Forsythe-French Inc/Kansas City, MO | 816-561-6678 |
| Frink, Chin, Casey Inc/Minneapolis, MN | 612-333-6539 |

## G
| | |
|---|---|
| Gellman, Stan Graphic Design Studio/St Louis, MO | 314-361-7676 |
| Gerhardt and Clements/Chicago, IL | 312-337-3443 |
| The Glen Smith Co/Minneapolis, MN | 612-871-1616 |
| Glenbard Graphics Inc/Carol Stream, IL | 312-653-4550 |
| Goldsholl Assoc/Northfield, IL | 312-446-8300 |
| Goldsmith Yamasaki Specht Inc/Chicago, IL | 312-266-8404 |
| Goose Graphics/Minneapolis, MN | 612-871-2671 |
| Gournoe, M Ltd/Chicago, IL | 312-787-5157 |
| Graphic Corp/Des Moines, IA | 515-247-8500 |
| Graphic Corporation/Troy, MI | 313-649-5050 |
| Graphic House Inc/Dearborn, MI | 313-336-8710 |
| Graphic Specialties Inc/Minneapolis, MN | 612-922-4000 |
| Graphics Group/Chicago, IL | 312-782-7421 |
| Graphics-Cor Associates/Chicago, IL | 312-332-3379 |
| Greenberg, Jon Assoc Inc/Southfield, MI | 313-559-2333 |
| Greenlee-Hess Ind Design/Cleveland, OH | 216-382-7570 |
| Greiner, John & Assoc/Chicago, IL | 312-644-2973 |
| Grusin, Gerald Design/Chicago, IL | 312-944-4945 |
| Gulick & Henry Inc/Minneapolis, MN | 612-341-4551 |

## H
| | |
|---|---|
| The Hanley Partnership/St Louis, MO | 314-621-1400 |
| Hans Design/Northbrook, IL | 312-272-7980 |
| Harley, Don E Associates/West St Paul, MN | 612-455-1631 |
| Herbst/Lazar Design Inc/Chicago, IL | 312-822-9660 |
| Higgins Hegner Genovese, Inc/Chicago, IL | |
| Hirsch, David Design Group Inc/Chicago, IL | 312-329-1500 |
| Hirsh Co/Skokie, IL | 312-267-6777 |
| Hoekstra, Grant Graphics/Chicago, IL | 312-641-6940 |
| Hoffman-York Inc/Minneapolis, MN | 612-835-5313 |
| Horvath, Steve Design/Milwaukee, WI | 414-271-3992 |

## I
| | |
|---|---|
| IGS Design, Div of Smith H & G/Detroit, MI | 313-964-3000 |
| ISD Incorporated/Chicago, IL | 312-467-1515 |
| Imagemakers/Cincinnati/Cincinnati, OH | 513-281-3511 |
| Indiana Design Consortium/Lafayette, IN | 317-423-5469 |
| Industrial Technological Assoc/Cleveland, OH | 216-771-4151 |
| Ing, Victor Design/Morton Grove, IL | 312-965-3459 |
| Intelplex/Maryland Hts, MI | 314-739-9996 |
| Interdesign Inc/Minneapolis, MN | 612-871-7979 |
| Interface Design Group/Milwaukee, WI | 414-276-6688 |

## J
| | |
|---|---|
| JMH Design Center/Indianapolis, IN | 317-639-2535 |
| James, Frank Direct Marketing/Clayton, MO | 314-726-4600 |
| Jansen, Ute/Chicago, IL | 312-922-5048 |
| Johnson, Stan Design Inc/Brookfield, WI | 414-783-6510 |
| Johnson, Stewart Design Studio/Milwaukee, WI | 414-265-3377 |
| Jones, Richmond Designer/Chicago, IL | 312-935-6500 |
| Joss Design Group/Chicago, IL | 312-828-0055 |

## K
| | |
|---|---|
| KDA Industrial Design Consultants Inc/Addison, IL | 312-495-9466 |
| Kaleidoscope Art Inc/Cleveland, OH | 216-932-4454 |
| Kaulfuss Design/Chicago, IL | 312-943-2161 |
| Kearns, Marilyn/Chicago, IL | 312-645-1888 |
| Kosterman, Wayne/Schaumburg, IL | 312-843-2378 |
| Krupp, Merlin Studios/Minneapolis, MN | 612-871-6611 |

## L
| | |
|---|---|
| LVK Associates Inc/St Louis, MO | 314-367-4824 |
| Lange, Jim Design/Chicago, IL | 312-527-4260 |
| Larson Design/Minneapolis, MN | 612-835-2271 |
| Lehrfeld/Ray Studio/Chicago, IL | 312-944-0651 |
| Lerdon, Wes Assoc/Columbus, OH | 614-486-8188 |
| Lesniewicz/Navarre/Toledo, OH | 419-243-7131 |
| Lipson & Jacobs Associates/Cincinnati, OH | 513-961-6225 |
| Lipson Associates Inc/Northbrook, IL | 312-291-0500 |
| Liska Design/Chicago, IL | 312-943-5910 |
| Loew, Dick & Assoc/Chicago, IL | 312-787-9032 |

| | |
|---|---|
| Lubell, Robert/Toledo, OH | 419-531-2267 |

## M
| | |
|---|---|
| Maddox, Eva Assoc Inc/Chicago, IL | 312-649-0092 |
| Manning Studios Inc/Cincinnati, OH | 513-621-6959 |
| Market Design/Cleveland, OH | 216-771-0300 |
| Marsh, Richard Assoc Inc/Chicago, IL | 312-236-1331 |
| McCoy, Steven/Omaha, NB | 402-554-1416 |
| McDermott, Bill Graphic Design/St Louis, MO | 314-862-6021 |
| McGuire, Robert L Design/Kansas City, MO | 816-523-9164 |
| McMurray Design Inc./Chicago, IL | 312-527-1555 |
| Media Corporation/Columbus, OH | 614-488-7767 |
| Medialoft/Minneapolis, MN | 612-831-0226 |
| Meyer Seltzer Design/Illustration/Chicago, IL | 312-348-2885 |
| Mid-America Graphics/Omaha, NB | 402-554-1416 |
| Minnick, James Design/Chicago, IL | 312-527-1864 |
| Moonink Inc/Chicago, IL | 312-565-0040 |
| Murrie White Drummond Leinhart/Chicago, IL | 312-943-5995 |

## N O
| | |
|---|---|
| Newcomb House Inc/St Louis, MO | 314-997-7262 |
| Nobart Inc/Chicago, IL | 312-427-9800 |
| Nottingham-Spirk Design Inc/Cleveland, OH | 216-231-7830 |
| Oak Brook Graphics, Inc/Elmhurst, IL | 312-832-3200 |
| Osborne-Tuttle/Chicago, IL | 312-565-1910 |
| Oskar Designs/Evanston, IL | 312-328-1734 |
| Our Gang Studios/Omaha, NB | 402-341-4965 |
| Overlock Howe & Co/St Louis, MO | 314-241-8640 |

## P
| | |
|---|---|
| Pace Studios/Lincolnwood, IL | 312-676-9770 |
| Painter/Cesaroni Design, Inc/Glenview, IL | 312-724-8840 |
| Palmer Design Assoc/Wilmette, IL | 312-256-7448 |
| Paramount Technical Service Inc/Cleveland, OH | 216-585-2550 |
| Patrick Redmond Design/St Paul, MN | 612-292-9851 |
| Perception Inc/Chicago, IL | 312-663-5040 |
| Perman, Norman/Chicago, IL | 312-642-1348 |
| Phares Associates Inc/Birmingham, MI | 313-645-9194 |
| Pinzke, Herbert Design/Chicago, IL | 312-528-2277 |
| Pitt Studios/Cleveland, OH | 216-241-6720 |
| Podall, Robert Assoc Inc/Northbrook, IL | 312-498-0230 |
| Polivka-Logan Design/Minnetonka, MN | 612-474-1124 |
| Porter-Matjasich/Chicago, IL | 312-670-4355 |
| Powell/Kleinschmidt Inc/Chicago, IL | 312-726-2208 |
| Pride and Perfomance/St Paul, MN | 612-646-4800 |
| Prodesign Inc/Plymouth, MI | 612-559-1884 |
| Purviance, George Marketing Comm/Clayton, MO | 314-721-2765 |
| Pycha and Associates/Chicago, IL | 312-944-3679 |

## Q R
| | |
|---|---|
| Quality Graphics/Akron, OH | 216-375-5282 |
| Quality Images/Akron, OH | 216-375-5282 |
| Richardson/Smith Inc/Worthington, OH | 614-885-3453 |
| Robertz, Webb and Co./Chicago, IL | 312-861-0060 |
| Ronald Kovach Design/Chicago, IL | 312-461-9888 |
| Ross & Harvey Inc./Chicago, IL | 312-467-1290 |
| Roth, Randall/Chicago, IL | 312-467-0140 |
| Rotheiser, Jordan I/Highland Park, IL | 312-433-4288 |

## S
| | |
|---|---|
| Samata Design Group Ltd/West Dundee, IL | 312-428-8600 |
| Savlin Assoc/Evanston, IL | 312-328-3366 |
| Schlatter Group Inc/Battle Creek, MI | 616-964-0898 |
| Schmidt, Wm M Assoc/Harper Woods, MI | 313-881-8075 |
| Schrin, Janet Interiors/Chicago, IL | 312-943-0010 |
| Schultz, Ron Design/Chicago, IL | 312-528-1853 |
| Sherman, Roger Assoc Inc/Dearborn, MI | 313-582-8844 |
| Shipley, R W Assoc Inc/Elmhurst, IL | 312-279-1212 |
| Simanis, Vito/St Charles, IL | 312-584-1683 |
| Simons, I W Industrial Design/Columbus, OH | 614-451-3796 |
| Skolnick, Jerome/Chicago, IL | 312-944-4568 |
| Slavin Assoc Inc/Chicago, IL | 312-944-2920 |
| Source Inc/Chicago, IL | 312-236-7620 |
| Space Design International Inc/Cincinnati, OH | 513-241-3000 |
| Spatial Graphics Inc/Milwaukee, WI | 414-545-4444 |
| Stepan Design/Mt. Prospect, IL | 312-364-4121 |
| Stromberg, Gordon H Visual Design/Chicago, IL | 312-275-9449 |

# GRAPHIC DESIGNERS CONT'D.

Please send us your additions and updates.

| | |
|---|---|
| Studio 1/Milwaukee, WI | 414-265-2565 |
| Studio One Graphics/Livonia, MI | 313-522-7505 |
| Studio One Inc/Minneapolis, MN | 612-831-6313 |
| Swanson, Gladys Graphics/Chicago, IL | 312-726-3381 |
| Swoger Grafik/Chicago, IL | 312-935-0755 |
| Synthesis/Chicago, IL | 312-787-1201 |

## TU
| | |
|---|---|
| T & Company/Chicago, IL | 312-463-1336 |
| Tassian, George Org/Cincinnati, OH | 513-721-5566 |
| Total Communications Inc./St Louis, MO | 314-421-3800 |
| Underwood, Muriel/Chicago, IL | 312-236-8472 |
| Unicom/Milwaukee, WI | 414-354-5440 |
| Unigraphics/Troy, MI | 313-528-0370 |
| Unimark International Corp/Schaumberg, IL | 312-843-3394 |

## V
| | |
|---|---|
| Vallarta, Frederick Assoc Inc/Chicago, IL | 312-944-7300 |
| Vanides-Mlodock/Chicago, IL | 312-663-0595 |
| Vann, Bill Studio/St Louis, MO | 314-231-2322 |
| Venture Graphics/Chicago, IL | 312-943-2900 |
| Vista Three Design/Minneapolis, MN | 612-920-5311 |
| Visual Image/St Paul, MN | 612-644-7314 |

## W
| | |
|---|---|
| Wallner Graphics/Chicago, IL | 312-787-6787 |
| Weiss, Jack Assoc/Evanston, IL | 312-864-7480 |
| Widmer, Stanley Assoc Inc/Staples, MI | 218-894-3466 |
| Wilkes, Jean/Chicago, IL | 312-332-5168 |
| Winbush Design/Chicago, IL | 312-527-4478 |
| Wise, Guinotte/Independence, MO | 816-836-1362 |
| Worrel, W Robert Design/Minneapolis, MN | 612-933-0303 |

## XZ
| | |
|---|---|
| Xeno/Chicago, IL | 312-327-1989 |
| Zender and Associates/Cincinnati, OH | 513-561-8496 |

# SOUTHWEST

## A
| | |
|---|---|
| A Worthwhile Place Comm/Dallas, TX | 214-946-1348 |
| A&M Associates Inc/Phoenix, AZ | 602-263-6504 |
| Ackerman & McQueen/Oklahoma City, OK | 405-843-9451 |
| The Ad Department/Ft Worth, TX | 817-335-4012 |
| Ad-Art Studios/Ft Worth, TX | 817-335-9603 |
| Advertising Inc/Tulsa, OK | 918-747-8871 |
| Art Associates/Irving, TX | 214-258-6001 |

## BC
| | |
|---|---|
| Beals Advertising Agency/Oklahoma City, OK | 405-848-8513 |
| The Belcher Group Inc/Houston, TX | 713-271-2727 |
| Brooks & Pollard Co/Little Rock, AR | 501-375-5561 |
| Cathey Graphics Group/Dallas, TX | 214-638-0731 |
| Central Advertising Agency/Fort Worth, TX | 817-390-3011 |
| Chesterfield Interiors Inc/Dallas, TX | 214-747-2211 |
| Clark, Betty & Assoc/Dallas, TX | 214-980-1685 |
| Coffee Design Co/Houston, TX | 713-780-0571 |
| Cranford-Johnson-Hunt & Assoc/Little Rock, AR | 501-376-6251 |

## DEF
| | |
|---|---|
| Design Enterprises, Inc/El Paso, TX | 915-594-7100 |
| Designmark/Houston, TX | 713-626-0953 |
| Ellies, David Industrial Design Inc/Dallas, TX | 214-742-8654 |
| Fedele Creative Consulting/Dallas, TX | 214-528-3501 |
| First Marketing Group/Houston, TX | 713-626-2500 |

## G
| | |
|---|---|
| GKD/Oklahoma City, OK | 405-232-2333 |
| The Goodwin Co/El Paso, TX | 915-584-1176 |
| Gore, Fred M & Assoc/Dallas, TX | 214-521-5844 |
| Graphic Designers Group Inc/Houston, TX | 713-622-8680 |
| Graphics Hardware Co/Phoenix, AZ | 602-242-4687 |
| Graphics Intern Adv & Des/Fort Worth, TX | 817-731-9941 |
| Graphics International Adv & Dsgn/Fort Worth, TX | 817-731-9941 |
| **GRIMES, DON/DALLAS, TX (P 116)** | **214-526-0040** |
| Grimm, Tom/Dallas, TX | 214-526-0040 |

## HIK
| | |
|---|---|
| Harrison Allen Design/Houston, TX | 713-771-9274 |
| Hood Hope & Assoc/Tulsa, OK | 918-749-4454 |

| | |
|---|---|
| ISD Incorporated/Houston, TX | 713-236-8232 |
| KCBN/Dallas, TX | 214-521-6400 |
| Konig Design Group/San Antonio, TX | 512-824-7387 |

## LMNO
| | |
|---|---|
| Lowe Runkle Co/Oklahoma City, OK | 405-848-6800 |
| Mantz & Associates/Dallas, TX | 214-521-7432 |
| McGrath, Michael Design/Dallas, TX | 214-361-1337 |
| Morales, Frank Design/Dallas, TX | 214-827-2101 |
| Neumann, Steve & Friends/Houston, TX | 713-629-7501 |
| Newhall, Leslie/Phoenix, AZ | 602-279-2933 |
| Owens & Assoc Advertising Inc/Phoenix, AZ | 602-264-5691 |

## PRS
| | |
|---|---|
| Pen N'Inc Studio/Ft Worth, TX | 817-332-7687 |
| Pirtle, Woody Inc/Dallas, TX | 214-522-7520 |
| Portzmann Design Inc/Houston, TX | 713-977-5700 |
| Reed Melnichek Gentry/Dallas, TX | 214-634-7337 |
| The Richards Group/Dallas, TX | 214-231-2500 |
| Strickland, Michael & Co/Houston, TX | 713-526-6654 |
| Sullivan, Jack Design Group/Phoenix, AZ | 602-271-0117 |
| Sunstar Designs/Prescott, AZ | 602-778-2714 |

## TVW
| | |
|---|---|
| 3D/International/Houston, TX | 713-871-7000 |
| Total Designers/Houston, TX | 713-688-7766 |
| Varner, Charles/Dallas, TX | 214-744-0148 |
| Weekley & Penny Inc/Houston, TX | 713-529-4861 |
| Winius Brandon/Bellaire, TX | 713-666-1765 |
| Witherspoon & Assoc/Fort Worth, TX | 817-335-1373 |

# WEST

## A
| | |
|---|---|
| ADI/Los Angeles, CA | 213-254-7131 |
| AGI/Los Angeles, CA | 213-462-0821 |
| Ace Design/Sausalito, CA | 415-332-9390 |
| Ad-Venture/Denver, CO | 303-771-6520 |
| Addison & Assoc/Santa Barbara, CA | 805-965-8188 |
| Adfiliation/Eugene, OR | 503-687-8262 |
| Advertising Design & Production Service/San Diego, CA | 714-483-1393 |
| Advertising Dsgn & Prod Services/San Diego, CA | 714-483-1393 |
| Advertising/Design Assoc/Littleton, CA | 415-421-7000 |
| Albertazzi, Mark/San Diego, CA | 704-452-9845 |
| Allied Artists/San Francisco, CA | 415-421-1919 |
| American Now Inc/Denver, CO | 303-573-1663 |
| Ampersand Studios/Denver, CO | 303-571-1446 |
| Amstutz Design/Los Angeles, CA | 213-652-7110 |
| Anaconda Studio/Santa Monica, CA | 213-454-2825 |
| Antisdel Image Group/Santa Clara, CA | 408-988-1010 |
| Arnold Design Inc/Denver, CO | 303-832-7156 |
| The Art Directors Club of Denver/Denver, CO | 303-837-1070 |
| The Art Zone/Honolulu, HI | 808-537-6647 |
| Artists In Print/San Francisco, CA | 415-673-6941 |
| Artmaster Studios/San Fernando, CA | 213-365-7188 |
| Artworks/Los Angeles, CA | 213-653-5683 |
| Asbury Tucker & Assoc/Long Beach, CA | 213-595-6481 |
| Aurora Borealis/San Francisco, CA | 415-392-2971 |

## B
| | |
|---|---|
| Baily, Robert Design Group/Portland, OR | 503-228-1381 |
| Banullos Design/Anaheim, CA | 714-978-1074 |
| Barnes, Herb Design/South Pasadena, CA | 213-682-2420 |
| Barnstorm Studios/Colorado Springs, CO | 303-630-7200 |
| Basic Designs Inc/Muir Beach, CA | 415-388-5141 |
| Bass, Yager and Assoc/Hollywood, CA | 213-466-9701 |
| Bean, Carolyn Associates Inc/San Francisco, CA | 415-957-9573 |
| Bennett, Douglas Design/Seattle, WA | 206-324-9966 |
| Bennett, Ralph Assoc/Van Nuys, CA | 213-782-3224 |
| Blanchard, D W & Assoc/Salt Lake City, UT | 801-484-6344 |
| Blazej, Rosalie Graphics/San Francisco, CA | 415-586-3325 |
| Bloch & Associates/Santa Monica, CA | 213-450-8863 |
| The Boardroom/Santa Monica, CA | 213-450-8343 |
| Boelter, Herbert A/Burbank, CA | 213-845-5055 |
| Boyd, Douglas Design/Los Angeles, CA | 213-655-9642 |
| Bright & Associates, Inc/Los Angeles, CA | 213-658-8844 |

# GRAPHIC DESIGNERS CONT'D.

Please send us your additions and updates.

| | |
|---|---|
| Briteday Inc/Mountain View, CA | 415-968-5668 |
| Brookins, Ed/Studio City, CA | 213-766-7336 |
| Brown, Bill & Assoc/Los Angeles, CA | 213-386-2455 |
| Brown, Steve/Northridge, CA | 213-349-0785 |
| Bruce, Joel Graphic Design/Santa Ana, CA | 714-641-2905 |
| Burns & Associates Inc/San Francisco, CA | 415-567-4404 |
| Burridge Design/Santa Barbara, CA | 805-965-8023 |
| Burridge, Robert/Santa Barbara, CA | 805-964-2087 |
| Business Graphics/Los Angeles, CA | 213-467-0292 |
| Busse and Cummins/San Francisco, CA | 415-957-0300 |

## C

| | |
|---|---|
| CAG Graphics/Van Nuys, CA | 213-901-1077 |
| Carlson, Keith Advertising Art/San Francisco, CA | 415-397-5130 |
| Carre Design/Santa Monica, CA | 213-395-1033 |
| Cassidy & Associates/Santa Clara, CA | 408-735-8443 |
| Cassidy Design/Santa Clara, CA | 408-735-8443 |
| Catalog Design & Production Inc/San Francisco, CA | 415-468-5500 |
| Chan Design/Santa Monica, CA | 213-393-3735 |
| Chandler Media Productions/Irvine, CA | 714-751-0880 |
| Chapman Productions/Los Angeles, CA | 213-460-4302 |
| Chartmasters Inc/San Francisco, CA | 415-421-6591 |
| Clark, Tim/Los Angeles, CA | 213-202-1044 |
| Coak, Steve & Pamela Designers/Altadena, CA | 213-797-5477 |
| The Coakley Heagerty Co/Santa Clara, CA | 408-249-6242 |
| Coates Creates/Portland, OR | 503-241-1124 |
| Cognata Associates/San Francisco, CA | 415-931-3800 |
| Communicreations/Denver, CO | 303-759-1155 |
| Conber Creations/Portland, OR | 503-288-2938 |
| Consortium West/Concept Design/Salt Lake City, UT | 801-278-4441 |
| Conversano, Henry & Assoc/Oakland, CA | 415-547-6890 |
| Corporate Graphics/San Francisco, CA | 415-474-2888 |
| Crawshaw, Todd Design/San Francisco, CA | 415-956-3169 |
| Creative Consultant/Venice, CA | 213-399-3875 |
| Cronan, Michael Patrick/San Francisco, CA | 415-398-2368 |
| CropMark/Los Angeles, CA | 213-388-3142 |
| Crouch, Jim & Assoc/Delmar, CA | 714-450-9200 |
| Cuerden Advertising Design/Denver, CO | 303-321-4163 |
| Cullimore, Jack M/Spokane, WA | 509-747-0905 |

## D

| | |
|---|---|
| DMR/Santa Clara, CA | 408-496-5010 |
| Danziger, Louis/Los Angeles, CA | 213-935-1251 |
| Dave Doane Studio/Newport Beach, CA | 714-548-7285 |
| Dellaporta Adv & Graphic/Santa Monica, CA | 213-394-0023 |
| DeMaio Graphics & Advertising/Van Nuys, CA | 213-785-6551 |
| Design & Direction/Torrance, CA | 213-320-0822 |
| Design Center/Salt Lake City, UT | 801-532-6122 |
| Design Corps/Los Angeles, CA | 213-651-1422 |
| Design Direction Group/Pasadena, CA | 213-792-4765 |
| Design Element/Los Angeles, CA | 213-656-3293 |
| Design Geometrics Inc/Santa Ana, CA | 714-557-1168 |
| Design Office/San Francisco, CA | 415-543-4760 |
| Design Projects Inc/Encino, CA | 213-995-0303 |
| Design Vectors/San Francisco, CA | 415-391-0399 |
| The Design Works/Los Angeles, CA | 213-556-2021 |
| Design/Graphics/Portland, OR | 503-227-7247 |
| Designamite/Santa Ana, CA | 714-549-8210 |
| The Designory Inc/Long Beach, CA | 213-432-5707 |
| Detanna Advertising Design/Los Angeles, CA | 213-852-0808 |
| Deutsch Design/Los Angeles, CA | 213-937-3521 |
| Dimensional Design/N Hollywood, CA | 213-769-5694 |
| Diniz, Carlos/Los Angeles, CA | 213-387-1171 |
| Dubow & Hutkin/Los Angeles, CA | 213-938-5177 |
| Dyer, Rod/Los Angeles, CA | 213-937-4100 |
| Dyna-Pac/San Diego, CA | 714-560-0117 |

## E F

| | |
|---|---|
| Earnett McFall & Assoc/Seattle, WA | 206-364-4956 |
| Ehrig & Assoc/Seattle, WA | 206-623-6666 |
| Ellies, Dave Industrial Design Inc/Santa Clara, CA | 408-727-0626 |
| Engle, Ray/Los Angeles, CA | 213-381-5001 |
| Entercom/Denver, CO | 303-393-0405 |
| Environetics Inc./San Francisco, CA | 415-392-7438 |
| Exhibit Design Inc/Burlingame, CA | 415-342-3060 |
| Farber, Melvyn Design Group/Venice, CA | 213-399-3242 |
| Farber, Rose Graphic Design/Venice, CA | 213-392-3049 |
| Finger, Julie/Los Angeles, CA | 213-653-0541 |
| First Impressions Design Studio/San Diego, CA | 714-226-1800 |
| Five Penguins Design/Burbank, CA | 213-841-5576 |
| Floyd, Richard Graphics/Lafayette, CA | 415-283-1735 |
| Flying Colors/San Francisco, CA | 415-563-0500 |
| Follis, John & Assoc/Los Angeles, CA | 213-735-1283 |
| Fox, BD & Friends/Hollywood, CA | 213-464-0131 |
| Frazier Design Assoc/Los Angeles, CA | 213-857-5500 |
| Freelance Design/Seattle, WA | 206-365-0065 |
| Furniss, Stephanie Design/San Geronomo, CA | 415-488-4692 |

## G

| | |
|---|---|
| Garner, Glenn Graphic Design/Seattle, WA | 206-323-7788 |
| Garnett, Joe Design/Illus/Los Angeles, CA | 213-381-1787 |
| General Graphics/Denver, CO | 303-832-5258 |
| Georgopoulos/Imada Design/Los Angeles, CA | 213-933-6425 |
| Gerber Advertising Agency/Portland, OR | 503-221-0100 |
| Gibby, John Design/Layton, UT | 801-544-0736 |
| Girvin, Tim Design/Seattle, WA | 206-623-7918 |
| Glickman, Abe Design/Van Nuys, CA | 213-989-3223 |
| The Gnu Group/Sausalito, CA | 415-332-8010 |
| Gohata, Mark/Gardena, CA | 213-327-6595 |
| Gould & Assoc/W Los Angeles, CA | 213-208-5577 |
| Graformation/N Hollywood, CA | 213-985-1224 |
| Graphic Concepts Inc/Salt Lake City, UT | 801-359-2191 |
| Graphic Data/Pacific Beach, CA | 714-274-4511 |
| Graphic Designers, Inc/Los Angeles, CA | 213-381-3977 |
| Graphic Designs by Joy/Newport Beach, CA | 714-642-0271 |
| Graphic Ideas/San Diego, CA | 714-299-3433 |
| Graphics One/Los Angeles, CA | 213-483-1126 |
| Greiman, April/Los Angeles, CA | 213-462-1771 |

## H

| | |
|---|---|
| Hale, Dan Ad Design Co/Woodland Hills, CA | 213-347-4021 |
| Hardbarger, Dave Design/Oakland, CA | 415-655-4928 |
| Harper and Assoc/Bellevue, WA | 206-885-0405 |
| Harrington and Associates/Los Angeles, CA | 213-876-5272 |
| Harte/Yamashita/Harte/Los Angeles, CA | 213-462-6486 |
| Hauser, S G Assoc Inc/Woodland Hills, CA | 213-884-1727 |
| Head & Hamilton/Los Angeles, CA | 213-937-8632 |
| Helgesson, Ulf Ind Dsgn/Woodland Hills, CA | 213-883-3772 |
| Hornall, John/Seattle, WA | 206-283-1856 |
| Horner, Pat/Seattle, WA | |
| Hosick, Frank Design/Seattle, WA | 206-789-5535 |
| The Howard Group/Woodland Hills, CA | 213-888-0505 |
| Hubert, Laurent/Menlo Park    CA, 94 | 5-321-5182 |
| Human Graphic/San Diego, CA | 714-299-0431 |
| Hyde, Bill/Foster City, CA | 415-345-6955 |

## I J

| | |
|---|---|
| Imag'Inez/San Francisco, CA | 415-398-3203 |
| Image Makers/Santa Barbara, CA | 805-965-8546 |
| Image Stream/Los Angeles, CA | 213-933-9196 |
| Imagination Creative Services/Santa Cruz, CA | 408-988-8696 |
| Industrial Design Affiliates/Beverly Hills, CA | 213-878-0808 |
| JFDO Design/Los Angeles, CA | 213-653-0541 |
| Jaciow Kelley Organization/Menlo Park, CA | 415-327-8210 |
| Jamieson, Tom Design/Claremont, CA | 714-626-8338 |
| The Jeff Dayne Studio/Portland, OR | 503-222-7144 |
| Jerde Partnership/Los Angeles, CA | 213-413-0130 |
| Johnson Rodger Design/Rolling Hills, CA | 213-377-8860 |
| Johnson, Jerry & Assoc/Burbank, CA | 213-849-1444 |
| Johnson, Paige Graphic Design/Palo Alto, CA | 415-327-0488 |
| Johnson, Scott Graphic Art/Emeryville, CA | 415-655-9673 |
| Joly Assoc/San Francisco, CA | 415-641-1933 |
| Jones, Steve/Venice, CA | 213-396-9111 |
| Jonson Pedersen Hinrichs & Shakery/San Francisco, CA | 415-981-6612 |
| Juett Dennis & Assoc/Los Angeles, CA | 213-385-4373 |

## K

| | |
|---|---|
| K S Wilshire Inc/Los Angeles, CA | 213-879-9595 |
| KLAC Metro Media/Los Angeles, CA | 213-462-5522 |
| Kageyama, David Designer/Seattle, WA | 206-622-7281 |
| Kano & Company Inc/Playa Del Rey, CA | 213-823-7772 |

# GRAPHIC DESIGNERS CONT'D.

Please send us your additions and updates.

| | |
|---|---|
| Keating & Keating/San Francisco, CA | 415-421-3350 |
| Keser, Dennis/San Francisco, CA | 415-387-6448 |
| Kessler, David & Assoc/Hollywood, CA | 213-462-6043 |
| Keylin, Richard/Denver, CO | 303-777-1300 |
| Klein/Los Angeles, CA | 213-278-5600 |
| Klein, Larry Designer/San Carlos, CA | 415-595-1332 |
| Kleiner, John A/Marina Del Rey, CA | 213-472-7442 |
| Kramer, Gideon Assoc/Seattle, WA | 206-623-0676 |
| Kuey, Patty/Yorba Linda, CA | 714-970-5286 |

## L

| | |
|---|---|
| LaFleur Design/Sausalito, CA | 415-332-3725 |
| Lanberger, Roy Assoc/Campbell, CA | 408-379-8822 |
| Landes & Assoc/Torrance, CA | 213-379-6817 |
| Landor Associates/San Francisco, CA | 415-955-1200 |
| Larson, Ron/Los Angeles, CA | 213-465-8451 |
| Laurence-Deutsch Design/Los Angeles, CA | 213-937-3521 |
| Leipzig, Dale/Huntington Beach, CA | 714-847-1240 |
| Leong, Russel Design Group/Palo Alto, CA | 415-321-2443 |
| Lesser, Joan/Etcetera/Santa Monica, CA | 213-450-3977 |
| Levine & Company, Steve Levine/Venice, CA | 213-399-9336 |
| Lipson, Marty & Assoc/Santa Monica, CA | 213-451-1421 |
| Littles, Dolores/Los Angeles, CA | 213-757-3622 |
| Logan Carey & Rehag/San Francisco, CA | 415-543-7080 |
| Loveless, J R Design/Santa Ana, CA | 714-754-0886 |
| Lum, Darell/Monterey Park, CA | 213-613-2538 |
| Lumco/Monterey Park, CA | 213-613-2538 |
| Lumel-Whiteman Assoc/North Hollywood, CA | 213-769-5332 |
| Lumel-Whiteman Assoc/Monterey Park, CA | 213-613-2538 |

## M

| | |
|---|---|
| Maddus, Patrick & Co/San Diego, CA | 714-238-1340 |
| Magnussen Design Inc/Walnut, CA | 714-595-2483 |
| Malmberg, Gary Assoc/Denver, CO | 303-777-5411 |
| Manhattan Graphics/Manhattan Beach, CA | 213-376-2778 |
| Manwaring, Michael Office/San Francisco, CA | 415-421-3595 |
| Mar, Vic Designs/North Shore, CA | 714-393-3968 |
| Marra, Ann Graphic Design/Portland, OR | 503-227-5207 |
| Martino Design/Portland, OR | 503-227-7247 |
| Matrix Design Consultants/Los Angeles, CA | 213-620-0828 |
| Matrix Design Inc/Denver, CO | 303-388-9353 |
| Media Services Corp/San Francisco, CA | 415-928-3033 |
| Mediate, Frank/Los Angeles, CA | 213-381-3977 |
| Mikkelson, Linda S/Los Angeles, CA | 213-937-8360 |
| Miura Design/Torrance, CA | 213-320-1957 |
| Mize, Charlie Advertising Art/San Francisco, CA | 415-421-1548 |
| Mizrahi, Robert/Buena Park, CA | 714-527-6182 |
| Mobius Design Assoc/Los Angeles, CA | 213-659-5330 |
| Molly Designs Inc/Irvine, CA | 714-751-6600 |
| Monahan, Leo/Los Angeles, CA | 213-463-3116 |
| Mortensen, Gordon/Santa Barbara, CA | 805-962-5315 |
| Multi-Media Inc/Englewood, CO | 303-741-4600 |
| Murphy, Harry & Friends/Mill Valley, CA | 415-383-8586 |
| Murray/Bradley Inc/Seattle, WA | 206-622-7082 |

## N

| | |
|---|---|
| N Lee Lacy/Assoc Ltd/Los Angeles, CA | 213-852-1414 |
| Naganuma, Tony K Design/San Francisco, CA | 415-433-4484 |
| Nagel, William Design Group/Palo Alto, CA | 415-328-0251 |
| New Breath Productions/Los Angeles, CA | 213-876-3491 |
| New Concepts Industrial Design Corp/Seattle, WA | 206-633-3111 |
| Newman, Rich Graphic/San Francisco, CA | 415-433-4977 |
| Nicholson Design/San Diego, CA | 714-235-9000 |
| Nicolini Associates/Oakland, CA | 415-531-5569 |
| Niehaus, Don/Westwood, CA | 213-279-1559 |

## O

| | |
|---|---|
| O'Brien, Stephanie/Long Beach, CA | 213-438-4367 |
| Odgers, Jayme/Los Angeles, CA | 213-484-9965 |
| Okland Design Assoc/Salt Lake City, UT | 801-484-7861 |
| Olson & Assoc/San Diego, CA | 714-235-9993 |
| Omega Productions/Santa Ana, CA | 714-547-5669 |
| Orr, R & Associates Inc/El Toro, CA | 714-770-1277 |
| Orsan, Lou Designs/Los Angeles, CA | 213-413-5300 |
| Osborn, Michael/San Francisco, CA | 415-495-4292 |
| Osborn, Stephen/San Francisco, CA | 415-495-4292 |
| Oshima, Carol/Covina, CA | 213-966-0796 |
| Overby, Robert/Santa Barbara, CA | 805-966-2359 |
| Overton, Chuck Designer/San Francisco, CA | 415-552-7090 |

## PQ

| | |
|---|---|
| Pacif Graphic Assoc/City of Industry, CA | 213-336-6958 |
| Pease, Robert & Co/San Francisco, CA | 415-775-4667 |
| Peddicord & Assoc/Santa Clara, CA | 408-727-7800 |
| Persechini & Moss/Los Angeles, CA | 213-559-0864 |
| Petzold & Assoc/Portland, OR | 503-221-1800 |
| Pilas Schmidt Westerdahl Co/Portland, OR | 503-228-4000 |
| Popovich, Mike c/o Pacific Graphic Assoc/City of Industry, CA | 213-336-6958 |
| Powers Design International/Newport Beach, CA | 714-645-2265 |
| Primo Angeli Graphics/San Francisco, CA | 415-974-6100 |
| Quatro Graphics Publishing Co/Seattle, WA | 206-881-7711 |
| The Quorum/Clinton, WA | 206-321-5868 |

## R

| | |
|---|---|
| RJL Design Graphics/Fremont, CA | 415-657-2038 |
| Radetsky Design Associates/Denver, CO | 303-629-7375 |
| Rainbow Graphics & Printing/San Diego, CA | 714-296-8242 |
| Regis McKenna Inc/Palo Alto, CA | 415-494-2030 |
| Rehag, Larry/San Francisco, CA | 415-543-7080 |
| Reid, Scott/Santa Barbara, CA | 805-963-8926 |
| Reineck & Reineck/San Francisco, CA | 415-566-3614 |
| Reis, Gerald & Co/San Francisco, CA | 415-543-1344 |
| Richard Reineman Industrial Design/Newport Beach, CA | 714-673-2485 |
| Richard Runyan Design/West Los Angeles, CA | 213-477-8878 |
| Rickabaugh Design/Portland, OR | 503-223-2191 |
| Ricks Ehrig Inc/Seattle, WA | 206-623-6666 |
| Robinson, David & Assoc/San Diego, CA | 714-298-2021 |
| Rogow & Bernstein/Los Angeles, CA | 213-936-9916 |
| Rolandesign/Woodland Hills, CA | 213-346-9752 |
| Ross, Deborah/Studio City, CA | 213-985-5205 |
| Roy Ritola Inc/San Francisco, CA | 415-788-7010 |
| Rubin, Marvin/Venice, CA | 213-392-2226 |
| Runyan, Robert Miles & Assoc/Playa Del Rey, CA | 213-823-0975 |
| Rupert, Paul Designer/San Francisco, CA | 415-391-2966 |

## S

| | |
|---|---|
| Sackheim, Morton Enterprises/Beverly Hills, CA | 213-652-0220 |
| Sanchez, Michael Assoc/Pasadena, CA | 213-793-4017 |
| Sandvick, John Studios/Los Angeles, CA | 213-685-7148 |
| Sant'Andrea, Jim/Compton, CA | 213-979-9100 |
| Saunders, Britt Design/Irvine, CA | 714-549-1274 |
| Schaefer, Robert Television Art/Hollywood, CA | 213-462-7877 |
| Schorer, R Thomas/Palos Verdes, CA | 213-377-0207 |
| Schulz, Margi Design Inc/Los Angeles, CA | 213-386-5261 |
| Schwab, Michael/San Francisco, CA | 415-546-7559 |
| Schwartz, Clem & Bonnie Graphic Design/San Diego, CA | 714-291-8878 |
| Schwartz, Daniel & Assoc/Santa Ana, CA | 714-633-1170 |
| Scroggin & Fischer Advertising/San Francisco, CA | 415-391-2694 |
| See Design & Production Inc/Salem, OR | 503-393-1733 |
| Seigle Rolfs & Wood Inc/Honolulu, HI | 808-531-6211 |
| Seiniger & Assoc/Los Angeles, CA | 213-653-8665 |
| Sellers, Michael Advertising/San Francisco, CA | 415-781-7200 |
| Sharon Shuman, Designer/Los Angeles, CA | 213-837-6998 |
| Shaw, Michael Design/Manhattan Beach, CA | 213-545-0516 |
| Shenon, Mike/Palo Alto, CA | 415-326-4608 |
| Shoji Graphics/Los Angeles, CA | 213-384-3091 |
| Shook & Assoc/Glendale, CA | 213-504-9623 |
| Sidjakov, Nicholas/San Francisco, CA | 415-543-9962 |
| Signworks Inc/Seattle, WA | 206-525-2718 |
| Smidt, Sam/Palo Alto, CA | 415-327-0707 |
| The Smith Group/Portland, OR | 503-224-1905 |
| Sorensen, Hugh E Industrail Design/Brea, CA | 714-529-8493 |
| Soyster & Ohrenschall Inc/San Francisco, CA | 415-956-7575 |
| Spangler Leonhardt & Hornall Inc./Seattle, WA | 206-624-0551 |
| Spear Design Associates/Santa Monica, CA | 213-395-3939 |
| Spivey, William Design/Newport Beach, CA | 714-752-1203 |
| The Stansbury Company/Beverly Hills, CA | 213-273-1138 |
| **STEINBERG, BRUCE/SAN FRANCISCO, CA (P 391)** | **415-864-0739** |
| Stine, Kym E/Seal Beach, CA | 213-431-9464 |
| Stockton, James & Assoc/San Francisco, CA | 415-929-7900 |
| Strong, David Design Group/Seattle, WA | 206-447-9160 |

# GRAPHIC DESIGNERS CONT'D.

Please send us your additions and updates.

| | |
|---|---|
| The Studio/San Francisco, CA | 415-928-4400 |
| Studio Artists Inc/Los Angeles, CA | 213-382-6281 |
| Sugi, Richard Design & Assoc/Los Angeles, CA | 213-385-4169 |
| Sullivan & Assoc/Los Angeles, CA | 213-384-3331 |
| Superior Graphic Systems/Long Beach, CA | 213-433-7421 |
| Sussman & Prejza/Santa Monica, CA | 213-829-3337 |

## T
| | |
|---|---|
| TOPS Talent Agency/Honolulu, HI | 808-537-6647 |
| Tamburello, Michael Graphic Design/Littleton, CO | 303-773-0128 |
| Tanner Laffitte Advertising Inc/Irvine, CA | 714-957-8591 |
| Tartak Libera Design/Los Angeles, CA | 213-477-3571 |
| Taylor, Robert W Design Inc/Boulder, CO | 303-494-8479 |
| Teitelbaum, William/Los Angeles, CA | 213-277-0597 |
| Thomas & Assoc/Santa Monica, CA | 213-451-8502 |
| Thomas, Keith M Inc/Santa Ana, CA | 714-979-3051 |
| Thompson, Larry Ltd/San Bernardino, CA | 714-885-4976 |
| Trade Marx/Seattle, WA | 206-623-7676 |
| Tribotte Design/Los Angeles, CA | 213-466-6514 |
| Trygg Stefanic Advertising/Los Altos, CA | 415-948-3493 |
| Tycer Fultz Bellack/Palo Alto, CA | 415-328-6300 |

## U V
| | |
|---|---|
| Unigraphics/San Francisco, CA | 415-398-8232 |
| Valentino Graphic Design/Los Angeles, CA | 213-386-9444 |
| Van Hamersveld Design/Los Angeles, CA | 213-656-3815 |
| Van Noy & Co Inc/Los Angeles, CA | 213-386-7312 |
| Vanderbyl Design/San Francisco, CA | 415-397-4583 |
| Vantage Advertising & Marketing Assoc/San Leandro, CA | 415-352-3640 |
| Vicom Associates/San Francisco, CA | 415-391-8700 |
| Village Design/Irvine, CA | 714-857-9048 |
| Visual Images Inc/Denver, CO | 303-388-5366 |
| Visual Resources Inc/Los Angeles, CA | 213-851-6688 |
| Voltec Associates/Los Angeles, CA | 213-467-2106 |

## W
| | |
|---|---|
| Walker Design Associates/Denver, CO | 303-773-0426 |
| Warner Design/Berkeley, CA | 415-658-0733 |
| Weideman and Associates/North Hollywood, CA | 213-769-8488 |
| West End Studios/Westwood, CA | 213-279-1539 |
| West End Studios/San Francisco, CA | 415-434-0380 |
| West, Suzanne Design/Palo Alto, CA | 415-324-8068 |
| White, Ken Design/Los Angeles, CA | 213-467-4681 |
| Whitely, Mitchell Assoc/San Francisco, CA | 415-398-2920 |
| Wilkerson, Haines/Manhattan Beach, CA | 213-372-3325 |
| Wilkins & Peterson Graphic Design/Seattle, WA | 206-624-1695 |
| Wilkins, Doug/Seattle, WA | |
| **WILLARDSON & WHITE/LOS ANGELES, CA (P 184,185)** | **213-656-9461** |
| Williams, Leslie/Norwalk, CA | 213-864-4135 |
| Williamson Clave Inc/Los Angeles, CA | 213-836-0143 |
| Wilton Coombs & Colnett Inc/San Francisco, CA | 415-981-6250 |
| Winters, Clyde Design/San Francisco, CA | 415-391-5643 |
| Woodard Racing Graphics Ltd/Boulder, CO | 303-443-1986 |
| Woodward Design Assoc/Hollywood, CA | 213-461-4141 |
| Woodward, Teresa/Pacific Palisades, CA | 213-459-2317 |
| Workshop West/Beverly Hills, CA | 213-278-1370 |
| Worthington, Carl A Partnership/Boulder, CO | 303-443-7271 |

## Y Z
| | |
|---|---|
| Yamaguma & Assoc/San Jose, CA | 408-279-0500 |
| Yanez, Maurice & Assoc/Los Angeles, CA | 213-938-3846 |
| Young & Roehr Adv/Portland, OR | 503-297-4501 |
| Yuguchi Krogstad/Los Angeles, CA | 213-383-6915 |
| Zamparelli Design/Pasadena, CA | 213-577-7292 |
| Zolotow, Milton/Westwood, CA | 213-279-1789 |

# PHOTO/FILM SERVICES

## LABS & RETOUCHERS

### NEW YORK CITY

| | |
|---|---|
| A M I/11 W 25th St | 212-255-8778 |
| A Z O Color Labs/149 Madison Ave | 212-982-6610 |
| ACS Studios/56 W 45th St | 212-575-9250 |
| ASAP Photolab Inc/40 E 49th St | 212-832-1223 |
| Accu-Color Group Inc/103 Fifth Ave | 212-989-8235 |
| Acorn Color Laboratories Inc/244 W 49th St | 212-265-4413 |
| Alchemy Color Ltd/125 W 45th St | 212-997-1944 |
| American Blue Print Co Inc/7 E 47th St | 212-751-2240 |
| American Photo Print Co/350 Fifth Ave | 212-736-2885 |
| American Photo Print Co/285 Madison Ave | 212-532-2424 |
| Andy's Place/17 E 48th St | 212-371-1362 |
| Anselmo Studio/211 E 51st St | 212-753-1606 |
| Apco-Apeda Photo Co/250 W 54th St | 212-586-5755 |
| Appel, Albert/9 E 40th St | 212-686-2830 |
| Art Way Photo & Stat Service/18 E 48th St | 212-755-7280 |
| Atlantic Blue Print Co/575 Madison Ave | 212-755-3388 |
| Authenticolor Labs Inc/227 E 45th St | 212-867-7905 |
| Bebell Inc/416 W 45th St | 212-245-8900 |
| Bellis, Dave Studios/155 E 55th St | 212-753-3740 |
| Berger, Jack/41 W 53rd St | 212-245-5705 |
| Berkey K & L/222 E 44th St | 212-661-5600 |
| Bishop, Bob/236 E 36th St | 212-889-3525 |
| Blae,Ken Tetouching Inc/1501 Broadway | 212-869-3488 |
| Bluestone Photoprint Co Inc/19 W 34th St | 212-564-1516 |
| Bonaventura Studio/307 E 44th St | 212-687-9208 |
| Broderson, Charles Backdrops/873 Broadway | 212-925-9392 |
| Brunel, Jean Inc/11 Jay St | 212-226-3009 |
| C C S Co/330 E 59th St | 212-752-2330 |
| CJS Enterprises Inc/420 Lexington Ave | 212-986-5153 |
| Cacchione & Sheehan/156 E 52nd St | 212-752-1143 |
| Canon/1114 Avenue of the Americas | 212-869-8350 |
| Carlson & Forino Studios/230 E 44th St | 212-697-7044 |
| Carroll Associates/441 Lexington Ave | 212-490-2455 |
| Chapman, Edwin W Studio/299 Madison Ave | 212-697-0872 |
| Chroma Copy/227 E 56th St | 212-421-5207 |
| Chrome Print/104 E 25th St | 212-228-0840 |
| Colmer, Brian-The Final touch/310 E 46th St | 212-682-3012 |
| Color By Pergament/305 E 47th St | 212-751-5367 |
| Color Design Studio/19 W 21st St | 212-255-8103 |
| Color Masters Inc/143 E 27th St | 212-889-7464 |
| Color Perfect Inc/200 Park Ave S | 212-777-1210 |
| Color Unlimited Inc/443 Park Ave S | 212-889-2440 |
| Color Vision Photo Finishers/29 W 38th St | 212-221-7040 |
| Colorama/311 W 43rd St | 212-757-7474 |
| Colprite Film Processing Labs/115 E 31st St | 212-532-2116 |
| Columbia Blue & Photoprint Co/14 E 39th St | 212-532-9424 |
| Commerce Photo Print Co/415 Lexington Ave | 212-986-2068 |
| Compo Stat Service/18 E 48th St | 212-758-1690 |
| Copy-Line Corp/40 W 37th St | 212-563-3535 |
| Copycolor/8 W 30th St | 212-725-8252 |
| Copytone Inc/8 W 45th St | 212-575-0235 |
| Corona Color Studios Inc/10 W 33rd St | 212-239-4990 |
| Cortese, Phyllis/306 E 52nd St | 212-421-4664 |
| Crandall, Robert Assoc/306 E 45th St | 212-661-4710 |
| Creative Color Inc/25 W 45th St | 212-582-3841 |
| The Creative Color Print Lab Inc/25 W 45th St | 212-582-6237 |
| Dai Nippon Printing/1633 Broadway | 212-397-1880 |
| The Darkroom Inc/222 E 46th St | 212-687-8920 |
| Davis-Ganes/15 E 40th St | 212-687-6537 |
| Diamond Art Studio Ltd/515 Madison Ave | 212-355-5444 |
| Diamond, Richard/50 E 42nd St | 212-697-4720 |
| Diane Studio/315 W 57th St #7D | 212-757-0445 |
| The Dick Sharkey Studio/315 W 57th St | 212-265-1036 |
| Dimension Color Labs Inc/28 W 39th St | 212-354-5918 |
| DiPierro-Turiel/210 E 47th St | 212-752-2260 |
| Duggal Color Projects Inc/9 W 20th St | 212-924-6363 |
| Dzurella, Paul Studio/15 W 38th St | 212-840-8623 |
| Edstan Studio/240 Madison Ave | 212-686-3666 |
| Egelston Retouching Services/45 W 45th St | 212-753-0017 |
| Eliopulos, Elias/75 E 55th St | 212-758-5280 |
| Estelle Friedman Retouchers/160 E 38th St | 212-532-0084 |
| Evans-Avedisian DiStefano Inc/29 W 38th St | 212-697-4240 |
| Filmstat/520 Fifth Ave | 212-840-1676 |
| Filorama, Jack/19 W 44th St | 212-944-6220 |
| Fine-Art Color Lab Inc/221 Park Ave S | 212-674-7640 |
| Finley Photographics Inc/488 Madison Ave | 212-688-3025 |
| Fodale Studio/247 E 50th St | 212-755-0150 |
| Forway Studios Inc/441 Lexington Ave | 212-661-0260 |
| Four Colors Photo Lab Inc/10 E 39th St | 212-889-3399 |
| Frenchys Color Lab/10 E 38th St | 212-889-7787 |
| Frey, Louis Co Inc/90 West St | 212-791-0500 |
| Fromia, John A/799 Broadway | 212-473-7930 |
| Gayde, Richard Assoc Inc/515 Madison Ave | 212-421-4088 |
| Geller, Fred Assoc Inc/325 E 64th St | 212-535-6240 |
| George Gray Studios/230 E 44th St | 212-661-0276 |
| George, Peter J/342 E 53rd St | 212-355-1840 |
| Goodman, Irwin Inc/1156 Avenue of the Americas | 212-944-6337 |
| Graphic Images Ltd/151 W 46th St | 212-869-8370 |
| Grubb, Louis D/155 Riverside Dr | 212-873-2561 |
| H-Y Photo Service/16 E 52nd St | 212-371-3018 |
| Hadar, Studio Eric/10 E 39th St | 212-889-2092 |
| Holt, Dolores/353 E 72nd St | 212-737-9250 |
| Housten Shields & Assoc/145 E 49th St | 212-753-7760 |
| Hudson Reproductions Inc/76 Ninth Ave | 212-989-3400 |
| J & R Color Lab/29 W 38th St | 212-869-9870 |
| J M W Studio Inc/230 E 44th St | 212-986-9155 |
| Jaeger, Elliot/49 W 45th St | 212-840-6278 |
| Jellybean Photographics Inc/99 Madison Ave 14th Fl | 212-679-4888 |
| Joe Ramer Associates/509 Madison Ave | 212-751-0894 |
| K-G Studio Inc/11 E 44th St | 212-697-0877 |
| Kaye Graphics Inc/151 Lexington Ave | 212-889-8240 |
| Kurahara, Joan/6 E 39th St #804 | 212-684-5099 |
| **LAFERLA, SANDRO/135 W 14TH ST (P 401)** | **212-620-0693** |
| Larson Color Lab/123 Fifth Ave | 212-674-0610 |
| Leon Appel Assoc/2 W 46th St | 212-840-6633 |
| Loonan, Matthew/121 Varick St | 212-255-7463 |
| Lucas, Bob/10 E 38th St | 212-725-2090 |
| Lukon Art Service Ltd/56 W 45th St 3rd Fl | 212-575-0474 |
| Lyons/Stevens Photographic Retouching/400 E 78th St | 212-628-6484 |
| Mancaruso, Ann/5 W 46th St 3rd Fl | 212-840-0215 |
| Mann & Greene Color Inc/320 E 39th St | 212-481-6868 |
| Manna Color Labs Inc/42 W 15th St | 212-691-8360 |
| Marshall, Henry/6 E 39th St | 212-686-1060 |
| Martin, Tulio G studio Inc/140 W 57th St | 212-245-6489 |
| Martin/Arnold Color Systems/150 Fifth Ave #429 | 212-675-7270 |
| Martini, Fred Studios Inc/575 Lexington Ave 24th Fl | 212-838-4503 |
| Mayer, Kurt Color Labs Inc/1170 Broadway | 212-532-3738 |
| McCurdy & Cardinale Color Lab/65 W 36th St | 212-695-5140 |
| McWilliams, Clyde/6 E 39th St | 212-532-5936 |
| Media Universal Inc/116 W 32nd St | 212-695-7454 |
| Medina Studios Inc/141 E 44th St | 212-867-3113 |
| Merril Photos Corp/1501 Broadway | 212-221-8211 |
| Modernage Photo Services/312 E 46th St | 212-661-9190 |
| Moser, Klaus T Ltd/127 E 15th St | 212-475-0038 |
| Motal Custom Darkrooms/25 W 45th St 3rd Fl | 212-757-7874 |
| Murray Hill Photo Print Inc/32 W 39th St | 212-921-4175 |
| My Own Color Lab/45 W 45th St | 212-391-8638 |
| National Reproductions/420 Lexington Ave | 212-687-8877 |
| National Reprographics Co/110 W 32nd St | 212-736-5674 |
| New York Flash Rental/156 Fifth Ave | 212-741-1165 |
| Ornaal Color Photos/24 W 25th St | 212-675-3850 |
| P I C Color Lab/25 W 45th St | 212-575-5600 |
| Paccione, E S Inc/150 E 56th St | 212-755-0965 |
| Palevitz, Bob/333 E 30th St | 212-684-6026 |
| Pastore dePamphilis Rampone/145 E 32nd St | 212-889-2221 |
| Pergament/305 E 47th St | 212-751-5367 |
| Photo Retouch Inc/160 E 38th St | 212-532-0084 |

# PHOTO/FILM SERVICES CONT'D.

Please send us your additions and updates.

| | |
|---|---|
| Photographic Color Specialists Inc./10-36 47th Rd | 212-786-4770 |
| Photorama/239 W 39th St | 212-354-5280 |
| Portgallo Photographic Services/72 W 45th St | 212-840-2636 |
| Positive Color Inc/342 Madison Ave | 212-986-2980 |
| Precision Chromes Inc/310 Madison Ave | 212-687-5990 |
| Preferred Photographic Co/165 W 46th St | 212-757-0237 |
| Procil Adstat Co Inc/7 W 45th St | 212-819-0155 |
| Prussack, Phil/155 E 55th St | 212-755-2470 |
| Quality Color Lab/305 E 46th St | 212-753-2200 |
| R & V Studio/32 W 39th St | 212-944-9590 |
| Rainbow Graphics/10 E 49th St | 212-869-2544 |
| Ram Retouching/152 E 35th St #6B | 212-599-0985 |
| Rasulo Graphics Service/36 E 31st St | 212-686-2861 |
| Regal Velox/25 W 43rd St | 212-840-0330 |
| Reiter Dulberg/157 W 54th St | 212-582-6871 |
| Reproduction Color Specialists/9 E 38th St | 212-683-0833 |
| Retouchers Gallery/211 E 53rd St | 212-751-9203 |
| Retouching Inc/9 E 38th St | 212-683-4188 |
| Rhina Color Services Ltd/10 E 39th St | 212-679-8718 |
| Rio Enterprises/321 E 53rd St | 212-758-9300 |
| Rivera and Schiff Assoc Inc/21 W 38th St | 212-354-2977 |
| Robotti, Thomas/5 W 46th St | 212-840-0215 |
| Rogers Color Lab Corp/165 Madison Ave | 212-683-6400 |
| Scala Fine Arts Publishers Inc/342 Madison Ave | 212-354-9646 |
| Schaeffer, Daniel/171 Madison Ave | 212-532-2263 |
| Scope Assoc/11 E 22nd St | 212-674-4190 |
| Scott Screen Prints/228 E 45th St | 212-697-8923 |
| Sharron Photographic Labs/260 W 36th St | 212-239-4980 |
| Simmons-Beal Inc/3 E 40th St | 212-532-6261 |
| Slide Shop Inc/220 E 23rd St | 212-725-5200 |
| Spano/Roccanova Retouching Inc/16 W 46th St | 212-840-7450 |
| Spector, Hy Studios/56 W 45th St | 212-221-3656 |
| Spectrakrome Division/216 E 45th St | 212-490-2345 |
| Spectrum Creative Retouchers Inc/230 E 44th St | 212-687-3359 |
| Stanley, Joseph/211 W 58th St | 212-246-1258 |
| Stathouse/41 E 42nd St | 212-867-6512 |
| Stewart Color Labs Inc/563 Eleventh Ave | 212-868-1440 |
| Studio 55/25 W 43rd St | 212-840-0920 |
| Studio Chrome Lab Inc/36 W 25th St | 212-989-6767 |
| Studio X/20 W 20th St | 212-989-9233 |
| Sunlight Graphics/2 E 37th St | 212-683-4452 |
| Super Photo Color Services/49 W 37th St | 212-221-3035 |
| T R P Slavin Colour Services/920 Broadway | 212-674-5700 |
| Tanksley, John Studios Inc/210 E 47th St | 212-752-1150 |
| Tartaro Color Lab/29 W 38th St | 212-840-1640 |
| Todd Photoprint Inc/1600 Broadway | 212-245-2440 |
| Trio Studio/18 E 48th St | 212-752-4875 |
| Ultimate Image/443 Park Ave S 7th Fl | 212-683-4838 |
| Van Chromes Corp/311 W 43rd St | 212-582-0505 |
| Vanderhoff, J A/500 Fifth Ave #2525 | 212-719-1290 |
| Verilen Reproductions/3 E 40th St | 212-686-7774 |
| Vidachrome Inc/25 W 39th St 6th Fl | 212-391-8124 |
| Vogue Wright Studios/225 Park Ave S | 212-254-3400 |
| Wagner Photoprint Co/121 W 50th St | 212-245-4796 |
| Ward, Jack Color Service/220 E 23rd St | 212-725-5200 |
| Way Color Inc/420 Lexington Ave | 212-687-5610 |
| Weber, Martin J Studio/171 Madison Ave | 212-532-2695 |
| Weiman & Lester Inc/21 E 40th St | 212-679-1180 |
| Welbeck Studios Inc/39 W 38th St | 212-869-1660 |
| Wind, Gerry & Assoc/265 Madison Ave | 212-686-1818 |
| Winter, Jerry Studio/333 E 45th St | 212-490-0876 |
| Wolf, Bill/420 Lexington Ave | 212-697-6215 |
| Wolsk, Bernard Inc/509 Madison Ave | 212-751-7727 |
| Zazula, Hy Inc/2 W 46th St | 212-581-2747 |

## NORTHEAST

| | |
|---|---|
| Able Art Service/77 Summer St, Boston, MA | 617-482-4558 |
| Adams & Abbott Inc/46 Summer St, Boston, MA | 617-542-1621 |
| Alfie Custom Color/155 N Dean St, Englewood, NJ | 201-569-2028 |
| Alves Photo Service/14 Storrs Ave, Braintree, MA | 617-843-5555 |
| Asman Custom Photo Service Inc/926 Pennsylvania Ave SE, Washington, DC | 202-547-7713 |
| Bateman Photo/200 E Lexington St, Baltimore, MD | 301-539-1256 |
| Blakeslee-Lane/916 N Charles St, Baltimore, MD | 301-727-8800 |
| Blow-Up/2441 Maryland Ave, Baltimore, MD | 301-467-3636 |
| Boris Color Labs Inc/35 Landsdowne St, Boston, MA | 617-261-1152 |
| Boston Photo Service/112 State St, Boston, MA | 617-523-0508 |
| Boston Photocopy Inc/235 Stuart St, Boston, MA | 617-266-1115 |
| Calverts Inc/938 Highland Ave, Needham Hts, MA | 617-444-8000 |
| Colorlab/5708 Arundel Ave, Rockville, MD | 301-770-2128 |
| Colortek/111 Beach St, Boston, MA | 617-451-0894 |
| Complete Photo Service/703 Mt Auburn St, Cambridge, MA | 617-864-5954 |
| Creative Color Inc/419 Boylston St, Boston, MA | 617-482-3651 |
| The Darkroom Inc/232 First Ave, Pittsburgh, PA | 412-261-6056 |
| Delbert, Christian/19 Linell Circle, Billerica, MA | 617-273-3138 |
| Dunigan, John V/62 Minnehaha Blvd, PO Box 70, Oakland, NJ | 201-337-6656 |
| Dunlop Custom Photolab Service/2321 4th St NE, Washington, DC | 202-526-5000 |
| Durkin, Joseph/25 Huntington, Boston, MA | 617-267-0437 |
| Foto Fidelity Inc/35 Leon St, Boston, MA | 617-267-6487 |
| G F I Printing & Photo Co/2 Highland St, Port Chester, NY | 914-937-2823 |
| Goldstein, Jerome/Box 421, Central Valley, NY | 914-928-2001 |
| Gould, David/76 Coronado St, Atlantic Beach, NY | 516-371-2413 |
| Industrial Color Lab/P O Box 563, Framingham, MA | 617-872-3280 |
| K E W Color Labs/112 Main St, Norwalk, CT | 203-853-7888 |
| Kennedy, Bruce/204 Westminster Mall, Provdence, RI | 401-273-8090 |
| Leonardo Printing Corp/529 E 3rd St, Mount Vernon, NY | 914-664-7890 |
| Lerner, Jerry/11 Lincoln Ave, West Orange, NJ | 201-325-0087 |
| Maglione, Marcia/381 Hanover St, Boston, MA | |
| Makepeace, B L Inc/1266 Boylston St, Boston, MA | 617-267-1292 |
| Mannis, Ben/22 Bassett St, Lynn, MA | 617-595-2998 |
| Media Lab Inc/440 Summer St, Boston, MA | 617-426-5655 |
| Modern Mass Media/Box 950, Chatham, NJ | 201-635-6000 |
| Moore's Photo Laboratory/1107 Main St, Charleston, WV | 304-343-8650 |
| Muggeo, Sam/63 Hedgebrook Lane, Stamford, CT | 212-838-4625 |
| National Color Labs Inc/306 W 1st Ave, Roselle, NJ | 201-241-1010 |
| Northeast Color Research/40 Cameron Ave, Somerville, MA | 617-666-1161 |
| Photo Dynamics/PO Box 731, 70 Jackson Dr, Cranford, NJ | 201-272-8880 |
| Professional Color Services Inc/77 N Washington St, Boston, MA | 617-367-9253 |
| Retouching Graphics Inc/205 Roosevelt Ave, Massapequa Park, NY | 516-541-2960 |
| Riter, Warren/2291 Penfield, Pittsford, NY | 716-381-4368 |
| Rothman, Henry/6927 N 19th St, Philadelphia, PA | 215-424-6927 |
| STone, Fred Reprographics/1033 Mass Ave, Cambridge, MA | 617-876-6900 |
| Spaulding Co Inc/301 Columbus, Boston, MA | 617-262-1935 |
| Stone Reprographics/44 Brattle St, Cambridge, MA | 617-876-4540 |
| Subtractive Technology/335 Newbury St, Boston, MA | 617-261-1887 |
| Superior Photo Retouching Service/1955 Mass Ave, Cambridge, MA | 617-661-9094 |
| Trama, Gene/35 Fairport Rd, Rochester, NY | 716-232-2270 |
| Van Iderstine/148 State Hwy 10, E Hanover, NJ | 201-887-7879 |
| Van Ryzin, Peter Assoc/173 June Rd, Cos Cob, CT | 203-322-3754 |
| Van Vort, Donald D/71 Capital Hts Rd, Oyster Bay, NY | 516-922-5234 |
| Vibrant Color Labs/1000 Highland Ave, Needham, MA | 617-444-6767 |
| Visual Horizons/180 Metropark, Rochester, NY | 716-424-5300 |
| Von Eiff, Damon/930 F St NW Suite 812, Washington, DC | 202-347-2788 |
| Weinstock, Bernie/162 Boylston, Boston, MA | 617-423-4481 |

## SOUTHEAST

| | |
|---|---|
| A A A Blue Print Co/3120 Maple Dr, Atlanta, GA | 404-261-1580 |
| Advance Color Processing Inc/1807 Ponce de Leon Blvd, Miami, FL | 305-443-7323 |
| Allen Photo/3808 Wilson Blvd, Arlington, VA | 703-524-7121 |
| Ampersand Graphics/1404 McCaullie Ave, Chattanooga, TN | 615-622-8366 |
| Ashley Studio/112 N 23rd St, Birmingham, AL | 205-251-4048 |
| Associated Photographers/19 SW 6th St, Miami, FL | 305-373-4774 |
| Atlanta Blue Print/1052 W Peachtree St N E, Atlanta, GA | 404-873-5911 |
| Barral, Yolanda/100 Florida Blvd, Miami, FL | 305-261-4767 |
| Bristow Photo Service/2018 Wilson Blvd, Hollywood, FL | 305-920-1377 |
| Clark Studio/6700 Sharon Rd, Charlotte, NC | 704-552-1758 |
| Color Graphic/3184 Roswell Rd, Atlanta, GA | 404-233-2174 |

# PHOTO/FILM SERVICES CONT'D.

Please send us your additions and updates.

| | |
|---|---|
| Color Image-Atlanta/478 Armour Circle, Atlanta, GA | 404-876-0209 |
| The Color Lab Inc/7190 NW 6th Court, Miami, FL | 305-751-1828 |
| Colorcraft Corporation-Savannah/5202 Paulsen, Savannah, GA | 912-232-1019 |
| Colorcraft of Columbia/331 Sunset Shopping Center, Columbia, SC | 803-252-0600 |
| Customlab/508 Armour Cr, Atlanta, GA | 404-875-0289 |
| Dixie Color Lab/520 Highland S, Memphis, TN | 901-458-1818 |
| Eagle Photographics/3612 Swann Ave, Tampa, FL | 813-870-2495 |
| Fidelity Color Labs/2420 Wake Forest Rd, Raleigh, NC | 919-834-6491 |
| Florida Color Lab/PO Box 10907, Tampa, FL | 813-877-8658 |
| Florida Photo Inc/781 NE 125th St, N Miami, FL | 305-891-6616 |
| Fordyce, R B Photography/4873 NW 36th St, Miami, FL | 305-885-3406 |
| Gables Blueprint Co/4075 Ponce De Leone Blvd, Coral Gables, FL | 305-443-7146 |
| General Color/80 Peachtree Park Dr. NE, Atlanta, GA | 404-355-8400 |
| General Color Corporation/604 Brevard Ave, Cocoa Beach, FL | 305-631-1602 |
| Janousek & Kuehl/3300 NE Expy # 8-T, Atlanta, GA | 404-458-8989 |
| Kilpatrick, Don/1516 Elizabeth Ave, Charlotte, NC | 704-374-0560 |
| Klickovich Retoucher/1638 Eastern Pkwy, Louisville, KY | 502-459-0295 |
| Lamson's Photographic Lab Service/45 N Texas Ave, Orlando, FL | 305-299-7731 |
| Mid-South Color Laboratories/496 Emmet, Jackson, TN | 901-422-6691 |
| PEC Laser Color Labs/Fairfield Dr, West Palm Beach, FL | 305-848-7211 |
| Par Excellence/2900 Youree Dr, Shreveport, LA | 318-869-2533 |
| Photo-Pros/635 A Pressley Rd, Charlotte, NC | 704-525-0551 |
| Plunkett Graphics/1052 W Peachtree St, Atlanta, GA | 404-873-5976 |
| Rich, Bob Photo/12495 NE 6th Ave, Miami, FL | 305-893-6137 |
| Rosenfeld, M B Photo Lab/P O Box 440524, Miami, FL | 305-443-2011 |
| Rothor Color Labs/1251 King St, Jacksonville, FL | 904-388-7717 |
| S & S Pro Color Inc/2801 S MacDill Ave, Tampa, FL | 813-831-1811 |
| Sheffield & Board/18 E Main St, Richmond, VA | 804-649-8870 |
| Spectrum Custom Color Lab/221 A E Davis Blvd, Tampa, FL | 813-251-0338 |
| Stat/Us/360 Greco Rd, Coral Gables, FL | 305-445-0553 |
| Studio Masters Inc/1398 NE 125th St, N Miami, FL | 305-893-3500 |
| Supreme Color Inc/71 NW 29th St, Miami, FL | 305-573-2934 |
| Taffae, Syd/3550 N Bayhomes Dr, Miami, FL | 305-667-5252 |
| Thomson Photo Lab Inc/4210 Ponce De Leon Blvd, Coral Gables, FL | 305-443-0669 |
| True Color Photo Inc/710 W Sheridan Ave, Oklahoma City, OK | 405-232-6441 |
| Viva-Color Labs/748 Willoughby Way NE, Atlanta, GA | 404-521-1688 |
| Williamson Photography/9501 SW 160th St, Miami, FL | 305-255-6400 |
| World Color Inc/P O Box 1327, Ormond Beach, FL | 904-677-1332 |

# MIDWEST

| | |
|---|---|
| A C Color Lab Inc/2160 Payne Ave, Cleveland, OH | 216-621-4575 |
| A-1 Photo Service/105 W Madison Ave, Chicago, IL | 312-346-2248 |
| Ad Photo/2056 E 4th St, Cleveland, OH | 216-621-9360 |
| Anderson Graphics/521 N 8th St, Milwaukee, WI | 414-276-4445 |
| Anro West/409 Green St, Rockford, IL | 815-962-0884 |
| Arrow Photo Copy Co/523 S Plymouth Ct, Chicago, IL | 312-427-9515 |
| Artstreet/25 E Delaware Pl, Chicago, IL | 312-664-3049 |
| Astra Photo Service/6 E Lake, Chicago, IL | 312-372-4366 |
| Astro Color Labs/61 W Erie St, Chicago, IL | 312-280-5500 |
| B G Studio/228 N La Salle Room 2245, Chicago, IL | 312-236-3378 |
| Boulevard Photo/333 N Michigan Ave, Chicago, IL | 312-263-3508 |
| Brookfield Photo Service/9146 Broadway, Brookfield, IL | 312-485-1718 |
| Buffalo Photo Co/60 W Superior, Chicago, IL | 312-787-6476 |
| Capps, Robert Studio/233 E Wacker # 602, Chicago, IL | 312-726-5642 |
| Carlson Studios/203 N Wabash, Chicago, IL | 312-263-5876 |
| Carriage Barn Studio/2360 Riverside Dr, Beloit, WI | 608-365-2405 |
| Chicago Color Center/335 W Lake St, Chicago, IL | 312-467-5634 |
| Chromatics Ltd/4507 N Kedzie Ave, Chicago, IL | 312-478-3850 |
| Color Central/612 N Michigan Ave, Chicago, IL | 312-321-1696 |
| Color Correct Studio/Route 1, Woodlawn, IL | 618-735-2420 |
| Color Darkroom Corp/3320 W Vliet St, Milwaukee, WI | 414-344-3377 |
| Color Detroit/533 W Congress St, Detroit, MI | 313-962-2370 |
| Color Graphics Inc/5809 W Divison St, Chicago, IL | 312-261-4143 |
| Color International Labs/365 W Lake St, Elmhurst, IL | 312-279-6632 |
| The Color Market/3000 Dundee Rd #201, Northbrook, IL | 312-564-3770 |
| Color Perfect Inc/24 Custer St, Detroit, MI | 313-872-5115 |
| Color Service Inc/325 W Huron St, Chicago, IL | 312-664-5225 |
| Color Systems/5719 N Milwaukee Ave, Chicago, IL | 312-763-6664 |
| Color Technique Inc/57 W Grand Ave, Chicago, IL | 312-337-5051 |
| Colorprints Inc/410 N Michigan Ave, Chicago, IL | 312-467-6930 |
| The Colour Works Inc/2871 E Grand Ave, Chicago, IL | 312-467-5171 |
| Commercial Colorlab Service/222 E Downer Pl, Aurora, IL | 312-892-9330 |
| Copy-Matics, Div Lith-O-Lux/6324 W Fond du Lac Ave, Milwaukee, WI | 414-462-2250 |
| Custom Color Processing Lab/1300 Rand Rd, Des Plaines, IL | 312-297-6333 |
| Cutler-Graves/535 N Michigan Ave, Chicago, IL | 312-828-9310 |
| Drake, Brady Copy Center/413 N 10th St, St Louis, MO | 314-421-1311 |
| Duncan, Virgil Studios/4725 E State Blvd, Ft Wayne, IN | 219-483-6011 |
| Dzuroff Studios/1020 Huron Rd E, Cleveland, OH | 216-696-0120 |
| Eastman Kodak Co/1712 S Prairie Ave, Chicago, IL | 312-922-9691 |
| Fotis Photo/25 E Hubbard St, Chicago, IL | 312-337-7300 |
| The Foto Lab Inc/160 E Illinois St, Chicago, IL | 312-321-0900 |
| Foto-Comm Corporation/215 W Superior, Chicago, IL | 312-943-0450 |
| Gamma Photo Lab Inc/314 W Superior St, Chicago, IL | 312-337-0022 |
| Gordy Thorstad Retouching Inc/512 Nicolas Mall Bldg, Minneapolis, MN | 612-338-2597 |
| Graphic Reproductions Inc/101 High Ave, Cleveland, OH | 216-861-6022 |
| Grignon Studios/1300 W Altgeld, Chicago, IL | 312-975-7200 |
| Grossman Knowling Co/5715 Woodward Ave, Detroit, MI | 313-832-2360 |
| Hill, Vince Studio/119 W Hubbard, Chicago, IL | 312-644-6690 |
| Imperial Color Inc/618 W Jackson Blvd, Chicago, IL | 312-454-1570 |
| J D H Inc/1729 Superior Ave, Cleveland, OH | 216-771-0346 |
| Jahn & Ollier Engraving/817 W Washington Blvd, Chicago, IL | 312-666-7080 |
| Janusz, Robert E Studios/1020 Huron Rd, Cleveland, OH | 216-621-9845 |
| John, Harvey Studio/823 N 2nd St, Milwaukee, WI | 414-271-7170 |
| K & S Photographics/180 N Wabash Ave, Chicago, IL | 312-782-0522 |
| K & S Photographics/1155 Handley Industrial Ct, St Louis, MO | 314-962-7050 |
| Kai-Hsi Studio/160 E Illinois St, Chicago, IL | 312-642-9853 |
| Kier Photo Service/1627 E 40th St, Cleveland, OH | 216-431-4670 |
| Kitzerow Studios/203 N Wabash, Chicago, IL | 312-332-1224 |
| Kloc Studio/202 S State St, Chicago, IL | 312-427-6837 |
| Kolorstat Studios/415 N Dearborn St, Chicago, IL | 312-644-3729 |
| Koopman-Neumer Inc/231 S Green St, Chicago, IL | 312-726-3508 |
| Kremer Photo Print/228 S Wabash, Chicago, IL | 312-922-3297 |
| LaDriere Studios/1565 W Woodward Ave, Bloomfield Hills, MI | 313-644-3932 |
| Lagasca, Dick & Others/203 N Wabash, Chicago, IL | 312-263-1389 |
| Langen & Wind Color Service Inc/2871 E Grand Blvd, Detroit, MI | 313-871-5722 |
| Lobeck & Assoc Inc/405 N Wabash, Chicago, IL | 312-726-5580 |
| Lubeck, Larry & Assoc/405 N Wabash Ave, Chicago, IL | 312-726-5580 |
| Merrill-David Inc/3420 Prospect Ave, Cleveland, OH | 216-621-0988 |
| Meteor Photo Company/1099 Chicago Rd, Troy, MI | 313-583-3090 |
| Midwest Litho Arts/5300 C McDermott Dr, Berkeley, IL | 312-449-2442 |
| Multiprint Co Inc/153 Ohio St, Chicago, IL | 312-644-7910 |
| Munder, Charles/2771 Galilee Ave, Zion, IL | 312-764-4435 |
| NCL Graphics/575 Bennett Rd, Elk Grove Village, IL | 312-593-2610 |
| National Photo Service/114 W Illinois St, Chicago, IL | 312-644-5211 |
| Norman Sigele Studios/25 E Hubbard St, Chicago, IL | 312-642-1757 |
| O'Connor-Roe Inc/111 E Wacker, Chicago, IL | 312-856-1668 |
| O'Donnell Studio Inc/333 W Lake St, Chicago, IL | 312-346-2470 |
| P-A Photocenter Inc/310 W Washington St, Chicago, IL | 312-641-6343 |
| Pallas Photo Labs/319 W Erie, Chicago, IL | 312-787-4600 |
| Parkway Photo Lab/57 W Grand Ave, Chicago, IL | 312-467-1711 |
| Photocopy Inc/104 E Mason St, Milwaukee, WI | 414-272-1255 |
| Photographic Specialties Inc/225 Border Ave N, Minneapolis, MN | 612-332-6303 |
| Photomatic Corp/59 E Illinois St, Chicago, IL | 312-527-2929 |
| Print Lab/29 W Hubbard, Chicago, IL | 312-644-5472 |
| Procolor/909 Hennepin Ave, Minneapolis, MN | 612-332-7721 |
| Proctor, Jack/2050 Dain Tower, Minneapolis, MN | 612-338-7777 |
| Professional Photo Colour Service/126 W Kinzie, Chicago, IL | 312-644-0888 |
| Quantity Photo Co/119 W Hubbard St, Chicago, IL | 312-644-8288 |
| Race Frog Stats/207 E Michigan Ave, Milwaukee, WI | 414-276-7828 |
| Reichart, Jim Studio/2301 W Mill Rd, Milwaukee, WI | 414-228-9089 |
| Repro Inc/912 N Washington Blvd, Chicago, IL | 312-666-3800 |
| Robb, Don Ltd/676 N La Salle, Chicago, IL | 312-943-2664 |
| Ross-Ehlert/225 W Illinois, Chicago, IL | 312-644-0244 |
| Schellhorn Photo Techniques/3916 N Elston Ave, Chicago, IL | 312-267-5141 |
| Sladek, Dean/6000 W Creek Rd, Cleveland, OH | 216-447-9028 |

# PHOTO/FILM SERVICES CONT'D.

Please send us your additions and updates.

| | |
|---|---|
| Sosin, Bill/415 W Superior, Chicago, IL | 312-751-0974 |
| Speedy Stat Service/343 S Dearborn St, Chicago, IL | 312-939-3397 |
| Standard Studios Inc/25 E Hubbard, Chicago, IL | 312-944-5300 |
| The Stat Center/The Illuminating Bldg, Cleveland, OH | 216-861-5467 |
| Superior Bulk Film Co Inc/442 N Wells St, Chicago, IL | 312-644-4448 |
| Uhlir, Louis J/2509 Kingston Rd, Cleveland Hts, OH | 216-932-4837 |
| Williams, Warren E & Assoc/233 E Wacker Dr, Chicago, IL | 312-565-2689 |

## SOUTHWEST

| | |
|---|---|
| A-1 Blue Print Co Inc/2220 W Alabama, Houston, TX | 713-526-3111 |
| Alamo Photolabs/5025 Broadway, San Antonio, TX | 512-828-9079 |
| Baster, Ray Enterprises/834 N 7th Ave, Phoenix, AZ | 602-258-6850 |
| The Black & White Lab/4930 Maple Ave, Dallas, TX | 214-528-4200 |
| Casey Color Inc/2115 S Harvard Ave, Tulsa, OK | 918-744-5004 |
| Century Copi-Technics Inc/710 N St Paul St, Dallas, TX | 214-741-3191 |
| Color Mark Laboratories/2202 E McDowell Rd, Phoenix, AZ | 602-273-1253 |
| The Color Place/1330 Conant St, Dallas, TX | 214-631-7174 |
| The Color Place/2927 Morton St, Fort Worth, TX | 817-335-3515 |
| The Color Place/4201 San Felipe, Houston, TX | 713-629-7080 |
| Commercial Color Corporation/1621 Oaklawn St, Dallas, TX | 214-744-2610 |
| Dallas Printing Co/4225 Office Pkwy, Dallas, TX | 214-826-3331 |
| Five-P Photographic Processing/2122 E Governor's Circle, Houston, TX | 713-688-4488 |
| Floyd & Lloyd Burns Industrial Artist/3223 Alabama Courts, Houston, TX | 713-622-8255 |
| H & H Blueprint & Supply Co/5042 N 8th St, Phoenix, AZ | 602-279-5701 |
| Hall/Photographers/6 Greenway Plaza, Houston, TX | 713-961-3454 |
| Hot Flash Photographics/5933 Bellaire Blvd #114, Houston, TX | 713-666-9510 |
| Hunter, Marilyn Art Svc/3200 Maple Ave Suite 313, Dallas, TX | 214-747-0512 |
| Kolor Print Inc/PO Box 747, Little Rock, AR | 501-375-5581 |
| Magna Professional Color Lab/2601 N 32nd St, Phoenix, AZ | 602-955-0700 |
| Master Printing Co Inc/220 Creath St, Jonesboro, AR | 501-932-4491 |
| Meisel Photochrome Corp/9645 Wedge Chapel, Dallas, TX | 214-350-6666 |
| Optifab Inc/1550 W Van Buren St, Phoenix, AZ | 602-254-7171 |
| The Photo Company/124 W McDowell Rd, Phoenix, AZ | 602-254-5138 |
| Photo Labs (etc)/1926 W Gray, Houston, TX | 713-527-9300 |
| Photo Processors Inc/909 Congress, Austin, TX | 512-472-6926 |
| Pounds Photo Lab Inc/2507 Manor Way, Dallas, TX | 214-350-5671 |
| Pro Photo Lab Inc/2700 N Portland, Oklahoma City, OK | 405-942-3743 |
| Quali-Color Laboratory/6300 Gulfton, Houston, TX | 713-785-5757 |
| Raphaele Chrome Retouching/3403 Roseland, Houston, TX | 713-524-7489 |
| Spectro Photo Labs Inc/4519 Maple, Dallas, TX | 214-522-1981 |
| Steffan Photographic Copying/1905 Skillman, Dallas, TX | 214-827-6128 |

## WEST

| | |
|---|---|
| ABC Color Corp/3020 Glendale Blvd, Los Angeles, CA | 213-662-2125 |
| Action Photo Service/719 Market St, San Francisco, CA | 415-543-1777 |
| Alan's Custom Lab/1545 Wilcox, Hollywood, CA | 213-461-1975 |
| Aristo Art Studio/636 N La Brea, Los Angeles, CA | 213-939-0101 |
| Art Craft Custom Lab/1900 Westwood Blvd, Los Angeles, CA | 213-475-2986 |
| Atkinson-Stedco Color Film Service/7610 Melrose Ave, Los Angeles, CA | 213-655-1255 |
| Banks, Harlan/920 W Glenoaks Blvd, Glendale, CA | 213-241-9031 |
| Black & White Color Reproductions/38 Mason, San Francisco, CA | 415-989-3070 |
| Bogle Graphic Photo/1117 S Olive, Los Angeles, CA | 213-749-7461 |
| CPS Lab/1759 Las Palmas, Los Angeles, CA | 213-464-0215 |
| Cardinale, Timothy J/6855 Costello Ave, Van Nuys, CA | 213-781-5222 |
| Chrome Graphics/449 N Huntley Dr, Los Angeles, CA | 213-657-5055 |
| Clark Photographic Inc/866 Sutter St, San Francisco, CA | 415-928-1022 |
| Coletti, John/251 Kearny, San Francisco, CA | 415-421-3848 |
| Collazo, Frank/649 Burnside Ave, Los Angeles, CA | 213-935-8429 |
| Color Quickly/604 Mission St, San Francisco, CA | 415-543-2515 |
| Colorscope/305 Parkman Ave, Los Angeles, CA | 213-487-6120 |
| Complete Negative Service/6007 Waring Ave, Hollywood, CA | 213-463-7753 |
| Cook, Gerald/403 Silver Lake Blvd, Los Angeles, CA | 213-383-5337 |
| Croxton, Stewart Inc/8736 Melrose, Los Angeles, CA | 213-652-9720 |
| Cudin, Lou/618 S Western Ave #202, Los Angeles, CA | 213-388-9465 |
| Custom Graphics/15162 Goldenwest Circle, Westminister, CA | 714-893-7517 |
| Custom Photo Lab/880 Folsom, San Francisco, CA | 415-777-1441 |
| Duographics Inc/1136 N Fairfax Ave, Los Angeles, CA | 213-656-5050 |
| Exposure/5940 College Ave, Oakland, CA | 415-658-7028 |
| Faulkner Color Lab/1200 Folsom St, San Francisco, CA | 415-861-2800 |
| Frosh, R L & Sons Scenic Studio/4144 Sunset Blvd, Los Angeles, CA | 213-662-1134 |
| G P Color Lab/215 S Oxford Ave, Los Angeles, CA | 213-386-7901 |
| Gamma Photographic Labs/555 Howard St, San Francisco, CA | 415-495-8833 |
| General Graphics/880 Folsom, San Francisco, CA | 415-777-3333 |
| Gibbons Color Lab/606 N Almont Dr, Los Angeles, CA | 213-275-6806 |
| Graphic Center/7386 Beverly, Los Angeles, CA | 213-938-3773 |
| Graphic Process Co/5635 Hollywood Blvd, Los Angeles, CA | 213-466-5396 |
| Graphic Services Inc/265 29th St, Oakland, CA | 415-832-7685 |
| Graphicolor/8132 W Third, Los Angeles, CA | 213-653-1768 |
| Hollywood Photo Reproduction/6413 Willoughby Ave, Hollywood, CA | 213-469-5421 |
| Imperial Color Lab/939 Howard St, San Francisco, CA | 415-777-4020 |
| Ivey-Seright/83 S Washington, Seattle, WA | 206-623-8113 |
| Jacobs, Ed/937 S Spaulding, Los Angeles, CA | 213-935-1064 |
| Jacobs, Robert Retouching/6010 Wilshire Blvd #505, Los Angeles, CA | 213-931-3751 |
| Johnston, Chuck/1111 Wilshire, Los Angeles, CA | 213-482-3362 |
| Kawahara, George/681 Market St, San Francisco, CA | 415-543-1637 |
| Kimbo Color Laboratory Inc/179 Stewart, San Francisco, CA | 415-989-6123 |
| Laursen Color Lab/1641 Reynolds, Irvine, CA | 714-546-6232 |
| Lee Film Processing/434 N LaBrea Ave, Los Angeles, CA | 213-938-3724 |
| Marin Color Lab/41 Belvedere St, San Rafael, CA | 415-456-8093 |
| Mark III Colorprints/7401 Melrose Ave, Los Angeles, CA | 213-653-0433 |
| Mercury Blueprint Co/414 S Brand Blvd, Glendale, CA | 213-241-8332 |
| Metz Air Art/2817 E Lincoln Ave, Anaheim, CA | 714-630-3071 |
| Modern Photo Studio/5625 N Figueroa, Los Angeles, CA | 213-255-1527 |
| Modernage/470 E Third St, Los Angeles, CA | 213-628-8194 |
| Newell Color Lab/165 Second, San Francisco, CA | 415-392-1776 |
| Olson, Bob Photo Blow-Up Lab/7775 Beverly Blvd, Los Angeles, CA | 213-931-6643 |
| Ostoin, Larry/22943 B Nadine Cr, Torrance, CA | 213-530-1121 |
| Pace Colorprints/1236 S La Cienega Blvd, Los Angeles, CA | 213-655-4322 |
| Paragon Photo/7301 Melrose Ave, Los Angeles, CA | 213-933-5865 |
| Peacock Color Lab/1014 N Sycamore, Hollywood, CA | 213-851-8281 |
| Personal Color Lab/1552 Gower, Los Angeles, CA | 213-467-0721 |
| Petron Corp/5443 Fountain Ave, Los Angeles, CA | 213-461-4626 |
| Pevehouse, Jerry Studio/3931 Tweedy Blvd, South Gate, CA | 213-564-1336 |
| Photoking Lab/6612 W Sunset Blvd, Los Angeles, CA | 213-466-2977 |
| Prisma Color Inc/5619 Washington Blvd, Los Angeles, CA | 213-728-7151 |
| Professional Color Labs/96 Jessie, San Francisco, CA | 415-397-5057 |
| Prolab/8276 Santa Monica, Los Angeles, CA | 213-654-5713 |
| Quantity Photos Inc/5432 Hollywood Blvd, Los Angeles, CA | 213-467-6178 |
| RGB Lab Inc/816 N Highland, Los Angeles, CA | 213-469-1959 |
| Rapid Color Inc/1236 S Central Ave, Glendale, CA | 213-245-9211 |
| Remos, Nona/4053 8th Ave, San Diego, CA | 714-692-4044 |
| Revilo Color/4650 W Washington Blvd, Los Angeles, CA | 213-936-8681 |
| Reynolds, Carol Retouching/1428 N Fuller Ave, Hollywood, CA | 213-874-7083 |
| Ro-Ed Color Lab/707 N Stanley Ave, Los Angeles, CA | 213-651-5050 |
| Roller, S J/6881 Alta Loma Terrace, Los Angeles, CA | 213-876-5654 |
| Rudy Jo Color Lab Inc/130 N La Brea, Los Angeles, CA | 213-937-3804 |
| Schroeder, Mark/70 Broadway, San Francisco, CA | 415-421-3691 |
| Snyder, Len/238 Hall Dr, Orinda, CA | 415-254-8687 |
| Staidle, Ted & Assocs/544 N Larchmont Blvd, Los Angeles, CA | 213-462-7433 |
| Stat House/8126 Beverly Blvd, Los Angeles, CA | 213-653-8200 |
| Still Photo Lab/1216 N LaBrea, Los Angeles, CA | 213-465-6106 |
| Technicolor Inc/2049 Century Park E, Los Angeles, CA | 213-553-5200 |
| Thomas Reproductions/1147 Mission, San Francisco, CA | 415-431-8900 |
| Timars/918 N Formosa, Los Angeles, CA | 213-876-0175 |
| Tom's Chroma Lab/5818 W Third St, Los Angeles, CA | 213-933-5637 |
| Tri Color Camera/1761 N Vermont Ave, Los Angeles, CA | 213-666-1855 |
| Vloeberghs, Jerome/333 Kearny St, San Francisco, CA | 415-982-1287 |
| Wild Studio/1311 N Wilcox Ave, Hollywood, CA | 213-463-8369 |
| Williams, Alan & Assoc Inc/8032 W Third St, Los Angeles, CA | 213-653-2243 |
| Wolf Color Lab/6416 Selma, Los Angeles, CA | 213-463-0766 |
| Zammit, Paul/5478 Wilshire Blvd #300, Los Angeles, CA | 213-933-8563 |
| Ziba Photographics/591 Howard St, San Francisco, CA | 415-543-6221 |

# PHOTO/FILM SERVICES CONT'D.

Please send us your additions and updates.

# LIGHTING

## NEW YORK CITY

| | |
|---|---|
| Altman Stage Lighting Co Inc/57 Alexander | 212-569-7777 |
| Artistic Neon by Gasper/76-19 60th Ln | 212-821-1550 |
| Balcar Lighting Systems/15 E 30th St | 212-889-5080 |
| Barbizon Electric Co Inc/426 W 55th St | 212-586-1620 |
| Bernhard Link Theatrical Inc/104 W 17th St | 212-929-6786 |
| Big Apple Cine Service/49-01 25th Ave | 212-626-5210 |
| Big Apple Lights Corp/533 Canal St | 212-226-0925 |
| Camera Mart/456 W 55th St | 212-757-6977 |
| Electra Displays/122 W 27th St | 212-924-1022 |
| F&B/Ceco Lighting & Grip Rental/315 W 43rd St | 212-974-4640 |
| Feature Systems Inc/512 W 36th St | 212-736-0447 |
| Ferco/707 11th Ave | 212-245-4800 |
| Filmtrucks, Inc/450 W 37th St | 212-868-7065 |
| Fiorentino, Imero Assoc Inc/44 West 63rd St | 212-246-0600 |
| Four Star Stage Lighting Inc/585 Gerard Ave | 212-993-0471 |
| Kliegl Bros Universal/32-32 48th Ave | 212-786-7474 |
| Lee Lighting America Ltd/534 W 25th St | 212-924-5476 |
| Litelab Theatrical & Disco Equip/76 Ninth Ave | 212-675-4357 |
| Lowel Light Mfg Inc/475 10th St | 212-949-0950 |
| Luminere/160 W 86th St | 212-724-0583 |
| Martorano, Salvatore Inc/9 West First St | 516-379-8097 |
| Metro-Lites Inc/750 Tenth Ave | 212-757-1220 |
| Movie Light Ltd/460 W 24th St | 212-989-2318 |
| New York Flash/156 Fifth Ave | 212-741-1165 |
| Paris Film Productions Ltd/213-23 99th Ave | 212-740-2020 |
| Photo-Tekniques/119 Fifth Ave | 212-254-2545 |
| Production Arts Lighting/636 Eleventh Ave | 212-489-0312 |
| Ross, Charles Inc/333 W 52nd St | 212-246-5470 |
| Stage Lighting Discount Corp/346 W 44th St | 212-489-1370 |
| Stroblite Co Inc/10 E 23rd St | 212-677-9220 |
| Tekno Inc/15 E 30th St | 212-887-5080 |
| Times Square Stage Lighting Co/318 W 47th St | 212-541-5045 |
| Vadar Ltd/150 Fifth Ave | 212-989-9120 |

## NORTHEAST

| | |
|---|---|
| Barbizon Light of New England/3 Draper St, Woburn, MA | 617-935-3920 |
| Blake, Ben Films/104 W Concord St, Boston, MA | 617-266-8181 |
| Capron Lighting & Sound/278 West St, Needham, MA | 617-444-8850 |
| Cestare, Thomas Inc/188 Herricks Rd, Mineola, NY | 516-742-5550 |
| Dyna-Lite Inc/140 Market St, Kenilworth, NJ | 201-245-7222 |
| Film Associates/419 Boylston St #209, Boston, MA | 617-266-0892 |
| Filmarts/38 Newbury St, Boston, MA | 617-266-7468 |
| Heller, Brian/200 Olney St, Providence, RI | 401-751-1381 |
| Lighting Products, GTE Sylvania/Lighting Center, Danvers, MA | 617-777-1900 |
| Limelight Productions/Yale Hill, Stockbridge, MA | 413-298-3771 |
| Lycian Stage Lighting/P O Box 68, Sugar Loaf, NY | 914-469-2285 |
| McManus Enterprises/111 Union Ave, Bala Cynwyd, PA | 215-664-8600 |
| Norton Assoc/53 Henry St, Cambridge, MA | 617-876-3771 |
| Packaged Lighting Systems/29-41 Grant, PO Box 285, Walden, NY | 914-778-3515 |
| R & R Lighting Co/813 Silver Spring Ave, Silver Spring, MD | 301-589-4997 |
| Reinhard, Charles Lighting Consultant/39 Ocean Ave, Massapequa, NY | 516-799-1615 |
| Stuart Cody Inc/300 Putnam Ave, Cambridge, MA | 617-661-4540 |

## SOUTHEAST

| | |
|---|---|
| Kupersmith, Tony/320 N Highland Ave NE, Atlanta, GA | 404-577-5319 |

## MIDWEST

| | |
|---|---|
| Duncan, Victor Inc/32380 Howard St, Madison Heights, MI | 313-589-1900 |
| Film Corps/3101 Hennepin Ave, Minneapolis, MN | 612-338-2522 |
| Frost, Jack/234 Piquette, Detroit, MI | 313-873-8030 |
| Grand Stage Lighting Co/630 W Lake, Chicago, IL | 312-332-5611 |
| Midwest Cine Service/304 W 79th Terr, Kansas City, MO | 816-333-0022 |
| Midwest Stage Lighting/2104 Central, Evanston, IL | 312-328-3966 |
| Studio Lighting/1345 W Argyle St, Chicago, IL | 312-989-8808 |

## SOUTHWEST

| | |
|---|---|
| ABC Theatrical Rental & Sales/825 N 7th St, Phoenix, AZ | 602-258-5265 |
| Astro Audio-Visual/1336 W Clay, Houston, TX | 713-528-7119 |
| Chase Lights/1942 Beech St, Amarillo, TX | 806-381-0575 |
| Dallas Stage Lighting & Equipment Co/2813 Florence, Dallas, TX | 214-827-9380 |
| Duncan, Victor Inc/2659 Fondren Dr, Dallas, TX | 214-369-1165 |
| FPS Inc/11250 Pagemill Rd, Dallas, TX | 214-340-8545 |
| Gable, Pee Wee Inc/PO Box 11264, Phoenix, AZ | 602-242-7660 |
| MFC-The Texas Outfit/5915 Star Ln, Houston, TX | 713-781-7703 |
| Southwest Film & TV Lighting/904 Koerner Ln, Austin, TX | 512-385-3483 |

## WEST

| | |
|---|---|
| Aguilar Lighting Works/3230 Laurel Canyon Blvd, Studio City, CA | 213-766-6564 |
| American Mobile Power Co/3218 W Burbank Blvd, Burbank, CA | 213-845-5474 |
| Astro Generator Rentals/2835 Bedford St, Los Angeles, CA | 213-838-3958 |
| B S Rental Co/18857 Addison St, North Hollywood, CA | 213-761-1733 |
| B S Rental Co/1082 La Cresta Dr, Thousand Oaks, CA | 805-495-8606 |
| Backstage Studio Equipment/5554 Fairview Pl, Agoura, CA | 213-889-9816 |
| Casper's Camera Cars/8415 Lankershim Blvd, Sun Valley, CA | 213-767-5207 |
| Castex Rentals/591 N Bronson Ave, Los Angeles, CA | 213-462-1468 |
| Ceco, F&B of CA Inc/7051 Santa Monica Blvd, Hollywood, CA | 213-466-9361 |
| Cine Turkey/2624 Reppert Ct, Los Angeles, CA | 213-654-6495 |
| Cine-Dyne Inc/9401 Wilshire Blvd #830, Beverly Hills, CA | 213-622-7016 |
| Cine-Pro/1037 N Sycamore Ave, Hollywood, CA | 213-461-4794 |
| Cinemobile Systems Inc/11166 Gault St, North Hollywood, CA | 213-764-9900 |
| Cineworks-Cinerents/5724 Santa Monica Blvd, Hollywood, CA | 213-464-0296 |
| Cool Light Co Inc/5723 Auckland Ave, North Hollywood, CA | 213-761-6116 |
| Denker, Foster Co/1605 Las Flores Ave, San Marino, CA | 213-799-8656 |
| Fiorentino, Imero Assoc Inc/6430 Sunset Blvd, Hollywood, CA | 213-467-4020 |
| Great American Market/PO Box 178, Woodlands Hill, CA | 213-883-8182 |
| Grosso & Grosso/7502 Wheatland Ave, Sun Valley, CA | 213-875-1160 |
| Hollywood Mobile Systems/7021 Hayvenhurst St, Van Nuys, CA | 213-782-6558 |
| Independent Studio Services/11907 Wicks St, Sun Valley, CA | 213-764-0840 |
| Kalani Studio Lighting/129-49 Killion St, Van Nuys, CA | 213-762-5991 |
| Key Lite/333 S Front St, Burbank, CA | 213-848-5483 |
| Leonetti Cine Rentals/5609 Sunset Blvd, Hollywood, CA | 213-469-2987 |
| Mobile Power House/3820 Rhodes Ave, Studio City, CA | 213-766-2163 |
| Mole Richardson/937 N Sycamore Ave, Hollywood, CA | 213-851-0111 |
| Pattim Service/10625 Chandler, Hollywood, CA | 213-766-5266 |
| Picture Package Inc/22236 Cass Ave, Woodland Hills, CA | 213-703-7168 |
| Producer's Studio/650 N Bronson St, Los Angeles, CA | 213-466-3111 |
| Production Systems Inc/5759 Santa Monica Blvd, Hollywood, CA | 213-469-2704 |
| RNI Equipment Co/7272 Bellaire Ave, North Hollywood, CA | 213-875-2656 |
| Rocky Mountain Cine Support/1332 S Cherokee, Denver, CO | 303-795-9713 |
| Skirpan Lighting Control Co/1100 W Chestnut St, Burbank, CA | 213-840-7000 |
| Tech Camera/6370 Santa Monica Blvd, Hollywood, CA | 213-466-3238 |
| Wallace Lighting/6970 Varna Ave, Van Nuys, CA | 213-764-1047 |
| Young Generations/8517 Geyser Ave, Northridge, CA | 213-873-5135 |

# STUDIO RENTALS

## NEW YORK CITY

| | |
|---|---|
| The 95th St Studio/206 E 95th St | 212-831-1946 |
| Astoria Motion Picture and TV Center/34-31 35th St | 212-392-5600 |
| Boken Inc/513 W 54th St | 212-581-5507 |
| C & C Visual/12 W 27th St 7th Flr | 212-684-3830 |
| Camera Mart Inc/456 W 55th St | 212-757-6977 |
| Cine Studio/241 W 54th St | 212-581-1916 |

# PHOTO/FILM SERVICES CONT'D.

Please send us your additions and updates.

| | |
|---|---|
| Control Film Service/321 W 44th St | 212-245-1574 |
| DeFilippo/215 E 37th St | 212-986-5444 |
| Duggal Color Projects/9 W 20th St | 212-243-1114 |
| Farkas Films Inc/385 Third Ave | 212-679-8212 |
| Greene St Dance Studio/350 Fifth Ave | 212-966-4916 |
| Horvath & Assoc Studios/306 E 38th St | 212-679-7384 |
| Matrix Studios Inc/727 Eleventh Ave | 212-265-8500 |
| Mothers Sound Stages/210 E 5th St | 212-260-2050 |
| National Video Industries/15 W 17th St | 212-691-1300 |
| New York Flash Rental/156 Fifth Ave | 212-741-1165 |
| Ninth Floor Studio/1200 Broadway | 212-679-5537 |
| North American Video/423 E 90th St | 212-369-2552 |
| Osonitsch, Robert/112 Fouth Ave | 212-533-1920 |
| Phoenix State Ltd/537 W 59th St | 212-581-7721 |
| Photo-Tekniques/119 Fifth Ave | 212-254-2545 |
| Production Center/221 W 26th St | 212-675-2211 |
| Reeves Teletape Corp/304 E 44th St | 212-573-8888 |
| Sherman Studios/881 Seventh Ave | 212-664-8470 |
| Stage 54 West/429 W 54th St | 212-757-6977 |
| Stages 1&2 West/460 W 54th St | 212-757-6977 |
| Studio 39/144 E 39th St | 212-685-1771 |
| Studio Rentals/873 Broadway | 212-677-0310 |
| 3G Stages Inc/236 W 61st St | 212-247-3130 |
| Trigon Video Works Inc/24 W 40th St | 212-921-9860 |
| VPS Inc/106 W 43rd St | 212-354-9553 |
| Vagnoni, A Devlin Productions/150 W 55th St | 212-582-5572 |
| Yellowbox/47 E 34th St | 212-532-4010 |

## NORTHEAST

| | |
|---|---|
| Allscope Inc/PO Box 4060, Princeton, NJ | 609-799-4200 |
| Bay State Film Productions Inc/35 Springfield St, Agawam, MA | 413-786-4454 |
| Cameo Stages Inc/188 Herricks Rd, Mineola, NY | 516-742-7153 |
| Centel/651 Beacon St, Boston, MA | 617-267-6400 |
| Color Leasing Studio/330 Rt 46 East, Fairfield, NJ | 201-575-1118 |
| D4 Film Studios Inc/109 Highland Ave, Needham, MA | 617-444-0226 |
| Pike Productions Inc/47 Galen St, Watertown, MA | 617-924-5000 |
| September Productions Inc/171 Newbury St, Boston, MA | 617-262-6090 |
| Studio B/419 Boylston St #209, Boston, MA | 617-266-5464 |
| Television Productions & Services/55 Chapel St, Newton, MA | 617-965-1626 |
| The Video Picture Company/1170 Commonwealth Ave, Boston, MA | 617-731-2990 |
| Videocom Inc/502 Sprague St, Dedham, MA | 617-329-4080 |
| WFEV - TV/430 County St, New Bedford, MA | 617-993-2651 |
| WHYN - TV/P.O. Box 3633, Springfield, MA | 413-785-1911 |

## SOUTHEAST

| | |
|---|---|
| Enter Space/20 14th St NW, Atlanta, GA | 404-885-1139 |
| The Great Southern Stage/15221 NE 21st Ave, North Miami Beach, FL | 305-947-0430 |
| Williamson Photography Inc/9501 SW 160th St, Miami, FL | 305-255-6400 |

## MIDWEST

| | |
|---|---|
| Emrich Style & Design/2461 N Clark, Chicago, IL | 312-871-4659 |
| Gard, Ron/2600 N Racine, Chicago, IL | 312-975-6523 |
| Hanes, Jim/1930 N Orchard, Chicago, IL | 312-944-6554 |
| Lewis, Tom/2511 Brumley Dr, Flossmoor, IL | 312-799-1156 |
| The Production Center/151 Victor Ave, Highland Park, MI | 313-868-6600 |
| Rainey, Pat/4031 N Hamlin Ave, Chicago, IL | 312-463-0281 |
| Sosin, Bill/415 W Superior St, Chicago, IL | 312-951-0974 |
| Stratford Studios Inc/2857 E Grand Blvd, Detroit, MI | 313-875-6617 |
| Zawaki, Andy & Jake/1830 W Cermak, Chicago, IL | 312-226-1749 |

## SOUTHWEST

| | |
|---|---|
| AIE Studios/3905 Braxton, Houston, TX | 713-781-2110 |
| Arizona Cine Equipment/1660 Winsett St, Tuscon, AZ | 602-623-8268 |
| Century Studios Inc/4519 Maple Ave, Dallas, TX | 214-522-3310 |
| Hayes Productions Inc/710 S Bowie, San Antonio, TX | 512-224-9565 |
| MFC Film Productions Inc/5915 Star Ln, Houston, TX | 713-781-7703 |
| Pearlman Productions Inc/2506 South Blvd, Houston, TX | 713-523-3601 |
| Stokes, Bill Assoc/5642 Dyer, Dallas, TX | 214-363-0161 |
| Take Two Productions of Houston/3900-A Osage, Houston, TX | 713-961-0234 |
| Tecfilms Inc/2856 Fort Worth Ave, Dallas, TX | 214-339-2217 |

## WEST

| | |
|---|---|
| Blakeman, Bob Studios/2032 Stoner Ave, Los Angeles, CA | 213-479-4327 |
| Carthay Studio/5907 W Pico Blvd, Los Angeles, CA | 213-938-2101 |
| Chris-Craft Video Tape/915 N LaBrea, Los Angeles, CA | 213-851-2626 |
| Cine-Rent West Inc/991 Tennessee St, San Francisco, CA | 415-864-4644 |
| Cine-Video/948 N Cahuenga Blvd, Los Angeles, CA | 213-464-6200 |
| Columbia Pictures/300 S Colgems Sq, Burbank, CA | 213-843-6000 |
| Design Arts Studios/800 N Seward, Hollywood, CA | 213-464-9118 |
| Disney, Walt Productions/500 S Buena Vista St, Burbank, CA | 213-845-3141 |
| Eliot, Josh Studio/706 W Pico Blvd, Los Angeles, CA | 213-742-0367 |
| Goldwyn, Samuel Studios/1041 N Formosa Ave, Los Angeles, CA | 213-650-2500 |
| Great American Cinema Co/10711 Wellworth Ave, Los Angeles, CA | 213-475-0937 |
| Hollywood General Studios/1040 N Las Palmas Ave, Los Angeles, CA | 213-469-9011 |
| Hollywood National Studios/6605 Eleanor Ave, Hollywood, CA | 213-463-2123 |
| Hollywood Stage/6650 Santa Monica Blvd, Los Angeles, CA | 213-466-4393 |
| Kelley, Tom Studios/8525 Santa Monica Blvd, Los Angeles, CA | 213-657-1780 |
| Kings Point Corporation/9336 W Washington, Culver City, CA | 213-836-5537 |
| Lewin, Elyse/820 N Fairfax Ave, Los Angeles, CA | 213-655-4214 |
| Liles, Harry Productions Inc/1060 N Lillian Way, Los Angeles, CA | 213-466-1612 |
| MGM Studios/10202 W Washington, Culver City, CA | 213-836-3000 |
| Miller, Donald Inc/2032 Stoner Ave, Los Angeles, CA | 213-477-2491 |
| 940 Photo/940 N Highland, Los Angeles, CA | 213-469-5567 |
| Norwood, David/4040 Del Ray Ave, Marina Del Ray, CA | 213-827-2020 |
| Paramount/5451 Marathon St, Los Angeles, CA | 213-463-0100 |
| Producers Studio/650 N Bronson Ave, Los Angeles, CA | 213-466-7778 |
| Rouzer Studio/7022 Melrose Ave, Los Angeles, CA | 213-936-2494 |
| Solaris T V Studios/2525 Ocean Park Blvd, Santa Monica, CA | 213-450-6227 |
| Studio AV/1227 First Ave S, Seattle, WA | 206-223-1007 |
| Studio Center CBS/4024 Radford Ave, Studio City, CA | 213-760-5000 |
| Sunset/Gower Studio/1438 N Gower, Los Angeles, CA | 213-467-1001 |
| Superstage/5724 Santa Monica Blvd, Los Angeles, CA | 213-464-0296 |
| Team Production Co Inc/10616 Moorpark St, North Hollywood, CA | 213-506-5700 |
| Television Center Studios/846 N Cahuenga Blvd, Los Angeles, CA | 213-466-1355 |
| Trans-American Video/1541 Vine St, Los Angeles, CA | 213-466-2141 |
| Tri-Ads/9260 Alden Dr, Los Angeles, CA | 213-278-6821 |
| Twentieth Centruy-Fox/10201 W Pico Blvd, Los Angeles, CA | 213-277-2211 |
| UPA Pictures/4440 Lakeside Dr, Burbank, CA | 213-842-7171 |
| Universal City Studios/Universal Studios, Universal City, CA | 213-985-4321 |
| The Videography Studios/8471 Universal Plaza, Universal City, CA | 213-204-2000 |
| Vine Street Video Center/1224 Vince St, Pasadena, CA | 213-462-1099 |
| Warner Brothers/4000 Warner Blvd, Burbank, CA | 213-843-6000 |
| Wolin/Semple Studio/520 N Western Ave, Los Angeles, CA | 213-463-2109 |

# ANIMATORS

## NEW YORK CITY

| | |
|---|---|
| A P A/230 W 10th St | 212-929-9436 |
| ALZ Productions/11 Waverly Pl | 212-473-7620 |
| Abacus Prod, Inc/475 Fifth Ave | 212-532-6677 |
| Abrahams, Marty/111 Hudson St | 212-431-8482 |
| Ani-Live Film Service Inc/45 W 45th St | 212-819-0700 |
| Animated Productions Inc/1600 Broadway | 212-265-2942 |
| Animation Camera Workshop/51 E 42nd St | 212-239-7112 |
| Animation Services Inc/47 W 57th St | 212-688-6225 |
| Animation Stand Inc/2 W 46th St | 212-719-1549 |

# PHOTO/FILM SERVICES CONT'D.

Please send us your additions and updates.

| | |
|---|---|
| Animus Films/15 W 44th St | 212-391-8716 |
| Ariel Productions Inc/210 Fifth Ave | 212-679-8554 |
| Backle, R J Prod/222 E 44th St | 212-867-4030 |
| Bakst, Edward/160 W 96th St | 212-666-2579 |
| Beckerman, Howard/45 W 45th St #300 | 212-869-0595 |
| Blechman, R O/2 W 47th St | 212-869-1630 |
| The Cartoon Co Films Inc/141 E 56th St | 212-935-1440 |
| Cel-Art Productions Inc/7 E 48th St | 212-751-7515 |
| Charisma Productions/32 E 57th St | 212-832-3020 |
| Charlex Inc/2 W 45th St | 212-719-4600 |
| Cinema/TV Design/321 W 44th St | 212-581-1667 |
| Clark, Ian/229 E 96th St | 212-289-0998 |
| Clark, Timothy P/35 W 45th St | 212-221-7428 |
| D & R Productions Inc/36 W 44th St | 212-730-1028 |
| Dale Cameragraphics Inc/12 W 27th St | 212-696-9400 |
| Darino Films/222 Park Ave S | 212-228-4024 |
| Devlin Productions Inc/150 W 55th St | 212-582-5572 |
| Diamond & Diaferia/12 E 44th St | 212-986-8500 |
| Digital Effects Inc/321 W 44 St | 212-581-7760 |
| Dolphin Productions Inc/140 E 80th St | 212-628-5930 |
| Doros Animation, Inc/475 Fifth Ave | 212-684-5043 |
| Elinor Bunin Productions Inc/30 E 60th St | 212-688-0759 |
| Fandango Productions Inc/124 E 40th St | 212-986-5676 |
| The Fantastic Animation Machine/12 E 46th St | 212-697-2525 |
| Feigenbaum Prod, Inc/25 W 43rd St #220 | 212-840-3744 |
| Film Planning Assoc/38 E 20th | 212-260-7140 |
| Gati, John/881 Seventh Ave #832 | 212-582-9060 |
| Granato Animation Photography/15 W 46th St | 212-869-3231 |
| Graphics Group, Inc/321 W 44th St | 212-582-8270 |
| Greenberg, R Assoc/240 Madison Ave | 212-689-7886 |
| Grossman, Robert/19 Crosby St | 212-925-1965 |
| Hankinson Studios/1156 Sixth Ave | 212-730-0434 |
| Harold Friedman Consortium/420 Lexington Ave | 212-697-0858 |
| Howard Graphics/36 W 25th St | 212-929-2121 |
| I F Studios/328 E 44th St | 212-697-6805 |
| Image Factory Inc/18 E 53rd St | 212-759-9363 |
| The Ink Tank/2 W 47th St | 212-869-1630 |
| International Production Center/514 W 57th St | 212-582-6530 |
| J C Productions/16 W 46th St | 212-575-9611 |
| Kim & Gifford Productions Inc/342 Madison Ave | 212-986-2826 |
| Kimmelman, Phil & Assoc Inc/50 W 40th St | 212-944-7766 |
| Kurtz and Friends/130 E 18th St | 212-777-3256 |
| Leo Animation Camera Service/25 W 43rd St | 212-997-1840 |
| Locomo Productions/875 West End Ave | 212-222-4833 |
| Marz Productions Inc/130 E 37th St | 212-686-2785 |
| Motion Picker Studio/416 Ocean Ave | 212-856-2763 |
| Murphy, Neil/208 W 23rd St | 212-691-5730 |
| Musicvision, Inc/185 E 85th St | 212-860-4420 |
| Ovation Films/49 W 24th St | 212-675-4700 |
| Paganelli, Albert/21 W 46th St | 212-719-4105 |
| Perpetual Animation/17 W 45th St | 212-953-9110 |
| Polestar Films & Assoc Arts/870 Seventh Ave | 212-586-6333 |
| Rankin/Bass Productions/1 E 53rd St | 212-759-7721 |
| Raul DaSilva & Other Film Makers/311 E 85th St | 212-925-8521 |
| Rebecca Singer Studio Inc/111 W 57th St | 212-541-4552 |
| Rembrandt Films/59 E 54th St | 212-758-1024 |
| Robinson, Keith Prod Inc/200 E 21st St | 212-533-9078 |
| Rowholt Animation Photo/35 W 45th St | 212-869-0010 |
| Seeger, Hal/45 W 45th St | 212-586-4311 |
| Shadow Light Prod, Inc/12 W 27th St 7th Fl | 212-689-7511 |
| Stanart Studios/1650 Broadway | 212-586-0445 |
| Stark, Philip/312 E 90th St | 212-534-0760 |
| Sunflower Films/15 W 46th St | 212-869-0123 |
| Swallow, Barbara Assoc/45 W 45th St | 212-840-6676 |
| Synthavision-Magi/3 Westchester Plaza | 212-733-1300 |
| Telemated Motion Pictures/77 Bleecker St | 212-475-8050 |
| Today Video, Inc/45 W 45th St | 212-391-1020 |
| Videart Inc/39 W 38th St | 212-840-2163 |
| Video Works/24 W 40th St | 212-869-2500 |
| Weiss, Frank Studio/66 E 7th St | 212-477-1032 |
| World Effects Inc/20 E 46th St | 212-687-7070 |
| Zander Animation Parlor/18 E 41st St | 212-725-1331 |

## NORTHEAST

| | |
|---|---|
| Advent Universal Studios/654 Kennebec Ave, Tacoma Park, MD | 301-587-4942 |
| The Animators/247 Ft Pitt Blvd, Pittsburgh, PA | 412-391-2550 |
| Animistic Flicks, Ltd/1069 Wisconsin Ave NW, Washington, DC | 202-338-8178 |
| Aviation Simulations International Inc/Box 358, Huntington, NY | 516-271-6476 |
| Aviations Simulations Intern Inc/Box 358, Huntington, NY | 516-271-6476 |
| Broadcast Arts, Inc/1005 E St NW, Washington, DC | 202-347-9315 |
| Com Corps, Inc/711 4th St NW, Washington, DC | 202-638-6550 |
| Consolidated Visual Center/2529 Kenilworth Ave, Tuxedo, MD | 301-772-7300 |
| Felix, Luisa/732 Willow Ave #10, Hoboken, NJ | 201-653-1500 |
| Friar Graphics/9232 Warren St, Silver Springs, MD | 301-588-5900 |
| Gary Hughes/Film Studio, Inc/PO Box 54, Cabin John, MD | 301-229-1100 |
| Myriad Communications, Inc/357 Robin Rd, Englewood, NJ | 201-871-0190 |
| Penpoint Prod Svc/331 Newbury St, Boston, MA | 617-266-1331 |
| Pilgrim Film Service/2504 50th Ave, Hyattsville, MD | 301-773-7072 |
| Symmetry T/A/13813 Willoughby Road, Upper Marlboro, MD | 301-627-5050 |
| West End Film Production/2141 Newport Pl NW, Washington, DC | 202-331-8078 |

## SOUTHEAST

| | |
|---|---|
| Bajus-Jones Film Corp/401 W Peachtree Summit #3, Atlanta, GA | 404-221-0700 |
| Cinetron Computer Systems Inc/6700 I-85 N, Norcross, GA | 404-448-9463 |
| March Brothers Inc/229 W Bute St, Norfolk, VA | 804-627-0415 |

## MIDWEST

| | |
|---|---|
| AGS & R Studios/425 N Michigan Ave, Chicago, IL | 312-836-4500 |
| Associated Audio-Visual Corp/2821 Central St, Evanston, IL | 312-866-6780 |
| Bajus-Jones Film Corp/203 N Wabash, Chicago, IL | 312-332-6041 |
| The Beach Productions Ltd/22 W Erie, Chicago, IL | 312-337-0688 |
| Boyer Studio/1324 Greenleaf, Evanston, IL | 312-491-6363 |
| Coast Prod/505 N Lake Shore Dr, Chicago, IL | 312-222-1857 |
| Filmack Studios, Inc/1327 S Wabash, Chicago, IL | 312-427-3395 |
| Freese & Friends, Inc/14 N Wells, Chicago, IL | 312-642-4475 |
| Goldsholl Assoc/420 Frontage Rd, Northfield, IL | 312-446-8300 |
| Goodrich Animation/230 E Ohio #206, Chicago, IL | 312-644-7786 |
| Heartland Prod Inc/1058 W Washington Blvd, Chicago, IL | 312-738-3338 |
| Kayem Animation Services/100 E Ohio, Chicago, IL | 312-664-7733 |
| Kinetics/303 E Wacker, Chicago, IL | 312-644-2767 |
| Optimation Inc/9055 N 51st St, Brown Deer, WI | 414-355-4500 |
| Pilot Prod/1819 Ridge Ave, Evanston, IL | 312-328-3700 |
| Quicksilver Assoc Inc/16 W Ontario, Chicago, IL | 312-943-7622 |
| Reel Directions/213 W Institute Pl, Chicago, IL | 312-649-9506 |
| Ritter Waxberg & Assoc/200 E Ontario, Chicago, IL | 312-664-3934 |
| Simott & Assoc./676 N La Salle, Chicago, IL | 312-440-1875 |
| Special Effects, Inc/610 N Fairbanks Ct, Chicago, IL | 312-266-0125 |

## SOUTHWEST

| | |
|---|---|
| Graphic Art Studio/5127 S Lewis Ave, Tulsa, OK | 918-743-3915 |
| Media Visions, Inc/2716 Bissonnet #408, Houston, TX | 713-521-0626 |

## WEST

| | |
|---|---|
| Abel, Bob & Assoc/953 N Highland Ave, Los Angeles, CA | 213-462-8100 |
| Animation Filmakers Corp/7000 Romaine St, Hollywood, CA | 213-851-5526 |
| Animedia Procuctions Inc/10200 Riverside Dr, North Hollywood, CA | 213-769-7469 |
| Bajus-Jones Film Corp/1831 Prosser Ave, Los Angeles, CA | 213-475-7794 |
| Bass, Saul & Assoc/7039 Sunset Blvd, Hollywood, CA | 213-466-9701 |
| Bosustow Entertainment/1649 11th St, Santa Monica, CA | 213-394-0218 |
| Braverman Productions Inc/8961 Sunset Blvd, Los Angeles, CA | 213-278-5444 |
| CPC Associates Inc/6309 Eleanor Ave, Hollywood, CA | 213-467-5900 |
| Carlson, Paul Cartoons Inc/4440 Lakeside Dr, Burbank, CA | 213-842-7174 |
| Cinema Research Corp/6860 Lexington Ave, Hollywood, CA | 213-461-3235 |
| Clampett, Bob Prod/729 Seward St, Hollywood, CA | 213-466-0264 |
| Cornerstone Productions/5915 Cantelope Ave, Van Nuys, CA | 213-994-0007 |
| Creative Film Arts/7026 Santa Monica Blvd, Hollywood, CA | 213-466-5111 |
| DePatie-Freleng Enterprises/6859 Hayvenhurst Ave, | |

# PHOTO/FILM SERVICES CONT'D.

Please send us your additions and updates.

| | |
|---|---|
| Van Nuys, CA | 213-873-7451 |
| Duck Soup Productions Inc/1026 Montana Ave, Santa Monica, CA | 213-451-0771 |
| Emotion Pictures/765 Hyperion Ave, Los Angeles, CA | 213-666-4720 |
| Energy Productions/846 N Cahuenga Blvd, Los Angeles, CA | 213-462-3310 |
| Excelsior Animated Moving Pictures/749 N LaBrea, Hollywood, CA | 213-938-2335 |
| Filmcore/849 N Seward, Hollywood, CA | 213-464-7303 |
| Filmfair/10900 Ventura Blvd, Studio City, CA | 213-877-3191 |
| Fred Craig Productions/932 S Pine, San Gabriel, CA | 213-287-6479 |
| Gallerie International Films Ltd/11320 W Magnolia Blvd, Hollywood, CA | 213-760-2040 |
| Hanna-Barbera/3400 W Cahuenga, Hollywood, CA | 213-466-1371 |
| The Holographic Animation Co/600 S Burnside, Los Angeles, CA | 213-934-3579 |
| Image West Ltd/845 N Highland Ave, Hollywood, CA | 213-466-4181 |
| The Jay Teitsell Company/201 The Grand Canal, Venice, CA | 213-822-9024 |
| Jean-Guy Jacque & Assoc/633 N LaBrea Ave, Hollywood, CA | 213-936-7177 |
| Kramer/Rockien/616 Westbourne, Los Angeles, CA | 213-659-9640 |
| Kurtz & Friends/1728 Whitley, Hollywood, CA | 213-461-8188 |
| Learning Garden Inc/7805 Sunset Blvd, Los Angeles, CA | 213-874-6632 |
| Littlejohn, William Prod Inc/23425 Malibu Colony Dr, Malibu, CA | 213-456-8620 |
| Luckey-Zamora Picture Moving Co/66 Broadway, San Francisco, CA | 415-421-2241 |
| Lumeni Productions/1727 N Ivar, Hollywood, CA | 213-462-2110 |
| Lyon Lamb Video Animation Syst/723 N Broadway, Laguna Beach, CA | 714-497-1135 |
| Marks & Marks/2690 Beachwood Dr, Los Angeles, CA | 213-464-6302 |
| Melendez, Bill Prod Inc/439 N Larchmont Blvd, Los Angeles, CA | 213-463-4101 |
| Murakami Wolf Swenson Films Inc/1463 Tamarind Ave, Hollywood, CA | 213-462-6474 |
| New Hollywood Inc/1302 N Cahuenga Blvd, Hollywood, CA | 213-466-3686 |
| Orsatti Productions/11466 San Vincente Blvd, Los Angeles, CA | 213-826-8235 |
| Pantomime Pictures Inc/12144 Riverside Dr, North Hollywood, CA | 213-980-5555 |
| Pegboard Productions/1310 N Cahuenga Blvd, Hollywood, CA | 213-469-7376 |
| Phillips, Stan & Assoc/865 Delaware, Denver, CO | 303-595-9911 |
| Quartet Films Inc/5631 Hollywood Blvd, Hollywood, CA | 213-464-9225 |
| R & B EFX/1802 Victory Blvd, Glendale, CA | 213-956-8406 |
| Raintree Productions Ltd/666 N Robertson Blvd, Hollywood, CA | 213-659-9620 |
| Richard Haboush Company/1514 N Formosa Ave, Hollywood, CA | 213-851-8955 |
| Richard Williams Animation/5631 Hollywood Blvd, Los Angeles, CA | 213-461-4344 |
| Ruby-Spears Productions/11240 Sherman Way, Sun Valley, CA | 213-764-7700 |
| S & A Graphics/3350 Barham Blvd, Los Angeles, CA | 213-874-2301 |
| Spungbuggy Works Inc/8506 Sunset Blvd, Hollywood, CA | 213-657-8070 |
| Story, Robert Moving Pictures/6922 Hollywood Blvd, Hollywood, CA | 213-467-6700 |
| Sullivan & Associates/3377 Barham Blvd, Los Angeles, CA | 213-874-2301 |
| Sunwest Productions Inc/1021 N McCadden Pl, Hollywood, CA | 213-461-2957 |
| Title House/800 N Cole Ave, Los Angeles, CA | 213-469-8171 |
| Triplane Film & Graphics Inc/1545 N Wilcox Ave, Hollywood, CA | 213-463-8131 |
| U P A Pictures Inc/4440 Lakeside Dr, Burbank, CA | 213-849-6666 |
| Wally Bulloch/Anicam/6315 Yucca St, Hollywood, CA | 213-465-4114 |
| Walt Disney Productions/500 S Buena Vista Terr, Burbank, CA | 213-845-3141 |

# MODELS & TALENT

## NEW YORK CITY

| | |
|---|---|
| Act 48 Mgt Inc/1501 Broadway #1713 | 212-354-4250 |
| Adair, Rose/250 W 57th St | 212-582-1957 |
| Adams, Bret/36 E 61st St | 212-752-7864 |
| Agency for Performing Arts/888 Seventh Ave | 212-582-1500 |
| Agents for the Arts/1650 Broadway | 212-247-3220 |
| Alexander, Willard/660 Madison Ave | 212-751-7070 |
| Ambrose Co/1466 Broadway | 212-921-0230 |
| American Intl Talent/166 W 125th St | 212-663-4626 |
| American Talent Inc/888 Seventh Ave | 212-977-2300 |
| Anderson, Beverly/1472 Broadway | 212-944-7773 |
| Ann Wright Assoc/136 E 57th St | 212-832-0110 |
| Arcara Bauman & Hiller/250 W 57th St | 212-757-0098 |
| Associated Booking/1995 Broadway | 212-874-2400 |
| Associated Talent Agency/41 E 11th St | 212-674-4242 |
| Astor, Richard/119 W 57th St | 212-581-1970 |
| Baldwin Scully Inc/501 Fifth Ave | 212-922-1330 |
| Barbizon Agency of Rego Park/95-20 63rd | 212-275-2100 |
| Barry Agency/165 W 46th St | 212-869-9310 |
| Beilin, Peter/230 Park Ave | 212-949-9119 |
| Big Beauties Unlimited/159 Madison Ave | 212-685-1270 |
| Bishop, Lola/160 W 46th St | 212-997-1836 |
| Bloom, J Michael/400 Madison Ave | 212-832-6900 |
| Buchwald, Don & Assoc Inc/10 E 44th St | 212-867-1070 |
| Case, Bertha/345 W 58th St | 212-541-9451 |
| Cataldi, Richard Agency/250 W 57th St | 212-245-6660 |
| Celebrity Lookalikes/235 E 31st St | 212-532-7676 |
| Coleman-Rosenberg/667 Madison Ave | 212-838-0734 |
| Columbia Artists/165 W 57th St | 212-397-6900 |
| Cunningham, W D/919 Third Ave | 212-832-2700 |
| D M I Talent Assoc/250 W 57th St | 212-246-4650 |
| DHKPR/165 W 46th St | 212-869-2880 |
| Deacy, Jane Inc/300 E 75th St | 212-752-4865 |
| DeVore, Ophelia/1697 Broadway | 212-586-2144 |
| Diamond Artists/119 W 57th St | 212-247-3025 |
| Dolan, Gloria Management Ltd/850 Seventh Ave | 212-246-1420 |
| Draper, Stephen Agency/37 W 57th St | 212-421-5780 |
| Eisen, Dulcina Assoc/154 E 61st St | 212-355-6617 |
| Elite Model Management Corp/150 E 58th St | 212-935-4500 |
| Fields, Marje/250 W 57th St | 212-581-7240 |
| Filor Models Inc/140 E 56th St | 212-832-1636 |
| Flight 485/575 Madison Ave | 212-751-6522 |
| Ford Models Inc/344 E 59th St | 212-688-8538 |
| Foster Fell Agency/26 W 38th St | 212-944-8520 |
| Funny Face/527 Madsion Ave | 212-752-6090 |
| Gage Group Inc/1650 Broadway | 212-541-5250 |
| Greco, Maria & Assoc/888 Eighth Ave | 212-757-0681 |
| H A Artists & Assoc/575 Lexington Ave | 212-935-8980 |
| Hadley, Peggy Ent/250 W 57th St | 212-246-2166 |
| Harth, Ellen Inc/515 Madison Ave | 212-593-2332 |
| Hartig, Michael Agency Ltd/527 Madison Ave | 212-759-9163 |
| Henderson-Hogan/200 W 57th St | 212-765-5190 |
| Henry, June/119 W 57th St | 212-582-8140 |
| Hesseltine Baker Assocs/165 W 46th St | 212-921-4460 |
| Hunt, Diana Management/44 W 44th St | 212-391-4971 |
| Hutto Management Inc/467 W 22nd St | 212-807-1234 |
| International Creative Management/40 W 57th St | 212-556-5600 |
| International Model Agency/232 Madison Ave | 212-686-9053 |
| Jacobsen-Wilder Inc/419 Park Ave So | 212-686-6100 |
| Jan J Agency/224 E 46th St | 212-490-1875 |
| Jerry Kahn Inc/853 Seventh Ave | 212-582-1280 |
| Jordan, Joe Talent Agency/200 W 57th St | 212-582-9003 |
| KMA Associates/303 W 42nd St | 212-581-4610 |
| Kennedy Artists/881 Seventh Ave | 212-675-3944 |
| Kid, Bonnie Agency/250 W 57th St | 212-246-0223 |
| King, Archer/1440 Broadway | 212-764-3905 |
| Kirk, Roseanne/527 Madison Ave | 212-888-6711 |
| Kolmar-Luth Entertainment Inc/1776 Broadway | 212-581-5833 |
| Kroll, Lucy/390 West End Ave | 212-877-0556 |
| L B H Assoc/1 Lincoln Plaza | 212-787-2609 |
| The Lantz Office/888 Seventh Ave | 212-586-0200 |
| Larner, Lionel Ltd/850 Seventh Ave | 212-243-3105 |
| Leach, Dennis/100 Fifth Ave | 212-691-3450 |
| Leaverton, Gary Inc/1650 Broadway | 212-541-9640 |
| Leighton, Jan/205 W 57th St | 212-757-5242 |
| Lenny, Jack Assoc/140 W 58th St, #1B | 212-582-0270 |
| Lester Lewis Assoc/110 W 40th St | 212-921-8370 |
| L'Image Model Management Inc/667 Madison Ave | 212-758-6411 |
| M E W Company/370 Lexington Ave | 212-889-7272 |
| MMG Ent/Marcia's Kids/250 W 57th St | 212-246-4360 |

# PHOTO/FILM SERVICES CONT'D.

Please send us your additions and updates.

| | |
|---|---|
| Mannequin Fashion Models Inc/730 Fifth Ave | 212-586-7716 |
| Martial Arts Talent & Models/30 W 90th St | 212-580-2236 |
| Martinelli Attractions/888 Eighth Ave | 212-586-0963 |
| Masterworks Glamour Management/135 E 55th St | 212-758-6295 |
| McDearmon, Harold/45 W 139th St | 212-283-1005 |
| McDermott, Marge/216 E 39th St | 212-889-1583 |
| Michael Amato Theatrical Ent/1650 Broadway | 212-247-4456 |
| Models Service Agency/1457 Broadway | 212-944-8896 |
| Morris, William Agency/1350 Sixth Ave | 212-586-5100 |
| New York Production Studio/250 W 57th St | 212-765-3433 |
| Nolan, Philip/134 W 58th St | 212-243-8900 |
| Oppenheim-Christie/565 Fifth Ave | 212-661-4330 |
| Oscard, Fifi/19 W 44th St | 212-764-1100 |
| Ostertag, Barna Agency/501 Fifth Ave | 212-697-6339 |
| Packwood, Harry Talent Ltd/342 Madison Ave | 212-682-5858 |
| Palmer, Dorothy/250 W 57th St | 212-765-4280 |
| Perkins Models/213 W 53rd St | 212-582-9511 |
| Pfeffer & Roelfs Inc/79 Madison Ave | 212-689-9020 |
| PlusModel Model Management Ltd/49 W 37th St | 212-997-1785 |
| Powers, James Inc/12 E 41st St | 212-686-9066 |
| Premier Talent Assoc/3 E 54th St | 212-758-4900 |
| Raglyn-Shamsky/60 E 42nd St | 212-661-6690 |
| Rogers, Wallace Inc/160 E 56th St | 212-755-1464 |
| Roos, Gilla Ltd/527 Madison Ave | 212-758-5480 |
| Rosen, Lewis Maxwell/1650 Broadway | 212-582-6762 |
| Rubenstein, Bernard/215 Park Ave So | 212-460-9800 |
| Ryan, Charles Agency/200 W 57th St | 212-245-2225 |
| STE Representation/888 Seventh Ave | 212-246-1030 |
| Sanders, Honey Agency Ltd/229 W 42nd St | 212-947-5555 |
| Sanford Leigh Agency/527 Madison Ave | 212-752-4450 |
| Schuller, William Agency/667 Madison Ave | 212-758-1919 |
| Silver, Monty Agency/200 W 57th St | 212-765-4040 |
| Smith, Friedman/850 Seventh Ave | 212-581-4490 |
| The Starkman Agency/1501 Broadway | 212-921-9191 |
| Stein, Lillian/1501 Broadway | 212-840-8299 |
| Stewart Artists Corp/215 E 81st St | 212-249-5540 |
| Stroud Management/18 E 48th St | 212-688-0226 |
| Summa/250 W 57th St #2231 | 212-582-7035 |
| Szold, Ruth Promo Models/644 Broadway | 212-777-4998 |
| Talent Reps Inc/20 E 53rd St | 212-752-1835 |
| Tatinas Models & Fitters Assoc/1328 Broadway | 212-947-5797 |
| Theater Now Inc/1515 Broadway | 212-840-4400 |
| Thomas, Michael Agency/22 E 60th St | 212-755-2616 |
| Tranum Robertson Hughes Inc/2 Dag Hammarskjold Plaza | 212-371-7500 |
| Troy, Gloria/1790 Broadway | 212-582-0260 |
| Universal Attractions/218 W 57th St | 212-582-7575 |
| Universal Talent/505 5th Ave | 212-661-3896 |
| Van Der Veer People Inc/225A E 59th St | 212-688-2880 |
| Waters, Bob Agency/510 Madison Ave | 212-593-0543 |
| Wilhelmina Models/9 E 37th St | 212-532-6800 |
| Witt, Peter Assoc Inc/215 E 79th St | 212-861-3120 |
| Zoli/146 E 56th St | 212-758-5959 |

## NORTHEAST

| | |
|---|---|
| American Residuals & Talent Inc/69 Newbury St, Boston, MA | 617-536-4827 |
| Cameo Models/392 Boylston St, Boston, MA | 617-536-6004 |
| Carnegie Talent Agency/300 Northern Blvd, Great Neck, NY | 516-487-2260 |
| Conover, Joyce Agency/33 Gallowae, Westfield, NJ | 201-232-0908 |
| Copley 7 Models & Talent/29 Newbury St, Boston, MA | 617-267-4444 |
| Danline Management Inc/260 N Michigan Ave, Kenilworth, NJ | 201-245-5900 |
| Faces Enterprises/One Investemen Pl, Baltimore, MD | 301-321-9512 |
| Ford Models of Boston/176 Newbury St, Boston, MA | 617-266-6939 |
| Hart Model Agency/137 Newbury St, Boston, MA | 617-262-1740 |
| Johnston Agency/4 Branble Lane, Riverside, CT | 203-637-5949 |
| Pennington Entertainment Ltd/72 Edmund St, Edison, NJ | 201-985-9090 |
| Rocco, Joseph Agency/Public Ledger Bldg, Philadelphia, PA | 215-923-8790 |
| Rosemary Brian Agency/50 E Palisades Ave, Engelwood, NJ | 212-564-8616 |

## SOUTHEAST

| | |
|---|---|
| A del Corral Model & Talent Agency/5830 Argonne Blvd, New Orleans, LA | 504-482-8963 |
| Act 1 Casting Agency/1460 Brickell Ave, Miami, FL | 305-371-1371 |
| The Agency South/1501 Sunset Dr, Coral Gables, FL | 305-667-6746 |
| Amaro Agency/1617 Smith St, Orange Park, FL | 904-264-0771 |
| Artists Rep of New Orleans/1012 Philip, New Orleans, LA | |
| Artists Representatives of New Orleans/1012 Philip, New Orleans, LA | 504-524-4683 |
| Atlanta Models & Talent Inc/3030 Peachtree Rd NW, Atlanta, GA | 404-261-9627 |
| Birmingham Models & Talent/1023 20th St, Birmingham, AL | 205-252-8533 |
| Brown, Bob Marionettes/1415 S Queen St, Arlington, VA | 703-920-1040 |
| Brown, Jay Theatrical Agency Inc/221 W Waters Ave, Tampa, FL | 813-933-2456 |
| Bruce Enterprises/1022 16th Ave S, Nashville, TN | 615-255-5711 |
| Burns, Dot Model & Talent Agcy/478 Severn St, Tampa, FL | 813-251-5882 |
| Byrd, Russ Assoc/9450 Koger Blvd, St Petersburg, FL | 813-577-1555 |
| Carolina Talent/600 Queens Rd, Charlotte, NC | 704-332-6601 |
| Cassandra Models Agency/635 N Hyer St, Orlando, FL | 305-423-7872 |
| Casting & Production Services/12434 Largo Drive, Savannah, GA | 912-927-3807 |
| The Casting Directors Inc/1524 NE 147th St, North Miami, FL | 305-944-8559 |
| Central Casting of FL/P O Box 154, Ft Lauderdale, FL | 305-379-7526 |
| Chez Agency/922 W Peachtree St, Atlanta, GA | 404-873-1215 |
| Creations Unlimited/3373 Columbia Woods Dr, Decatur, GA | 404-289-4216 |
| Creative Enterprises Talent Agency/2863 1st Ave S, St Petersburg, FL | 813-823-3700 |
| Dassinger, Peter International Modeling/1018 Royal, New Orleans, LA | 504-525-8382 |
| Directions Talent Agency/400 State St Station #C, Greensboro, NC | 919-373-0955 |
| Dodd, Barbara Studios/3508 Central Ave, Nashville, TN | 615-385-0740 |
| Faces, Ltd/2915 Frankfort Ave, Louisville, KY | 502-893-8840 |
| Falcon, Travis Modeling Agency/17070 Collins Ave, Miami, FL | 305-947-7957 |
| Fashioncrest International/777 NW 72nd Ave, Miami, FL | 305-261-6821 |
| Flair Models/PO Box 17372, Nashville, TN | 615-361-3737 |
| Florida Talent Agency/2631 E Oakland Pk, Ft Lauderdale, FL | 305-565-3552 |
| Glyne Kennedy Ltd Inc/1828 NE 4th Ave, Miami, FL | 305-358-5998 |
| House of Talent of Cain & Sons/996 Lindridge Dr NE, Atlanta, GA | 404-261-5543 |
| Jo-Susan Modeling & Finishing School/3415 West End Ave, Nashville, TN | 615-383-5850 |
| Kline, Maezie Murphy/220 Sunrise Ave, Palm Beach, FL | 305-833-3052 |
| Mar Bea Talent Agency/104 Crandon Blvd, #305, Key Biscayne, FL | 305-361-1144 |
| Marilyn's Modeling Agency/823 N Elm St, Greensboro, NC | 919-275-7947 |
| McQuerter, James/3204 Bay to Bay, Tampa, FL | 813-839-8335 |
| Millie Lewis Modeling School/3022 Millwood Ave, Columbia, SC | |
| Parker, Sarah Models & Talent/425 S Olive Ave, West Palm Beach, FL | 305-659-2833 |
| Patricia Stevens Modeling Agency/3330 Peachtree Rd NW, Atlanta, GA | 404-261-3330 |
| Poison Apple/465 Hammond Dr NE, Atlanta, GA | 404-252-4300 |
| Polan, Marian Talent Agency/PO Box 7154, Ft Lauderdale, FL | 305-525-8351 |
| Powers, John Robert School/828 SE 4th St, Fort Lauderdale, FL | 305-467-2838 |
| Professional Models Guild & Workshop/210 Providence Ave, Charlotte, NC | 704-377-9299 |
| Serendipity Models and Talent/3130 Maple Dr NE, Atlanta, GA | 404-237-4040 |
| Signature Talent Inc/PO Box 221086, Charlotte, NC | 704-542-0034 |
| Sims, Lynn Fashion College/1925 Marion St, Columbia, SC | 803-252-3914 |
| Spivia, Ed/PO Box 38097, Atlanta, GA | 404-292-6240 |
| Studio Productions/17070 Collins Ave, Miami, FL | 305-893-5611 |
| Take One Talent/3330 Peachtree St NE, Atlanta, GA | 404-231-2315 |
| Talent & Model Land, Inc/1501 12th Ave S, Nashville, TN | 615-385-2723 |
| Talent Enterprises Inc/148-75 NE 20th Ave, North Miami, FL | 305-949-6099 |
| The Talent Shop Inc/3379 Peachtree Rd NE #606, Atlanta, GA | 404-261-0770 |
| Theatrics Etcetera/PO Box 11862, Memphis, TN | 901-278-7454 |
| Thompson, Jan Agency/1800 East Blvd, Charlotte, NC | 704-377-5987 |
| Top Billing Inc/PO Box 121089, Nashville, TN | 615-327-1133 |
| Universal Personalities, Inc/520 Virginia Dr, Orlando, FL | 305-896-9800 |

# PHOTO/FILM SERVICES CONT'D.

Please send us your additions and updates.

## MIDWEST

| | |
|---|---|
| A-Plus Talent Agency Corp/666 N Lakeshore Dr, Chicago, IL | 312-642-8151 |
| Advertisers Casting Service/15 Kercheval Ave, Grosse Point Farms, MI | 313-881-1135 |
| Affiliated Talent & Casting Service/28860 Southfield Rd, #100, Southfield, MI | 313-559-3110 |
| Arlene Willson Agency/9205 W Center St, Milwaukee, WI | 414-259-1611 |
| Creative Casting Inc/430 Oak Grove, Minneapolis, MN | 612-871-7866 |
| Gem Enterprises/5100 Eden Ave, Minneapolis, MN | 612-927-8000 |
| Glamour/140 N Main St, Dayton, OH | 513-222-8321 |
| Hamilton, Shirley Inc/620 N Michigan Ave, Chicago, IL | 312-644-0300 |
| Hogan, Frank J/307 N Michigan Ave, Chicago, IL | 312-263-6910 |
| Lee, David Models/64 E Walton, Chicago, IL | 312-649-0500 |
| Limelight Assoc Inc/3460 Davis Lane, Cincinnati, OH | 513-631-8276 |
| MOore, Eleanor Agency/1610-B W Lake St, Minneapolis, MN | 612-827-3823 |
| Marx, Dick & Assoc Inc/101 E Ontario St, Chicago, IL | 312-440-7300 |
| The Model Shop/415 N State St, Chicago, IL | 312-822-9663 |
| Monza Talent Agency/911 Main St, Commerce Tower, Kansas City, MO | 816-421-0222 |
| New Faces Models & Talent Inc/310 Groveland Ave, Minneapolis, MN | 612-871-6000 |
| Powers, John Robert/5900 Roche Dr, Columbus, OH | 614-846-1047 |
| SR Talent Pool/206 S 44th St, Omaha, NE | 402-553-1164 |
| Schucart, Norman Ent/1417 Green Bay Rd, Highland Park, IL | 312-433-1113 |
| Sharkey Career Schools Inc/1299-H Lyons Rd Governours Sq, Centerville, OH | 513-434-4461 |
| Station 12-Producers Express/1759 Woodgrove Ln, Bloomfield Hills, MI | 313-569-7707 |
| Talent & Residuals Inc/303 E Ohio St, Chicago, IL | 312-943-7500 |
| Talent Phone Productions/612 N Michagan Ave, Chicago, IL | 312-664-5757 |
| Verblen, Carol Casting Svc/323 W Webster, Chicago, IL | 312-348-0047 |
| White House Studios/229 Ward Parkway, Kansas City, MO | 816-931-3608 |

## SOUTHWEST

| | |
|---|---|
| Accent Inc/900 NE 63rd St, Oklahoma City, OK | 405-843-1303 |
| Actors Clearinghouse/501 N IH 35, Austin, TX | 512-476-3412 |
| American Talent Assoc/7331 Harwin #116, Houston, TX | 713-975-8380 |
| Ball, Bobby Agency/808 E Osborn, Phoenix, AZ | 602-264-5007 |
| Barbizon School & Agency/1647-A W Bethany Home Rd, Phoenix, AZ | 602-249-2950 |
| Bennett, Don Agency/4630 Deepdale, Corpus Christi, TX | 512-854-4871 |
| Blair, Tanya Agency/3000 Carlisle St, Dallas, TX | 214-748-8353 |
| Butler, Beverly Freelance Talent/PO Box 5158, Little Rock, AR | 501-664-1641 |
| Creative Entertainment Assoc/1629 E Sahara Ave, Las Vegas, NV | 702-733-7575 |
| Creme de la Creme/5643 N Pennsylvania, Oklahoma City, OK | 405-843-6679 |
| Dawson, Kim Agency/PO Box 585060, Dallas, TX | 214-638-2414 |
| Flair-Career Fashion & Modeling/11200 Menaul Rd, Albuquerque, NM | 505-296-5571 |
| Fosi's Talent Agency/2777 N Campbell Ave, #209, Tucson, AZ | 602-795-3534 |
| Fullerton, Jo Ann/923 W Brittom Rd, Oklahoma City, OK | 405-848-4839 |
| Hall, K Agency/503 W 15th St, Austin, TX | 512-476-7523 |
| Halpin, Gerri Agency/3606 Montrose St, Houston, TX | 713-526-5747 |
| Harrison-Gers Modeling Agency/1707 Wilshire Blvd NW, Oklahoma City, OK | 405-840-4515 |
| Heina Modeling Agency/1100 W 34th St, Little Rock, AR | 501-375-3519 |
| The Mad Hatter/7349 Ashcroft Rd, Houston, TX | 713-995-9090 |
| Mannequin Modeling Agency/204 E Oakview, San Antonio, TX | 512-224-4231 |
| Melancon, Joseph Studios/2934 Elm, Dallas, TX | 214-742-2982 |
| Models and Talent of Tulsa/4528 S Sheridan Rd, Tulsa, OK | 918-664-5340 |
| Models of Houston Placement Agency/1305 South Voss, Houston, TX | 713-789-4973 |
| New Faces Inc/5108-B N 7th St, Phoenix, AZ | 602-279-3200 |
| Plaza Three Talent Agency/4343 N 16th St, Phoenix, AZ | 602-264-9703 |
| Powers, John Robert Agency/3005 S University Dr, Fort Worth, TX | 817-923-7305 |
| Scarbrough, Charlie/1201 N Pierce, #62, Little Rock, AR | 501-666-7838 |
| Shaw, Ben Modeling Studios/5353 W Alabama, Houston, TX | 713-850-0413 |
| Simorgh Modeling & Talent Agcy/4150 N 19th Ave, #16, Phoenix, AZ | 602-274-8532 |
| Southern Arizona Casting Co/2777 N Campbell Ave, #209, Tucson, AZ | 602-795-3534 |
| Strawn, Libby/3612 Foxcroft Rd, Little Rock, AR | 501-227-5874 |
| TOPS Talent Agency/4104 San Jacinto #130, Houston, TX | 713-522-1160 |
| Taylor, Peggy Talent Inc/3616 Howell, Dallas, TX | 214-526-4800 |
| The Texas Cowgirls Inc/4300 N Central, #109C, Dallas, TX | 214-696-4176 |
| Universal Models/953 E Sahara, Las Vegas, NV | 702-732-2499 |
| Wyse, Joy Agency/6318 Gaston Ave, Dallas, TX | 214-826-0330 |

## WEST

| | |
|---|---|
| Adrian, William Agency/520 S Lake Ave, Pasadena, CA | 213-681-5750 |
| Anthony's, Tom Precision Driving/1231 N Harper, Hollywood, CA | 213-462-2301 |
| Artists Management Agency/2232 Fifth Ave, San Diego, CA | 714-233-6655 |
| Barbizon Modeling & Talent Agy/15477 Ventura Blvd, Sherman Oaks, CA | 213-995-8238 |
| Barbizon School of Modeling/452 Fashion Valley, San Diego, CA | 714-296-6366 |
| The Blair Bunch Inc/7561 Woodman Pl, Van Nuys, CA | 213-994-8811 |
| Blanchard, Nina/1717 N Highland Ave, Hollywood, CA | 213-462-7274 |
| Celebrity Look-Alikes/9000 Sunset Blvd #407, W Hollywood, CA | 213-273-5566 |
| Character Actors/935 NW 19th Ave, Portland, OR | 503-223-1931 |
| Citywide Modeling Agency/3656 Scadlock La, Sherman Oaks, CA | 213-906-8316 |
| Commercials Unlimited/7461 Beverly Blvd, Los Angeles, CA | 213-937-2220 |
| The Coordinator/2130 Fourth Ave, San Diego, CA | 714-234-7911 |
| Crosby, Mary Talent Agency/2130 Fourth Ave, San Diego, CA | 714-234-7911 |
| Cunningham, William D/261 S Robertson, Beverly Hills, CA | 213-855-0200 |
| Demeter and Reed Ltd/445 Bryant, San Francisco, CA | 415-777-1337 |
| Franklin, Bob Broadcast Talent/10325 NE Hancock, Portland, OR | 503-253-1655 |
| Frazer-Nicklin Agency/3600 Cruz Ridge Ave, Santa Clara, CA | 408-554-1055 |
| Garrick, Dale Intern'l Agency/8831 Sunset Blvd, Los Angeles, CA | 213-657-2661 |
| Grimme Agency/214 Grant Ave, San Francisco, CA | 415-392-9175 |
| Hansen, Carolyn Agency/1516 6th Ave, Seattle, WA | 206-622-4700 |
| Illinois Talent/2664 S Krameria, Denver, CO | 303-757-8675 |
| International Creative Management/8899 Beverly Blvd, Los Angeles, CA | 213-550-4000 |
| The Jack Hampton Agency/Beverly Hills, CA | 213-274-6075 |
| Joseph, Jaye Agency/439 S LaCienega Blvd, Los Angeles, CA | 213-273-2000 |
| Kelman, Toni Agency/8537 3/8 Sunset Blvd, Los Angeles, CA | 213-851-8822 |
| L'Agence Models/100 N Winchester Blvd #370, San Jose, CA | 408-985-2993 |
| Leonetti, Ltd/6526 Sunset Blvd, Los Angeles, CA | 213-462-2345 |
| Liebes School of Modeling Inc/1807 Broadway, San Francisco, CA | 415-673-7171 |
| The Light Company Talent Agcy/1443 Wazee St, Denver, CO | 303-572-8363 |
| Longenecker, Robert Agency/11704 Wilshire #200, Los Angeles, CA | 213-477-0039 |
| Mack, Jess Agency/111 Las Vegas Blvd S, Las Vegas, NV | 702-382-2193 |
| Media Talent Center/1928 NE 41st St, Portland, OR | 503-281-2020 |
| Model Management Inc/1400 Castro St, San Francisco, CA | 415-282-8855 |
| Pacific Artists, Ltd/515 N La Cienega, Los Angeles, CA | 213-657-5990 |
| Playboy Model Agency/8560 Sunset Blvd, Los Angeles, CA | 213-659-4080 |
| Powers, John Robert/1610 6th Ave, Seattle, WA | 206-624-2495 |
| Schwartz, Don Agency/8721 Sunset Blvd, Los Angeles, CA | 213-657-8910 |
| Seattle Models Guild/1610 6th Ave, Seattle, WA | 206-622-1406 |
| Shaw, Glen Agency/3330 Barham Blvd, Los Angeles, CA | 213-851-6262 |
| Stern, Charles Agency/9220 Sunset Blvd, Los Angeles, CA | 213-273-6890 |
| Stunts Unltd/3518 Cahuenga Blvd W, Los Angeles, CA | 213-874-0050 |
| Tanner, Herb & Assoc/6640 W Sunset Blvd, Los Angeles, CA | 213-466-6191 |
| Tina Real/3108 Fifth Ave, San Diego, CA | 714-298-0544 |
| Williams Agency/158 Thomas #35, Seattle, WA | 206-223-0777 |
| Wormser Iteldford & Joseph/1717 N Highland Ave, Los Angeles, CA | 213-466-9111 |

# CASTING

# PHOTO/FILM SERVICES CONT'D.

Please send us your additions and updates.

## NEW YORK CITY

| | |
|---|---|
| BCI Casting/1500 Broadway | 212-221-1583 |
| Brinker, Jane/51 W 16th St | 212-924-3322 |
| Brown, Deborah Casting/250 W 57th St | 212-581-0404 |
| Burton, Kate/226 W 11th St | 212-243-6114 |
| Carter, Kit & Assoc/160 W 95th St | 212-864-3147 |
| Cast Away Casting Service/14 Sutton Pl S | 212-755-0960 |
| Central Casting Corp of NY/200 W 54th St | 212-582-4933 |
| Cereghetti Casting/119 W 57th St | 212-765-5260 |
| Claire Casting/118 E 28th St | 212-889-8844 |
| Complete Casting/45 W 45th St | 212-944-5724 |
| Comtemporay Casting Ltd/16 W 46th St | 212-575-9450 |
| Deron, Johnny/30-63 32nd St | 212-728-5326 |
| Digiaimo, Lou/581 Sixth Ave | 212-691-6073 |
| Donna DeSeta Casting/424 W 33rd St | 212-239-0988 |
| Fay, Sylvia/71 Park Ave | 212-889-2626 |
| Feuer & Ritzer Casting Assoc/1650 Broadway | 212-765-5580 |
| Greco, Maria Casting/888 Eighth Ave | 212-757-0681 |
| Herman & Lipson Casting, Inc/114 E 25th St | 212-777-7070 |
| Hughes/Moss Assoc/1515 Broadway | 212-840-2474 |
| Iredale Assoc Inc/271 Madison Ave | 212-889-7722 |
| Jacobs, Judith/336 E 81st St | 212-744-3758 |
| Johnson/Liff/850 Seventh Ave | 212-757-9420 |
| Kressel, Lynn Casting/250 W 57th St | 212-581-6990 |
| L 2 Casting, Inc/106 E 19th St | 212-505-0480 |
| McCorkle-Sturtevant Casting Ltd/240 W 44th St | 212-888-9160 |
| Navarro-Bertoni Casting Ltd/25 Central Park West | 212-765-4251 |
| Pulvino and Howard, Ltd/215 Park Ave So | 212-477-2323 |
| Reed/Sweeney/Reed Inc/1780 Broadway | 212-265-8541 |
| Reiner, Mark Contemporary Casting/16 W 46th St | 212-575-9450 |
| Schneider, Joseph/119 W 57th St | 212-265-1223 |
| Shapiro, Barbara Casting/111 W 57th St | 212-582-8228 |
| Shulman/Pasciuto, Inc/1457 Broadway #308 | 212-944-6420 |
| Silver, Stan/113 E 31st St | 212-683-8280 |
| Todd, Joy/211 W 58th St | 212-765-1212 |
| Wollin, Marji/233 E 69th St | 212-472-2528 |
| Woodman, Elizabeth Roberts/1650 Broadway | 212-541-9431 |

## NORTHEAST

| | |
|---|---|
| American Residuals & Talent/69 Newbury St, Boston, MA | 617-536-4827 |
| Booking Agent Lic/860 Floral Ave, Union, NJ | 201-353-1595 |
| Central Casting/1000 Connecticut Ave NW, Washington, DC | 202-659-8272 |
| Dilworth, Francis/496 Kinderkamar Rd, Oradell, NJ | 201-265-4020 |
| Holt/Belajac & Assoc Inc/The Bigelow #1924, Pittsburgh, PA | 412-391-1005 |
| Kara, Michael Casting/2100 N Central Rd, Fort Lee, NJ | 201-592-8309 |
| Lawrence, Joanna Agency/82 Patrick Rd, Westport, CT | 203-226-7239 |
| Levine, Eli/860 Floral Ave, Union, NJ | 201-353-1595 |

## SOUTHEAST

| | |
|---|---|
| Central Casting/PO Box 7154, Ft Lauderdale, FL | 305-379-7526 |
| DiPrima Barbara Casting/3332 Virginia St #B, Coconut Grove, FL | 305-445-7630 |
| Elite Artists, Inc/3285 Airways #128, Memphis, TN | 901-346-1800 |
| Manning, Maureen/1283 Cedar Hts Dr, Stone Mt, GA | 404-296-1520 |
| Snyder/Whalen Enterprises, Inc/905 W Main St, Durham, NC | 919-683-3033 |
| Taylor Royal Casting/1425 Stevenson Rd, Stevenson, MD | 301-621-5555 |

## MIDWEST

| | |
|---|---|
| Station 12 Producers Express Inc/1759 Woodgrove Ln, Bloomfield Hills, MI | 313-569-7707 |

## SOUTHWEST

| | |
|---|---|
| Abramson, Shirley/321 Valley Cove, Garland, TX | 214-272-3400 |
| Austin Actors Clearinghouse/501 North 1H 35, Austin, TX | 512-476-3412 |
| Blair, Tanya Agency/Artists Managers/3000 Carlisle, #101, Dallas, TX | 214-265-4020 |
| Chason, Gary & Assoc/5645 Hillcroft St, Houston, TX | 713-789-4003 |
| Greer, Lucy & Assoc Casting/600 Shadywood Ln, Richardson, TX | 214-231-2086 |
| Jr Black Acad of Arts & Letters/723 S Peak St, Dallas, Tx | 214-526-1237 |
| KD Studio/2300 Stemmons #1643, Dallas, TX | 214-638-0484 |
| Kegley, Liz/Shari Rhodes/2021 Southgate, Houston, TX | 713-522-5066 |
| Kegley, Liz/Shari Rhodes/5737 Everglade, Dallas, TX | 214-272-6069 |
| Kent, Rody/5338 Vanderbilt Ave, Dallas, TX | 214-827-3418 |
| MBA Productions/8914 Georgian Dr, Austin, TX | 512-836-3201 |
| New Visions/Box 14 Whipple Station, Prescott, AZ | 602-445-3382 |
| Schermerhorn, Jo Ann/3032 Gessner, Houston, TX | 713-939-1805 |

## WEST

| | |
|---|---|
| Abrams-Rubaloff & Associates/9012 Beverly Blvd, Los Angeles, CA | 213-273-5711 |
| Associated Talent International/8816 Burton Way, Beverly Hills, CA | 213-271-4662 |
| BCI Casting/9200 Sunset Blvd, Los Angeles, CA | 213-550-0156 |
| Brandt, Werner/9034 W Sunset Blvd, Los Angeles, CA | 213-273-8554 |
| C H N International/7428 Santa Monica Blvd, Los Angeles, CA | 213-874-8252 |
| The Carey-Phelps-Colvin Agency/1407 N LaBrea, Los Angeles, CA | 213-874-7780 |
| Celebrity Look-Alikes/9000 Sunset Blvd, #407, West Hollywood, CA | 213-273-5566 |
| Commercials Unlimited/7461 Beverly Blvd, Los Angeles, CA | 213-937-2220 |
| Creative Artists Agency Inc/1888 Century Park E, Los Angeles, CA | 213-277-4545 |
| Cronin, Bernyce & Assoc/439 S LaCienega Blvd, Los Angeles, CA | 213-273-8144 |
| Cunningham, William & Assocs/261 S Robertson Blvd, Beverly Hills, CA | 213-855-0200 |
| Davis, Mary Webb/515 N LaCienega, Los Angeles, CA | 213-652-6850 |
| Garrick, Dale Internat'l Agency/8831 Sunset Blvd, Los Angeles, CA | 213-657-2661 |
| Grady, Mary Agency/Children/10850 Riverside Dr, North Hollywood, CA | 213-985-9800 |
| The Granite Agency/1920 S LaCienega Blvd, #20, Los Angeles, CA | 213-934-8383 |
| Greco, Maria Casting/9200 Sunset Blvd #414, Los Angeles, CA | 213-273-5563 |
| Hecht, Beverly Agency/8949 Sunset Blvd, #203, Los Angeles, CA | 213-278-3544 |
| Kelman, Toni Agency/7813 Sunset Blvd, Los Angeles, CA | 213-851-8822 |
| Kjar, Tyler Agency/9229 Sunset Blvd, Los Angeles, CA | 213-278-0912 |
| Leonetti, Caroline Ltd/6526 Sunset Blvd, Los Angeles, CA | 213-462-2345 |
| Lien, Michael Casting/336 N Foothill, Beverly Hills, CA | 213-550-7381 |
| Loo, Bessi Agency/8235 Santa Monica, W Hollywood, CA | 213-650-1300 |
| Mangum, Johr Agency/8831 Sunset Blvd, Los Angeles, CA | 213-659-7230 |
| Michelle Unlimited/8060 Melrose, #225, Los Angeles, CA | 213-653-9610 |
| Morris, William Agency/151 El Camino Dr, Beverly Hills, CA | 213-274-7451 |
| Pacific Artists Limited/515 N LaCienega Blvd, Los Angeles, CA | 213-657-5990 |
| REB-Sunset International/6912 Hollywood Blvd, Hollywood, CA | 213-464-4440 |
| Rose, Jack/6430 Sunset Blvd, #1203, Los Angeles, CA | 213-463-7300 |
| Schaeffer, Peggy Agency/10850 Riverside Dr, North Hollywood, CA | 213-985-5547 |
| Schwartz, Dor & Assoc/8721 Sunset Blvd, Los Angeles, CA | 213-657-8910 |
| Stern, Charles H Agency/9220 Sunset Blvd, Los Angeles, CA | 213-273-6890 |
| Sutton Barth & Venari/8322 Beverly Blvd, Los Angeles, CA | 213-653-8322 |
| Tannen, Herb & Assoc/6640 Sunset Blvd, #203, Los Angeles, CA | 213-466-6191 |
| Turco, Terri Agency/6732 N Lankershim, North Hollywood, CA | 213-982-6130 |
| Wilhelmina/West/1800 Century Park E #504, Century City, CA | 213-553-9525 |
| Wormser Heldford & Joseph/1717 N Highland, #414, Hollywood, CA | 213-466-9111 |
| Wright, Ann Assoc/8422 Melrose Place, Los Angeles, CA | 213-655-5040 |

## ANIMALS

# PHOTO/FILM SERVICES CONT'D.

Please send us your additions and updates.

## NEW YORK CITY

| | |
|---|---|
| All-Tame Animals Inc/37 W 57th St | 212-752-5885 |
| Canine Academy of Ivan Kovach/3725 Lyme Ave | 212-682-6770 |
| Captain Haggertys Theatrical Dogs/1748 First Ave | 212-410-7400 |
| Chateau Theatrical Animals/608 W 48th St | 212-246-0520 |
| Clove Lake Stables Inc/1025 Clove Rd | 212-448-1414 |
| Dawn Animal Agency/160 W 46th St | 212-575-9396 |
| Mr Lucky Dog Training School Inc/27 Crescent St | 212-827-2792 |

## NORTHEAST

| | |
|---|---|
| Animal Actors Inc/RD 3, Box 221, Washington, NJ | 201-689-7539 |
| Carriages for Occasions/339 Warburton Ave, Hastings-on-Hudson, NY | 914-478-4045 |
| Long Island Game Farm & Zoo/Chapman Blvd, Manorville, NY | 516-727-7443 |
| Morgan, Bill/Box 159T, RD 2, Greenville, NY | 518-966-8229 |
| Parrots of the World/239 Sunrise Hwy., Rockville Center, NY | 212-343-4141 |

## MIDWEST

| | |
|---|---|
| Plainsmen Zoo/Rt 4, Box 151, Elgin, IL | 312-697-0062 |

## SOUTHWEST

| | |
|---|---|
| Bettis, Ann J/Rt 1-A Box 21-B, Dripping Springs, TX | 512-264-1952 |
| Dallas Zoo in Marsalis Park/621 E Clarendon, Dallas, TX | 214-946-5155 |
| Estes, Bob Rodeos/PO Box 962, Baird, TX | 915-854-1037 |
| Fort Worth Zoological Park/2727 Zoological Park Dr., Fort Worth, TX | 817-870-7050 |
| International Wildlife Park/601 Wildlife Parkway, Grand Prairie, TX | 214-263-2203 |
| Newsom's Varmints N' Things/13015 Kaltenbrun, Houston, TX | 713-931-0676 |
| Scott, Kelly Buggy & Wagon Rentals/Box 442, Bandera, TX | 512-796-3737 |
| Taylor, Peggy Talent Inc/3616 Howell, Dallas, TX | 214-526-4800 |
| Wild West Stunt Company/Lee Preston/Box T-789, Stephenville, TX | 214-526-4800 |
| Y O Ranch/Dept AS, Mountain Home, TX | 512-640-3222 |

## WEST

| | |
|---|---|
| American Animal Enterprises/PO Box 338, Little Rock, CA | 805-944-3011 |
| The American Mongrel/PO Box 2406, Lancaster, CA | 805-269-1865 |
| Animal Action/PO Box 824, Arleta, CA | 213-767-3003 |
| Animal Actors of Hollywood/864 Carlisle Rd, Thousand Oaks, CA | 805-495-2122 |
| Birds and Animals/25191 Riverdell Dr, El Toro, CA | 714-830-7845 |
| The Blair Bunch/7561 Woodman Pl, Van Nuys, CA | 213-994-1136 |
| Casa De Pets/11814 Ventura Blvd, Studio City, CA | 213-761-3651 |
| Cougar Hill Ranch/PO Box 132, Little Rock, CA | 805-944-3549 |
| Di Sesso's, Moe Trained Wildlife/24233 Old Road, Newhall, CA | 805-255-7969 |
| Frank Inn Inc/12265 Branford St, Sun Valley, CA | 213-896-8188 |
| Gentle Jungle/3815 W Olive Ave, Burbank, CA | 213-841-5300 |
| Griffin, Gus/11281 Sheldon St, Sun Valley, CA | 213-767-6647 |
| Martin, Steve Working Wildlife/PO Box 65, Acton, CA | 805-268-0788 |
| Pyramid Bird/1407 W Magnolia, Burbank, CA | 213-843-5505 |
| Randall Ranch/2370 Pine St, Newhall, CA | 805-259-8990 |
| Schumacher Animal Rentals/14453 Cavette Pl, Baldwin Park, CA | 213-338-4614 |
| The Stansbury Company/9304 Santa Monica Blvd, Beverly Hills, CA | 213-273-1138 |
| Weatherwax, Robert/16133 Soledad Canyon Rd, Canyon Country, CA | 805-252-6907 |

# HAIR & MAKE-UP

## NEW YORK CITY

| | |
|---|---|
| Abrams, Ron/126 W 75th St | 212-580-0705 |
| Barba, Olga/201 E 16th St | 212-533-6385 |
| Beauty Booking/130 W 57th St | 212-977-7157 |
| Blake, Marion/130 W 57th St | 212-977-7157 |
| Boushelle/444 E 82nd St | 212-861-7225 |
| Braithwaite, Jordan/130 W 57th St | 213-977-7157 |
| Cinandre/11 E 57th St | 212-758-4770 |
| Costantini, Raymond/444 E 82nd St | 212-861-7225 |
| DeVega, Leonardo/444 E 82nd St | 212-861-7225 |
| Downey, Martin/130 W 57th St | 212-977-7157 |
| Duffy, Susan/130 W 57th St | 212-977-7157 |
| Garcia, A/240 E 27th St | 212-889-3028 |
| Gordon, Robert/444 E 82nd St | 212-861-7225 |
| Hammond, Claire/440 E 57th St | 212-838-0712 |
| Imre, Edith Beauty Salon/20 W 56th St | 212-758-0233 |
| Keller, Bruce Clyde/422 E 58th St | 212-593-3816 |
| Lane, Judy/444 E 82nd St | 212-861-7225 |
| Longobardi, Gerard/444 E 82nd St | 212-861-7225 |
| Malle, William Inc/440 Park Ave(Drake Hotel) | 212-753-2326 |
| Masterworks/135 E 55th St | 212-758-6295 |
| Multiple Artists/42 E 23 St | 212-473-8020 |
| Pamela Jenrette/300 Mercer St | 212-673-4748 |
| Pattner, Emily/130 W 57th St | 212-977-7157 |
| Pittman, Jane/130 W 57th St | 212-977-7157 |
| Reece, Debra/756 Seventh Ave | 212-489-8870 |
| Richardson, John Ltd/119 E 64th St | 212-772-1874 |
| Rodriguez, Thomas/130 W 57th St | 212-977-7157 |
| Sansone, Barbara/444 E 82nd St | 212-861-7225 |
| Tamblyn, Thom Inc/240 E 27th St | 212-683-4514 |

## SOUTHEAST

| | |
|---|---|
| Colby, Terry/957 Virginia Ave N E, Atlanta, GA | 404-876-6676 |

## MIDWEST

| | |
|---|---|
| Adams, Jerry Hair Salon/420 West Huron, Chicago, IL | 312-642-7986 |
| Alderman, Frederic/Rt 2 Box 205, Mundelein, IL | 312-438-2925 |
| Bianco, Cherie/908 W Armitage, Chicago, IL | 312-935-5212 |
| Bobak, Ilona/300 N State, Chicago, IL | 312-321-1679 |
| Carnylle/112 E Oak, Chicago, IL | 312-943-1120 |
| Collins Chicago, Inc/67 E Oak, Chicago, IL | 312-266-6662 |
| Curtis, Linell/2408 N Surrey Ct, Chicago, IL | 312-549-5644 |
| International Guild of Make-Up/6970 N Sheridan, Chicago, IL | 312-271-6900 |
| Simmons, Sid Inc/2 E Oak, Chicago, IL | 312-943-2333 |

## SOUTHWEST

| | |
|---|---|
| Kim Dawson Agency/PO Box 585060, Dallas, TX | 214-638-2414 |
| Rockwell, Janis A/1131 Allston St, Houston, TX | 713-862-6573 |

## WEST

| | |
|---|---|
| Andre, Maurice/9426 Santa Monica Blvd, Beverly Hills, CA | 213-274-4562 |
| Antovniov/11908 Ventura Blvd, Studio City, CA | 213-763-0671 |
| Armando's | 213-657-5160 |
| Bjorn/Goldbeg-Ehrlich/9701 Wilshire Blvd N, #800, Beverly Hills, CA | 213-550-5935 |
| Bourget, Lorraine/559 Muskingum Pl, Pacific Palisades, CA | 213-454-3739 |
| Cassandre 2000/18386 Ventura Blvd, Tarzana, CA | 213-881-8400 |
| Craig, Kenneth/13211 Ventura Blvd, Studio City, CA | 213-995-8717 |
| Design Pool/11936 Darlington Ave, #303, Los Angeles, CA | 213-826-1551 |
| Evonne | 213-275-1658 |
| Exley, Susan/6448 Santa Monica Blvd, Hollywood, CA | 213-467-7693 |
| Francisco/PO Box 49995, Los Angeles, CA | 213-826-3591 |
| Geiger, Pamela | 213-274-5737 |
| HMS/1541 Harvard St, #A, Santa Monica, CA | 213-829-5700 |
| Hamilton, Bryan J/909 N Westbourne Dr, Los Angeles, CA | 213-654-9006 |
| Hirst, William | 213-501-0993 |
| Johns, Arthur/8661 Sunset Blvd, Hollywood, CA | 213-855-9306 |
| Jordan, Sandra Kartoon | 213-876-2552 |
| Loretta/109 N Clark Dr, Los Angeles, CA | 213-275-7872 |
| Ohen/139 S Kings Rd, Los Angeles, CA | 213-655-4452 |

# PHOTO/FILM SERVICES CONT'D

Please send us your additions and updates.

| | |
|---|---|
| Pauli, Denise/1232 1/2 N Flores, W Hollywood, CA | 213-654-6155 |
| Pearson, Kandace/7731 White Oak Ave, Reseda, CA | 213-705-4276 |
| Ray, David Frank/15 Wave Crest, Venice, CA | 213-392-5640 |
| Samuel, Martin/6138 W 6th, Los Angeles, CA | 213-930-0794 |
| Serena, Eric/840 N Larabee, Bldg 4, W Hollywood, CA | 213-652-4267 |
| Towsend, Jeanne/433 N Camden Dr, Beverly Hills, CA | 213-851-7044 |
| Turnage, Jerry/1326 N Laurel, Los Angeles, CA | 213-656-0734 |
| Wachtel, Cotty/1647 Los Angeles Ave, Simi, CA | 805-526-4189 |
| Welsh, Franklyn/704 N LaCienega Blvd, Los Angeles, CA | 213-656-8195 |

# HAIR

## NEW YORK CITY

| | |
|---|---|
| Albert-Carter/Hotel St Moritz | 212-688-2045 |
| Benjamin Salon/104 Washington Pl | 212-255-3330 |
| Davian Salon Hair Styling/833 Madison Ave | 212-535-1563 |
| DePalma, Lawrence/444 E 82nd St | 212-861-7225 |
| George V Hair Stylist/501 Fifth Ave | 212-687-9097 |
| Harrison, Hugh/130 W 57th St | 212-977-7157 |
| Moda 700/700 Madison Ave | 212-935-9188 |
| Monsieur Marc Inc/22 E 65th St | 212-861-0700 |
| Pearson, Robert/130 W 57th St | 212-977-7157 |
| Peter's Beauty Home/149 W 57th St | 212-247-2934 |
| Pierro, John/130 W 57th St | 212-977-7157 |
| Raena/276 First Ave | 212-679-7037 |
| Richard at the Carlton/22 E 62nd St | 212-751-6240 |
| Suarez, Jorge/130 W 57th St | 212-977-7157 |

## NORTHEAST

| | |
|---|---|
| Brocklebank, Tom/149 Emily Ave, Elmont, NY | 516-775-5356 |

## SOUTHEAST

| | |
|---|---|
| Yellow Strawberry/1021 E Las Olas Blvd, Ft Lauderdale, FL | 305-463-4343 |

## MIDWEST

| | |
|---|---|
| Adams, Joyce/420 West Huron, Chicago, IL | 312-642-7986 |
| Anthony, Carey/420 West Huron, Chicago, IL | 312-642-7986 |
| Kenny, Kevin/420 West Huron, Chicago, IL | 312-642-7986 |
| Rodriguez, Ann/420 West Huron, Chicago, IL | 312-642-7986 |

## SOUTHWEST

| | |
|---|---|
| Southern Hair Designs/3563 Far West Blvd, Austin, TX | 512-346-1734 |

## WEST

| | |
|---|---|
| Anatra, M Haircutters/7509 Melrose Ave, Los Angeles, CA | 213-655-7160 |
| Barronson Hair/11908 Ventura, Studio City, CA | 213-763-4337 |
| Beck, Shirley | 213-763-2930 |
| Blondell, Kathy | 213-342-6490 |
| City Lights Hair Design/2845 Wyandot, Denver, CO | 303-458-0131 |
| Coma B/530 N LaCienega, Los Angeles, CA | 213-657-4551 |
| Drake, Leonard | 213-851-6333 |
| Ely, Shannon | 213-392-5832 |
| Fisher, Jim/c/o Rumours, 9018 Beverly Blvd, Los Angeles, CA | 213-550-5946 |
| Francisco/PO Box 49995, Los Angeles, CA | 213-826-3591 |
| Frier, George | 213-393-0576 |
| Germaine, Susan | 213-874-5179 |
| Grieve, Ginger | 213-347-2947 |
| Grill, Damion | 213-841-2206 |
| Gurasich, Lynda | 213-981-6719 |
| HMS/1541 Harvard St, #A, Santa Monica, CA | 213-829-5700 |
| The Hair Conspiracy/11923 Ventura Blvd, Studio City, CA | 213-985-1126 |
| Henderson, Dalee/925 W Mount Dr, W Hollywood, CA | 213-659-0352 |
| Hjerpe, Warren/c/o Rumours 9018 Beverly Blvd, Los Angeles, CA | 213-550-5946 |
| Iverson, Betty | 213-462-2301 |
| John, Michael Salon/414 N Camden Dr, Beverly Hills, CA | 213-278-8333 |
| Kemp, Lola | 213-293-8710 |
| Linterman's/9641 Little Santa Monica Blvd, Beverly Hills, CA | 213-276-3109 |
| Lorenz, Barbara | 213-657-0028 |
| Malone, John | 213-246-1649 |
| Menage a Trois/8822 Burton Way, Beverly Hills, CA | 213-278-4431 |
| Miller, Patty | 213-843-5208 |
| Mizu, Andrea | 213-363-4813 |
| Morrissey, Jimie | 213-657-4318 |
| Payne, Allen | 213-395-5259 |
| Peter, Jon Hair Salon/400 N Rodeo Dr, Beverly Hills, CA | 213-274-8575 |
| Phillips, Marilyn | 213-923-6996 |
| Reilly, Jean Burt | 213-766-4716 |
| Rigney, Robert/1326 N Laurel, Los Angeles, CA | 213-876-8500 |
| Rizzuto, Peter/316 E Hopkins, Aspen, CO | 303-925-4434 |
| Robinette, Steve | 213-204-3168 |
| Sami/1230 N Horn Ave, #525, Los Angeles, CA | 213-652-5816 |
| Sassoon, Vidal Inc/1801 Century Park E, #1805, Los Angeles, CA | 213-553-6100 |
| Torres, Richard/530 N LaCienega Blvd, Los Angeles, CA | 213-657-4551 |
| Trainoff, Linda | 213-769-0373 |
| Vecchio, Faith | 213-345-6152 |
| Zenobia, Keith/465 S Beverly Dr, Beverly Hills, CA | 213-858-1401 |

# MAKE-UP

## NEW YORK CITY

| | |
|---|---|
| Adams, Richard/130 W 57th St | 212-977-7157 |
| Bertoli, Michele/264 Fifth Ave | 212-684-2480 |
| Berzjon, Robert/130 W 57th St | 212-977-7157 |
| Bonzignor's Cosmetics/110 Fulton | 212-267-1108 |
| Lawrence, Rose/444 E 82nd St | 212-861-7225 |
| Make-Up Center Ltd/150 W 55th St | 212-977-9494 |
| Nasso, Vincent/P.O. Box 511, Canal St Sta | 212-925-6594 |
| Nutriance/217 E 76th St | 212-288-2951 |
| Place, Stan/130 W 57th St | 212-977-7157 |
| Richardson, John Ltd/119 E 64th St | 212-772-1874 |
| Ross, Rose Cosmetics/16 W 55th St | 212-586-2590 |
| Sartin, Janet of Park Ave Ltd/480 Park Ave | 212-751-5858 |
| Stage Light Cosmetics Ltd/630 Ninth Ave | 212-757-4851 |
| Suzanne de Paris/509 Madison Ave | 212-838-4024 |

## NORTHEAST

| | |
|---|---|
| Damaskos, Zoe E/13 Follen St, Cambridge, MA | 617-547-4080 |
| Gemelli, Michael/6 Ware Corner Rd, Oakham, MA | 617-882-3041 |
| Gilmore, Robert Assoc Inc/990 Washington St, Dedham, MA | 617-329-6633 |
| Meth, Miriam/96 Greenwood Ln, White Plains, NY | 212-787-5400 |
| Minassian, Amie/62-75 Austin St, Rego Park, NY | 212-446-8048 |
| Phillipe, Louise Miller/46 Gardner Rd, Brookline, MA | 617-566-3608 |
| Phillipe, Robert/46 Gardner Rd, Brookline, MA | 617-566-3608 |
| Pisces Unlimited, Inc/46 Gardner Rd, Brookline, MA | 617-566-3608 |
| Ross, Penny/809 Thayer Ave, Silver Spring, MD | 301-565-5025 |
| Something Special/1601 Walter Reed Dr S, Arlington, VA | 703-892-0551 |
| Zack, Sandra/94 Orient Ave, East Boston, MA | 617-567-7581 |

## SOUTHEAST

| | |
|---|---|
| Ellyn Krieger Fineman/7521 SW 57th Terrace, Miami, FL | 305-666-1250 |
| Star Styled of Miami/475 NW 42nd Ave, Miami, FL | 305-541-2424 |
| Star Styled of Tampa/4235 Henderson Blvd, Tampa, FL | 813-872-8706 |

## SOUTHWEST

| | |
|---|---|
| ABC Theatrical Rental & Sales/825 N 7th St, Phoenix, AZ | 602-258-5265 |
| Chelsea Cutters/One Chelsea Pl, Houston, TX | 713-529-4813 |

# PHOTO/FILM SERVICES CONT'D.

Please send us your additions and updates.

| | |
|---|---|
| Copeland, Tom/502 West Grady, Austin, TX | 512-835-0208 |
| Corey, Irene/4147 Herschel Ave, Dallas, TX | 214-528-4836 |
| Dobes, Pat/1826 Nocturne, Houston, TX | 713-465-8102 |
| Ingram, Marilyn Wyrick/10545 Chesterton Drive, Dallas, TX | 214-349-2113 |
| Jenicci/2709 McKinney Ave, Dallas, TX | 214-748-0939 |
| Messersmith, Christopher/1949 Stemmons, Dallas, TX | 214-522-1430 |
| Stamm, Louis M/721 Edgehill Dr, Hurst, TX | 817-268-5037 |

## WEST

| | |
|---|---|
| Angell, Jeff | 213-278-6565 |
| Astier, Guy c/o Design Pool/11936 Darlington Ave, #303, Los Angeles, CA | 213-826-1551 |
| Blackman, Charles F/12751 Addison, N Hollywood, CA | 213-761-2177 |
| Blackman, Gloria/12751 Addison, N Hollywood, CA | 213-761-2177 |
| Case, Tom/5150 Woodley, Encino, CA | 213-788-5268 |
| Cooper, David/3616 Effie, Los Angeles, CA | 213-660-7326 |
| Cosmetic Connection/9484 Dayton Way, Beverly Hills, CA | 213-550-6242 |
| Dawn, Wes/11113 Hortense St, N Hollywood, CA | 213-761-7517 |
| The Design Pool/11936 Darlington Ave #303, Los Angeles, CA | 213-826-1551 |
| DiBella, Joe | 213-347-0068 |
| D'Ifray, T J/468 N Bedford Dr, Beverly Hills, CA | 213-274-6776 |
| Fradkin, Joanne c/o Pigments/8822 Burton Way, Beverly Hills, CA | 213-858-7038 |
| Francesca | 213-787-6618 |
| Francisco/PO Box 49995, Los Angeles, CA | 213-826-3591 |
| Freed, Gordon | 213-360-9473 |
| Frier, George | 213-393-0576 |
| Geike, Ziggy | 213-789-1465 |
| Grant, Lani Centers/616 Washington, Denver, CO | 303-837-1015 |
| Henrriksen, Ole/8601 W Sunset Blvd, Los Angeles, CA | 213-854-7700 |
| Howell, Deborah/291 S Martel Ave, Los Angeles, CA | 213-935-7543 |
| Inzerella, John | 213-654-4159 |
| Jones, Jeffrey/4573 Round Top Dr, Los Angeles, CA | 213-256-4404 |
| Koelle, c/o Pigments/8822 Burton Way, Beverly Hills, CA | 213-668-1690 |
| Kruse, Lee C | 213-894-5408 |
| Laurent, c/o Menage a Trois/8822 Burton Way, Beverly Hills, CA | 213-278-4430 |
| Logan, Kathryn | 213-988-7038 |
| Malone, John E | 213-247-5160 |
| Manges, Delanie (Dee) | 213-763-3311 |
| Manges, Ed c/o Creative Network/8440 Sunset Blvd, #218, N Hollywood, CA | 213-656-2604 |
| Maniscalco, Ann S | 213-894-5408 |
| Maxwell, Nora | 213-376-3950 |
| McLynn, Patrick/4733 Orion, #11, Sherman Oaks, CA | 213-986-1827 |
| Menage a Trois/8822 Burton Way, Beverly Hills, CA | 213-278-4431 |
| Minch, Michelle/339 S Detroit St, Los Angeles, CA | 213-484-9648 |
| Moon Sun Emporium/2019 Broadway, Boulder, CO | 303-443-6851 |
| Natasha,/4221 1/2 Avocado St, Los Angeles, CA | 213-663-1477 |
| Nielsen, Jim | 213-461-2168 |
| Nye, Dana | 213-477-0443 |
| Odessa/1448 1/2 N Fuller Ave, W Hollywood, CA | 213-876-5779 |
| Palmieri, Dante | 213-396-6020 |
| Penelope, | 213-654-6747 |
| Pigments/8822 Burton Way, Beverly Hills, CA | 213-858-7038 |
| Romero, Bob/5030 Stern Ave, Sherman Oaks, CA | 213-784-4583 |
| Rumours/9018 Beverly Blvd, Los Angeles, CA | 213-550-5946 |
| Sanders, Nadia | 213-465-2009 |
| Schoenfeld, Don | 213-849-3669 |
| Schultz, Lisa c/o Rumours/9018 Beverly Blvd, Los Angeles, CA | 213-550-5946 |
| Sharah, Richard c/o The Design Pool/11936 Darlington Ave #303, Los Angeles, CA | 213-826-1551 |
| Shatsy/9008 Harratt St, Hollywood, CA | 213-464-8381 |
| Shulman, Sheryl Leigh | 213-760-0101 |
| Sidell, Bob | 213-360-0794 |
| Simon, Davida/11154 Agua Vista, N Hollywood, CA | 213-469-5126 |
| Smith-Simmons, Hallie | 213-658-6267 |
| Striepke, Danny/4800 No C Villa Marina, Marina Del Rey, CA | 213-823-5957 |
| Tuttle, William | 213-454-2355 |
| Vincent, Antonia | 213-826-0982 |
| Wardell, Marie-Claude c/o Shatsy/9008 Harratt St, Hollywood, CA | 213-464-8381 |
| Warren, Dodie | 213-763-3172 |
| Westmore, Marvin | 213-908-0780 |
| Westmore, Michael | 213-763-3158 |
| Westmore, Monty | 213-762-2094 |
| Wilder, Brad | 213-985-1010 |
| Winston, Stan | 213-886-0630 |
| Winters, Jean | 213-766-6382 |
| Wolf, Barbara | 213-466-4660 |

# STYLISTS

## NEW YORK CITY

| | |
|---|---|
| Abbe, Kathryn/Brookville Rd | 212-369-4660 |
| Baldassano, Irene/16 W 16th St | 212-255-8567 |
| Bandiero, Paul/P O Box 121-FDR Station | 212-586-3700 |
| Batteau, Sharon/130 W 57th St | 212-977-7157 |
| Beauty Bookings/130 W 57th St | 212-977-7157 |
| Benner, Dyne/311 E 60th St | 212-688-7571 |
| Berman, Benicia/399 E 72nd St | 212-737-9627 |
| Bodian, Betty/199 Second Ave | 212-473-4413 |
| Bromberg, Florence/350 Third Ave | 212-255-4033 |
| Cheverton, Linda/131 E 15th St | 212-533-3247 |
| Chin, Fay/ | 212-254-7667 |
| Cohen, Susan/233 E 54th St | 212-755-3157 |
| Connolly, Mary T/210 E 68th St | 212-861-5263 |
| D'Arcy, Timothy/43 W 85th St | 212-580-8804 |
| DeJesu, Joanna/101 W 23rd St | 212-255-3895 |
| Edwards, Linda/130 W 57th St | 212-977-7157 |
| Eller, Ann/7816 Third Ave | 212-238-5454 |
| Final Touch/55-11 13th Ave | 212-435-6800 |
| George, Georgia A/404 E 55th St | 212-759-4131 |
| Goday, Dale/55 E 11th St | 212-586-6300 |
| Golden, Charlie/220 E 79th St | 212-288-6907 |
| Greene, Jan/200 E 17th St | 212-233-8989 |
| Haddock, Sherry/350 E 62nd St | 212-888-7937 |
| Herman, Joan/15 W 84th St | 212-724-3287 |
| Hirsche, Maureen/1325 Third Ave | 212-288-3783 |
| Hoffman, Terese/11 Fifth Ave | 212-673-4100 |
| Jackson, Ophelia/45 Fifth Ave | 212-868-3330 |
| Joffe, Carole Reiff/233 E 34th St | 212-725-4928 |
| Jorrin, Sylvia/130 W 57th St | 212-977-7157 |
| Kimmel, Lily/12 E 86th St | 212-532-2925 |
| Klein, Mary Ellen/330 E 33rd St | 212-683-6351 |
| Lakin, Gaye/345 E 81st St | 212-861-1892 |
| Lee, Gretta/130 W 57th St | 212-977-7157 |
| Levin, Laurie/55 Perry St | 212-691-7950 |
| Lopes, Sandra/444 E 82nd St | 212-249-8706 |
| Magidson, Peggy/182 Amity St | 212-570-6252 |
| McCabe, Christine/200 W 79th St | 212-799-4121 |
| Meyers, Pat/436 W 20th St | 212-620-0069 |
| Minch, Deborah Lee/175 W 87th St | 212-873-7915 |
| Morgan, Alida/130 W 57th St | 212-977-7157 |
| Murphy, Vanessa/265 W 81st St | 212-799-0004 |
| Murray, Diana/444 E 82nd St | 212-861-7225 |
| Nagle, Patsy/242 E 38th St | 212-682-0364 |
| Norton, Sally/250 E 39th St | 212-867-1579 |
| Nosoff, Frank/50 Riverside Dr | 212-873-4214 |
| Ouellette, Dawn/336 E 30th St | 212-799-9190 |
| Puskarcik, Joann/1200 Broadway | 212-679-5537 |
| Rapp, Nancy/160 E 38th St, #27 H | 212-986-4393 |
| Reilly, Veronica/60 Gramercy Park N | 212-840-1234 |
| Robins, Joan C/130 W 57th St | 212-977-7157 |
| Sampson, Linda/431 W Broadway | 212-925-6821 |
| Seymour, Celeste/130 E 75th St | 212-744-3545 |
| Siciliano, Jeanne/125 Fifth Ave | 212-673-8721 |
| Silverblatt, Joanna/130 W 57th St | 212-977-7157 |
| Slote, Ina/7 Park Ave | 212-679-4584 |

# PHOTO/FILM SERVICES CONT'D.

Please send us your additions and updates.

| | |
|---|---|
| Smith, Helen/99 E 4th St | 212-533-5384 |
| Specht, Meredith/166 E 61st St | 212-832-0750 |
| Staley, Etheleen/151 Central Park West | 212-362-6428 |
| Stockland, Jillayne/576 Sixth Ave | 212-243-6493 |
| Willis, Barbara/1060 Park Ave | 212-582-4240 |
| Wilson, Patti/444 E 82nd St | 212-861-7225 |

## NORTHEAST

| | |
|---|---|
| Bailey Designs/110 Williams St, Malden, MA | 617-321-4448 |
| Baldwin, Katherine/109 Commonwealth Ave, Boston, MA | 617-267-0508 |
| Case, Carol/Brenner Pl, Alpine, NJ | 201-767-1041 |
| Gold, Judy/40 Sulgrave Rd, Scarsdale, NY | 914-723-5036 |
| Immerman, Kathy/519 Remsen Ln, Oyster Bay, NY | 516-922-3360 |
| Judy/13 Karsten Dr, Suffern, NY | 914-357-7494 |
| Rosemary's Cakes Inc/299 Rutland Ave, Teaneck, NJ | 201-833-2417 |
| Sheeran, Kay/530 Valley Rd, Upper Montclair, NJ | 201-744-0333 |
| Zabel/125 Washington Pl, New York, NY | 212-242-2459 |

## SOUTHEAST

| | |
|---|---|
| Colby, Terry/957 Viginia Ave N E, Atlanta, GA | 404-876-6676 |
| Cox, Ann/1104 Toddington Dr., Murfressboro, TN | 615-890-1972 |
| Foodworks/1541 Colonial Ter, Arlington, VA | 703-524-2606 |
| Gaffney, Janet D/464 W Wesley N W, Atlanta, GA | 404-355-7556 |
| Kupersmith, Tony/320 N Highland Ave NE, Atlanta, GA | 404-577-5319 |
| Marina Polvay Assoc/9250 NE 10th Ct, Miami Shores, FL | 305-759-4375 |
| Torres, Martha/3904 Camp, New Orleans, LA | 504-895-6570 |

## MIDWEST

| | |
|---|---|
| Alan, Jean/1032 W Altgeld, Chicago, IL | 312-929-9768 |
| Bledsoe, Bonnie/957 W Belden, Chicago, IL | 312-871-2327 |
| Camylle,/112 E Oak, Chicago, IL | 312-579-0100 |
| Carlson, Susan/255 Linden Park Pl, Highland Park, IL | 312-433-2466 |
| Carter, Karen/3323 N Kenmore, Chicago, IL | 312-935-2901 |
| Chevaux Ltd/908 W Armitage, Chicago, IL | 312-935-5212 |
| Emruh Style Design/714 W Fullerton, Chicago, IL | 312-871-4659 |
| Erickson, Emily/2 E Oak, Chicago, IL | 312-642-5865 |
| Guerra, Paul/17 N Elizabeth, Chicago, IL | 312-243-8764 |
| Heller, Nancy/2021 N Mohawk, Chicago, IL | 312-549-4486 |
| Hill, Tina/315 W Walton, Chicago, IL | 312-266-8029 |
| Jacobs, Roger/676 W LaSalle, Chicago, IL | 312-787-1541 |
| Johnson, Karen/2695 Forest Ct, Deerfield, IL | 312-664-6919 |
| Lapin, Kathy Santis/925 Spring Hill Dr, Northbrook, IL | 312-272-7487 |
| Larson Associates/1726 Barnhart Rd, Troy, MI | 512-339-9289 |
| Mary, Wendy/719 W. Wrightwood, Chicago, IL | 312-871-5476 |
| Pace, Leslie/3420 N Lake Shore Dr #4L, Chicago, IL | 312-281-1017 |
| Perry, Lee Ann/640 W. Willow, Chicago, IL | 312-649-1815 |
| Rabert, Bonnie/2230 W Pratt, Chicago, IL | 312-743-7755 |
| Sager, Sue/875 N Michigan, Chicago, IL | 312-642-3789 |
| Seeken, Christopher | 312-944-4311 |
| Shaver, Betsy/3714 N Racine, Chicago, IL | 312-327-5615 |
| Stancik, Ilene/540 Briar, #7A, Chicago, IL | 312-929-7605 |
| Style Vasilak and Nebel/750 N Dearborn, Chicago, IL | 312-280-8516 |
| Szymarek, Nancy/3405 N Ozark, Chicago, IL | 312-625-9323 |
| Trainor, Jan/2112 Bissell, Chicago, IL | 312-472-1894 |
| Twolips/715 W Belmont, Chicago, IL | 312-472-6550 |
| Uttich, Linda/1320 Wellington, Chicago, IL | 312-935-0636 |
| Weber-Mack, Kathleen/2119 Lincoln, Evanston, IL | 312-869-7794 |
| Witmer, Diane/462 Madison Ave, Glencoe, IL | 312-835-3236 |

## SOUTHWEST

| | |
|---|---|
| Bishop, Cindy/6101 Charlotte, Houston, TX | 713-666-7224 |
| Janet-Nelson/PO Box 143, Tempe, AZ | 602-968-3771 |
| Jenicci/2809 McKinney Ave, Dallas, TX | 214-748-0939 |
| Stamm, Louis M/721 Edgehill, Hurst, TX | 817-268-5037 |
| Taylor, John Michael/2 Dallas Commun. Complex #, Irving, TX | 214-823-1333 |
| Vickers, Jon L./700 E 4th, Austin, TX | 512-472-8043 |

## WEST

| | |
|---|---|
| Akimbo Prod/801 Westbourne, W Hollywood, CA | 213-657-4657 |
| Alaimo, Doris/8800 Wonderland Ave, Los Angeles, CA | 213-851-7044 |
| Allen, Jamie R/Los Angeles, CA | 213-655-9351 |
| Altbaum, Patti/244-CS Lasky Dr, Beverly Hills, CA | 213-553-6269 |
| Anabel's Diversified Services/PO Box 532, Pacific Palisades, CA | 213-454-1566 |
| Anderson, Jane/8113 1/2 Melrose Ave, Los Angeles, CA | 213-655-8743 |
| Azzara, Marilyn/3165 Ellington Drive, Los Angeles, CA | 213-876-2551 |
| Banks, Robbi | 213-763-7916 |
| Biles, Suzanne/10840 Lindbrook Dr, West Los Angeles, CA | 213-475-6338 |
| Castaldi, Debbie/10518 Wilshire Blvd #25, Los Angeles, CA | 213-475-4312 |
| Chinamoon/642 S Burnside Ave, #6, Los Angeles, CA | 213-937-8251 |
| Coro, Margaret/914-18th St, Santa Monica, CA | 213-453-1200 |
| Corwin-Hankin, Aleka/1936 Cerro Gordo, Los Angeles, CA | 213-665-7953 |
| Craig, Kenneth/13211 Ventura Blvd, Studio City, CA | 213-995-8717 |
| Davis, Rommie/4414 La Venta Dr, West Lake Village, CA | 213-889-9680 |
| Design Pool/11936 Darlington Ave, #303, Los Angeles, CA | 213-826-1551 |
| Eis, Margie/4501 Gable Dr, Encino, CA | 213-345-9258 |
| Evonne | 213-275-1658 |
| Ferry, Patricia/2047 Paramount Dr, Hollywood, CA | 213-874-6372 |
| Flating, Janice/8113 1/2 Melrose Ave, Los Angeles, CA | 213-653-1800 |
| Frank, Tobi/1269 N Hayworth, Los Angeles, CA | 213-552-7921 |
| Gaffin, Lauri/1123-12th St, Santa Monica, CA | 213-451-2045 |
| Glesby, Ellen | 213-477-4648 |
| Governor, Jucy/963 North Point, San Francisco, CA | 415-861-5733 |
| Graham, Victory/24 Ave 26, Venice, CA | 213-934-0990 |
| Granas, Marilyn/200 N Almont Dr, Beverly Hills, CA | 213-278-3773 |
| Griswald, Sandra/963 North Point, San Francisco, CA | 415-775-4272 |
| HMS/1541 Harvard St, #A, Santa Monica, CA | 213-829-5700 |
| Hamilton, Bryan J/1269 N Hayworth, Los Angeles, CA | 213-654-9006 |
| Hewett, Julie/7551 Melrose Ave, Los Angeles, CA | 213-651-5172 |
| Hirsch, Lauren/858 Devon, Los Angeles, CA | 213-271-7052 |
| Howell, Deborah/219 S Martel Ave, Los Angeles, CA | 213-935-7543 |
| James, Elizabeth/5320 Bellingham Ave, N Hollywood, CA | 213-761-5718 |
| Jordan, Sandra Kartoon | 213-876-2552 |
| Kimball, Lynnda/133 S Peck Dr, Beverly Hills, CA | 213-656-5500 |
| King, Max/308 N Sycamore Ave, Los Angeles, CA | 213-938-0108 |
| Lawson, Karen/6836 Lexington Ave, Hollywood, CA | 213-464-5770 |
| Lynch, Jody/19130 Pacific Coast Hwy, Malibu, CA | 213-456-2383 |
| MacGregor, Helen/1406 1/2 Havenhurst Dr, Los Angeles, CA | 213-656-8766 |
| Magana, Saundra K | 213-938-4975 |
| Marell, Gail Has Style/833 Market St, San Francisco, CA | 415-543-3314 |
| Maxwell, Susan/443 Cloverdale, #3, Los Angeles, CA | 213-933-3067 |
| Miller, Freyda/1412 Warner Ave, Los Angeles, CA | 213-474-5034 |
| Moore, Francie/842 1/2 N Orange Dr, Los Angeles, CA | 213-462-5404 |
| Morrow, Suzanne/26333 Silver Spur, Palos Verdes, CA | 213-378-2909 |
| Mougin, Maeera/6603 Whittley Terr, Los Angeles, CA | 213-464-0497 |
| Neal, Robin Lynn/3105 Durand, Hollywood, CA | 213-465-6037 |
| Olsen, Eileen/1619 N Beverly Dr, Beverly Hills, CA | 213-273-4496 |
| Parshall, Mary Ann/19850 Pacific Coast Hwy, Malibu, CA | 213-456-8303 |
| Pearson, Kardace/7731 White Oak Ave, Reseda, CA | 213-705-4276 |
| Peiffer, Frederique/3121 Ellington Dr, Los Angeles, CA | 213-855-7895 |
| Pre Production West/1406 1/2 Havenhurst Dr, Los Angeles, CA | 213-656-8766 |
| Prindle, Judy Peck/6057 Melrose Ave, Los Angeles, CA | 213-650-0962 |
| Russo, Leslie/377 10th, Santa Monica, CA | 213-395-8461 |
| Shatsy/9008 Harratt St, Hollywood, CA | 213-275-2413 |
| Skinner, Jeanette/1622 Moulton Pkwy #A, Tustin, CA | 714-730-5793 |
| Skinner, Randy/920 S Wooster St, Los Angeles, CA | 213-659-2936 |
| Sloane, Hilary/6351 Ranchito, Van Nuys, CA | 213-855-1010 |
| Smith, Carol Center/6621 Green Valley Circle, Fox Hills, CA | 213-641-3719 |
| Style, by Michels & Young/1437 N Highland Ave, Los Angeles, CA | 213-484-1852 |
| Surkin, Helen/2100 N Beachwood Dr, Los Angeles, CA | 213-464-6847 |
| Thomas, Lisa/9029 Rangely Ave, W Hollywood, CA | 213-858-6903 |
| Townsend, Jeanne/433 N Camden Dr, Beverly Hills, CA | 213-851-7044 |
| Tucker, Joan/1402 N Fuller St, Los Angeles, CA | 213-876-3417 |
| Tyre, Susan | 213-877-3884 |
| Valade | 213-659-7621 |
| Vincent, Antonia | 213-826-0982 |
| Walters, Candace | 213-462-5955 |

# PHOTO/FILM SERVICES CONT'D.

Please send us your additions and updates.

| | |
|---|---|
| Watje, Janice Fox/626 S Detroit St, Los Angeles, CA | 213-935-8650 |
| Weiss, Fredda/9595 Wilshire Blvd, #410, Beverly Hills, CA | 213-476-6275 |
| Weiss, Sheri/2170 N Beverly Glen, Los Angeles, CA | 213-470-1650 |
| Young, Pamela/1611 Lakeshore Ave, Los Angeles, CA | 213-484-1852 |
| Zeitsoff, Leslie/630 N Plymouth Blvd, Los Angeles, CA | 213-466-7126 |

# COSTUMES

## NEW YORK CITY

| | |
|---|---|
| A M Costume Wear/135-18 Northern Blvd | 212-358-8108 |
| Academy Clothes Inc/1703 Broadway | 212-765-1440 |
| Barris Alfred Wig Maker/165 W 46th St | 212-354-9043 |
| Brooks-Van Horn Costume Co/117 W 17th St | 212-989-8000 |
| Capezio Dance Theater Shop/755 Seventh Ave | 212-245-2130 |
| Chenko Studio/167 W 46th St | 212-944-0215 |
| David's Outfitters Inc/36 W 20th St | 212-691-7388 |
| Eaves Costume Co Inc/423 W 55th St | 212-757-3730 |
| G Bank's Theatrical & Custom/320 W 48th St | 212-586-6476 |
| Grace Costumes Inc/254 W 54th St | 212-586-0260 |
| Havona Designs/110 Thompson St | 212-966-0062 |
| Herbert Danceware Co/902 Broadway | 212-677-7606 |
| Ian's Botique Inc/1151-A Second Ave | 212-838-3969 |
| Karinska/16 W 61st St | 212-247-3341 |
| Kulyk/84-E Seventh Ave | 212-674-0414 |
| Lane Costume Co/507 Fifth Ave | 212-697-3664 |
| Manwaring Studio/232 Atlantic Ave | 212-855-2796 |
| Martin, Alice Manougian/239 E 58th St | 212-688-0117 |
| Meyer, Jimmy & Co/428 W 44th St | 212-246-5769 |
| Michael-Jon Costumes Inc/353 W 12th St | 212-675-4508 |
| Mincou, Christine/405 E 63rd St | 212-838-3881 |
| Nostalgia Alley Antiques/380 Second Ave | 212-988-3949 |
| Pavlova's Pointe Ltd/35 W Eighth St | 212-260-7885 |
| Purcell, Elisabeth/105 Sullivan St | 212-925-1962 |
| Rubie's Costume Co/86-15 Jamaica Ave | 212-846-1008 |
| Selva Retail Center/1776 Broadway | 212-586-5140 |
| Star Costumers Co/600 W 57th St | 212-581-1246 |
| Stivanello Costume Co Inc/102 Fifth Ave | 212-651-7715 |
| Tint, Francine/1 University Pl | 212-233-8989 |
| Trudi Seligman Antique Arts/82 W 12th St | 212-929-8944 |
| Universal Costume Co Inc/1540 Broadway | 212-575-8570 |
| Weiss & Mahoney Inc/142 Fifth Ave | 212-675-1915 |
| Winston, Mary Ellen/11 E 68th St | 212-879-0766 |
| Ynocencio, Jo/302 E 88th St | 212-348-5332 |

## NORTHEAST

| | |
|---|---|
| At-A-Glance Rentals/712 Main, Boonton, NJ | 201-335-1488 |
| Baldwin, Katharine/109 Commonwealth Ave, Boston, MA | 617-267-0508 |
| Costume Armour Inc/Stewart Airport P O Box 6086, Newburgh, NY | 914-564-7100 |
| House of Costumes Ltd/166 Jericho Tpk, Mineola, NY | 516-294-0170 |
| Westchester Costume Rentals/540 Netterhan Ave, Yonkers, NY | 914-337-6674 |

## SOUTHEAST

| | |
|---|---|
| ABC Costume/185 NE 59th St, Miami, FL | 305-757-3492 |
| Atlantic Costume Co/2089 Monroe Dr, Atlanta, GA | 404-874-7511 |
| Carol, Lee Inc/2145 NW 2nd Ave, Miami, FL | 305-573-1759 |
| Costumes by Faye/213 Clematis St, West Palm Beach, FL | 305-832-1723 |
| Dixon Costume Shop/1828 Biscayne Blvd, Miami, FL | 305-371-8418 |
| Fun Stop Shop/1601 Biscayne Blvd Omni Int F-, Miami, FL | 305-358-2003 |
| Goddard, Lynn Prod Svcs/712 Pelican Ave, New Orleans, LA | 504-367-0348 |
| Miami Dancewear/352 NE 167th St, N Miami Beach, FL | 305-940-1762 |
| Ponciana Sales/2252 W Flagler St, Miami, FL | 305-642-3441 |
| Quality Costumes/7441 NW 72nd Ave, Miami, FL | 305-885-9136 |
| Star Styled/475 NW 42nd Ave, Miami, FL | 305-649-3030 |

## MIDWEST

| | |
|---|---|
| Advance Theatrical Co/2451 N Sacramento, Chicago, IL | 312-772-7150 |
| Backstage Enterprises/1525 Ellinwood, Des Plaines, IL | 312-692-6159 |
| Be Something Studio/5533 N Forest Glen, Chicago, IL | 312-685-6717 |
| Broadway Costumes Inc/932 W Washington, Chicago, IL | 312-829-6400 |
| Bruesser, F Co/441 Macomb St, Detroit, MI | 313-962-8266 |
| Brune, Paul/6330 N Indian Rd, Chicago, IL | 312-763-1117 |
| Chicago Costume Co Inc/725 W Wrightwood Ave, Chicago, IL | 312-528-1264 |
| Cindy Makes Things/1035 W Barry, Chicago, IL | 312-929-1060 |
| Costumes Unlimited/814 N Franklin St, Chicago, IL | 312-642-0200 |
| Ennis, Susan/2772 N Lincoln Ave, Chicago, IL | 312-525-7483 |
| Hollywood-Costumes/22135 Michigan St, Dearborn, MI | 313-563-9111 |
| House of Rulah/6000A W Irving Park Rd, Chicago, IL | 312-286-0958 |
| Kaufman Costumes/5117 N Western, Chicago, IL | 312-561-7529 |
| Magical Mystery Tour, Ltd/110 Waukegan Rd, Deerfield, IL | 312-291-0920 |
| Magical Mystery Tour, Ltd/6010 Dempster, Morton Grove, IL | 312-966-5090 |
| Marcella Costumes/2048 W Lawrence, Chicago, IL | 312-878-1723 |
| Masters Costume/8820 S Commercial Ave, Chicago, IL | 312-768-2432 |
| N Y Costume Co/P O Box 483, De Kalb, IL | 815-756-1188 |
| Okains Costume & Theater/380 S Jefferson, Joliet, IL | 815-741-9303 |
| Stechman's Creations/1920 Koehler, Des Plains, IL | 312-827-9045 |
| Taylor, Corinna/1700B W Granville, Chicago, IL | 312-472-6550 |
| Toy Gallery/1640 N Wells, Chicago, IL | 312-944-4323 |

## SOUTHWEST

| | |
|---|---|
| A & J Costume Rental, Dsgn & Const/304 White Oaks Dr, Austin, TX | 512-836-2733 |
| ABC Theatrical Rental & Sales/825 N 7th St, Phoenix, AZ | 602-258-5265 |
| Abel, Joyce/Rt 1 Box 165, San Marcos, TX | 512-392-5659 |
| Ann Lind - Second Childhood/3010 Windsor Rd, Austin, TX | 512-472-9696 |
| Campioni, Freddrick/1920 Broken Oak, San Antonio, TX | 512-342-7780 |
| Corey, Irene/4147 Herschel Ave, Dallas, TX | 214-528-4836 |
| Grafica: A Total Design Co/3110 Fairmount, Dallas, TX | 214-741-3810 |
| Incredible Productions/3327 Wylie Dr, Dallas, TX | 214-350-3633 |
| Jill's Costume & Specialty Shoppe/2460 Harry Wurzbach, San Antonio, TX | 512-824-1814 |
| Lucy Greer & Assoc. Casting/600 Shadywood Ln, Richardson, TX | 214-231-2086 |
| Moreau, Suzanne/1007-B West 22nd St, Austin, TX | 512-477-1532 |
| Nicholson, Christine/c/o Lola Sprouse, Carrollton, TX | 214-245-0926 |
| Paul Osborne and Associates, Inc/1162 Security Dr, Dallas, TX | 214-630-7800 |
| Rosebud, I M Inc/531 Main St, Rosebud, TX | 817-583-7951 |
| Second Childhood/604 W 16th St, Austin, TX | 512-472-9696 |
| Smith, Jo Karen/222 East Riverside Dr #333, Austin, TX | 512-441-6955 |
| Thomas, Joan S/6904 Spanky Branch Court, Dallas, TX | 214-931-1900 |
| Welch, Virginia L./3707 Manchaca #138, Austin, TX | 512-447-1240 |

## WEST

| | |
|---|---|
| AAA Cinema Costumers/5514 Hollywood Blvd, Hollywood, CA | 213-464-9894 |
| Aardvark/7579 Melrose Ave, Los Angeles, CA | 213-655-6769 |
| Adele's of Hollywood/5059 Hollywood Blvd, Hollywood, CA | 213-663-2231 |
| American Costume Corp/12980 Raymer, N Hollywood, CA | 213-764-2239 |
| And Sew On-Jila/2017 Broadway, Boulder, CO | 303-442-0130 |
| Auntie Mame/1102 S La Cienaga Blvd, Los Angeles, CA | 213-652-8430 |
| Boserup House of Canes/1636 Westwood Blvd, W Los Angeles, CA | 213-474-2577 |
| The Burbank Studios Wardrobe Dept/4000 Warner Blvd, Burbank, CA | 213-843-6000 |
| CBS Wardrobe Dept/7800 Beverly Blvd, Los Angeles, CA | 213-852-2345 |
| California Surplus Mart/6263 Santa Monica Blvd, Los Angeles, CA | 213-465-5525 |
| Can Do Fabrications/35 Stratton Pl Suite 2, Pasadena, CA | 213-449-7553 |
| Capezio Dancewear/1777 Vine St, Hollywood, CA | 213-465-3744 |
| Courtney, Elizabeth/8636 Melrose Ave, Los Angeles, CA | 213-657-4361 |
| Crystal Palace (Rentals)/835 N Fairfax, Los Angeles, CA | 213-651-5458 |
| Crystal Palace (Sales)/8457 Melrose Ave, Hollywood, CA | 213-653-6148 |
| Design Studio/6685-7 Sunset Blvd, Hollywood, CA | 213-469-3661 |
| E C 2 Costumes/431 S Fairfax, Los Angeles, CA | 213-934-1131 |
| Fantasy Fair Inc/4310 San Fernando Rd, Glendale, CA | 213-245-7367 |

# PHOTO/FILM SERVICES CONT'D.

Please send us your additions and updates.

| | |
|---|---|
| International Costume Co/1269 Sartori, Torrance, CA | 213-320-6392 |
| J&M Costumers/5010 Sunset Blvd, Los Angeles, CA | 213-660-5153 |
| Kings Western Wear/6455 Van Nuys Blvd, Van Nuys, CA | 213-785-2586 |
| Krofft Enterprises Inc/7200 Vineland Ave, Sun Valley, CA | 213-875-3250 |
| LA Uniform Exchange/5239 Melrose Ave, Los Angeles, CA | 213-469-3965 |
| MGM Studios Wardrobe Dept/10202 W Washington Blvd, Culver City, CA | 213-836-3000 |
| Military Antiques & War Museum/208 Santa Monica Ave, Santa Monica, CA | 213-393-1180 |
| Myers Costume/5538 Hollywood Blvd, Hollywood, CA | 213-465-6589 |
| Nudies Rodeo Tailor/5015 Lanskershim Blvd, N Hollywood, CA | 213-762-3105 |
| Paramount Studios Wardrobe Dept/5451 Marathon St, Hollywood, CA | 213-468-5000 |
| Peabodys/1102 1/2 S La Cienega Blvd, Los Angeles, CA | 213-352-3810 |
| Piller's, Jerry/8163 Santa Monica Blvd, Hollywood, CA | 213-654-3038 |
| Raggedy Ann Clothes Emporium/1213 E Evans Ave, Denver, CO | 303-733-7937 |
| Tuxedo Center/7360 Sunset Blvd, Los Angeles, CA | 213-874-4200 |
| Valu Shoe Mart/5637 Santa Monica Blvd, Los Angeles, CA | 213-469-8560 |
| Western Costume Co/5335 Melrose Ave, Los Angeles, CA | 213-469-1451 |
| Workroom 27/425 W Los Feliz Rd, Glendale, CA | 213-245-0222 |

# PROPS

## NEW YORK CITY

| | |
|---|---|
| Abet Rent-A-Fur/307 Seventh Ave | 212-989-5757 |
| Abstracta Structures Inc/38 W 39th St | 212-944-2244 |
| Adirondack Direct/219 E 42nd St | 212-687-8555 |
| Alice's Antiques/552 Columbus Ave | 212-874-3400 |
| Alpha-Pavia Bookbinding Co Inc/55 W 21st St | 212-929-5430 |
| Archer Surgical Supplies Inc/217 E 23rd St | 212-689-3480 |
| Artisan's Studio/232 Atlantic Ave | 212-855-2796 |
| Artistic Neon by Gasper/70-19 60th Ln | 212-821-1550 |
| Arts & Crafters/175 Johnson St | 212-875-8151 |
| Arts & Flowers/234 W 56th St | 212-247-7610 |
| Associated Theatrical Designer/145 W 71st St | 212-362-2648 |
| Austin Display/139 W 19th St | 212-924-6261 |
| Baird, Bill Marionettes/41 Union Square | 212-989-9840 |
| Baker, Alex/30 W 69th St | 212-799-2069 |
| Bill's Flower Mart/816 Ave of the Americas | 212-889-8154 |
| Brandon Memorabilia/222 E 51st St | 212-593-2794 |
| Breitrose, Mark/156 Fifth Ave | 212-242-7825 |
| Brooklyn Model Works Inc/60 Washington Ave | 212-834-1944 |
| Browsers Welcome/380 Columbus Ave | 212-724-0688 |
| California Artificial Flower Co/225 Fifth Ave | 212-679-7774 |
| Carroll Musical Instrument Svc/351 W 41st St | 212-868-4120 |
| Centre Fire Arms/51 W 46th St | 212-246-7307 |
| Chateau Stables Inc/608 W 48th St | 212-246-0520 |
| Churchill Furniture Rental Inc/1421 Third Ave | 212-535-3400 |
| Clove Lake Stables Inc/1025 Clove Rd | 212-448-1414 |
| Cycle Service Center Inc/74 Sixth Ave | 212-925-5900 |
| Doherty Studios/252 W 46th St | 212-840-6219 |
| Eclectic Properties Inc./204 W 84th St | 212-799-8963 |
| Encore Studio/410 W 47th St | 212-246-5237 |
| FHM Food Arts Inc/79 W 12th St | 212-691-5853 |
| Florenco Foliage Systems Inc/30-28 Starr Ave | 212-729-6600 |
| The Focarino Studio/156 E 23rd St | 212-533-9872 |
| Furs, Valerie/150 W 30th St | 212-947-2020 |
| Golden Equipment Co Inc/422 Madison Ave | 212-838-3776 |
| Gordon Novelty Co/933 Broadway | 212-254-8616 |
| Gossard & Assocs Inc/801 E 134th St | 212-665-9194 |
| Gothic Color Co Inc/727 Washington St | 212-929-7493 |
| Greely Sign & Design/35 W 36th St | 212-736-8683 |
| Guccione/6 W 37th St | 212-279-3602 |
| Harra, John Wood & Supply Co/39 W 19th St, 11th Fl | 212-741-0290 |
| Harrison/Erickson/95 Fifth Ave | 212-929-5700 |
| Hart Scenic Studio/35-41 Dempsey Ave | 212-947-7264 |
| Irving's Food Center/867 Ninth Ave | 212-757-3220 |
| Jeffers, Kathy-Modelmaking/106 E 19 St | 212-475-1756 |
| Joyce, Robert Studio Ltd/321 W 44th St, #404 | 212-586-5041 |
| Kaplan, Howard/35 E 10th St | 212-674-1000 |
| Karpen, Ben/212 E 51st St | 212-755-3450 |
| Kempler, George J/160 Fifth Ave | 212-989-1180 |
| Kenmore Furniture Co Inc/156 E 33rd St | 212-683-1888 |
| Manhattan Model Makers/131 W 23rd St | 212-620-0398 |
| The Manhattan Model Shop/40 Great Jones St | 212-473-6312 |
| Manwaring Studio/232 Atlantic Ave | 212-855-2796 |
| Marc Modell Associates/430 W 54th St | 212-541-9676 |
| Mason's Tennis Mart/911 Seventh Ave | 212-757-5374 |
| Matty's Studio Sales/543 W 35th St | 212-757-6246 |
| Mendez, Raymond A/220 W 98th St, #12B | 212-864-4689 |
| Messmore & Damon Inc/530 W 28th St | 212-594-8070 |
| Metro Scenery Studio Inc/215-31 99th Ave | 212-464-6328 |
| Modern Miltex Corp/280 E 134th St | 212-585-6000 |
| Movie Cars/825 Madison Ave | 212-288-6000 |
| Newell Art Galleries Inc/425 E 53rd St | 212-758-1970 |
| Nostalgia Alley Antiques/380 Second Ave | 212-988-3949 |
| Novel Pinball Co/593 Tenth Ave | 212-736-3868 |
| The Place for Antiques/993 Second Ave | 212-475-6596 |
| Plant Specialists Inc/524 W 34th St | 212-279-1500 |
| Plexability Ltd/200 Lexington Ave | 212-679-7826 |
| Porter-Rayvid/19 Second Ave | 212-677-9502 |
| Portobello Road Antiques Ltd/370 Columbus Ave | 212-724-2300 |
| The Prop House Inc/76 Ninth Ave | 212-691-9099 |
| Ray Beauty Supply Co Inc/721 Eighth Ave | 212-757-0175 |
| Ridge, John Russell/531 Hudson St | 212-929-3410 |
| Siciliano, Frank/125 Fifth Ave | 212-620-4075 |
| Simon's Dir of Theatrical Mat/1501 Broadway | 212-354-1840 |
| Smith & Watson/305 E 63rd St | 212-355-5615 |
| Smith, David/ | 212-730-1188 |
| Solco Plumbing Suplies & Bathtubs/209 W 18th St | 212-243-2569 |
| Special Effects/40 W 39th St | 212-869-8636 |
| State Supply Equipment Co Inc/68 Thomas St | 212-233-0474 |
| The Theater Machine/174 Cook Street | 212-366-8853 |
| Theater Technology Inc/37 W 20th St | 212-929-5380 |
| Times Square Theatrical & Studio/318 W 47th St | 212-245-4155 |
| Uncle Sam's Umbrella/161 W 57th St | 212-582-1976 |
| Weiss, David Importers Inc/969 Third Ave | 212-755-1492 |
| Westside Exchange Furn & Antiq/441 Columbus Ave | 212-874-9347 |
| Whole Art Inc/114 W 27th St | 212-255-6229 |
| William Rogers-Paint Backdrops/26 Bowery | 212-732-3355 |
| Wizardworks/67 Atlantic Ave | 212-349-5252 |
| Zakarian, Robert Prop Shop Inc/26 College Pl | 212-522-4606 |
| Zeller, Gary & Assoc/Special Effects/40 W 39th St | 212-869-8636 |

## NORTHEAST

| | |
|---|---|
| Antique Bicycle Props Service/113 Woodland Ave, Montvale, NJ | 201-391-8780 |
| Arawak Marine/P O Box 762, St Thomas, VI | 809-775-1858 |
| Atlas Scenic Studios Ltd/46 Brokfield Ave, Bridgeport, CT | 203-334-2130 |
| Baily Designs/110 Williams St, Malden, MA | 617-321-4448 |
| Baldwin, Katherine/109 Commonwealth Ave, Boston, MA | 617-267-0508 |
| Bestek Theatrical Productions/92 Field St, W Babylon, NY | 516-293-9010 |
| Big Apple Scenic Studios Inc/502-10 Madison Ave, Hoboken, NJ | 212-227-8775 |
| Cadillac Convertible Owners/Thiells, NY | 914-947-1109 |
| Dewart, Tim Assoc/83 Old Standley St, Beverly, MA | 617-922-9229 |
| Geiger, Ed/12 Church St, Middletown, NJ | 201-671-1707 |
| George M. Creations/Route 6, Mohegan Lake, NY | 914-528-1616 |
| L I Auto Museum/Museum Square, South Hampton, NY | 516-283-1880 |
| Mallie, Dale & Co/40 Stevens Pl, Lawrence, NY | 516-239-8782 |
| Master & Talent Inc/1139 Foam Place, Far Rockaway, NY | 516-239-7719 |
| Newbery, Tornas/Ridge Rd, Glen Cove, NY | 516-759-0880 |
| Rindner, Jack N Assoc/112 Water St, Tinton Falls, NJ | 201-542-3548 |
| Stewart, Chas H Stewart Co/6 Clarendon Ave, Sommerville, MA | 617-625-2407 |
| Theater Production Service Inc/26 S Highland Ave, Ossining, NY | 914-941-0357 |

# PHOTO/FILM SERVICES CONT'D.

Please send us your additions and updates.

## SOUTHEAST

| | |
|---|---|
| Alderman Company/325 Model Farm Rd, High Point, NC | 919-889-6121 |
| Dangar, Jack/3640 Ridge Rd, Smyrna, GA | 404-434-3640 |
| Dunwright Productions/15281 NE 21st Ave, N Miami Beach, FL | 305-944-2464 |
| Enter Space/20 14th St NW, Atlanta, GA | 404-885-1139 |
| hen's teeth/1206 Clifton Rd NE, Atlanta, GA | 404-378-6076 |
| Kupersmith, Tony/320 N Highland Ave NE, Atlanta, GA | 404-577-5319 |
| Manning, Maureen/1283 Cedar Heights Dr, Stone Mountain, GA | 404-296-1520 |
| Miller, Lee/Rte 1, Box 98, Lumpkin, GA | 912-838-4959 |
| Player, Joanne/3403 Orchard St, Hapeville, GA | 404-767-5542 |
| S C Educational TV/2712 Millwood Ave, Columbia, SC | 803-758-7284 |
| Smith, Roscoe/15 Baltimore Pl NW, Atlanta, GA | 404-252-3540 |
| Sugar Creek Studio Inc/16 Young St, Atlanta, GA | 404-522-3270 |
| Sunshine Scenic Studios/1370 4th St, Sarasota, FL | 813-366-8848 |
| Winslow, Geoffrey C/1027 North Ave, Atlanta, GA | 404-522-1669 |

## MIDWEST

| | |
|---|---|
| Advance Theatrical/125 N Wabash, Chicago, IL | 312-772-7150 |
| Becker Studios Inc/2824 W Taylor, Chicago, IL | 312-722-4040 |
| Bregstone Assoc/440 S Wabash, Chicago, IL | 312-939-5130 |
| Cadillac Plastic/1924 N Paulina, Chicago, IL | 312-342-9200 |
| Channon Corp/1343 W Argyle, Chicago, IL | 312-275-4700 |
| Chicago Scenic Studios Inc/2217 W Belmont Ave, Chicago, IL | 312-477-8362 |
| The Emporium/1551 N Wells, Chicago, IL | 312-337-7126 |
| Essanay Studio Stage/1345 W Argyle, Chicago, IL | 312-334-9510 |
| Furniture Leasing Service/819 N Clark, Chicago, IL | 312-642-0600 |
| Hartman Furniture & Carpet Co/220 W Kinzie, Chicago, IL | 312-664-2800 |
| Hatcher Associates/502 N Wells, Chicago, IL | 312-644-3065 |
| Hollywood Stage Lighting/5850 N Broadway, Chicago, IL | 312-271-4915 |
| House of Drane/410 N Ashland Ave, Chicago, IL | 312-829-8686 |
| Merrick Models Ltd/1426 W Fullerton, Chicago, IL | 312-281-7787 |
| Midwest Stage Lighting Co/2104 Central, Evanston, IL | 312-328-3966 |
| The Model Shop/415 N State St, Chicago, IL | 312-822-9663 |
| Scroungers Inc/401 N 3rd St, Minneapolis, MN | 612-332-0441 |
| Steve Starr Studios/2654 N Clark St, Chicago, IL | 312-525-6530 |
| Studio Specialties/409 W Huron, Chicago, IL | 312-337-5131 |
| Tim Dewart Assoc/706 W McNichols Rd, Detroit, MI | 313-863-0197 |
| White House Studios/4810 McGee, Kansas City, MO | 816-931-3608 |

## SOUTHWEST

| | |
|---|---|
| Creative Video Productions/5933 Bellaire Blvd, #110, Houston, TX | 713-661-0478 |
| Desert Wren Designs, Inc/7340 Scottsdale Mall, Scottsdale, AZ | 602-941-5056 |
| Doerr, Dean/11321 Greystone, Oklahoma City, OK | 405-751-0313 |
| Eats/P O Box 52, Tempe, AZ | 602-966-7459 |
| Janet-Nelson/PO Box 143, Tempe, AZ | 602-968-3771 |
| Marty, Jack/2225 South First, Garland, TX | 214-840-8708 |
| Melancon, Joseph Studios/2934 Elm, Dallas, TX | 214-742-2982 |
| Merrick Models Ltd/4302 N 30th, Phoenix, AZ | 602-955-8962 |
| Southern Importers/4825 San Jacinto, Houston, TX | 713-524-8236 |
| Young Film Productions/PO Box 50105, Tucson, AZ | 602-623-5961 |

## WEST

| | |
|---|---|
| A & A Special Effects/7021 Havenhurst St, Van Nuys, CA | 213-782-6558 |
| Abbe Rents/600 S Normandie, Los Angeles, CA | 213-384-5292 |
| Aldik Artificial Flowers Co/7651 Sepulveda Blvd, Van Nuys, CA | 213-988-5970 |
| Allen, Walter Plant Rentals/5500 Melrose Ave, Hollywood, CA | 213-469-3621 |
| Altbaum, Patti/244-CS Lasky Dr, Beverly Hills, CA | 213-553-6269 |
| Anabel's Diversified Services/PO Box 532, Pacific Palisades, CA | 213-454-1566 |
| Antiquarian Traders/8483 Melrose Ave, Los Angeles, CA | 213-658-6394 |
| Arnelle Sales Co Prop House/7926 Beverly Blvd, Los Angeles, CA | 213-930-2900 |
| Asia Plant Rentals/1215 225th St, Torrance, CA | 213-775-1811 |
| Astrovision, Inc/16800 Roscoe Blvd, Van Nuys, CA | 213-989-5222 |
| Backings, c/o 20th Century Fox/10201 W Pico Blvd, Los Angeles, CA | 213-277-0522 |
| Baronian Manufacturing Co/1865 Farm Bureau Rd, Concord, CA | 415-671-7199 |
| Barris Kustom Ind/10811 Riverside Dr, N Hollywood, CA | 213-877-2352 |
| Barton Surrey Svc/518 Fairview Ave, Arcadia, CA | 213-447-6693 |
| Basch, Joseph Galleries/5755 Santa Monica Blvd, Hollywood, CA | 213-463-5116 |
| Beverly Hills Fountain Center/8574 Monica Blvd, Los Angeles, CA | 213-652-5297 |
| Bischoff's/449 S San Fernando Blvd, Burbank, CA | 213-843-7561 |
| Briles Wing & Helicopter/3011 Airport Ave, Santa Monica, CA | 213-390-3554 |
| Brown, Mel Furniture/5804 S Figueroa St, Los Angeles, CA | 213-778-4444 |
| Buccaneer Cruises/Berth 76W-33 Ports O'Call, San Pedro, CA | 213-548-1085 |
| The Burbank Studios Prop Dept/4000 Warner Blvd, Burbank, CA | 213-843-6000 |
| Cinema Float/447 N Newport Blvd, Newport Beach, CA | 714-642-6600 |
| Cinema Mercantile Co/5857 Santa Monica Blvd, Hollywood, CA | 213-467-1151 |
| Cinema Props Co/6161 Santa Monica Blvd, Hollywood, CA | 213-464-3191 |
| City Lights/404 S Figueroa, Los Angeles, CA | 213-680-9876 |
| Colors of the Wind/2900 Main St, Santa Monica, CA | 213-399-8044 |
| Corham Artifical Flowers/11800 Olympic Blvd, Los Angeles, CA | 213-479-1166 |
| Custom Neon/3804 Beverly Blvd, Los Angeles, CA | 213-386-7945 |
| D'Andrea Glass Etchings/3671 Tacoma Ave, Los Angeles, CA | 213-223-7940 |
| Danny Rouzer Studio/7022 Melrose Ave, Hollywood, CA | 213-936-2494 |
| Decorative Paper Productions/1818 W 6th St, Los Angeles, CA | 213-484-1080 |
| Deutsch Inc/426 S Robertson Blvd, Los Angeles, CA | 213-273-4949 |
| Disco Sight & Sound Entertainment Co/14653 Aetna St, Van Nuys, CA | 213-780-5840 |
| Ellis Mercantile Co/169 N LaBrea Ave, Los Angeles, CA | 213-933-7334 |
| Featherock Inc/2890 Empire, Burbank, CA | 213-849-6723 |
| First Street Furniture Store/1123 N Bronson Ave, Los Angeles, CA | 213-462-6306 |
| Flower Fashions/9960 Santa Monica Blvd, Beverly Hills, CA | 213-272-6063 |
| Games Unltd/9059 Venice Blvd, Los Angeles, CA | 213-836-8920 |
| Golden Bear Ent/PO Box 3682, Glendale, CA | 805-942-5406 |
| Golden West Billiard Supply/6326 Laurel Canyon Blvd, North Hollywood, CA | 213-877-4100 |
| Grand American Fare/2941 Main St, Santa Monica, CA | |
| Haltzman Office Furniture/1417 S Figueroa, Los Angeles, CA | 213-749-7021 |
| The Hand Prop Room/5700 Venice Blvd, Los Angeles, CA | 213-931-1534 |
| The High Wheelers Inc/109 S Hidalgo, Alhambra, CA | 213-576-8648 |
| Hollywood Toys/6562 Hollywood Blvd, Los Angeles, CA | 213-465-3119 |
| House of Props Inc/1117 N Gower St, Hollywood, CA | 213-463-3166 |
| Hume, Alex R/140 N Victory Blvd, Burbank, CA | 213-849-1614 |
| Independent Studio Svcs/11907 Wicks St, Sun Valley, CA | 213-764-0840 |
| Iwasaki Images/19330 Van Ness Ave, Torrance, CA | 213-533-5986 |
| Jack Pill & Associates/6370 Santa Monica Blvd, Los Angeles, CA | 213-466-1665 |
| Jackson Shrub Supply/9500 Columbus Ave, Sepulveda, CA | 213-893-6939 |
| Johnson, Ray M Studio/5555 Sunset Blvd, Hollywood, CA | 213-465-4108 |
| Krofft Ent/7200 Vineland Ave, Sun Valley, CA | 213-875-3250 |
| Laughing Cat Design Co/723 1/2 N La Cienega Blvd, Los Angeles, CA | 213-855-8088 |
| Living Interiors/7273 Santa Monica Blvd, Los Angeles, CA | 213-874-7815 |
| MGM Studios Prop Dept/10202 W Washington Blvd, Culver City, CA | 213-836-3000 |
| The Magazine/14350 Millbank, Sherman Oaks, CA | 213-990-7124 |
| Malibu Florists/21337 Pacific Coast Hwy, Malibu, CA | 213-456-2014 |
| Marina Activities/13816 Bora Bora Way #140A, Marina del Rey, CA | 213-823-4377 |
| Marina Del Rey Small Craft Harbor/13837 Fiji Way, Marina del Rey, CA | 213-823-4571 |
| Marvin, Lennie Ent Ltd/1105 N Hollywood Way, Burbank, CA | 213-841-5882 |
| McDermott, Kate/1114 S Point View, Los Angeles, CA | 213-935-4101 |
| Mercury Archives/1574 Crossroads of the World, Hollywood, CA | 213-463-8000 |
| Modelmakers/216 Townsend St, San Francisco, CA | 415-495-5111 |
| Modern Furniture Rentals/5418 Sierra Vista Ave, Los Angeles, CA | 213-462-6545 |
| Mole-Richardson/937 N Sycamore Ave, Hollywood, CA | 213-851-0111 |
| Moskatels/733 S San Julian St, Los Angeles, CA | 213-627-1631 |
| Motion Picture Marine/616 Venice Blvd, Marina del Rey, CA | 213-822-1100 |
| Music Center/5616 Santa Monica Blvd, Hollywood, CA | 213-469-8143 |
| Omega Studio Rentals/5757 Santa Monica Blvd, Hollywood, CA | 213-466-8201 |

# PHOTO/FILM SERVICES CONT'D.

Please send us your additions and updates.

| | |
|---|---|
| PJM Traffic Consultants/1322 N Cole St, Los Angeles, CA | 213-466-7778 |
| Pacific Palisades Florists/15244 Sunset Blvd, Pacific Palisades, CA | 213-454-0337 |
| Paramount Studios Prop Dept/5451 Marathon St, Hollywood, CA | 213-468-5000 |
| Photo Productions/400 Montgomery St, San Francisco, CA | 415-392-5985 |
| The Plantation/1595 E El Segundo Blvd, El Segundo, CA | 213-322-7877 |
| Post, Don Studios/8211 Lankershim Blvd, N Hollywood, CA | 213-768-0811 |
| Producers Studio/650 N Bronson Ave, Los Angeles, CA | 213-466-7778 |
| Professional Scenery Inc/7311 Radford Ave, N Hollywood, CA | 213-875-1910 |
| Prop City/9336 W Washington, Culver City, CA | 213-559-7022 |
| Prop Service West/6223 Santa Monica Blvd, Hollywood, CA | 213-461-3371 |
| Rent-A-Mink/6738 Sunset Blvd, Hollywood, CA | 213-467-7879 |
| Roschu/6514 Santa Monica Blvd, Hollywood, CA | 213-469-2749 |
| Scale Model Co/401 W Florence, Inglewood, CA | 213-679-1436 |
| School Days Equipment Co/973 N Main St, Los Angeles, CA | 213-223-3474 |
| Shafton Inc/5500 Cleon Ave, North Hollywood, CA | 213-985-5025 |
| Sierra Railroad Company/3745 E Colorado Blvd, Pasadena, CA | 213-887-8657 |
| Silvestri Studios/1733 W Cordova St, Los Angeles, CA | 213-735-1481 |
| Snakes/6100 Laurel Canyon Blvd, North Hollywood, CA | 213-985-7777 |
| Special Effects Unlimited/752 N Cahuenga Blvd, Hollywood, CA | 213-466-6361 |
| Spellman Desk Co/6159 Santa Monica Blvd, Hollywood, CA | 213-467-0628 |
| Stage Right/Box 2265, Canyon Country, CA | 805-251-4342 |
| Star Sporting Goods/1645 N Highland Ave, Hollywood, CA | 213-469-3531 |
| Stembridge Gun Rentals/5451 Marathon St, Hollywood, CA | 213-468-5000 |
| Studio Specialties/249 N Reno St, Los Angeles, CA | 213-480-3101 |
| Stunts Unlimited/3518 Cahuenga Blvd W, Los Angeles, CA | 213-874-0050 |
| Surf, Val/4807 Whitsett, N Hollywood, CA | 213-769-6977 |
| Transparent Productions/3410 S Lacienaga Blvd, Los Angeles, CA | 213-938-3821 |
| Tri-Tronex Inc/2921 W Alameda Ave, Burbank, CA | 213-849-6115 |
| Tropizon Plant Rentals/1401 Pebble Vale, Monterey Park, CA | 213-269-2010 |
| UPA Pictures/4440 Lakeside Dr, Burbank, CA | 213-842-7171 |
| Western Costume Company/5335 Melrose Ave, Hollywood, CA | 213-469-1451 |
| Wizards Inc/18624 Parthenia Bldgs 3&4, Northridge, CA | 213-368-8974 |
| Woolf, Billy/1112 N Beachwood St, Hollywood, CA | 213-469-5335 |

# LOCATIONS

## NEW YORK CITY

| | |
|---|---|
| Act Travel/310 Madison Ave | 212-697-9550 |
| Carmichael-Moore, Bob Inc/141 Charles St | 212-255-0465 |
| Dancerschool/400 Lafayette St | 212-260-0453 |
| Full View Scouting/180 Duane Street | 212-925-7212 |
| Honeywagons, Inc/Pier 62 North River | 212-807-1919 |
| Howell, T J Interiors/301 E 38th St | 212-532-6267 |
| Juckes, Geoff/295 Bennett Ave | 212-567-5676 |
| Leach, Ed Inc/100 Fifth Ave | 212-691-3450 |
| Location Connection/31 E 31st St | 212-684-1888 |
| Location Locators/225 E 63rd St | 212-832-1866 |
| Loft Locations/50 White St | 212-966-6408 |
| Marks, Arthur/140 E 40th St | 212-685-2761 |
| The Perfect Place Ltd/182 Amity St | 212-570-6252 |
| Scenes Unlimited/850 Third Ave | 212-532-9400 |
| Terrestris/409 E 60th St | 212-758-8181 |
| This Must Be The Place/2119 Albermarle Terrace | 212-282-3454 |
| Unger, Captain Howard/80 Beach Rd | 212-639-3578 |

## NORTHEAST

| | |
|---|---|
| Bell, Kenneth/Curtis St, Somerville, MA | 617-628-6931 |
| Berkshire Services, Inc/W Rowe Box 1036, Stockbridge, MA | 413-298-3072 |
| Boston Location Services/Boston, MA | 617-536-7975 |
| C-M Associates/268 New Mark, Rockville, MD | 301-340-7070 |
| Cinemagraphics/101 Trowbridge St, Cambridge, MA | 617-491-0966 |
| Connecticut State Travel Office/210 Washington St, Hartford, CT | 203-566-3383 |
| Cooper Productions/175 Walnut St, Brookline, MA | 617-738-7278 |
| Delaware State Travel Service/630 State College Rd, Dover, DE | 302-736-4254 |
| Dobush, Jim/148 Mountain Rd, Ridgefield, CT | 203-431-3718 |
| Duda, Jules/24 Edison Dr, Huntington Sta, NY | 516-427-5863 |
| Florentine Films, Inc/25 Main St, Northampton, MA | 413-584-0816 |
| Forma, Belle/433 Claflin Ave, Mamaroneck, NY | 914-698-2598 |
| Gilmore, Robert Assoc Inc/990 Washington St, Dedham, MA | 617-329-6633 |
| Girl/Scout Locations/One Hillside Ave, Port Washington, NY | 516-883-8409 |
| Goldstein, Marty Triangle Prod/36 Vernon St, Brookline, MA | 617-232-1934 |
| Great Locations/97 Windsor Road, Tenafly, NJ | 201-567-2809 |
| Hackerman, Nancy Prod Inc/6 East Eager St, Baltimore, MD | 301-685-2727 |
| Hampton Locations/109 Hill Street, South Hampton, NY | 516-283-2160 |
| The Hermitage/PO Box 4, Yorktown Heights, NY | 914-632-5315 |
| Jurgielewicz, Annie/P O Box 422, Cambridge, MA | 617-628-1141 |
| Krause, Janet L/43 Linnaean St, #26, Cambridge, MA | 617-492-3223 |
| Lewis, Jay/87 Ripley St, Newton Center, MA | 617-332-1516 |
| The Location Hunter/16 Iselin Terr, Larchmont, NY | 914-834-2181 |
| Location Scouting Service/153 Sidney St, Oyster Bay, NY | 516-922-1759 |
| Location Services/269 Lyons Plains Rd, Weston, CT | 203-227-1477 |
| Location Unlimited/90 Brayton St, Englewood, NJ | 201-567-2809 |
| Magro, Bob/44 Ashford St, Allston, MA | 617-783-0980 |
| Maine State Development Office/193 State St, Augusta, ME | 207-289-2656 |
| Marlin, Glen/44 Ashford St, Allston, MA | 617-783-0980 |
| Marrs, Deborah/42 Allen St, Arlington, MA | 617-646-5168 |
| Maryland State Economic Division/2525 Riva Rd, Annapolis, MD | 301-269-2051 |
| Massachusetts State Film Bureau/100 Cambridge St, Boston, MA | 617-727-3330 |
| McGlynn, Jack/34 Buffum St, Salem, MA | 617-745-8764 |
| Mettler, Judy/90 Brayston St, Englewood, NJ | 201-567-2809 |
| Myriad Communications, Inc/357 Robin Rd, Englewood, NJ | 201-871-0190 |
| NJ State Motion Pic Dev/Gateway One, Newark, NJ | 201-648-6279 |
| Nassau Farmer's Market/600 Hicksville Rd, Bethpage, NY | 516-931-2046 |
| New Hampshire Vacation Travel/P O Box 856, Concorde, NH | 603-271-2666 |
| New Locations/247 N Wyoming Ave, South Orange, NJ | 201-762-5433 |
| Norcross, Gail E/140 Mt Vernon St, Boston, MA | 617-723-8374 |
| Nozik, Michael/9 Cutler Ave, Cambridge, MA | 617-783-4315 |
| PA Div of Film Promotion/South Office Bldg, Harrisburg, PA | 405-521-3981 |
| PhotoSonics/1116 N Hudson St, Arlington, VA | 703-522-1116 |
| Proteus Location Services/9225 Baltimore Blvd, College Park, MD | 301-441-2928 |
| RenRose Locations, Ltd/4 Sandalwood Dr, Livingston, NJ | 201-992-4264 |
| Rhode Island State Tourist Division/7 Jackson Walkway, Providence, RI | 401-277-2601 |
| Strawberries Finders Service/Buck County, Reigelsville, PA | 215-346-8000 |
| Terry, Karen/131 Boxwood Dr, Kings Park, NY | 516-724-3964 |
| Triangle Prod/36 Vernon St, Brookline, MA | |
| USVI Film Promotion Office/St Thomas, VI | 809-774-1331 |
| Upstate Production Services, Inc/277 Alexander St #510, Rochester, NY | 716-546-5417 |
| Verange, Joe - Century III/545 Boyston St, Boston, MA | 617-267-9800 |
| Vermont State Travel Division/61 Elm St, Montpelier, VT | 802-828-3236 |
| Washington DC Public Space Committee/415 12th St, N W Washington, DC | 202-629-4084 |
| West Virginia State Film Department/1900 Washington St E, Charleston, WV | 304-348-3977 |
| Wood, Carol/7 Merritt St, Marblehead, MA | 617-631-4232 |

## SOUTHEAST

| | |
|---|---|
| Alabama State Film Commission/532 S Perry St, Montgomery, AL | 800-633-5898 |
| Baker, Sherry/1823 Indiana Ave, Atlanta, GA | 404-373-6666 |
| Bruns, Ken & Gayle/7810 SW 48th Court, Miami, FL | 305-666-2928 |
| Dangar, Jack/3640 Ridge Rd, Smyrna, GA | 404-434-3640 |
| Darracott, David/1324 Braircliff Rd #5, Atlanta, GA | 404-872-0219 |
| Fl State Motion Picture/TV Svcs/107 W Gaines St, Tallahassee, FL | 904-487-1100 |
| Georgia State Film Office/P O Box 1776, Atlanta, GA | 404-656-3591 |
| Harris, George/2875 Mabry Lane NE, Atlanta, GA | 404-231-0116 |
| hen's teeth/1206 Clifton Rd NE, Atlanta, GA | 404-378-6076 |
| Kentucky Film Commission/Capital Plaza Tower, Frankfort, KY | 502-564-2240 |
| Kupersmith, Tony/320 N Highland Ave NE, Atlanta, GA | 404-577-5319 |

# PHOTO/FILM SERVICES CONT'D.

Please send us your additions and updates.

| | |
|---|---|
| McDonald, Stew/6905 N Coolidge Ave, Tampa, FL | 813-886-3773 |
| Miller, Lee/Rte 1, Box 98, Lumpkin, GA | 912-838-4959 |
| Mississippi State Film Commission/P O Box 849, Jackson, MS | 601-354-6715 |
| NC State Motion Pic Dev/430 N Salisbury St, Raleigh, NC | 919-733-7651 |
| Player, Joanne/3403 Orchard St, Hapeville, GA | 404-767-5542 |
| Reel Wheels/21320 NE 20th Ave, Miami, FL | 305-935-2462 |
| South Florida Location Finders/1214 Cortez St, Coral Gables, FL | 305-445-0739 |
| TN State Econ & Comm Dev/1007 Andrew Jackson Bldg, Nashville, TN | 615-741-1888 |
| Virginia State Travel Service/6 N Sixth St, Richmond, VA | 804-786-2051 |

## MIDWEST

| | |
|---|---|
| Illinois State Film Office/205 W Wacker Dr, Chicago, IL | 213-793-3600 |
| Indiana State Tourism Development/440 N Meridian, Indianapolis, IN | 317-232-8860 |
| Iowa State Development Commission/250 Jewett Bldg, Des Moines, IA | 515-281-3251 |
| KS State Dept/Economic Div/503 Kansas Ave, Topeka, KS | 913-296-3481 |
| Location Services Film/Vileo/417 S 3rd St, Minneapolis, MN | 612-338-3359 |
| Manya Nogg Co/9773 Lafayette Plaza, Omaha, NB | 402-397-8887 |
| Michigan State Travel Bureau/P O Box 30226, Lansing, MI | 517-373-0670 |
| Minnesota State Tourism Division/480 Cedar St, St Paul, MN | 612-296-5017 |
| Missouri State Tourism Commission/308 E High St, Jefferson City, MO | 314-751-3051 |
| ND State Business & Industrial/513 E Bismarck Ave, Bismarck, ND | 701-224-2810 |
| Nebraska State Film Assistance Bureau/1819 Farnam St, Omaha, NB | 402-444-5001 |
| Ohio Film Bureau/30 E Broad St, Columbus, OH | 614-466-2284 |
| Station 12 Producers Express Inc./24333 Southfield Rd, Southfield, MI | 313-569-7707 |
| Stock Photography Outdoor Studio/4211 Flora Place, St Louis, MO | 314-773-2298 |

## SOUTHWEST

| | |
|---|---|
| Aero-Country Aviation/Rt 1, Box 201, McKinney, TX | 214-347-2416 |
| Alamo Village/PO Box 528, Brackettville, TX | 512-563-2580 |
| Arkansas State Dept of Economics/ #1 Capital Mall, Little Rock, AR | 501-371-1121 |
| Beverly Nichols/Skipper Richardson/6043 Vanderbilt Avenue, Dallas, TX | 214-824-7054 |
| Blair, Tanya Agency/2320 N Griffin St, Dallas, TX | 214-748-8353 |
| Burns, Robert A/113 West Johanna, Austin, TX | 512-444-6858 |
| Cinema America/Box 56566, Houston, TX | 713-780-8819 |
| DCB&R Film Productions/3627 Howell, Suite 244, Dallas, TX | 214-361-1525 |
| Desert Wren Designs, Inc/7340 Scottsdale Mall, Scottsdale, AZ | 602-941-5056 |
| Duncan, S Wade/PO Box 140273, Dallas, TX | 214-828-1367 |
| Edwards, Kathy Price/3764 South 99th East Avenue, Tulsa, OK | 918-663-7388 |
| El Paso Film Liaison/5 Civic Center Plaza, El Paso, TX | 915-544-3650 |
| Epic Film Productions/4314 Medical Parkway Suite 2, Austin, TX | 512-452-9461 |
| Fashion Consultants/262 Camelot Center, Richardson, TX | 214-234-4006 |
| Flach, Bob/3513 Norma, Garland, TX | 214-272-8431 |
| Fowlkes, Rebecca W/412 Canterbury Hill, San Antonio, TX | 512-826-4142 |
| Grapevine Productions/3214-A Hemlock Avenue, Austin, TX | 512-472-0894 |
| Greenblatt, Linda/6722 Waggoner, Dallas, TX | 214-691-6552 |
| Griffin, Gary Productions/12667 Memorial Dr Ste 4, Houston, TX | 713-465-9017 |
| Hendricks, Bruce/14907 Woodbriar, Dallas, TX | 214-233-2563 |
| Herod, Thomas Jr/9727 Lynbrook, Dallas, TX | 214-343-8088 |
| Kessel, Mark/3631 Granada, Dallas, TX | 214-526-0415 |
| Kim Dawson Agency/PO Box 585060, Dallas, TX | 214-638-2414 |
| Lively Enterprises, Inc/Star Route F-13, San Saba, TX | 214-462-1600 |
| MacLean, John/10017 Woodgrove, Dallas, TX | 214-343-0181 |
| Maloy, Buz/Rt 1 Box 155, Kyle, TX | 512-442-6665 |
| Maloy, John W/718 W 35th St, Austin, TX | 512-453-9660 |
| McLaughlin, Ed M/3512 Rashti Court, Ft. Worth, TX | 817-927-2310 |
| Murray Getz Commer & Indust Phot/2310 Genessee, Houston, TX | 713-526-4451 |
| OK State Tourism-Rec Dept/500 Will Rogers Bldg, Oklahoma City, OK | 405-521-3981 |
| Phillips, Michael/8133 Chadbourne Road, Dallas, TX | 214-358-0857 |
| Putman, Eva M/202 Dover, Richardson, TX | 214-630-4018 |
| Quinlivan, Joe/3205 Cortez Dr, Ft. Worth, TX | 817-244-1188 |
| Ranchland - Circle R/Rt 3, Box 229, Roanoke, TX | 817-430-1561 |
| Ray, Al/2304 Houston Street, San Angelo, TX | 915-949-2716 |
| Ray, Rudolph/2231 Freeland Avenue, San Angelo, TX | 915-949-6784 |
| Reinninger, Laurence H/501 North IH 35, Austin, TX | 512-478-8593 |
| Republic of Texas Film Prod & Svcs/316 W Main, Fredricksburg, TA | 512-734-7183 |
| San Antonio Zoo & Aquar/3903 N St Marys, San Antonio, TA | 512-734-7183 |
| Senn, Loyd C/P O Box 6060, Lubbock, TX | 806-792-2000 |
| Summers, Judy/1504 Harvard, Houston, TX | 713-861-7265 |
| TBK Talent Enterprises/5255 McCullough, San Antonio, TX | 512-822-0508 |
| Taylor, Peggy Talent, Inc/Two Dallas Comm Complex, Dallas, TX | 214-869-1515 |
| Texas Film Commission/P O Box 12428, Austin, TX | 512-475-3785 |
| Texas Pacific Film Video, Inc/501 North IH 35, Austin, TX | 512-478-8585 |
| Wild West Stunt Company/Box T-789, Stephenville, TX | 817-965-4114 |
| Young Film Productions/PO Box 50105, Tuscon, AZ | 602-623-5961 |
| Zimmerman and Associates, Inc/710 Avenue E, San Antonio, TX | 512-225-6708 |
| Zuniga, Tony/2616 North Flores #2, San Antonio, TX | 512-735-5441 |

## WEST

| | |
|---|---|
| Anabel's Diversified Services/PO Box 532, Pacific Palisades, CA | 213-454-1566 |
| Briles Wing & Helicopter, Inc/3011 Airport Ave, Santa Monica, CA | 213-390-3554 |
| CA State Motion Picture Council/6725 Sunset Blvd, Hollywood, CA | 213-736-2465 |
| California State Motion Picture Council/6725 Sunset Blvd, Hollywood, CA | 213-736-2465 |
| Chimera Antiques/1807 Polk St, San Francisco, CA | 415-441-0326 |
| City Lights/404 S Figueroa, Los Angeles, CA | 213-680-9876 |
| Daniels, Karil, Point of View Prod/2477 Folsom St, San Francisco, CA | 415-821-0435 |
| Design Art Studios/800 Seward, Hollywood, CA | 213-464-9118 |
| Film Permits Unlimited/8058 Allott Ave, Van Nuys, CA | 213-997-6197 |
| Herod, Jr, Thomas/PO Box 2543, Hollywood, CA | 213-353-0911 |
| The Location Co/8646 Wilshire Blvd, Beverly Hills, CA | 213-855-7075 |
| Location Enterprises Inc/6725 Sunset Blvd, Los Angeles, CA | 213-469-3141 |
| Mindseye/394 Greenwood Beach, Tiburon, CA | 415-383-7839 |
| Newhall Ranch/27050 Henry Mayo Rd, Valencia, CA | 213-362-1515 |
| Producers Location Service/1617 El Centro, Los Angeles, CA | 213-462-1133 |
| San Francisco Conv/Visitors Bur/1390 Market St #260, San Francisco, CA | 415-626-5500 |

# SETS

## NEW YORK CITY

| | |
|---|---|
| Abstracta Structures/38 W 39th St | 212-944-2244 |
| Alcamo Marble Works/220 E 24 St | 212-255-5224 |
| Associated Theatrical Designers Ltd/220 W 71st St | 212-362-2648 |
| Baker, Alex/30 W 69th St | 212-799-2069 |
| The Focarino Studio/156 E 23rd St | 212-533-9872 |
| Golden Office Interiors/574 Fifth Ave | 212-719-5150 |
| **LAFERLA, SANDRO/135 W 14TH ST (P 401)** | **212-620-0693** |
| Lincoln Scenic Studios/440 W 15th St | 212-255-2000 |
| Plexability Ltd/200 Lexington Ave | 212-679-7826 |
| Set Shop/3 W 20 St | 212-929-4845 |
| Siciliano, Frank/125 Fifth Ave | 212-620-4075 |
| Theater Technology Inc/37 W 20th St | 212-929-5380 |
| Variety Scenic Studio/25-19 Borden Ave | 212-392-4747 |
| Yurkiw, Mark/225 E 11th St | 212-475-8718 |

# PHOTO/FILM SERVICES CONT'D.

Please send us your additions and updates.

## NORTHEAST

| | |
|---|---|
| Foothills Theater Company/PO Box 236, Worcester, MA | 617-754-0546 |
| Fox, Charles W III/6 Oldham Rd, West Newton, MA | 617-527-8979 |
| George M. Creations/Rt 6, Mohegan Lake, NY | 914-528-1616 |
| RK0 East/RK0 General Building Governmen, Boston, MA | 617-725-2816 |
| Silverman, Hannah/265 A Elm St, #3, Somerville, MA | 617-625-5743 |
| Trapp, Patricia/33 Stanton Rd, Brookline, MA | 617-734-9321 |
| Video Picture Company/1170 Commonwealth Ave, Boston, MA | 617-731-2990 |
| Videocom, Inc/502 Sprague St, Dedham, MA | 617-329-4080 |
| White Oak Design/286 Congress St, Boston, MA | 617-426-7171 |

## SOUTHEAST

| | |
|---|---|
| Enter Space/20 14th St NW, Atlanta, GA | 404-885-1139 |
| The Great Southern Stage/15221 NE 21 Ave, N Miami Beach, FL | 305-947-0430 |
| Kupersmith, Tony/320 N Highland Ave NE, Atlanta, GA | 404-577-5319 |
| Sugar Creek Scenic Studio, Inc/441 Memorial Dr, Atlanta, GA | 404-523-0962 |

## MIDWEST

| | |
|---|---|
| Becker Studio/2824 W Taylor, Chicago, IL | 312-722-4040 |
| Centerwood Cabinets/3700 Centerwood Rd, New Brighton, MN | 612-786-2094 |
| Chicago Scenic Studio Inc./213 N Morgan, Chicago, IL | 312-942-1483 |
| Dimension Works/4130 W Belmont, Chicago, IL | 312-545-2233 |
| Grand Stage Lighting Co/630 W Lake, Chicago, IL | 312-332-5611 |
| White House Studios/4810 McGee, Kansas City, MO | 816-931-3608 |

## SOUTHWEST

| | |
|---|---|
| Bradford, Bill/3103 Oak Hill Rd, Carrollton, TX | 214-827-9380 |
| Country Roads/701 Ave B, Del Rio, TX | 512-775-7991 |
| Crabb, Ken/3066 Ponder Pl, Dallas, TX | 214-352-0581 |
| Dallas Stage Lighting & Equipment/2813 Florence, Dallas, TX | 214-827-9380 |
| Dallas Stage Scenery Co, Inc/2804 Live Oak St, Dallas, TX | 214-821-0002 |
| Dunn, Glenn E/7412 Sherwood Rd, Austin, TX | 512-441-0377 |
| Edleson, Louis/6568 Lake Circle, Dallas, TX | 214-823-7180 |
| Eschberger, Jerry/6401 South Meadows, Austin, TX | 512-447-4795 |
| Freeman Design & Display Co/2233 Irving Blvd, Dallas, TX | 214-638-8800 |
| Grafica: A Total Design Company/3627 Howell, Dallas, TX | 214-521-7550 |
| H & H Special Effects/2919 Chisholm Trail, San Antonio, TX | 512-826-8214 |
| Houston Stage Equipment/2301 Dumble, Houston, TX | 713-926-4441 |
| Howard, Kay Design/3809-D Manchaca, Austin, TX | 512-441-3883 |
| Lewallen, Robert Hugh/2810 South 1st St, Austin, TX | 512-442-4120 |
| Reed, Bill Decorations/333 First Ave, Dallas, TX | 214-823-315 |
| Texas Scenic Co, Inc/P O Box 28297, San Antonio, TX | 512-684-0091 |

## WEST

| | |
|---|---|
| Act Design & Execution/P.O. Box 5054, Sherman Oaks, CA | 213-788-4219 |
| American Scenery/18555 Eddy St, Northridge, CA | 213-886-1585 |
| Backings, J C/10201 W Pico Blvd, Los Angeles, CA | 213-277-0522 |
| CBS Special Effects/7800 Beverly Blvd, Los Angeles, CA | 213-852-2345 |
| Carthay Set Services/1036 N Cole Ave, Hollywood, CA | 213-469-5618 |
| Carthay Studio/5907 W Pico, Los Angeles, CA | 213-938-2101 |
| Cinema Scenic Services/5907 W Pico, Los Angeles, CA | 213-469-3240 |
| Erecter Set Inc/1150 S LaBrea, Hollywood, CA | 213-938-4762 |
| Get Set Inc/650 N Bronson, Hollywood, CA | 213-461-4041 |
| Grosh, RL & Sons/4144 Sunset Blvd, Los Angeles, CA | 213-662-1134 |
| Hollywood Scenery/665 Eleanor Ave, Hollywood, CA | 213-463-2123 |
| Hollywood Stage/6650 Santa Monica Blvd, Los Angeles, CA | 213-466-4393 |
| Krofft Ent/7200 Vineland Ave, Sun Valley, CA | 213-982-2920 |
| Pacific Studios/8315 Melrose Ave, Los Angeles, CA | 213-653-3093 |
| Producers Studio/650 N Bronson Ave, Los Angeles, CA | 213-466-3111 |
| R J Set Service Inc/6006 Eleanor Ave, Hollywood, CA | 213-467-2127 |
| Serrurier & Assoc/61 W Mountain St, Pasadena, CA | 213-798-0951 |
| Shafton Inc/5500 Cleon Ave, N Hollywood, CA | 213-985-5025 |
| Show Time Scenery/1777 N Main, Los Angeles, CA | 213-227-4101 |
| Superstage/5724 Santa Monica Blvd, Los Angeles, CA | 213-464-0296 |
| Triangle Scenery/1215 Bates Ave, Los Angeles, CA | 213-661-1262 |
| Zoetrope Studios/1040 N Las Palmas Ave, Los Angeles, CA | 213-463-7191 |

**NOTES:**

**NOTES:**

**NOTES:**

**NOTES:**

**NOTES:**

**NOTES:**

**NOTES:**

**NOTES:**

**NOTES:**

# INDEX

## A

| | |
|---|---|
| Abel, Wilton | 256 |
| Abraham, Russell | 344 |
| Alexander, Jules | 47 |
| Allen, Jim | 48 |
| Alt, Howard | 49 |
| Ambrose, Paul | 345 |
| Arnold, Peter | 398,399 |
| Aubry, Daniel | 38 |

## B

| | |
|---|---|
| brt Photographic Illustrations | 206,207 |
| Bagshaw, Cradoc | 317 |
| Baker, Joe | 50 |
| Baker, Kipp | 318 |
| Barley, Bill | 257 |
| Barrow, Scott | 51 |
| Bartone, Laurence | 33 |
| Bartz, Carl | 301 |
| Bator, Joe | 347 |
| Beaudin, Ted | 52 |
| Becker Bishop Studios, Inc. | 332,333 |
| Bedford Photo-graphic | 208 |
| Benn, Nathan | 240 |
| Berkun, Phil | 53 |
| Bevilacqua | 54 |
| Bezushko | 55 |
| Bilby, Glade II | 258 |
| Blakeley, Jim | 334,335 |
| Blaustein, John | 348,349 |
| Brimacombe, Gerald | 302,303 |
| Browne, Warren | 350 |
| Buchanan, Craig | 351 |
| Byers, Bruce | 56 |

## C

| | |
|---|---|
| Cadge, Bill | 57 |
| Cannon, Gregory | 58 |
| Cantor, Phil | 59 |
| Carriker, Ronald C. | 259 |
| Carroll, Don | 60,61 |
| Carroon, Chip | 352 |
| Cassidy Photographic Design | 353 |
| Certo, Rosemarie | 63 |
| Chaney, Brad | 354,355 |
| Chapple, Ron | 250 |
| Click! Chicago | 289-291 |
| Clifford, Geoffrey C. | 64,65 |
| Clintsman, Dick | 319 |
| Clough, Terry | 66,67 |
| Collins, Fred | 209 |
| Cook, Irvin | 68 |
| Cook, Kathleen Norris | 356 |
| Cowan, Ralph | 292 |
| Crane, Tom | 69 |

## D

| | |
|---|---|
| Dahlstrom Photography, Inc. | 357 |
| Davidson, Jerry | 358,359 |
| Deahl, David | 276,277 |
| DeBold, Bill | 284 |
| de Gennaro, George | 360,361 |
| De Lessio, Len | 70 |
| De Sciose, Nicholas | 362 |
| De Vault, Jim | 260,261 |
| Digital Transparencies, Inc. | 320 |
| D'Innocenzo, Paul | 71 |
| Dreyer, Peter | 210 |
| Dunbar, Clark | 342 |
| Dunn, Phoebe | 72 |
| Dunoff, Rich | 73 |
| Duran, Mark | 314 |
| Dwiggins, Gene | 211 |

## E

| | |
|---|---|
| Elkins, Joel | 34 |
| Elliott, Peter | 278,279 |
| Elmore, Steve | 75 |

## F

| | |
|---|---|
| Fader, Bob | 363 |
| Faustino | 321 |
| Ferro, Daniel J. | 364 |
| Fishbein, Chuck | 76,77 |
| Fishman, Chuck | 78 |
| Flatow, Carl | 79 |
| Forelli, Chip | 81 |
| Foster, Frank | 213 |
| Francekevich, Al | 82,83 |
| Fraser, Douglas | 85 |
| Funk, Mitchell | 86,87 |
| Furman, Michael | 88,89 |

## G

| | |
|---|---|
| Gardner, Robert | 365 |
| Gayle, Rick | 322 |
| Gerczynski, Tom | 323 |
| Giese, Al | 91 |
| Gladstone, Gary | 92,93 |
| Gleasner, Bill | 262 |
| Glentzer, Don | 324 |
| Gordon, Joel | 95 |
| Gottlieb, Mark | 367 |
| Green-Armytage, Stephen | 96,97 |
| Greenberg, David | 98 |
| Gscheidle, Gerhard | 99 |
| Gupton, Lee | 263 |

## H

| | |
|---|---|
| Hamilton, Jeffrey Muir | 325 |
| Hansen, Steve | 214,215 |
| Harrington, Marshall | 368,369 |
| Harrington, Phillip A. | 100 |
| Harris, Bart | 285 |
| Harris, Brownie | 101 |
| Hashi | 102,103 |
| Haviland, Brian | 104 |
| Hedrich, David | 35 |
| Heffernan, Terry | 336,337 |
| Heilman, Grant | 400 |
| Henderson, Chip | 264 |
| Hetisimer, Larry | 293 |
| Hix, Steve | 304 |
| Hood, Robin | 255 |
| Horowitz, Ryszard | 105 |

## J

| | |
|---|---|
| Jamison, Chipp | 253 |
| Joachim, Bruno | 198,199 |
| Joern, James | 106 |
| Johansky, Peter | 107 |
| Johns, Douglas | 265 |
| Jones, Jerry | 326 |
| Jones, Lou | 217 |

## K

| | |
|---|---|
| Kahn, Dick | Back Cover |
| Kalfus, Lonny | 108 |
| Kaluzny, Zigy | 315 |
| Kaplan, Peter B. | 109 |
| Katz, Arni | 254 |
| Kazu | 294,295 |
| Kawalerski, Ted | 218,219 |
| Kearney, Mitchell | 251 |
| Keeling, Robert | 283 |
| Keenan, Larry | 370 |
| Kent, Karen | 110 |
| King, Ralph | 200,201 |
| Kohanim, Parish | 248,249 |
| Korsh, Ken | 111 |

## L

| | |
|---|---|
| La Ferla, Sandro | 401 |
| Landsman, Gary D. | 112,113 |
| Lane, Whitney | 114 |
| La Riche, Michael | 220,221 |
| Lee, Larry | 371 |
| Leeds, Karen | 115 |
| Leighton, Thomas | 116,117 |
| Lerner, Richard | 104 |
| Leung, Jook | 118 |
| Livzey, John | 372,373 |
| Long, James L. | 402 |
| Luria, Dick | 119 |

continued

# INDEX

## M

| | |
|---|---|
| Manarchy, Dennis | 280,281 |
| Marchese, Jim | 120,121 |
| Maresca, Frank | 122,123 |
| Marshall, Jim | 327 |
| Marshall, Lee | 124 |
| Martin, Butch | 125 |
| Martin, Marilyn | 222 |
| Masterson, Ed | 375 |
| McAllister, Bruce | 376,377 |
| McCoy, Dan | 223 |
| McGrail, John | 126 |
| McKean, Tom | 224 |
| Melgar Photographers | 378 |
| Mellor, D.W. | 127 |
| Meola, Eric | 128-133 |
| Mervar, Louis | 36,37 |
| Meyler, Dennis | 328 |
| Miller, Donald L. | 134,135 |
| Miller, Randy | 266,267 |
| Mishler, Clark | 379 |
| Morgan, Frank | 241 |
| Mulligan, Joseph | 32 |
| Munson, Russell | 136 |
| Murray, Steve | 268 |
| Musto, Tom | 137 |
| Myers Studio, Inc. | 138 |

## N

| | |
|---|---|
| Nadelson, Jay | 139 |
| Nathan, Simon | 141 |
| Noble, Inc. | 238,239 |
| Northlight Group | 203 |

## O

| | |
|---|---|
| Obremski, George | 142,143 |
| O'Brien, Tom | 341 |
| Ochi | 46 |
| Orenstein, Ronn | 144 |

## P

| | |
|---|---|
| Palmer, Gabe | 145 |
| Parik, Jan | 146 |
| Peacock, Christian | 147 |
| Pease, Greg | 242,243 |
| Peltz, Stuart | 148 |
| Percey, Roland | 380 |
| Peregrine, Paul | 381 |
| Perry, David | 382 |
| Peterson, Bruce | 316 |
| Petrey, John | 269 |
| Photofile International, Ltd. | 44,45 |
| Photographic Communications | 383 |
| Photography Associates | 225 |
| Photoscope | 149 |
| Pitzner, Al | 305 |
| Pohuski, Michael | 237 |
| Pottle, Jock | 150 |
| Powers, Guy | 151-156 |
| Pribula, Barry | 157 |

## R

| | |
|---|---|
| Ressmeyer, Roger | 384 |
| Rezny, Aaron | 159 |
| Rizzo, Alberto | 160 |
| Robinson, George A. | 226 |
| Rockhill, Morgan | 205 |
| Rohman, Jim | 306 |
| Rosner, Eric H. | 161 |
| Roth, Peter | 162 |
| Rotman, Jeffrey L. | 227 |
| Rubin, Laurie | 288 |
| Rusing, Rick | 40,41 |
| Rysinski, Edward | 163 |

## S

| | |
|---|---|
| Sadlon, Jim | 385 |
| Sanderson, Glenn | 307 |
| Sandone, A.J. | 164 |
| Sauter, Ron | 228 |
| Schleipman, Russ | 229 |
| Schoenfeld, Michael | 386 |
| Schoon, Tim | 244 |
| Schridde, Charles | 308 |
| Scott, Denis | 282 |
| Sherman, Ron | 271 |
| Shore, Stephen | 165 |
| Simmons, Erik Leigh | 230 |
| Simpson, Jerry | 166 |
| Skalski, Ken | 167 |
| Smith, Charles J. | 387 |
| Smith, Gordon E. | 168 |
| Smith, R. Hamilton | 309 |
| Smith, Richard W. | 252 |
| Smith, William Edward | 169 |
| Smyth, T. Kevin | 170 |
| Sochurek, Howard | 171 |
| Solomon, Marc | 388,389 |
| Sööt, Olaf | 173 |
| Southern Stock Photos | 403 |
| Sports Illustrated Pictures | 404 |
| Springmann, Christopher | 340 |
| Standart, Joe | 39 |
| Steinberg, Bruce | 391 |
| Steiner, Peter | 231 |
| Stock Imagery | 405 |
| The Stock Market | 406 |
| Stratos, Jim | 174,175 |
| Strongin, Jeanne | 176 |
| Stuart, John | 177 |
| Stuart, Stephen | 179 |
| The Studio Inc. | 202 |
| Swarthout, Walter | 392,393 |

## T

| | |
|---|---|
| Tcherevkoff, Michel | 180,181 |
| Togashi | 183 |
| Touchton, Ken | 245 |
| Tucker, Bill | 286 |

## V

| | |
|---|---|
| Vance, David | 272,273 |
| Vaughan, Ted | 232,233 |

## W

| | |
|---|---|
| Waine, Michael | 184,185 |
| Warkenthien, Dan | 296 |
| Watson, H. Ross | 187 |
| Weidman, H. Mark | 188,189 |
| Weigand, Tom | 190 |
| Weinberg, Michael | 191 |
| Weitz, Allan | 192 |
| Welzenbach, John | 287 |
| Werts Studios, Inc. | 338,339 |
| West, Charles | 193 |
| Westerman, Charlie | 310,311 |
| Wick, Walter | 194,195 |
| Wilcox, Shorty | 42,43 |
| Wood, James B. | 394 |
| Wortham, Robert | 395 |

## Y

| | |
|---|---|
| Yablon, Ron | 234 |
| Young, Ed | 343 |

## Z

| | |
|---|---|
| Zak, Ed | 330,331 |
| Zann, Arnold | 297 |
| Zenreich, Alan | 196 |